D0080085

Advance praise for *Who Built America?*

"*Who Built America?* stands out from other textbooks in the clarity of its focus. The labor theme serves as an excellent framework, allowing the authors to synthesize most of the events in the standard chronology of history while still providing a distinctive perspective."

— Lawrence A. Peskin, *Morgan State University*

"*Who Built America?* is a textbook of remarkable scope and diversity, with the narrative drive of a good novel. This is how it should be."

— Betty Mitchell, *University of Massachusetts, Dartmouth*

"A history of American society must begin and end with its people and *Who Built America?* excels at this."

— Gordon Harvey, *University of Louisiana, Monroe*

"The new subheadings in the table of contents are a wonderful addition. Students need a way to organize material, and these subdivisions make the chapters easier to follow."

— Diane Barnes, *Youngstown State University*

"The visual materials in *Who Built America?* have always been terrific. The pictures, for example, are often unique to this text, while one sees the same things over and over in others. *WBA?*'s successful search for materials on working people in particular make it especially captivating for students in search of a fresh perspective on the American past."

— Jama Lazerow, *Wheelock College*

American Social History Project
The City University of New York

Christopher Clark
University of Connecticut

Nancy A. Hewitt
Rutgers University

Visual Editors: Joshua Brown, Graduate Center, City University of New York, and David Jaffee, Bard Graduate Center for Studies in The Decorative Arts, Design, and Culture

Executive Editor: Stephen Brier, Graduate Center, City University of New York

Supervising Editor: Ellen Noonan, Graduate Center, City University of New York

Based on previous editions authored by: Bruce Levine, Stephen Brier, David Brundage, Edward Countryman, Dorothy Fennell, and Marcus Rediker

Who Built America?

Working People and the Nation's History

THIRD EDITION

Volume One
To 1877

BEDFORD / ST. MARTIN'S

BOSTON ✦ NEW YORK

For Bedford/St. Martin's

Publisher for History: Mary V. Dougherty
Director of Development for History: Jane Knetzger
Executive Developmental Editor for History: William J. Lombardo
Developmental Editor: Shannon Hunt
Production Editors: Deborah Baker and Annette Pagliaro Sweeney
Production Supervisor: Jennifer Peterson
Executive Marketing Manager: Jenna Bookin Barry
Editorial Assistants: Holly Dye and Adrianne Hiltz
Production Assistants: Lindsay DiGianvittorio and Katherine Caruana
Copyeditor: Barbara Willette
Text and Cover Design: Joyce Weston
Indexer: James O'Brien
Cover Art: Battery Rogers. © Corbis
Cartography: Mapping Specialists Limited
Composition: Pine Tree Composition
Printing and Binding: R. R. Donnelley & Sons Company

President: Joan E. Feinberg
Editorial Director: Denise B. Wydra
Director of Marketing: Karen Melton Soeltz
Director of Editing, Design, and Production: Marcia Cohen
Managing Editor: Elizabeth M. Schaaf

Library of Congress Control Number: 2007934299

Copyright © 2008 by Bedford/St. Martin's

All rights reserved. No part of this book may be reproduced, stored in a retrieval system, or transmitted in any form or by any means, electronic, mechanical, photocopying, recording, or otherwise, except as may be expressly permitted by the applicable copyright statutes or in writing by the Publisher.

Manufactured in the United States of America.

2   1   0   9   8   7

f   e   d   c   b   a

For information, write: Bedford/St. Martin's, 75 Arlington Street, Boston, MA 02116
(617-399-4000)

ISBN-10: 0-312-44691-8 (Vol. One)   ISBN-10: 0-312-44692-6 (Vol. Two)
ISBN-13: 978-0-312-44691-8   ISBN-13: 978-0-312-44692-5

For Roy Rosenzweig (1950–2007), trusted friend and collaborator, world-class historian, and coauthor and coeditor, who was with us every step of the way for the past twenty-five years and who helped us understand that to recover a meaningful past, we needed to give voice to ordinary people, embrace innovation in all its forms, and possess, as he always did, a great sense of humor.

Preface

Who built the seven towers of Thebes?
The books are filled with the names of kings.
Was it kings who hauled the craggy blocks of stone? . . .
In the evening when the Chinese wall was finished,
Where did the masons go? . . .

—Bertolt Brecht, "Questions from a
Worker Who Reads" (1935)

*W*HO BUILT AMERICA? surveys the nation's past from an important but often neglected perspective: the transformations wrought by the changing nature and forms of work and the role that working people played in the making of modern America. In an age when globalizing economies, profound technological changes, and ever more remote exercises of power are altering the nature of life and labor, *Who Built America?*'s distinctive interpretation of the nation's past is more necessary than ever. Not merely a documentation of the country's presidents, politics, and wars, *Who Built America?* focuses on the fundamental social and economic conflicts that have shaped U.S. history and challenges the notion that the vast majority of America's citizens have always been united in a broad consensus about the nation's basic values and shared in its extraordinary prosperity. This emphasis puts the history of the workplace, community, family, gender roles, race, and ethnicity at the center of the more familiar textbook narrative of politics and economic development; in doing so, it renders more intelligible the beliefs and actions of the nation's economic, political, and intellectual elites. By taking up the central questions of how the nation's work has changed and how workers have changed the nation, *Who Built America?* offers an indispensable guide to the historical developments that have brought us to the present day.

Approach

We have defined the category of "working people" broadly. Throughout much of its history, the nation's actual workforce embraced a wide spectrum of people laboring in very different conditions and settings. Answering the question "Who built America?" therefore requires attention not only to wage-earning industrial employees but also to indentured servants, slaves, tenant farmers, sharecroppers, independent farm families, artisans, small proprietors, day laborers, clerks, domestic workers, outworkers, service and technical workers, and women and children performing unpaid family labor—in short, the great majority of the American population at every phase of the country's development.

This book grew out of the now four-decades-old effort to reinterpret American history from the bottom up—drawing on studies of workers, women, consumers, farmers, African Americans, and immigrants—that has helped to transform our understanding of the past. The American Social History Project (ASHP) was founded in 1981 at the City University of New York by Herbert Gutman (a pioneer of what was then the "new social history") and Stephen Brier to bring this history to the broadest possible audience. In addition to this book, ASHP has produced over the past quarter-century a wide range of accessible educational materials in print, video, and digital media and has worked closely with college, high school, and adult and labor education teachers to help them use these resources effectively in their classrooms.

Who Built America?, now in its third edition, retains its distinctive interpretation and strong point of view. We continue to tackle controversial issues and offer opinions that are sometimes critical of celebrated figures or dominant beliefs. Our view is that readers would rather encounter a clearly stated perspective, even if they disagree with it, than bland platitudes about the past.

Organization and Coverage

This volume of *Who Built America?* is divided into three parts. The principal theme is the rise and subsequent decline of various precapitalist labor systems, especially racial slavery, and the parallel development and ultimate dominance of capitalism and its system of wage labor. Each part is preceded by a brief essay that lays out the events, changes, and ideas covered in the chapters to come. These essays help students to think synthetically and thematically about the material.

• Part One covers three centuries, beginning with the often-violent encounters among peoples in the Americas as Europeans first occupied the land of Native Americans and subsequently enslaved Africans to work the plantations they established. It examines the different patterns of European colonization in North America, the growing importance of the English colonies on the continent's Atlantic seaboard, and the evolution of these colonies, North and South. It culminates in the colonists' successful war for independence and the establishment of the United States.

- Part Two, covering the decades between the ratification of the Constitution and the onset of the tumultuous 1850s, departs slightly from a strictly chronological organization by alternating focus between the labor systems developing in the South and the North. This structure emphasizes the changing nature of work and the changing conditions, experiences, outlooks, and conduct of working people themselves as the two systems followed diverging paths that led the United States into civil war. Profound economic, social, and political changes—including the Industrial Revolution, the growth of the cotton kingdom, westward expansion and war with Mexico, and the deepening conflict between the free-labor North and proslavery South over the status of slavery in the growing nation—sparked movements among a wide array of Americans, including many who did not yet have access to formal political rights but who nonetheless sought to shape the American nation.

- Part Three examines the intensifying political struggle over the West and the coming of the Civil War—America's Second Revolution. It also looks at the conflict itself, the aftermath of the South's defeat, and the hopes and fears engendered among all Americans, including four million newly freed slaves, during the era of Reconstruction. The volume concludes with the formal end of Reconstruction and the explosive wave of railroad strikes that shook the nation in 1877. Together, the dramatic events of that year signal the close of one major epoch in American social, economic, and political history and the beginning of another.

New to This Edition and Distinctive Features

The most visible change in the third edition is a reorganized chapter structure that makes *Who Built America?* work better as a textbook. Each chapter now has several main sections with subsections, enabling students to navigate the chapters more efficiently. New outlines at the beginning of each chapter show coverage at a glance. All section headings have been revised for clarity, all chapter and section introductions have been strengthened to help students focus on key ideas, and each chapter ends with a conclusion that reinforces the main points and eases the transition to the next chapter. Detailed timelines (Years in Review) are provided at the end of each chapter to ensure that key events are not lost in the narrative flow and to facilitate review. For instructors and students seeking to explore topics in greater depth, there is also at the end of each chapter a list of Additional Readings that encompass the topics covered in that chapter.

Just as important for the third edition, we have taken into account the vast outpouring of recent scholarship to explore more deeply the histories of American Indians, Spanish-speaking peoples, women, and the West. At the same time, we have linked these histories both to changing class and racial dynamics in the broader society and to the decisions made by economic and political elites. We have also expanded discussions of the global context in which the American nation was built, particularly in the colonial period, which stretched from the sixteenth to the nineteenth centuries and from what would become the southwestern United States to the Atlantic Coast and the far Northwest. Where new historical evidence has come to light, we have modified our interpretation.

Instructors familiar with *Who Built America?* will also note that Volume One includes thirteen chapters rather than the previous edition's twelve. Here, we have returned to the organization of the first edition and present two chapters covering the years 1865–1877. Chapter 12 provides an overview of Reconstruction in the South, and Chapter 13 presents a fuller discussion about the rapidly growing West as well as the industry-driven East after the Civil War.

In response to user feedback, this edition of *Who Built America?* also contains more "Voices" in each chapter — excerpts from letters, diaries, autobiographies, poems, songs, journalism, fiction, official testimony, oral histories, and other historical documents. These primary sources convey the experiences and beliefs of working people who lived through the events recounted in the text and offer instructors additional opportunities for assignments and discussions. In the interest of clarity, we have modernized some of the spelling, punctuation, and (especially in the case of the earliest documents) usage in these records.

Visual Program

The drawings, paintings, prints, cartoons, photographs, objects, and other visual media that we have selected to illustrate *Who Built America?* supplement the book's themes and narrative, showing the people, places, and events discussed in the text. In this new edition, we have included examples of material culture — from implements used in the workshop or office to furniture used in the home — to show how everyday objects embodied significant changes in social life. But in keeping with our approach in the first two editions of the book, our illustrations also address subjects not included in the narrative; they offer perspectives on the past that were often not articulated in the written record or were conveyed in a wholly different way from "the word" via visual media. Throughout U.S. history, ideas, experiences, events, and conditions were recorded and expressed in evocative and provocative images and objects that Americans treated with as much seriousness and enjoyment as they did text. Sometimes tainted by racism or chauvinism and marked by invidious caricatures, Americans challenged these images as part of their larger longstanding struggles to achieve equality. In short, images mattered, and the illustrations and captions in each chapter of *Who Built America?* offer readers a parallel narrative that, in juxtaposition to the text, demonstrates how different visual media interpreted and thus helped shape beliefs about the people, events, and ideas of the time.

Supplements

NEW   Computerized Test Bank for *Who Built America?* Written by Steven H. Jaffe, Ph.D. (Volume 1), and John Spencer of Ursinus College (Volume 2), the new Test Bank for *Who Built America?* offers multiple-choice, short answer, and essay questions for each chapter, providing opportunities for ongoing assessments and cumulative exams.

NEW   Instructor's Resource CD-ROM. Includes PowerPoint presentations built around chapter outlines, maps, figures, and selected images from the textbook, plus JPEG versions of all maps and figures and selected images.

NEW   Book Companion Site at bedfordstmartins.com/whobuiltamerica The companion Web site gathers all the electronic resources for *Who Built America?* at a single Web address, providing convenient links to assignment and research materials such as the libraries at Make History and the resources provided by the American Social History Project/Center for Media and Learning.

Acknowledgments

Despite the major changes implemented by the authors and editors of this edition, the narrative of *Who Built America?* rests heavily on the labors of the authors of the previous two editions: David Bensman, Susan Porter Benson, Stephen Brier, Joshua Brown, David Brundage, Bret Eynon, Joshua Freeman, Bruce Levine, Nelson Lichtenstein, Bryan Palmer, and Susan Strasser. We want to note with regret the passing of Susan Porter Benson, who was one of the original authors and contributors to the American Social History Project. In addition, we want to thank the many people who helped to bring forth this edition, especially our colleagues at Bedford/St. Martin's: Joan Feinberg, Mary Dougherty, Jane Knetzger, William Lombardo, Donna Dennison, Shelby Disario, Jenna Bookin Barry, Patricia Rossi, Shannon Hunt, Amy Leathe, Holly Dye, Adrianne Hiltz, Elizabeth Schaaf, Deborah Baker, and Annette Pagliaro Sweeney.

We are deeply grateful to Jim O'Brien for his superb work on the index. We thank Jeannette Gabriel, Tom Harbison, Madeleine Lopez, Vernon

Lucas, David Parsons, Leah Potter, Tabitha Tally, and Andrea Ades Vásquez for research and advice. We especially thank Will Menaker for research assistance and help in locating and captioning illustrations. We reiterate our sincere thanks to the many people who helped on the first two editions (and are acknowledged in those volumes). And we thank Lynn Hunt for her abiding faith in and commitment to the American Social History Project.

To the following colleagues who gave us encouragement and valuable feedback at various stages during the preparation of this edition, we are most grateful: Gregg Andrews, Texas State University, San Marcos; Jay Antle, Johnson County Community College; Diane Barnes, Youngstown State University; Michael Botson, Houston Community College; Tracy Campbell, University of Kentucky; Robert Cassanello, University of Central Florida; Elizabeth Clement, University of Utah; Gregory Dorr, University of Alabama; Laurence Gross, University of Massachusetts Lowell; Gordon Harvey, University of Louisiana at Monroe; Robert Harmon, Elgin Community College; Martin Halpern, Henderson State University; Patricia Knol, Triton College; Jama Lazerow, Wheelock College; Norman Markowitz, Rutgers University; Betty Mitchell, University of Massachusetts Dartmouth; Jason Newman, Cosumnes River College; Greg O'Brien, University of Southern Mississippi; Lawrence Peskin, Morgan State University; Dona Reaser, Columbus State Community College; Steve Rosswurm, Lake Forest College; Victor Silverman, Pomona College; Ashley Sousa, West Valley College; and Steve Stein, University of Memphis.

Finally, we would be remiss if we ended our acknowledgments without noting the role of the late Herbert Gutman (1929–1985) in creating the American Social History Project, which gave birth to this book, and in shaping the generation of historical scholarship on which it is based. Our collective and individual debts to Herb are immeasurable. We hope that this new edition of *Who Built America?* meets the high standards he set for himself throughout his rich but too brief career.

Contents

4. Toward Revolution, 1750–1776   160

5. Revolution, Constitution, and the People, 1776–1815   210

Part Two. Free Labor and Slavery, 1790–1850   264

6. The Consolidation of Slavery in the South, 1790–1836   270

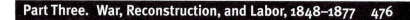

12. Reconstructing the Nation, 1865–1877   588

13. New Frontiers: Westward Expansion and Industrial Growth, 1865–1877   632

About the Authors and Editors

Christopher Clark is Professor of History at the University of Connecticut. He received the Frederick Jackson Turner Award from the Organization of American Historians for *The Roots of Rural Capitalism: Western Massachusetts, 1780–1860* (1990). His other publications include *The Communitarian Moment: The Radical Challenge of the Northampton Association* (1995) and *Social Change in America: From the Revolution through the Civil War* (2006), together with articles on rural history and the social roots of American economic development in the *Journal of Social History*, *American Quarterly*, the *Journal of the Early Republic,* and in several essay collections. He has also been the co-recipient of the Cadbury Schweppes Prize for innovative teaching in the humanities.

Nancy A. Hewitt is Professor of History and Women's and Gender Studies at Rutgers University. She has received many awards and prizes, including the Jerome T. Krivanek Distinguished Teaching Award and the Julia Cherry Spruill Book Prize, as well as fellowships from the National Endowment for the Humanities, the Andrew W. Mellon Foundation, and the John Simon Guggenheim Memorial Foundation. Professor Hewitt has been involved in a number of teaching projects, including Teaching American History projects in Florida and in New York City. Her publications include *Women's Activism and Social Change: Rochester, New York, 1822–1872* (1984); *Visible Women: New Essays on American Activism*, coedited with Suzanne Lebsock (1993); and *Southern Discomfort: Women's Activism in Tampa, Florida, 1880s-1920s* (2001). She has published numerous articles on women's history and women's activism in journals such as *Feminist Studies*, *Radical History Review*, and *Social History* and edited *A Companion to American Women's History* (2002). Her current research includes a biography of antebellum activist Amy Post and an edited volume, *No Permanent Waves: Recasting Histories of American Feminism.*

Stephen Brier, Executive Editor, cofounded the American Social History Project in 1981 with the late Herbert Gutman and served as its Executive Director until 1998. He was the supervising editor and coauthor of the first edition of the *Who Built America?* textbook and executive editor of the second edition. He also coauthored the two *Who Built America?* CD-ROMs and was the executive producer of ASHP's award-winning *Who Built America?* video series and the Web site *History Matters: The U.S. Survey Course on the Web*. Dr. Brier is the Vice President for Information Technology and External Programs, the co-director of the New Media Lab, and the coordinator of the doctoral Certificate Program in Interactive Technology and Pedagogy at the Graduate Center of the City University of New York. He has written numerous scholarly and popular articles on race, class, and ethnicity in U.S. labor history and on the educational impact of instructional media and information technology.

Joshua Brown, Visual Editor, is the Executive Director of the American Social History Project/Center for Media and Learning and Professor of History at the Graduate Center of the City University of New York. He was visual editor of the first edition of *Who Built America?* and also coauthored the accompanying CD-ROMs and video documentary series. He has served as executive producer on many digital and Web projects, including *Liberty, Equality, Fraternity: Exploring the French Revolution, History Matters: The U.S. Survey Course on the Web, The Lost Museum: Exploring Antebellum American Life and Culture,* and *The September 11 Digital Archive.* Brown is author of *Beyond the Lines: Pictorial Reporting, Everyday Life, and the Crisis of Gilded Age America* (2002), coauthor (with Eric Foner) of *Forever Free: The Story of Emancipation and Reconstruction* (2005), and coeditor of *History from South Africa: Alternative Visions and Practices* (1991), as well as numerous essays and reviews on the history of U.S. visual culture. He serves on the editorial boards of *Common-place*, *Labor*, and the *Encyclopedia of American Studies* and is a member of the American Antiquarian Society. His cartoons and illustrations appear regularly in academic and popular publications in print and online.

Pennee Bender, Supervising Editor, is the Associate Director and a Media Producer with the American Social History Project/Center for Media and Learning at the Graduate Center of the City University of New York. She was a co-creator of the Web site *History Matters: The U.S. Survey Course on the Web* and of two CD-ROMs: *Who Built America? From the Great War of 1914 to the Dawn of the Atomic Age* and *Liberty, Equality, Fraternity: Exploring the French Revolution*. She also served as Web producer of *The Lost Museum: Exploring Antebellum American Life and Culture* and *What Exit: New Jersey and Its Turnpike*. Her film and video credits include *Savage Acts: Wars, Fairs, and Empire; Heaven Will Protect the Working Girl; The West Bank: Whose Promised Land; Bitter Cane; Missing Persons/Personas Ausentes;* and *Labor Produces*. She has a Ph.D. in U.S. history from New York University and teaches working women's history at the Cornell Institute for Industrial and Labor Relations.

Ellen Noonan, Supervising Editor, works as a director of education programs and a media producer at the American Social History Project/Center for Media and Learning at the Graduate Center of the City University of New York. While with ASHP/CML, she has helped to conceptualize and write for the Web sites *History Matters: The U.S. Survey Course on the Web, The Lost Museum: Exploring Antebellum American Life and Culture*, and *The September 11 Digital Archive*. She has also designed and implemented faculty development programs serving hundreds of New York City public school social studies teachers. She served as Managing Editor and member of the Editorial Collective of *Radical History Review*, and she received her Ph.D. in U.S. History from New York University.

David Jaffee teaches American material culture at the Bard Graduate Center for Studies in the Decorative Arts, Design, and Culture. He is the author of *People of the Wachusett: Greater New England in History and Memory, 1630–1860* (1999) and is completing a book titled *Craftsmen and Consumers in Early America, 1760–1860*. He has also written many essays on artists and artisans in early America as well as on the use of new media in the history classroom. He was the project director of two NEH grants at the City College of New York to develop multimedia resources for the teaching of U.S. history. He has been the recipient of various fellowships from organizations including the Metropolitan Museum of Art, the Winterthur Museum, and the Huntington Library.

Who Built America?

THIRD EDITION

Volume One
To 1877

Part One

Colonization and Revolution

1492–1815

THE END OF THE FIFTEENTH CENTURY marked the beginning of modern America, as explorers from Europe encountered the inhabitants of the Americas and Africa. Spurred by crises in their own societies, European rulers, adventurers, and merchants commenced a frenetic search for new sources of wealth, and Christian rulers sent missionaries to convert the native peoples their countrymen encountered. They created a vast new system of expropriation and trade across the Atlantic, linking together and dramatically transforming Africa, the Americas, and Europe itself. The quest for riches and the accompanying search for souls to convert to Christianity prompted both creativity and destruction.

The settlement and growth of European societies in the Americas was part of a broader process of empire building. The colonies made possible a massive accumulation of wealth for the elites of Europe and for some of the colonists themselves. It underlay in both North America and Europe the development of capitalism — a new economic system based on private ownership and free trade that redefined social classes and fostered distinctive political ideologies and societal values. Many of the peoples who were caught up in the overseas expansion of European empires, however, saw their own worlds crumble as a result of disease, death, and intrusion. Colonists violently seized land from the native inhabitants of the Americas and forcibly enslaved millions of Africans to provide labor for their New World settlements. Even the white people who crewed trading vessels and slave ships or labored in the fields and towns of the New World faced hardship, danger, and premature death.

Spain, France, Holland, and England all staked claims in North America as they sought to expand their Atlantic-based empires, establishing trading ports, missions, plantations, and settlements in varying stages of permanence. From the mid-seventeenth century onward, however, England's Chesapeake Bay and New England colonies attracted the most settlers, achieved the fastest population growth, and destroyed or disrupted native American groups that stood in the way of their expanding settlements. The English also settled in the Carolinas, captured land claimed by the Dutch, and continued their expansion into the Mid-Atlantic region, from New York to Pennsylvania. During the eighteenth century, the success of their colonies helped Britain achieve a dominant position over France and Spain in North America.

Colonies developed according to the varied objectives of their investors and settlers. The South proved attractive to those who sought profit from the land itself; its favorable soils and climate fostered the emergence of plantation agriculture sustained by the labor first of indentured servants and then of African slaves. Indentured servants, slaves, and wage workers toiled in the North as well, but the aims of northern colonists — many seeking religious ideals and independent land ownership unattainable in Britain — led to the creation of smaller-scale farming and craft economies based primarily on family labor. Distinct labor systems — free and unfree — increasingly defined the ways of life of the two regions.

All the American colonies, however, faced political, economic, religious, and racial conflicts. Colonists' expansion meant increasing conflict with native groups whose land they sought, periodically inciting full-scale wars. Slaveholders struggled with enslaved Africans, who proved unwilling laborers. Colonists also struggled with each other over who would own the land, who would govern society, and how to conduct religious life. For the many less wealthy European settlers in America, their own aspirations for economic independence and liberty from oppression led them to clash with wealthier colonists who sought to exploit or control them. Just as slaves tried to resist their enslavement, ordinary colonists adopted methods of protest and political organization to assert what they saw as their natural rights. British settlers and their descendants especially, influenced by the radical ideologies of the English Civil War in the mid-seventeenth century, claimed political rights as "freeborn Englishmen" and nurtured a belief in social equality.

By the 1760s, internal conflicts had merged with the larger issue of the colonies' continuing relationship with their "mother country." Colonial activists took steps to secure their rights as subjects of the British empire. When their protests led to war with Britain in the 1770s, they found themselves pursuing complete independence from British rule. A broad coalition of Americans — rich, middling, and poor; northern and southern; men and women — supported independence and finally secured it in 1783, achieving the first successful New World colonial revolution.

People of the newly independent United States sought to establish a system of government based on republican principles, avoiding the formal social inequalities and hierarchies of European societies. However, particularly when determining what shape their national government would take, Americans disagreed as to who was best fitted to govern in a postrevolutionary society. Advocates of both elite and popular rule disputed this issue well into the nineteenth century. What was made clear, however, was that political rights would extend only to certain Americans. Women, slaves, and even many free men of color found themselves partly or wholly excluded from the benefits of citizenship in the new republic.

Throughout the colonial and revolutionary periods, then, tension existed in America between those with full access to economic and political rights and those who had those rights denied them. This tension and the aspirations of laboring Americans shaped America's early history and defined its emergence as an independent nation. Famous political leaders did not always control events. They were constantly challenged, and events themselves profoundly influenced, by the aspirations and experiences of the ordinary men and women of all cultures who built America.

1

A Meeting of Three Worlds

Europe, Africa, and American Colonization

1492–1680

America

The natural bounty of the New
World was put on display in this
seventeenth-century Flemish
painting. On the left of the
central panel, America is represented by Indians who lounge
alongside the favored object of
European desire: a collection of
gold weights. Jan van Kessel the
Elder, *America*, oil on copper, 19 1/8
× 26 5/8 inches, 1664–66—Alte
Pinakothek, Bayerische Staats-
gemäldesammlungen, Munich.

I N 1492, THE GENOESE-BORN sea captain Christopher Columbus
and his Spanish crewmen landed on a small island in the Bahamas after
a two-month Atlantic voyage and met the inhabitants, who called the island
Guanahaní. The encounter was friendly, but Columbus had plans for these
people. Leaving a Spanish encampment on a large nearby island he had
renamed "Hispaniola," he captured six native men and brought them back
with him to Spain. Columbus's appropriation of these men and of the territories he encountered indicated the European intention to gain wealth and
power from overseas exploration.

Columbus had sailed in the service of King Ferdinand and Queen
Isabella of Spain, searching for a western route to the Indies, the Asian
source of spices and other valuable goods. Thinking that he had reached the
Indies, Columbus and Europeans after him called the native inhabitants
"Indians." Columbus made three subsequent voyages and apparently
believed to his death, in 1506, that he had reached Asia. But other explorers
had already questioned this belief. One of them, Amerigo Vespucci, calculated that these lands were part of a continent unknown to Europeans. In
1507, in Vespucci's honor, a German mapmaker named this continent
"America."

Columbus and his crew were not, in fact, the first Europeans in America. In the eleventh century, Scandinavians had reached Labrador and Newfoundland, where they built a short-lived settlement. But other Europeans

had no knowledge of that venture; to them, Columbus's 1492 voyage marked the "discovery" of a "New World" that they would compete avidly with natives and with each other to possess. Seeking wealth or land, they commenced a process of conquest and settlement that would alter or destroy the lives of the peoples who already lived there. To Native Americans, it marked the beginning of a long invasion that would see them colonized, conquered, and in many places almost wiped out.

Tragedy tinged even the first contacts. Columbus took his six captives to the royal court at Barcelona, where they excited much curiosity, were baptized into the Catholic Church, and were given Spanish names. But they did not live long in Spain. Some were taken back to the Caribbean; one man became a page at court but soon died. Columbus, meanwhile, returned to Hispaniola to find his crewmen vanished. Intentionally or accidentally, disease, malnutrition, violence, murder, and destruction would in places reach catastrophic proportions.

Europe's encounter with the Americas would transform both continents and soon would involve Africa, too. Traders, warriors, missionaries, and adventurers would forge commercial, political, and religious changes on all three continents, bringing new wealth to some people and exposing others to great brutality and misery. Even in Europe, the chief beneficiary of contact with the New World, conquest and colonization would contribute to inequality and social conflict.

Europeans dreamed of finding wealth in the New World but knew that to do so, they would need much labor. Columbus predicted that the natives he encountered "should be good and intelligent servants." The history of the Americas would be shaped by the efforts of conquerors and settlers to use first Native American and then European and African labor to exploit the continent's riches. In the process, most of these laborers had to endure poverty and untimely death, but they were the people who built America.

Peoples of the New World

None of those involved in the encounter between Europe, the Americas, and Africa were a single people. Most varied of all were the inhabitants of the Americas. Evidence about their origins is thin and uneven, and archaeologists continue to debate it hotly. Until recently, it was conventional to trace the earliest Americans to a period approximately 13,000 years ago, late in the last Ice Age, when groups from Siberia migrated across the dry land that linked Asia with Alaska before rising sea levels separated the continents. Recent findings suggest that people may also have reached the Americas by sea from Southeast Asia via Polynesia as much as 20,000 or more years ago and that several different migrations populated the continents before about 4000 B.C.E. At any event, migrants and their descendants spread across

North and South America and to the Caribbean islands, building a vast array of cultures and languages. By 1492, there may have been as many as 50 or 100 million people in the Americas, perhaps one-seventh of the world's population. But their isolation from the rest of the world—particularly their lack of immunity to European diseases—left them vulnerable as Europeans started coming to the Americas in the late fifteenth century.

Centralized Empires in Central and South America   Some Central and South American societies had developed strong states. That of the Incas, centered in present-day Peru and Bolivia, had expanded in the fifteenth century into an empire stretching far along the Andes Mountains and South America's western coast. Common peoples' obligatory labor supported a royal family surrounded by aristocrats. Women wove cloth that was prized in commerce and religious ritual. Men grew crops and built extensive road and canal systems that united the empire and irrigated arid land.

The Aztecs of Mexico, too, forged a loosely confederated empire during the fifteenth century, conquering the descendants of earlier Olmec, Mayan, and Toltec empires and exacting tribute payments from outlying tribes. Fifteen to twenty million strong, the Aztecs boasted impressive achievements in irrigation, metallurgy, and city-building. Tenochtitlán, the capital, had over a quarter of a million inhabitants. Aztec society was based on clans that organized farming, much of it on communal lands. Its upper ranks, headed by a figure the Spanish would call an "emperor," included priests, generals, and wealthy merchants. But most Aztec people were craft workers, farmers, laborers, soldiers, or slaves.

Dispersed Societies to the North   America north of Mexico was more sparsely populated. Archaeologists disagree as to how many people inhabited its vast land area. Estimates vary from one million to eighteen million, but most suggest that there were around five million in 1500. These groups, smaller than those farther south, spoke some 375 different languages, many of which also had mutually unintelligible dialects. Native American societies had long been based on hunting, fishing, and gathering wild plant foods. Starting around 3000 B.C.E. in the Southwest and spreading northward and eastward over nearly three thousand years, the cultivation of maize (corn) and other crops had also evolved. In most cases, women performed the main tasks of raising and preparing food. The Hohokam culture (300 B.C.E. to 800 C.E.) of present-day Arizona and the later pueblo peoples of the

The New Chronicle and Good Government

This drawing by an Andean nobleman, Felipe Guamán Poma de Ayala, depicts the Incan view of the world. The kingdom of Peru, the capital city of Cuzco in its center, is situated at the top of the world, overshadowing Spain below. Guamán Poma's 1200-page *Nueva corónica y buen gobierno*, illustrated with 400 quill drawings, was written between 1587 and 1615. It comprises a unique Andean interpretation of Peruvian history from the Creation through the Spanish conquest. Felipe Guamán Poma de Ayala, *El primer nueva corónica y buen gobierno* (1936)—American Social History Project.

highlands north of Mexico built irrigation systems not unlike those that the Incas and Aztecs would subsequently construct.

Farming meant more dependable food supplies and population growth. Groups that cultivated crops became more stable and often more powerful than neighbors who still relied on hunting and gathering. Pueblo societies of the Southwest were among the most complex. By the twelfth century, the inhabitants of Chaco Canyon had twelve towns and over two hundred villages, each built of contiguous rooms, that altogether housed 15,000 people. Corn-cultivating societies in the Mississippi Valley built urban centers and became socially stratified. The largest town, at Cahokia, near present-day St. Louis, covered around 6 square miles and housed at least 10,000 people before it went into decline in the thirteenth century.

Some groups, such as the Jumanos of the Southwest and the Ottawas of the Great Lakes region, were known as traders. On the plains and prairies of the West, groups hunted buffalo; some, like the Pawnees, exchanged meat for grain with corn-growing societies nearby. Eastward to the Atlantic coast, where most of the early encounters with Europeans took place, people combined horticulture, hunting, and trade.

Gathering the Harvest

A drawing from Guamán Poma's *Nueva corónica* depicts Incans gathering the annual May harvest before the Spanish conquest. Felipe Guamán Poma de Ayala, *El primer nueva corónica y buen gobierno* (1936)—American Social History Project.

Eastern Woodland Indians Most Eastern woodland peoples lived in family-based societies with little organized hierarchy. Except in the far Northeast, where the climate and poor soil prevented farming, they relied on cultivated crops—typically corn, beans, and squashes—for half or more of their food. Women worked the fields, located close to villages so that they could coordinate crop raising with other tasks. Villages, each with up to a few hundred inhabitants, contained easily moved shelters and could relocate according to seasonal and ecological changes. Strong kinship ties bound individuals to one another. Land and water were the common property of each village, and all inhabitants shared in the yield of hunt and harvest. "Every proprietor knows his own," an English observer noted, "yet all things . . . are used in common amongst them."

The absence of accumulated personal property ensured a roughly equal distribution of wealth. The Iroquois, wrote a French missionary, had no poorhouses "because there are neither mendicants nor paupers. . . . A whole village must be without corn before any individual can be obliged to endure privation." Sharing goods reinforced individuals' sense of group belonging,

Ancient Cliff Dwellers

The Ancestral Pueblo people occupied the Four Corners area (where the present-day states of Arizona, New Mexico, Colorado, and Utah meet) from approximately 1 to 1300 C.E. They developed extensive irrigation works and apartment complexes in the arid Southwest. The remains of one of their settlements, in southwestern Colorado's Mesa Verde National Park, features an amazing array of architectural styles. First, pit houses were dug into the hilltop mesas; as the population increased, two- and three-story houses followed. Around 1200, for reasons not entirely known, "cliff houses"—large, multistory apartment complexes fashioned of sandstone blocks—were built in alcoves on the canyon walls. More than six hundred cliff houses exist in Mesa Verde today. Residents left the settlements during an extended drought in the late thirteenth century. Horace Swartley Poley, 1901—Denver Public Library.

and there were strong sanctions against unacceptable behavior, from public disapproval or ridicule to expulsion and exile.

Many groups were matrilineal; identity and status descended from mothers to children. Eastern woodland groups tended also to be matrilocal—after marriage, men moved into their wives' households. Leadership in these groups was not restricted to men. Some women enjoyed a degree of personal independence and power. Prominent Iroquois women controlled

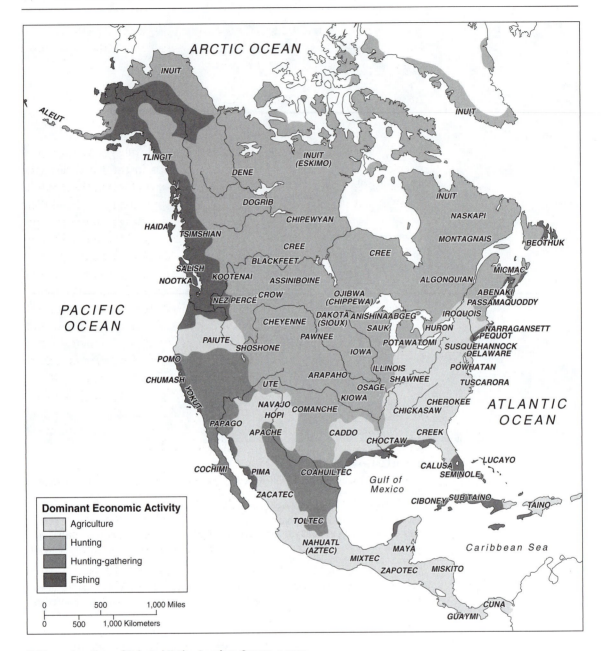

MAP 1.1 Locations of Selected Native American Groups, c. 1500

This map shows just some among the great number and variety of Indian societies in North America at the time of European contact, including several of the East Coast groups that would come into conflict with the first English colonists in the seventeenth century.

their own homes and fields, could divorce at will, and had the right to choose leaders from among their menfolk. They supervised their appointees and could remove them for misdeeds or incompetence.

America's Peoples at Contact   Native American societies were not static but had faced long periods of change and conflict (Map 1.1). Between the twelfth and fifteenth centuries, large settlements such as Chaco Canyon and Cahokia declined, and their populations dispersed to villages. Wars erupted over access to land and resources. Five groups in the Northeast (the Mohawk, Oneida, Cayuga, Onondaga, and Seneca) formed the Iroquois Confederacy in the fifteenth century, apparently to reduce such conflicts between them. The Confederacy, though, aggravated tensions with other groups. Martial prowess became so prized that Iroquois leadership commonly passed to those who were reputed to be the best warriors.

Two common factors influenced the terms on which indigenous societies would face contact with Europeans. The fact that no society north of Mexico had an overarching state like those of the Aztecs and Incas had advantages and disadvantages. When the Spanish invaded Central and South America after 1518, they had quickly toppled the Aztec and Inca empires. Few North American groups faced such rapid collapse. However, their dispersion and disunity made cohesive response or resistance to invasion difficult to attain.

A second factor was the process that scholars now call the Columbian Exchange. European contact with Africa and the Americas initiated an exchange of flora, fauna, and microorganisms between ecosystems that had hitherto been isolated from one another. New World crop seeds were carried to Europe, along with diseases such as syphilis, which spread there rapidly after arriving in the 1520s. But the effect of European organisms on America was more dramatic. Newly introduced grasses drove out existing species, and domesticated livestock flourished on a continent where they had been unknown. Most damaging was the fact that new human diseases had disastrous effects on populations that lacked immunity to them. In some areas, typhus, influenza, measles, and smallpox wiped out 90 percent of native peoples by 1600. Such devastation—by reducing native populations and undermining their societies—would help conquerors and settlers shape their colonies to serve their own purposes.

The Background to Overseas Expansion: Europe and Africa

Led by Hernán Cortés, a Spanish expedition set out in 1518 to conquer Mexico. Successive waves of conquistadors followed. One wrote that he did so "for King, God, and Gold," summing up the motivations that drove Europeans to explore and seize overseas territory. Changes in Europe over the centuries before 1500 had initiated political consolidation, religious division, and commercial development. These in turn fostered overseas trade and conquest, which led first to closer links between Europe and West Africa and then to the colonization of Atlantic islands. As Europe's interest in the Americas deepened, it drew Africa more tightly into the process.

Politics, Religion, and Commerce in Western Europe   Early in the fourteenth century, European population growth peaked. Wars and changes in climate hampered food production just as growing populations were stretching resources to their limits. The consequent famine was followed in the 1340s by plague—the Black Death—that ravaged many parts of the continent. Between 1300 and 1400, Europe lost two-fifths or more of its people.

Aristocratic landlords held most of the land in Europe, and they controlled the labor of peasant serfs who were legally bound to the land. Population loss weakened these feudal ties between landlords and serfs and challenged or toppled monarchical dynasties. As population and wealth grew again in the fifteenth century, however, some monarchs created new military and administrative structures that asserted their power over unruly nobles. The uniting of the crowns of Aragon and Castile in 1469 created a strong Spanish monarchy, while the ascent of the Tudor dynasty in England in 1485 ended the long baronial feuding known as the Wars of the Roses and began a consolidation of royal administration. Such "new monarchies" formed nation-states that would soon compete for wealth and territory overseas.

As monarchies consolidated, Roman Christendom began to fragment. Discontent with the wealth and corruption of the papacy and clergy fostered religious dissent in some regions and efforts at church renewal and reform elsewhere. Spain produced a revitalized Catholicism symbolized by the piety of King Ferdinand and Queen Isabella, but in Germany and other parts of northern Europe from 1517 on, Martin Luther and other reformers sparked a revolt, known as the Protestant Reformation, that led many churches to break with Rome. In Sweden and many German principalities, the Reformation secured the adherence of rulers who saw religion as a vehicle for state power. The English king Henry VIII, too, severed ties with Rome in 1534, in a clash with the papacy over his wish for a divorce, and declared himself head of a separate Church of England. From midcentury onward, as Catholic reform turned into an effort to regain lost ground, wars between Protestants and Catholics wracked France, Germany, and the Netherlands.

This turmoil added a religious dimension to overseas exploration and colonization. Especially in Catholic Europe, the pursuit of territory was

The Beak Doctor

An illustration from a seventeenth-century medical history shows the recommended outfit to be worn by doctors during the "plague years." The long-nosed mask filled with perfumes and disinfectants, along with the gogglelike lenses covering the eyes, was supposed to protect doctors from the deadly airborne "miasmas" that were believed to spread the Black Death. Thomas Bartholin, *Historiarum anatomicarum medicarum rariorum* (1661)—Prints and Photographs Division, Library of Congress.

clothed in the imperative to convert "heathen" indigenous peoples to Catholicism. Spain revitalized religious orders such as the Franciscans and Dominicans, making them spearheads of the Faith in the New World. Struggles against Protestantism spurred a redoubling of efforts to save souls overseas as priests belonging to new orders, such as the Society of Jesus (Jesuits), also became missionaries.

Political and religious impulses for expansion were underpinned by developments in trade and shipping that marked Europe's recovery from the crisis of the Black Death. Banking spread to northern Europe from its origins in Italy, strengthening a commercial revival that accompanied the growth of urban populations from 1400 onward. Merchants accumulated capital to invest in the rich trade in luxury goods from Asia. But the expansion of the Islamic Ottoman empire and the dominance of the Asian trade by states such as Venice hampered their efforts. Accordingly, they sought alternative routes to the sources of this trade and of the gold and silver that could purchase the goods. Monarchs wanting to pay for their new governments and armies were also eager for new sources of wealth.

Society and Trade in West Africa   The search for wealth first drew Europeans into increasing contact with trading societies in Africa. Africa's total population may have exceeded eighty million, four-fifths of it located south of the Sahara. From the Islamic traders of the Indian Ocean port of Mombasa to the farmers of the fertile forest regions of what is now Nigeria to the food-collecting San and cattle-keeping Khoi-Khoi of the south, the continent contained a wide diversity of cultures and economies. In complexity and prosperity, many African societies compared with those of Europe and Central America (Map 1.2).

West Africa, which would have the most importance for New World developments, had roughly eleven million inhabitants in 1500. Towns such as Timbuktu, Gao, and Benin were significant trading centers, home to merchants, craft workers, scholars, and priests and to handicrafts, the arts, education, and legal systems. Most West Africans, however, were rural dwellers, belonging to groups organized around kinship networks. Families raised livestock and cultivated crops with iron tools of a type made in the region for more than a thousand years.

Kin groups owned land communally, and households often cooperated to produce food. Women dominated food production and were active in the marketplaces, where they sold surplus produce. Polygyny, whereby one man had several wives, was common, especially among the wealthy. Family and clan leaders exercised authority in the collective leadership of villages and larger political confederations. Religious beliefs varied from place to place, but most West Africans believed that they were part of a spiritual world

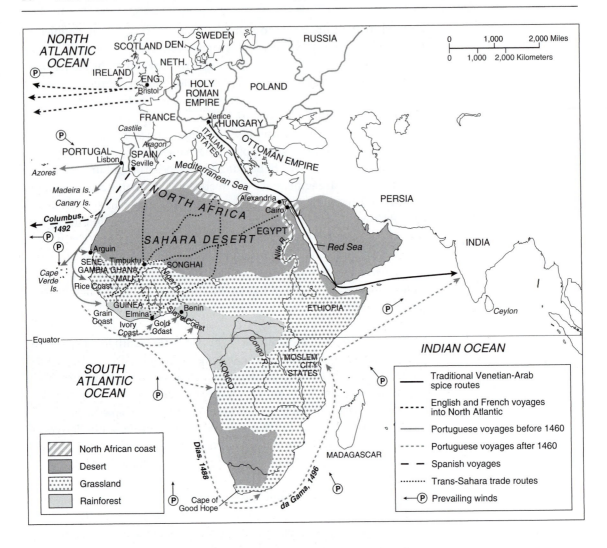

MAP 1.2 Europe and Africa, c. 1492

Trade centers in West Africa had long-standing links with the Mediterranean coast, the Middle East, and the lands along the Indian Ocean. Portuguese explorers established direct European links with West Africa, building trading forts like that at Elmina that would subsequently become important centers of the transatlantic slave trade.

shaped by the cycles of nature, the legacy of ancestors, and an all-knowing Creator. In the towns and grasslands south of the Sahara, there was growing adherence to Islam.

The labor of slaves often supplemented that of family members. Slavery was an ancient system, with roots in ancient Greece and Rome, in Africa and Byzantium, under Islam and under Christianity. It had largely died out in Western Europe but was common in West Africa, where slaves were attached to kinship or family groups and worked in the fields or at household tasks. Some slaves had been captured in warfare, some were debtors, others were criminals. Many slaves had some rights, and slave status rarely passed from parent to child. Some slaves could work for their freedom; some married into the families that held them; some even owned property. But slavery had

Benin

An engraving from a seventeenth-century Dutch survey of Africa features the royal court of Benin in the foreground, while the expansive city stretches into the distance. Olfert Dapper, *Naukeurige Beschrijvinge der Afrikaensche Gewesten van Egyptien, Barbaryen, Libyen . . .* (1676) — Rare Books and Manuscript Division, New York Public Library, Astor, Lenox and Tilden Foundations.

harsher aspects too. Some societies put slaves to sacrificial death, and there was a growing slave trade with trans-Saharan and Indian Ocean markets, where women and children, especially, were in demand for their labor or for sexual purposes.

Most West African societies were stateless, but warfare and slavery had led villages and kin groups to increase reliance on kingdoms, whose rulers offered protection and fostered commerce in return for tribute and taxes. The Mali empire, centered in the Niger River valley, was one of the world's largest empires in the early fifteenth century but then was eclipsed first by the Songhai empire and later by smaller but powerful kingdoms — Benin, Dahomey, and Kongo — that rose to prominence after 1600.

Such states encouraged West Africa's important trading networks. Merchants exercised significant economic and political power. Commercial towns exported gold, ivory, cotton goods, leather, spices, and slaves to

"Our Land Is Uncommonly Rich and Fruitful . . .": Olaudah Equiano Describes Benin

According to his autobiography, The Interesting Narrative of the Life of Olaudah Equiano, *Olaudah Equiano was kidnapped at age eleven from his home in the Benin Empire on the Guinea coast in southern Nigeria, sold into slavery, and brought to the New World. During his decade as a slave, Equiano served an English naval officer and worked in the shipping business of a Montserrat merchant, finally purchasing his freedom with money earned by trading on his own. Published in London in 1789, his autobiography includes this description of the West African world of his childhood. Although some scholars question whether Equiano was in fact born in Africa, most still consider his account a rare source of information about Africa in this period, one that is probably based on a mixture of his own and others' experiences.*

The Kingdom of Benin . . . is divided into many provinces or districts, in one of the most remote and fertile of which I was born, in the year 1745, situated in a charming, fruitful vale named Essaka. The distance of this province from the capital of Benin and the seacoast must be very considerable; for I had never heard of white men or Europeans, nor of the sea; and our subjection to the king of Benin was little more than nominal. . . .

We are almost a nation of dancers, musicians, and poets. Thus every great event, such as a triumphant return from battle, or other cause of public rejoicing, is celebrated in public dances, which are accompanied with songs and music suited to the occasion. The assembly is separated into four divisions [or age grades]. . . . Each represents some interesting scene of real life, such as a great achievement, domestic employment, a pathetic story, or some rural sport. . . . This gives our dances a spirit and a variety which I have scarcely seen elsewhere. We have many musical instruments, particularly drums of different kinds, a piece of music which resembles a guitar, and another much like a stickado [xylophone].

Our manner of living is entirely plain; for as yet the natives are unacquainted with those refinements in cookery which debauch the taste: bullocks, goats, and poultry supply the greatest part of their food. These constitute likewise the principal wealth of the country, and the chief articles of its commerce. The flesh is usually stewed in a pan. To make it savory we sometimes use also pepper and other spices; and we have salt made of wood ashes. Our vegetables are mostly plantains [bananas], yams, beans, and Indian corn. The head of the family usually eats alone; his wives and slaves have also their separate tables. . . .

Our land is uncommonly rich and fruitful, and produces all kinds of vegetables in great abundance. We have plenty of Indian corn, and vast quantities of cotton and tobacco. . . . All our industry is exerted to improve those blessings of nature. Agriculture is our chief employment; and every one, even the children and women, are engaged in it. Thus we are all habituated to labor from our earliest years. Every one contributes something to the common stock; and, as we are unacquainted with idleness, we have no beggars. The benefits of such a mode of living are obvious.

Olaudah Equiano, *The Interesting Narrative of the Life of Olaudah Equiano* (1789).

markets in North Africa, the Middle East, and Europe. A European visitor to Benin city found a rich array of goods in its markets:

> Pepper and elephant teeth, oil of palm, cloth made of cotton wool very curiously woven, and cloth made of the bark of palm trees . . . iron works of sundry sorts, Manillos or bracelets of copper, glass beads and coral. . . . They have good store of soap . . . also many pretty fine mats and baskets that they make, and spoons of elephant's teeth very curiously wrought with divers proportions of fowls and beasts made upon them.

Looking for the goods that West Africa's trading networks had to offer, Portuguese sea captains ventured down its coast. In 1470, they reached the Gold Coast (now mostly in Ghana), later establishing a trading post at Elmina and fortifying it against European rivals. Before 1492, trade with the Gold Coast provided two-thirds of Europe's gold supply. By 1600, Portugal

West Africa

This 1606 Venetian map emphasizes the coastal trading centers of Western Africa, incorrectly portraying the interior as largely uninhabited. Giovanni Battista Ramusio, *Della navigationi et viaggi raccolte* . . . (1606)—Rare Books and Manuscript Division, New York Public Library, Astor, Lenox and Tilden Foundations.

was shipping out 170,000 gold coins each year, obtained in payment for wheat, cloth, and metal goods.

West African societies' strength and commercial sophistication enabled them to trade with Europeans while confining these outsiders largely to river and coastal centers. The disease-riddled environment also proved harsh for Europeans, who succumbed at alarming rates to malaria and other fatal tropical afflictions. Consequently, Europeans made little effort to establish extensive colonial settlements in West Africa. But they did use African commerce and slavery as instruments in their encounters with the newly found Americas.

The Invasion of the Americas Begins: Portugal, Spain, and the Need for Labor

The immediate cause of Europeans' interest in the Americas lay in developments in Spain and Portugal. Since early in the fifteenth century, Portuguese fishing and trading vessels had probed the Atlantic. In time, they established the island colonies of Madeira, the Cape Verde Islands, and the island of São Tomé off the African coast. Navigational experience and trade with West Africa after 1470 led to a concerted effort to reach the East Indies. In 1487, a voyage led by Bartholomeu Dias rounded southern Africa; ten years later, Vasco da Gama and his crew sailed all the way to India.

The Spanish empire grew out of conquest at home. On and off since the twelfth century, Spain's Catholic rulers and nobles had attempted to drive out or convert Islamic settlers in the south of Spain. This *reconquista*, renewed around 1450, culminated in the Spanish monarchy's defeat of the kingdom of Granada in 1492 and the expulsion or forced conversion of its Muslim and Jewish population. From the 1470s to 1496, Spanish troops also fought to create a colony in the Canary Islands, exploiting indigenous labor and annihilating the inhabitants in the process.

Both Spain and Portugal commenced practices that they would carry to the New World. As early as 1444, Portuguese traders were purchasing slaves in West Africa for transport to Portugal as lifelong domestic servants. After they established settlements on Madeira and other islands off the African coast, the Portuguese took slaves there, too, and as settlers developed plantations for growing sugarcane, they purchased African slaves to work them, building a prototype for forced labor in the growing Atlantic economy.

Columbus Discovers . . . ?
A plate from a 1493 edition of Columbus's letters depicts an explorer landing somewhere — but not in America. The galley ship in the foreground, which could never have endured an ocean voyage, bears no resemblance to Columbus's vessels. The illustration probably derived from an older publication about Mediterranean exploration. Christopher Columbus, *Letter to Sanchez* (1493) — Rare Books and Manuscript Division, New York Public Library, Astor, Lenox and Tilden Foundations.

Oxema y Juanteo de los templos idolaticos de la prouin° de Taxcala
por los frayles y Españoles y consentim° de los naturales

Implanting a New Faith

A sixteenth-century Spanish drawing approvingly documents the destruction of Aztec temples in Tlaxcala, Mexico. Glasgow University Library.

Overseas Expansion and Conquest King Ferdinand and Queen Isabella authorized Columbus's voyage just after the fall of Granada. Their aim was to extend westward the militancy that Spain had successfully employed at home. Landing on Guanahaní, Columbus at once claimed the island as a Spanish possession and gave it a Spanish name (San Salvador), an act he and other Spaniards would repeat whenever they came across new territory.

Columbus's voyage spurred exploration and its associated mission of Christian conversion. In 1493, Pope Alexander VI granted Spain the right to spread the gospels in the Americas. The next year, Spain and Portugal signed the treaty of Tordesillas, in which they divided the entire world between them, an act of arrogance that was soon marred for Spain when Brazil was discovered in the Portuguese zone. Portugal laid claim to Brazil in 1500 and over the next half-century prepared to extend its Atlantic island plantation labor system to South America (Map 1.3).

Spain, meanwhile, extended its exploration of the Caribbean. In 1502, Spanish families were settled on Hispaniola, and soon they were colonizing Cuba, Puerto Rico, Jamaica, and other islands. After 1508, there were ventures onto the Central American mainland, and in 1513, Vasco Núñez de Balboa crossed the Isthmus of Panama, became the first European to see the Pacific Ocean, and confirmed that the Americas were a separate continent. The Aztec emperor learned promptly of this Spanish activity but punished priest-diviners who foretold an invasion of Mexico. Within a few years, however, Hernán Cortés and his troops marched on Tenochtitlán and captured it.

Spanish slaughtering and looting provoked a revolt, and the Aztecs drove Cortés and his men back. But they recaptured Tenochtitlán in 1521, assisted by fire and disease, which killed or dispersed much of the population. The capital's fall started the collapse of the Aztec empire itself, a process that was hastened by revolts among tribes the Aztecs had subdued. The conquerors soon established Spanish rule, put ordinary men and women to forced labor, hunted down nobles and priests, and set about destroying the knowledge and learning that had sustained what the Spaniards considered a "heathen" civilization.

Moving beyond the valley of Mexico, the invaders conquered the Maya of the Yucatan and pressed into South America. From 1524 onward, Francisco Pizarro led explorations of the Pacific coast, and in 1532–1533, his

MAP 1.3 Spanish and Portuguese Possessions in the Americas, to c. 1610

This map conveys the rapidity and scale of Spanish colonization in South and Central America and the Caribbean, and smaller incursions into North America. Spain and Portugal's 1494 treaty attempting to divide the globe between them gave the latter Brazil, which the Portuguese turned into an important plantation slave society in the sixteenth and seventeenth centuries.

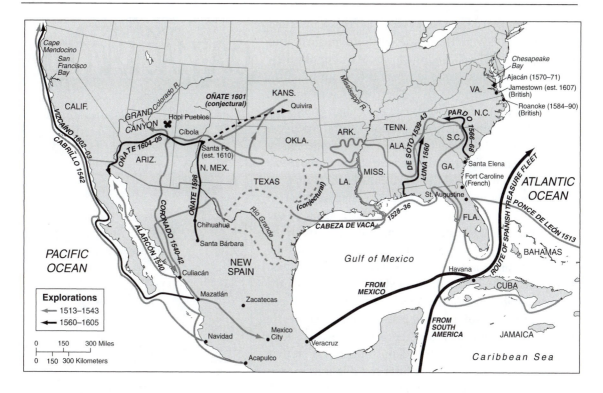

MAP 1.4 Spanish Exploration in North America, 1513–1610

The gold-seeking expeditions of Hernando de Soto, Francisco Vázquez de Coronado, and others before the mid-sixteenth century laid the foundation of settlements in Florida and New Mexico.

forces invaded the Incas' heartland in the Peruvian Andes (Map 1.4). The capture of the Incan capital, Cuzco, provoked a political collapse, and despite rebellions against the invaders, the Incan empire folded as rapidly as that of the Aztecs.

If conquistadors fought for "King" and "God," they also envied Portuguese access to African gold and wanted their own. Rumors abounded of fabulous wealth in the Americas. "Those lands do not produce bread or wine," claimed a Spanish writer, "but they do produce large quantities of gold, in which lordship consists." The Spanish first looted the treasures from Aztec and Inca temples and palaces but soon exhausted these riches and began searching for new sources. In 1545, they discovered huge silver ore deposits at Potosí in the Bolivian Andes; they found smaller ore fields in northern Mexico and elsewhere. The Spanish forced many thousands of indigenous people to work in these mines to send a flow of precious metals into Spanish coffers. Between 1500 and 1650, more than 180 tons of gold and 16,000 tons of silver extracted by Spain from the Americas significantly augmented the supply of capital available in Europe.

The search for gold also took the Spanish northward from Mexico. Two military expeditions around 1540 failed to find any riches, but soldiers brutally attacked the Indians who resisted them. Francisco Vásquez de

Coronado explored from New Mexico as far as Kansas and the Arkansas River. Hernando de Soto pushed into Florida, the Southeast, and the lower Mississippi valley, fighting one pitched battle in which thousands of native and Spanish combatants died. These incursions and the diseases they introduced weakened the Indian groups the Spaniards encountered. In what is now central Arkansas, Coronado found thriving towns that had disappeared by the time French explorers reached the region in the 1670s.

Spain then ignored the North until others took an interest in it. In 1562, some French Protestants settled on the Florida coast, but they had withdrawn again by the time the Spanish, fearing attacks on their treasure fleets, sent a force to remove them. In 1565, Spain founded the town of St. Augustine, now the oldest continually occupied European settlement in the United States. Subsequently, they explored as far as Chesapeake Bay, and in northern Florida, Spanish soldiers and priests established nearly forty mission stations. By 1600, the Spaniards were making similar efforts farther westward, pushing into what they named New Mexico, building forts and missions to subdue and convert the indigenous pueblos and, in 1608, founding the town of Santa Fe.

The Need for Labor   New territory could enhance a nation's power and prestige. Conquered peoples could be converted to Christianity. New land could provide wealth from mining, farming, or trade for governments, investors, and settlers. The Spanish crown, keen to use colonization as a means of rewarding, and thus controlling, Spain's lesser nobility, placed the conduct of overseas conquest under central control, creating the Council of the Indies in 1524 to administer the whole Spanish empire from the port city of Seville. But success depended on obtaining and directing the labor of millions of people.

Conquistadors and noble settlers did not intend to do any work themselves, nor could they attract sufficient emigrants from Spain or Portugal to work for them in the Americas. From Columbus onward, they hoped that labor would be provided by native peoples who could be forced to work for their new masters. Whether the Europeans were priests seeking souls to convert, planters seeking crops to export, or officials seeking taxes to collect, forced labor helped to give them what they wanted.

Adapting practices both from southern Spain and the Canary Islands and from Aztec society, the Spanish crown granted conquistadors in Mexico and Peru rights to share in the forced labor of native settlements. Cortés

"Yes, We Eat It"
This drawing from Guamán Poma's *Nueva corónica* depicts a meeting between an Incan king and one of the Spaniards left behind by Pizarro after his first voyage to Peru. Curious about the Spanish obsession with gold, the Incan used sign language to ask his visitor whether the Spaniards ate the metal. "Yes," the Spaniard answered, misunderstanding, "we eat it." According to Guamán Poma, to satisfy this strange diet, the Incans began to offer gold to the Spaniards. Felipe Guamán Poma de Ayala, *El primer nueva corónica y buen gobierno* (1936)—American Social History Project.

Bearing the Cross

After Franciscan friars arrived in Florida in 1573, they established a string of missions that extended 250 miles westward beyond coastal St. Augustine. Among them was the mission town of San Luis de Talimali in the heartland of the Apalachee people. This community of 1,400 residents was the largest of the mission towns, situated within the bounds of present-day Tallahassee. Archaeologists recently found a carved quartz crystal cross at the mission church, which is believed to have been produced by Native Americans for their burial rites. Mission San Luis, Florida Division of Historical Resources.

alone had 23,000 workers under this *encomienda* system by the mid-1520s, and in parts of Spanish America, it was used until the late seventeenth century to provide labor for missions, mines, and large farms. In Florida and New Mexico, missionaries resettled natives into peasant communities, forcing them to work erecting buildings and growing crops. The missions in Florida, with just seventy priests among them, claimed to have over 25,000 Christianized natives working for them by the mid-seventeenth century. Colonial governors exploited native labor to obtain private income. Church and government disputed over the right to put native inhabitants to work. In the Southwest, pueblo peoples came into the missions in part to evade harassment by marauding Spanish soldiers.

But native labor frequently did not fulfill colonists' hopes, even though distance from colonial authority often enabled them to treat indigenous populations mercilessly with little fear of restraint. Disease and the harsh demands of forced labor killed large numbers of natives in Spanish America throughout the sixteenth century. The Timucuans of Florida were about 350,000 strong in 1500, but a century later, only 7,000 remained; four out of every five New Mexican pueblos or villages were abandoned as populations declined. The *encomienda* provoked Indian resistance, and from the 1570s on, the Spanish partly replaced it with a less harsh system, known as the *repartimiento*, that obliged natives to provide involuntary but compensated labor on public works.

Some Spaniards criticized forced labor. In 1511, the Dominican priest Antonio Montesinos challenged the exploitation of natives, asking conquistadors "with what right and with what justice do you keep these poor Indians in such cruel and horrible servitude?" He influenced another priest, Bartolomé de Las Casas, who for half a century denounced the slaughter and ill treatment of New World peoples and the common Spanish assumption that natives were "slaves by nature."

Yet Las Casas knew that the work in the colonies had to be done and that Europeans could not be found to do it. For him and for many other Spanish and Portuguese, the solution was to import slaves from Africa instead. As they opened up Brazil in the sixteenth century, the Portuguese adapted the sugar plantation system they had established in Madeira and the Cape Verde Islands. Finding the indigenous people of Brazil difficult to control, the Portuguese drove them deep into the tropical forests and brought laborers from Africa and the islands to work for them. The Spanish had also begun substituting Africans for Native American labor. So began a transatlantic trade in slaves that would last for almost four centuries.

Africa and the American Slave Trade

For Europeans, slaves purchased in West Africa were an ideal solution to their New World labor problems. In 1510, the Spanish crown legalized the sale of Africans in the Americas, and eight years later, a Spanish ship carried the first full cargo of Africans across the Atlantic. By the 1540s, slaves were distributed around all the Spanish and Portuguese colonies. Cortés himself had 68 African slaves in 1547 in addition to 169 Mexican slaves. A century later, there were 30,000 African slaves working in the valleys around Lima in Peru and more in the mines of Mexico. But slaves would be used most in the plantation economies of Brazil and the Caribbean. By 1600, the Spanish and Portuguese had forcibly removed over 250,000 Africans to the Americas, and the numbers grew rapidly as French, English, and Dutch merchants also entered the slave trade (Map 1.5).

Slave trading would prove extremely lucrative, becoming part of a larger commerce — referred to as the *triangular trade* — that took European goods to Africa, slaves to America, and New World produce back to Europe. But the Europeans who were involved did not share the rich pickings equally. Many rulers, merchants, and shipowners made money, but most

MAP 1.5   Atlantic Trade Patterns, in the Early 1700s

This map shows the principal routes in use by the eighteenth century by which slaves, colonial products, and manufactured goods traveled through the Atlantic trade system. At this stage, the British North American colonies focused primarily on oceanic trade rather than seeking trading opportunities inland.

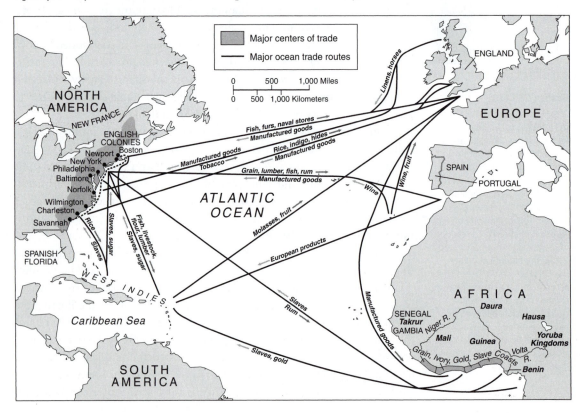

The Spanish Treatment of Fugitive Black Slaves

This is an engraving from the Frankfurt edition of Girolamo Benzoni's widely read sixteenth-century history of America, *Historia del mondo nuovo*. The Milanese author denounced Spanish treatment of Indians and, more unusually, of African slaves in the New World. Theodor de Bry, ed., *America pars quinta Nobilis & admiratione plena Hieronymi Benzoni . . .* (1595) — British Library.

minor officials and ships' crews endured poor pay and harsh conditions. Of Dutch West India Company employees in the slave trade, for instance, only one in twenty made a fortune, and another two made more modest profits; the rest made little or nothing.

Some West African rulers, such as the *obas* (kings) of Benin after 1550, used their power to curb the American slave trade. Resistance to the trade fostered revolts, such as the one headed by Muslim inhabitants on the Senegal River around 1670. But many rulers willingly took part. From Senegal to Angola, they organized the capture of people, usually from the interior and from ethnic groups other than their own, for delivery to European traders on the coast. They purchased European guns to help fight wars and augment the number of their captives. The Ashanti and the king of Dahomey increased their power and wealth as a result. Some African merchants also did well: Abee Coffu Jantie Seniees, the leading trader of Cape Coast, and

"... Our Country Is Being Completely Depopulated": King Nzinga Mbemba on the Slave Trade

In a 1526 letter from King Nzinga Mbemba of the Congo (baptized King Afonso I) to King João III of Portugal, the African ruler condemns the impact of the slave trade on his own people, an impact that would only intensify in the next century. The slave trade had a profound effect not only on the people who were enslaved, but also on the African societies from which they came. While many African societies engaged in slavery and slave trading, it was frequently quite different in nature from the sort of slavery that Europeans instituted in the New World.

Sir, your highness should know how our Kingdom is being lost in so many ways. . . . We cannot reckon how great the damage is, since [your Portuguese] merchants are taking every day our natives, sons of the land and the sons of our noblemen and vassals and our relatives. . . . So great, Sir, is the corruption and licentiousness that our country is being completely depopulated, and Your Highness should not agree with this or accept it as in your service. . . . That is why we beg of Your Highness to help and assist us in this matter, commanding your factors [representatives] that they should not send here either merchants or wares, because it is our will that in these Kingdoms there should not be any trade of slaves nor outlet for them. . . .

Moreover, Sir, in our Kingdoms there is another great inconvenience which is of little service to God, and this is that many of our people [are] keenly desirous . . . of the wares and things of your Kingdoms, which are brought here by your people. In order to satisfy their voracious appetite, [they] seize many of our people, freed and exempt men, and very often it happens that they kidnap even noblemen and the sons of noblemen, and our relatives, and take them to be sold to the white men who are in our Kingdoms. . . .

Basil Davidson, *The African Past: Chronicles from Antiquity to Modern Times* (1964).

John Kabes, the main middleman between the Ashanti and the port of Komenda, made fortunes selling slaves in the seventeenth century.

European nations competed fiercely for a share in the slave trade, but strong local rulers prevented any of them from monopolizing it. At Ouidah in the kingdom of Dahomey, the king's powerful viceroy kept the port open to all Europeans equally, setting rules by which they could do business. The Dahomean state relied on the slave trade, both for the exercise of policy and as a source of revenue.

However, in the long run, the slave trade debilitated West Africa. Up to twelve million people were sold to Europeans and shipped to the Americas between the fifteenth and nineteenth centuries. European goods imported to pay for slaves drove local artisans out of business, and people fled coastal regions to avoid slave hunters, ruining Africa's trading economies. Slave traders primarily sought young, healthy men who could be sold in the Americas as field hands, so in time, women came to outnumber men in West Africa, altering family and marriage patterns and causing populations to fall. Meanwhile, local demand for labor from women slaves increased, so the Atlantic slave trade strengthened African, as well as American, slavery.

Captivity and the Middle Passage   Local traders seized most slaves inland and marched them, enchained, for as long as a year to the coastal forts. Hunger, sickness, or exhaustion killed many on the way. Survivors reaching the coast were locked up to await shipment in prisons known as barracoons, slaveholds, or trunks. At the English fort of Cape Coast, these were underground caves, able to hold a thousand or more people each. A French trader, Jean Barbot, described the slave pens at Ouidah in the 1680s:

> [T]he slaves . . . are put into a booth or prison, built for that purpose near the beach, all of them together; and when the Europeans are to receive them, they are brought out into a large plain, where the ships' surgeons examine every one of them, to the smallest member, men and women being all stark naked. Such as are allowed [judged] good and sound are set on one side . . . [each] is marked on the breast with a red-hot iron, imprinting the mark of the French, English, or Dutch companies so that each nation may distinguish their own property, and so as to prevent their being changed by the sellers for others that are worse.

Branded by their new owners, captives were chained below decks in ships designed to carry the largest number of people in the smallest

Strange Cargo

A diagram from an 1808 abolitionist report on the African slave trade shows the interior of a "slaver," with human beings packed below deck and no room left to move. Conditions on earlier slave ships were even more foul and cramped. Thomas Clarkson, *The History of the Rise, Progress, and Accomplishment of the African Slave-Trade by the British Parliament* (1808)—American Social History Project.

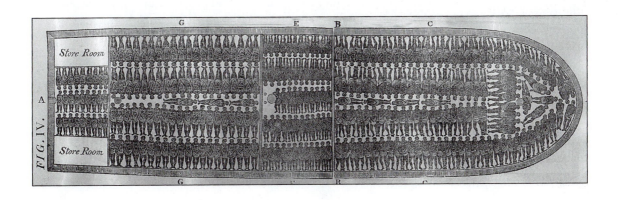

"A Most Horrible Scene": Ottobah Cugoano Describes Being Taken Captive by Slave Traders

When Ottobah Cugoano was about thirteen years old, he, along with a group of his friends, was captured by slave traders and transported to the coast of Africa. This excerpt from his "Narrative of the Enslavement of Ottobah Cugoano, a Native of Africa," published in 1787, recounts the brutal days of his transport and experiences on a slave vessel off the coast of West Africa. He was subsequently transferred to another ship for the Middle Passage journey to the Caribbean island of Grenada. Set free by his owner in 1772, Cugoano became an abolitionist and a leader of London's African community.

Next day we travelled on, and in the evening came to a town, where I saw several white people, which made me afraid that they would eat me, according to our notion, as children, in the inland parts of the country. This made me rest very uneasy all the night, and next morning I had some victuals brought, desiring me to eat and make haste, as my guide and kidnapper told me that he had to go to the castle with some company that were going there, as he had told me before, to get some goods. After I was ordered out, the horrors I soon saw and felt, cannot be well described; I saw many of my miserable countrymen chained two and two, some handcuffed, and some with their hands tied behind. We were conducted along by a guard, and when we arrived at the castle, I asked my guide what I was brought there for, he told me to learn the ways of the browfow, that is, the white-faced people. I saw him take a gun, a piece of cloth, and some lead for me, and then he told me that he must now leave me there, and went off. This made me cry bitterly, but I was soon conducted to a prison, for three days, where I heard the groans and cries of many, and saw some of my fellow-captives. But when a vessel arrived to conduct us away to the ship, it was a most horrible scene; there was nothing to be heard but the rattling of chains, smacking of whips, and the groans and cries of our fellow-men. Some would not stir from the ground, when they were lashed and beat in the most horrible manner. I have forgot the name of this infernal fort; but we were taken in the ship that came for us, to another that was ready to sail from Cape Coast. When we were put into the ship, we saw several black merchants coming on board, but we were all drove into our holes, and not suffered to speak to any of them. In this situation we continued several days in sight of our native land; but I could find no good person to give any information of my situation to Accasa at Agimaque [Cugoano's home city]. And when we found ourselves at last taken away, death was more preferable than life; and a plan was concerted amongst us, that we might burn and blow up the ship, and to perish all together in the flames: but we were betrayed by one of our own countrywomen, who slept with some of the headmen of the ship, for it was common for the dirty filthy sailors to take the African women and lie upon their bodies; but the men were chained and pent up in holes. It was the women and boys which were to burn the ship, with the approbation and groans of the rest; though that was prevented, the discovery was likewise a cruel bloody scene.

"Narrative of the Enslavement of Ottobah Cugoano, a Native of Africa; published by himself, in the Year 1787," in *The Negro's Memorial, or, Abolitionist's Catechism*, 1825, 123–124.

possible space for the transatlantic voyages that became known as the Middle Passage. A German ship's surgeon noted that "some of these poor people obeyed . . . without . . . any resistance," but "others . . . filled the air with heartrending cries which . . . cut me to the quick." Barbot recalled one man, a *marabou*, or Muslim teacher, who spoke not one word on the two-month Atlantic crossing, "so deep was his sorrow." (Barbot sold him in the Caribbean.)

Shipboard conditions were ghastly. Men, women, and children were crammed together in their own excrement; it was said that a slave ship could be smelled downwind long before it came into sight. Traders accepted that perhaps one in six slaves would die from disease, malnutrition, or suicide during the voyage. Occasionally, they died in shipboard revolts that the European crews brutally suppressed. Sailors lived barely more comfortably than the slaves they carried, and their death rates from disease could be even higher.

Slaves began their journey to the Americas not as "Africans," but as members of many different societies and ethnic groups, speaking an array of languages and holding to a variety of customs and beliefs (Map 1.6). Even in the 1540s, Cortés's slaves came from many places, from Gambia to Mozambique. Shippers often mixed captives from different places to reduce the risk of mutiny. Still, many slaves shared common skills and common assumptions about religion, kinship, and social life. Many had some connections with the trading cultures of the African seaboard, and some had knowledge of trading languages. Aboard ship, the things they had in common enabled them to begin to cooperate, despite the differences among them. Forced across the ocean, they became "African" and started a long, painful transition to a distinctly African American culture that would help to shape the New World.

Early Colonization Efforts in North America

Spain's colonization of Central and South America extended to the Americas the process of formal conquest that had occurred in Spain itself in previous centuries. In contrast, northwestern Europeans' ventures in America

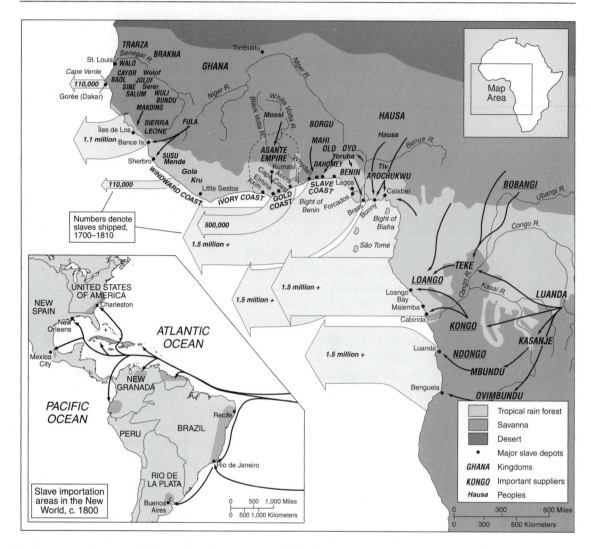

MAP 1.6   Slave Exports from West Africa to the Americas in the Eighteenth Century

Over six and a half million people were forcibly removed from Africa as slaves between 1700 and 1810, the majority of them shipped to work on plantations in the Caribbean and Brazil. This map identifies the regions from which they came, the main West African kingdoms and slaving ports, and some of the ethnic groups that lost a large number of people to slavery.

grew out of fishing and commerce and initially made a more tentative impact on the continent. There were no powerful empires to be conquered, as Spain had overrun the Aztecs or the Incas. French, Dutch, and English explorers and traders pursued varied ambitions. During the seventeenth

A New World Beast

Illustrations that appeared in sixteenth-century accounts of European exploration of the Americas often showed exotic wildlife that owed as much to imagination as to observation. This woodcut, from a book by a French Franciscan friar whose two-month visit to Brazil in 1555 was spent largely in a sickbed, probably represents a North American bison. André Thevet, *Les singularitez de la France Antarctique, autrement nommé Amérique* (1557)—Rare Books and Manuscript Division, New York Public Library, Astor, Lenox and Tilden Foundations.

century, however, they established settlements that transformed this part of the continent as surely as the Spanish did farther south.

Exploration   Early European contact with North America came with voyages of exploration. A French-sponsored venture under Giovanni da Verrazano in 1524 sailed the East Coast from the Carolinas to Maine (where, Verrazano wrote, some Abenakis "made all the signs of scorn and shame . . . such as showing their buttocks and laughing"). A decade later, the Frenchman Jacques Cartier explored the St. Lawrence River. French and Dutch ventures looked for furs and other trade goods. The English began their contact as state-licensed pirates, attacking Spanish shipping in the hope of seizing some of the New World's wealth for themselves.

The first settlements arose from fishing. From the French and English coasts, men braved the Atlantic to catch cod in the rich fishing grounds off Newfoundland. They established semipermanent camps ashore for shelter and for processing their catches. By 1620, these camps dotted the coastline from Newfoundland southwestward to what would become New England.

Meanwhile, English adventurers sought more permanent North American settlements. In 1583, Sir Humphrey Gilbert, who had already helped to found colonies in Ireland, claimed Newfoundland for England before his ship sank, with all hands, on its way home. The next year, Sir Walter Raleigh planned a base from which to conduct raids on Spanish treasure fleets and sent a small force of soldiers to Roanoke Island on North Carolina's Outer Banks. In 1587, over 100 people arrived to start a colony at Roanoke, but war with Spain delayed a ship that was to bring supplies to the colony. By the time it arrived, in 1590, the settlers had disappeared without a trace.

Warfare continued to hinder ventures to North America until, after a peace settlement in 1604, the French, Dutch, and English resumed efforts to create permanent colonies. The English established a precarious settlement at Jamestown, Virginia, in 1607. The following year, the French founded Quebec, which would become the center of their colony of New France; and in 1614, the Dutch established Fort Orange (later Albany) on the Hudson River. In 1620, English religious dissenters known as the Pilgrims arrived, in the *Mayflower*, at what became Plymouth, Massachusetts. Ten years later, the first fleet of English Puritans, who were also seeking to establish a religious colony, sailed into Massachusetts Bay. By this time, several thousand English settlers were living on the shores of Chesapeake Bay in Virginia. By 1640, tens of thousands more had come to both Massachusetts and the

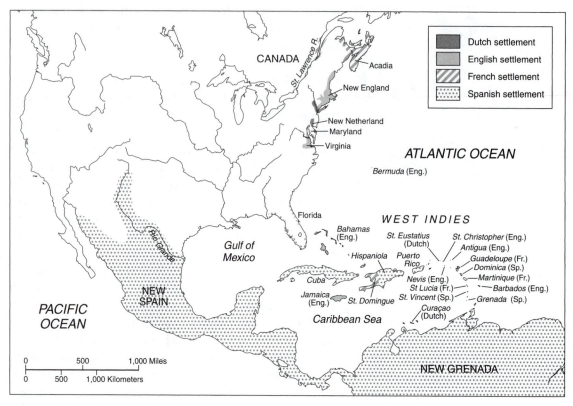

MAP 1.7   North and Central American Colonies, c. 1660
This map illustrates the land claimed by the major European colonizing powers in the seventeenth century. Though tiny in size, the Caribbean colonies, with their rich sugar plantations, would remain highly important—especially to Britain and France—throughout the seventeenth and eighteenth centuries.

Chesapeake. The English, French, and Dutch competed to secure their claims to parts of North America (Map 1.7).

The French and Dutch   In some respects, French and Dutch colonization efforts differed. France aimed to dominate a vast sweep of territory from the St. Lawrence River valley through the Great Lakes region and down the Mississippi River. The French state backed merchants and missionaries who penetrated far into the backcountry, establishing close relationships with Native Americans and converting many to Catholicism. Dutch interest, primarily commercial and organized by the Dutch West India Company, focused on the Mid-Atlantic region, especially the Hudson River valley. Dutch merchants and settlers stayed closer to the coast. They brought their Protestant churches with them; but with a lesser commitment to missions,

Dutch religious beliefs had a smaller impact on Indian life than did those of the French.

In other ways, however, French and Dutch efforts were comparable. Both established agricultural settlements, but though the French government and the Dutch West India Company tried hard to recruit colonists, social conditions in France and Holland did not induce large numbers of people to want to become farmers in America. Half of the Dutch population were town dwellers, many of whom shared in Holland's considerable commercial prosperity. France was poorer, and mainly rural, but had low rates of internal migration and hence relatively few potential overseas emigrants. There were only 3,000 French people in New France by the early 1660s.

More important to both countries was the fur trade. Dutch traders stayed close to their posts at Fort Orange and Nieuw Amsterdam (later New York City), but they obtained large quantities of furs in trade with the Iroquois and other native groups. French fur traders and scouts (known as *coureurs de bois*, or "forest runners") traveled far into the interior. The fur trade overwhelmingly employed men, many of whom intermarried with Indians, creating a substantial mixed-race (*métis*) population.

French and Dutch colonization efforts significantly influenced North American development. Dutch families, legal structures, place names, and expressions helped to shape early New York. The French presence in the Great Lakes region and the Mississippi Valley is still marked by hundreds of place names, while the descendants of French settlers retain their distinct identity in Quebec and other parts of Canada. But the most lasting North American colonies would be English.

Though the English took part in fishing and the fur trade, they became more concerned than the French or the Dutch with establishing settlements that occupied and cultivated the land. After the English captured New Netherland and renamed it New York in 1664, during one of several wars against Holland's commercial empire, the Dutch relinquished their colony to secure more valuable territories elsewhere. Similarly, when British forces seized New France a century later, in the French and Indian War (see

New Amsterdam

This satirical English print shows the 1647 arrival of Dutch troops, led by Governor Peter Stuyvesant (left), in New Amsterdam. Prints and Photographs Division, Library of Congress.

Chapter 4), the French chose to give it up in return for keeping wealthier Caribbean sugar islands.

The English Colonial Experience

The English colonies that came to occupy North America's eastern seaboard were more than just land claims or commercial outposts. They became permanent homes for streams of migrants from the British Isles and elsewhere. Between 1620 and 1640 alone, almost 40,000 men and women left England to live in North America. Some English colonists, including the merchants who organized and financed expeditions, sought to make their fortunes. But a majority probably had more modest hopes: to achieve economic independence or religious or political freedoms that were denied them at home. All were influenced by changes that had been taking place in England over the previous two centuries. The conditions that impelled them to leave for the New World shaped the character of English colonies and the variations among them.

The Roots of English Migration to America   In England, as elsewhere in Europe, the Black Death caused a catastrophic population decline in the fourteenth century. The resultant shortage of labor led, in time, to the collapse of English serfdom. Feudal landlords could no longer compel labor services from peasants, who resisted or fled to the comparative freedom of the towns. Lacking labor, landlords divided their fields, rented out plots to peasants, and began to live on the rents. Hired laborers benefited from rising wages. Though still dogged by poverty and disease, people working on the land were supported by a web of customary rights, including access to common land, where they might graze livestock, grow vegetables, or cut timber. Markets were also regulated, so profiteering was restricted and the price of bread controlled during times of shortage.

But changing circumstances once more undermined peasants' security. Population growth resumed in the fifteenth century. By 1500, landlords were demanding higher rents, usually in cash, and evicting tenants who could not pay. When Henry VIII broke with the Roman Church in the 1530s, he confiscated vast amounts of church land and granted it to his supporters among the aristocracy and gentry. Henry, and later his daughter Elizabeth I, also enhanced the lawmaking powers of Parliament, in which many nobles and gentry sat. Large landowners found their wealth and status increasing.

They also had opportunities to squeeze higher earnings from their lands. As the textile industry expanded, wool growing became more profitable, so many landlords evicted tenants to make room for sheep or—by a practice called *enclosure*—fenced off common land on which tenants had

"They Live Like Beasts, Voide of Lawe and All Good Order." England's subjugation of Ireland during the reign of Elizabeth I served as a rehearsal for the colonization of Virginia in the seventeenth century. As in the later New World colony, the crown licensed private individuals and companies to undertake conquest and settlement for their own profit. Protestant colonists expropriated Irish Catholic lands and rationalized their violence against the Irish by branding them as savage pagans. In this sixteenth-century woodcut, English soldiers returned to their camp carrying a grisly trophy of conquest. John Derricke, *The Image of Irelande* (1581) — Folger Shakespeare Library.

relied for part of their livelihoods. Smallholders in Kent petitioned that "they were greatly relieved by [their] common and would be utterly undone if it should be unjustly taken from them." Some tenants moved to woodland or upland areas where they could eke out a living. Thousands more became hired farmhands or weavers, left the land for the towns, or went to work as miners, sailors, or soldiers. Many single women were obliged to spin wool into yarn in isolated drudgery. By 1600, 40 percent of English people were working for wages.

Between 1520 and 1580 alone, England's population grew from 2.5 million to 3.5 million, helping to keep wages low. Yet prices for food, rent, and fuel rose fivefold between 1530 and 1640, an inflation helped by the influx of Spanish American gold and silver. War in the 1590s disrupted the cloth trade, throwing many people out of work in textile districts, and poor harvests in the 1590s and 1620s caused hunger and even famine in a few places. Men and women tramped the countryside or flocked to towns, seeking work. London's population quadrupled between 1500 and 1600, reaching at least 200,000. A clergyman wrote in 1622 that the city was crowded with "people who rose early, worked all day and went late to bed, yet were scarce able to put bread in their mouths . . . [or] clothes on their backs." In the view of England's governing classes, poverty threatened to bring social disorder. Laws prohibited vagrancy or punished "idleness" with imprisonment or public whipping, effectively compelling the poor to work for low pay and long hours in harsh conditions.

Widespread poverty contrasted with the prosperity, not just of landowners but also of urban merchants who had grown rich from textile manufacture or trade and were willing to invest in new ventures. In return for supporting the monarchy, groups of merchants were granted special privileges, including monopolies on trade with particular parts of the world. Beneficiaries included the founders of the Muscovy Company (1553), the Spanish Company (1577), the Senegal Adventurers (1588), the East India Company (1600), the Virginia Company (1607), and the Massachusetts Bay Company (1629). These companies organized exploration and trade, and some began also to sponsor attempts at overseas settlement.

From the 1560s onward, the government had promoted English and Scottish "plantations" in parts of Ireland, displacing Catholic peasants from fertile land to make way for Protestant settlers. Some commentators came to see overseas colonization as a solution to English poverty. The poet John Donne suggested that it would "sweep your streets, and wash your doors, from idle persons, and the children of idle persons, and employ them," while Sir Francis Bacon saw it as a cure for "rebellions of the belly" brought on by the reorganization of agriculture.

By the early seventeenth century, the elements of English overseas colonization were in place: merchants, shipowners, and landholders ready to seek out new sources of profit; a crown that was prepared to grant special rights to promote English and Protestant expansion; and a sizable population of mobile poor, who might provide the labor for schemes of settlement. Poor people migrating to towns in search of work encountered promoters who offered passage to the New World in exchange for a few years' labor. Many men and some women opted to travel to North America as "indentured servants" (bound to labor by contracts called indentures). They took with them a legacy of hardship and injustice, a suspicion of landlords, hope for some land of their own, and a determination to defend popular rights.

Colonizing the Chesapeake   The first English settlement at Jamestown, Virginia, established in 1607 by the Virginia Company of London, mimicked the fantasies of easy wealth that had first driven the Spanish to the Americas. Virginia, its promoters hoped, would furnish precious metals or valuable plants. Explorers' accounts misled settlers into expecting a paradise where they could gather food without effort, would need little clothing or shelter, and could make docile native people work for them. The 104 men and boys who founded Jamestown had no idea how to build a permanent farming settlement. About one in five were "gentlemen," who considered manual labor to be beneath them. Most of the rest were unskilled laborers, military recruits, and servants. The few craftsmen included clockmakers, jewelers, and gentlemen's perfumers.

A Festive Dance

John White drew this "green corn" celebration in the Indian village of Secoton sometime around 1585. The Indians in his drawings appear exotic yet also reassuringly familiar. Their poses, resembling figures in classical antiquity, and their discreetly draped clothes may have been intended to calm English fears of Indian violence and immorality. White, who was appointed governor of the unsuccessful Virginia colony of Roanoke in 1587, underplayed or omitted many aspects of Indian life that would disturb English sensibilities and deter potential colonists. John White, watercolor over black lead, touched with white, c. 1585, 10 3/4 × 14 1/8 inches—British Museum.

Instead of the paradise they had expected, they found a harsh, disease-ridden place. One of its leaders, John Smith, remarked that early Jamestown was "a miserie, a ruine, a death, a hell." Supplies dwindled and fields remained uncultivated while starving gentlemen passed the time playing bowls. Far from being willing to work for them, watching Indians waited for the English intruders to die. Most did. The thirty-five who survived until spring 1608 were about to abandon the colony when new settlers and supplies arrived.

For the next decade, Virginia Company officers sought to impose order. They introduced harsh military discipline, divided servants into work gangs, and viciously punished infractions of the rules. Punishments varied according to rank. For lesser crimes, the wealthy paid fines while the poor were whipped, branded, or had body parts cut off. Serious offenses were punished by death, and servants were often mutilated before and after execution. Men worked in the fields; the handful of women, such as Ann Leyden and June Wright, stitched shirts and performed other household tasks. When their work was judged inadequate, an eyewitness recorded, the women were "whipped, and Ann Leyden being then with child, the same night thereof miscarried." Settlers could not return to England without permission, and their often pitiful letters home were censored. Coercive methods maintained the colony in a bleak, precarious existence, setting precedents for the later introduction of slavery.

"What Can You Get by War . . . ?": Powhatan Addresses Captain John Smith

In 1612 (only five years after the colony's founding) Powhatan, a leader of the Algonquian-speaking people in colonial Virginia, addressed Captain John Smith, governor of the Virginia colony. Powhatan's remarks (in this version written down by two of Smith's associates), reflected eloquently on the rapidly deteriorating relations between the first colonists and the Indians on whom the English were so dependent in the colony's early years.

Captain Smith, you may understand that I . . . know the difference of peace and war better than any in my Country. But now I am old, and ere long must die. My brethren, namely Opichapam, Opechankanough, and Kekataugh, my two sisters, and their two daughters, are distinctly each other's successors. I wish their experiences no less than mine, and your love of them, no less than mine to you: but this bruit [noise] from Nansamund, that you are come to destroy my Country, so much affrighteth all my people, as they dare not visit you. What will it avail you to take [by force] that you may quietly have with love, or to destroy them that provide you food? What can you get by war, when we can hide our provisions and fly to the woods, whereby you must famish, by wronging us your friends? And why are you thus jealous of our loves, seeing us unarmed . . . and are willing still to feed you with that [which] you cannot get but by our labors? Think you I am so simple not to know it is better to eat good meat, lie well, and sleep quietly with my women and children, laugh, and be merry with you, have copper, hatchets, or what I want being your friend; than be forced to fly . . . , and thus with miserable fear end my miserable life, leaving my pleasures to such youths as you? . . . Let this therefore assume you of our loves, and every year our friendly trade shall furnish you with corn; and now also if you would come in friendly manner to see us, and not thus with your guns and swords, as [if] to invade your foes.

Lyon Gardiner Tyler, ed., *Narratives of Early Virginia, 1606–1625* (New York: Charles Scribner's Sons, 1907), 163–66.

Soon, however, the Virginia Company found that it could use its servants to make money. In 1611, the company began to grow tobacco, which had become popular in England for its supposed medicinal properties. Demand soared. Within a few years, the company, and those who acquired land from it, turned wholeheartedly to tobacco cultivation. Virginia's fertile soil and long growing season were suited to tobacco. Tidal rivers made the interior accessible to the vessels that would carry the crop across the Atlantic. The colony boomed. Tobacco exports rose from 2,000 pounds in 1615 to 1.5 million pounds just fifteen years later.

To entice more people to go to Virginia and grow tobacco, the Virginia Company offered land in return for labor or other services. Skilled artisans would receive "a house and four acres as long as they plied their trades." A

John Smith and the Indians

Smith, one of the first governing councillors of the Virginia colony, took a less benevolent view of the Indians than did John White. This engraving from his *Generall Historie of Virginia*, published in 1624, shows the Chesapeake tribes as threatening giants. Smith recommended repression: "bring them to be tractable, civil, and industrious . . . that the fruit of their labor might make us some recompense." (Robert Vaughan) John Smith, *The Generall Historie of Virginia* (1624)—Call Number STC 22790. By permission of the Houghton Library, Harvard University.

man willing to cultivate new land could receive fifty acres for himself and another fifty for every person he brought to the colony. Indentured servants were promised land at the end of their terms of service. For a settlement whose population was overwhelmingly male, young, and single, the company shipped in women to sell as wives to men who could pay 120 pounds of tobacco for them.

The company also took steps to foster support from landowning settlers. It softened martial law. In 1619, it set up the House of Burgesses, an assembly to which all adult freemen could elect representatives to share

Ætatis suæ 21. Aº. 1616.

Matoaks als Rebecka daughter to the mighty Prince
Powhatan Emperour of Attanoughkomouck als Virginia
converted and baptized in the Christian faith, and
Wife to the wor.ᵈ Mr Tho: Rolff.

Pocahontas

This is a portrait of the daughter of Chief Powhatan, at the age of twenty-one, soon after her arrival in London. The caption gives her name as "Matoaks als [alias] Rebecka"— Matoaka was her given Algonquian name (Pocahontas was a nickname), and she adopted the name Rebecka after her conversion to Christianity. According to John Smith, Pocahontas saved him from execution when he was captured by the Algonquians in 1607. She subsequently married an English gentleman and became the first Indian of "royal blood" to be brought to England for the edification and entertainment of the nobility—and the first to succumb to England's inhospitable climate, probably dying of tuberculosis. Anonymous (after an engraving by Simon van de Passe), after 1616, oil on canvas, 30 1/4 × 25 1/4 inches—National Portrait Gallery, Smithsonian Institution.

government with company officers. Between 1619 and 1625, nearly 5,000 new settlers arrived. But such numbers outgrew the Virginia Company's military organization, and in 1624, King James I dissolved the company, making Virginia a royal colony under his direct supervision.

Early Virginia was an armed camp where individualism, competition, and fear prevailed. Men scrambling for wealth had little time for public spirit or civic cooperation. Rather than building towns or villages, tobacco planters scattered along the navigable rivers. The most successful owned hundreds of acres, but most lived like their servants in crude shacks, miles from neighbors. Planters abused servants with "intolerable oppression and hard usage." Death rates stayed high. Over 7,000 people migrated to Virginia between 1607 and 1625, but the colony's population was only 1,200 when the Virginia Company was abolished.

As well as hunger and disease, settlers faced the risk of massacre by Indians. The first colonists had provoked the local Algonquian speakers by stealing food from them, and within two years, the natives' leader, Powhatan, declared war, noting that the English "comming hither is not for trade, but to invade my people, and possesse my country." In the diplomacy that patched up this dispute in 1614, Powhatan permitted his daughter Pocahontas to marry the Englishman John Rolfe, though she fell ill and died while visiting England in 1617. Meanwhile, the Virginia colony continued to grow, and so did its demand for land. Conflicts twice more erupted into war, as Powhatan's brother and successor Opechancanough led campaigns against the settlers. During the first, in 1622, his men killed 347 colonists, prompting the English to promise not to encroach on tribal land. But by 1644, with the Virginia colony's population at 8,000, settlers' encroachments again caused hostilities. More than 500 colonists died in the struggle before Opechancanough was captured and killed in 1646 and the Powhatans signed a treaty acknowledging English authority.

By this time, the colony of Maryland had been founded adjacent to Virginia in the upper part of Chesapeake Bay, under a royal charter granted in the early 1630s to the Earl of Baltimore. Baltimore, a Catholic convert, sought a refuge for fellow Catholics facing persecution in England. His family planned to establish feudal manors, with land leased to tenant farmers. But the promise of land and of profits from tobacco cultivation attracted migrants, both Protestant and Catholic. To obtain support, the proprietors had to modify their plans, offering land to own as well as rent, and permitting the formation of a representative assembly of freemen. Migration to both Chesapeake colonies continued to grow. By 1660, about 50,000 people had crossed the Atlantic to settle there.

Mr. Richard Mather

This 1670 portrait of the Puritan leader was the first woodcut printed in the colonies. Mather, a minister who arrived in the Massachusetts Bay Colony in 1635, was father to Increase Mather and grandfather to Cotton Mather, both influential Massachusetts clergymen. John Foster, woodcut, 6⅛ x 4⅞ inches, 1670 — American Antiquarian Society.

Mr. Richard Mather.

Colonizing New England The Virginia Company had hoped to attract members of the English gentry to America and recruited servants from among the poor, single, and young. But many among the "middling sort," too, were discontented in England. The Protestant reformers known as Puritans, especially, distrusted the policies of the Stuart kings James I and Charles I and faced a measure of persecution.

Puritans included gentry, village craftsmen and small landowners, and urban merchants and artisans. Their difficulties arose from theological disputes thrown up by the Reformation. They followed John Calvin's doctrine that one's fate after death was predestined by God, rejecting the "Arminian" doctrine (named for a Dutch theologian, Jacobus Arminius) that human actions could influence whether one was saved or damned. Although most Puritans worshiped in the Church of England, they objected to its ornateness, its ritual, and the authority of Arminian bishops.

They emphasized the authority of God's Word in the Bible and feared that the Stuarts were leading a return to Catholicism.

Puritans loathed England's disorder, its extremes of wealth and poverty, and what they saw as its sinfulness. Regarding churches as communities of the godly, they assembled for preaching, not ritual, and sought to choose their own ministers. Some who advocated separation from the English church had already faced persecution. These included the Pilgrims, who had spent ten years in voluntary exile in Holland before sailing to New England in 1620. After 1625, Archbishop of Canterbury William Laud pressed for conformity in the Church, and other Puritans began to look for a place where they could avoid England's evils and build their own godly society for the world to see.

When investors formed the Massachusetts Bay Company in 1629, a group of Puritans led by John Winthrop turned it into a vehicle for their plans. The company's charter granted it political and economic rights in New England and, unusually, failed to require that company meetings be held in England. Taking advantage of this technicality, Winthrop and his recruits sailed in 1630 to found a colony in Massachusetts armed with the right to govern their own affairs. The charter would remain the colony's legal basis until 1684.

Once arrived in Massachusetts, Winthrop and his followers abandoned the plan to make profits, closed membership in the Massachusetts Bay Company to investors, and reserved it instead for male members of an organized Puritan church. The political leadership of Massachusetts comprised Winthrop, the colony's governor, and the General Court, its governing body. A tax protest in 1632 obliged Winthrop to make the General Court a representative body. Over the next decade, more than 20,000 English migrants, mainly Puritan families with their children and servants, arrived to establish new farms and communities on New England's rocky soil, aiming to build for themselves a way of life that England denied them.

Civil War

The frontispiece illustration from a 1645 book by the English religious poet Francis Quarles portrays King Charles defending the tree of Religion from Cromwell's Puritan followers. Francis Quarles, *The Shepherd's Oracles* (1645)—Prints and Photographs Division, Library of Congress.

"Their Extraordinary Great Labour": Roger Williams on Indian Women

In comparison to the frequent disapproval by Europeans of the work and leadership roles of Indian women, the separatist minister Roger Williams was a more sympathetic observer. Williams helped to found the colony of Rhode Island after he was expelled from neighboring Massachusetts Bay for questioning its leaders' authority. Critical of English claims to natives' land, Williams set about studying the nearby Narragansett Indians, and he compiled a handbook of their vocabulary and phrases which he published in London in 1643. This Key into the Language of North America *also contains vivid observations of Indian life.*

. . . from their extraordinary great labour (even above the labour of men) as in the Field, they sustain the labour of it, in carrying of mighty Burthens, in digging clammes and getting other Shelfish from the Sea, in beating all their corne in Morters: &c. Most of them count it a shame for a Woman in Travell [labor and childbirth] to make complaint, and many of them are scarcely heard to groane. I have often knowne in one Quarter of an houre a Woman merry in the House, and delivered and merry againe: and within two dayes abroad, and after foure or five dayes at worke, &c . . .

The Women set or plant, weede, and hill, and gather and barne all the corne, and Fruites of the field: Yet sometimes the man himselfe (either out ouf love to his Wife, or care for his Children, or being an old man) will help the Woman which (by the custome of the Countrey) they are not bound to.

When a field is to be broken up, they have a very loving sociable speedy way to dispatch it: All the neighbours men and Women forty, fifty, a hundred &c, joyne, and come in to help freely.

With friendly joyning they breake up their fields, build their Forts, hunt the Woods, stop and kill fish in the Rivers, it being true with them as in all the World in the Affaires of Earth or Heaven: By concord little things grow great, but discord the greatest come to nothing.

Colin G. Calloway, ed., *The World Turned Upside Down: Indian Voices from Early America* (1995).

Winthrop and his followers began by establishing Boston and a ring of towns around it. They incorporated ramshackle camps previously set up on the coast by English fishing crews, forming towns such as Salem, Marblehead, and Gloucester. They also made connections with the Pilgrims' Plymouth Colony, which would remain separate from Massachusetts Bay until 1691.

By the mid-1630s, political disputes and growing numbers led the Puritan colonists to expand their settlements to the south and west. When the government expelled him in 1635 for questioning its authority, the minister Roger Williams led followers into nearby Rhode Island to found a colony that would become a haven for exiles from Puritan orthodoxy. Migrants from Plymouth and Massachusetts established the separate colonies of Connecticut and New Haven. Outbreaks of smallpox in 1633 had devastated native populations in these areas. "It pleased God to visite these Indians with a great sickness," wrote Plymouth governor William Bradford; so many died that "many of them did rott above ground for want of buriall."

More than profits, the Puritans were pursuing religious and community ideals. They were attached to owning their own property, but they set up community institutions to regulate one another. For most of these hardworking men and women, the ideal society revolved around cooperation rather than individualism. When two Puritan noblemen inquired in 1635 about migrating to Massachusetts, they were told that they would be welcome but would receive no special privileges. Neither came. Establishing their towns and farms in a land that they saw as a "wilderness," New Englanders created one of the important templates for early American society in the northern colonies.

The English Revolution and Its Effects on the Colonies   In England, meanwhile, economic dislocation, religious conflict, and political instability were deepening and, by 1642, had brought on a civil war, a period of upheaval called the English Revolution that was to have important ramifications both in England and in the colonies. Since 1629, Charles I had ruled without calling Parliament into session, asserting a monarch's "divine right" to govern and levy taxes. Puritans were among many in England who opposed such arbitrary rule and insisted that Parliament be consulted. Forced to recall Parliament in 1640 to raise taxes in order to quell a rebellion in Scotland, Charles found Parliament resistant and within two years had provoked open warfare by attempting to suppress it. After two periods of bitter fighting, the king was arrested and, in early 1649, executed. England became a republic, led by the Puritan Oliver Cromwell until his death in 1658.

The Civil War brought social upheaval and an upsurge of religious and political debate in England. As it began, Puritans stopped leaving for Massachusetts, and some returned home from the colony, since England itself might now become (as one minister put it) "a land of saints and a pattern of holiness to all the world." Radicals questioned almost every facet of established society. Poor and middling men and women, calling themselves Levellers, Diggers, Seekers, or Ranters, attacked the Church's right to levy tithes (a one-tenth share of crops or income) and questioned enclosures, wage labor, and even property itself. They asked why more people should not have the vote and whether heaven and hell were inventions of the rich to keep the poor in subjection. A growing sect known as Quakers, who stressed the authority of the divine "inner light" in all believers, condemned religious, civil, and social hierarchy. Quaker women as well as men preached and prophesied.

Faced with what they saw as expressions of anarchy, England's propertied classes brushed aside many of these radical voices and, after Cromwell's death, closed ranks to arrange for the restoration of the monarchy under Charles II in 1660. But the English Revolution left a rich legacy of ideas for those who, in the future, would criticize monarchy or rule by the rich. Even as they put a king back on the throne, English elites recognized that rulers had obligations to their people and that a people could justifiably depose a monarch who failed to honor these. English people who shared such attitudes, including many Quakers, were among those who took passage to America later in the seventeenth century.

The Revolution also accelerated England's commercial development and social polarization. It limited the monarch's taxing power and abolished many aspects of feudal land ownership, but it confirmed the property rights of landowners and cleared the way for further enclosure and agricultural improvement, strengthening ties between agriculture, commerce, and moneyed interests.

Both Cromwell and the restored monarchy pursued vigorous policies to regulate trade, promote colonies, and fight wars with commercial rivals, particularly the Dutch. Guided by economic doctrines loosely known as "mercantilism," which held that overall wealth was roughly fixed and that states could enrich themselves only by diverting flows of income from rival nations, English governments passed trade laws, including the Navigation Acts, aimed at ensuring a net inflow of wealth into the country. Overseas colonies would be an important source of commodities and raw materials for England's development. Later policies would also seek to expand colonial markets for English goods, again with the aim of assuring profits for the mother country.

Native Americans: Decline, Resistance, Exchange

English attitudes to American colonization had been shaped by their earlier conquest and settlement of parts of Ireland. "Planters" in Ireland disdained the Gaelic Irish peasants whose land they occupied, considering them to be "savages." Some early settlers in America compared the native peoples they encountered favorably with the hated Irish, but often the settlers' view of the Irish prepared them to have similar contempt for Native Americans.

Many Virginians and New Englanders perceived Native Americans as inferior because they spoke in strange tongues, cultivated with hoes rather than plows, and had no concept of property accumulation. William Simmonds wrote of Virginia in 1612 that "we found only an idle, improvident, scattered people, ignorant of the knowledge of gold, or silver, or any

"The Iroquois Were Much Astonished That Two Men Should Have Been Killed So Quickly": Samuel de Champlain Introduces Firearms to Native Warfare

Samuel de Champlain was a trader, soldier, explorer, diplomat, and author. He set up a small trading post at Quebec, the capital of the colony of New France, in 1608. In June 1609, Champlain and nine French soldiers joined a war party of Montagnais, Algonquian, and Hurons to fight their enemies, the Iroquois. While in this instance only the white soldiers wielded firearms, Native Americans also traded with the French for their own guns, adding a deadly new dimension to native conflicts.

. . . As soon as we landed, our Indians began to run some two hundred yards towards their enemies, who stood firm and had not yet noticed my white companions who went off into the woods with some Indians. Our Indians began to call to me with loud cries; and to make way for me they divided into two groups, and put me ahead some twenty yards, and I marched on until I was within some thirty yards of the enemy, who as soon as they caught sight of me halted and gazed at me and I at them. When I saw them make a move to draw their bows upon us, I took aim with my arquebus and shot straight at one of the three chiefs, and with this shot two fell to the ground and one of their companions was wounded who died thereof a little later. I had put four bullets into my arquebus. As soon as our people saw this shot so favourable for them, they began to shout so loudly that one could not have heard it thunder, and meanwhile the arrows flew thick on both sides. The Iroquois were much astonished that two men should have been killed so quickly, although they were provided with shields made of cotton thread woven together and wood, which were proof against their arrows. This frightened them greatly. As I was reloading my arquebus, one of my companions fired a shot from within the woods, which astonished them again so much that, seeing their chiefs dead, they lost courage and took to flight, abandoning the field and their fort, and fleeing into the depth of the forest, whither I pursued them and laid low still more of them. Our Indians also killed several and took ten or twelve prisoners. The remainder fled with the wounded. Of our Indians fifteen or sixteen were wounded with arrows, but these were quickly healed.

After we had gained the victory, our Indians wasted time in taking a large quantity of Indian corn and meal belonging to the enemy, as well as their shields, which they had left behind, the better to run. Having feasted, danced, and sung, we three hours later set off for home with the prisoners. The place where this attack took place is in 43° and some minutes of latitude, and was named Lake Champlain.

Samuel de Champlain, *The Works of Samuel de Champlain* (Toronto, 1925), Vol. 2, 89–101. For Champlain's publications and maps, see: http://www.loc.gov/exhibits/treasures/trr009.html and http://www.sunysb.edu/libmap/img2cap.htm.

commodities; and carelesse of anything but from hand to mouth." To the English, such attitudes justified misunderstandings over theft, the seizure of native land, and the subjugation or expulsion of native peoples they found in their way. These attitudes also influenced reactions to the destruction of Indians by disease. Local inhabitants, wrote one of the first Massachusetts settlers in 1630, "above twelve years since were swept away by a great & grievous Plague . . . so that there are verie few left." Like many Puritans, he saw the epidemic as part of God's design to clear the land for His chosen people.

Yet Indians were not simply victims of disease and conquest. What happened to Native Americans depended not only on what settlers demanded of them, but also on their own actions and the character of their own societies. Even on North America's eastern seaboard, where native cultures would be largely eradicated by the nineteenth century, over two hundred years of conflict and negotiation followed European contact.

Adaptation and Negotiation   Indians first tried to incorporate settlers into their own systems of authority. At Jamestown in 1607 and 1608, Powhatan treated Virginia leaders just like the other local chiefs who owed allegiance to him, and his offer of Pocahontas in marriage to John Rolfe in 1614 was part of an effort to control the English. Opechancanough's challenges to the growing Virginia settlements aimed to set bounds on the colony's expansion and on unreasonable English behavior. A Wicomesse leader told Maryland's governor in 1633 that "since . . . you are heere strangers and come into our Countrey, you should rather confine yourselves to the Customes of our Countrey, than impose yours upon us."

To some groups, neighboring tribes posed more problems than Europeans, and they saw settlers as allies in their rivalries. Apaches attacking pueblo Indians in the Southwest made them more vulnerable to Spanish domination. Algonquian speakers in the St. Lawrence valley, under pressure from hostile Iroquois, turned to the French for help and built an alliance that enabled the Algonquians to hold the Iroquois back and reach a settlement with them in the 1690s. English settlers found themselves used for similar ends.

Yet the growth of European settlements did oblige native cultures to adapt. From bands based on kinship they formed more structured "tribes." The fur trade brought irreversible changes. The Micmacs of Nova Scotia found themselves trapped by it. Dependent entirely on hunting and fishing, the Micmacs had ensured their survival by avoiding overhunting. But when European traders offered guns, cloth, ironware, and alcohol, the Micmacs increased their hunting to obtain the pelts to trade for these goods. Soon their beaver were gone, the traders and their goods moved on, and the Micmacs were unable to support themselves.

As hunters depleted beaver populations in coastal regions, they moved inland to search for fresh supplies, in the process colliding with other groups. Demand for pelts set tribe against tribe, and competing Europeans were usually pleased to sell arms to the rivals. Along the Hudson River, Dutch traders at first obtained furs from local Mahicans. But as their beaver dwindled, the Mahicans were pushed aside by Mohawks, who set up a regular supply of furs from the Iroquois interior.

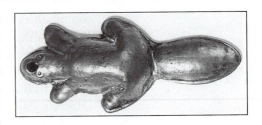

Worth Its Weight in Copper? This small copper beaver was equal in value to one beaver pelt in the Hudson Bay fur trade. George Gustav Heye Center of the National Museum of the American Indian, Smithsonian Institution, photo number 240737.000. Photo by NMAI Photo Services Staff.

Wars among Indians not only caused many deaths, but also reshaped tribes' territories and alliances. Greater reliance on hunting and warfare widened the gap between male and female roles, reducing the importance of agriculture, strengthening the power of men at the expense of women, and enhancing the claims of hunters and warriors to leadership.

Such changes often left Indians with stark alternatives. They could labor for their European conquerors, or they could (like some Mahicans and Susquehannocks) move inland and be assimilated into more powerful groups that might successfully resist European encroachment. Natives of Nantucket Island took the first path. Puritan traders advanced them goods, but they fell into debt, which they were obliged to work off by going to sea as crewmen on fishing vessels or whaling boats. But they found that they could never earn enough to settle their accounts and were trapped in a cycle of debt and forced labor that weakened their community. In 1600, they were about 2,500 strong; two centuries later only 22 of them remained. The Catawba of the Carolinas negotiated their survival by making themselves useful to colonists, accepting in the process significant changes to their own culture and forming alliances with the English against neighboring tribes.

Resistance and Warfare   Few coastal peoples managed to resist colonial encroachment successfully. Their groups were small and fragmented. On the southern New England coast, the Pequots were at first strengthened by European contact. They traded furs from the interior to Dutch and English shippers and built up their military power. The 1630s, however, brought epidemics and then encroachment by English settlers moving west from Massachusetts Bay. To resist the English, the Pequots joined with other tribes and attacked colonists' farms and towns. But the English made their own alliances with the Pequots' rivals, including the Narragansetts. Attacking a Pequot village in 1637, English soldiers burned or hacked to death more than four hundred men, women, and children, while their Indian allies encircled the site to prevent any Pequots from escaping. When the Pequot War ended, the English executed many captured warriors, sold women and children into slavery, and dispersed the remaining Pequots to other tribes.

PHILIP. *KING* of Mount Hope.

King Philip

This fanciful 1772 engraving by the Boston silversmith Paul Revere was copied from a portrait of the Mohawk chief Thayendanegea, or Joseph Brant (see page 223). Despite its inaccuracy, Revere's picture influenced print and stage portrayals of Metacom through the mid-nineteenth century. American Antiquarian Society.

The Narragansetts, who had helped the English destroy the Pequots, soon began to ponder their own prospects for survival. One leader, Miantonomi, traveled across southern New England and Long Island in the early 1640s to arrange a pact, warning of what would be lost if the English were not turned back. But the colonists, helped by Mohegan allies, silenced Miantonomi. The Mohegans captured him, delivered him to a Massachusetts court for trial on a trumped-up murder charge, and then executed him when the court convicted him and returned him to them for punishment.

Other natives sought greater association with the colonists. Puritan missionaries in Massachusetts established towns for "praying Indians," who were converted to Christianity and settled on farms. There were fourteen such towns by the early 1670s. Yet even these converts never allayed English suspicion of Indians. In time, the choice of the "praying Indians" to seek a form of assimilation with the colonists would help little to preserve their own communities.

The Wampanoag tribe, which had so far maintained cordial relations with both the Massachusetts and Plymouth colonies, came under pressure from new settlements in the 1650s and 1660s. Under their leader Metacom, whom the English called "King Philip," they sought to reverse such encroachment decisively. After repeated provocations, the Wampanoags began attacking outlying eastern Massachusetts towns in 1675, at first acting alone, then in alliance with the Nipmucks of the Connecticut Valley and with the Abenaki and others on the Maine coast. When colonial soldiers searching for Wampanoags massacred 300 people, mostly women and children, in Narragansett settlements, they pushed the Narragansetts into Metacom's alliance, too. Colonists suffered heavily in consequence. Of their ninety towns, twelve were wiped out and forty more were damaged. One-tenth of New England's adult white male population was killed or captured. It looked as if Metacom might succeed in turning back English settlement.

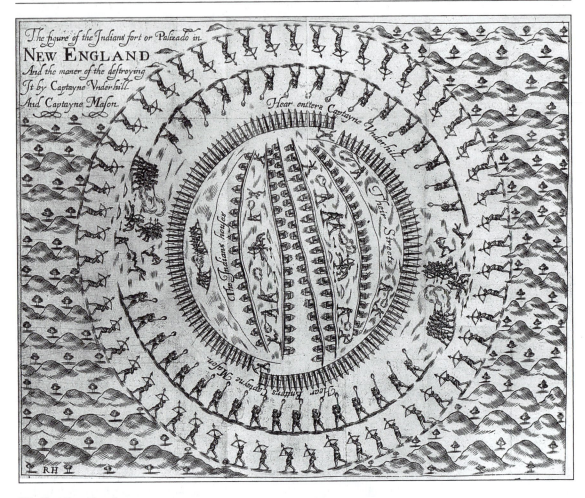

"We Must Burn Them"

An engraving from a contemporary account of the Pequot war shows the dawn raid on the Pequot fort at Mystic, Connecticut, on May 26, 1637. "Many were burnt in the fort, both men, women, and children. Others forced out, . . . twenty and thirty at a time, which our soldiers received and entertained with the point of the sword. Down fell men, women, and children; those that scaped us fell into the hands of the Indians that were in the rear of us." John Underhill, *Newes from America: or a New Discoverie of New England* (1638) — Rare Books and Manuscript Division, New York Public Library, Astor, Lenox and Tilden Foundations.

Yet the colonists proved too well established to dislodge. New Englanders forged their own alliances and took harsh measures. Distrusting even the "praying Indians," the Massachusetts government forcibly interned them on an island in Boston Harbor. Mohawks allied with the colonists weakened Metacom's forces in battle, and in 1676, colonial fighters cornered Metacom in a swamp and killed him. Most native resistance then collapsed, although in Maine, the Abenaki sustained their attacks into 1677. "King

Philip's War," as the English called it, marked the defeat of armed native resistance in eastern and southern New England, though conflicts continued in the region's interior for some decades to come.

In the Spanish territories, extreme labor demands and missionary efforts provoked more successful resistance. Florida tribes rebelled against missions repeatedly from the 1590s to the 1650s. Although it was difficult to coordinate their attacks, the tribes nevertheless survived in the swamps and, after 1680, even began to drive the missions out. New Mexican pueblo Indians only partially submitted to Spanish conversion efforts and demands for forced labor. Christian "converts" covertly adhered to their native beliefs. Sporadic revolts from the 1630s onward took advantage of the Spanish remoteness from their Mexican bases and the rivalry between missions and farming estates.

In 1680, under a leader called El Popé, a concerted uprising swept the eastern pueblo villages, killing settlers and priests and driving the Spanish out of New Mexico in panic. For over a decade, the pueblos were free from intrusion, until a campaign in 1692–1693 reconquered them. Even then, the pueblos continued to resist, rebelling when participants in the revolt were executed, preventing the reimposition of the *encomienda* system, and so obliging Spanish settlers to take up ranching rather than farming. The pueblos, now weakened by population decline and by Apache and Comanche raids from the north, worked out a way of coexisting with the Spanish that largely preserved their own identity.

Coexistence on the Middle Ground   Coexistence, rather than collapse or resistance, was indeed common for Indians whose lands were not directly subject to European settlement. Among the most successful at holding settlers at arm's length were the Iroquois, whose organization and coherence increased under European pressure. Until the mid-eighteenth century, much of upland eastern North America, the Great Lakes, and Mississippi Valley formed an arena of exchange and interaction between natives and Europeans that historians now term "the middle ground." After early setbacks and consolidations, some tribes stabilized control over their fields and hunting grounds and probably even achieved modest population growth. Many regarded themselves as superior to the invading Europeans, whose actions they saw as uncivilized. In these societies, too, women initially retained much of their status and authority.

The fur trade with English, French, or Dutch merchants provided Indians with metalware, guns, blankets, or rum. These exchanges could lead to dependency, and many Europeans and some native leaders saw alcohol especially as a source of exploitation. Settlers enjoyed stories of natives accepting trinkets in payment for furs or even land. But trade was often not as one-sided as it appeared. Indians sought goods that were useful to them;

"Now They Were as They Had Been in Ancient Times": The Pueblo Revolt of 1680

Captured during the Pueblo Revolt of 1680, a Keresan Pueblo man named Pedro Naranjo described the rebellion's plans and causes in this testimony, recorded by his Spanish captors. The Pueblo Revolt against Spanish rule in New Mexico was probably the most successful of all Native American efforts to turn back the European colonists of North America. As the Spanish sought to retake the territory they had lost—and punish the rebels harshly—they captured and interrogated Indian prisoners.

Finally, in the past years, at the summons of an Indian named Popé who is said to have communication with the devil, it happened that in an estufa [kiva] of the pueblo of Los Taos there appeared to the said Popé three figures of Indians who never came out of the estufa. They told him to make a cord of maguey fiber and tie some knots in it which would signify the number of days that they must wait before the rebellion. He said that the cord was passed through all the pueblos of the kingdom so that the ones which agreed to it [the rebellion] might untie one knot in sign of obedience, and by the other knots they would know the days which were lacking; and this was to be done on pain of death to those who refused to agree to it. The said cord was taken from pueblo to pueblo by the swiftest youths under the penalty of death if they revealed the secret. Everything being thus arranged, two days before the time set for its execution, because his lordship had learned of it and had imprisoned two Indian accomplices from the pueblo of Tesuque, it was carried out prematurely that night, because it seemed to them that they were now discovered; and they killed religious, Spaniards, women, and children. This being done, it was proclaimed in all the pueblos that everyone in common should obey the commands of their father whom they did not know, which would be given through El Caydi or El Popé. This was heard by Alonso Catití, who came to the pueblo of this declarant to say that everyone must unite to go to the villa to kill the governor and the Spaniards who had remained with him, and that he who did not obey would, on their return, be beheaded; and in fear of this they agreed to it. Finally, the señor governor and those who were with him escaped from the siege, and later this declarant saw that as soon as the Spaniards had left the kingdom an order came from the said Indian, Popé, in which he commanded all the Indians to break the lands and enlarge their cultivated fields, saying that now they were as they had been in ancient times, free from the labor they had performed for the religious and the Spaniards, who could not now be alive. He said that this is the legitimate cause and the reason they had for rebelling.

Albert L. Hurtado and Peter Iverson, eds., *Major Problems in American Indian History* (1994).

knives, guns, pans, and cloth made hunting or survival easier. And Europeans could seem naive. "[T]he English have no sense," laughed a member of the Montagnais tribe on the St. Lawrence River; "they give us twenty knives for this one beaver skin." Although frontier exchange could provoke antagonism and conflict, natives conducted their dealings with whites as equals or superiors and demanded a measure of deference from them. Until circumstances changed, many Indians would hold their ground.

Conclusion: The Remaking of Three Worlds

Europeans' intrusion into the Americas profoundly altered the ways of life of three previously independent worlds. New World exploration, trade, and settlement linked the peoples of Europe, Africa, and the Americas in patterns of commerce, conflict, and labor coercion.

Africa was the most evident loser. The slave trade, with its grievous drain of population and cultural dislocation, profited some powerful Africans, but few others except Europeans benefited. It impoverished much of the African continent, disrupted trade, and altered political structures. Before 1500, West African economies had living standards comparable with those of much of Europe. Slavery, external and internal, greatly weakened them, leaving Africa susceptible to colonization by European powers in the nineteenth century. The forced movement of slaves from Africa to the Americas long exceeded the scale of European transatlantic migration. Until about 1800, six out of every seven people arriving in the Americas were enslaved Africans. Most were taken to Brazil, Central America, or the West Indies. Only about 5 percent went to British North America.

On the Americas themselves, the European impact was mixed. Major Central and South American empires collapsed and were rapidly incorporated into colonial societies. As Europeans established new settlements, vast numbers of Native Americans were killed by disease or war or were driven to find new places to live. In North America, most eastern seaboard groups declined or retreated in the face of invasion, disease, and dispossession. Those in the interior and in the Spanish borderlands had some success in resisting deeper invasion and in adapting their cultures to the new situation. But even peoples who had little direct contact with Europeans felt their influence.

Not surprisingly, Europeans were the main beneficiaries of colonization. To notables who received land grants, absentee planters who controlled crop production, and merchants in the Atlantic trade, it brought new wealth, though this also sustained social divisions in European societies. Colonial goods changed European tastes. Sugar from the Caribbean and Brazil brought confections to Europeans of middling rank that had previously been enjoyed only by the very wealthy. Virginia tobacco swept Holland and England early in the seventeenth century, and its popularity continued to mount. The period of early colonial settlement initiated a lasting dependence on overseas commodities that would affect all levels of European society in the centuries to come.

Profits from colonial trade helped to transform European economies. By 1600, two hundred ships each year were arriving in Spain, laden with treasure from the Spanish empire. This increasingly found its way to the trading cities of northern Europe, inflating prices but boosting commerce and urban growth and helping to finance further overseas expansion. Spain, France, and Britain all saw North America as an arena for territorial acquisition and rivalry; throughout the eighteenth century, they would fight wars to gain greater control of the continent.

White settlers in Spanish, French, and English America, meanwhile, built an array of new societies. All started to see their interests as different from those of the countries they had come from. In Spanish colonies, where high officials rotated through offices in order to make careers back home, distinctions emerged between Spanish-born *peninsulares* and American-born *criollos* (creoles). Settlers and Native Americans intermarried at a high rate. Mixed-race mestizos outnumbered the Spanish in Mexico after 1650 and among the "Spanish" who migrated northward into New Mexico.

In the English colonies, the distinction between English- and American-born settlers was never as formal as that in the Spanish empire. English–Native American intermarriage was also much rarer. Still, population growth and migration increased the proportion of American-born "English" people with no direct ties to England. In the context of colonial rivalry and wars from the mid-eighteenth century on, these American-born colonists would radically alter their relationships both with England and with Native Americans.

The settlers of North America continued, above all, to need labor. The differences in the ways they procured it would have profound implications for the future. This was particularly true of the different labor patterns that developed in the northern and southern colonies of British North America.

The Years in Review

C. 13,000 B.C.E.

- Asian peoples, who are later called Indians, migrate to North America.

3000 B.C.E.

- Settled agriculture begins among Indians of the Southwest.

1000 C.E.

- Norsemen led by Leif Ericsson "discover" the Western Hemisphere. They call it "Vinland" ("Wineland") because of the grapes growing there.

1340
- Plague ravages Europe, which loses two-fifths of its population between 1300 and 1400.

1444
- Portuguese traders purchase West African slaves to work as lifelong domestic servants in Portugal—the beginnings of the European slave trade.

1492
- Christopher Columbus sails in search of a westerly route to the East, to Asia, but instead lands in the Bahamas, "discovering" a "New World." This leads to the European exploration of the Americas, home to 75 to 100 million people, perhaps one-seventh of the world's population.

1493
- Europeans first taste pineapples, which have been brought back by Columbus; other foods and crops discovered by Columbus are maize, sweet potatoes, and tobacco.

1494
- Spain and Portugal sign the treaty of Tordesillas, in which they agree to divide the entire world between them.

1497
- Vasco da Gama of Portugal rounds Africa and reaches India.

1502
- The first Spanish families settle on the Caribbean island of Hispaniola.

1507
- A German mapmaker names the New World "America" in honor of explorer Amerigo Vespucci.

1513
- Spanish explorer Vasco Núñez de Balboa becomes the first European to see the Pacific Ocean.

1517
- The Protestant Reformation begins in Germany.

1518
- A Spanish ship carries the first full cargo of Africans across the Atlantic, initiating the highly lucrative slave trade and one of the largest forced migrations in history.
- Hernán Cortés and Spanish conquistadors set out for Mexico; within three years, they conquer the Aztec Empire. Within thirty years, the native population drops by almost half as the result of Spanish exploitation and new diseases.

- Conquistadors discover foods that will transform the European palate, including chocolate, peanuts, tortillas, turkeys, and tomatoes.

1524
- A French expedition led by Giovanni da Verrazano explores the east coast of North America; while willing to trade with the newcomers, Maine's Abenaki Indians exhibit what Verrazano describes as "signs of scorn," such as "showing their buttocks and laughing."

1532–1533
- Spanish conquistador Francisco Pizarro, aided by horses and firearms and facing Indians weakened by civil war, invades the Peruvian Andes, defeats the Incas, and conquers Peru.

1534
- Jacques Cartier of France explores the St. Lawrence River.

1545
- The Spanish discover silver in the Andes; between 1500 and 1650, Spaniards (often using forced labor of indigenous peoples) extract 180 tons of gold and 16,000 tons of silver from the Americas.

1565
- The Spanish found St. Augustine (Florida), which has become the oldest continually occupied European settlement in North America.

1583
- Sir Humphrey Gilbert claims Newfoundland for England.

1587
- One hundred English settlers arrive on Roanoke Island, in North Carolina's Outer Banks; by 1590, when a delayed supply ship finally arrives, the colonists have disappeared without a trace.
- England and Spain embark on seventeen years' worth of intermittent armed conflict, which delays English settlement in North America until after the war's conclusion in 1604.

1607
- The first permanent English settlement in the New World is created at Jamestown (Virginia); fewer than half of the new arrivals survive their first year.

1608
- The French establish the colony of Quebec.
- The Spanish, heading north from Mexico in an effort to subdue and convert Indians, found Santa Fe in what they call "New Mexico."

1614
- The Dutch establish Fort Orange (later Albany) on the Hudson River.

1619
- The Virginia House of Burgesses (the first colonial legislature) meets for the first time; colonists have discovered tobacco, and the colony is booming; Indians teach them how to cultivate tobacco, which is popular in England as medicine.

1620
- Pilgrims (religious dissenters) establish a colony at Plymouth, Massachusetts.

1624
- James I dissolves the Virginia Company and establishes Virginia as a royal colony.

1626
- The Dutch settlement of Nieuw Amsterdam is established on Manhattan Island.

1630
- The Massachusetts Bay Company establishes a colony of English Puritans.
- Lemonade is invented in Paris, one of many effects of the availability of cheap sugar grown by slaves and imported from the West Indies.

1635
- Roger Williams, expelled from Massachusetts Bay, founds Providence, Rhode Island.

1637
- English and Indian allies wage war against the Pequot tribe of Connecticut, leading to the virtual extermination of the Pequots.

1638
- Swedish settlers create a short-lived colony at Fort Christina (now Wilmington, Delaware).

1640
- The first book is published in New England: *The Whole Booke of Psalmes faithfully Translated into English Metre* (commonly called *Bay Psalm Book*).

1642–46
- The first English Civil War occurs.

1648
- The second English Civil War begins; King Charles I is beheaded in 1649, and a Commonwealth with Cromwell as its leader is created.

1658

- Cromwell dies.

1660

- Charles II is restored to the throne.

1670

- Muslim inhabitants on the Senegal River revolt in resistance to the slave trade.

1680

- Pueblo Indians led by El Popé drive the Spanish from New Mexico; the Spanish do not reconquer the pueblos for a dozen years.

Additional Readings

For a fine, broad overview of early North American history before 1800, see: Alan Taylor, *American Colonies: The Settling of North America* (2001).

For more on the peoples of the New World prior to contact with Europeans, see: Alvin F. Josephy, ed., *America in 1492: The World of the Indian Peoples before the Arrival of Columbus* (1993); Roger G. Kennedy, *Hidden Cities: The Discovery and Loss of Ancient North American Civilization* (1994); Shepard Krech, *The Ecological Indian: Myth and History* (1999); and Daniel K. Richter, *Facing East from Indian Country: A Native History of North America* (2001).

For more on the European contexts for New World exploration and conquest, see: Nicholas P. Canny and Peter J. Marshall, eds., *The Oxford History of the British Empire, Vol. I* (1998); Norman Davies, *Europe: A History* (1996); Anthony Pagden, *European Encounters with the New World: From Renaissance to Romanticism* (1993); Simon Schama, *The Embarrassment of Riches: An Interpretation of Dutch Culture in the Golden Age* (1987); David Underdown, *A Freeborn People: Politics and the Nation in Seventeenth-Century England* (1996); and Keith Wrightson, *English Society, 1580–1680* (1982).

For more on West African societies and the African slave trade, see: Bonbacar Barry, *Senegambia and the Atlantic Slave Trade* (1998); Robin Blackburn, *The Making of New World Slavery: From the Baroque to the Modern, 1492–1800* (1997); Basil Davidson, *West Africa before the Colonial Era: A History to 1850* (1998); David Brion Davis, *Challenging the Boundaries of Slavery* (2003); David Eltis, *The Rise of African Slavery in the Americas* (2000); Herbert S. Klein, *The Atlantic Slave Trade* (1999); Robin Law, *The Slave Coast of West Africa, 1550–1750: The Impact of the Atlantic Slave Trade* *on an African Society* (1991); Patrick Manning, *Slavery and African Life: Occidental, Oriental and African Slave Trades* (1990); Hugh Thomas, *The Slave Trade: The History of the Atlantic Slave Trade, 1440–1870* (1997); and John Thornton, *Africa and Africans in the Making of the Atlantic World, 1400–1680* (1992).

For more on the early conquest and colonization of the Americas, see:
Joyce E. Chaplin, *Subject Matter: Technology, the Body, and Science on the Anglo-American Frontier, 1500–1676* (2001); Alfred W. Crosby, *Ecological Imperialism: The Biological Expansion of Europe, 900–1900* (1986); Thomas D. Hall, *Social Change in the Southwest, 1350–1880* (1989); Karen Ordahl Kupperman, *Roanoke: The Abandoned Colony,* Second Edition (2007); D. W. Meinig, *The Shaping of America: A Geographical Perspective on 500 Years of History, Vol. 1, Atlantic America, 1492–1800* (1986); Patricia Seed, *Ceremonies of Possession in Europe's Conquest of the New World, 1492–1640* (1995); and David J. Weber, *The Spanish Frontier in North America* (1992).

For more on the English colonial experience, see: David Cressy, *Coming Over: Migration and Communication between England and New England in the Seventeenth Century* (1987); Philip D. Curtin, *The Rise and Fall of the Plantation Complex: Essays in Atlantic History,* Second Edition (1998); David Hackett Fischer, *Albion's Seed: Four British Folkways in America* (1989); James Horn, *A Land as God Made It: Jamestown and the Birth of America* (2005); James Horn, *Adapting to a New World: English Society in the Seventeenth-Century Chesapeake* (1994); and Edmund S. Morgan, *American Slavery, American Freedom: The Ordeal of Colonial Virginia* (1975).

For more on responses by Native Americans to European contact, see:
Virginia DeJohn Anderson, *Creatures of Empire: How Domestic Animals Transformed Early America* (2004); James Axtell, *After Columbus: Essays in the Ethnohistory of Colonial North America* (1988); Kristina Bross, *Dry Bones and Indian Sermons: Praying Indians in Colonial America* (2004); Colin G. Calloway, *New Worlds for All: Indians, Europeans, and the Remaking of Early America* (1997); Karen Ordahl Kupperman, *Indians and English: Facing Off in Early America* (2000); Jill Lepore, *The Name of War: King Philip's War and the Origins of American Identity* (1998); Neal Salisbury, *Manitou and Providence: Indians, Europeans, and the Making of New England, 1500–1643* (1982); Jack Weatherford, *Indian Givers: How the Indians of the Americas Transformed the World* (1988); and Richard White, *The Middle Ground: Indians, Empires, and Republics in the Great Lakes Region, 1650–1815* (1991).

2

Servitude, Slavery, and the Growth of the Southern Colonies

1620–1760

Below Decks

This sketch shows the interior of a Spanish slave ship called the *Albanez*, bound for the West Indies. After a British naval frigate captured the slaver, one of its officers descended below decks to record the horrible conditions of the Africans' Middle Passage.

Francis Meynell, *The Slave Deck of the* Albanez, watercolor, c. 1860 — National Maritime Museum.

ANTHONY JOHNSON arrived in Virginia early in the 1620s, one of the first African slaves to be brought to the colony, and was set to work on the land, like other Africans and thousands of English servants. He married Mary, another slave. By the 1650s, both had obtained their freedom, and he owned 250 acres of land on Virginia's Eastern Shore. Their son and grandson also became landowners, and Anthony Johnson may have been the first black Virginian to possess a slave of his own. Asserting that "I know myne owne ground[.] I will worke when I please and play when I please," Johnson expressed aspirations for economic independence held by many migrants. But in the mid-seventeenth century, such opportunities were reserved increasingly for whites. Harassed by white landowners, Anthony and Mary Johnson sold their acreage in the 1660s and moved to a settlement in Maryland where they were more welcome. Their experience exemplified a growing racial rigidity that would see the emergence of racially based slavery as a distinctive labor system and its extension from Virginia and Maryland into the new English Lower South colonies of the Carolinas and Georgia.

Originating as commercial ventures, England's North American colonies were all open to settlers from the British Isles and other parts of Europe. By 1700, an estimated 130,000 migrants had journeyed from the British Isles to the Chesapeake colonies of Virginia and Maryland alone. After the near-disastrous early settlement in Jamestown, English men and women learned to survive in Virginia; to make their colony and its neighbor, Maryland, economically viable; to organize local governments; and to adapt their Old World values, habits, and expectations to New World realities. They used the land to grow tobacco for export to Europe, making the

Chesapeake a prototype staple-crop producer and tobacco the crop around which their entire economy revolved (Map 2.1).

Tobacco was a "poor man's crop" in that it could be produced on small landholdings with a limited supply of labor. Most tobacco farmers were men of modest but independent means, although some were tenants of larger landholders and a few were servants hoping to acquire land of their own. But at the top of the social hierarchy were large tobacco planters, who could harness the labor of others to grow their crops for them. For half a century or so after 1620, most laborers were indentured servants; only a small proportion were African slaves. After the injustices and instability of early colonial life sparked open rebellion among Virginia servants in the 1670s, however, planters began to rely more and more on slave labor, and the number of slaves increased. Initially, the Chesapeake had been what historians call a "society with slaves," but by the early eighteenth century, it had been transformed into a "slave society," in which slavery was essential to the economic and social fabric and in which the two most significant groups were slaves and the master class who owned them. This change, the single most important development in the early Chesapeake region, set a pattern for the other southern colonies as they too expanded.

Tobacco Plant

This woodcut in *Stirpium Adversaria Nova*, a botanical study published in 1570, was the first published illustration of the plant. (Pierre van der Borcht?) Pierre Pena and Mathias de Lobel, *Stirpium Adversaria Nova* (1570) — Arents Collection, New York Public Library, Astor, Lenox and Tilden Foundations.

By the time David George was born into slavery in Surry County, Virginia, around 1740, the slave system was well entrenched. Put to work in the tobacco fields with members of his family, he experienced slavery's cruelty firsthand. He was whipped by his owners "many a time on my naked skin . . . sometimes until the blood has run down over my waist band," had to watch his mother and sister being whipped, and saw a brother tortured for trying to run away. David himself escaped but was re-enslaved by Indians, and later by a South Carolina planter. Growing up during the religious revivals known as the Great Awakening, which stirred both white and black communities, David George was one of a increasing number of slaves who embraced Christianity. In due course, he became a pioneering Baptist minister. His life reflected one of the many ways in which, even as they were confined by the shackles of slavery, African Americans in the South carved out a degree of cultural autonomy.

The Development of the Southern Colonies

The southern colonies' reliance on the exporting of crops tied them closely to the broader trading patterns of the Atlantic, to British policies for regulating commerce, and to overseas sources of labor and manufactured goods. They had important links with the growing number of British colonies on the islands of the West Indies such as Barbados and Jamaica; after the Dutch introduced sugar cane to Barbados in 1636, sugar plantations worked by African slaves came to dominate these islands. As in all British American colonies, the inhabitants lived alongside Native Americans and the neighboring territories of other European powers, especially France and Spain. Despite crucial differences between the French, Spanish, and British colonies, their proximity to one another would influence the British colonies' development. Elite British colonists needed labor to extract the profits they envisioned in this new land, and they turned to indentured servants to supply it. But large disparities in wealth and opportunity soon resulted in challenges from within colonial society.

The Southern Colonies in Context French and Spanish settlements in North America represented marked contrasts to the patterns that evolved in English colonies, including those of the South. Neither the French nor the Spanish government successfully encouraged large numbers of its own people to move to the colonies. The Hispanic population of Spanish North America, in particular, remained tiny and predominantly male.

France established permanent agricultural settlements in Quebec and an extensive trading network that extended far across the Great Lakes region and ultimately down the Mississippi Valley to the colony of Louisiana, where the port and administrative center of New Orleans was established in 1718. French missionaries sought to convert Indians across this vast territory to Christianity. Since, except in Quebec and in parts of Louisiana, the French were primarily traders rather than settlers on the land, they often established reciprocal relations with the indigenous peoples they encountered.

Spanish missionaries also sought religious converts in New Mexico and Florida but with less harmonious consequences. Spain's military conquests and efforts to harness native labor often provoked resistance, including the Pueblo Revolt of 1680, which temporarily drove Spanish settlers out of New Mexico (see Chapter 1). From the viewpoint of the Spanish government, the missions and fortifications of Florida and New Mexico, even the military bases, or *presidios*, that they later established in their North American territories, were marginal northern outposts of Spain's richer, more important colonies in Mexico and South America.

Nevertheless, the European powers jockeyed for position in North America, not least to restrain their rivals' influence. French traders in the Mississippi Valley and Louisiana, for instance, made contact with native Apaches and Comanches of the Southwest, providing them with horses and firearms that they used to attack settlements in New Mexico. Partly to

Recording an Ambush

These paintings on buffalo hide, produced by an anonymous New Mexican artist sometime between 1720 and 1750, are the first known depictions of Spanish colonial life in the United States. In the summer of 1720, Lt. Governor Pedro de Villasur led Spanish soldiers northward from the New Spain capital of Santa Fe to attack French forces that, with their Apache allies, planned to seize the colony. In this detail of the hide painting, the Spaniards are shown surrounded by their Indian and French foes in an ambush that killed one-third of the Santa Fe garrison. Detail, Segesser II Hide Painting, Villasur expedition, battle of August 13, 1720, painted c. 1720–29 — Palace of the Governors (MNM/DCA), Neg. 158345.

counter the French, Spain extended its military and missionary activity into Texas in the eighteenth century. Spain and Britain, meanwhile, eyed one another warily over Florida; the Spanish were keen to protect their sea routes to the Caribbean and Central America, and the English were anxious about their colonies in the Carolinas and Georgia, fearing them vulnerable to Spanish influence. Early in the eighteenth century, the English helped Florida Indians attack and roll back the Spanish network of missions. The Spanish towns of St. Augustine and Pensacola, however, for a while remained potential refuges for fugitive slaves from the Lower South colonies.

While the French and Spanish monarchies sought close control of their empires and were unwilling to admit to their colonies immigrants from other European powers, English governments permitted much freer migration. In the South, arrivals from England and the West Indies, as well as the

MAP 2.1 The Chesapeake Colonies, 1607–1700

Early English colonists in Virginia and Maryland kept close to the easily navigable coastal inlets around Chesapeake Bay that facilitated travel between the settlements. As Native Americans were pushed back from the bay and the colonial population expanded, settlement spread across much of the low-lying region known as the Tidewater. By the eighteenth century, small farmers and larger planters were settling land in the higher piedmont region above the fall line.

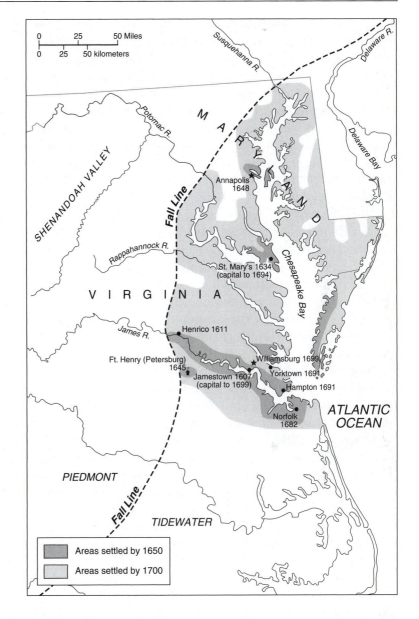

importation of slaves, ensured relatively rapid population growth and expanding settlements. By increasing the demand for land, however, such growth fueled the potential for conflict with Native Americans. Plans to establish missions and schools for southern tribes rarely came to much. Largely unable to exploit Indians' labor and often uninterested in saving their souls, English settlers became increasingly bent on removing or destroying them. As Virginia's English population grew, it pushed well to the west most of the area's Indian inhabitants.

The Demand for Labor: Servitude in the Chesapeake New North American colonies faced an inescapable fact: The availability of land made gathering and keeping a labor force difficult. People who could make a living for themselves from the land had little reason to work for others. For hunters and small farmers whose family members provided sufficient labor, this posed few problems, but owners of large plantations could not work their fields solely with their own labor and that of wives and children. In tobacco, the leaders of the Chesapeake colonies had found a staple crop that could make them prosperous if they could grow it on a large scale, but to do that, they needed to find and discipline a labor force that would make their land yield its wealth.

Virginia's first promoters expected to make Native Americans the colony's labor force. They hoped that English goods and civility would seduce and domesticate a native population that they regarded as inferior to themselves. When the Powhatan people refused to play this role, planters considered enslaving them. But for four decades after 1607, the Chesapeake tribes were too well armed, too numerous, and too familiar with the countryside to be easily enslaved, and the 1622 and 1644 wars with the Powhatans convinced planters to drive them away from areas of English settlement.

So planters had to look elsewhere for laborers. English authorities assisted by forcibly transporting some of London's orphans to work in the tobacco fields. Between 1617 and 1624, several hundred orphans, scores of whom had declared "their unwillingness to go to Virginia," were turned over to planters to be worked until they reached the age of twenty-one. Having been "brought to goodness under severe Masters," they could then be set free. Most of these involuntary migrants, however, died prematurely after months or years of hard labor. The crown also proposed shipping convicts to Virginia, but planters opposed the plan. Not wishing to employ men and women who had already demonstrated a readiness to break the law, they were until the next century able to limit the number of convicts transported to Virginia.

Planters had little choice but to recruit young, poor English adults as servants. Population growth, economic depression, and enclosures had worsened poverty and unemployment in England and produced a supply of recruits who were willing to sign an indenture, a contract by which they agreed to work for a term of four to seven years in exchange for passage to the colonies. At the end of their period of service, each would get freedom, a set of new clothes, some tools, and fifty acres of land. Over half of early indentured servants came from agricultural backgrounds, and another 20 percent were from the textile or clothing trades. Few had any other prospect of acquiring that much land.

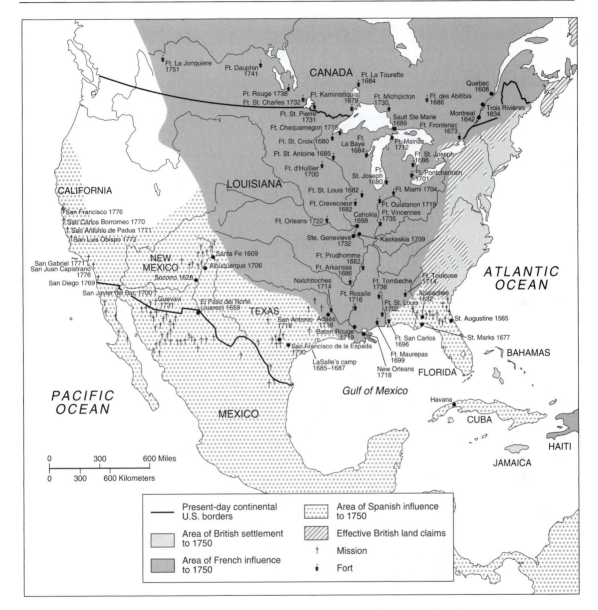

MAP 2.2   Spanish and French Settlements in North America before 1750

Early Spanish mission building in Florida and New Mexico was followed in the first half of the eighteenth century by the occupation of parts of Texas (and, from 1769, of the coast of California, too). Meanwhile, the far-flung activities of French fur traders in the Great Lakes and Mississippi Valley led to the establishment of numerous forts and trading centers, such as New Orleans. British colonies were confined to the eastern part of the continent.

THE INCONVENIENCIES
THAT HAVE HAPPENED TO SOME PERSONS WHICH HAVE TRANSPORTED THEMSELVES

from *England* to *Virginia*, vvithout prouisions necessary to sustaine themselues, hath greatly hindred the *Progresse* of that noble *Plantation*: For preuention of the like disorders heereafter, that no man suffer, either through ignorance or misinformation; it is thought requisite to publish this short declaration: wherein is contained a particular of such necessaries, as either priuate families or single persons shall haue cause to furnish themselues with, for their better support at their first landing in Virginia: whereby also greater numbers may receiue in part, directions how to prouide themselues.

Apparrell.

Apparrell for one man, and so after the rate for more.

	li.	s.	d.
One Monmouth Cap	00	01	10
Three falling bands	—	01	03
Three shirts	—	07	06
One waste-coate	—	02	02
One suite of Canuase	—	07	06
One suite of Frize	—	10	00
One suite of Cloth	—	15	00
Three paire of Irish stockins	—	04	—
Foure paire of shooes	—	08	08
One paire of garters	—	00	10
One doozen of points	—	00	03
One paire of Canuase sheets	—	08	00
Seuen ells of Canuase, to make a bed and boulster, to be filled in *Virginia* 8.s.			
One Rug for a bed 8.s. which with the bed seruing for two men, halfe is	08	00	
Fiue ells coorse Canuase, to make a bed at Sea for two men, to be filled with straw, iiij.s.			
One coorse Rug at Sea for two men, will cost vj.s. is for one	05	00	
	04	00	00

Victuall.

For a whole yeere for one man, and so for more after the rate.

	li.	s.	d.
Eight bushels of Meale	02	00	00
Two bushels of pease at 3.s.	—	06	00
Two bushels of Oatemeale 4.s. 6.d.	—	09	00
One gallon of *Aquauitæ*	—	02	06
One gallon of Oyle	—	03	06
Two gallons of Vineger 1.s.	—	02	00
	03	03	00

Armes.

For one man, but if halfe of your men haue armour it is sufficient so that all haue Peeces and swords.

	li.	s.	d.
One Armour compleat, light	—	17	00
One long Peece, fiue foot or fiue and a halfe, neere Musket bore	01	02	—
One sword	—	05	—
One belt	—	01	—
One bandaleere	—	01	06
Twenty pound of powder	—	18	00
Sixty pound of shot or lead, Pistoll and Goose shot	—	05	00
	03	09	06

Tooles.

For a family of 6. persons and so after the rate for more.

	li.	s.	d.
Fiue broad howes at 2.s. a piece	—	10	—
Fiue narrow howes at 16.d. a piece	—	06	c8
Two broad Axes at 3.s. 8.d. a piece	—	07	c4
Fiue felling Axes at 18.d. a piece	—	07	06
Two steele hand sawes at 16.d. a piece	—	02	08
Two two-hand sawes at 5. s. a piece	—	10	—
One whip-saw, set and filed with box, file, and wrest	—	10	—
Two hammers 12.d. a piece	—	02	00
Three shouels 18.d. a piece	—	04	06
Two spades at 18.d. a piece	—	03	—
Two augers 6.d. a piece	—	01	00
Six chissels 6.d. a piece	—	03	00
Two percers stocked 4.d. a piece	—	00	08
Three gimlets 2.d. a piece	—	00	06
Two hatchets 21.d. a piece	—	03	06
Two frowes to cleaue pale 18.d.	—	03	00
Two hand bills 20. a piece	—	03	04
One grindlestone 4.s.	—	04	00
Nailes of all sorts to the value of	02	00	—
Two Pickaxes	—	03	—
	06	02	c8

Houshold Implements.

For a family of 6. persons and so for more or lesse after the rate.

	li.	s.	d.
One Iron Pot	—	07	—
One kettle	—	06	—
One large frying-pan	—	02	c6
One gridiron	—	01	c6
Two skillets	—	05	—
One spit	—	02	—
Platters, dishes, spoones of wood	—	04	—
	01	08	00

For Suger, Spice, and fruit, and at Sea for 6 men — 12 c6

So the full charge of Apparrell, Victuall, Armes, Tooles, and houshold stuffe, and after this rate for each person, will amount vnto about the summe of — 12 10 —

The passage of each man is — 06 00

The fraight of these prouisions for a man, will bee about halfe a Tun, which is — 01 10 —

So the whole charge will amount to about — 20 00 00

Nets, hookes, lines, and a tent must be added, if the number of people be greater, as also some kine.

And this is the vsuall proportion that the Virginia Company doe bestow vpon their Tenants which they send.

Whosoeuer transports himselfe or any other at his owne charge vnto *Virginia*, shall for each person so transported before Midsummer 1625. haue to him and his heires for euer fifty Acres of Land vpon a first, and fifty Acres vpon a second diuision.

Imprinted at London by FELIX KYNGSTON. 1622.

Inconveniences

Directed to British free men and their families, this 1622 notice lists the necessities that prospective voluntary immigrants should obtain before embarking for Virginia — or risk becoming a detriment to the colony. John Carter Brown Library, Brown University.

Between 75 and 85 percent of those who migrated to Virginia and Maryland in the seventeenth century did so as indentured servants, and three-fourths of these were single men between the ages of fifteen and twenty-four. Most worked with one or two other indentured servants on tobacco farms, performing the routine but delicate tasks of sprouting, transplanting, and curing tobacco. During growing season, the fields had to be hoed often, and much additional work was required to eke out a subsistence through gardening, hunting, and foraging.

"To Be in England Again": An Indentured Servant in Virginia

On March 20, 1623, Richard Frethorne, an indentured servant, wrote to his parents in England; he had landed in Virginia three months earlier. The dangers posed by disease and hostile Indians, the pain of separation from home, and the persistent problem of securing adequate food left many new settlers in a state of despair. Two-thirds of Frethorne's fellow ship passengers had died since arriving in the colony. Frethorne asks his parents to "redeem," that is, buy out, his indenture.

Loving and kind father and mother . . . this is to let you understand that I your child am in a most heavy case by reason of the nature of the country [which] is such that it causeth much sickness, [such] as the scurvy and the bloody flux, and diverse other diseases, which maketh the body very poor and weak. And when we are sick there is nothing to comfort us, for since I came out of the ship, I never ate anything but peas and loblollie (that is water gruel); as for deer or venison I never saw any since I came into this land; there is indeed some fowl, but we are not allowed to go and get it, but must work hard both early and late for a mess of water gruel, and a mouthful of bread and beef. A mouthful of bread, for a penny loaf must serve for 4 men which is most pitiful if you did know as much as I, when people cry out day and night— Oh! that they were in England without their limbs—and would [sacrifice] any limb to be in England again. . . .

We live in fear of the enemy every hour, yet we have had to combat with them . . . and we took two alive, and make slaves of them . . . for we are in great danger, for our Plantation is very weak, by reason of the dearth, and sickness, of our company. . . .

But I am not half, a quarter so strong as I was in England, and all is for want of victuals, for I do protest unto you that I have eaten more in a day at home then I have allowed me here for a week. . . . If you love me you will redeem me suddenly, for which I do entreat and beg, and if you cannot get the merchants to redeem me for some little money then for God's sake get a gathering or entreat some good folks to lay out some little sum of money, in meal, and cheese and butter, and beef. . . .

Good father do not forget me, but have mercy and pity my miserable case. I know if you did but see me you would weep to see me, for I have but one suit, but it is a strange one, . . . and as for my part I have set down my resolution that . . . the answer of this letter will be life or death to me, therefore good father send as soon as you can . . .

Susan Kingsbury, ed., *The Records of the Virginia Company of London* (1935).

Indentured women, who accounted for nearly all unmarried female immigrants from England, made up only a small percentage of the population. Only a few hundred went to Maryland, where in the early decades of settlement, men outnumbered women six to one. More women went to Virginia, but the sex ratio was still unbalanced: men outnumbered women

by four to one in 1625 and remained in the majority for most of the century. An indentured woman's work depended on the social status of her employer. If indentured to a small planter, she labored in the fields. Wealthier planters and merchants employed their female servants in domestic tasks such as washing clothes, sewing, preparing food, and child rearing.

Some planters also purchased slaves and set them to work alongside English indentured servants. Nearly all the earliest slaves in North America were male Africans who had been enslaved for several years on the tobacco or sugar plantations of the Caribbean and so arrived in the Chesapeake already "seasoned." Many of this first generation of American slaves were from the trading societies of the West African coast and had some familiarity with the commercial system that had ensnared them, as well as with the languages (English or various pidgins) that were spoken in the English Atlantic world.

Although the first slaves reached Virginia in 1619, their numbers remained small for decades. By 1660, the English population of the Chesapeake had reached 30,000, but there were probably fewer than 1,500 people of African birth or descent in the region. Though most of them labored as slaves for life, some worked as indentured servants and were freed when their terms of service expired. Black and white servants worked together, but

From Rags to Riches

This British engraving represents a fictional colonial success story. Polly Haycock, pregnant and unmarried, was sentenced to transportation to Virginia as an indentured servant. Brutalized by her master, Polly was released from her servitude by a Virginia magistrate, whom she married. The end of the tale depicts Polly as a rich plantation mistress who mistreats her own servants. Anonymous, *The Fortunate Transport. Rob Theif: or the Lady of ye Gold Watch Polly Haycock*, engraving, 1760–80, 11 1/4 × 15 3/4 inches — Colonial Williamsburg.

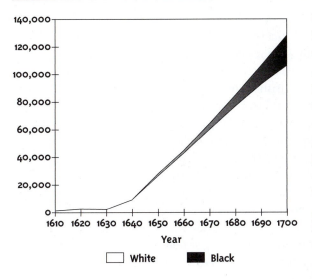

Figure 2.1 Population in the Seventeenth-Century Southern Colonies

This chart illustrates the slow population growth among whites during the early decades of settlement, followed by steady growth after 1640; it also shows the population increase among the initially small black population from the 1670s on as slavery expanded.

black servants' terms of service tended to be longer, and punishments for infractions tended to be more severe. Nevertheless, there were still chances to obtain freedom. By 1650, a small free black population had grown up in the Chesapeake, finding employment as craft workers, laborers, and tenants or—like Anthony Johnson—acquiring land and becoming independent farmers.

Between the 1620s and the 1650s, as the tobacco economy expanded, thousands of English immigrants flocked to Virginia and Maryland (Figure 2.1). Servants and slaves found themselves scattered on farms and plantations across the Tidewater, the low-lying region that lay close to Chesapeake Bay's many navigable rivers and inlets, where crops could easily be loaded onto ships. Virginia's elected assembly, the House of Burgesses, emerged as the protector of the interests of large planters. Yet because planters' lives revolved so completely around the competitive scuffle for tobacco and money, public institutions often remained scanty or neglected. One member of the House of Burgesses was so busy getting rich from tobacco that he attended only one session in eight years. Schooling was poor or nonexistent, and no public provision for education would be made for generations. Some planters could not even be persuaded to organize, much less to participate in, a militia.

To ensure that their servants actually worked, masters exercised considerable power. Colonial laws gave them wider authority over servants than they would have enjoyed in England. Unlike their English counterparts, Virginia servants lacked, for example, the right to take masters to court for maltreatment or breach of contract, and the local magistrates to whom they might have appealed were in any case often the very men who employed them. Labor discipline was maintained largely by brute force. One woman was beaten "like a dogge," another "sore beaten and her body full of sores and holes." Even when the authorities did act to protect servants, masters could show their contempt. A Captain William Odeon, on being convicted in 1662 of repeated maltreatment of servants, promptly "struck and abused his servant" right there in the courtroom.

Colonial indentured servants, unlike English servants, could be repeatedly bought and sold, and those who were accused of insubordination could be fined, branded, or whipped or have their terms of service extended. Serious offenders faced execution, usually at a public ceremony attended by fellow servants, staged to act as an example to the discontented among them. The Virginia House of Burgesses required each county court to install a ducking stool (a chair in which offenders were ducked in water) with which to punish misbehaving women. Combined with the fact that most servants had no family in the Chesapeake, such conditions often resulted in lives of abject misery. "So the truth is," the servant Edward Hill wrote to his brother in England, "we live in the fearfullest age that ever Christians lived in."

Disease, poor diet, and maltreatment meant that before 1650, nearly two-thirds of servants died before their indentures expired, so planters often escaped the obligation to provide land to servants on completion of their terms. Even in Maryland, where survival rates exceeded those in Virginia, only one in three of the servants who arrived before 1642 eventually acquired land. After midcentury, however, although labor remained harsh, improvements in diet and living conditions did produce a higher survival rate among indentured servants.

The Chesapeake colonies also faced the problem of regulating sexual contacts and marriages with scarce white women in a predominantly male society. Unmarried servant women who became pregnant, as did an esti-mated 20 percent, were punished by additional years of service. It took Virginia until 1662 to recognize the obvious incentive this gave owners to impregnate their own servants; the House of Burgesses then passed a law requiring that the extra service be with a new master. Some women had their infants taken from them and sold, for a few pounds of tobacco, to another master. Masters permitted these female servants to marry only if the servants compensated them for the loss of their labor, a financial obliga-tion that was beyond most servants' means.

Only rarely did female servants acquire property or political rights after gaining their freedom. For a time, however, it was possible for freed men who obtained land to aspire to minor political offices and to vote for the prominent planters who filled nearly all important public positions. Nev-ertheless, the planter elite continued to protect its own interests. In both Virginia and Maryland, new laws lengthened the years of indentured serv-ice, denied freed men their promised fifty acres, or narrowed economic and political opportunities for small landowners. As more servants survived their terms and clamored for the land they had been promised, the system of indentured servitude began to lose its attractiveness to planters. Unwill-ing to share wealth and power with their former servants, planters found this growing group of free, landless people menacing. Their geographical isolation on Tidewater plantations heightened planters' sense of vulnerabil-ity. After midcentury, their lives would be dominated by a constant balanc-ing of their need for labor against their fear of social disorder.

Power and Society in the Chesapeake: 1650s–1670s At the top of this fragile new society were the men who had been most successful at reaping wealth from the fertile soil through the hard work of their servants. Many of those who sat in the House of Burgesses and on the judicial bench had married the widows of wealthy planters, made the best deals, or paid the highest bribes to other men to do their bidding. By midcentury, some planters had obtained thousands of acres of land apiece. Colonel Philip Ludwell acquired his land simply by altering documents so that he received ten times the acreage he was entitled to. Planters' exercise of power through government and law was an unconcealed effort to use the tools of civil authority to keep the upper hand in a continuing battle for profit.

The Chesapeake colonies' reputation improved as they achieved a measure of stability. Rather backhandedly, an English pamphleteer noted in 1656 that they were no longer "a nest of Rogues, whores, desolate and rooking persons" but somewhere planters might prosper. The Chesapeake attracted a new group of men: immigrants who were richer and better connected with the aristocracy in England. They acquired assembly seats, joined court benches, and obtained other important positions. Many were the younger sons of English gentry. Barred from their fathers' status and wealth by England's laws of primogeniture, by which an eldest son inherited his father's whole estate, these men found in America the chance to begin life at the top of society. Some had inherited thousands of acres originally purchased from the Virginia Company; others arrived with the cash to buy plantations or uncleared land. In the 1660s and 1670s, these men formed a new ruling elite, using their wealth as tobacco planters to make political connections and filling political offices with relatives. By 1700, 90 percent of Virginia's burgesses were linked by ties of blood or marriage.

The rise of this new colonial elite took place during a time of great turmoil in England. Between 1640 and 1660, England had been too preoccupied with its civil war to pay much attention to what was happening in the colonies. Virginia planters turned to Dutch merchants to carry tobacco to Europe and ship cattle to the West Indies, and access to Caribbean markets encouraged them to shift some land from growing tobacco to raising cattle and grains, which they traded for rum, sugar, and slaves, largely without paying duties to the English government. Planters came to regard free trade as a right and any English law not ratified by their own assemblies as invalid.

Their notions did not survive challenge from England, both before and after the restoration of Charles II to the throne in 1660. Commercial rivalry between England and Holland provoked three wars between the 1650s and 1670s and led English governments to curb colonists whose trade conflicted with England's interests. New trade regulations known as the Navigation Acts, introduced in 1651 and extended in the early 1660s, required colonial products to be carried in vessels built, owned, and crewed by Englishmen or English colonials. Tobacco, whatever its ultimate destination, had to be shipped to England, Ireland, or another English colony, where it incurred an import duty, and cargoes shipped on from there were assessed export duties as well. These rules enriched the crown and English merchants but burdened Chesapeake planters. To make matters worse, overproduction of tobacco in the 1660s and 1670s drove the price of the crop to an all-time low, just as the second and third Anglo-Dutch wars disrupted trade and colonists were obliged to raise taxes to pay for troops and fortifications.

To ensure that planters paid the taxes they owed, Charles II relied on his friend and supporter, Virginia's governor William Berkeley. Royal officialdom in Virginia, often at odds with the House of Burgesses, comprised Berkeley and those he chose to favor with office. Though officials and burgesses overlapped in membership and goals, the crown and planters faced a basic conflict of interests. Planters' fortunes rose and fell with the price of tobacco and the consequent profits they could earn from the crop; overproduction, which drove prices down, was a major concern to them. Crown revenues depended on the quantity, not the price, of tobacco shipped, so officials had no interest in curbing output or promoting agricultural diversification.

In many respects, the Chesapeake colonies were more successful by the mid-seventeenth century than they had been in their early years. Life expectancy for the second generation of colonists was at least as good as the forty years enjoyed by their English cousins. Immigrants found opportunities in the colonies, and the crown and merchants benefited financially from them. Still, the Chesapeake was far from idyllic. Death rates were still such that one in four white newborns died within a year, and half of white Virginians did not live to be twenty-one. Men outnumbered women by at least three to one in 1660, and by six to one in some areas, so marriages were not the rule, and mortality often disrupted those that did occur: two out of three marriages lasted less than ten years. Orphans were common; half of seventeenth-century Virginia children had lost one or both parents by the age of nine. Society still seemed crude and unstable.

It was also unequal. The great majority of colonists were either landowners or servants. Wealthy planters stacked the odds in their own favor and against their poorer neighbors. They made up 5 percent or less of the landowners, but they reserved the best land for themselves and their children, including much of the fertile Tidewater. They had pushed westward most of the region's Indians, who maintained uneasy contacts with English traders and the colonists who settled near them.

Plantation House

The architect Benjamin Latrobe sketched Virginia's first great plantation house in 1796. At the time, the principal part of the house, built by Sir William Berkeley, was more than 147 years old. Benjamin Henry Latrobe, *View of "Greenspring," home of William Ludwell Lee*—Maryland Historical Society.

Planters' need for a large workforce did not lead them to improve conditions for their laborers. Instead, like most English employers of the period, they tried to exploit to the full the men and women they could recruit. Of the servants who survived long enough to achieve their freedom, only a small proportion were able to acquire land—between 9 and 17 percent in Virginia in the 1670s, depending on the county. Even these fortunates often had land that was of poor quality, controlled by Indians, or too far from navigable water to permit tobacco to be marketed. Large planters often controlled the shipping that took tobacco to market and could gouge smaller competitors, and the planter-dominated House of Burgesses fixed taxes and fees to the disadvantage of small landholders. These conditions combined to create a large group of frustrated, debt-ridden small farmers who also, if they lived on the frontier of settlement, faced conflicts with nearby Indians.

Bacon's Rebellion of 1676: A Turning Point For Governor Berkeley and wealthy planters, this discontent posed a threat. Small landowners, Berkeley told the Privy Council in London, set a bad example for servants and alienated both from the colonial government, which, he wrote in 1667 during one of the Anglo-Dutch wars, was "pressed at our backes with Indians, in our Bowills with our servants . . . and invaded from without by the Dutch." He feared that free smallholders and servants would rise together to support the Dutch "in hopes of bettering their condition by sharing the Plunder of the Country with them." Six years later, he thought that even without foreign provocation, the population, of whom "Six parts of Seven at least are Poore, Indebted, Discontented, and Armed," might rebel at any time. These fears were grounded in growing numbers of servant runaways and small revolts in the early 1660s, one of which (led by Isaac Friend) resulted in several executions and laws tightening curbs on servants' and slaves' freedom of movement.

Freemen and servants resented not just the elite as such, but also the colonial government's perceived indifference to their interests. By 1675, skirmishes with Indians had intensified, and many frontier settlers had come to see all Indians, friendly or not, as enemies. Governor Berkeley and the burgesses planned measures against local tribes but hesitated for fear of igniting a widespread Indian war. The following spring, armed groups of small farmers pressing for action adopted as their leader Nathaniel Bacon, a young and well-to-do member of the gentry who, with other prosperous planters, was frustrated by Berkeley's leniency. With a mixed group of farmers and planters, Bacon led an unauthorized assault on a native village in May 1676, massacring friendly as well as hostile Indians and seizing stocks of pelts.

"The Declaration of the People": Bacon's Rebellion

In announcing the rebellion in 1676, Nathaniel Bacon issued "The Declaration of the People," in which he detailed a set of grievances of the common people against Governor Berkeley's administration and argued the revolutionary notion that Berkeley's authority could not be considered legitimate without the people's consent.

For having upon specious pretenses of Public works raised unjust Taxes upon the Commonality for the advancement of private Favorites and other sinister ends. . . .

For having abused and rendered Contemptible the Majesty of Justice, [by] advancing to places of judicature scandalous and Ignorant favorites.

For having wronged his Majesty's Prerogative and Interest by assuming the monopoly of the Beaver Trade.

By having in that unjust gaine Bartered and sold his Majesty's Country and the lives of his Loyal Subjects to the Barbarous Heathen [the Indians].

For having protected, favored, and Imboldened the Indians against his Majesty's most Loyal subjects, never contriving, requiring, or appointing any due or proper means [to prevent] their many Invasions, Murders, and Robberies Committed upon us. . . .

For having . . . forged a Commission by we know not what hand, not only without but against the Consent of the People, for raising and effecting of Civil Wars and distractions. . . .

Of these the aforesaid Articles we accuse Sir William Berkeley, as guilty of each and every one of the same, and as one, who has Traitorously attempted, violated and Injured his Majesty's Interest here. . . .

These are therefore in his Majesty's name, to Command you forthwith to seize the Persons above mentioned as Traitors to your King and Country, . . . and if you want any other Assistance, you are forthwith to demand it in the Name of the People of all the Counties of Virginia.

Virginia Magazine of History and Biography, I (1893–94).

Bacon sought a military commission from the governor to pursue further attacks, but Berkeley declared him and his followers to be rebels and had Bacon captured. Having made Bacon write a confession, Berkeley nevertheless pardoned him in an effort to conciliate Bacon's followers and reassert his own authority. Instead, during the summer of 1676, Bacon's supporters drove Berkeley out of Virginia, tried to capture Maryland's governor, plundered the estates of their prosperous opponents, and continued to attack Indians. In September, when Berkeley tried to restore his government in Virginia, Bacon and over five hundred armed men attacked Jamestown and burned it to the ground. The ranks swollen by servants and slaves, including those of Berkeley's supporters who had joined the cam-

Bacon's Castle, Surrey, Va.
No portrait of Nathaniel Bacon survived. This engraving in an 1866 weekly newspaper shows a house that Bacon and his followers reputedly used as a stronghold in 1676. Albert Berghaus, *Frank Leslie's Illustrated Newspaper*, September 8, 1866 — American Social History Project.

BACON'S CASTLE, SURREY, VA.—SEE PAGE 391.

paign on being promised their freedom, Bacon's movement had become a full-scale rebellion against Virginia's rulers. Women such as the affluent Sarah Drummond helped to stir Bacon's supporters to action.

Bacon's sudden death from dysentery in October 1676 blunted the rebellion, and the subsequent arrival of armed vessels from England cooled the enthusiasm of his more prosperous supporters, but many servants, slaves, and "Freemen that had but lately crept out of the condition of Servants" fought on for a period. By January 1677, the rebellion was over, and Berkeley's restored government exacted punishment by hanging twenty-three rebels, including Sarah Drummond's husband, the governor. But although the rebellion had collapsed, it marked an important turning point in the emergence of a distinctly southern form of colonial society. Having almost succeeded in toppling the Virginia elite, Bacon's Rebellion alerted colonial leaders to the dangers they faced from the concerted actions of freeholders, servants, and slaves in opposition to them.

Nathaniel Bacon was himself no social leveler. In fact, he was related by marriage to Berkeley and was a member of the governor's council. But in rallying supporters against Berkeley, he drew no distinctions between whites and blacks, freemen and slaves, speaking only of a "common people" united by oppression from "unworthy favourites and juggling parasites" among the colony's rulers. Bacon's own resentment toward the governor's ruling clique became the vehicle for a more popular uprising of the poor against the wealthy. As many as one in ten of all Virginia's black males joined the rebellion, and among the last rebels to surrender were eighty slaves and four hundred white laborers. Leading planters, terrified by such interracial and interclass solidarity, were determined that no such challenge should threaten them again.

The Making of Southern Slave Societies

Population growth and the westward migration of former servants, who settled in the backcountry, increased pressure on the frontiers and intensified demands from white settlers for military action against Indians. Tensions between rich and poor and between backcountry settlers and Tidewater inhabitants threatened to divide Chesapeake society along class lines. The elite saw particular danger in the potential for a union of poorer whites and blacks to rise up against them. They resolved to place less reliance on white servants and to recruit increasing numbers of black slave laborers. Such changes altered landowners' plans for working their properties. Thomas Gerard, lord of the manor of St. Clement's in St. Mary's County, Maryland, had expected to make his money from renting land to tenants, as he might have done in England. He purchased indentured servants to work on his farms and recruited settlers and freed servants who were willing to rent land from him. But this increasingly became a difficult venture. Freed servants with means wished to purchase their own land, and the poor could neither buy nor rent. By 1670, Gerard had sold much of his manor to freeholders and was preoccupied with purchasing slaves to work other land he owned in Virginia. In previous decades, Virginia and Maryland had been societies with slaves, in which slaves had provided some of the labor. By the end of the seventeenth century, they were being transformed into slave societies, in which slaves formed the bulk of the subordinate labor force.

From Servitude to Slavery in the Chesapeake

Demographic changes and a new sense of permanence contributed to the emergence of a new labor system. White farmers, artisans, tenants, and laborers — the men among them, at least — secured some rights and economic opportunities that were denied to the growing number of black slaves, who would increasingly be kept in racially based subjugation.

Among the first steps taken after Bacon's Rebellion were efforts to reduce social tensions among whites. Disagreements between local and royal authorities diminished as Charles II limited the power of his council in Virginia and extended that of the House of Burgesses. Freed servants' access to land was improved. New laws curbed land speculation, such as that practiced by the king himself when he granted two friends all the public lands in Virginia. There was a campaign to drive the Indians over the mountains into present-day Kentucky and Tennessee. The English Parliament began investigating the treatment of indentured servants. The crown now prosecuted recruiters who used illegal tactics such as kidnapping, misrepresentation, and fraud.

Continuing a process begun before the rebellion, a series of measures sought to place black people—both free and slave—in greater subjection and to break the ties between white and black laborers. Free blacks faced new restrictions on their legal and political rights. Laws passed in the 1660s had formally recognized slavery and begun to define it in racial terms. Any child born to a slave woman would be enslaved, too. Although "Christians" could not be slaves, Africans were to be excluded from this principle; in 1682, those whose parents or homeland were not Christian at the time of their purchase were defined as slaves. Other laws prohibited interracial cohabitation or marriage, banned "Negroes and other slaves" from carrying arms or joining the militia, made freeing slaves more difficult, and prevented slaves from owning land. Laws against rape excluded slave women from their protection. By 1705, the contempt earlier generations of planters had shown for Indians and English indentured servants had reached its logical culmination in a slave code that gave masters unrestricted power over a permanently unfree labor force.

As many blacks lost what freedom they had, whites now benefited from preferential treatment. Guaranteed their own freedom, even poor whites could see themselves as superior to blacks. With laws that placed all whites above and separate from blacks, Virginia's elite fostered racial bonds among whites that overcame the economic and political inequalities between them and reduced the chance that poor whites would join blacks against their masters. Planters drove a wedge between slaves and white servants and so ensured their own continued dominance.

Other changes reinforced these efforts to differentiate white from black labor. Opportunities elsewhere curbed both the free white migration to the region and the supply of new white indentured servants. A revival of the English economy improved opportunities for the poor in England, while the attraction of newly opening colonies, such as Pennsylvania (see Chapter 3), also reduced the flow of servants available to do farm and craft labor in the South. Indentured servants continued to come to the Chesapeake, but an increasing proportion were young women, purchased to perform domestic work in prosperous households.

As white labor became scarcer, more and more planters followed Thomas Gerard's lead in buying slaves to work as field hands. Until 1698, the Royal Africa Company held a monopoly on the slave trade with English colonies, and although company slave shipments increased after 1672, the Chesapeake planters' demand for slaves induced them to resort to illegal purchases whenever they could. Abolition of the monopoly increased the supply, and the number of slaves imported from Africa continued to rise markedly. Virginia's slave population rose from 3,000 in 1680 to 13,000 in 1700, of whom half had been brought from Africa and the remainder were born either locally or in the Caribbean. By 1720, there were 27,000 slaves in Virginia, and imports from Africa exceeded 1,000 a year. In St. Mary's County, Maryland, where servants outnumbered slaves by almost four to one in 1680, by 1710 slaves outnumbered servants by five to one. Instead of the society of landlords, tenants, and servants that wealthy settlers had once envisioned, the Chesapeake Tidewater was turning into a society of large and small landowners, poor white laborers, and African slaves.

Unlike many among the first American slaves, newly imported slave men and women spoke no English and had had no experience of even near-equality with whites. Most came from the African interior, where there was little contact with the languages or commerce of the Atlantic trade system, as there was in coastal West Africa. After suffering capture and a brutal voyage, they reached the Chesapeake to be put on sale. According to one observer around 1700, "slaves can be selected according to pleasure, young and old, men and women. They are entirely naked when they arrive, having only corals of different colors around their necks and arms." They were usually dispersed singly or in small groups among different slave owners.

The strange society into which they were forced was becoming increasingly comfortable for its white inhabitants. After two generations of imbalanced sex ratios and high mortality, the Chesapeake's white population was growing naturally, as well as through immigration, by the late seventeenth century. A better food supply and improved living conditions increased life expectancy. The proportion of women rose: in St. Mary's County, Maryland, where men outnumbered women by three or four to one before 1670, the ratio had reached 1.22 to 1 by 1712. Marrying young, women bore considerable numbers of children, an increasing proportion of whom survived infancy. Marriages, less frequently broken by death, lasted longer; among the gentry, the average length of marriage rose from fifteen years in the late seventeenth century to twenty-five years for those commenced after 1700. Planters and small farmers began to build more permanent houses and farm buildings. A settled southern society, based on slavery, was starting to take shape.

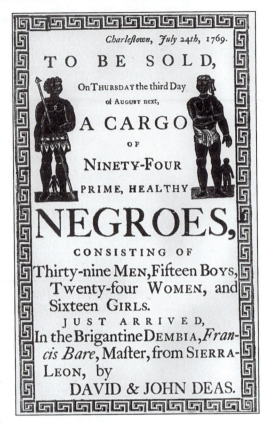

"To Be Sold"
This handbill announcing an auction of African captives was posted around the city of Charleston in 1769. American Antiquarian Society.

The Lower South   As these changes were taking place in the Chesapeake, immigrants began to colonize the Lower South. They settled in the area that at first was called Carolina, granted to a company of proprietors by Charles II after his restoration to the throne in 1660. From this original grant, the colonies of North and South Carolina (formally separated in 1719) and Georgia would eventually be formed.

At first, the Lower South differed from the Chesapeake. Although migrants from Virginia brought tobacco and slavery to the Albemarle region, which became North Carolina, early South Carolinians rejected both tobacco and exclusive reliance on slave labor. They grew a variety of crops with a mixed workforce that, in addition to slaves, included family members, indentured servants, and wage laborers. By the early eighteenth century, however, South Carolina too was making the transition from a society with slaves to a slave society.

The original principles of government for Carolina, the Fundamental Constitutions, were drawn up in the late 1660s, chiefly by the English political philosopher John Locke. He envisaged a harmonious agricultural society with an economy based on mixed farming, cattle raising, and a trade in deerskins with local natives. Though his subsequent writings helped to inspire, among a later generation of Americans, the belief that all men were created equal, here Locke proposed an ordered, hierarchical society in which the right of large landowners to govern would receive the formal assent of the majority of settlers. However, despite repeated attempts, the colony's proprietors failed to persuade settlers to approve the Fundamental Constitutions. Carolina society would indeed be unequal and hierarchical but along lines of race and class quite different from those Locke had projected.

Carolina's proprietors planned to recruit only "seasoned" colonists from the Caribbean who would pay their own passage, be offered land at a low price, and be encouraged to form communities of self-sufficient family farms. The crown granted all colonists political and religious freedom and promised adult white males the right to vote for assemblymen, who were to govern the colony with the help of noblemen drawn from England.

Migrants flocked to Carolina. Children of some of the richest planters of the Caribbean sugar islands came, bringing hundreds of slaves and the customs of the West Indian gentry. Still, independent, non–slave-owning white farmers at first outnumbered slave owners, indentured servants, propertyless laborers, and slaves. Many migrants were Barbadians who owned too few slaves and too little land on Barbados to make a success of sugar growing and who by the 1650s had few prospects on their already crowded, overcultivated island. They were generally older than the first Chesapeake colonists, and many had families. Immigrant families from Scotland, Germany, and Ireland likewise took up mixed-crop farming in Carolina. Most

"All Things Are Very Dear in the Town": An Early South Carolina Settler Writes Home

In this letter, the Oxford University–educated Thomas Newe describes to his father his first impressions of the South Carolina colony. Not surprisingly, Newe focuses on the issues that were most pressing to colonists in the growing settlement: subsistence and relations with local Indian groups.

. . . As for the Countrey I can say but little of it as yet on my one [own] knowledge, but what I hear from others. The Town which two years since had but 3 or 4 houses, hath now about a hundred houses in it, all which are wholy built of wood, tho here is excellent Brick made, but little of it. All things are very dear in the Town . . . the common drink of the Countrey is Molossus [molasses] and water, I don't hear of any malt that is made hear as yet . . . Severall in the Country have great stocks of Cattle and they sell so well to new comers that they care not for killing, which is the reason provision is so dear in the Town, whilst they in the Country are furnisht with Venison, fish, and fowle by the Indians for trifles, and they that understand it make as good butter and cheese as most in England. The land near the sea side is generally a light and sandy ground, but up in the Country they say there is very good land, and the farther up the better, but that which at present doth somewhat hinder the selling [settling] farther up, is a war that they are ingaged in against a tribe of Barbarous Indians being not above 60 in number, but by reason of their great growth and cruelty in feeding on all their neighbours, they are terrible to all other Indians, of which, there are above 40 severall Kingdoms, the strength and names of them all being known to our Governer who upon any occasion summons their Kings in. We are at peace with all but those common enemies of mankind, those man eaters before mentioned, by name the Westos, who have lately killed two eminent planters that lived far up in the Country, so that they are resolved now if they can find their settlement (which they often change) to cut them all off. There is a small party of English out after them, and the most potent Kingdome of the Indians armed by us and continually in pursuit of them. . . .

Alexander S. Salley, Jr., ed., *Narratives of Early Carolina, 1650–1708* (New York, 1911), 181–87.

colonists lived on modest farms, close to the coast, where they grew their own food and raised cattle for export to the Caribbean.

Mixed subsistence farming generated little revenue, however, and the hoped-for deerskin trade with Indians failed to materialize. Instead, some colonists organized a new slave trade, capturing Indians to sell in the West Indies in exchange for rum and sugar. Meanwhile, the small minority of wealthy migrants acquired huge tracts of land and seized political control, many of them settling in Charleston, which soon became the largest port town in the South. Before 1705, these Charleston families owned most of the colony's slaves. But successful traders and farmers also employed laborers, some American-born whites, some indentured servants from England and Ireland, and some African-born slaves brought from the Caribbean.

Settling the Carolina coastal region, or low country, involved interactions with Indian groups. As elsewhere, early cooperation was followed by colonists' provocations that caused first resentment against whites and then resistance to them. In what would become North Carolina, settlers captured Tuscarora women and children to sell as slaves and then encroached on the group's lands. After a two-year war, beginning in 1711, settlers defeated the Tuscarora, displacing them inland. In South Carolina, English settlers removed the Westo people in the 1680s with the help of the neighboring Yamasees, who then formed a thirty-year-long alliance with English governments, directed in part against Spanish Florida farther down the coast. But English demands and encroachments eventually sparked Yamasee resistance as well. Shifting their alliance to the Spanish and the Creeks, the Yamasee attacked South Carolina settlements in 1715, but they were defeated, and the survivors were sold into slavery. The English formed a new alliance with the stronger inland Cherokees, who for another half-century held their position, trading in slaves and establishing settled agriculture while maintaining some of their traditional ways; Cherokee women, for instance, maintained rights over land and agricultural produce. By the 1760s, however, the English and the Cherokees were themselves coming into conflict.

Conditions in early South Carolina were difficult for all settlers, white and black. Work was hard. All suffered from inadequate shelter, poor nutrition, and semitropical diseases. Even those who survived their first few years had a relatively short life expectancy. For instance, Judith Manigault, who settled with her husband on the Santee River in 1689 and worked with him to clear and plant land, died in 1711, aged 42. Though mortality rates fell with each generation, only after 1750 did births outnumber deaths.

Some harsher aspects of the Chesapeake's labor regime were absent from South Carolina, however. Restrictions placed on masters in 1676 and the availability of land in other colonies gave prospective indentured servants some bargaining power. Slaves, too, had slightly more freedom of action than was the case in Virginia or Maryland. Commercial cattle farmers, unlike tobacco planters, needed a mobile, self-reliant labor force, and they recognized the skill of Africans at raising livestock in a subtropical climate. Cattle were unfenced, and slaves who tended them had to move with the herds and run down strays. Male servants and slaves also had some access to public life. As late as 1706, petitioners complained that in "the last election Jews, Strangers, Sailors, Servants, Negroes, and almost every French Man came down to elect, and their votes were taken." The need to defend the colony from hostile Spanish troops in Florida even required—in

Establishing the Colony of Georgia

An illustration from a 1733 book that advocated colonization depicts Georgia as an idyllic, bountiful land — the perfect setting for the creation of a well-ordered, hierarchical society. Note the well-dressed gentleman in the lower right corner supervising the work. B. Martyn, *Reasons for Establishing the Colony of Georgia* (1733) — Rare Books and Manuscript Division, New York Public Library, Astor, Lenox and Tilden Foundations.

contrast to Virginia — that slaves sometimes be mobilized and armed. A Carolina official noted in 1710 that "enrolled in our Militia [are] a considerable Number of active, able, Negro Slaves; and Law gives everyone of those his freedom, who in Time of an Invasion kills an Enemy."

In 1732, the southernmost territory of the original Carolina grant was organized as the new colony of Georgia. Initially, Georgia was to be a military buffer between South Carolina and Spanish Florida, and its founders hoped for a colony not based on slavery. Early settlers were Englishmen who had signed up for the colony's militia as an alternative to debtor's prison. The colony's promoters, led by James Oglethorpe, recruited skilled workers from Italy, who they hoped would develop a silk industry, and unskilled laborers from Scotland, Ireland, and Germany. Women and children were not included in their original plans because they could not contribute to the colony's defense. In 1735, slavery was prohibited on military grounds as a potential source of internal rebellion, and some Georgia settlers also expressed moral objections to slavery. Whites, wrote some petitioners to the king in 1738, would one day pay a heavy price for enslaving men and women who held freedom as "dear" as they did.

The Growth of Slavery in the Carolinas and Georgia   But in the Lower South, as in the Chesapeake, various factors led to the expansion and hardening of slavery. After 1680, the number of white indentured servants arriving in the Carolinas fell. Determined to reap profits from staple-crop production, the wealthy planters who had migrated from Barbados consolidated their low-country farms into large plantations and concentrated on growing rice, thus squeezing out mixed-crop farmers and cattle raisers. By the early eighteenth century, the rice grown on these plantations became

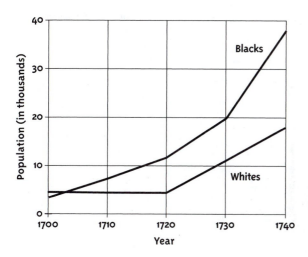

FIGURE 2.2 The Emergence of a Black Majority in South Carolina

As planters imported more and more slaves to grow rice and other crops, South Carolina's black population quickly exceeded that of whites, growing rapidly into the mid-eighteenth century.

South Carolina's chief export, and planters turned almost exclusively to imported African slaves for their workforce. Some of these slaves had grown rice as free men and women in West Africa. South Carolina's slave population rose from 2,400 in 1700 to 12,000 in 1720, of whom nearly three-fifths were African-born (Figure 2.2). Moreover, by 1708, for the first time in any North American colony, Carolina's blacks outnumbered the white population.

Rice cultivation also spread quickly to the Georgia low country after the colony's founding, and in 1749, Georgia rescinded its ban on slavery. A plantation economy then developed, and the lure of profits helped to overcome the original proprietors' military and moral objections to slavery. In addition, slave owners in other colonies had objected to Georgia's prohibition of slavery, viewing it as an enticement to their own slaves to escape.

Slaves growing rice were not subject to the regimentation and close supervision that were imposed on those in the tobacco regions. Rice did not, like tobacco, require constant daily attention. Slaves spent part of the year repairing dams, building canals, and mending fences. Many had done similar work in Africa, and their experience helped both to shape the system of labor and to enhance their bargaining position with English masters who did not know how to grow rice. Even so, conditions were very difficult. Planting and harvesting rice in water-filled fields involved backbreaking, unhealthy labor; work on dikes and canals was heavier still. Hard work, poor diet, disease, and maltreatment contributed to high mortality rates. Masters had unrestricted authority over their slaves and did not hesitate to use it. Brute force maintained discipline. In South Carolina, the law prescribed amputation as the punishment for recaptured runaway slaves: females could have their ears cut off, males their testicles.

As the rice economy spread and a structured, race-bound society emerged, slavery became more rigid. An English immigrant wrote in 1711 that freemen could do well in the colony if they could "get a few slaves and beat them well to make them work hard." Slaves had little chance of obtaining freedom. Free black servants, too, could expect extended terms of bondage, and free black women were forced to "apprentice" their children who were born during their servitude, which often lasted into their early thirties. Opportunities for escape became scarcer as the loose supervision of cattle farms gave way to a tighter plantation regime and the Yamasee war wiped out the runaway slaves' chief allies.

View of Mulberry House and Grounds

In this painting of a rice plantation near Charleston in the 1770s, the master's house is framed by the slave quarters. The artist probably depicted the size of the slave cabins inaccurately, suggesting a height and spaciousness that the one-room cabins did not possess. Thomas Coram, oil on paper — Gibbes Art/Carolina Art Association, Charleston, 1968.18.01.

Beginning in the 1720s, successful South Carolina rice planters left over-seers in charge of their plantations and moved to Charleston, where the climate was pleasanter, diseases such as malaria less prevalent, and the society more stimulating than that in the countryside. In Charleston, they formed an aristocracy at least as wealthy and elegant as that of Virginia. Many slaves in Charleston were hired out, working for master craft workers as ship-builders, rope makers, leather workers, and carpenters or as dock workers or general laborers. In contrast to those on plantations, many urban slaves were literate, worked as artisans, and were of mixed English and African origin. Women also formed a higher proportion of urban slaves than of slaves in the countryside. By 1776, half of Charleston's 12,000 inhabitants were black. Interaction with their masters, more frequent than on the plantations, also provided the occasional opportunity to buy or be granted freedom.

African American Culture in the South

By 1760, the American slave system, which would last another century, was firmly in place. It defined most black people as the property of white men, yet within slavery's confines, blacks created their own fragile institutions through which to assert their dignity and humanity. They established kinship and community networks that extended beyond the limits of any one plantation and strove to survive the slave sales that separated husband from wife and parent from child. African Americans also practiced their own religions, composed songs, created dances, devised ceremonies, and established ways of thinking that distinguished them from both their masters and their

Group of Negroes Imported to Be Sold as Slaves
A late-eighteenth-century engraving from a British abolitionist report shows newly arrived captive Africans being driven to an auction. (William Blake) John Gabriel Stedman, *Narrative of a five-years expedition against the revolted Negroes of Surinam . . . from the year 1772, to 1777* (1796) — Rare Books and Manuscript Division, New York Public Library, Astor, Lenox and Tilden Foundations.

African ancestors. African American culture evolved as some half-million transported Africans and their descendants learned to resist the degradation and oppression of their enslavement and to assert some control over their day-to-day existence. This culture was neither English nor African, neither imposed by the master class nor simply a relic of a lost African past, but was instead a blend of cultures, adapted to the peculiar needs of a people in bondage. Slaves retained what they could of their African heritage and reconciled it with what they were forced to do, or had learned to do, to survive in America.

The First African American Generation This evolving African American culture contrasted with the experiences of the first two generations of slaves and free blacks in the Chesapeake. For early slaves, a distinctive new culture had been impossible. Their numbers were small, and contact among them was limited by their dispersal among a much larger English population. Closely supervised by their masters, slaves had little time for themselves. There were also no rigid barriers yet to divide white from black laborers, and some slaves could expect to gain their freedom. So slaves adopted the culture of their English fellow servants, with whom they drank, "frolicked," conspired, and escaped.

A distinctly African American culture began to emerge only as the number of Africans increased, as racial laws began restricting their contact with whites, and as the chances of freedom from slavery dwindled. Wrenched from different societies in Africa, most newly arrived slaves faced a life among strangers. They had been robbed of their land, tools, and possessions, so they could not ply their trades or even dress as they had previously done. Separated from others from their own societies, they could not speak their native languages, play their assigned kinship roles, or practice their religions — the things that had distinguished them as belonging to diverse African villages and regions. Forcibly separated from their families, most slaves began life in America without kin or other acquaintances around them.

As the number of slaves grew rapidly in the first half of the eighteenth century, different circumstances in the Chesapeake and the Lower South determined how long it would take for new arrivals to establish relationships with one another and with those who had preceded them (Figure 2.3).

In the Chesapeake, many slaves were sold to small planters and so lived separately from each other. Perhaps as many as one in three Chesapeake slaves lived in groups of five or fewer, and they had quite close contact with whites. As slavery spread across the Virginia piedmont region in the eighteenth century, only about one-third of slaves lived on plantations with more than twenty slaves each. South Carolina rice plantations were larger, on average, than Chesapeake tobacco farms. Here, newly imported slaves were more often sold in large groups to single planters and so were less likely to be separated from one another and more likely to live apart from whites. Consequently, slaves in the Chesapeake tended to speak English, while those in South Carolina and Georgia combined various African languages with English to form Gullah, which became a common and unifying language among low-country slaves.

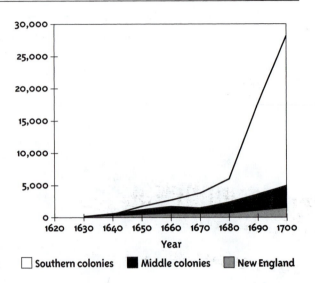

FIGURE 2.3   The Distribution of African Americans in the Seventeenth-Century Colonies
Even though slavery existed throughout the colonies, its rapid expansion in the South after the 1670s meant that the great majority of African Americans lived there, rather than in New England or the Middle Colonies.

Conditions of Work and Kinship   Differences between tobacco and rice production also shaped regional patterns in slave life. Work on large Chesapeake tobacco farms was fairly continuous, conducted by gangs of slaves who worked for long hours under the supervision of overseers. Carolina rice cultivation, by contrast, involved more strenuous but more varied work and was not suited to gang labor. Rice planters introduced a task system, in which slaves remained more free of direct supervision; upon the completion of allocated jobs, they were allowed time to hunt, fish, or cultivate their own "provision grounds" (garden plots). As a result, South Carolina slaves found themselves with greater relative autonomy and greater responsibility for providing their own food than those in the Chesapeake. At the same time, though, they were more vulnerable to the whims of overseers left in charge by absentee planters who had taken up residence in Charleston.

Despite these differences, slave cultures throughout the South also developed much in common with one another. The strong emphasis African societies placed on kinship, and especially on ties between brothers and sisters, helped uprooted people to survive enslavement. Even aboard slave ships, unrelated captives began to refer to each other as brothers and sisters, and sexual intercourse between such "siblings" was forbidden. Children were taught to call former shipmates "aunt" and "uncle." Over several generations, kinship practices helped slaves from diverse backgrounds to order their lives and maintain connections that extended beyond a single slave quarter, plantation, or county.

These bonds were easily strained by the constant arrival of new immigrants and by the sending of slaves from one plantation to another, fracturing communities. Even so, because such movements often occurred within the same geographical area, kin connections and knowledge of family histories could, with effort, be maintained. In southern Maryland in the 1760s, between 120 and 300 slaves claimed their descent from a couple called Butler, who had started having children eighty years before. After 1720 in the Chesapeake and 1760 in the Lower South, various impediments to slave family life diminished: death rates fell, the number of men and women equalized, and slave importation from Africa declined in relative importance. Among Robert "King" Carter's slaves in Virginia, over half lived in households with children by 1733, including almost all the women. Of fifty-five slaves belonging to a North Carolina owner in 1761, only eight were single; the rest lived in six families.

Accordingly, by contrast with the slaves of Caribbean and Brazilian plantation societies, where sex ratios and mortality remained unfavorable, the Chesapeake's slave population began to sustain its numbers by natural increase — the first in the Americas to do so. By the 1740s, a majority of Chesapeake slaves were native-born, and this would be the case throughout the South by 1800. Increasingly, young black Americans were not "seasoned" by white masters like their predecessors, but were raised by African American parents in an emerging African American culture.

Yet masters still defined the character of daily life and limited the ways in which slaves could act. Masters set working conditions, enforced slave codes, and ultimately held the power of life and death. They could break up slaves' families at will, and their indebtedness, bankruptcy, or death could do so unintentionally. However, if slavery was to work for them, masters had to depend on their slaves' ability to take care of each other, to raise children, to learn English, to perform a variety of tasks, and, in some cases, to manage other slaves. Slaves did all of these things and taught their children to do likewise.

Slaves' living arrangements also evolved. In the seventeenth century, when the majority of field hands were men, many lived together in rough barracks. But as the sex ratio became more balanced in the early eighteenth century and many slaves established families, an increasing number lived in separate dwellings. Cabins sprang up in the slave settlements near plantation houses. They reminded one visitor to South Carolina of the "wooden cottages [of] poor villagers" in England, but many that were constructed by slaves themselves reflected an African influence. Often scantily built, these dwellings offered basic shelter but little material comfort or adornment. Still, in the family cabin, slaves enjoyed a space that was mostly theirs, where to some extent they could shape their own lives. Within this private sphere, they took last names that were different from their masters' and named

Advertisements for Slaves in the *Maryland Gazette*

Although most slaves worked as field hands, there was also demand for men and women slaves with craft skills, particularly in districts with large plantations. Some male slaves were trained as carpenters, shoemakers, blacksmiths, and masons or as coopers who made barrels for shipping tobacco and other goods. A smaller number of women slaves escaped field labor to become household servants or to work at spinning yarn and weaving cloth. These advertisements from the Maryland Gazette *reflect the market in skilled slaves.*

[April 27, 1748]

TO BE SOLD BY THE SUBSCRIBER, IN ANNAPOLIS

A brisk likely Country-born Negro Wench about 18 or 19 years of Age, who is a good Spinner; with a Child, about 18 months Old. William Reynol

Very good Nutmegs, by the Pound, or Ounce, to be sold by the same Reynolds.

[May 29, 1751]

TO BE SOLD

A likely, strong Negro Girl, about 16 Years of Age, fit for Plantation Work, or very capable of making a Good House Wench, having for some Months served as such in a small Family. For further Particulars, Enquire of the Printer Hereof.

[May 28, 1752]

TO BE SOLD BY PUBLIC VENDOR

At the House of Mr. Samuel Middleton, in Annapolis, on Wednesday the 10th Day of June next at 4 o'clock in the afternoon:

The Hull of a New Vessel lying now at the Town Dock, together with her Masts, and some of her Yards. . . .

Also at the same time will be sold a Blacksmith and a Wheelright, with their Tools; both being excellent workmen. Also a Collier and a Sawyer, who have each about 5 Yeares to Serve. . . .

Likewise a Country-born Negro Wench, About 27 Years of Age, very sober and healthy; and understands Household Business very well, with a Mulatto Boy about a year and a half old, who is the said Negro's Child.

Whoever is inclinable to purchase, on giving security (if required), may have two Months time for Payment.

[December 17, 1761]

TO BE SOLD BY THE SUBSCRIBER, being near Upper Marlborough, in Prince George's County, on the Second Day of January next, for good Bills of Exchange:

A Choice Parcel of Country-born Slaves, consisting of Men, Women, Boys, and Girls, all Young and healthy, chief between 10 and 20 years of Age; among these Slaves there are two Wenches about 16 or 17 Years of Age, who Understand Spinning and Knitting, and a young Fellow of 20 Years of Age, a good Plowman and Cartman.

The Sale to be on a Plantation now Mr. William Beall's. William Parker

Allan Kulikoff, *Tobacco and Slaves: The Development of Southern Cultures in the Chesapeake, 1680–1800* (University of North Carolina Press, 1986), 405.

The Old Plantation
This unusual late-eighteenth-century painting by an unknown artist indicates the blending of cultural influences in the slaves' quarters. African and American culture merge in the slaves' dress, dance, and musical instruments (a drum and banjo). The ceremony shown is probably a wedding at which, by African custom, the bride and groom jump over a stick. Anonymous, watercolor, c. 1800 — Abby Aldrich Rockefeller Folk Art Center, Williamsburg, Virginia.

children for grandparents and great-grandparents—Cuffee, Quash—linking them to an African past and the memory of freedom.

Many masters, intent on destroying the remnants of their chattels' free identities, discouraged African customs and languages, so the work habits, family arrangements, and religious beliefs that were most similar to English practices were those most likely to survive. Even so, slaves retained non-Christian beliefs, dances, songs, and funeral practices. African influences persisted in foodways; child-rearing practices; the work of artisans who made pottery, musical instruments, and metal goods; and the objects slaves placed in the graves of their dead. By building bonds of family and kinship and by preserving aspects of African culture, slaves fashioned a social identity that enabled them to maintain their dignity despite captivity and oppression.

Slave Resistance and Rebellion   In addition to forging social and cultural bonds, slaves tried actively to resist captivity. By 1760, African Americans accounted for about two-fifths of the Chesapeake's population. In South Carolina, with its larger rice plantations, they were a substantial majority, and here, particularly, the threat of slave rebellion led plantation owners to create more repressive arrangements. But wherever slavery existed, the fear and actuality of resistance produced harsh laws and institutions designed to impose order on potentially unruly slaves.

"A Bloody Tragedy": Slave Insurrection Averted in Charleston

Full-scale rebellion was rare, but the very possibility of such insurrection terrified southern whites, as this letter, printed in the October 22, 1730, issue of the Boston Weekly News-Letter, *reveals. A slave uprising planned to begin in Charleston, South Carolina, on August 15, 1730, was uncovered in advance. This report hints at how slaves planned to spread their actions out of the city into the countryside.*

I shall give an Account of a bloody Tragedy which was to have been executed here last Saturday night (the 15th Inst.) by the Negroes, who had conspired to Rise and destroy us, and had almost brought it to pass: but it pleased God to appear for us, and confound their Councils. For some of them proposed that the Negroes of every Plantation should destroy their own Masters; but others were for Rising in a Body, and giving the blow at once on surprise; and thus they differed. They soon made a great Body at the back of the Town, and had a great Dance, and expected the Country Negroes to come & join them; and had not an overruling Providence discovered their Intrigues, we had been all in Blood. . . . The Chief of them, with the others, is apprehended and in Irons, in order to a Tryal, and we are in Hopes to find out the whole Affair.

Boston Weekly News-Letter, October 22, 1730.

From time to time, slaves did overtly rebel. As many as two hundred slaves took part in a revolt near Norfolk, Virginia, in 1730. Four of them were executed, and whites enlarged local militias. The Stono Rebellion in South Carolina in 1739 began when about twenty slaves marched off in the direction of Florida from the Stono River, not far from Charleston. Many of them had recently arrived from Angola and may have been prompted to resist their enslavement by an outbreak of war between England and Spain. After stealing arms and decapitating two storekeepers, they began burning buildings and murdering whites at the plantations they passed, while recruiting an additional fifty or more slaves into their ranks. At the Edisto River, a white militia confronted them, shooting fourteen slaves dead immediately and killing two dozen more after they had surrendered. In the brutal repression that followed, fleeing rebels were rounded up and executed. Their heads were displayed at mileposts along the roadsides as a warning to others.

Such outright rebellion was rare. But fear of it was common, and periodic panics gripped the white population. Planters were also wary of "intestine enemies" and "dangerous domestics." Women employed as cooks, who were intimately connected to their white owners and in a unique position to harm them, came under suspicion. Slaves were known to have brought

"Barns Being Burnt . . .": Slave Resistance in South Carolina

Slaves' resistance took many forms. In South Carolina, slaves involved in rice production often burned down the barns where the harvested rice was stored. This October 14, 1732, letter, printed in the South Carolina Gazette, *reveals how common the slave "custom" of barn-burning had become in one part of the colony.*

I have taken notice for Several Years past, that there has not one Winter elapsed, without one or more Barns being burnt, and two Winters since, there was no less than five. Whether it is owing to Accident, Carelessness, or Severity, I will not pretend to determine; but am afraid, chiefly to the [latter two causes]. I desire therefore, as a Friend to the Planters, that you'll insert the following Account from Pon Pon, which, I hope, will forewarn the Planters of their Danger, and make them for the future, more careful and human:

About 3 Weeks since, Mr. James Gray worked his Negroes late in his Barn at Night, and the next Morning before Day, hurried them out again, and when they came to it, found it burnt down to the Ground, and all that was in it.

South Carolina Gazette, October 14, 1732.

---

the knowledge of poisons from Africa, and those who were suspected of plotting to use it faced savage punishment.

Slaves resisted in less violent ways as well. As their numbers grew and a sense of community developed among them, they worked together to protect one another and reduce the harshness of labor. Though whippings for disobedience or insolence were a near-certainty, slaves conspired to break tools, feign illness, slow down or neglect work, and avoid learning new tasks. When a Virginia planter skimped on his field hands' clothing so that they were almost naked, one of his neighbors noted that he got "nothing by his injustice but the scandal of it," because the slaves produced poor crops. The Virginia planter Landon Carter railed at the frequency with which his slaves fell ill on Mondays.

Slaves also made bids for freedom. Running away, individually or in small groups, was common. Most left only for short periods, to visit kin on other farms or escape punishment. Much truancy occurred during planting, hoeing, or harvesting seasons. The majority of runaways were men, though women frequently harbored fugitives. Returned runaways could expect a whipping, but some persistent fugitives had their toes cut off; one planter wrote that "nothing less than dismemberment" would "reclaim" an "incorrigible rogue" who kept absconding. Some escapees paid with their lives. Twenty-one-year-old Henry Carter, sold to a new master with a fearsome reputation, ran away, only to be stoned to death by an overseer who caught him crossing a river.

Suppression of a Runaway Slave Community

In a letter to the Board of Trade in London, written in 1729, Virginia's lieutenant-governor, Sir William Gooch, describes measures taken by planters and colonial governments to curb slave runaways.

My Lords:

. . . Sometime after my Last a number of Negroes, about fifteen, belonging to a new Plantation on the head of James River formed a Design to withdraw from their Master and to fix themselves in the fastness of the neighboring Mountains. They had found means to get into their possession some Arms & Ammunition, and they took along with them some Provisions, their Cloaths, bedding and working Tools; but the Gentleman to whom they belonged with a Party of Men made such diligent pursuit after them, that he soon found them out in their new Settlement, a very obscure place among the Mountains, where they had already begun to clear the ground, and obliged them after exchanging a shot or two by which one of the Slaves was wounded, to surrender and return back, and so prevented for this time a design which might have proved as dangerous to this Country, as is that of the Negroes in the Mountains of Jamaica to the Inhabitants of that Island. Tho' this attempt has happily been defeated, it ought nevertheless to awaken us into some effectual measures for preventing the like hereafter, it being certain that a very small number of Negroes once settled in those Parts, would very soon be encreas'd by the Accession of other Runaways and prove dangerous Neighbours to our frontier Inhabitants. To prevent this and many other Mischiefs I am training and exercising the Militia in the several counties as the best means to deter our Slaves from endeavouring to make their Escape, and to suppress them if they should.

Sally E. Hadden, *Slave Patrols: Law and Violence in Virginia and the Carolinas* (Harvard University Press, 2001), 30.

Unlike some Caribbean islands, such as Jamaica, whose black majority populations and mountainous terrain sheltered communities of escaped slaves (known as maroons), the southern colonies provided only slender chances for permanent escape. Hostile whites inhabited land surrounding Chesapeake plantation districts, for example. Near present-day Lexington, Virginia, in 1728–1729, one group of runaway slaves did create a village. They built homes like those they had known in Africa, established a government under a chief, and (with stolen implements) grew crops using African methods. Whites soon destroyed the village, killed the chief, and returned the residents to their masters. The Carolinas held somewhat more promise, but not much. Escape to Indians such as the Cherokee or Creeks might offer a

Ran Off

The September 18, 1762, edition of the *South Carolina Gazette* includes notices about escaped slaves, stray animals, and runaway wives. *South Carolina Gazette*, Supplement, September 18, 1762 — Prints and Photographs Division, Library of Congress.

chance for assimilation but was equally likely to lead to re-enslavement by the tribe to which they fled. Small groups of maroons did survive in the swamps behind rice plantations but in isolated and harsh conditions.

The Spanish in Florida gave Carolina slaves one other chance of escape. In 1693, Spain promised freedom to fugitives who would convert to Catholicism. Some slaves evaded capture on the dangerous march south, and in Florida, groups of runaways lived among Native Americans or in their own communities. Even so, they were vulnerable. English troops seized the largest maroon village, Santa Teresa de Mose near St. Augustine, in 1740. Although the Spanish later recaptured it, Mose never regained its former size and disintegrated when Florida became a British possession in 1763.

Prosperity, Inequality, and Shifting Ideas in Slave Societies

By the 1750s, the population of the southern colonies numbered just over 300,000 whites and about 200,000 black slaves, together with small numbers of free blacks and Indians who had not yet been forced west. Nearly two-thirds of all southerners lived in Virginia and Maryland, and a third lived in the two Carolinas; only about 5,000 people had settled in Georgia by this time. Each colony had a colonial assembly and court system that governed in accordance with English precedents. The king's representatives included a royal governor in each colony, customs collectors, and other officials charged with overseeing trade. The Church of England had become part of the fabric of life; as in England, it was closely identified with the elite and with the enforcement of social hierarchy. Southern customs and lifestyles no longer horrified English visitors as they had in earlier decades. Though few of the increasing numbers of white people born in the South would ever see England, many shared an English cultural identity and to some extent duplicated the social norms of their English peers. The availability of abundant land meant that more white men

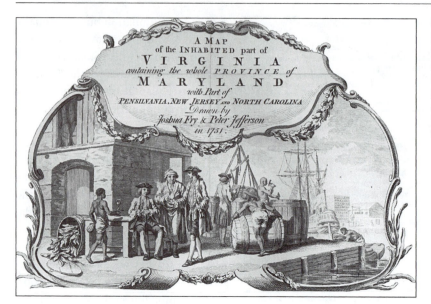

Exporting Tobacco

A detail from a map published in 1775 shows slaves packing tobacco in barrels on a Virginia wharf for shipment abroad. Joshua Frye and Peter Jefferson, *A Map of the Most Inhabited Part of Virginia . . . (1775)* — Maryland Historical Society.

owned land than in England, yet great disparities in wealth remained. A small network of wealthy families, mainly located in coastal regions, largely dominated politics and society and demanded deference, but inland settlers and later the rise of evangelical religious beliefs frequently challenged this elite authority.

Hierarchy and Society   Men no longer outnumbered women in the southern colonies, and the family became the center of social life. Like their counterparts in England, many white women contributed to the family income by spinning, weaving, gardening, and selling dairy products. Slavery and the plantation economy were securely in place. There had been some diversification of agriculture. Chesapeake farmers and planters exported cattle and wheat. From the Lower South went shipments of the dyestuff indigo — first grown on the plantation of a resourceful young woman planter, Eliza Lucas Pinckney — as well as naval stores such as pitch, tar, and timber. But the main staple crops of each region remained dominant. In the Chesapeake, tobacco production rose from twenty-eight million pounds in 1700 to eighty million in 1760; from coastal South Carolina and Georgia, rice exports rose from ten thousand barrels in 1720 to one hundred thousand in 1760.

Export crops and slave labor gave the southern colonies a prosperity unmatched elsewhere in eighteenth-century North America. White wealth per capita in Virginia and South Carolina was double that in New England or the Middle Colonies. Land was easier to acquire in the South than in England, and European visitors noted the abundance of food and prevalence of landownership. In Virginia, about two in three white families

"Pity Your Distressed Daughter": Inequality in the Eighteenth-Century South

In this 1756 letter to her parents in England, Elizabeth Sprigs, a female servant in Maryland, describes the harsh conditions of her life and labor. Well into the eighteenth century, many women committed themselves to indentured servitude in exchange for passage to the North American colonies.

Honored Father

My being forever banished from your sight will I hope pardon the boldness I now take of troubling you with these [words]. . . . O Dear Father, believe that I am going to relate the words of truth and sincerity, and balance my former bad conduct [to] my sufferings here, and then I am sure you'll pity your distressed daughter. What we unfortunate English people suffer here is beyond the probability of you in England to conceive. Let it suffice that I, one of the unhappy number, am toiling almost day and night, and very often in the horses' drudgery, with only this comfort that "you bitch you do not half enough," and then tied up and whipped to that degree that you'd not serve an animal. Scarce anything but Indian corn and salt to eat and that even begrudged nay many Negroes are better used, almost naked no shoes nor stockings to wear, and the comfort after slaving during Master's pleasure, what rest we can get is to wrap ourselves up in an blanket and lay upon the ground. This is the deplorable condition your poor Betty endures, and now I beg if you have any bowels of compassion left show it by sending me some relief, clothing is the principal thing wanting, which if you should condescend to, may easily send them to me by any ships bound to Baltimore Town, Patapsco River, Maryland, and give me leave to conclude in duty to you and Uncles and Aunts, and respect to all friends, Honored Father

Your undutiful and disobedient child

ELIZABETH SPRIGS

Elizabeth Sprigs, "Letter to Mr. John Sprigs in White Cross Street near Cripple Gate, London, September 22, 1756," in Isabel Calder, ed., *Colonial Captivities, Marches, and Journeys* (New York: MacMillan Company, 1935), 151–152. Reprinted by permission of the Connecticut Chapter of the National Society of Colonial Dames of America.

farmed their own land in 1750, consuming roughly 60 percent of what they produced and bartering the surplus for tools and other goods they could not make. In the Carolinas, the proportion of white households with land was higher still.

Yet the South's wealth was very unequally distributed. Dramatic distinctions existed between rich and poor. Those at the lower end of the scale slipped easily into poverty, and at least one-fifth of the white population owned little more than the clothes they wore. Owning slaves enhanced the advantages of the rich over the poor. Tobacco and rice, speculation in western land, slave trading, and shipping had made a few southerners very wealthy. When he died in 1732, Virginia's richest planter, Robert "King" Carter, owned 300,000 acres and almost one thousand slaves. Across the southern colonies, the richest 10 percent of the population owned half of all wealth, including one-seventh of the people.

Wealthy planters mimicked the English gentry. By the 1720s, they were building spacious brick mansions in parklike surroundings, and Charleston's elite built elegant townhouses too. The rich imported elaborate furnishings, adorned their wives and daughters in European fashions, and maintained large numbers of slaves as house servants. They hired tutors for their sons or sent

Charleston Entertainment, 1760
Having served supper and then after-dinner drinks, a young slave dozes while members of Charleston's merchant-planter elite carouse around the dining room table. The drawing is set in the home of Peter Manigault (seated at the left center), scion of one of the wealthiest families in colonial Carolina. George Roupell, *Peter Manigault and His Friends*, c. 1760, black ink and wash, 10 3/16 × 13 3/16 inches — Henry Francis duPont Winterthur Museum.

them to be educated in Scotland or England. They raised their children to exercise authority, sometimes by purchasing young slaves to be their personal servants.

Most white southerners lived in humbler surroundings. Their houses were small and built of wood; they had no servants, slaves, or silverware and relied on their own labor. Though many had land, significant numbers of whites in the Chesapeake owned none. In Maryland, a majority of small farmers were tenants, renting land from large landholders and living in relative poverty. Landless whites relied on intermittent work or settled and hunted on marginal land or in frontier areas. Landless men worked as tenants on large estates or as wage laborers in agriculture, shipping, or craft trades; most landless women worked as domestic servants.

Also in humble surroundings were the growing numbers of white men and women who lived in the less-settled areas of the South, away from the coast. This backcountry attracted both the children of poorer native-born southerners and recent immigrants from Ireland, Scotland, and Germany. A midcentury visitor to the South Carolina backcountry found many inhabitants who "have nought but a Gourd to drink out of, nor a Plate, Knive or Spoon, a Glass, Cup, or anything." Many were tenants who rented from large landowners and speculators. Backcountry society was less structured and authority less established than on the coast. There were few great plantations or large concentrations of slaves. In western North Carolina, for example, only about 12 percent of the white population owned slaves, and very few of those owned more than five.

Frontier land was cheaper than land on the coast, and thousands of white people obtained legal title through squatter's rights — that is, by building a cabin, clearing a number of acres, and planting a crop. Permitting

Nondescripts . . . near Oaks, Virginia

"A family of poor White children," architect Benjamin Henry Latrobe noted in his sketchbook, "observed from the Stage carrying peaches to a neighboring Barbecue for Sale." The woman and children in this 1796 sketch wore large, stiff bonnets common to that part of Virginia. Benjamin Henry Latrobe, *Nondescripts attracted by a neighbouring barbecue, near the Oaks, Virginia*, 1796, pencil, pen and ink, wash, 6 15/16 × 10 15/16 inches — Maryland Historical Society.

settlement to expand in this way could help a colonial government bolster its claims to the interior against the counterclaims of Indians, English speculators, or other colonies. Though few settlers achieved more than a decent subsistence, they established communities in which a rough equality prevailed. The backcountry could also provide the opportunity for social mobility. In Virginia's newly settled Southside, for instance, John Hix and George McLaughlin were landless laborers in 1748, but by 1769, McLaughlin owned two hundred and fifty acres, and Hix had acquired almost four hundred acres and two slaves.

Deference and Conflict   Along with crown officials, the South's wealthy men controlled government, courts, and church, forming a stable gentry class. By the eighteenth century, the Beverlys, Randolphs, Carters, Harrisons, Lees, and Byrds, with their relatives and connections, had secure hold of Virginia's House of Burgesses. Between 1700 and 1760, members of just nine families held one-third of places in the Virginia governor's council. John Randolph wrote that "person[s] of note in [Virginia] . . . are almost all related, or so connected in our interests, that whoever of a Stranger presumes to offend any one of us will infallibly find an enemy of the whole." Pinckneys, Rutledges, Draytons, and some others gained even greater relative prominence in South Carolina.

Gentry power was locally rooted. Planters controlled the vestries, or governing bodies, of the established Church of England (or Anglican church), and individual parishes levied taxes to pay clergymen, who were mostly educated and ordained in England. County courts, the local centers of political as well as legal power, were dominated by the gentry too. Planters' houses were centers of social and political activity, of hospitality and patronage for farmers and voters, and of sociable rituals of gambling, horse racing, and other entertainment.

It was assumed that in an unequal society, the wealthy and powerful were owed deference and respect by the majority. One Virginian recalled that "we were accustomed to look upon . . . gentle folks as beings of a superior order." Nonelite white men could participate in the benefits of privilege. By the mid-eighteenth century, the proportion of small slaveholders was rising, particularly in coastal regions. About half the white farmers in coastal Maryland owned one or more slaves, as did a majority of Charleston's white artisans. Property holding or taxpaying was widespread enough that many white men qualified for the vote — between 60 and 90 percent across the

Three-Decker Authority
The Aquia Church in northern Virginia's Stafford County (built in 1754–57) offered its congregants light and space while also reinforcing the colony's social hierarchy. Its imposing three-decker pulpit, of a style that made its appearance in Virginia by the late seventeenth century, accentuated the authority of the clergy and heightened the respectability of the gentry. Aquia Church, Stafford County, Virginia, Harold Wickliffe Rose Papers — Yale University Library.

South. The 10 to 40 percent of men who could not qualify were disenfranchised, as were all blacks and women. Even elite single women, such as the pioneer landowner Mistress Margaret Brent, were unable to translate financial and political influence into the formal right to vote. But no white men, however poor, shared the inferior economic and political status of women or the burdens and penalties of slavery. These circumstances sustained notions of deference.

But powerful as the gentry were, their relationship with the poorer whites around them was not just one of domination. The Chesapeake gentry had noted the lessons of Bacon's Rebellion, dispensing credit and employment to the less affluent and making court sessions and elections a theater in which white property owners enjoyed a measure of equality. Sociability at taverns, racecourses, militia musters, and court days and the hospitality of the planter houses bridged distinctions between rich and poor whites and reflected their interdependence.

Even so, sharp conflicts over religion, politics, and economic issues arose between whites. Elites were divided by political differences. Wealthy planters and royal officials vied for power and the spoils of office. Planters complained about the "exorbitant" salaries they had to pay governors and other officials and thought them too eager to exploit the region. Struggles over land and markets often pitted wealthy landowners and speculators against middling and poorer whites. In the 1730s, Virginia planters secured the passage of tobacco inspection laws that threatened to squeeze out smaller growers of the crop. Small farmers protested, burning down tobacco warehouses in several counties, but in vain.

In the Carolinas, there was conflict between the dominant coastal elites and poorer inhabitants of the backcountry. Frontier settlers claimed the right of all freeborn Englishmen to oppose illegitimate authority. People expected the wealthy to rule but also to protect the larger interests of the community. When they did not, ordinary men and women claimed the right to take action on the community's behalf. Backcountry people in the Lower South seriously challenged coastal elites in the 1760s. Grievances mostly concerned access to the land and representation in colonial assemblies. Complaints readily escalated into violent confrontations because frontier dwellers were already organized into armed militias for action against the Indians in the area. Though coastal authorities in the Carolinas and Georgia accused frontier dwellers of living "out of the bounds of the law," such people were not overly violent or reckless. They were simply less deferential, more irreverent, and more egalitarian than their low-country peers.

The Challenge of the Great Awakening   A less violent but broader challenge emerged in the 1740s, when poor and politically disenfranchised whites joined a religious movement—called "the Great Awakening" by historians—that spread rapidly across the northern and southern colonies (see Chapter 3). For decades, the Anglican clergy and educated colonists had adopted the view, increasingly current among secular intellectuals in Europe, that God was rational and kind. This stance fit well with elite concepts of a decorous form of religious observance in which popular participation would pose no threat to social order or the authority of rulers. But evangelicals, many from the middling and lower classes, rejected the rationalists' refined, philosophical religious discourse. Their God was wrathful and disgusted at humankind's sinfulness. Individuals could be saved only by recognizing their own helplessness and depravity in the face of God's might and by surrendering to God through an emotional conversion and begging forgiveness.

Figures who were at the heart of profound religious changes in England during the 1730s helped to spread the Great Awakening in America. John Wesley, the founder of Methodism, preached in Georgia in 1736, and a tour of the colonies three years later by his colleague George Whitefield prompted widespread revivals. From early revival meetings grew new sects that challenged Anglicanism and appealed to people of moderate and poor means. "New Lights," as they were known, disputed with the clergy; attacked gambling, horse racing, and other leisured activities as sinful; and proclaimed the spiritual equality of all men and women before God. In Virginia, small farmers enthusiastically denounced the gentry's way of life. Itinerant preachers taught their growing flocks that ordinary folk were more likely candidates for divine inspiration than were the gentry and educated clergymen who led them.

The egalitarianism of the Great Awakening challenged more than planters' habits. It called their control into question, and it also threatened to break through the racial barriers that had become an essential facet of slave societies. Although Whitefield did not question slavery itself, he did condemn the mistreatment of slaves and referred to the recent Stono Rebellion as God's judgment on planters. Others went further. In 1741, Hugh Bryan, a South Carolina planter and politician who had been converted in the revival, began prophesying a day of doom that would bring "Deliverance of the Negroes from servitude." The colonial assembly forced him to retract and apologize for his remarks because, as another planter put it, "we dreaded the consiquence of such a thing being put in to the head of the slaves and the advantage they might take of us." The doctrine of spiritual equality had subversive potential in a slave society.

Revivalist religion, unlike Anglican hierarchicalism, spread Christianity among slaves, as well as poor whites, in the mid-eighteenth century. Slaves like David George converted in large numbers, and the proportion of Christianized slaves would rise, though faster in the Chesapeake than in the Lower South. Some evangelicals — considered by Virginia's well-to-do to be "continual fomenters of discord" — held the radical belief that equality before God extended to all men and women, black and white; all could surrender to God and be saved. In the Virginia backcountry, the Presbyterian preacher Samuel Davies attracted growing numbers of black and white members to his churches in the 1750s, while Methodist churches regularly became forums of biracial worship. The evangelical movement as a whole, white and black, raised the level of religious involvement in the colonies and was particularly influential among women.

Davies assured leading Virginians that he was not seeking to undermine the social order. By turning human minds to spiritual matters, revivalism was potentially a conservative force. But by democratizing salvation, preachers

Bunn, the Blacksmith, at a Campmeeting near Georgetown
In 1809, Benjamin Henry Latrobe attended a Virginia Methodist revival meeting, at which he sketched the effective performance of a self-educated, artisan preacher. "A general groaning was going on," Latrobe wrote in his journal, "in several parts of the Camp, women were shrieking, and just under the stage there was an uncommon bustle, and cry, which I understood arose from some persons who were under conversion." Benjamin Henry Latrobe, *Bunn, the blacksmith, at a Campmeeting near Georgetown,* August 6, 1809, pencil, pen and ink, 8 × 12 3/4 inches — Maryland Historical Society.

An Overseer Doing His Duty

A relaxed overseer watches two slave women at work in a Virginia scene sketched by Benjamin Henry Latrobe in 1798. Latrobe (who would become one of the most influential architects in nineteenth-century America) had been in the United States only two years, but during that brief time, he grew to detest slavery (as suggested in the sarcastic title of the sketch). Benjamin Henry Latrobe, *An overseer doing his duty. Sketched from life near Fredericsburg, March 13, 1798,* pencil, pen and ink, watercolor, 7 × 10 1/4 inches — Maryland Historical Society.

helped to erode some of the deference with which blacks and most whites were expected to regard the gentry. Groups such as the Separate Baptists became open critics of slavery and slave trading. Calling slavery into question and bringing white and black worshippers together on an equal footing, the Awakening weakened the gentry's formula, worked out in the aftermath of Bacon's Rebellion, for preserving order in a slave society.

The Awakening also helped to popularize the belief that government was merely the human mechanism through which God would ensure equality among individuals from various classes. In this belief, illiterate craft workers, backwoods farmers, and female servants sought salvation for themselves and for society. Disdaining planters' excessive comforts and pleasures, evangelicals questioned the legitimacy of their rule and the superiority of their culture.

Conclusion: Southern Society at Mid-Eighteenth Century

Social tensions in the English southern colonies did not undermine their position with regard to the Indians or other European powers whose territory lay adjacent to them. Population growth and frontier settlement maintained pressure on Native American groups. Wars and skirmishes across the border to the South weakened Spanish control of Florida and would lead to the British acquisition of East Florida in 1763. Meanwhile, in the Mississippi Valley, the French were also having difficulty sustaining their projected plantation society. Having imported several thousand African slaves to Louisiana in the decade or so after founding New Orleans, they found themselves unable to build the kind of slave society that had emerged in the English South. Slaves and members of the local Natchez tribe revolted in 1729, weakening an already tenuous French control of society. The European population grew more slowly than the African, and Louisiana soon had a black majority. Slaveholding was concentrated in the hands of a small elite of planters and merchants, but racial distinctions were weakly defined, and intermarriage became frequent. In contrast with the English slave colonies, Louisiana ceased to be dominated by the existence of slavery; it became a "society with slaves."

From Maryland to Georgia, by contrast, wealthy landowners convinced many poor whites that the division between white and black meant more than that between rich and poor. The existence of slavery shaped virtually all social relations in the English southern colonies, where planters held sway over economic and political activity and exercised relatively unconstrained power. This made the South different, not only from Florida and Louisiana, but also from the other English settlements to the north.

The Years in Review

1607
- The first permanent English settlement in the New World is created at Jamestown (Virginia).

1611
- Tobacco production is introduced in Virginia; Indians teach whites how to cultivate the crop.

1617
- Several hundred London orphans are forcibly transported to Virginia to work in the tobacco fields.

1619
- The first African slaves arrive in America.
- The Virginia House of Burgesses (the first colonial legislature) meets for the first time.

1622
- Powhatan Indians attack white settlers in Virginia in the War of 1622.

1634
- Lord Baltimore establishes a colony in Maryland that welcomes both Protestants and Catholics.

1636
- The Dutch introduce sugar cane into Barbados; it soon becomes the major crop in the West Indies; by 1645, Barbados has 6,000 slaves, most of them working on sugar plantations.

1651

- The first of the English government's trade regulations on colonists, known as Navigation Acts, are passed; they are extended further in 1660s.

1660

- Slavery gains official sanction in colonial law.

- Charles II is restored to English throne after the Civil War and the Commonwealth; he reasserts the crown's authority over the American colonists.

1661

- Indentured servants in Virginia led by Isaac Friend plan rebellion, but their plot is quashed when officials learn of it.

1663

- The Carolina colony is chartered.

- Officials stop a rebellion of indentured servants in Gloucester County, Virginia, and execute several of the conspirators.

1672

- The Royal Africa Company, which has a monopoly on the slave trade with the English colonies, increases its slave shipments from Africa.

1676

- Indentured servants, discontented free farmers, slaves, and others led by Nathaniel Bacon rebel against propertied elites and Indians, whom they see as keeping them from land they want. Bacon's Rebellion is crushed, and twenty-three of his followers are hanged.

1693

- The Spanish government offers freedom to slaves in its territory who convert to Catholicism.

1699

- Virginia law declares that an owner who killed his slave could not be guilty of murder because he would not intentionally destroy his own property.

1700

- Massachusetts Puritan Samuel Sewall publishes *The Selling of Joseph*, probably the first antislavery tract in the colonies.

1708

- Blacks outnumber whites (in Carolina) for the first time in any of the colonies.

1711

- The Tuscarora Indians in northern Carolina are defeated and pushed inland.

1715
- The Yamasee Indians attack English settlements encroaching on their territory. The Yamasees are defeated and sold into slavery.

1719
- North and South Carolina are formally separated into two colonies.

1728
- Runaway slaves create a village, establish tribal government, and grow crops in Lexington, Virginia. Whites destroy the village the following year.

1730
- Two hundred slaves revolt near Norfolk, Virginia; the defeat leads to the enlargement of local militias.

1732
- The colony of Georgia is established.

1735
- Slavery is banned in Georgia.

1739
- An uprising of South Carolina slaves, known as the Stono Rebellion, is brutally suppressed with executions and the display of severed heads as warning to others.
- Preaching by the Methodist George Whitefield helps to set off religious revivals known as the Great Awakening.

1740
- English troops capture a village of escaped slaves near St. Augustine, Florida.

1749
- Georgia rescinds its ban on slavery.

Additional Readings

For more on the colonial South in the continental context, see: Alan Taylor, *American Colonies: The Settling of North America* (2001).

For more on slavery and African American culture, see: Ira Berlin, *Many Thousands Gone: The First Two Centuries of Slavery in North America* (1998); Ira Berlin, *Generations of Captivity: A History of African American Slavery* (2003); Sylvia R. Frey and Betty Wood, *Come Shouting to Zion: African American Protestantism in the American South and British Caribbean to 1830* (1998); and Gwendolyn M. Hall, *Africans in Colonial Louisiana: The Development of Afro-Creole Culture in the Eighteenth Century* (1992).

For more on slavery in the Chesapeake colonies, see: Rhys Isaac, *Landon Carter's Uneasy Kingdom: Revolution and Rebellion on a Virginia*

Plantation (2004); Edmund S. Morgan, *American Slavery, American Freedom: The Ordeal of Colonial Virginia* (1975); Philip D. Morgan, *Slave Counterpoint: Black Culture in the Eighteenth-Century Chesapeake and Lowcountry* (1998); Anthony S. Parent, Jr., *Foul Means: The Formation of a Slave Society in Virginia, 1660–1740* (2003); and Lorena S. Walsh, *From Calabar to Carter's Grove: The History of a Virginia Slave Community* (1997).

For more on the Carolinas, see: Tom Hatley, *The Dividing Paths: Cherokees and South Carolinians Through the Revolutionary Era* (1993); Johanna Miller Lewis, *Artisans in the North Carolina Backcountry* (1995); Daniel C. Littlefield, *Rice and Slaves: Ethnicity and the Slave Trade in Colonial South Carolina* (1981); Robert Olwell, *Masters, Slaves, and Subjects: The Culture of Power in the South Carolina Low Country* (1998); and Peter H. Wood, *Black Majority: Negroes in Colonial South Carolina from 1670 through the Stono Rebellion* (1974).

For more on the Chesapeake, see: Richard R. Beeman, *The Evolution of the Southern Backcountry: A Case Study of Lunenburg County, Virginia, 1746–1832* (1984); T. H. Breen, *Tobacco Culture: The Mentality of the Great Tidewater Planters on the Eve of Revolution* (1985); Kathleen M. Brown, *Good Wives, Nasty Wenches, and Anxious Patriarchs: Gender, Race, and Power in Colonial Virginia* (1996); Lois G. Carr, et al., *Robert Cole's World: Agriculture and Society in Early Maryland* (1991); April Lee Hatfield, *Atlantic Virginia: Intercolonial Relations in the Seventeenth Century* (2004); James Horn, *Adapting to a New World: English Society in the Seventeenth Century Chesapeake* (1994); Rhys Isaac, *The Transformation of Virginia, 1740–1790* (1982); Allan Kulikoff, *Tobacco and Slaves: The Development of Southern Cultures in the Chesapeake* (1986); Linda L. Sturtz, *Within Her Power: Propertied Women in Colonial Virginia* (2002); and Terri L. Snyder, *Brabbling Women: Disorderly Speech and the Law in Early Virginia* (2003).

For more on Indians, see: James H. Merrell, *The Indians' New World: Catawbas and Their Neighbors from European Contact Through the Period of Removal* (1989); Jane T. Merritt, *At the Crossroads: Indians and Empires on a Mid-Atlantic Frontier, 1700–1763* (2003); Timothy Silver, *A New Face on the Countryside: Indians, Colonists, and Slaves in South Atlantic Forests, 1500–1800* (1990); Daniel H. Usner, Jr., *Indians, Settlers, and Slaves in a Frontier Exchange Economy: The Lower Mississippi Valley Before 1783* (1992); and Peter H. Wood, et al., eds., *Powhatan's Mantle: Indians in the Colonial Southeast* (1989).

For more on the Great Awakening, see: Sylvia R. Frey, *Water from the Rock: Black Resistance in a Revolutionary Age* (1991); Michael J. McClymond, ed., *Embodying the Spirit: New Perspectives on North American Revivalism* (2004); and Mark A. Noll, *America's God: From Jonathan Edwards to Abraham Lincoln* (2002).

3

Family Labor and the Growth of the Northern Colonies

1640–1760

Straw Hat Maker.

A Cooper.

Spinner.

A Carpenter.

A Bricklayer.

Type Founder.

Shipwright.

Hat-maker.

Colonial Trades
These illustrations were published in the American edition of *The Book of Trades*, a British survey of crafts that were practiced in the colonies. *The Book of Trades, or Library of the Useful Arts* (1807) — American Social History Project.

AFTER MICHAEL AND HANNAH Emerson married in 1657 and settled on a small farm in Haverhill, Massachusetts, they worked at shoemaking as well as running the farm and household. To Hannah fell much of the work of raising a growing family, and for her, this work would have been long and arduous, for she eventually gave birth to fifteen children. This was an unusual number even for colonial New England, where large families were common. Five of the Emerson children died before adulthood, but the other ten survived to expect to marry and begin their own families. In New England, as elsewhere in the northern colonies, family households were at the center of society and of economic activity.

New England, growing from the Puritan settlements of the 1620s and 1630s, developed differently from the Chesapeake and Lower South. There were no tobacco or rice plantations. Rather than extracting wealth through the forced labor of others, the majority of colonists sought a "decent competency" by steady family toil on the land. Family labor was also important in the Middle Colonies — New York, New Jersey, and Pennsylvania — that developed to the south of New England. New York, originally the Dutch territory of New Netherland, was seized by the English in 1664. King Charles II gave it to his brother the Duke of York, who renamed it after himself. In the 1670s and 1680s, further land grants by the English crown led to the settlement of New Jersey and Pennsylvania. Though the Middle Colonies differed from New England in important respects, all the northern colonies came to share the same economic foundation: family-run farming.

Like the colonies to the south, the northern colonies attracted diverse peoples. Most came from the British Isles, among them English, Highland Scots, Scots-Irish, Welsh, and a few Catholic Irish, but substantial numbers migrated from mainland Europe: Dutch (in New Netherland), Huguenot (Protestant) French, and many Protestant Germans. A few Sephardic Jews also arrived from the Mediterranean. Scandinavians, who settled in the Delaware Valley, introduced the log house to North America. Many northern settlers were working people of moderate means who migrated more or less willingly, hoping to obtain land and become independent farmers or to secure independence as skilled artisans, small merchants, midwives, or dressmakers. Puritan migrants to Massachusetts Bay, Quakers who settled Pennsylvania, and the Amish who later followed them there were prominent among those who sought to build societies that could embody their religious ideals.

But though rural families formed its backbone, northern colonial society was not made up solely of independent yeoman farmers. In some areas, such as New York's Hudson River Valley, ambitious, privileged men were assembling great estates on which they would earn wealth from the labor of tenants. There were also, along the coasts and estuaries, port towns whose inhabitants linked the rural interior to the commerce and fishing grounds of the Atlantic Ocean.

Most northern colonists were free, but not all. Many poorer white immigrants, especially in Pennsylvania and the northern Chesapeake, had signed on for periods of indentured servitude. At times in the eighteenth century, indentured servants made up half of the immigration from Europe. There were also slaves in the North. In 1645, Emmanuel Downing of Salem, Massachusetts, urged Governor John Winthrop to sponsor slave imports, arguing: "I do not see how we can thrive until we get a stock of slaves sufficient to do all our business." New York imported sizable numbers of slaves, and in the mid-eighteenth century, over one-fifth of New York City's population was of African origin, either enslaved or free. Northern slavery could be as harsh and oppressive as that in the South but was much less widespread. In the absence of staple crops and with the prevalence of family farming, slavery never became the crucial underpinning of society that it did in southern plantation regions.

Many parts of the northern colonies grew rapidly in population, and some became very prosperous. As in the South, growth entailed conflict. The spread of settlement provoked confrontations with Indians, many of whom resented and tried to resist the European incursion. The nations that were well inland, such as the Iroquois, managed to hold off the colonists' encroachment. Conflict with Indians became entwined with fierce international rivalries, first between the Dutch and the English and then, for almost a century, between the English and the French in Canada. Repeated wars put New Englanders and other frontier settlers under arms. Social and religious tensions, some arising from the religious revivals known as the Great Awakening, and disputes between colonies meant that the northern settlers were far from united.

Early New England

From the start of European migration to the northern colonies, most settlers found themselves in a healthier, less economically exploitative environment than did their counterparts in the South. Early migrants to the Chesapeake faced high mortality from disease (see Chapter 2) and harsh treatment, but those who reached New England soon established stable, flourishing societies. The availability of land and food enabled the first generation of Massachusetts settlers to enjoy life expectancies that were longer than any in Europe. Even as Indians died from Europeans' diseases, white northern settlers began to build large families and doubled their populations every twenty years or so.

The goals held by their organizers also explain why the northern colonies became quickly established. While Virginia's founders had come to the New World intending to get rich and get out, the founders of New England—and later Pennsylvania—intended to build stable communities for which families were essential. Seven out of eight migrants to Massachusetts in the 1630s traveled with at least one relative, and three out of four came in a family group.

Women were present in significant numbers from the start. In the Chesapeake, men outnumbered women by three to two even in 1700, but in New England, the ratio was almost balanced half a century earlier. This was another reason for rapid population growth. Most men and women found marriage partners, women bore an unprecedented number of children, and children survived infancy at an unprecedented rate. Husbands, wives, and children supplied most basic requirements for labor. Men and women divided tasks between them, and children worked for the family, too. If a family obtained other assistance, as often happened, it was usually to supply a need that, for the time being, the family could not meet itself. Even though the flow of emigrants to New England ceased in the early 1640s as England became embroiled in civil war, high birth rates and low mortality enabled the settlements there to survive and thrive. In these stable, growing colonies, the majority of white men owned land, and the colonies' Puritan leaders enforced strict social and religious boundaries. Yet the colonists' attitudes about the meaning of land ownership and their desire for ever more land led to increasing conflict with local Indian groups.

A Freeholders' Society One key to New England's survival was the widespread availability of land that was not monopolized by the wealthy or by those with the right connections (Map 3.1). Landownership in New England usually conferred outright title, or "freehold," to a property. In England, most land had been held by large landholders, who might lease it in portions to tenant farmers in return for rent or who even retained feudal or manorial rights to payments, labor services, and other obligations from the people who occupied and worked it. New Englanders took pride in their absolute property rights and in the freedom this conferred to pass on their land as they wished without owing tribute to landlords. They came to see freeholding as an essential part of their "English liberties."

Yet largely rejecting competitive individualism and aiming to shape their lives to achieve spiritual grace and social harmony, most early New Englanders avoided the kind of free-for-all that had marked planters' acquisition of land in Virginia. In Massachusetts, the government usually made grants of land not to individuals but to whole communities, known as "towns." Sometimes at meetings of all freemen in the town and sometimes through special committees, townsmen themselves decided how to allocate the grant. Dedham, Massachusetts, and other early towns divided land into large open fields rather than separate enclosed farms, a pattern that was familiar especially to those who had come from eastern England. People lived together in central villages, offering one another mutual support and defense. Each landowner had individual strips in the different fields, but townspeople collaborated at work, from the first plowing to the harvest.

Requests for town grants met with generous response from the colonial government. Andover's founders received more than 38,000 acres of land for a population that, as late as 1662, numbered only forty families. Towns often held most of their land in reserve. When the town of Sudbury made its first division, it handed out only 751 acres, in grants ranging from 4 acres to 76 acres. Individuals — almost always male household heads — received their land on the basis of the town's judgment about how much each needed. A man's prestige (being the minister or having a good name from England), community need (for a miller or a blacksmith), and individual necessity (the number of children in a family) all influenced the allocation. Towns held back undivided land for distribution to newcomers and, especially, for the next generation of townspeople. The towns' distribution of land helped to secure the authority and economic position of male property owners.

Equality and Inequality in Puritan Society But towns were much more than devices for managing land. Town meetings of all freemen were the basic unit of local government, while to Puritan leaders, towns were also the means for gathering communities of believers. Each town had an

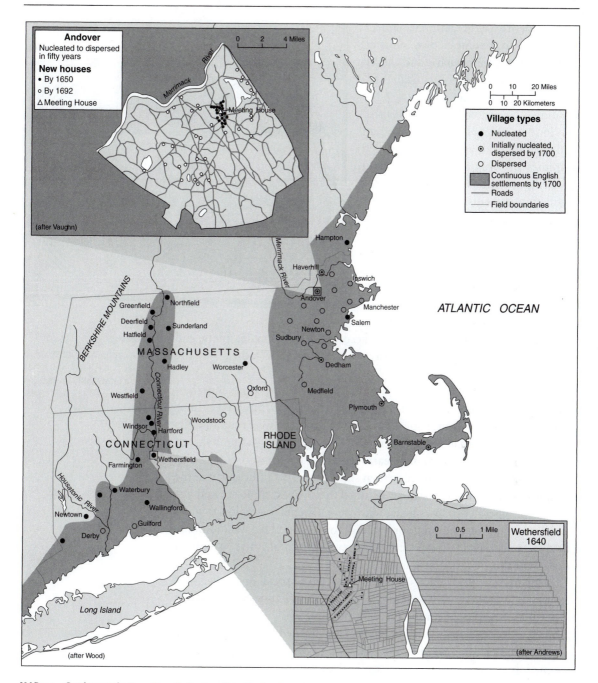

MAP 3.1 Settlement in Seventeenth-Century New England

New England colonists quickly spread out from their initial settlements of Plymouth and Boston, reaching down to Long Island Sound, up the Connecticut River valley, and up the coast toward what became New Hampshire and Maine. But warfare and continued Indian resistance helped to prevent the further spread of settlement beyond these areas until the next century. Meanwhile, within New England, settlement patterns changed. Early nucleated towns such as Wethersfield were succeeded by towns such as Andover, where most residents lived on dispersed farms.

independent Congregational church with power to appoint its own minister. Although town membership and church membership were never identical, Puritans saw their churches as central to the creation of an ordered commonwealth.

Puritan society had both egalitarian and hierarchical aspects. It avoided extremes of wealth and poverty and rejected ostentation or formal hereditary distinction. Yet it also stressed authority and hierarchy as instruments of social order. Even in New England, wrote Governor John Winthrop, "some must be rich some poore, some highe and eminent in power and dignitie; others meane and in subjeccion." At public worship, people were seated according to their rank in town. Respect was to be accorded to age, gender, piety, and social standing. Clergy and magistrates were cast as "fathers" to the community.

Harvesting

A woodcut from a Pennsylvania almanac published in the 1760s shows a farm family at work in the fields. *Father Abraham's 1760 Almanac* (1759) — American Antiquarian Society.

Only men with property exercised influence in towns and churches, and they curbed the voices of women and youths. Though Puritans regarded men and women as spiritual equals and women were economically vital, this did not mean that women were socially equal. Puritans shared the patriarchal assumptions of all early settlers that men were superior to women and that property-owning men should exercise authority over the members of their families, which included their wives, children, and any servants or other dependents living with them. Parents or employers could lawfully administer whippings or beatings for wrongdoing, and although the courts punished excessive cruelty, they also admonished parents or masters for showing too much laxity.

Puritans saw orderly households as the germ of social order. Personal freedom and individuality were suspect. To ensure that everyone resided under the discipline of family life, young single men and women were obliged to live with families as servants. They formed up to one-third of New England's workforce before 1650, although their relative importance declined after that. Servants were obliged to remain with uncongenial employers and could be returned to them if they ran away, and the law looked with similar disfavor on wives who sought to escape cruel husbands or neglected the household duties they were expected to perform.

Women who spoke up or stood out posed a threat to social order. In 1637, Anne Hutchinson, a prominent Boston woman, was tried and

"The 7th of this month I sowed turnips": A Farmer's Diary

Thomas Minor was a prosperous farmer in the coastal Connecticut town of Stonington, who attended to town and other public affairs as well as his own farm. His diary for the summer and autumn months of 1660 reflects the variety of farming tasks, the produce and livestock Minor traded, the use of family and locally hired labor, and exchanges with neighbors. The butter Minor delivered would have been made by his wife, Grace, or by another female member of the household. Until the mid-eighteenth century, the English colonists started the New Year in March—hence Minor's numbering of the months in his diary.

The fifth month is July 31 days & Sabbath day the first. This week I agreed with Rogers about John's 2 Cows & a calf & Sabbath day the 8. The 7th of this month I sowed turnips. The 13 there was a town meeting & Sabbath day the 15. I pulled hemp. Ephraim & Joseph [Thomas Minor's sons] mowed in the orchard Friday & Saturday 20 and 21. We had a court at Captain Denison's Sabbath day 22. 23 I looked horses fetched one load of hay & Saturday the 28 I cut peas & Sabbath day 29 & Tuesday the 31.

The sixth month is August 31 days and Wednesday the first. I cut fence & carried them Wednesday the 8. I carried my wheat Thursday the 9. I carried the Ram to the Island & Wednesday the 15. Friday 17 Thomas & Ephraim [Thomas Minor's sons] was at Samuel Cheesbrough's. The 13 day I had the gelding at Captain Denison's. The 20th day John Tower came here & Wednesday the 22 we Carried 5 loads of hay & made a rick next to the barn. Wednesday 29 I was at town & took up things for John. I was at Prentice to show the horse Friday 31.

The seventh month is September 30 days & Saturday the first. Mr. Winthrop [John Winthrop, Jr., son of the Massachusetts Bay leader and a governor of Connecticut] was at New London. . . .

The eight month is October 31 days & Monday the first. This day Hannah her child [possibly Grace Minor's sister Hannah] died before day & Monday the 8 the moon was Eclipsed. I was to go with Mr. Bridgen [sic] toward Mohegan & Monday the 29 I carried the firkin of butter to Mr. Smith for Amos. . . .

The ninth [month] is November 30 days & Thursday the first. Friday the 2 I weighed Amos his firkin of butter at Mr. Smith's. It was 70 pounds & there is 13 pounds to pay. The 8 day being Thursday we had Carried 45 loads of muck out of the yards. There was a meeting to be at Smith's of the whole Town & Thursday the 15. This week we killed the steer. I was at New London & had the axes & guns mended. The steer came to six pounds. The 20 we began the little house. Thursday 22 it snowed the second time. Thursday the 29 we appointed a meeting to be at Cheesbrough's. That day fortnight I began to clean clapboards. Friday the 30 we had home all the timber for the little house.

Thomas Minor, *The Diary of Thomas Minor of Stonington, Connecticut,* 1653–84 (New London, CT: The Day Publishing Co., 1899).

banished from Massachusetts after attracting a religious following and "casting reproach upon the faithful Ministers of this Country." Governor John Winthrop claimed that she had "a very voluble tongue, more bold than a man" and feared that her opinions would "spread like a Leprosie, and infect farr and near." When a few Quaker preachers, including women, entered Massachusetts in the late 1650s, they were jailed, whipped, and banished. Four of them were executed, including Mary Dyer, who was hanged in 1660 after she defied the courts and returned to Boston from exile in Rhode Island to preach.

Women who were seen as too independent or assertive also faced suspicion of witchcraft or complicity with the devil, a crime that was punishable by death. Eighty percent of accused witches in seventeenth-century New England were women, many of them widowed or in some sense independent. The fear of disorder such women instilled helped to bring about the notorious Salem Village trials of 1692, when magistrates put credence in rampant accusations of witchcraft in a local community. Of nineteen alleged witches who were eventually hanged at Salem, fourteen were women. The first three to be accused—a West Indian slave, a poor widow, and an old semi-invalid woman who lived on the edge of town—were at the margins of Salem society, but among the others were women of means who had exercised some discretion over their own affairs.

There were also substantial inequalities among men, however. Not all towns developed in the manner of Dedham, Sudbury, or Andover. The ports and fishing camps northeast of Boston were dominated by traders and shipowners, for whom poorer men worked as crews on fishing boats and as seamen. Such places were never as egalitarian as some of the inland towns. In mid-seventeenth-century Ipswich, 75 percent of families owned less than 90 acres of land each, almost 25 percent owned more than 100 acres, and five men owned over 1,000 acres. Yet most New Englanders upheld the ideal of a society based on widespread freehold landownership by independent households. This ideal helped to seal the fate of New England's Indians; it also shaped colonists' attitudes to English rule in the later seventeenth century.

Conflict with Indians   The destruction of the Pequot tribe in the late 1630s (see Chapter 1) did not end the friction between growing populations of settlers and native groups. Most settlers wanted to clear the forest; fence in their fields; build houses and barns, meetinghouses and stores; plant English crops; and raise livestock. Native Americans and Europeans had very different understandings of what it meant to possess and work the land. For most Native Americans, a land title was collective and relative. All members of a tribe owned the land; there was no such thing as rent or purchase. But

Witchcraft

Women were accused, prosecuted, and occasionally executed for the crime of witchcraft in seventeenth-century New England. Although Anne Hutchinson was never accused outright of being a witch, the Puritan fathers interpreted the delivery of a stillborn and allegedly deformed infant to one of her female associates, Mary Dyer, in 1637 as the Devil's work. This illustration from an eighteenth-century chapbook (a cheaply printed pamphlet) presents a "monstrous" birth as a sign of witchcraft. John Ashton, *Chap-books of the Eighteenth Century* (1882) — Prints and Photographs Division, Library of Congress.

for New England's freeholders, ownership was individual and absolute. Colonists asserted that Indians did not, according to English law, actually own their land but merely occupied it, because they built no permanent buildings and used no draft animals. No fences and hedges marked where one person's fields ended and another's began. Native men, settlers claimed, were idle while women tended crops and exerted themselves only to hunt or fish, activities that were suitable for aristocrats or poachers but unworthy of sturdy independent yeomen.

Differing assumptions had tragic consequences. To Europeans, land that natives had not actually cleared was not really theirs. To natives, "selling" the land to Europeans merely meant allowing them to use it. Even the settlers' introduction of livestock had huge effects. Following English custom, colonists let their animals roam free in the woods, to be rounded up when needed, and they built fences to keep the animals out of their own crops. But their pigs and cattle invaded Indians' unfenced fields and destroyed their crops. Roger Williams, a founder of Rhode Island, was one of the few early colonists to acknowledge the violation of natives' rights: "Swine," he noted, "are most hateful to all Natives, and they call them filthy cutthroats." But many settlers convinced themselves that natives would have to move out of their way or be removed.

Their defeat of the Pequots helped colonists to expand across southern New England. They established Connecticut and the small colony of New Haven and soon began to settle Long Island. Making alliances with some native groups against others, they were able to hold off any united resistance to their expansion. They made deals, often with minor sachems (chiefs), by which native groups agreed to cede land or pay tribute in return for protection.

The responses of natives to this intrusion varied. Some ceded land simply because they were outnumbered. At New Haven, five dozen or so Quinnipiacs and others, their population depleted by disease and displacement, faced 2,500 arriving colonists. In eastern Connecticut, however, the large Mohegan tribe made an alliance with the English so as to strengthen their own hold over smaller native groups and in hope of protecting themselves against encroachment. Inhabitants of the fourteen "praying Indian" towns in Massachusetts accepted greater association with colonists until King Philip's War (see Chapter 1) breached the bonds of trust between them

"We Must Be One as They Are . . .": The Narragansett Seek Alliances

In the Pequot War of the late 1630s, the Narragansett Indians of Rhode Island had allied with the English, and they had absorbed some of the surviving Pequots into their settlements after the war ended. Soon, however, Narragansett leaders became alarmed at continued English incursions on their land and hunting grounds. In 1642, the Narragansett sachem Miantonomi traveled to Long Island to forge alliances with members of the Montauk and other groups. Outmaneuvered by the English and their Mohegan allies, Miantonomi was eventually captured, tried, and executed. Though this English account of Miantonomi's efforts to form an Indian alliance was part of the case against him, it amply summarizes New England Indians' grievances.

A while after this came Miantenomie from Block-Island to Mantacut with a troop of men . . . ; and instead of receiving presents, which they used to do in their progress, he gave them gifts, calling them brethren and friends, for so are we all Indians as the English are, and say brother to one another; so must we be one as they are, otherwise we shall be all gone shortly, for you know our fathers had plenty of deer and skins, our plains were full of deer, and also our woods, and of turkies, and our coves full of fish and fowl. But these English having gotten our land, they with scythes cut down the grass, and with axes fell the trees; their cows and horses eat the grass, and their hogs spoil our clam banks, and we shall all be starved; therefore it is best for you to do as we, for we are all the Sachems from east to west, both Moquakues and Mohauks joining with us, and we are all resolved to fall upon them all, at one appointed day; and therefore I am come to you privately first, because you can persuade the Indians and Sachem to what you will, and I will send over fifty Indians to Block-Island, and thirty to you from thence, and take an hundred of Southampton Indians with an hundred of your own here; and when you see the three fires that will be made forty days hence, in a clear night, then do as we, and the next day fall on and kill men, women, and children, but no cows, for they will serve to eat till our deer be increased again. . . .

Collections of the Massachusetts Historical Society, third series, volume 3 (1833), 152–155.

and caused many Indians to be banished. Defensive alliances to stem the settlers' invasion, such as that attempted by the Narragansetts in the 1640s, could be outmaneuvered by the English in conjunction with other Indian groups, such as the Mohegans. King Philip's War itself marked the high tide and then collapse of native resistance in southern New England. Subsequently, native peoples were dispersed across this region, obliged to live on marginal lands, hunting and fishing where they could or supporting themselves by laboring for white communities, their children often put into white families as servants. By the eighteenth century, many Indians lived like the parents of the Mohegan Samson Occom, who "Chiefly Depended upon Hunting, Fishing and Fowling for their Living and had no connection with the English except to Traffic with them in their small Trifles." They preserved a degree of independence but had largely lost control of their lands.

America and England in the Late Seventeenth Century

Overcoming native resistance did not, however, assure New Englanders that they would be secure on their freehold lands. The ending of the English civil war by the restoration of the monarchy in England in 1660 (see Chapter 1) brought renewed aristocratic visions of great landed estates in the New World, threatening the freehold ideal. New Englanders' ambition to build a Puritan commonwealth and their sympathy with English Puritans brought them under scrutiny by the restored monarchy of Charles II. English Puritans now faced a hostile political climate, and the crown seemed likely to undermine New England's distinctiveness and relative independence, including its freehold land titles.

Developments in the territory south of New England and north of the Chesapeake soon demonstrated the fragility of the freehold ideal as huge areas became the subject of royal grants to favored landed proprietors. The creation of great proprietorships in the Middle Colonies suggested that English North America might become a society of great estates on the English pattern, in which aristocrats would, for their own benefit and profit, employ tenant farmers and other dependents to cultivate the land. While English colonists controlled ever greater amounts of land in coastal areas, the strength and diplomacy of some Indian groups in the interior, such as the Iroquois, meant that settlers and Indians negotiated various forms of cooperation and exchange.

The Establishment of the Middle Colonies   The small population of New Netherland could do little to discourage the land-hungry English from invading Dutch claims. When Charles II granted land including the Dutch colony to his brother James, Duke of York, James moved quickly to take power from the governor, Peter Stuyvesant. After three English attacks, the Dutch relinquished control of New Netherland in 1664, and it became the English colonies of New York and later New Jersey. The Dutch had already created large landholdings, known as patroonships, in New Netherland. The English did the same, granting large tracts of land on feudal terms to manor lords, who gained the right to hold court and sit in judgment over their

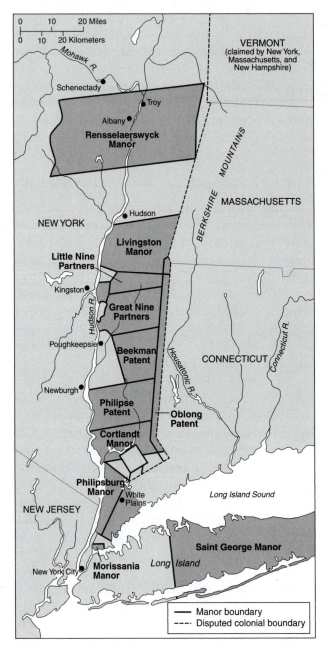

MAP 3.2 The Manors of the Hudson River Valley

From the seventeenth century, large manorial grants occupied most of the eastern side of the Hudson River valley after first the Dutch, then the English awarded them to wealthy landowners. Farmed by tenants, not freeholders, the manors both blocked migration from crowded parts of New England and fed New England farmers' greatest fear — that they, too, might be "reduced to lord-ships."

tenants. No landowner actually exercised that right, but three manorial families would control what amounted to private seats in the New York colonial assembly.

The development of great estates in the Hudson and Mohawk river valleys was a notable feature of New York society over the next several decades

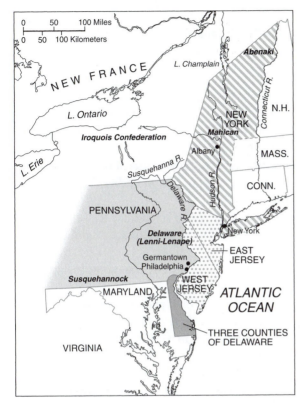

MAP 3.3   The Middle Colonies in the Late Seventeenth Century

This map shows the principal land grants made by the government of King Charles II after the English capture of Dutch New Netherland, with some of the main Indian groups that lived there. Colonial settlements soon surrounded or displaced the Mahicans and Delawares, but the Iroquois successfully resisted white encroachments until the American Revolution in the 1770s. Robert A. Divine, et al., *America: Past and Present*, 5th edition (1999).

(Map 3.2). Families such as the Van Rensselaers, the Johnsons, the Livingstons, the Schuylers, the Philipses, and the Morrises acquired large manors derived from Dutch or English land-grants. Livingston Manor, some forty miles south of Albany, grew to occupy 160,000 acres of prime farmland. Landlords rented farms to tenants, over whom they acquired considerable power. The result was class division and landlords' expectation of deference from their tenants. Sir William Johnson, the eighteenth-century "Mohawk Baronet," owned the local courthouse, jail, and Anglican church on his estate. A tenant could sell his leasehold only with the landlord's consent. When one landlord's daughter was married, "tenants gathered before the manor hall" in deferential attendance, "as on rent day."

The Duke of York had meanwhile given New Jersey to his close associates, Lord John Berkeley and Sir George Carteret. In 1676, William Penn and three other Quaker gentlemen acquired Carteret's share. By the early 1680s, the well-connected Penn had negotiated control of even more territory, accepting a large mass of land, which he named "Pennsylvania," in return for forgiving a large debt owed him by the king. The Penns became hereditary proprietors of their new province, and its governorship descended in their family until the American Revolution. Having created an American proprietorship on a grand scale, William Penn drew up an ambitious scheme of settlement, advertising for colonists in 1681. A year later, his first party of emigrants reached the Delaware River, founding the city of Philadelphia and settling the land nearby (Map 3.3).

Pennsylvania, however, did not follow the Hudson Valley pattern. William Penn was primarily concerned with creating a prosperous haven for oppressed Quakers and an experiment in religious toleration, so he never set up the lesser lordships permitted by his charter. Instead, the Penns encouraged migrants by selling them land directly, fixing only modest sums for the annual "quitrents" to which their grant entitled them, and setting aside fifty-acre allotments of land for male servants completing their terms. In practice, Pennsylvania's land system worked little differently from the freehold tenure of New England. Purchasers who did become landlords in their own right never enjoyed the power of a New York manor patroon.

"The Air Is Sweet and Clear, the Heavens Serene": William Penn Advertises for Colonists for Pennsylvania

William Penn, a well-placed English gentlemen and a Quaker, took great pains in setting up his colony; twenty drafts survive of his First Frame of Government, the colony's 1682 constitution. Penn was determined to deal fairly with the Lenni Lenape or Delaware Indians and maintain friendly relations with them. He sent back glowing accounts of the colony to his English friends and patrons. This Letter to the Free Society of Traders, *published in 1683, has been recognized as the most effective of Penn's promotional tracts. And it proved successful; by 1700, Pennsylvania's population reached 21,000.*

I. The country itself in its soil, air, water, seasons, and produce, both natural and artificial, is not to be despised. The land contains divers sorts of earth, as sand, yellow and black, poor and rich; also gravel, both loamy and dusty; and in some places a fast fat earth, like to our best vales in England, especially by inland brooks and rivers. God in His wisdom having ordered it so, that the advantages of the country are divided, the back lands being generally three to one richer than those that lie by navigable waters. . . .

II. The *air* is sweet and clear, the heavens serene, like the south parts of France, rarely overcast; and as the woods come by numbers of people to be more cleared, that itself will refine.

III. The *waters* are generally good, for the rivers and brooks have mostly gravel and stony bottoms, and in number hardly credible. . . .

XI. The NATIVES I shall consider in their persons, language, manners, religion, and government, with my sense of their original. For their persons, they are generally tall, straight, well built, and of singular proportion; they tread strong and clever, and mostly walk with a lofty chin. Of complexion black, but by design, as the gypsies in England. They grease themselves with bear's fat clarified, and using no defense against sun or weather, their skins must needs be swarthy. Their eye is little and black, not unlike a straight-looked Jew. . . .

XVII. If a European comes to see them, or calls for lodging at their house or wigwam, they give him the best place and first cut. If they come to visit us, they salute us with an *Itah,* which is as much as to say "Good be to you," and set them down, which is mostly on the ground, close to their heels, their legs upright. . . .

XIX. But in liberality they excel; nothing is too good for their friend. Give them a fine gun, coat, or other thing, it may pass twenty hands before it sticks; light of heart, strong affections, but soon spent, the most merry creatures that live, [they] feast and dance perpetually; they never have much, nor want much. Wealth circulates like the blood, all parts partake; and though none shall want what another has, yet [they are] exact observers of property. . . .

William Penn, *A Letter from William Penn, Proprietary and Governor of Pennsylvania in America, to the Committee of the Free Society of Traders of that Province, residing in London* (London, 1683), 2–9.

The Glorious Revolution of 1688–1689

After 1660, New Englanders were apprehensive that the crown would seek greater control of their colonies and impose on them some form of aristocracy or enforce the practices of the Anglican church. Royal officials began to scrutinize colonists' conformity to trade regulations, including the new Navigation Acts (see Chapter 2), and the close connections—except in Rhode Island—between Puritan churches and colonial governments. Complaints reached England from people who were denied political rights because they were not members of a Puritan church or who had been punished for infractions of tight Puritan laws. Massachusetts in particular feared that the crown would overturn the colony's original charter and bring the Puritan experiment in godly government to an end.

The crown suspended the Massachusetts charter in 1684 and the next year placed the colony with Plymouth, Maine, and New Hampshire in a united "Dominion of New England." Connecticut and Rhode Island were also pressed to join, under the royal governor of New York, Sir Edmund Andros. Massachusetts lost its elected General Court and was ruled by a council appointed by Andros. The Dominion's creation followed the Duke of York's accession to the English throne as James II in 1685; that James was suspected of autocratic designs and Catholic sympathies underscored colonists' fears for the future of their religious and political autonomy and of their freehold land titles.

Events in England helped the colonies to evade disaster. Protestant Whig opposition to James mounted, and in what its supporters came to call the "Glorious Revolution," he was deposed and forced to flee to France in 1688. Parliament confirmed James's son-in-law, the Protestant Dutch ruler William III, as the new king and passed laws to secure its own powers and exclude Catholics from the English throne. News of James's flight touched off rebellions in Maryland and New York, while Massachusetts leaders ousted Governor Andros, reinstituted their own government, and petitioned London for a new charter. By 1689, the Dominion of New England was shattered. All awaited a new political settlement.

Two years later, Massachusetts received its new charter, which ended the Puritans' autonomy, reduced the churches' influence in government, and created a royal governorship like those in New York and Virginia. But the charter also restored Massachusetts' elected assembly, the General Court, and confirmed the colony's freehold land titles. After decades of uncertainty, New Englanders could celebrate their escape from the "reduction to lordships" that the English Restoration had threatened.

Iroquois Diplomacy and the Limits of Colonial Expansion By the early eighteenth century, many Indians along the East Coast acknowledged the king of England's sovereignty over his colonies, but they also insisted that this sovereignty did not confer control over native peoples or how they used their lands. In most seaboard regions, unfortunately, such insistence did little to prevent the conquest and near-destruction of native cultures.

In the interior, however, more powerful groups such as the Iroquois held off European settlement remarkably well. In the 150 years before the American Revolution, the boundary of white settlement moved inland by at most a few hundred miles. Beyond it, Native Americans imposed limits on the seizure and occupation of their land and exploited alliances with both the English and the French as they fought colonial wars with one another. In northern New England, native groups harassed colonial villages and held back the spread of settlement until the 1720s and 1730s. Raids, like that of Indians and French fighters on Deerfield in western Massachusetts in 1704, resulted in the death or capture of dozens of whites and discouraged frontier expansion. Of some 300 people captured between 1690 and 1730, over one in ten of males and one in four of females chose to adopt their captors' way of life. Neither native nor settlers' culture could simply dominate the other.

The Iroquois-speaking Mohawks, Senecas, Onondagas, Oneidas, and Cayugas played a key part in containing white settlement. Their territory stretched from Canada to New York's Finger Lakes, and in the seventeenth century, the Iroquois used their power mainly to expel other native groups from the region. Controlling the fur-rich Adirondack Mountains and key routes toward the west, they could induce both the French in Montreal and the Dutch and English at Albany to pay court to them. Meanwhile they continued to absorb other groups. In 1716, they adopted a sixth Iroquois-speaking tribe, the Tuscaroras, who had been driven out of North Carolina by white settlement. By the 1740s and 1750s, after a deal with the Pennsylva-

Captivity

In 1676, during King Philip's War, Mary Rowlandson was captured by Indians raiding Lancaster, Massachusetts. After being held for three months, she was ransomed and freed. She later wrote *The Sovereignty and Goodness of God: A Narrative . . .*, which was published in 1682 and often reprinted (here in a 1773 edition). It was the first of many "captivity" narratives, which portrayed captivity as a test of the protagonists' Puritan faith. Mary Rowlandson, *A Narrative of the Captivity, Sufferings and Removes of Mrs. Mary Rowlandson* (1773) — Rare Books and Manuscript Division, New York Public Library, Astor, Lenox and Tilden Foundations.

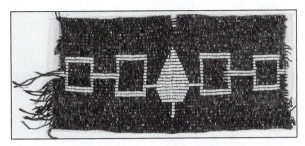

Hiawatha Wampum Belt
This belt depicted the Haude-no-saunee, "the people of the Longhouse," called the Iroquois Confederacy by the French. The Great Tree of Peace was the central symbol, unifying the five Iroquois-speaking nations. Courtesy of the Onondaga Nation and the New York State Museum.

nia government, the Iroquois were taking Delawares under their supervision in the upper Susquehanna valley.

The Iroquois learned much from observing the subjugation or destruction of other tribes. Because French Jesuit missionaries respected Iroquois culture, they had some success in converting them to Christianity. The grave of Kateri Tekakwitha, a Mohawk woman noted for her penitent life, became an object of Catholic pilgrimage after her death in Canada in 1680. But knowing how the "praying Indians" of Massachusetts had been crushed by Puritans who had converted them and then changed their way of life, the Iroquois remained wary of Protestant missionaries well into the eighteenth century.

The Iroquois could fight fiercely and might severely torture men they captured in war, but they also adopted captives into the tribe. Such people might rise to high rank. Hendrick Peters, born around 1680, adopted by the Mohawk as Tee Yee Neen No Ga Row, became a prominent leader at Canajoharie, west of Albany. Women elders usually determined the fate of captives. Female prisoners were not sexually molested, and those who accepted adoption sometimes became honored matriarchs in a society in which women wielded considerable power. Both Eunice Williams, taken from Deerfield as a child by the Mohawks, and Mary Jemison, captured by the Senecas in 1758, refused to return to their white families and lived out long lives in their new Native American communities.

Using the advantages of their position, the Iroquois became as adept at diplomacy as any European nation, playing off the rival contenders for their lands against each other. For well over a century, they balanced the Dutch against the French, then the French against the English, and finally the English against their own colonists. Iroquois fighters played an important part in the succession of wars between English and French colonies that took place from the 1680s to the 1760s. The Iroquois Confederacy held together and managed to curb colonial expansion. Only later, when the American Revolution decisively altered the balance of power against them, would the Iroquois' diplomacy finally fail.

Rural Societies in the Eighteenth Century

By the eighteenth century, the rural population of the northern colonies was growing, both in absolute numbers and as a proportion of the total. The rural North was divided between the relatively small areas of New York and New Jersey, where tenancy and large estates were common, and the bulk of New England and Pennsylvania, where most land was controlled by independent farmers. Though landownership patterns varied, the majority of farms in all these regions were maintained by the families who lived on them, and this shaped the opportunities and constraints they faced.

New York and Pennsylvania Though geographically close to one another, the colonies of New York and Pennsylvania developed very differently. At first, when their land was still unsettled by whites, New York's proprietary landlords made tenancy attractive so as to secure scarce labor. They provided mills, roads, help with livestock, and rent-free periods in order to lure new settlers onto uncultivated land grants. But such benefits came at a price. Some manors obliged tenants to work a certain number of days for the landlord, give the landlord first option to buy their crops, and grind their grain at his mill. Landlords could require tenants to plant certain kinds of trees or build certain kinds of houses. Tenants could not buy the land they farmed. They could expect payment from the landlord for any improvements they made, but if they wanted farms of their own, they were obliged to sell their leases and move to freehold land elsewhere. When a lease was sold, the landlord could demand up to one-third of the purchase price. For some landlords, the manorial system created immense wealth.

Landlords' relations with tenants varied. Some, including Frederick Philipse at Philipse Manor and Sir William Johnson in the Mohawk Valley, tried to create stable, paternalistic communities. Although Philipse raised rents when he inherited his manor in 1760, he promised never to do so again and kept his word. But others were out to gain all they could. While Philipse held rents steady, his brother-in-law Colonel Beverly Robinson raised his rents three times. Tenants resented the shaky legal basis of some estate grants. Only 6,000 of Livingston Manor's 160,000 acres had been included in the original grant to the first manor lord. Poorly drawn surveys and outright fraud had contributed the rest, and the tenants knew it.

Poor conditions for many tenants served to limit New York colony's growth. In 1770, its population stood at approximately 162,000. By contrast, Pennsylvania, founded decades later, had by then already surpassed 240,000. By making land relatively attractive and affordable, William Penn had sown the seeds of rapid growth. Most settlers created small or moderately sized family farms. At first, they raised cattle and other livestock, but they soon switched to grain farming, which on modest farms could better provide livelihoods for their children. To a significant degree, settlers realized William Penn's founding vision of a middling rural society in which family and neighborhood cooperation would be complemented by the commerce generated by grain exports.

Pennsylvania's people were especially diverse, including English Quakers of the "middling sort," many of them skilled artisans; Germans of peasant origin who came to found religious communities on Pennsylvania's rich farmland; and tens of thousands of Protestant Scots-Irish migrants from the

"Oak Tree Stumps Are Just as Hard in America . . .": A German Emigrant's Story

Though many poor Europeans were attracted to Pennsylvania, some travelers, like Gottlieb Mittelberger, warned that the vision of prosperity there was exaggerated. Mittelberger came to America from Germany in 1750, experiencing the hardships of the Atlantic crossing and of indentured servitude in Pennsylvania. He returned home after four years and wrote a book urging his countrymen not to emigrate to America. His descriptions of shipboard conditions, the sale of servants at Philadelphia, and farm work bear strong similarities to accounts of the African slave trade.

When the ships have weighed anchor for the last time, usually off Cowes in Old England, then both the long sea voyage and misery begin in earnest. For from there the ships often take eight, nine, ten, or twelve weeks sailing to Philadelphia, if the wind is unfavorable. But even given the most favorable winds, the voyage takes seven weeks.

During the journey the ship is full of pitiful signs of distress— smells, fumes, horrors, vomiting, various kinds of sea sickness, fever, dysentery, headaches, heat, constipation, boils, scurvy, cancer, mouth-rot, and similar afflictions, all of them caused by the age and the highly salted state of the food, especially of the meat, as well as by the very bad and filthy water, which brings about the miserable destruction and death of many. Add to all that shortage of food, hunger, thirst, frost, heat, dampness, fear, misery, vexation, and lamentation as well as other troubles. Thus, for example, there are so many lice, especially on the sick people, that they have to be scraped off the bodies. All this misery reaches its climax when in addition to everything else one must also suffer through two to three days and nights of storm, with everyone convinced that the ship with all aboard is bound to sink. In such misery all the people on board pray and cry pitifully together. . . .

When the ships finally arrive in Philadelphia after the long voyage only those are let off who can pay their sea freight or can give good security. The others, who lack the money to pay, have to remain on board until they are purchased. . . .

This is how the commerce in human beings on board ship takes place. Every day Englishmen, Dutchmen, and High Germans come from Philadelphia and other places, some of them very far away, . . . and go on board the newly arrived vessel that has brought people from Europe and offers them for sale. From among the healthy they pick out those suitable for the purposes for which they require them. Then they negotiate with them as to the length of the period for which they will go into service in order to pay off their passage, the whole amount of which they generally still owe. When an agreement has been reached, adult persons by written contract bind themselves to serve for three, four, five, or six years, according to their health and age. The very young, between the ages of 10 and 15, have to serve until they are 21, however. . . .

Our Europeans, who are purchased, must always work hard, for new fields are constantly laid out; and so they learn that stumps of oak-trees are in America certainly as hard as in Germany. . . .

Linda R. Monk, ed., *Ordinary Americans: U.S. History Through the Eyes of Ordinary People* (1994).

A German Wardrobe — with a Dash of English Drawers
German immigrants formed the largest non-British white community in the colonies by the time of the Revolution. Many managed to balance their German ethnicity and the English culture they encountered — in religious institutions, residential patterns, marriage partners, and the furniture they used every day. David Hottenstein built this wardrobe (or *shrank* in German) to store clothing and other household items in Berks County, Pennsylvania, in 1781. While the wardrobe's shape, decoration, and mode of construction were inspired by styles that were common in Germany at the time, Hottenstein added a set of drawers, an English innovation. Winterthur Museum.

northern part of Ireland, many of whom — like the Germans — came as indentured servants. As they migrated to the colonial frontier, friction with Indians and other settlers often led to trouble. Pennsylvanians had a reputation for sturdy independence. When the gentleman pamphleteer John Dickinson wanted to emphasize Americans' independence of spirit during one of the 1760s disputes with Britain, he could find no better way than to style himself "a farmer in Pennsylvania."

Rural Families and Independence   Wherever they lived and whether they were tenants or freeholders, northern farm families shared many common circumstances. In most places, the open-field villages of the earliest New England settlements had given way to dispersed settlements and scattered farmsteads, though ideals of social harmony persisted. Church membership, town government, family ties, and the mutual exchange of goods and labor sustained a sense of "neighborhood" in much of New England. In the

Middle Colonies, too, tenants and farmers maintained ties to their neighborhoods and to the wider commercial world. For all farm families, a central concern was how to pass on land and livelihoods to their children.

In a pre-contraceptive age, almost every married woman spent a good part of her life pregnant and caring for children. The women of Andover, Massachusetts, had more than five births per marriage in every decade between 1650 and 1720, and between 1690 and 1710, the rate was higher than seven. Yet, though childbirth risked women's lives in some cases, the life expectancy of women in New England was better than that in England or the southern colonies and almost as good as that of men. In four out of every five early New England marriages, both partners survived to at least the end of normal childbearing years. In legal terms, a colonial woman ceased to exist as an independent being when she married. Unless there were special prenuptial arrangements, a wife could not control her own property or make a binding contract. Her husband controlled the family's property, whether he had purchased it himself, inherited it, or acquired it through her. In day-to-day life, however, a wife was her husband's partner. The operation of a household depended heavily on women's work—not just the raising of children, but also a host of other tasks. Women made cheese and butter, which were vital sources of cash income; women also made the beer or cider and much of the food that sustained the family's members. Women made and repaired clothing, produced the soap that kept the family clean, and made the tallow candles that provided lighting. During harvest, farm

Untimely Deaths

Although women in colonial New England could expect to live longer than their counterparts in England or the southern colonies, early American graveyards testify to the hazards of childbirth for colonial women and their babies. Edmund Vincent Gillon, Jr., *Early New England Gravestone Rubbings* (1966).

women joined in gathering crops. An artisan's wife was likely to acquire some of her husband's craft skills and take a hand in production.

In a rural community, unmarried women faced great hardships. Some did venture outside the conventional expectations of their roles, daring (as one put it) to be "as independent as circumstances will admit [i.e., permit]." But often the best they could hope for was to have a room in a relative's house in exchange for performing household chores. Widows also encountered difficulties. The law guaranteed the "widow's portion," usually one-third, of a husband's real estate, but her right was not to the freehold, only to the use of it during her lifetime; in some colonies, even this right eroded over time. Many widows were as dependent on their sons or sons-in-law as they had once been on their fathers and husbands.

Farm Work

An engraving from a 1760 New York almanac showed one woman milking a cow and another churning butter. Women typically took charge of the dairy on rural farms, making cheese and butter to sell or trade. *Hutchin's Improved: being an Almanack for 1761* (1760) — American Antiquarian Society.

Children were expected to submit to parental authority. As they grew older, children became important to the work of most rural households, first performing simple tasks, then assuming the roles that, according to their sex, would fall to them as adults. Unmarried daughters usually assisted with household and garden tasks and undertook dairy work or home manufacturing. Boys and young men, as well as helping with farm work, often provided crucial labor for felling trees, clearing land, and other tasks involved in creating and maintaining new settlements. Fathers could use the promise of land to keep their sons at home and working for the household until well into the sons' adulthood. It was a form of labor control that shaped and fitted the family life cycle and the transmission of economic power from one generation to another in families with property. Poor or orphaned children were often sent to live with and work for other families, where their labor earned them no future security.

Some farm neighborhoods were largely self-sufficient, with families growing or making much of what they needed and swapping labor, or "'changing works," among households. Farmers grew mixed crops and built local networks of exchange, in which a tradesman might accept "wheat, rye, Indian corn, as well as cash, or anything that is good to eat," in return for his services. Farm wives traded cloth, butter, and beer as well as nursing, midwifery, and child care. Many farmers also bought and sold land to build holdings large enough to provide for their children and to set them up for similar lives of modest prosperity and independence, which contemporaries often referred to as a "competency."

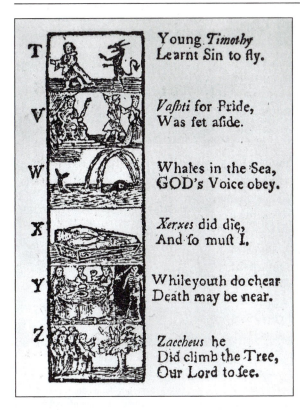

T   Young *Timothy*
Learnt Sin to fly.

V   *Vashti* for Pride,
Was set aside.

W   Whales in the Sea,
GOD's Voice obey.

X   *Xerxes* did die,
And so must I.

Y   While youth do chear
Death may be near.

Z   *Zaccheus* he
Did climb the Tree,
Our Lord to see.

New England Primer

As a page from a 1767 edition of the widely used schoolbook demonstrates, children learning the alphabet also received lessons in obedience and restraint. *New England Primer* (1767) — Rare Books and Manuscript Division, New York Public Library, Astor, Lenox and Tilden Foundations.

Constraints in Rural Society   For most country people, competency also involved producing surpluses to be marketed. The role of this surplus produce in broader patterns of commerce and in farm families' own strategies varied according to circumstances. In much of eastern and southern New England by the mid-eighteenth century, settlements were becoming crowded, and families were dividing up landholdings. Of farms in Andover, Massachusetts, only one in three exceeded 200 acres in size. The land in many parts of New England was relatively infertile, and crop surpluses there were low. Families seeking land on which to settle their offspring might well look to frontier regions. From the 1730s onward, their demand for land led to a powerful outward migration from old to new areas of North America.

In the Middle Colonies, many landholdings were larger, and more fertile land was available. In the Delaware Valley in the mid-eighteenth century, two-thirds of farms exceeded 500 acres in size. By concentrating their efforts on grain production, farmers there were able to raise market income from the sale of wheat and other crops, and they used these resources to provide for their children. Eighty percent of Pennsylvania farms had crop surpluses, and 40 percent of the total crop was sent to market for export. By the 1760s, wheat from New York, Pennsylvania, and the northern Chesapeake fed people all around the Atlantic basin. Farm women, too, contributed to marketable surpluses through dairying and raising poultry.

But the demands of wheat farming also altered patterns of labor, especially on the larger farms in Pennsylvania's English-speaking areas. An increasing number of servants, some of them indentured to work off the cost of transatlantic passages, were employed to assist with crop raising. Many were German or Scots-Irish and were unrelated to their employers. Conflicts arose over harsh treatment or monotonous work. Servants—like George Owens of Chester County, Pennsylvania, who was driven to despair because his only work was chopping wood—often ran away. Married servants known as "inmates" occupied cottages on farm lands. Others worked as day laborers. In Chester County in 1750, there was one inmate or free laborer for roughly every four householders, but a decade later, the proportion had risen to nearly one for every two. Wage labor was a growing part of the grain-exporting rural economy.

Although independent farm families dominated northern agriculture, slavery also became important in a few localities: along Rhode Island's

Narragansett Bay and in parts of southern Connecticut, Long Island, and New Jersey. Around 1700, 13 percent of Long Island's inhabitants were slaves, while slaves and free black people accounted for one-fifth of the population of Bergen County, New Jersey. In contrast to southern plantations, however, most northern slaveholders owned only one slave. As a result, northern slaves often lived separate lives, without their own families or distinctive culture.

Social stratification among rural whites also grew in the eighteenth century. The Connecticut River valley in western Massachusetts became dominated politically by wealthy families, whose influence earned them the title of "River Gods." Members of these families intermarried, filled town delegations to the General Court in Boston, secured provincial appointments as colonels of militia or county court judges, and became pastors of some of the region's churches. Although the New England freeholding ethos sometimes bred resentment against the powerful and well-to-do, deference toward age, wealth, and family remained common. Only during times of political crisis was it sometimes disrupted.

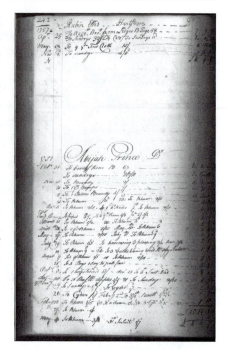

Urban America

By 1770, about 93 percent of all colonists lived in places with populations under 2,500. However, one way in which the northern colonies differed from most parts of the South was in the relative significance of the port towns that grew up along their coasts and river estuaries.

In 1700, even the largest of these towns — Boston, New York City, and Philadelphia — had been little more than overgrown villages, with a few thousand inhabitants each. But by 1760, they were substantial places whose people lived differently from their rural counterparts. In these port towns, merchants and shipowners rubbed shoulders with professional men, with master artisans and their apprentices, with the day laborers who worked on the wharves, and with seamen from many places who crewed cargo ships and fishing vessels. Public emblems still commemorate the work of these early colonists. In Boston's State House hangs the gilded image of a codfish, symbol of New England's early wealth from fishing and the sea. New York City's official seal bears the sails of a windmill, two barrels, a beaver, and the figures of a Native American and a white man. It recalls the port's initial prosperity from the trade in native-trapped furs and from grain grown by farmers, ground by millers, and shipped in barrels made by coopers. In towns, as in the country, many economic activities were organized around families and households. But all who worked in the port towns were not free, and not all had their own families and households. A growing number of slaves and indentured servants worked as laborers, domestic servants,

Accounting for Trade

Account books are the most common documents left by ordinary people who lived in eighteenth-century rural communities. Historians rely on these valuable sources to reconstruct the economic world of preindustrial societies. As shown in the 1756 and 1757 accounts of merchant Elijah Williams of Deerfield, Massachusetts — chronicling his transactions with Abijah Prince, a free black town resident — rural shopkeepers, farmers, and craftsmen used these books to keep track of their customers' indebtedness. Williams sold textiles, food, spirits, and other wares; he accepted cash, labor, and agricultural products in return. Account book of Elijah Williams, Ledger C, Vol. 4 — Pocumtuck Valley Memorial Association Library, Deerfield, MA.

and dock workers; slaves in particular tended to live in their masters' houses, isolated from other African Americans.

Cities by the Sea   Even so, Boston, New York, and Philadelphia had established themselves as places where trade and manufacturing, rather than farming, formed the essential basis of life (Map 3.4). Lesser centers, such as Newport, Albany, and Baltimore, which expanded in the eighteenth century, developed in the same direction. None was large by modern standards. Even the biggest were "walking towns," easily crossed on foot, full of places and faces familiar to their residents.

Boston occupied no more than a small peninsula that jutted into Massachusetts Bay, linked to the mainland by a narrow spit called Boston Neck. Although the town grew steadily for a century, around 1750 its population leveled off at about 15,000. It governed itself by the same town meetings of freemen that were used in the smallest New England settlements. Ordinary Bostonians highly valued these open meetings, in which they had a voice. As early as 1708, they resoundingly defeated a proposal to abandon town meetings and create a mayor and a board of aldermen, not least because people objected to the 1,000-pounds wealth qualification for holders of the new

MAP 3.4   British and American Atlantic Trade Patterns in the Eighteenth Century

American merchants based in the North carved out for themselves a substantial share of Anglo-American trade. The Navigation Acts gave British traders dominance over many routes, but merchants from the northern port towns captured business with the Mediterranean and the West Indies, shipping crops produced in the southern colonies and importing slaves for sale.

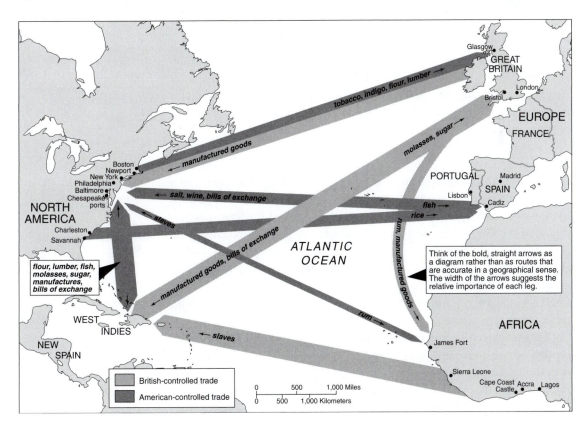

Shipbuilding

A late-eighteenth-century engraving depicts work in a Philadelphia shipyard. Construction of a ship usually took about a year, employing large numbers of men with various skills that focused on different parts of the vessel. "[A]bove 30 Denominations of Tradesmen and Artificers," according to one 1749 observer, were involved in building a ship, including carpenters who worked on the hull and masts, joiners who constructed the interior, and ropemakers and sailmakers. William Birch, *Preparation for War to defend Commerce*, line engraving, 11 1/2 × 13 5/8 inches, 1800 — Free Library of Philadelphia.

offices. As one pamphleteer argued, "The rich will exert that right of Dominion, which they think they have exclusive of all others . . . and then the Great Men will no more have the Dissatisfaction of seeing their Poorer Neighbours stand up for equal Privileges with them." Boston would retain its town meeting until 1821, when it was deemed large enough for a city form of government.

New York and Philadelphia exceeded Boston in size but not by much. As late as 1770, New York filled only the southernmost part of Manhattan Island, where the financial district now stands, and boasted a mere 21,000 inhabitants. Philadelphia was North America's fastest-growing city. Its population of 25,000 in 1770 made it, after London, one of the largest settlements in the English-speaking world. Even so, its people occupied little more than the modern downtown area. Both cities were governed differently from Boston. In New York, a mayor was picked by the colony's royal governor, but aldermen were chosen by election. Philadelphia, like many English boroughs, was run by a "closed" corporation, a body of officials who picked their own successors.

Port towns fulfilled many functions. They were important commercial centers, whose merchants dispatched and received ships and their cargoes over thousands of miles. Colonial ships carried fish from the Grand Banks, flour from Pennsylvania, barrel staves from New York's forests, flaxseed for Irish linen growers, lemons, salt, oil, and wine. They also carried slaves; from the 1720s onward, merchants in Boston, Providence, Newport, and other New England ports became active in the Atlantic slave trade. After the mid-eighteenth century, Newport was the largest slave port in North America; its ships carried slaves from Africa either to the West Indies or to the mainland for sale to southern planters. As their commerce grew, the port towns increasingly became centers of wealth as well, and some of their richest merchants enjoyed fortunes that were respectable even by British standards.

The main ports were also centers of politics and the arts. They were provincial capitals, where men with a claim to rule gathered to conduct public business. They were home to colleges, playhouses, concerts, and artists, such as the painters Benjamin West and John Singleton Copley, who matched Europe's best. Philadelphia in particular was emerging as an intellectual hub, noted for its contributions to science and high-quality craftsmanship.

Colonial towns fostered manufactures as well as upper-class culture. Shipyards, ropewalks, iron foundries, and sailmaking shops arose in Boston and other New England ports to build, equip, and supply fishing boats and cargo-carrying vessels. Skilled artisans and laborers ran the yards and shops, and the ships they built earned a high reputation around the Atlantic. By 1760, American shipyards were building one-third of all new British commercial ships, and their growing number of employees with wages to spend attracted other occupations. Towns became hives of activity, where craft workers, wagoners, seamstresses, laborers, coopers, dressmakers, midwives, and prostitutes plied their trades.

FIGURE 3.1 Growing Inequality in the Northern Port Towns

This chart illustrates the urban elites' expanding share of wealth and the decreasing shares enjoyed by the middling and poorer sections of the towns' populations. By 1775, the poorest three-fifths of urban inhabitants owned less than one-twentieth of taxable wealth.

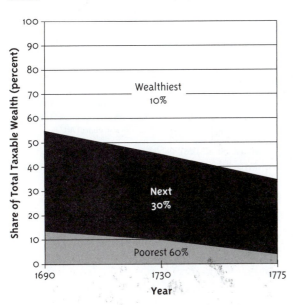

Urban Elites Northern towns developed their own social order, with different classes following distinct ways of life. Wealthy "elites," or upper classes, emerged, enjoying connections in international networks and colonial administrations. The richest were likely to be merchants trading across the Atlantic; others, usually less wealthy, conducted trade along the American coast and to the Caribbean. A professional class, too, began to take shape, starting with the Protestant ministry. In the eighteenth century, lawyers emerged as a second group, using their specialized skills to serve landowners and merchants as laws became more elaborate and business expanded. Ministers and lawyers formed an intellectual elite, producing much of early America's writing and scholarship.

Merchant elites varied in character. Boston's divided between Puritan descendants of early settlers and more recent arrivals, many of whom were Anglican. Philadelphia's early Quaker merchants were joined later by those of other faiths. Boston and Philadelphia merchants were relatively uninvolved in rural landholding, since New England's and Pennsylvania's independent farming economies kept them at arm's length. Some of New York's prominent merchant families, however, were also among the colony's manorial estate holders.

Some women, mostly widows, succeeded in business, most of them running small stores. A few of these "she-merchants" prospered as long-distance traders. Perhaps the most notable was the Bostonian Elizabeth Murray Smith, whose wealth enabled her, as she proudly put it, "to live and act as I please." But even she did not attain public positions. In 1733, some New York businesswomen complained to the governor that "We are Housekeepers, Pay our Taxes, carry on Trade and most of us are she Merchants, and as we in some measure contribute to the Support of Government, we ought to be entitled to some of the Sweets of it." Even when financial independence was not a factor, gender remained an obstacle to political power.

During the eighteenth century, urban elites increased their share of colonial wealth (Figure 3.1). In 1687 in Philadelphia, the top 5 percent of taxpayers owned 30 percent of all property, but by 1774, they owned 55 percent. In Boston, the share of wealth held by the top 10 percent of taxpayers rose from 46 percent in 1687 to 63 percent in 1771. A few had connections to the highest circles in England. By 1750, a daughter of New York's DeLancey family had married a knighted British admiral, and one of the DeLancey sons was close to the Archbishop of Canterbury. Such families lived in a cosmopolitan world in which events thousands of miles away were just as important as those close at hand and where men and women adopted European customs and fashions to demonstrate that they were not mere colonists.

Clothes Make the Man

In colonial New England, merchants commissioned paintings that would display not only their faces but their place in society as well. Made of fine imported fabric, Boston merchant Joseph Sherburne's ostentatious outfit signaled his social rank and wealth in this portrait by John Singleton Copley, painted in the late 1760s. John Singleton Copley, *Joseph Sherburne*, oil on canvas, 1767–70, 50 × 40 inches — Metropolitan Museum of Art.

Artisans, Laborers, and Seamen

Most townspeople, however, were not merchants, ministers, or lawyers but belonged to the "laboring classes" and worked with their hands. Workmen's practical dress—leather work-aprons and long trousers—contrasted with the elite's satin coats, wigs, and knee

Commerce Makes the Man
Other merchants, such as James Tilley in this 1757 painting attributed to Copley, preferred to emphasize the source of their wealth: the shipping wharf and ropewalk glimpsed through the window in the portrait. John Singleton Copley, *James Tilley*, oil on copper, 1757, 13 3/4 × 10 1/4 inches — M. Knoedler and Company, New York.

breeches. Women's clothing that was made for the rigors of kitchen work, sewing, and washing was clearly distinct from the silk garments of well-to-do women.

Seamen lived in a shipboard world with its own conditions and customs. Inhabitants of the ocean as much as any port town, they faced low pay, constant discomfort, and harsh discipline, as well as the danger of shipwreck and the fear that the British navy might forcibly "impress" them into its service or that a privateer or enemy warship might capture them. Landsmen, too, worked in connection with maritime commerce, though often under considerably better circumstances. Shipwrights and ironworkers employed in the largest manufacturing establishments had skills and status that gave them considerable freedom and control of their own time.

Most laboring townsmen aimed to become master artisans or "mechanics," which meant serving several years of apprenticeship, learning the skills of a trade while legally bound in service to a master. On completing an apprenticeship, the laborer became a journeyman, hired for a time as he

"Plough Deep, While Sluggards Sleep": *Poor Richard's Almanack*

Benjamin Franklin's Poor Richard's Al-manack was perhaps the most popular advice book published in colo-nial America. Although many of Franklin's proverbs and homilies are now clichés, at the time, they reflected the abiding belief of farmers and skilled artisans in the dignity and impor-tance of their labor in northern colonial society.

Industry need not wish, as Poor Richard says, and he that lives upon Hope will die fasting. There are no Gains without Pains; then Help Hands, for I have no Lands, or if I have, they are smartly taxed. And, as Poor Richard likewise observes, He that hath a Trade hath an Estate; and he that hath a Calling, hath an Office of Profit and Honour; but then the Trade must be worked at, and Calling well followed, or neither the Estate nor the Office will enable us to pay our taxes. If we are industrious, we shall never starve; for, as Poor Richard says, At the working Man's House Hunger looks in, but dares not enter. Nor will the Bailiff or the Constable enter, for Industry pays Debts, while Despair encreaseth them, say Poor Richard. What though you have no Treasure, nor has any rich Relation left you a Legacy, Diligence is the Mother of Goodluck, as Poor Richard says, and God gives all Things to Industry. Then plough deep, while Sluggards sleep, and you shall have Corn to sell and to keep, says Poor Dick. . . . If you were a Servant, would you not be ashamed that a good Master should catch you idle? Are you then your own Master, be ashamed to catch yourself idle, as Poor Dick says. When there is so much to be done for yourself, your Family, your Country, and your gracious King, be up by Peep of Day; Let not the Sun look down and say, Inglorious here he lies.

Richard Saunders, ed., *Poor Richard: The Almanacks for the Years 1753–1758* (1964).

saved to acquire a shop of his own. A master in his own right had to be many things: a producer, using his tools to turn out goods; a businessman, buying raw materials and selling finished products; a teacher, training apprentices; and an employer, hiring journeymen as he himself had once been hired. Just as on farms, urban work was based in households. Most master craftsmen had the support of a hardworking wife who provided housing, food, clothing, and laundry services for her husband and his apprentices.

Some master artisans, such as the Boston silversmith Paul Revere, achieved considerable comfort. Under special circumstances, an artisan might claim international fame; the Philadelphia printer Benjamin Franklin, for example, became one of the foremost scientific figures of the eighteenth century. The mottoes he printed in *Poor Richard's Almanack* showed Franklin's belief that hard work and self-discipline would carry a man far in the world. Yet more typical was the life of the Boston shoemaker George Robert Twelves Hewes, who never grew wealthy. Financial uncer-

Crafts Make the Man
Boston silversmith Paul Revere was one of the few colonial craftsmen painted by Copley. In this painting, dating from about 1770, Revere poses at his workbench, wearing the artisan's plain linen shirt and vest and displaying his engraving tools and an unfinished teapot. John Singleton Copley, *Paul Revere*, oil on canvas, 1768–70, 35 × 28 1/2 inches — Gift of Joseph W., William B., and Edward H. R. Revere, Museum of Fine Arts, Boston.

tainty and poverty were very real for someone like Hewes, for whom one bad year could mean the humiliation of debtors' prison or the poorhouse. Such difficulties were worse still for the day laborers who loaded and unloaded ships or carted goods and for the growing numbers of widows and orphans who could barely support themselves adequately in the absence of a male wage earner. For them, economic insecurity was part of life.

Larger towns offered women more options than the countryside did. Women took in lodgers, ran taverns, made fashionable clothes for the well-to-do, or practiced midwifery. One Boston midwife, a Mrs. Phillips, was said to have delivered over 3,000 babies by the time she died in her early forties in 1761. Widows of artisans quite often took charge of their husbands' shops. Elizabeth Holt succeeded her husband as the publisher of the *New York Journal*, and she became New York State's official printer during the Revolution. But most working women were confined to tasks that paid little money or just bed and board. Some women worked as prostitutes. In smaller ports, such as Salem, Massachusetts, women formed a majority of the working population because many men were away at sea. Rarely able to obtain well-paid employment, women also formed a significant proportion of the poor in port towns. With their husbands at sea amid the hazards of accident, disease, and shipwreck, many of these women could also expect to face the trials of premature widowhood.

Indeed, poverty was increasingly common in eighteenth-century towns. In Boston, the problem was economic stagnation. In the 1760s, the town spent almost six times as much per person for poor relief as it had forty years before. But Philadelphia's expanding economy also provided a struggle for laboring people, as a constant flow of migrants from the countryside and overseas competed for jobs. Of Philadelphia laborers and journeymen who got married in 1756, for example, one-fifth owned no property at all, and another three-fifths owned only the bare necessities for setting up a home. Over the next eleven years, only about one in four of them improved their position. The share of property held by the bottom 30 percent of Philadelphia taxpayers fell from 2.6 percent in 1687 to barely 1 percent in 1774.

Poor though they might be, laborers and journeymen could console themselves that they were at least free. At the bottom of the colonial

The Centenarian
Despite its title, George Robert Twelves Hewes was ninety-three when Joseph G. Cole painted this portrait in 1835. On the basis of Hewes's clothes and demeanor, viewers of the painting probably did not know about his artisanal background or that he was destitute. Bostonian Society, Old State House, Boston.

social scale were many people—white and black, indentured servants and slaves—who were not.

The Unfree: Servants and Slaves Indentured servants came to the Middle Colonies, as they did to the South, throughout the colonial period. At first, most were single males from London and the south of England, who reached colonial ports such as Philadelphia, where they worked off their indentures and stayed on. More than half were artisans, and another quarter were laborers and personal servants. The iron and construction industries were hungry for skilled workers, and some servants bargained themselves into good situations. By the mid-eighteenth century, a growing proportion of bound servants arriving in Pennsylvania were from places other than England, especially the north of Ireland and Germany.

Young families also came as indentured servants. They tended to work off their indentures in agricultural areas such as western New York, at the edges of colonial settlement, where they hoped to find land of their own

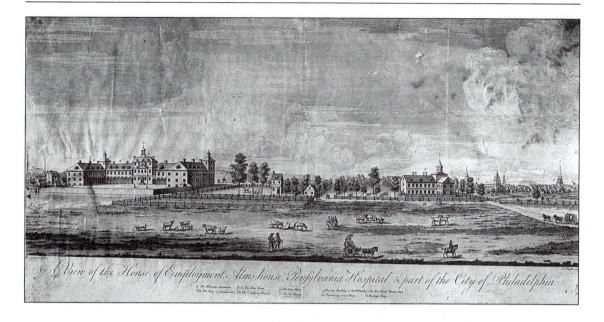

Poverty Incarcerated

Increasing numbers of urban poor taxed the resources of northern colonial towns and cities. Many were incarcerated in almshouses and workhouses, but these institutions grew overcrowded. This 1767 engraving commemorated the opening of new facilities on the outskirts of Philadelphia. Typically, the print emphasizes the institution's bucolic setting rather than the less picturesque activities within its walls. James Hulett, *A View of the House of Employment, Almshouse, Pennsylvania Hospital, & part of the City of Philadelphia*, line engraving, c. 1767, 13 1/2 × 18 5/8 inches — Library Company of Philadelphia.

when their service was complete. These were people whose circumstances in Europe were so hard that they were willing to sell a portion of their adult lives to escape, knowing that in America, they would be sold to a stranger who would govern them for four to seven years. Not surprisingly, their "fondness for freedom" often led to disputes with their masters, complaints of harsh treatment, or bids to escape.

Unlike the majority of indentured servants, most northern slaves were town dwellers. In the late seventeenth century, they were often employed as domestics, but their functions broadened with the North's involvement in the slave trade. From 1710 to 1742, the number of slaves in Boston quadrupled, to about 1,300, or 8.5 percent of the population. Slaves made up 18 percent of New York's population in 1731 and 21 percent in 1746. Perhaps half of New York City households owned a slave by the 1740s.

These urban slaves usually lived in their master's house without the company of other slaves. Most were men, working as general laborers, porters, or dockworkers; women slaves tended to work in domestic service, meaning that they were particularly isolated. One New Yorker advertised his slave for sale, noting that "she drinks no Strong Drink, and gets no Children" and was, consequently, "a very good Drudge." A few blacks lived as freemen in northern cities, although they could neither vote nor own property.

Many whites were hostile toward this growing African American population, fearing slave insurrection. In 1712, twenty New York slaves set a

FIVE SHILLINGS REWARD.

RUNAWAY from the fubfcriber living in Fourth-ftreet, a little above Race-ftreet, the 25th ult. a girl named Chriftiana Lower, 13 years of age: Had on a blue calimancoe cap, blue and white checked handkerchief, a fhort red gown, blue and white ftriped linfey petticoat, an old pair of black ftockings and new fhoes. Whoever takes up faid girl and brings her home, fhall have the above reward and reafonable charges.

CHRISTIAN LOWER.

THREE POUNDS REWARD.

RUN AWAY from the Subfcriber, living at Warwick furnace, Minehole, on the 23d ult. an Irifh fervant man, named DENNIS M'CALLIN, about five feet eight inches high, nineteen years of age, has a freckled face, light coloured curly hair. Had on when he went away, an old felt hat, white and yellow ftriped jacket, a new blue cloth coat, and buckfkin breeches; alfo, he took with him a bundle of fhirts and ftockings, and a pocket piftol; likewife, a box containing gold rings, &c. Whoever takes up faid fervant and fecures him in any goal, fo as his mafter may get him again, fhall have the above reward and reafonable charges paid by JAMES TODD.

N. B. All mafters of veffels, and others, are forbid from harbouring or carrying him off, at their peril.

Reward

These reward notices for the capture of runaway servants appeared in a 1772 edition of a Pennsylvania newspaper. *Pennsylvania Packet and General Advertiser*, February 10, 1772 — Historical Society of Pennsylvania.

blaze and then fired on a group of whites who arrived to put it out, touching off a major panic. The white militia quickly routed the slaves, but for weeks, there were arrests, trials, suicides, and executions. Nineteen convicted slaves were hanged or burned alive and cut into pieces. But even such brutal punishment did little to quell the fear of slave revolt, and the New York events spurred efforts by Pennsylvanians to curb slave imports into their province. In another episode in 1741, New York slaves accused of arson and theft were alleged to have conspired with Irish and free black laborers to kill white inhabitants. Eighteen blacks were hanged or burned to death along with four white servants who were implicated in the conspiracy.

"Forty Shillings Reward": Advertisements for Runaway Servants

Indentured servants had an extremely difficult time in colonial America, as evidenced by the number of servants who ran away from their masters. Masters were often reduced to placing advertisements in local newspapers to announce the disappearance of their servants, as these notices—from a New York shipmaster in 1737 and from an Albany merchant in 1761—suggest.

Run away from the Brigantine Joanna . . . an Irish Servant man, named Charles McCammel, aged about 25 Years, a tall lusty Man, wearing his own black Hair. . . . N.B. The Servant having been offr'd 8 shillings for his Hair, it's suppos'd he may have cut it off. He speaks very good English.

New-York Weekly Journal, August 29, 1737.

FORTY SHILLINGS REWARD. For taking up and securing Mary Brown, alias Edwards, a Pennsylvania born indented Servant, who ran away from the Service of . . . her Master a few days ago: She is a so-so-sort of a looking Woman, inclinable to Clumsiness, much Pock pitted, which gives her an hard Favour and a frosty Look, wants several of her Teeth, yet speaks good English and Dutch, about 26 or 28 Years old, perhaps 30. Had on and about her when she went off a red quilted Pettycoat, a crossbarr'd brown and white Josey [jersey], a sorry red Cloak and the making of a new stuff Wrapper, supposed to be gone towards Philadelphia, via New York. — James Crofton, Albany

New-York Mercury, March 19, 1761.

Hierarchy and Equality in Northern Societies

By modern standards, the northern colonies were not democratic. Most people had no official part to play in public life. Only men who owned some property and who could claim to be independent of others' authority had the right to vote or hold political office. This excluded slaves, servants, women, youths, and adult men who did not meet the minimum property requirements. The last group amounted to almost half of free adult males. Altogether, up to 80 or 90 percent of the population was disenfranchised.

War and economic fluctuations in the mid-eighteenth century added to the strains already emerging in rural and urban societies, tending to reinforce and even enhance the inequalities contained within them. At the same time, however, there were patterns of opportunity in both towns and the countryside that helped the northern colonies to avoid the wider economic disparities that were evident farther south. And changes in both political and religious culture produced challenges to the most hierarchical assumptions of colonial life and to the power of rural and urban elites.

Government and Power Even men who did vote frequently deferred to their social "betters"—the merchants, planters, lawyers, and large landowners who occupied most seats in the colonial assemblies. Rarely did genuine farmers or artisans reach the circles that wielded real political power. In New England, where each organized town normally chose its own assembly delegate, farmers were frequently elected, but even there, the voices that counted most belonged to great merchants, to graduates of Harvard and Yale, and to the well-connected "River Gods" of the Connecticut River valley. In New York's provincial government, there was little pretense of democracy. The assembly had fewer than thirty seats, three of them effectively hereditary, and members of the landed and mercantile elite expected to fill them. In 1761, Abraham Yates, an Albany shoemaker turned lawyer, tried to win a seat in the New York assembly but was defeated by no less a figure than Sir William Johnson. This rebuff would spur Yates to try, during the American Revolution, to overturn the elite's hold on government.

Head of a Negro

This portrait painted in the late 1770s by John Singleton Copley, possibly of a London dock-worker, was unusual in this era in portraying a person of color as an individual. John Singleton Copley, *Head of a Negro*, oil on canvas, 1777–78, 21 × 16 1/4 inches — The Detroit Institute of the Arts. Founders Society Purchase, Gibbs-Williams Fund.

Much power in fact lay with wealthy men who held appointive rather than elective offices. These included the royal governor in most colonies, whichever member of the Penn family occupied the Pennsylvania proprietorship, and members of the governors' councils (except in Massachusetts, Connecticut, and Rhode Island) as well as mayors, judges, sheriffs, and the members of Philadelphia's closed corporation.

Yet in comparison with almost anywhere else in the eighteenth century, the northern colonies were quite democratic. Following the Glorious Revolution and the granting of new charters for these colonies, voting rights in New England were no longer tied to church membership, and eligibility to vote followed the same basic rule that held in England: a man had to have a freehold valued at 40 pounds or a tenancy worth 40 shillings per year. In England, this limit was high enough to deny the vote to the vast majority, but in America, where land was more easily obtained, a little over half of free adult males met the requirement. This included most of the tenants on New York's great estates, although there was no secret ballot and voice voting meant that the landlord's candidate rarely lost. There were other ways to be eligible to vote as well. In New York City and in Albany, the status of "free-

A Seat Fit for a Merchant Prince
Moses Gill was a hardware merchant who married well, becoming one of the largest landowners in Worcester County, Massachusetts. When he built one of the first mansion houses in the mid-eighteenth-century colonies, he chose a Georgian style with four chimneys, a central hall, gardens, and fences set on a 3,000-acre tract with a magnificent view of Boston. Samuel Hill, *View of the Seat of the Hon. Moses Gill Esq. at Princeton, in the County of Worcester, MASS*, reproduced in *Massachusetts Magazine* (November 1792) and Francis Blake, *History of Princeton, Massachusetts* (Boston, 1915) — American Social History Project.

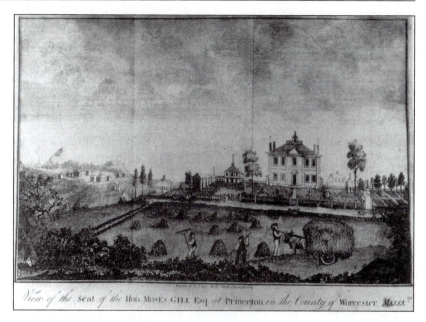

View of the Seat of the Hon. Moses Gill Esq. at Princeton, in the County of Worcester, Mass.

man," open to most male craft workers, conferred voting rights and was an important avenue to political expression among urban workingmen.

For women, no such possibilities for voting existed. They found the churches their best arena for public involvement. The radical sects of seventeenth-century England had flirted boldly with the idea of gender equality. Quaker women could preach. Even some mainstream Puritans leaned toward the notion of equality. Puritan women were sometimes members of a church while their husbands were not. Though this gained the women no formal voice in church affairs, such as men enjoyed, they nevertheless had the prestige of being "visible saints" and publicly affirming their faith. Yet they still risked censure if they overstepped their "proper" roles, and they remained unable to preach or to exercise authority.

Outside their churches, colonists governed themselves under their own version of the British political system. In each colony, a governor represented the king, and in most, he was appointed by the king. Often, he was a fortune hunter intent on increasing his own wealth. But he found himself having to placate both his royal master, who issued detailed instructions, and the leading figures of the province, who often had distinct interests of their own. The other main political institutions were the council, a pale imitation of the House of Lords, and the assembly, whose members liked to compare themselves with the House of Commons and to assert similar constitutional privileges. The governor had an absolute veto on colonial laws, as did the crown (a power it ceased to exercise in Britain itself after the early eighteenth century). Some governors also exercised considerable patronage through grants of land and appointments to public offices.

Although most colonists, particularly urban dwellers, depended in one way or another on commerce, the Navigation Acts and other British regulations meant that they were not free to organize trade as they chose. Although in theory colonial economies were meant to supply the mother country with goods that it needed, the northern colonies posed more of a challenge to Britain than did the South, with its staple export crops. A higher proportion of northern output was either of little use to, or duplicated goods produced in, Britain. As colonial manufacturing grew and threatened to undercut British producers, Parliament sought to restrain it. An act of 1699 banned the export of woolen goods from the colonies, and in 1732, Parliament prohibited the sale of hats across provincial boundaries. By 1750, colonial ironworks, mainly in the Middle Colonies, were producing one-eighth of the world's crude iron. Parliament that year prohibited the colonies from refining iron, requiring that it be shipped to Britain for further processing. Yet these restrictions did little to alter the pattern of colonial work or production. The laws were poorly enforced, and in some instances, they directly benefited the colonies. Laws defining colonial-built ships as "British," for instance, enabled American shipyards to become important suppliers to British as well as colonial shipowners.

Colonial governments also regulated commerce, particularly in urban areas. European thinkers debated the advantages of letting an open market determine supplies and prices. The foremost proponent of free markets, the Scottish political economist Adam Smith, would publish his arguments in a book called *Inquiry into the Nature and Causes of the Wealth of Nations* in 1776. But these were new and uncommon ideas. Most colonists accepted an older view of trade: that government had an obligation to see that the market provided what people needed at a quality they would accept and at a price they could afford.

In New York, both the Dutch and English authorities set up controlled markets, in which it was illegal to influence or speculate on price changes by "engrossing" (buying a crop that was still in the fields), "forestalling" (buying provisions on their way to market), or "regrating" (buying in the market in order to sell again). Cities also regulated the price and weight of an ordinary loaf of bread. Such measures aimed to provide farmers and bakers with a decent return on their work and to protect purchasers — especially the poor — against sudden price rises or unscrupulous dealing when supplies were scarce. In crises, the authorities took even stronger steps. In 1748, New York's mayor and aldermen warned that "great and unusual exportations" of wheat had made it "most excessive dear, to the very great oppression of all degrees of people, but more especially to the industrious poor" of the city and its surroundings. They asked the provincial assembly to lay an embargo on export shipments to conserve the city's supplies and keep the price of wheat within people's means. Their call expressed a traditional concept of justice: that private profit should not take priority over public needs.

Popular Politics and Direct Action   If the authorities failed to uphold these principles, ordinary people sometimes took matters into their own hands. "Food riots" were common in eighteenth-century North America, as they were in Britain and elsewhere. Most often, food rioters aimed to prevent suppliers from taking advantage of scarcity at the expense of the poor. When, in 1713, the Boston merchant Andrew Belcher ignored Boston selectmen's pleas not to ship his grain to the Caribbean and so create a shortage in the town, two hundred women and men broke into Belcher's stores and seized the grain. The lieutenant-governor was wounded when he tried to intervene. The rioters' object was not to steal supplies outright but to regulate distribution at a price they deemed fair.

Similar crowd actions demonstrated popular opinion about a variety of other issues, exerting the people's presence and the threat or actuality of violence at individuals or officials who were regarded as unjust or incompetent. As in many food riots, participants often included women. In 1704, Boston women fed up with a failed military campaign doused returning soldiers with the contents of their chamber pots. Bostonians resisted elite efforts to curb street vendors and restrict the sale of produce to public market-houses; in the 1730s, women led protests to get the public markets abolished, culminating in a riot in 1737. Private actions, such as a creditor's efforts to collect debts, also provoked collective resistance if they were perceived as unjust. Violence was rarely indiscriminate. There was a common view that, despite being outside the law, crowd action could be justified. Even the Massachusetts chief justice and lieutenant-governor Thomas Hutchinson observed that "Mobs, a sort of them at least, are constitutional."

Crowd protests were often ritualized, forming part of a broader tradition of unofficial popular participation in public life. Poorer Bostonians gathered each November 5th to commemorate "Pope's Day," when in 1605 English Catholic conspirators had been discovered preparing to blow up the King and Parliament. Laborers, seamen, and artisans, demonstrating their Protestantism and claim to the benefits of "English liberty," paraded effigies through the streets and burned them on a bonfire. New York and Albany slaves gathered for the annual festival of "Pinkster," whose name derived from the feast of Pentecost but that incorporated African traditions, while slaves in several parts of New England had initiated annual "Negro Election Days," which enacted and satirized the political activities from which slaves were excluded. Crowd actions also extended other avenues by which ordinary people—men in particular—could take part in northern public life. Militia units, sheriff's posses, and volunteer fire companies were vehicles for

An Exhortation to young and old to be cautious of small Crimes, left they become habitual, and lead them before they are aware into thofe of the moft heinous Nature. Occafioned by the unhappy Cafe of *Levi Ames*, Executed on *Bofton*-Neck, *Ochober* 21ft, 1773, for the Crime of Burglary.

I.

BEWARE young People, look at me,
  Before it be too late,
And fee Sin's End is Mifery :
  Oh ! fhun poor *Ames*'s Fate.

II.

I warn you all (beware betimes)
  With my now dying Breath,
To fhun Theft, Burglaries, heinous Crimes ;
  They bring untimely Death.

III.

Shun vain and idle Company ;
  They'll lead you foon aftray ;
From ill-fam'd Houfes ever flee,
  And keep yourfelves away.

IV.

With honeft Labor earn your Bread,
  While in your youthful Prime ;
Nor come you near the Harlot's Bed,
  Nor idly wafte your Time.

V.

Nor meddle with another's Wealth,
  In a defrauding Way :
A Curfe is with what's got by ftealth,
  Which makes your Life a Prey.

VI.

Shun Things that feem but little Sins,
  For they lead on to great ;
From Sporting many Times begins
  Ill Blood, and poifonous Hate.

VII.

The Sabbath-Day do not prophane,
  By wickednefs and Plays ;
By needlefs Walking Streets or Lanes
  Upon fuch Holy days.

VIII.

To you that have the care of Youth,
  Parents and Mafters too,
Teach them betimes to know the Truth,
  And Righteoufnefs to do.

IX.

The dreadful Deed for which I die,
  Arofe from fmall Beginning ;
My Idlenefs brought poverty,
  And fo I took to Stealing.

X.

Thus I went on in finning faft,
  And tho' I'm young 'tis true,
I'm old in Sin, but catcht at laft,
  And here receive my due.

XI.

Alas for my unhappy Fall,
  The Rigs that I have run !
Juftice aloud for vengeance calls,
  Hang him for what he's done.

XII.

O may it have fome good Effeft,
  And warn each wicked one,
That they God's righteous Laws refpeft,
  And Sinful Courfes Shun.

Crowd Justice

Public executions were occasions for common people to express approval of the punishment of those who broke the moral code. This broadside, printed and distributed in Boston in 1773, tells the story of a twenty-one-year-old convicted burglar, Levi Ames. The ritual of execution extended over a period of two months. On Sundays, Ames was conveyed in shackles through the streets of Boston, followed by crowds of men, women, and children. Each Sabbath journey ended at a different church, where Ames stood while the minister delivered a moralizing sermon. Historical Society of Pennsylvania.

popular public involvement, as were craft societies, such as the Carpenters' Company founded by Philadelphia builders in 1724, which were formed to assist members in difficulty but also began to regulate prices, decide who could enter the trade, and set rules for apprenticeship.

Popular involvement also became part of formal politics. In New England town meetings, participants could discuss whatever issues they chose.

Several times in eighteenth-century Boston, popular efforts prevented the town meeting from becoming a preserve of the wealthy and privileged. Between 1718 and his death in 1733, the physician Elisha Cooke, Jr., helped form the Boston Caucus to represent artisans and small shopkeepers in the town meeting, backed policies to promote local manufacturing, and helped to mobilize opposition to market reforms. After Cooke died, the Massachusetts governor tacitly acknowledged his success at being a thorn in the side of privilege, referring to Cooke as "the late . . . head of the scum." After 1750, however, Boston's economic decline put popular participation at risk by sinking many men below the property qualification for voting. New York had no town meeting, but public life there was more open than that in any other city. New York had the highest proportion of men able to vote, and laboring men were a powerful presence at elections. Thirty percent of the councilmen chosen in New York in the early 1760s were artisans — three times the proportion in Boston.

Workingmen in the northern port towns found themselves neither wholly included nor wholly excluded from the political arena. They might be courted at election time by popular politicians like Cooke or even by rich men such as New York's Morrises, DeLanceys, and Livingstons. They made their voices heard in the parades that often accompanied elections. A politician who scorned the popular element, such as Boston's Thomas Hutchinson, might find himself despised. "Let it burn," a crowd shouted when Hutchinson's house caught fire in 1750. More prudent political leaders let it be known that they would find it "an honour to receive a visit from the meanest freeholder, nay condescend to shake hands with the dirtiest mechanic in the country." Public power remained a privilege of elites, but popular politics was becoming more important.

Social and Political Tensions By 1760, the northern colonies were mature societies with rapidly growing populations. Two of the great ports in particular, New York and Philadelphia, grew increasingly prosperous as international and domestic trade increased dramatically in midcentury. A colonial elite of landlords, lawyers, and merchants had emerged and was busily consolidating its power. Its members treated themselves to elegant houses, fine furniture, and imported carriages. The new colleges they founded — Princeton, Brown, the College of Philadelphia, and King's College in New York — joined Harvard and Yale as places at which to educate their sons. Colonial writers praised America as a good place to live, and immigration from Europe, especially to the Middle Colonies, rose.

But maturity brought poverty and conflict as well as prosperity. War was part of the problem. Since the 1680s, a great struggle had been under way between England and France for mastery of the Atlantic world. Four major wars occupied no fewer than forty-one of the seventy-five years from

1689 to 1763. Colonial farmers' sons and workingmen fought in all of them. In the French and Indian War that began in 1754, one-third of all Massachusetts men of fighting age served in the military. Some perceived that wartime suffering was not shared equally, that some grew rich—or even richer—in war years, and that some elite achievements came at the expense of working people.

In eastern New England, population densities approached English levels, and the agricultural system could not support all the inhabitants. The small, worn-out farms that some would inherit would not permit all New Englanders to remain in the places where they had been born. Laborers without property or regular work and male and female servants seeking employment swelled the slowly rising numbers of the "strolling poor."

From the second quarter of the eighteenth century, rigid patriarchal controls over women and children were also starting to weaken. In longer-settled regions, such as eastern Massachusetts and the outskirts of Philadelphia, few household heads now controlled enough land to promise farms for all their sons. Young men had to turn to other occupations than their fathers' to seek their livelihoods. This led many young people to challenge their parents' authority.

Parents, for instance, expected to control their children's choice of marriage partners, but many sons and daughters circumvented their parents and chose for themselves. A growing number of young Quakers were "disowned" by the sect for marrying outside it. In Massachusetts by the 1720s and 1730s, between one-third and one-half of brides were pregnant at marriage, almost always by the prospective husband, obliging parents to accept spouses of whom they might otherwise have disapproved.

Migrant New Englanders opened up new town sites in the Massachusetts and Connecticut highlands and trekked northward to New Hampshire, Maine, and an ill-defined region, claimed by both New Hampshire and New York, that lay between the upper Connecticut River valley and Lake George and Lake Champlain. Moving helped to solve some of the migrants' problems, for they found land in abundance. But migration created new problems, too: disputes over control of newly settled land and conflict with the natives already living there.

The Great Awakening in the North   These social tensions both encouraged and were intensified by the spread of the Great Awakening in the northern colonies. The movement first took root in New England, following publication of the minister Jonathan Edwards's account of a religious revival in his church at Northampton, Massachusetts. Edwards's sermon "Sinners in the Hands of an Angry God" remains one of the masterpieces of American preaching. A Scots-Irish Pennsylvanian, Gilbert Tennent, encouraged religious fervor among Presbyterians in the Middle Colonies. Edwards

"There Was a Great Multitude . . . Assembled Together"

This account by a Connecticut farmer, Nathan Cole, captures the spiritual frenzy of the Great Awakening, as thousands flocked to hear the preaching of the English evangelical preacher George Whitefield in 1740. Cole and his wife, riding double, dashed twelve miles on their horse in little more than an hour to join the throng gathered at Middletown, Connecticut.

Now it pleased God to send Mr. Whitefield into this land; and my hearing of his preaching at Philadelphia, like one of the old apostles, and many thousands flocking to hear him preach the Gospel, and great numbers were converted to Christ. I felt the Spirit of God drawing me by conviction; I longed to see and hear him and wished he would come this way. . . .

Then on a sudden, in the morning about 8 or 9 of the clock there came a messenger and said Mr. Whitefield preached at Hartford and Wethersfield yesterday and is to preach at Middletown this morning at ten of the clock. I was in my field at work. I dropped my tool that I had in my hand and ran home to my wife, telling her to make ready quickly to go and hear Mr. Whitefield preach at Middletown, then ran to my pasture for my horse with all my might, fearing that I should be too late. . . .

When we got to Middletown old meeting house, there was a great multitude, it was said to be 3 or 4,000 of people, assembled together. We dismounted and shook off our dust, and the ministers were then coming to the meeting house. I turned and looked towards the Great River and saw the ferry boats running swift backward and forward bringing over loads of people, and the oars rowed nimble and quick. Everything, men, horses, and boats seemed to be struggling for life. The land and banks over the river looked black with people and horses; all along the 12 miles I saw no man at work in his field, but all seemed to be gone. When I saw Mr. Whitefield come upon the scaffold, he looked almost angelical; a young, slim, slender youth, before some thousands of people with a bold undaunted countenance. And my hearing how God was with him everywhere as he came along, it solemnized my mind and put me into a trembling fear before he began to preach; for he looked as if he was clothed with authority from the Great God, and a sweet solemn solemnity sat upon his brow, and my hearing him preach gave me a heart wound. By God's blessing, my old foundation was broken up, and I saw that my righteousness would not save me.

George Leon Walker, *Some Aspects of the Religious Life of New England* (New York: Silver, Burdett, and Company, 1897), 89–92.

Baptism on the Schuylkill

The frontispiece to *Materials Towards a History of the American Baptists*, published in Philadelphia in 1770, depicts the ritual immersion of adults baptized into the church. (James Smithers) Morgan Edwards, *Materials Towards a History of the American Baptists*, I (1770) — Library Company of Philadelphia.

and Tennent, along with such men as the Englishman George Whitefield and James Davenport of Connecticut, abandoned the dry, logical arguments of the traditional Puritan sermon style and reached straight for the heart. Their message was simple: only sinners who cast themselves on God's mercy would be saved. This message was particularly appealing to people whose communities were undergoing upheaval and who were anxious to measure up to the standards of an earlier generation.

Preachers and worshippers influenced by the revival challenged the authority of their established ministers. Whitefield, Tennent, Davenport, and others were "itinerants," who traveled from place to place to preach. Their audiences could be huge. Whitefield's last appearance in Boston in 1740 was before a crowd of 20,000 on the Common. Where itinerants went, disruption often followed. Connecticut passed a law against wandering preachers, and a number of them were jailed.

Like their counterparts in the southern colonies, northern revivalists began to recapture the visions of equality that had seized the poor of England during the Civil War a century earlier. Their sermons addressed contentious political and economic questions, especially whether Massachusetts should set up a land bank, which would serve ordinary people, or a silver bank, which would serve the rich. Men without formal religious training became exhorters and preachers; in some cases, women did so, too. Churches split. New denominations such as the Baptists began to grow, challenging the established Congregational churches. Church separations exacerbated the divisions within towns and spurred migration to new regions. Antirevivalist ministers were outraged at the challenge that the Awakening posed to their authority and the threat that it implied to established patterns of cultural and political hierarchy.

Conclusion: Prosperity and Inequality at Midcentury

Yet even as tensions spread across the north, the colonies themselves continued to expand in both population and trade (Table 3.1). Pressure to occupy more land for farm settlements remained strong. Traders, farmers, and artisans with control of their own property and households valued their personal independence and their "English liberties." They carefully guarded their freehold rights. They sought obedience and respect from the dependents in their own households, and this helped to preserve their deference for officials and colonial rulers. But this public deference was conditional on the recognition of their own rights and interests. As prosperity and inequality grew in the eighteenth century, challenges to authority became more common. In politics, in their churches, and in direct action to uphold what they saw as just, ordinary people had started to make their influence felt.

The 1750s would bring renewed war between Britain and France, the climax of their long rivalry for empire in North America. The war would tie the people of the colonies more closely than ever before to the web of British colonial interests, but it would also intensify the inequalities and disputes that had been growing in colonial life. People who were already used to challenging others' power would start to question the very nature of their colonies' connections with Britain. Ordinary people and popular politics would play a crucial part in the crisis that ensued.

TABLE 3.1 Estimated Population of the British American Colonies, 1720–1760

Estimated Population of the British American Colonies, 1720–1760				
Year	Race	New England Colonies	Middle Colonies	Southern Colonies
1720	White	166,937	92,259	138,110
	Black	3,956	10,825	54,098
1730	White	211,233	135,298	191,893
	Black	6,118	11,683	73,220
1740	White	281,163	204,093	270,283
	Black	8,541	16,452	125,031
1750	White	349,029	275,723	309,588
	Black	10,982	20,736	204,702
1760	White	436,917	398,855	432,047
	Black	12,717	29,049	284,040

New England Colonies New Hampshire, Massachusetts, Rhode Island, and Connecticut

Middle Colonies New York, New Jersey, Pennsylvania, and Delaware

Southern Colonies Maryland, Virginia, North Carolina, South Carolina, and (after 1740) Georgia

Source: *The American Colonies* by R.C. Simmons © 1976 by R. C. Simmons. Reprinted by permission of Harold Matson Company, Inc.

The Years in Review

1637
- Massachusetts Bay Colony banishes Anne Hutchinson for religious heresy. Six years later, she is killed in New York by Mahican Indians.

1648
- Massachusetts Bay Colony authorizes shoemakers to create the first labor organization in America.

1649
- The English Civil War results in the arrest and beheading of King Charles I by parliamentary forces; England becomes a republic under Oliver Cromwell.

1653
- Dutch colonists in Nieuw Amsterdam build a wall across Manhattan to stop English attacks; it later becomes the source of the name "Wall Street."

1658
- Oliver Cromwell dies.

1660
- Charles II restores the English monarchy.
- Mary Dyer, a Quaker, is hanged after she defies the courts by trying to preach in Boston.
- A Massachusetts law forbids the celebration of Christmas.

1664
- New Netherland is captured by English and renamed New York.
- The colony of New Jersey is chartered.

1675
- In King Philip's War, Mohawk Indians led by Metacom (called "King Philip") attack English settlements in New England in an effort to reclaim their land; one-tenth of the adult white male population of New England is captured or killed, but colonial forces ultimately triumph in 1676.

1680
- The colony of New Hampshire is chartered.

1681
- William Penn founds the colony of Pennsylvania.

1684
- Massachusetts' charter is suspended; the next year, Massachusetts is placed with Plymouth, Maine, and New Hampshire in a united "Dominion of New England."

1685
- King James II succeeds to the English throne; he is suspected of autocratic designs and Catholic sympathies.

1688
- In what becomes known as the Glorious Revolution, Parliament removes James II from the throne and replaces him with a new Protestant king, William III.

1691
- Massachusetts receives a new colonial charter, which ends Puritan autonomy but restores the elected assembly.

1692
- Salem witchcraft trials result in the hanging of nineteen alleged witches, fourteen of them women.

1699
- In an effort to restrain colonial manufacturing, England bans the export of woolen goods from the colonies.

1704
- An Indian raid on Deerfield, Massachusetts, leads to the death or capture of dozens of whites and discourages frontier expansion.

1705
- Massachusetts outlaws intermarriage between blacks and whites; the law is not repealed until 1843.

1712
- Twenty New York slaves light a blaze and then fire on a group of whites who try to put it out; in the aftermath, nineteen convicted slaves are hanged or burned alive.

1719
- America's first streetlight (a single lantern in Boston) is a sign of the growth of towns in the New World.

1724
- Philadelphia builders found the Carpenters' Company, a voluntary association that assists members in difficulty, regulates prices, decides who can enter the trade, and sets rules for apprenticeship.

1740
- The Great Awakening, a wave of evangelical religious fervor, sweeps over the American colonies in the late 1730s and early 1740s.

1741
- New York slaves are accused of arson and theft and of conspiracy to kill whites; eighteen blacks are hanged or burned to death.

- Jonathan Edwards preaches his famous sermon, "Sinners in the Hands of an Angry God," at Enfield, Connecticut.

1754
- The French and Indian War starts.

1776
- Adam Smith's *The Wealth of Nations* makes arguments for a free market.

Additional Readings

For more on the New England colonies, see: Virginia DeJohn Anderson, *New England's Generation: The Great Migration and the Formation of Society and Culture in the Seventeenth Century* (1991); Richard Archer, *Fissures in the Rock: New England in the Seventeenth Century* (2001); Stephen Innes, *Creating the Commonwealth: The Economic Culture of Puritan New England* (1995); David Jaffee, *People of the Wachusett: Greater New England in History and Memory, 1630–1860* (1999); Jane Kamensky, *Governing the Tongue: The Politics of Speech in Early New England* (1997); Gloria L. Main, *Peoples of a Spacious Land: Families and Cultures in Colonial New England* (2001); Margaret Ellen Newell, *From Dependency to Independence: Economic Revolution in Colonial New England* (1998); and Daniel Vickers, *Farmers and Fishermen: Two Centuries of Work in Essex County, Massachusetts, 1630–1830* (1994).

For more on the Middle Colonies, see: Edwin G. Burrows and Mike Wallace, *Gotham: A History of New York City to 1898* (1999); Adrienne D. Hood, *The Weaver's Craft: Cloth, Commerce, and Industry in Early Pennsylvania* (2003); James T. Lemon, *The Best Poor Man's Country: A Geographical Study of Early Southeastern Pennsylvania* (1972); Barry Levy, *Quakers and the American Family: British Settlement in the Delaware Valley* (1988); Peter C. Mancall, *Valley of Opportunity: Economic Culture Along the Upper Susquehanna* (1991); Cathy Matson, *Merchants and Empire: Trading in Colonial New York* (1998); Donna Merwick, *Death of a Notary: Conquest and Change in Colonial New York* (1999); and A. G. Roeber, *Palatines, Liberty, and Property: German Lutherans in Colonial British America* (1993).

For more on urban workers, see: Ira Berlin, *Many Thousands Gone: The First Two Centuries of Slavery in North America* (1998); W. Jeffrey Bolster, *Black Jacks: African American Seamen in the Age of Sail* (1997); Leslie M. Harris, *In the Shadow of Slavery: African-Americans in New York City, 1626–1863* (2003); Gary B. Nash, *The Urban Crucible: Social Change, Political Consciousness, and the Origins of the American Revolution* (1979); and

Marcus Rediker, *Between the Devil and the Deep Blue Sea: Merchant Seamen, Pirates, and the Anglo-American Maritime World, 1700–1750* (1987).

For more on encounters between settlers and Indian groups, see: Colin G. Calloway, *New Worlds for All: Indians, Europeans, and the Remaking of Early America* (1997); John Demos, *The Unredeemed Captive: A Family Story from Early America* (1994); Allan Greer, *Mohawk Saint: Catherine Tekakwitha and the Jesuits* (2005); Evan Haefeli and Kevin Sweeney, *Captors and Captives: The 1704 French and Indian Raid on Deerfield* (2003); Jill Lepore, *The Name of War: King Philip's War and the Origin of American Identity* (1998); Daniel K. Richter, *The Ordeal of the Longhouse: The Peoples of the Iroquois League in the Era of European Colonization* (1992); and Ian K. Steele, *Warpaths: Invasions of North America* (1994).

For more on women, see: Cornelia H. Dayton, *Women Before the Bar: Gender, Law, and Society in Connecticut* (1995); Carol F. Karlsen, *The Devil in the Shape of a Woman: Witchcraft in Colonial New England* (1987); Barbara E. Lacy, ed., *The World of Hannah Heaton: The Diary of an Eighteenth Century New England Farm Woman* (2003); Mary Beth Norton, *Founding Mothers and Fathers: Gendered Power and the Forming of American Society* (1996); Elizabeth Reis, *Damned Women: Sinners and Witches in Puritan New England* (1997); Laurel Thatcher Ulrich, *Good Wives: Image and Reality in the Lives of Women in Northern New England, 1650–1750* (1982); and Helena M. Wall, *Fierce Communion: Family and Community in Early America* (1990).

For more on culture and religion, see: Bernard Bailyn and Philip D. Morgan, eds., *Strangers Within the Realm: Cultural Margins of the First British Empire* (1991); Richard L. Bushman, *The Refinement of America: Persons, Houses, Cities* (1992); David Hackett Fischer, *Albion's Seed: Four British Folkways in America* (1989); Richard P. Gildrie, *The Profane, the Civil, and the Godly: The Reformation of Manners in Orthodox New England, 1679–1749* (1994); Frank Lambert, *Inventing the "Great Awakening"* (1999); and Mary Beth Norton, *In the Devil's Snare: The Salem Witchcraft Crisis of 1692* (2002).

4

Toward Revolution

1750–1776

JOIN, or DIE.

Join, or Die

As war with France approached, this woodcut appeared in a 1754 edition of Benjamin Franklin's *Pennsylvania Gazette* as a call to Britain's colonies to form a unified defense. Eleven years later, when Britain attempted to enforce the Stamp Act, Paul Revere, looking for an effective image for resistance, appropriated the old symbol. Benjamin Franklin, *Pennsylvania Gazette*, May 9, 1754 — Rare Books and Manuscript Division, New York Public Library, Astor, Lenox and Tilden Foundations.

GEORGE ROBERT TWELVES HEWES was born in Boston in 1742. His father had been sent to Boston from a country town "to learn a mechanical trade" because the family lacked the means to support him. But the elder Hewes had not prospered, so at age fourteen, George had to apprentice himself to any artisan who would take him on. He became a shoemaker. Although he eventually obtained his own shop, he could make only a meager living in the Boston of the 1760s, and he even went on fishing voyages for extra income. In 1771, he lived in lodgings with his wife and children and owned no taxable property. Nearby, Jane Mecom struggled to raise her children, earning money by making soap and selling clothes. She, too, was from an artisan family but was able to get help from her successful brother, Benjamin Franklin, the printer who had left Boston to find his fortune in Philadelphia. Though Hewes's and Mecom's paths might never have crossed, both were drawn with thousands of others in the 1770s into the shattering events of the American Revolution and the colonies' pursuit of independence from Britain.

Neither Hewes nor Mecom held a prominent role in society (although at the end of his long life, Hewes would be fêted as one of the last survivors of the revolutionary generation). (See his portrait on page 142.) Fame was reserved for the political and military leaders who were honored as the founders of a new nation. But the Revolution could not have begun, and independence could not have been achieved, without the involvement of countless ordinary American colonists.

The colonies' prosperity and rapid growth led Benjamin Franklin and a few other colonists to predict that within a century, America, not the British Isles, would be the center of the British empire. To Britain, the North

American colonies were economically important parts of an expanding empire. Their shipping, agricultural exports (rice and indigo from the Carolinas, tobacco from Virginia, wheat from the Middle Colonies), demand for manufactured goods, and imports of African slaves all contributed to a steadily growing Atlantic economy. After 1750, Britain's trade with North America exceeded that with its Caribbean sugar colonies. By the early 1770s, the Americas would contribute two-fifths of Britain's total overseas trade.

The mainland colonies also gave Britain a strong foothold on the North American continent with which to pursue rivalries with other European powers. In the war fought between 1754 and 1763, known in North America as the French and Indian War, Britain successfully extended its influence. With active help from the colonies and Native American allies such as the Iroquois, British forces drove the French out of Canada and established control over much of the eastern part of the continent. It was a triumph that, with other gains in the Atlantic and Indian Oceans, consolidated what is often called the First British Empire.

Yet within little more than a decade, British ambitions in North America were shattered. In 1775, thirteen of the American colonies rose in rebellion against British rule and joined together in another war, this time to achieve their independence. How did Britain's American triumph turn so quickly to disaster? The story centers on two themes: the conflicts that arose in colonial society itself and the impact on the colonies of imperial wars and policies. In a colonial society already wracked by tensions and whose citizens were mindful of their political rights, British policies provoked increasing popular unrest and protest. When popular movements became allied with colonial elites, resistance became revolution. The goals and actions of people such as George Hewes helped to undermine Britain's rich transatlantic empire and bring into being a new, vigorous republic.

The Colonial Roots of Rebellion

When, in 1776, the people of the thirteen colonies declared independence from Britain and formed the United States of America, they transformed both the history and the geography of North America. As the United States secured its independence, grew, and prospered, its presence on the map would come to seem inevitable. But to most people in the middle of the eighteenth century, the union of Britain's North American colonies into a single nation would have seemed almost inconceivable. The thirteen colonies that would later form the United States — New Hampshire, Massachusetts, Rhode Island, Connecticut, New York, Pennsylvania, New Jersey, Delaware, Maryland, Virginia, North Carolina, South Carolina, and Georgia — were all distinct from each other and separately governed. There was little unity between them, and there were few institutions to foster it.

In 1754, Benjamin Franklin and others put forward the Albany Plan for a union of colonies to conduct defense and Indian affairs, but this came to nothing. Most colonies had closer, more regular ties with Britain than they had with each other, and to leading colonists, the British connection seemed largely beneficial.

British policies and colonists' responses to them after the French and Indian War generated the sparks of colonial rebellion. But those events and policies worked upon a social and political context that had already been shaped by the character of colonial developments and the tensions it had produced. Important roots of rebellion already lay in British American societies, as ordinary colonists (especially those in frontier regions) struggled with elites to gain fair access to freehold land and the right to self-government.

Why Were the Thirteen Colonies Ready to Revolt?   These were only thirteen among dozens of colonies—belonging to Britain, Spain, France, or other European countries—strung out across the Americas and the Caribbean (Map 4.1). Why did these colonies in particular, and not the others, come to rebel against European rule in the 1760s and 1770s? Answers to that question lie in the varied character of colonial societies and economies and in the different relationships these societies had with their mother countries in Europe. Although there were many contrasts among them, the thirteen colonies that rebelled did have things in common, characteristics that they shared with no other New World colonies at the time. By the mid-eighteenth century, they displayed collectively several traits that other settlements in the Americas shared only partly or not at all.

The thirteen colonies were successful centers of European settlement and economic activity to which British policy had permitted virtually unlimited immigration. Many people from the British Isles and parts of Germany, pressed by population growth, agricultural change, and political events, had taken the risk of resettling there. The thirteen colonies had their own political institutions, and they had ruling groups whose homes were in America rather than in Europe. Since the late seventeenth century, British governments had largely left these colonies to their own devices and relatively free of political direction or interference from the mother country. Political liberty and colonial expansion were connected. As South Carolina's Christopher Gadsden remarked, colonists proudly shared the "natural liberties of British subjects," without which "the sons of Britain would have been . . . very thinly scattered on this side of the Atlantic."

A brief look around the mid-eighteenth-century Americas demonstrates the thirteen colonies' distinctiveness. Spain's empire remained under central control, and Spanish colonial governors were expected to follow instructions from the royal Council of the Indies in Seville. Although

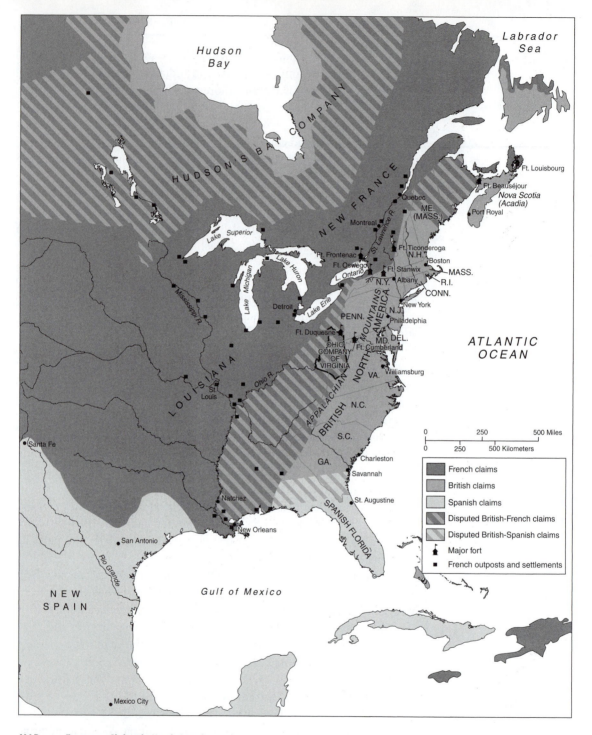

MAP 4.1 European Claims in North America, c. 1750

Britain, France, and Spain competed for influence in North America, each laying claim to vast areas of land and seeking alliances with the Native Americans who occupied most of it to secure their positions. The Indians, for their part, played the Europeans against one another as part of a strategy for holding on to their territories. Note the comparatively small area occupied by the thirteen colonies of mainland British North America.

"How Blest Is That Interpreter of Laws"

Colonists' pride in the institution of the law was demonstrated by this woodcut depicting a courtroom scene (with the presiding judge seated on the right). An accompanying poem celebrated the impartiality of the colonial court system:

How blest is that
INTERPRETER OF LAWS
Who rich and Poor make
equal in a Cause!
Who dares with steady hand
the Balance hold,
And ne'er inclines it to one
Side for Gold.

Prints and Photographs Division, Library of Congress.

distance often enabled governors to adapt or ignore their orders ("I obey, but I do not comply" was the legendary evasion), autonomous political institutions were weak or nonexistent in the Spanish colonies. Ruling groups remained divided between colonial-born *creoles* and Spanish-born *peninsulares*. Most prominent merchants were based in Spain, while to Spanish administrators, the North American provinces still seemed peripheral to their main possessions in Central and South America and the Caribbean.

French colonies, similarly, lacked the conditions for political independence. The one settler society, Quebec, had a small elite but little political autonomy. Elsewhere, across the Great Lakes and down the Mississippi Valley, France had built missionary and trading networks, but except at the port of New Orleans, there was no settler society or basis for a political culture. After France lost its American territories during the war of 1754–1763, most French inhabitants came under British or Spanish control, but no successful independence movements resulted. Spain ruthlessly put down rebels in Louisiana, while the British occupiers of Quebec pursued policies designed to avoid revolt among their new French Canadian subjects.

Preconditions for political independence were also scarce in British America outside the thirteen colonies. Newfoundland was a colony of fishing outposts, with little political cohesion, and Nova Scotia was only recently and sparsely settled. Many of Britain's Caribbean island possessions, however, were well populated. The largest, Jamaica, had its own provincial assembly that was often in dispute with the government in London. Yet there was little chance that Jamaica or other islands would rebel against British rule. White elites in the Caribbean were much more closely tied to Britain than were those on the mainland. Unlike Chesapeake or

Carolina planters, many wealthy Caribbean planters lived in England and had relatives or agents manage their plantations. The vast majority (90 percent in some cases) of the sugar islands' populations were African slaves. In economies dominated by sugar plantations, there was little land or activity to sustain individual farmers, artisans, or laborers, so the islands attracted few European settlers. Living in constant fear of slave insurrections, the islands' small white populations relied on Britain to suppress rebellion and to keep order.

Only the thirteen British mainland colonies, then, shared conditions that could foster a separate political identity. Locally rooted elites, significant populations of free working people, political institutions, and a degree of economic diversity all contributed to the possibility of independence from Europe. But in 1750, British Americans still had little sense of separateness from England. Over the next quarter century, that separation would be generated first by social and political conflicts within the colonies and then by mounting conflicts with Britain as well. Popular participation figured greatly in these events.

Political and Social Tensions By the mid-eighteenth century, each of the British American colonies had developed its own distinctive pattern of tensions and political disputes. In New York, factions that formed around the rival DeLancey and Livingston families competed for preeminence in the provincial legislature and city governments. In Pennsylvania, different ethnic and religious groups began to challenge the political dominance of Quakers and of the colony's proprietors. In Virginia, the popular evangelism of the Great Awakening produced social and political challenges to the Anglican gentry, while in New England, these challenges helped to break the tradition of consensus in town government that had been built up since the seventeenth century (see Chapters 2 and 3).

In port towns, market prices, trade fluctuations, poor relief, and the impressment of seamen into service in the Royal Navy provoked contention, even riots. The interests of town-based merchants often clashed with those of farmers and planters. Massachusetts, for instance, was divided in 1740–1741 by conflict over the establishment of a land bank, a scheme to issue paper currency backed by the mortgages on farmland that was widely supported in the colony because it promised to ease the payment of debts. Urban merchants, however, preferred being paid in silver or gold and used their influence with the colonial governor to have the land bank defeated. Massachusetts farmers remained wary of potential threats to their freehold system of property ownership and protective of the local institutions, including town meetings, that guaranteed them a degree of self-government.

Land Rioters and Demands for Freehold Rights The land bank dispute remained peaceful, but various causes did spark protests and rioting across

"Stones and Brickbats": Efforts to Halt Impressment

On December 1, 1747, Massachusetts governor William Shirley wrote this letter to the Lords of Trade, revealing Boston's reaction to the British habit of impressment (to supply men for its navy, the British government regularly employed "press gangs" to seize colonial merchant seamen). Boston was plagued by these press gangs in the 1740s; trade suffered as seamen fled the port to avoid forced military service. Shirley describes a November 16, 1747, incident in which several hundred Boston sailors and laborers, white and black, tried to halt an impressment by taking British officers hostage.

The mob now increased and joined by some inhabitants came to the Town House (just after candle light) and armed as in the morning, assaulted the Council Chamber . . . by throwing stones and brickbats in at the windows, and having broke all the windows of the lower floor . . . forcibly entered into it. . . .

In this confusion . . . the Speaker of the House and others of the Assembly pressed me much to speak two or three words to the mob . . . ; and in this parley one of the mob, an inhabitant of the town, called upon me to deliver up the Lieutenant of the Lark, which I refused to do; after which among other things, he demanded of me why a boy, one Warren now under sentence of death in jail for being [involved] in a press gang which killed two sailors in this town in the act of impressing, was not executed; and I acquainted 'em his execution was suspended by his Majesty's order till his pleasure shall be known upon it; whereupon the same person, who was the mob's spokesman, asked me "if I did not remember Porteous's case who was hanged upon a sign post in Edinburgh." I told 'em very well, and that I hoped they remembered what the consequence of that proceeding was to the inhabitants of the city; after which I thought it high time to make an end of parleying with the mob, and retired into the Council Chamber. . . .

In the evening the mob forcibly searched the Navy Hospital upon the Town Common in order to let out what seamen they could find there belonging to the King's ships; and [searched] seven or eight private houses for [British] officers, and took four or five petty officers; but soon released 'em without any ill usage . . . their chief intent appearing to be, from the beginning, not to use the officers ill any otherwise than by detaining 'em, in hopes of obliging [British commodore Charles] Knowles to give up the impressed men.

Charles Henry Lincoln, ed., *Correspondence of William Shirley* (1912).

the countryside from northern New England to South Carolina. Aspirations for freehold land and self-government were significant features of these upheavals, which, because the colonies were predominantly rural, often had broad political implications (Map 4.2).

In several areas, such as New Jersey and New York's Hudson River valley, conflict arose between large landholders and tenants. Small farmers, who believed they had the right to freeholds of their own, confronted landowners who, as one protester put it, wanted to lord it over "amiable and innocent tenants." Landlords' claims to vast tracts of land enjoyed the authority of the crown and the law. Against this, small farmers asserted a moral right to secure ownership of land they themselves had cleared and improved.

New Jersey witnessed a long-running campaign against the "East Jersey Proprietors," who, on the basis of a seventeenth-century grant from the Duke of York, claimed a large area around present-day Newark. The proprietors tried to collect overdue rent from farmers and began evicting those who refused to pay up. Arguing that this land had been granted illegally, without the consent of the Indians who held title to it, protesters released fellow farmers from jail, and rioters tore down the fences and houses of people who had accepted titles from the proprietors. One prisoner, Samuel Baldwin, was rescued in 1746 by 150 men armed "with clubbs, Axes, and Crow barrs." As though they were running their own government, land rioters collected taxes from their supporters, formed militia companies, and opened courts of their own in which to try their enemies.

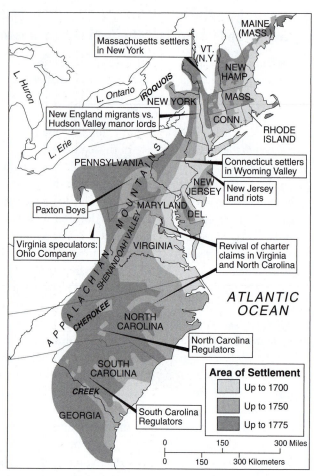

MAP 4.2 Conflicts over Land in the Mid-Eighteenth Century

From northern New England to South Carolina, struggles over land and rights erupted between the 1740s and 1770s as backcountry settlers fought with provincial governments, land speculators, or Indians.

In New York, protest focused on the great manors of the Hudson River valley, some of whose landlords were raising rents and reducing tenants' entitlements. Angry tenants knew that the titles to some of these estates, most notably Livingston Manor, were fraudulent, and they challenged the very basis of landownership in the colony, seeking to demolish its quasi-feudal structure. In 1766, the valley erupted in an insurrection that spread from Manhattan to Albany, as tenants withheld rent payments and claimed freehold title to the land they farmed. Their leader, William Prendergast, declared that they "sought the good of the country" and that "it was hard they were not allowed to have any property." New York's government sent British troops against the rioters in 1766, suppressed the revolt, and sentenced Prendergast to death.

This Hudson River valley conflict also involved New England migrants who were settling on land adjacent to New York, including the Green Mountains. Most of these settlers took up land under titles from New Hampshire that granted freehold ownership. But New York disputed New

Gathering at the Catamount Tavern

The Green Mountain Boys used the Catamount Tavern in Bennington as their headquarters. Bennington, named after New Hampshire's royal governor Benning Wentworth, was in the southeastern part of what is now Vermont, only a short distance from the seat of New York's government in Albany. The tavern was built around 1769 and featured a sign with a stuffed catamount or mountain lion. Stereograph, Special Collections, Bailey/Howe Library, University of Vermont.

Hampshire's claim to the region. The boundary between New York and Massachusetts had never been fixed, and Hudson River valley landholders were eager to expand their estates eastward. Settlers feared that if New York's claims were successful, proprietors would gain title to their farmland, turning them into tenants. After 1764, when the Privy Council in London decided that the Green Mountains did indeed belong to New York, New England settlers calling themselves the Green Mountain Boys waged sporadic guerrilla warfare against the New York authorities. Agreeing with William Prendergast that "there was no law for poor men," they tried to provide one that would guarantee the rights of independent small farmers against the claims of the wealthy, and they pursued their campaign into the American Revolution.

Conflict on the Frontier Farther south, immigration from Britain, Ireland, and Germany, as well as local population growth, prompted demand for new farmland. Migration to the frontier produced conflict between new settlers and leaders in older regions. Settlers demanded both better political representation and government help to remove Indians from the land they wanted to occupy.

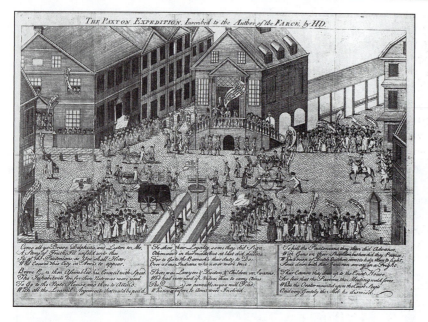

The Paxton Expedition

A contemporary engraving satirized Quaker Philadelphia's military preparations as the Paxton Boys neared the city in 1763. An accompanying poem concluded:

> To kill the Paxtonians, they
>   then did Advance,
> With Guns on their Shoul-
>   ders, but how did they
>   Prance;
> When a troop of Dutch Butch-
>   ers came to help them to
>   fight,
> Some down with their Guns,
>   ran away in a Fright.
> Their Cannon they drew up to
>   the Court House,
> For fear that the Paxtons the
>   Meeting would force,
> When the Orator mounted
>   upon the Court Steps
> And very Gently the Mob he
>   dismis'd.

Henry Dawkins, *The Paxton Expedition, Inscribed to the Author of the Farce, by HD*, line engraving, 1764, 13 11/16 × 7 5/16 inches — Library Company of Philadelphia.

In Pennsylvania, frontier settlers — many of them Scots-Irish — encroached on the territory of tribes with which the colonial government had so far largely managed to deal peacefully. Fraud and violence accompanied these encounters, making frontier life dangerous and precarious. Like Bacon's rebels in Virginia in 1676 (see Chapter 2), settlers sought to kill or remove natives, and in 1763, when the Pennsylvania government did not protect them from Indian counterattacks, frontiersmen formed their own army, the Paxton Boys. Sixty men raided a settlement of Christianized Indians at Conestoga, killing six inhabitants on the spot and later murdering fourteen others who had sought shelter in the jail at Lancaster. Two hundred and fifty frontiersmen then marched on Philadelphia, where assemblymen conceded many of their demands.

South Carolina frontier farmers and planters protested the lack of governmental institutions in the backcountry. They were unrepresented and had no effective officers or courts to protect them or to prosecute bandits who threatened them. Claiming equal rights with fellow colonists ("We are Free-men — British subjects — Not Born Slaves"), they appealed to the colonial assembly, which was dominated by coastal planters and had ignored them. Frontiersmen formed vigilante groups that called themselves Regulators and seized control of the backcountry from 1767 to 1769. They hanged, whipped, or banished suspected thieves and burned their homes. Although the leaders came from the small minority of ambitious, commercially oriented slave owners, thousands of small farmers supported them. At length, the assembly responded to their grievances. In 1769, it provided for

"Have Not Your Purses Been Pillaged . . . ?": The North Carolina Regulators

Herman Husband, the author of this tract, was the most prominent agitator in the North Carolina Regulator movement. A man of great contradictions, he held land grants of over 8,000 acres yet also advanced new democratic ideas in his writings. His September 1769 letter is addressed "to the inhabitants of the Province of North-Carolina" and appeals to farmers to vote for representatives of their own kind.

Dear Brethren,

Nothing is more common for Persons who look upon themselves to be injured than to resent and complain. These are sounded aloud, and plain in Proportion to the Apprehension of it. . . .

The late Commotions and crying Dissatisfactions among the common People of this Province, is not unknown nor unfelt by any thinking Person. No Person among you could be at a Loss to find out the true Cause. I dare venture to assert you all advised [as] to the Application of the Public Money; these you saw misapplied to the enriching of Individuals, or at least embezzled in some way without defraying the public Expenses. Have not your Purses been pillaged by the exorbitant and unlawful Fees taken by Officers, Clerks, &c? . . .

The Exorbitant, not to say unlawful Fees, required and assumed by Officers; the unnecessary, not to say destructive Abridgement of a Court's Jurisdiction; the enormous Encrease of the provincial Tax unnecessary; these are Evils of which no Person can be insensible, and which I doubt not has been lamented by each of you. . . .

I need not inform you that a Majority of our Assembly is composed of Lawyers, Clerks, and others in Connection with them, while by our own Voice we have excluded the Planter. . . . We have not the least Reason to expect the Good of the Farmer, and consequently of the Community, will be consulted by those who hang on Favour, or depend on the Intricacies of the Laws. . . .

But you will say, What is the Remedy against this malignant Disease?

I will venture to prescribe a sovereign one if duly applied; that is, as you have now a fit Opportunity, choose for your Representatives or Burgesses such Men as have given you the strongest Reason to believe they are truly honest: Such as are disinterested, publick spirited, who will not allow their private Advantage once to stand in Competition with the public Good. . . .

William K. Boyd, ed., *Some Eighteenth Century Tracts Concerning North Carolina* (1927).

extra representatives and two new inland parishes (counties) with legal and political institutions, including the courts, jails, and sheriffs that frontier settlers wanted. Having achieved their aims, the South Carolina Regulators disbanded.

In North Carolina, however, a separate Regulator movement faced a more hostile colonial government. A group of lawyers and land speculators had recently moved to the frontier, taking over local offices and accumulating large tracts of land. Their arrival shut out middling and poor whites, who had previously been able to acquire backcountry land and hold political office but now faced evictions, high taxes, and indebtedness as well as excessive court fees charged by corrupt officials. From 1765 on, many of these farmers, tenants, and laborers rose in rebellion. But the government, dominated by the coastal elite, resisted them and their demands. In 1771, when hundreds of armed Regulators clashed with colonial militia at the Alamance River, twenty Regulators were killed, one hundred were wounded, and the rest dispersed. Five Regulator leaders were executed, including one summarily on the battlefield, and their movement collapsed.

Unlike most town riots, which were short-lived and sporadic affairs over the price of bread or similar matters, unrest and rebellion in rural and frontier areas concerned fundamental issues: who would own land; how rights would be distributed and upheld; and whether society would tend toward hierarchy or equality. A recurrent theme was rural people's assertion of a right to self-government and to legal and political structures that would allow them to live without subservience to the wealthy and well connected.

The First British Empire: Triumph and Crisis

During the 1750s and 1760s, these same themes emerged in conflicts arising out of Britain's control over its empire. Questions of rights, freedom, and self-government came to alter colonists' views of their relationship to Britain. When imperial and internal conflicts became entangled, and particularly when rural people became involved in disputes with Britain, the mix proved explosive.

Over the first half of the eighteenth century, the British government had rarely intervened in colonial business. It usually left governors and provincial assemblies to handle matters themselves. For decades, colonial elites had controlled the taxation and administration of their colonies, imitating in their assemblies the practices of the English House of Commons. They told themselves and their people that they were the guardians of British liberties. They had become used to acting as a ruling class and to arguing that their rule was in the common interest. Still, the continent's increasingly important role in overseas trade and in Britain's rivalries with other European powers meant that the British were by no means indifferent to North America. Commercial development and war caused Britain's interest in the colonies to grow. The war of 1754 to 1763—its achievements and its consequences—would reshape British views of its colonial empire and its colonists' views of the mother country. Britain's greater involvement in the colonies' frontier land policies and relations with Indian tribes, coupled with a postwar economic slump that only exacerbated existing inequality, left many colonists resentful and prepared to question British intentions.

Economic Developments and Constant Warfare   Since the seventeenth century, Britain's trading regulations, especially the Navigation Acts, had directed colonial products in ways that best served British interests. In the eighteenth century, new regulations tried to ensure that colonial manufactured goods did not compete with those of Britain's burgeoning industrial producers. As the colonies expanded and matured, their economies became increasingly interdependent with Britain's. The southern and middle colonies exported agricultural goods, whereas the Northeast exported fish, ships, and forest products. Growing prosperity in the colonies meant increased demand for European manufactured items as well as for materials to supply colonial manufacturers. Colonists, moreover, were purchasing increasing amounts of luxury or ornamental products: fashionable cloths and furnishings, tableware, and beverages such as tea. Such items were being consumed across a growing spectrum of colonial society.

British merchants were keen to meet colonial demand but were also wary of acquiring bad debts if payments were not forthcoming. Like the bigger colonial merchants, they disliked paper currency schemes, such as the Massachusetts Land Bank or currency issued by colonial governments, because they feared that it would lose value. Twice, Parliament legislated against colonial paper money: a 1751 act prohibited it in New England, and the Currency Act of 1764 extended the ban to other colonies. Such laws provoked little opposition by themselves, but as events unfolded, a growing number of colonists regarded them as indications of a dangerous British interest in regulating colonial affairs for Britain's own purposes.

American colonists were also repeatedly embroiled in wars, not usually of their own making, for which they had to raise armies and pay taxes. Often arising out of European concerns, these wars nevertheless started in or spread to North America. Colonists took pride in their "English liberties" — voting for representatives, protection from arbitrary power, common law rights such as that to trial by jury — and were content enough to support wars against France or Spain, which they saw as "tyrannies" unblessed by such privileges. Their support for war was greatest when colonial and British ambitions coincided. New England's Protestants enthusiastically backed campaigns against the Catholic French in Quebec. In 1745, during King George's War between Britain and France, Massachusetts forces captured the French fortress of Louisbourg, on Cape Breton Island, which controlled the entrance to the St. Lawrence River. The victory prompted jubilation among New Englanders because it promised an end to their long-standing fear of their Catholic neighbors.

But joy later turned to dismay when Britain—pursuing its own interests at peace negotiations in 1748—returned Louisbourg to the French, exchanging it for a valuable Caribbean sugar island. A few colonists began to question their subordinate relationship to Britain. In a 1750 sermon, preached in Boston on the anniversary of Charles I's execution, Reverend Jonathan Mayhew argued that obedience to rulers was required only as long as they "perform the duty of rulers, by exercising a reasonable and just authority for the good of human society." Condemning as "slavish" the prevailing doctrine of unlimited submission to government, Mayhew suggested that the public good might "make us withhold from our rulers that obedience and subjection which it would, otherwise, be our duty to render."

The French and Indian War   American events soon broke the peace of 1748 between Britain and France. France saw Virginia settlers and Pennsylvania traders, who were pushing west across the Appalachian Mountains, as a threat to its territorial interests. When the French tried to build forts in the Ohio Valley, British and colonial governments warned them off. In western Pennsylvania in 1754, a Virginia militia unit under a young colonel named George Washington blundered into a skirmish with French troops and touched off a war that would spread from North America to Europe, India, and the Caribbean. By the time peace came in 1763, France's power in North America had been destroyed.

At first, though, the French were successful. The British general Edward Braddock led an expedition in 1755 to drive the French from Fort Duquesne in western Pennsylvania but was ambushed and killed, along with much of his force. However, the British were securing their hold on Nova Scotia, and in 1755, they forcibly deported thousands of Acadians, the region's French-speaking settlers. Some were dispersed to other British colonies, but after much hardship, many made their way to Louisiana, forming the nucleus of its Cajun (Acadian) community. After 1757, the British prepared to invade French Canada itself, with colonial assistance. They retook Louisbourg, captured Quebec in 1759, and seized Montreal the following year, shattering the French hold on North America. At the peace negotiations in Paris, Britain chose to keep Canada, ending France's threat to New England and the western frontier. Obtaining Florida from Spain too, Britain gained control of the continent's entire east coast.

The war was successful for Britain and its American colonies but also exposed disagreements between them. Colonists disliked having British troops "quartered" (compulsorily housed) in their homes. The British did not view colonists as their equals; until 1758, all British officers were formally superior to colonial officers, regardless of rank. The British looked down on colonial militias as less effective than their own regular soldiers because the militias did not embody what they believed to be proper social

The Death of General Wolfe

This 1770 painting by the Pennsylvania-born painter Benjamin West shows an incident that occurred during the Battle of Quebec in September 1759. This painting transformed the way in which artists depicted historical events. West, who settled in England and became court painter to King George III, portrayed the death of the commander of the English forces, Major General James Wolfe, at the height of the battle that would end in a French defeat. When the painting was exhibited, it stirred great controversy because its subjects wore contemporary dress instead of the ancient Greek and Roman costumes that were usually deemed appropriate for a history painting. West confronted his critics, declaring, "The same truth that guides the pen of the historian should govern the pencil of the artist . . . if instead of the facts . . . represent classical fictions, how shall I be understood by posterity? I want to mark the date, the place, and the parties engaged in the event." However, West's painting included men who were not with Wolfe when he died, including the lone Indian figure. No Indians fought with British forces in Quebec. Benjamin West, *The Death of General Wolfe*, 1770, oil on canvas, 60 × 84 1/2 inches — National Gallery of Canada, Ottawa; transfer from the Canadian War Memorials, 1921 (gift of the Second Duke of Westminster, Eaton Hall, Cheshire, 1918).

subordination. Most British officers were aristocrats and gentlemen who commanded soldiers drawn from among the poor and disadvantaged. Many colonial militia units reflected the greater democracy of New World settlements, with much less social distance between officers and men. In

1758, Governor Thomas Pownall of Massachusetts claimed that "most of these soldiers . . . are Freeholders, who pay taxes, [or] are the sons of some of our Militia colonels, and the sons of many of our Field Officers, now doing duty as Privates." Some units elected their company commanders. British officers, incredulous at practices that, to them, signaled unreliability, often treated colonial troops as mere auxiliaries, and the French and Indian War left them with a poor impression of Americans' fighting capabilities.

Prejudice blinded the British to military achievements that were in fact boosting colonials' self-confidence. Virginia militiamen, commanded by the same George Washington whose mistake the previous year had ignited hostilities, were prominent survivors of Braddock's defeat in 1755. Washington's good reputation for saving his unit would be recalled twenty years later, when the colonies sought a commander to lead their own forces against the British. Colonial soldiers took pride in their contributions to British victories. They still saw themselves as belonging to their own specific provinces, but many had served alongside units from other colonies, and this fostered a new sense of unity. Some spoke of themselves for the first time as "Americans."

The Consequences of War The war spurred British political interest in the colonies and a shift toward greater intervention in colonial affairs. It had been costly, and Britain looked to the colonies to foot part of the bill. The war's end, meanwhile, brought a decline in demand for military goods and services, which in turn caused suffering for many working people in the ensuing economic depression. Coupled with existing social tensions in the colonies, these economic changes led to a dramatic crisis in Anglo-American relations.

None were more affected by the French defeat in North America than Indians. The war's outcome opened the prospect of renewed colonial settlement and pressure on Indian lands. Previously able to play the French and British off against each other, many native groups feared having to deal with a single dominant European power. Native Americans from Maine to the Carolinas had taken the opportunity offered by the war to try and push back white settlements. The Chippewa chief Minevavana told the British that "although you have conquered the French, you have not yet conquered us. These lakes, these woods and mountains . . . are our inheritance; and we will part with them to no one."

By 1763, former French allies in the Ohio Valley and Great Lakes regions were mounting a concerted effort to hold off Anglo-American expansion. Ottawas, Hurons, Shawnees, and Delawares had switched alliances from the French to the British in 1759, hoping that the British would withdraw from west of the Appalachians and leave them alone. When

"Another Race of White Men Come Amongst Us": British Replace the French in the Lower Mississippi Valley

Native groups under-stood the dramatic consequences of the French and Indian War, as Alibamon Mingo, elderly leader of the Choctaw nation, indi-cated in his meetings with the British in Mo-bile in 1765. Mingo remembered the French fondly and spoke of his expectations of fair trade with and just treatment by the British.

When I was Young the White Men came amongst us bearing abundance along with them, I took them by the hand & have ever remained firm to my Engagements, in return all my wants & those of my Warriors & Wives & Children have been Bountyfully Supplied. I now See another Race of White Men Come amongst us bearing the Same abundance, & I expect they will be equally Bountyfull which must be done if they wish equally to gain the affection of my people. . . .

I cannot Immagine the Great King could Send the Superintendant to deceive us. In case we deliver up our French Medals & Commissions we expect to receive as good in their place, and that we Should bear the Same Authority & be entitled to the Same presents, If you wish to Serve your Old Friends you may give New Medals & Commissions & presents, but the worthy cannot bear to be disgraced without a fault, Neither will the Generous Inflict a Punishment without a Crime. . . .

I am not of opinion that in giving Land to the English, we deprive ourselves of the use of it, on the Contrary, I think we shall share it with them, as for Example the House I now Speak in was built by the White people on our Land yet it is divided between the White & the Red people. Therefore we need not be uneasy that the English Settle upon our Lands as by that means they can more easily Supply our wants.

Mississippi Department of Archives and History, *Mississippi Provincial Archives: English Dominion*, compiled and edited by Dunbar Rowland (Nashville, Tenn.: Brandon Printing Co., 1911), 240–41.

this did not happen, the Delaware prophet Neolin called for the expulsion of "the dogs clothed in red." The Ottawa chief Pontiac led an uprising aimed at dislodging British troops from the Great Lakes region, but disease quickly depleted his forces, and they had to abandon their campaign. Pontiac's rebellion nevertheless created conditions for a serious breakdown in relations between Britain and its colonists.

Frontier settlers and land speculators were quickly moving through the mountains into what would become Ohio, Kentucky, and Tennessee. The British wanted to impose order on this movement, to secure its own influence and end conflict between settlers and Indians. In a Proclamation of 1763, Britain prohibited settlement west of a line drawn along the ridge of the Appalachian Mountains (Map 4.3). The ban would be enforced by troops permanently stationed for the purpose.

MAP 4.3   British North America, 1763–1774
This map illustrates British policy in North America after the conquest of French Canada. The Proclamation Line of 1763 limited colonial settlements west of the Appalachian Mountains, whereas the Quebec Act of 1774 — passed at the same time as the Coercive Acts — fueled colonial anger by extinguishing several provinces' western land claims, extending the boundary of Quebec, and denying Quebec an elected assembly.

By itself, the Proclamation Line provoked some anger. Frontier settlers found their land titles in question. Investors in land companies (who included men such as George Washington and Benjamin Franklin) found their hopes of speculative profits jeopardized. Colonial pamphleteers denounced the specter of tyranny that arose from Britain's intention to keep a "standing army" in America. More important, these writers saw Britain's new frontier policy as evidence that Parliament was embarking on a determined effort to make the colonies serve British interests.

The Three Cherokees, came over from the head of the River Savanna to London 1762 & their Interpreter that was Poisoned.

2 Outacite or Man-killer; who Sets up the War Whoop, as, (Woach Woach ha ha hoch Waoch) with his Wampum.

3 Austenaco or King, a great Warrior who has his Calumet or Pipe, by taking a Whiff of which, is their most Sacred emblem of Peace.

4 Hostofees & Great Hunter, or Scalper; as the Character of a Warrier depends on the Number of Scalps he has them without Number.

Three Cherokees in London

The Cherokees began the Seven Years' War as one of Britain's staunchest Indian allies, but broken promises about land boundaries and gift exchanges tore apart that alliance. The Indians and British moved to open warfare in 1759, leading to decimation of the Cherokees' South Carolina homelands before they sued for peace. After the war, in 1762, three Cherokee chiefs visited London to meet the new English monarch, George III, and obtain assurances about their security. They were fêted but returned home empty-handed. This engraving depicts the Cherokee chiefs, with leading war chief Ostenaco in the center and their interpreter on the left. This is one of the few Indian portraits drawn from life during the colonial era, providing a more accurate depiction of the figures and their clothing. *Three Cherokees Came Over from the Head of the River Savannah to London, 1762* — National Anthropological Archives, Smithsonian Museum.

Strains Within the Empire: Trade and Taxes The French and Indian War benefited colonists who were in a position to profit from it. Colonial merchants who won wartime government contracts grew very rich. In New York City, Britain's American military headquarters, Oliver DeLancey used his political connections to boost his fortune to well over 100,000 pounds, the equivalent of many millions today. Lesser folk also prospered. Farmers found that the army needed their crops; gunsmiths made weapons; blacksmiths fashioned ironware; shipyard workers produced vessels; carpenters built barracks and fortresses; women brewers sold beer to soldiers; respectable widows provided bed and board for officers. But prosperity was not equally shared. Many colonists saw no gain from the war, and the disparity between rich and poor became more obvious.

The end of the war ended the prosperity it had generated. The slump was worst in Boston, which had sunk into an economic stagnation that the war had only temporarily alleviated. Boston's population ceased to grow around 1750, and some of its trade was drawn away by other ports, especially the rapidly growing towns of Philadelphia and New York. Boston was thrown into a severe postwar depression as work disappeared and many people found themselves without employment. Almshouses filled up with new inmates, many of them women and children. Wages fell but prices remained high, so even those who could find work were hardly better off.

The postwar slump also affected New York, Philadelphia, and Charleston. A New York rum seller regretted that "the Tipling Soldiery that used to help us out . . . are gone," and it was reported that the depression in the city had "reduced very many Families and poor People to great Distress." Charleston shipwrights and tanners found their work halved, while laborers faced irregular work and rising food prices. In all the port cities, the combination of inequality and hardship influenced the political events that were soon to unfold, although hard-hit Boston would play a particularly prominent role.

Imperial Conflict Grows

The French and Indian War also laid a heavy financial burden on Britain. The government of Prime Minister William Pitt had spent lavishly and raised taxes to conduct the fighting in the late 1750s. The new prime minister, George Grenville, faced enormous debts as well as expenditures for the navy, army, and officials essential to keeping Britain's newly expanded empire intact. Reluctant to raise taxes still further at home, Grenville's unstable administration looked to the American colonies to provide some of the necessary revenues.

Grenville was one of many British politicians who reasoned that the colonists had gained most from the war, which had removed their French enemy and enhanced their access to furs and other trade. Moreover, it seemed that the colonists had won these gains at little cost to themselves. Provincial assemblies had withheld contributions of men and resources or refused to pay governors' salaries unless they were given control of military appointments and supplies. Colonists had traded with the enemy under flags of truce or by smuggling. They so disregarded trading regulations that the customs service in the colonies cost more to run than it collected in revenue.

Unlike most other European monarchies, the British crown could not tax or make laws without Parliament's consent. This principle was celebrated as one of the safeguards of British liberties. In Grenville's view, the American colonists were, like all Britons, subject to Parliament's authority. Their own provincial assemblies were subordinate to Parliament, which alone could legislate for the general good. The general good now required that colonists start paying their own way within the empire.

Grenville and his successors discovered that colonists did not share this view. Parliamentary efforts to levy taxes in the colonies met with repeated resistance. Between 1765 and 1775, successive crises, each more serious than the last, drew increasing numbers of people from all levels of American society into a struggle that would eventually lead to independence. Animating this struggle was a growing belief that the British intended to remove their "liberties" and subject them to the tyranny of arbitrary government—to "enslave" them, as many colonists started to say.

The Stamp Act and Townshend Duties Grenville began his effort to increase revenues from the colonies with the Sugar Act of 1764, designed to end the notoriously inefficient enforcement of the navigation laws. Since 1733, a high duty had been imposed on molasses imported to North America from foreign colonies, but none had been imposed on molasses from British colonies. Smuggling was easy, and revenues suffered. The Sugar Act imposed a new, low duty on imported molasses, making smuggling less lucrative, and provided for more customs officers to be sent to America to enforce the law, with the right to receive one-third of the value of every vessel and cargo they condemned for smuggling. Smuggling cases would be removed from local courts, whose juries were often the defendants' friends and neighbors, to juryless vice-admiralty courts. Measures against smuggling caused some resentment, but the erosion of the entitlement to trial by jury was more serious to many colonists, who saw it as undermining their English liberties.

Grenville's next step ignited a serious crisis. In the Stamp Act of 1765, he extended to the colonies a measure that was already used in Britain: the requirement that a stamp be purchased for many documents and printed items (land titles, contracts, court documents, playing cards, books and newspapers). The tax had to be paid in hard currency, which was difficult to come by in the economic slump. The money that was raised would remain in the colonies to pay for troops and administration, but it would be controlled by colonial governors, not the elected assemblies.

The Stamp Act provoked widespread anger because it affected almost everyone. Apprentices signing indentures, young couples getting married, merchants making contracts, people making wills, those buying or selling land or slaves, newspaper readers—all would have to pay the new tax. The act also hit at the power of colonial political elites. The Stamp Act was Parliament's first attempt to levy a widespread colonial tax over the heads of colonial assemblies. The assemblies began to resist parliamentary initiatives. As they were quick to point out, the Stamp Act threatened to make colonists pay for their own subjection

to British rule. By giving royal governors an independent revenue, it promised to cut them free from restraint by the assemblies that voted their salaries. The rest of the tax would go to pay for the soldiers and officials who were enforcing unpopular British laws.

Political instability in Britain led to the ousting of Grenville and to the repeal of the Stamp Act early in 1766. Parliament, however, emphasized in a Declaratory Act that it retained the right to "make laws and statutes . . . to bind the colonies and people of America . . . in all cases whatsoever." Although this act contained no specific measures, its implications paved the way for further conflicts with the colonies.

In 1767, Parliament and a new chancellor of the exchequer, Charles Townshend, tried to tax the colonies again, both to raise money and to exercise parliamentary supremacy. Believing that colonists had rejected the Stamp Act because it was an "internal" tax, collected within the colonies themselves, Townshend sought to levy "external" taxes on goods brought into the colonies. The Revenue Act of 1767 (the "Townshend Duties") taxed paint, paper, lead, glass, and tea as they reached America. Colonists regarded the distinction between internal and external taxes as invalid, so these duties again provoked fierce opposition.

Colonists objected to British taxes because without representation in Parliament, they had no say in levying them, and because they saw taxation as part of a broader British plan to curb their liberties. Further resentment arose when Britain first suspended the New York assembly after it refused to vote for supplies for British troops in the province and then passed a Quartering Act obliging New Yorkers to board soldiers in their houses when required. The British also established a board of commissioners in Boston to run the colonial customs service and in 1768 posted two regiments of troops to Boston to protect the commission, aggravating colonists' fears of a standing army. This was the first time a garrison had been stationed out-

The Colonies Reduced

Britannia, surrounded by her amputated limbs — marked Virginia, Pennsylvania, New York, and New England — contemplated the decline of her empire in this 1767 engraving published in Britain. The cartoon, attributed to Benjamin Franklin, warned of the consequences of alienating the colonies through enforcement of the Stamp Act (the Latin phrase, meaning "Give a coin to Bellisarius," referred to the popular apocryphal tale of the noble Roman general Bellisarius, who, unjustly exiled by the Emperor Justinian, was forced to beg). Franklin, who was in England representing the colonists' claims, arranged to have the image printed on cards that he distributed to members of Parliament. *The Colonies Reduced. Design'd and Engrav'd for the Political Register*, 2 3/8 × 3 7/8 inches, 1767 — Prints and Photographs Division, Library of Congress.

affix the STAMP.

This is the Place to

"This Is the Place"

This protest against the Stamp Act was printed in the bottom right-hand corner of the October 24, 1765, *Pennsylvania Journal and Weekly Advertiser.* *The Pennsylvania Journal and Weekly Advertiser*, October 24, 1765 — Prints and Photographs Division, Library of Congress.

side New York or frontier outposts. The army erected a guard post at Boston Neck to catch deserters, putting everyone entering or leaving town under the sentries' scrutiny.

Meanwhile it seemed to colonists as if the customs service itself was at war with the American economy. Minor officials enforcing trade regulations regarded colonists as disloyal or criminal. They worked for the rewards they could earn by catching smugglers, using laws so complex that almost any vessel or traveler violated some technicality. A minor discrepancy in a ship's papers could result in the seizure of the vessel and its contents. All involved in commerce, from great merchants such as John Hancock of Boston to the ordinary seamen who crewed the ships, fell afoul of the rules.

Elite Protest Prominent in the arguments over British policy were colonial political leaders, who gathered in the provincial assemblies to debate what action to take. In 1765, the Stamp Act provoked prompt opposition. In June, the Virginia House of Burgesses passed strongly worded resolutions against the act, and eight other colonial assemblies followed suit. In October, official delegations from nine colonies gathered in New York City for a Stamp Act Congress, which adopted resolutions condemning the measure, called for a boycott of British goods, and sent petitions to Parliament and an address to the king.

Concerned about British policy, gentlemen, lawyers, clergymen, and merchants began to write essays and treatises on constitutional rights. The imperial crisis unleashed a decade-long outpouring of such works. At first, writers were hesitant, aware that they were toying with dangerous ideas by debating Parliament's power to tax and to interfere with colonial assemblies. These debates pushed them toward new conceptions of the colonies' relationship with Britain.

Colonists initially claimed that Parliament could not tax them for revenue because they were not represented in the House of Commons. The Virginia House of Burgesses argued that "taxation of the People by themselves or by persons chosen by themselves . . . is the distinguishing Characteristick of British freedom." For the burgesses, the "persons chosen" by Virginians would be the members of their own House, the only people for whom Virginians could vote. Some pamphleteers came to suggest that Parliament might have no authority in the colonies and that the colonial assemblies governed in its place, under the direct authority of the king. But this theory contradicted the British constitutional principle that the king ruled in and through Parliament and held no authority separate from it.

Gradually, pamphleteers undermined virtually everything colonists had once believed about their relationship with Britain, reaching increasingly radical conclusions, so that by 1774, Thomas Jefferson could insist that by migrating to the colonies, settlers had placed themselves beyond the sovereignty of Parliament. In *A Summary View of the Rights of British America*, Jefferson argued that the Navigation Acts were "void" because "the British Parliament has no right to exercise authority over us." Recent British measures in the colonies were "acts of power, assumed by a body of men, foreign to our constitutions and unacknowledged by our laws." Taken one by one, the measures might appear "accidental," but together, they "too plainly prove a deliberate and systematical plan of reducing us to slavery." Jefferson and like-minded colonial leaders were but a few steps short of regarding the American colonies as independent from Britain.

Popular Protest   Yet Jefferson and his fellow pamphleteers did not conduct political argument in a vacuum. Attitudes toward Britain became radicalized in light of events acted out on the colonies' streets and farmlands and in its households, as well as in the colonial assemblies. British taxes and British troops intruded on the lives of ordinary men and women. In Boston, Jane Mecom wrote to her brother Benjamin Franklin of the "confusion and distress those Opresive Actts have thrown us poor Americans into." Crowd action had long been an integral part of colonial life (see Chapter 3). Now women and men deployed these traditions against the symbols of British rule. In New York alone, fifty-seven crowd risings took place between 1764 and 1775, and numerous similar episodes occurred across the colonies. As popular crowds joined political elites in protesting British policy, they asserted their own sense of rights and justice and helped to turn protest into resistance.

In Boston, a small group of men calling themselves the "Loyal Nine," who included a painter, a printer, a jeweler, and two braziers (makers of brasswork), initiated popular resistance to the Stamp Act in the summer of 1765. They made August 14 a day of political theater to show Bostonians what the Stamp Act would mean when it went into effect that November. They hanged from a tree near Boston Neck effigies of George Grenville and of Andrew Oliver, the Boston merchant who had accepted the office of stamp distributor. Naming this the Liberty Tree, one of many that would appear in the next decade, the Nine set up a mock stamp office, where they ceremoniously stamped the goods of farmers and carters coming to town with produce and of passersby on foot and on horseback. A crowd then cut down the effigies, paraded and burned them, demolished a small building that was thought to be Oliver's stamp office, and then marched to Oliver's

"In Praise of Liberty": Colonial Crowds Protest the Stamp Act

Colonists' protests against the Stamp Act took many forms, including hanging and burning effigies of British officials and destroying their offices and houses, as well as those of colonial Stamp Act commissioners. The following account—from the Patriot newspaper The Boston Gazette—*of an attack on Boston's stamp collector Andrew Oliver shows how effective such dramatic crowd actions could be.*

Early on Wednesday morning last, the effigy of a gentleman sustaining a very unpopular office, viz, that of Stamp Master, was found hanging on a tree in the most public part of the town, together with a boot, wherein was concealed a young imp of the Devil represented as peeping out of the top. On the breast of the effigy was a label, "IN PRAISE OF LIBERTY," and announcing vengeance on the subverters of it. And underneath was the following words: He That Takes This Down Is an Enemy to His Country. The owner of the tree . . . endeavored to take it down; but being advised to the contrary by the populace, lest it should occasion the demolition of his windows, if not worse, desisted from the attempt. The diversion it occasioned among the multitude of spectators who continually assembled the whole day, is surprising: not a peasant was suffered to pass down to the market . . . till he had stopped and got his articles stamped by the effigy. Towards dark some thousands repaired to the said place of rendezvous, and having taken down the pageantry, they proceeded with it along the main street to the town house, thru which they carried it, and continued their route thru Tilby Street to Oliver's dock, where there was a new brick building just finished; and they imagining it to be designed for a Stamp Office, instantly set about demolishing of it, which they thoroughly effected in about half an hour.

Boston Gazette, *August 19, 1765.*

house, where they broke some windows, tore down fencing, and built a bonfire. The following day, Oliver resigned his position.

The August 14 protesters confined themselves to denouncing the British ministry, the Stamp Act, and its local agent. But protestors also touched on social divisions. A second Stamp Act riot on August 26 revealed the class antagonism that underlay Boston life in the wake of war and depression. This riot targeted symbols of wealth, culminating in a furious attack on the home of Lieutenant Governor Thomas Hutchinson. The crowd ransacked the house and, with considerable effort, demolished the cupola that had made it one of the town's grandest residences. The destruction marked popular resentment not just of British policy, but also of the power and privilege colonial rule gave to a few men.

Alarmed at the crowd's excesses on August 26, popular leaders tried to avoid further attacks on symbols of wealth. But they could not prevent social differences and tensions from finding expression. In November, a crowd sacked a fine mansion in New York, and the governor's chariot, sedan chair, and sleighs were "burnt in the Bowling Green with effigies and Gallows." In Charleston, a Stamp Act protest revealed not only opposition to British taxes, but also the fragility of the South's social fabric. As a white crowd paraded to the shout of "Liberty! Liberty! and [no] stamped paper," a group of African Americans provoked a panic when they took up the cry of "Liberty!" from the sidelines.

Opposition to the Stamp Act produced an unprecedented degree of political organization among colonists. Groups with names such as "Sons of Liberty" emerged in several towns and cities; the name later became a generic term for similar groups that provided the nucleus of a revolutionary movement. Their members came from a variety of backgrounds and included, like Boston's Loyal Nine, many artisans. Wealthy merchants protested as well, making up an important segment of the revolutionary leadership. Most famous was the Boston merchant and smuggler John Hancock. These groups also included men who were neither wealthy nor worked with their hands for a living. They included Samuel Adams of Boston, Isaac Sears of New York, and Dr. Thomas Young, who turned up in Albany, Boston, Newport, and finally Philadelphia. Samuel Adams was a Harvard graduate who dreamed of turning America into a "Christian Sparta"—a rigorous republican commonwealth—and who courted a popular following in the Boston town meeting. Thomas Young was a religious freethinker and self-taught physician who primarily treated the poor. Isaac Sears was the son of a Cape Cod oysterman who, after going to sea early in life, worked his way up to become a ship's captain before settling down ashore as a trader and marrying the daughter of a tavern keeper. As such men devoted themselves to building popular resistance to British authority, they started to transform American political life.

Colonists took Parliament's repeal of the Stamp Act early in 1766 as a sign that their protests had been successful, so when the Townshend Duties were enacted in 1767, protest resumed, lasting this time for over two years. Campaigners in the main ports organized nonimportation agreements binding merchants not to purchase goods from Britain. Violators were publicly denounced as "Enemies to their Country," were tarred and feathered, or had their houses daubed with the contents of cesspits (known as "Hillsborough paint" after the British minister for the colonies). Symbols of wealth were once again targets. In Marlborough, Massachusetts, the merchant Henry Barnes saw his carriage (one of the very few in town) vandalized when he refused to comply with nonimportation. Abstaining from imported products or fashions became a mark of patriotic willingness to give up luxuries for the public good.

Women as well as men supported the boycotts, and their support became important patriotic symbols. They organized spinning bees to pro-

Resistance to the Stamp Act
A generation after the event, an etching in a 1784 German pocket almanac imaginatively celebrated the Boston crowd (including women, African Americans, and artisans wearing leather aprons) burning stamped papers. Daniel-Nicholas Chodowiecki, *Historisch-genealogischer Calender, oder Jahrbuch der merkwürdigsten neuen Welt* (1784) — Prints and Photographs Division, Library of Congress.

duce yarn for cloth that would substitute for British textiles and announced their refusal to purchase or drink the tea imported by traders. In Massachusetts, over three hundred women agreed to "totally abstain" from drinking tea, and women at one spinning bee expressed the hope that they "may vie with the men in contributions to the preservation and prosperity of their country, and equally share the honor of it." For women, usually barred from a formal public role, the patriotic cause offered an opening into political events, and some claimed that their support for it should earn them political rights.

At first, nonimportation agreements formed a rallying point for popular political cohesion, but as the campaign dragged on, it revealed the divisions in colonial society. Never popular with colonial merchants, nonimportation was not fully enforceable. Bostonians loyal to Britain scored a propaganda victory by publishing lists of goods imported by supposedly patriotic merchants. By early 1770, merchants anxious not to break the boycott were also eager to resume trade with England as soon as nonimportation ended. That year, by repealing all but one of the import duties (that on tea), the British government succeeded both in breaking the boycott and in exacerbating divisions within the radical movement.

Artisans were the strongest supporters of nonimportation because it increased the demand for locally made goods, a boon for them during a time of depression. In 1770, after the boycott collapsed and this demand diminished, the shoemaker George Hewes was among many who ended up in debtors' prison. But artisans were not just protecting their material self-interest. They were also asserting a right to participate in political decisions. Nothing could be "more flagrantly wrong," said one New Yorker, "than the assertion of some of our mercantile dons, that the Mechanics have no right to give their Sentiments."

Seamen and laborers viewed the resistance to Britain differently. For them, nonimportation meant hardship: less trade, fewer ships at sea, and fewer jobs ashore. Some sailors tried to persuade merchants to support the resistance not by refusing to carry goods, but by evading the duties on them. Poorer colonists also gained their own perspective on the evils of a standing army. As competition among out-of-work seamen and laborers for scarce waterfront jobs grew tougher, the presence of ill-paid, idle British troops made matters still worse. In New York and Boston, friction between local workers and British soldiers hunting for jobs became commonplace.

In New York in January 1770, a two-day street fight, dubbed "the Battle of Golden Hill," broke out between soldiers and laborers. Events in Boston soon overshadowed it. There, resentments came to a head as demonstrations against the Townshend Duties continued. On February 22, a customs official fired his gun at some rioters and killed an eleven-year-old boy. The boy's funeral was observed throughout the town. Feelings were still running high when, on March 5, a crowd confronted a detachment of troops guarding the customs house on King Street, throwing snowballs and brickbats at them. Frightened by what seemed to be a bloodthirsty mob, the soldiers retaliated. George Hewes, who was in the crowd, was struck by a private's gun. Then, amid the confusion, troops opened fire, killing four Bostonians and fatally wounding a fifth. All five were laboring men: Crispus Attucks, a half-Indian, half-African sailor; Patrick Carr, an Irish journeyman leathermaker; Samuel Gray, a ropemaker;

A SOCIETY of PATRIOTIC LADIES.

Samuel Maverick, an ivory turner's apprentice; and James Caldwell, a ship's mate. As Caldwell was shot in the back and fell, the injured Hewes—who knew him—caught him in his arms.

Bostonians were incensed at what they soon came to call the "Boston Massacre," and radical propaganda ensured that, unlike the Battle of Golden Hill, the Massacre would remain firmly lodged in public memory. Paul Revere's engraving of the scene, widely copied and distributed, became the most familiar depiction of the event. Showing an orderly rank of redcoats discharging their muskets into the crowd, Revere presented the massacre not as the result of panic, but as a deliberate act of murder by the British army.

In the short run, the incident marked the end of a phase in the resistance to British policies. Within months, Britain had removed its troops from the town of Boston to Castle Island in Boston Harbor and had repealed most of the Townshend Duties. With the radicals already divided, the nonimportation movement collapsed. In time, though, the Boston Massacre came to seem a turning point in the conflict with Britain. For the next

A Society of Patriotic Ladies

Cheap prints depicting current events were in great demand in both England and the colonies. This 1775 British print mocks the Edenton, North Carolina, Ladies' Patriotic Guild, a group of fifty-one women who signed a declaration in support of nonimportation, swearing not to drink tea or purchase other British imports. The artist treated the women with scorn, portraying them as ugly, impressionable, and neglectful of their children. Philip Dawe (?), *A Society of Patriotic Ladies, at Edenton in North Carolina*, mezzotint, 1775, 13 3/4 × 10 inches — Prints and Photographs Division, Library of Congress.

The Bloody Massacre

Paul Revere issued his version of the Boston Massacre three weeks after the incident. The print (which Revere plagiarized from a fellow Boston engraver) was widely circulated and repeatedly copied (over twenty-four times). The print was the official Patriot version of the incident. British soldiers actually did not fire a well-disciplined volley; white men were not the sole actors in the incident; and the Bostonians provoked the soldiers with taunts and thrown objects before shots were fired. Paul Revere, *The Bloody Massacre perpetrated in King Street Boston on March 5th, 1770. . . .*, etching (handcolored), 1770, 7 3/4 × 8 3/4 inches — Prints and Photographs Division, Library of Congress.

thirteen years, until the end of the Revolutionary War, Boston observed March 5 as a day of public mourning. Radicals used the event to rebuild popular opposition to British rule. The Massacre's victims came to be viewed as the first martyrs of a revolutionary cause, and the fact that they were laborers built popular support for that cause. An event that had grown out of the nonimportation movement and reflected divisions in Boston society instead became a basis for building a united coalition.

Resistance Becomes Revolution

Although concerted opposition to Britain receded, attacks on customs officers and other officials continued sporadically. In 1772, a government revenue vessel, the *Gaspée*, ran aground in Narragansett Bay, and a crowd from Providence burned it, erecting liberty poles to mark the event. But these protests chiefly involved urban residents, not people in the countryside. This pattern changed during a further, still more serious imperial crisis, which began in 1773 with Parliament's passage of the Tea Act. Protest again began in the towns, but this time, it spread to rural regions, where the vast majority of colonists lived. When rural people became engaged in the struggle, resistance turned to revolution.

Since fleeing England in the seventeenth century and settling on land they could call their own, rural New Englanders had feared any measure that might threaten their freeholds and return them to some form of feudalism. Urban radicals played on this fear in the hope of igniting rural opposition to Britain. In 1772, the Boston town meeting appointed a Committee of Correspondence to rouse the interior, warning that if "a British house of commons can originate an act for taking away our money, our lands will go next or be subject to rack rents from haughty and relentless landlords who will ride at ease, while we are trodden in the dirt." At first, these efforts met with apathy. Some of the people to whom the committee wrote thought that relations with Britain were none of their business. But the campaign over the Tea Act of 1773 prompted country people to respond, and they did so with vigor. Along with protesters in the port towns they helped initiate a chain of colonial challenges and British responses that would forge unity between colonies, bring on outright war with Britain, and lead to the colonies' declaration in 1776 that they were an independent country.

From the Tea Act to Continental Resistance   The Tea Act was not intended as a colonial taxation measure. Parliament was trying to solve the financial troubles of the British East India Company, permitting it to raise money by selling tea directly to America through chosen agents in each

The Boston Massacre, c. 1868
Artists continued to redraw, repaint, and reinterpret the Boston Massacre. This engraving based on a painting by Alonzo Chappel still omitted Crispus Attucks, but it showed the chaos of the confrontation and captured the horror of soldiers shooting down unarmed citizens. American Social History Project.

"Let Every Man Do His Duty . . .": George Hewes Describes the Boston Tea Party

George Robert Twelves Hewes, a poor shoemaker who had also been at the scene of the Boston Massacre three years earlier, participated in the Boston Tea Party. In a memoir taken down by James Hawkes in 1834, Hewes describes the meeting of "the Whole body of the People" that deliberated on the action and then tells of the disciplined destruction of the tea.

On the day preceding the seventeenth [of December], there was a meeting of the citizens of the county of Suffolk, convened at one of the churches in Boston, for the purpose of consulting on what measures might be considered expedient to prevent the landing of the tea, or secure the people from the collection of the duty. At that meeting a committee was appointed to wait on Governor Hutchinson, and [to ask] whether he would take any measures to satisfy the people on the object of the meeting. . . . When the committee returned and informed the meeting of the absence of the Governor, there was a confused murmur among the members, and the meeting was immediately dissolved, many of them crying out, "Let every man do his duty, and be true to his country"; and there was a general huzza for Griffin's wharf. . . .

When we arrived at the wharf, there were three of our number who assumed an authority to direct our operations, to which we readily submitted. They divided us into three parties, for the purpose of boarding the three [tea] ships. . . . We were immediately ordered by the respective commanders to board all the ships at the same time, which we promptly obeyed. The commander of the division to which I belonged, as soon as we were aboard the ship, appointed me boatswain, and ordered me to go the [ship's] captain and demand of him the keys to the hatches and a dozen candles. I made the demand accordingly, and the captain promptly . . . delivered the articles; but requested me at the same time to do no damage to the ship or rigging. We then were ordered by our commander to open the hatches and take out all the chests of tea and throw them overboard, and we immediately proceeded to execute his orders, first cutting and splitting the chests with our tomahawks, so as thoroughly to expose them to the effects of the water.

In about three hours from the time we went on board, we had thus broken and thrown overboard every tea chest to be found in the ship, while those on the other ships were disposing of the tea in the same way, at the same time. We were surrounded by British armed ships, but no attempt was made to resist us.

James Hawkes, *A Retrospect of the Boston Tea Party* (1834).

colonial port. Its prices would be low enough that, even after paying the Townshend Duty on tea (which the act cut in half), the company could undercut other merchants who had, as John Adams put it, "honestly smuggled" their tea from Holland.

The Act should have made everyone happy: Britain would get taxes, the East India Company would get revenue, and colonists would get cheap tea. Instead, it reignited American outrage at British policy. Colonists spurned the attempt to bribe them into accepting the tax on tea. Charleston landed its first cargo of tea, but Philadelphia and New York refused to let tea ships even enter their harbors. In Boston in November 1773, the first vessels carrying tea docked because Thomas Hutchinson, who was now governor (and whose sons were Boston agents for the East India Company), insisted that the cargo should land and the tea duty be paid. Daylong protest meetings of "the whole Body of the People" convened, choosing leaders to persuade Hutchinson to desist. Talks broke down. On the night of December 16, parties of Patriot leaders and workingmen boarded the ships and dumped the tea overboard into the harbor. The shoemaker George Hewes led one of the groups.

This "Boston Tea Party" became a powerful emblem of American resistance. The men who carried it out were disguised as "Mohawks." Hewes had blackened his face with a piece of charcoal and thrown a blanket around his shoulders. When another tea ship reached New York a few months later, another group of "Mohawks" prepared to reenact the event but were beaten to it by a crowd that surged onto the ship, destroyed the tea themselves, then paraded the empty tea chests to "the Fields" outside the city walls and burned them. Rioters disguised themselves in Indian dress not for practical reasons (secrecy was unnecessary in a sympathetic neighborhood), but as a symbol of their identity as Americans rather than Englishmen living in America. They were shifting from being "freeborn Englishmen" to becoming "American freemen."

Britain responded severely to the Bostonians' destruction of a valuable tea cargo. Parliament passed four measures, which colonists called the Coercive Acts or the Intolerable Acts. These acts closed Boston Harbor until the town paid for the tea, cutting off Boston's main source of livelihood; altered Massachusetts government, revoking the 1691 charter that had given the colony the unique privilege of electing its own council and limiting town meetings to one each year for the election of local officers; allowed British officials accused of wrongdoing to face trial in another province or in Britain itself, away from Boston's charged atmosphere; and made it easy for the British to billet troops in colonial homes. Soon after the Coercive Acts were announced, in May 1774, Thomas Gage, the general in charge of Britain's army in America, replaced Hutchinson as governor, and Gage's troops reoccupied Boston.

The Able Doctor, or America Swallowing the Bitter Draught

Many British prints sympathized with the colonists' claims. In this engraving, published in the April 1774 *London Magazine*, America (depicted as an Indian woman) was assaulted by several recognizable British statesmen — principally Lord North, the Prime Minister, who was shown forcing tea down her throat (only to have it spat back into his face). Meanwhile, France and Spain looked on, and Britannia averted her eyes in shame. By June 1775, the engraving had reached the colonies, where it was copied and reproduced by Paul Revere. *London Magazine*, April 1774 — Rare Books and Manuscript Division, New York Public Library, Astor, Lenox and Tilden Foundations.

The able Doctor, or America Swallowing the Bitter Draught.

Britain meant to show that it would retreat no further in the face of American protests and would restore its authority in the colonies. But the Coercive Acts had exactly the opposite effect, redoubling the radical movement in Boston. Many Bostonians who had once been sympathetic to the crown began to change their views. Benjamin Franklin's sister Jane Mecom, who a few years before had regarded Thomas Hutchinson as "the Gratest ornament of our Country," was now angered by "the town[']s being so full of Proflegate soulders [profligate soldiers] . . . and "the[ir] Profane language."

More important, the British measures spread colonial resistance from town to countryside far more effectively than the Boston Committee of Correspondence had managed. By interfering with town meetings and county courts, the Coercive Acts carried Britain's quarrel with Boston to every corner of Massachusetts. Rural people, many of whom had been reluctant to oppose British policies, now acted to prevent the new measures from taking effect. In doing so, they turned their province away from the path of submission to royal authority and onto the road to revolution.

When the first court to convene under the provisions of the Coercive Acts was due to open in Worcester County in August 1774, its judges arrived to find virtually the whole male population of the county armed and assembled in their militia units near the courthouse. The crowd remained in place until each of the judges had read a public statement resigning his post. The Worcester court never opened; nor did any of the other county courts in the province. Prominent men appointed to the new provincial council under the Acts were also "persuaded" by assembled crowds to resign or were subjected to humiliating treatment. One councilor resigned only after being locked up for the night in a smokehouse.

By late summer 1774, royal government in Massachusetts had virtually collapsed, and the governor's authority ran no farther than his troops could march. Defying the governor's order that it dissolve, the province's General Court met in Salem, and militia units drilled under officers who now acknowledged the authority of this extralegal provincial assembly. Massachusetts people created their own political institutions and took over the province. Defying the British laws, town meetings and county conventions met to direct affairs, no longer conducting their business in the name of the king, but in the name of the "commonwealth" or "the people of Massachusetts." A revolution was under way.

Most significant of all, the Coercive Acts prompted popular action in other colonies too. By late 1774, much of New England was united behind Massachusetts. So was the white population of Virginia, where, despite the evangelical challenge to its leadership since the Great Awakening, the planter class remained firmly in control. Having suffered from weak tobacco prices in the 1760s and indebtedness to British merchants, many Virginia planters were reconsidering the benefits of being part of the British empire and coming to see colonial status as a disadvantage. Meanwhile, the colony's popular leaders, such as Patrick Henry, forged links between the gentry and others in the population, denouncing "luxury" and proclaiming the "virtue" of the Patriot cause. From 1774 to mid-1776, the combination of New Englanders and Virginia gentlemen led a drive for strong measures against Britain that would forge a path to independence.

These leaders found their forum in two Continental Congresses, formed of representatives from the different colonies gathered to resist British policies. Although intercolonial cooperation had been attempted in response to the Stamp Act, it was less far-reaching than this. The first Continental Congress met in Philadelphia for six weeks in the autumn of 1774, and the second commenced in May 1775. Convened to rally to the aid of Massachusetts, delegates came to the first congress from twelve, then thirteen colonies. They included participants in popular protests, such as artisan members of the Charleston Sons of Liberty who were among South Carolina's delegation. Led by radicals keen to make the rest of America see that they shared Massachusetts's problems, this congress drafted and

The Bostonian's Paying the EXCISE-MAN, or TARRING & FEATHERING
Plate I.

The Bostonians Paying the Excise-Man, or Tarring and Feathering
A 1774 British print depicts the tarring and feathering of Boston Commissioner of Customs John Malcolm. Tarring and feathering was a ritual of humiliation and public warning that stopped just short of life-threatening injury. In this print, Malcolm was attacked under the Liberty Tree by several Patriots, including a leather-aproned artisan, while the Boston Tea Party occurred in the background; in fact, the Tea Party had taken place four weeks earlier. This anti-Patriot print may have been a response to the sympathetic "The Able Doctor" published earlier the same year. Philip Dawe (?), mezzotint, 1774, 14 × 9 1/2 inches — Prints and Photographs Division, Library of Congress.

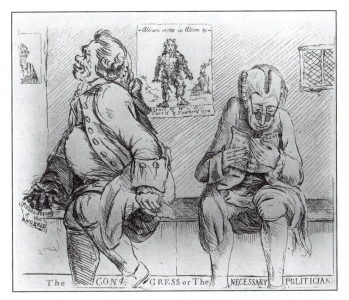

The "Necessary Politicians"
A particularly derisive comment on colonial demands, this 1775 British etching shows two Tory politicians evaluating Patriot documents in a privy (or "necessary" house). A tarred-and-feathered figure decorates the outhouse wall. *The Congress or Necessary Politicians*, etching, 1775?, 8 × 6 1/2 inches — Prints and Photographs Division, Library of Congress.

adopted the Continental Association, a measure that decreed a complete boycott of European products and called for the creation of committees throughout the colonies to enforce it. In Boston, Jane Mecom regarded "the Uniteing of the Colonies" as "a token of God[']s design to deliver us out of all our tro[u]bles."

Linking the colonies together in a common cause and providing for local support, the Continental Association harnessed popular action to the beginnings of a national movement. Sometimes against opposition, local Patriot committees started to enforce the Association's provisions. Even more than in the boycotts against the Townshend Duties, support for the Patriot cause entailed forgoing European goods and fashions and adopting symbols of domestic frugality. Following Massachusetts, other colonies set up extralegal institutions to take over effective government.

War Begins Before the Second Continental Congress could meet, fighting with Britain broke out in Massachusetts. During the fall and winter of 1774–1775, New Englanders had collected weapons and organized their town militias to defend their extralegal committees and conventions. In September 1774, a mere rumor that British troops had left Boston to capture a provincial powder store set thousands of rural Massachusetts men marching eastward until they could be recalled. An observer reported women in their houses along the way "making Cartridges, [and] running Bullets . . . animating their Husbands and Sons to fight for their Liberties." It was a sign of what would come. In occupied Boston, a committee of artisans watched troop movements closely. The extralegal provincial congress began planning to raise an army of 15,000 men. But this army did not yet exist when, on the night of April 18–19, 1775, General Gage dispatched troops to capture militia supplies hidden at Concord, some eighteen miles inland.

The artisans' committee sent Paul Revere and other riders to warn the interior. When the British detachment reached Lexington, the town's militia was drawn up on the green to face it. They probably intended only a symbolic confrontation, but someone's gun went off, the two sides exchanged fire, and soon eight militiamen were dead. The British troops marched on, completed their task at Concord, and set out back to Boston. Their outward march had been easy, but the return was not. Farmers and workmen

The Battle of Lexington
This picture was one of a set of four prints based on drawings sketched shortly after the battle of Lexington by Amos Doolittle, a twenty-one-year-old engraver who visited the site as a member of the Connecticut militia. Although the location was rendered with accuracy, the drawing misrepresented the behavior of British troops, whose discipline was less than perfect. The four prints, on sale by December 1775, were the first American illustrations of warfare during the Revolution. Amos Doolittle, *The Battle of Lexington, April 19th, 1775*, line engraving (hand-colored), 1775, 13 × 17 1/2 inches — Print Collection, Miriam and Ira Wallach Division of Art, Prints, and Photographs, New York Public Library, Astor, Lenox and Tilden Foundations.

rallied from the surrounding towns and attacked the British from the fields and woods along their route, scoring heavy casualties. Once the British had reached Boston, militia units—citizen-soldiers, poorly trained, and mostly without uniforms or good weapons—threw up siege lines around the city and kept the army penned up there. The British, commented Jane Mecom, "were much mistaken in the people they had to Deal with."

In June, the colonial militia again showed that they could fight. Gage decided to dislodge them from Breed's (now Bunker) Hill overlooking Charlestown. He did so, but only at great cost. Determined to demonstrate the superiority of regular soldiers over the provincial forces that he regarded as ill-disciplined, Gage launched a nearly suicidal uphill frontal assault on the defenses at the top. Before retreating to new positions, the militia killed or wounded nearly half of Gage's men. The British made no more such attacks, and when, in the winter of 1775–1776, the provincials were reinforced by cannons captured from Ticonderoga, New York, Gage was obliged to withdraw from Boston altogether.

During the summer of 1775, the Continental Congress took steps to support the New England armies and ready the colonies for war. It appointed George Washington to head a new Continental Army that would fight alongside the provincial militias and ensure that the cause was not fragmented by individual provinces' own interests. The choice of Washington was based partly on his reputation from the French and Indian

The Retreat

This print, possibly made in America, presents the plundering retreat of British troops on April 19, 1775. The unknown artist chose to portray the King's soldiers as donkeys and the advancing Massachusetts troops in disciplined ranks (in fact, they fought as guerrillas, harassing the British from the shelter of houses, trees, and rocks). British Museum.

The Retreat

From Concord to Lexington of the Army of Wild Irish Asses Defeated by the Brave American Militia

War, but it was also political. The appointment of a southerner such as Washington was essential if the war was to become more than a New England affair. Moreover, Washington was a wealthy member of Virginia's ruling class, and he would bring prestige to this new position.

The Second Continental Congress remained in session for over a decade, until well after the war itself was over. In July 1775, it issued a "Declaration of the Causes and Necessity of Taking Up Arms," summarizing the injuries that Britain had inflicted on the colonies, condemning the "cruel aggression . . . commenced by the British troops," and declaring that the "united colonies" faced a stark choice between "an unconditional submission to . . . tyranny" and "resistance by force." Although Virginia and New England were effectively united, much of the rest of America was not. Within a matter of months, however, events would bring Congress to face the issue of independence.

The People Take Sides Between 1774 and 1776, as the dispute with Britain grew, many people in the colonies were forced to take sides. Among those who formed the revolutionary coalition, there was a powerful feeling of belonging to a grand cause. But what some found exhilarating many others feared. Some of them decided to go along with revolution, as one New Yorker expressed it, by "swimming with a stream it is impossible to stem." Others decided that life would be unimaginable without a king and the social order for which he stood.

Loyalism to Britain was strong in some places. In the prosperous farming country around New York City, Loyalists formed a majority. In the Hudson and Mohawk valleys, parts of New Jersey, Maryland's eastern shore,

"Good for Nothing": A Shopkeeper Is Accused of Toryism

As Roelof Eltinge discovered, the divisions between those who supported the war against Britain, those who did not (known as Tories or Loyalists), and those attempting to remain neutral impinged on family and community life in a variety of ways. Eltinge was a shop owner in New Paltz, New York, and member of a wealthy family. His local Committee of Safety (one of many established by the Continental Congress in 1774 to enforce the boycott against British goods) suspected him of Toryism. Brought before the committee in 1776 to explain why he refused to accept the currency issued by the Continental Congress, Eltinge was arrested and eventually banished by the state of New York for his Tory sympathies, which, this excerpt from his testimony suggests, seemed motivated more by pragmatism than by politics.

Mr. Roelof Eltinge, being summoned by the Sub Committee, appeared accordingly and says in his Defence, on the first Emmitting the Continental Money there was Sundry Disputes about the Money. Some said it was Good, others said it was Good for Nothing. However, when he found he Could pass it readily he received it in payment, but to tell the truth of the matter, for it was a Folly to Lie about it, I Never liked it for I always thought if the King Got the better of the Country the money would be Good for Nothing. Farther, that a certain Mrs. Wirtz, wife of Doctor Wirtz, Came to my house in Order to purchase Some Goods out of my store, when I told Mrs. Wirtz that I did not like to take Congress money for my Goods, as I supposed She intended to pay me in that money, and that I would rather Trust her for the Goods. . . .

After this, our Troops Retreating from Long Island, there was a General rumour amongst the people of my Neighborhood that in a Little time Congress money would be Good for Nothing, as the King was likely to overcome, and at this Time numbers of People came to pay me money who, I do believe, would not have thought of doing it, had they not been afraid the money would be Good for Nothing, on which I told them I would not receive the money.

Catherine S. Crary, *The Price of Loyalty: Tory Writings from the Revolutionary Era* (McGraw-Hill Book Company, 1973), 146–147.

The Destruction of the Royal Statue

An incident in New York City in 1776 inspired this German engraving. After a public reading of the Declaration of Independence, Patriots marched to a statue of George III standing in the city's Bowling Green and pulled it off its pedestal. The lead statue was reputedly melted down and used for ammunition. Francois Xavier Habermann — Prints and Photographs Division, Library of Congress.

LA DESTRUCTION DE LA STATUE ROYALE A NOUVELLE YORK.

Die Zerstorung der Koniglichen Bild Saule zu New Yorck | La Destruction de la Statue royale a Nouvelle Yorck

and much of the Carolina backcountry, Loyalists were numerous enough to turn the struggle between Britain and the colonies into a civil war.

Inhabitants in and around Manhattan knew that they were vulnerable to attack by the British army headquartered there. Some Hudson Valley tenants followed their Loyalist landlords; others became Loyalists when landlords they hated chose the Patriot cause. Poor white Marylanders were suspicious of the planter elite. One wheelwright asserted that "The gentlemen were intending to make us all fight [the British to protect] their land and Negroes. . . . If I had a few more white people to join me I could get all the Negroes to back us, and they would do more good in the night than the white people could do in the day." Some Virginia slaves rallied to the king because the royal governor, Lord Dunmore, promised freedom to those who would serve in the army. Many whites in the North and South Carolina backcountry supported the crown because their provinces' Patriot leaders were the same men who had opposed the Regulator movements a few years before. Because only British restraints stood between them and land-hungry Americans, many Indians, too, remained allied to the crown. Tens of thousands of Loyalists would ultimately emigrate from their homes — some back to Britain, some to British colonies in the Caribbean, and many more to Nova Scotia or New Brunswick, where they remained British colonists.

Many who sided with the revolution did so only after long hesitation. Before independence, the greatest disunity existed in Pennsylvania and New York, where political leaders were sharply divided. Pennsylvania's Joseph Galloway, a longtime political ally of Benjamin Franklin, led a sizable portion of the Philadelphia elite to oppose any effort by Congress to do more than petition the king for redress of grievances. New York's DeLancey family and the political faction associated with it quickly chose Loyalism. These men, including wealthy import merchants, decided that the gathering revolutionary movement posed more danger than British policies. Much of the rest of New York's upper class, along with men such as Pennsylvania's John Dickinson, foremost of the pamphleteers against the Townshend Duties, hesitated on the brink long after Virginians such as Washington and Jefferson and New Englanders such as John Hancock and John and Abigail Adams had made up their minds for independence. After independence, these hesitant leaders did their best to obtain a new political order that would be secure for their own class.

Gradually, popular organization pushed New York and Philadelphia in a radical direction. In 1774, as those at a New York City meeting debated how to respond to the Coercive Acts, an astute young gentleman named Gouverneur Morris looked on from a balcony. On one side of the debate were merchants and property owners, men like Morris himself. On the other side were "all the tradesmen, etc. who thought it worthwhile to leave daily labor for the good of the country. . . . The mob begin to think and to reason." He called them "poor reptiles" but "with fear and trembling" predicted that "'ere noon they will bite." Morris overdramatized, but he understood what he saw. Nine years of resistance to Britain had given working people a political identity and a voice that would not be silenced.

The Two Meanings of Radicalism   The notion of radicalism had two dimensions that often, but not necessarily, coincided. On one hand, it entailed firm opposition to British measures and a willingness to take steps that would lead, by 1776, to a complete break with British rule. On the other, some radicals went further, advocating social and political change within America itself.

Between 1774 and 1776, committees that were formed to take on governmental functions became a new forum for urban artisans. New York City's Committee of Fifty-One was at first broadly based, containing both fiery radicals and men who would soon declare their loyalty to the crown. But enforcing the Continental Association and coordinating a war effort shifted the membership, and by early 1776, the same types of patriotic men who had formed the Sons of Liberty ten years earlier dominated urban committees. Obscure farmers often controlled rural committees. Women, too, became involved in popular action, helping committee searches, enforcing boycotts, raising funds, and making clothing and supplies. A young New Yorker, Charity Clarke, claimed that America, helped by a "fighting army of amazons . . . armed with spinning wheels," would be able to "retire beyond the reach of arbitrary power." These developments unleashed a greater militancy and radicalism, bringing new figures into public life and altering the way it was conducted.

"Remember the Ladies . . ."

Some American women were fired by the possibilities of the revolution, among them Abigail Adams, wife of John Adams, a Boston lawyer who was attending the Continental Congress in Philadelphia. Abigail Adams read Thomas Paine's Common Sense *and agreed with its plea for independence. She wrote to her husband, raising the question of revising laws that affected the status of women. John Adams's response, despite its bantering tone, shows the fears of elite patriots that subordinate people of all sorts were throwing off their deference to their social "betters."*

Abigail Adams to John Adams, Braintree [Mass.], March 31, 1776

I long to hear that you have declared an independency—and by the way in the new Code of Laws, which I suppose it will be necessary for you to make, I desire you would Remember the Ladies, and be more generous and favorable to them than your ancestors. Do not put such unlimited power into the hand of the Husbands. Remember all Men would be tyrants if they could. If particular care and attention is not paid to the Ladies we are determined to foment a Rebellion, and will not hold ourselves bound by any Laws in which we have no voice, or Representation.

That your Sex are Naturally Tyrannical is a Truth so thoroughly established as to admit of no dispute, but such of you as wish to be happy willingly give up the harsh title of Master for the more tender and endearing one of Friend. Why then, not put it out of the power of the vicious and the Lawless to use us with cruelty and indignity with impunity? Men of Sense in all Ages abhor those customs which treat us only as the vassals of your Sex. Regard us then as Beings placed by providence under your protection and in imitation of the Supreme Being make use of that power only for our happiness.

John Adams to Abigail Adams, Philadelphia, April 14, 1776

As to your extraordinary Code of Laws. I cannot but laugh. We have been told that our Struggle has loosened the bands of Government everywhere. That Children and Apprentices were disobedient—that schools and Colleges were grown turbulent—that Indians slighted their Guardians and Negroes grew insolent to their Masters. But your Letter was the first Intimation that another Tribe more numerous and powerful than all the rest were grown discontented. This is rather too coarse a Compliment but you are so saucy, I won't blot it out.

Depend upon it, We know better than to repeal our Masculine systems. . . . Rather than give up this, which would completely subject Us to the Despotism of the Petticoat, I hope General Washington, and all our brave Heroes would fight.

L. H. Butterfield and Wendell D. Garrett, eds., *Adams Family Correspondence*, Vol. 1 (1963).

Pennsylvania Patriots, including rural Germans and Scots-Irish and members of the urban popular movement, pressed for more equal political representation in the province and for a reduction in the property qualifications for voting. In Virginia and the Carolinas, radical political leaders found that patriotism involved compromising with popular demands for equality. When gentry in Fairfax County, Virginia, first formed a volunteer militia in September 1774, they adopted a gentlemen's uniform of blue coats, breeches, waistcoats, and stockings. Five months later, reorganized as the Fairfax County militia and "Embodying the people," they wore hunting shirts and trousers, the working clothes of ordinary men. The royal governor of South Carolina noted, "the People . . . have Discovered their own strength and importance" and would not be "so easily governed by their former Leaders."

Philadelphia's popular movement gained special importance because of the city's size and the fact that it was the seat of the Continental Congress. As the city's elite retreated, divided and confused, radical committees secured support for the revolutionary cause, drawing on the lively political culture of the city's artisans. The revolution's most powerful pamphleteer, the English radical Thomas Paine, had arrived in Philadelphia only in 1774 but quickly immersed himself in political journalism. Early in 1776, as the Continental Congress was wavering over whether or not to pursue independence from Britain, Paine's pamphlet *Common Sense* struck a powerful blow in favor.

Common Sense embodied radicalism in both senses, arguing both for American independence and for a new form of politics and society in the former colonies. "We have it in our power," Paine wrote, "to begin the world over again." He used plain language, addressing the political concerns of Patriot elites whom he urged to sever ties to Britain, but he aimed particularly at artisans and farmers, whom he urged to join the political discussion. Britain's military attacks on colonists, he argued, made reconciliation impossible. Americans' future would be jeopardized by retaining their colonial dependence on Britain. Independence would be not only just ("a government of our own is our natural right"), but also expedient: America's prosperity would follow from having "the legislative powers in her own hands."

Above all, Paine ridiculed the idea of a monarchy and the principle of government by hereditary succession. He laid out instead a plan for an inde-

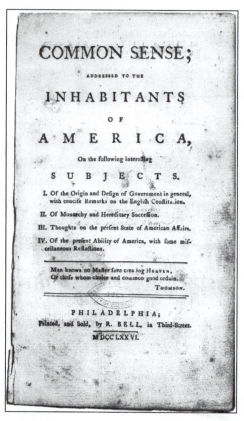

Common Sense

The cover of Thomas Paine's 1776 pamphlet. Prints and Photographs Division, Library of Congress.

pendent America under republican government, in which annually elected provincial assemblies based on "more equal . . . representation" would be overseen by an elected congress governed by a Continental Charter. Paine's pamphlet won wide acclaim; up to 150,000 copies were printed. From Georgia to New Hampshire, people read and applauded Paine's argument for independence and his vision of a great popular democracy freed from the ties of European monarchy.

Declaring Independence As the crisis deepened, the case for independence made increasing sense. Loyalists and those urging moderation found their arguments weakening as fellow colonists faced not only political oppression but also actual attack by the British army. The popularity of Paine's argument and of other calls for independence helped to move the cause forward, and the existence of the Continental Army gave Congress the political strength to contemplate such a step. In the early summer of 1776, the Continental Congress appointed Thomas Jefferson and others to draft a declaration of independence, which, after making amendments, it adopted in early July.

The Declaration's chief purpose was to explain and justify the severing of ties with Britain. It catalogued a long list of grievances against the king that amounted to "a history of repeated injuries and usurpations, all having in direct object the establishment of an absolute Tyranny over these States." If a people were suffering under oppressive rule, the Declaration proclaimed, "It is their right, it is their duty, to throw off such Government" and to set up a new political system.

By declaring independence and forming a new entity—the United States—Americans markedly raised the political and military stakes in their struggle with Britain. If it wanted to prevail, Britain would no longer have to suppress a rebellion; it would have to reconquer what had become an independent people. With independence, American radicals took the final step in redefining themselves and their protest against Britain. They no longer saw themselves as "colonists," as rebels against British authority, or as protecting their "rights and privileges [as] freeborn Englishmen." They were now free Americans defending their independent states against an overseas power.

Conclusion: What Sort of American Society?

Independence did much more than alter Americans' relationship to Britain. The Declaration of Independence proclaimed universal rights, rooted not in British precedents, but in the laws of nature. It suggested a radical vision of a new American society. It affirmed that the ultimate source of authority should lie not with kings or rulers, but with "the good People of these Colonies." Its bold statement "that all men are created equal" reflected the popular attempt to wrest self-government and self-determination from the hierarchical power of an imperial monarchy. Alongside liberty and political rights, it placed the concept of equality. Paine had written that "Whenever I use the words freedom or rights, I . . . mean a perfect equality of them. . . . The floor of Freedom is as level as water."

Yet Americans were not all agreed that equality or popular government should be the basis of their new nation. The citizen militias of New England had brought them to war and revolution, but Americans were divided as to whether New Englanders should provide a model for continuing the war or for forming new governments. When Washington arrived in Massachusetts in 1775 to take command of the Continental Army, he regarded his soldiers with the disdain a British officer could have mustered, as "generally speaking the most indifferent kind of people I ever saw . . . an exceedingly dirty and nasty people." New York Patriot generals cursed at having New England soldiers to command. "It is extremely difficult," wrote Philip Schuyler, "to introduce a proper subordination among a people where so little distinction is kept up," and Richard Montgomery complained that "New England troops are the worst stuff imaginable. There is such an equality among them."

George Washington's goal from the start was to build "a respectable army," and he gradually made conditions more like those of the British regulars his troops were fighting. The rough, often unruly democracy of the war's beginning was superseded by harsher discipline, and Washington's template for the Continental Army reflected the wishes of many members of Congress for an independent America. Once the British were finally removed, they hoped, they could build an ordered, disciplined society under the control of an American upper class. James Duane, a future mayor of New York, urged that leadership should be "in the hands of property and rank who . . . will preserve . . . authority over the minds of the people." The tension between popular and elite conceptions of the new United States would be a recurrent theme throughout the revolution and the events that were to follow.

The Years in Review

1744–1748

- New England Protestants enthusiastically support British campaigns against the French Catholic colonists in Quebec during King George's War between Britain and France.

1751

- Britain prohibits the New England colonies from making paper currencies legal tender in payment of debts; some see the ban as a dangerous intrusion on colonial affairs.

1754

- The French and Indian War begins, lasting for seven years and not settled until the Peace of Paris, 1763. Spreading to Europe in 1756, the war is known there as the Seven Years' War.

- Benjamin Franklin and others put forward the Albany Plan to create a union of colonies to conduct defense and Indian affairs; it is unsuccessful.

1763

- At the Peace of Paris, Great Britain acquires Canada from France and Florida from Spain.

- Britain issues a proclamation prohibiting settlement west of a line drawn along the ridge of the Appalachian mountains; the "Proclamation Line" is enforced by troops permanently stationed for the purpose.

- Scots-Irish frontiersmen (the Paxton Boys) raid a settlement of Christianized Indians at Conestoga and kill twenty, then march on Philadelphia to force the government to remove Indians from the land they want.

1764

- The Green Mountain Boys from New Hampshire wage sporadic guerrilla warfare against New York land speculators.

- The colonies strongly oppose the Sugar Act, passed by Parliament as a revenue-raising measure.

- The Currency Act demands that all American colonies cease printing paper money.

- A French fur trader establishes St. Louis as a Mississippi trading post.

1765

- The Stamp Act, which requires a stamp on printed materials ranging from wills and newspapers to playing cards, sparks colonial protest and political organization.

- A Boston protest against the Stamp Act results in a mob attack on Lieutenant Governor Thomas Hutchinson's house.

- Official delegations from nine colonies gather in New York City for a Stamp Act Congress, which adopts resolutions condemning the measure, calls for a boycott of British goods, and sends petitions to Parliament and an address to the king.

- Parliament passes the first Quartering Act (the second is passed in 1774), which obliges colonists to board British soldiers in their houses if required.

1766

- Parliament repeals the Stamp Act but declares its authority over the American colonies in the Declaratory Act.
- In New York's Hudson River valley, tenants led by William Prendergast revolt against landowners by withholding rent payments and claiming freehold title to the land they farmed. New York's government sends British troops against the rioters, suppresses the revolt, and sentences Prendergast to death.

1767

- The Revenue Act (Townshend Duties) places a duty on goods imported by the American colonies. In protest, activists in port cities organize nonimportation campaigns to convince merchants not to purchase goods from Britain.
- Frontier settlers in South Carolina form vigilante groups to seize control of the colony's backcountry; after two years, the colonial assembly provides for extra representatives and two new inland parishes (counties) with legal and political institutions, including courts, jails, and sheriffs.

1768

- The British government posts two regiments of troops to Boston to protect customs officials, for the first time establishing a garrison outside New York or frontier outposts.

1770

- On March 5, panicked British troops fire into a crowd of Bostonians protesting their presence in the city and kill five workingmen; the event becomes known as the Boston Massacre.

1771

- The Battle of the Alamance ends a six-year conflict in the North Carolina backcountry between disenfranchised middling and poor whites, known as Regulators, and the provincial government dominated by the coastal elite.

1772

- Boston town meeting establishes the Committee of Correspondence to build a coalition between town and country.

- Angry Rhode Islanders burn the British schooner *Gaspée.* The British government overrides the authority of the colonial courts by appointing a special commission to investigate.

1773

- The Tea Act gives the British East India Company a monopoly on tea imported to America.

- On December 16, Patriot leaders and workingmen board East India Company ships docked in Boston Harbor and dump their tea overboard to protest Massachusetts Governor Thomas Hutchinson's compliance with the Tea Act; this "Boston Tea Party" becomes an important symbol of American resistance.

1774

- In May, Parliament passes four measures designed to regain control over the colonies after the Boston Tea Party; colonists call these measures the Intolerable or Coercive Acts.

- The First Continental Congress meets in Philadelphia from September 5 to October 26 and passes the Continental Association, a measure that decrees a complete boycott of European products and calls for the creation of committees throughout the colonies to enforce it.

- Thomas Jefferson publishes the pamphlet *A Summary View of the Rights of British America,* which argues that "the British Parliament has no right to exercise authority over us."

1775

- The American War of Independence begins on April 19 at the Battles of Lexington and Concord.

- The Second Continental Congress convenes in Philadelphia in May.

1776

- Thomas Paine publishes the pamphlet *Common Sense,* which rapidly gains popularity among artisans and farmers.

- The Continental Congress declares independence from Britain on July 2. The Declaration of Independence is adopted on July 4, although most delegates do not sign it until August 2.

Additional Readings

For more on the factors that predisposed the colonies to revolution, see: T. H. Breen, *The Marketplace of Revolution: How Consumer Politics Shaped American Independence* (2004); Jon Butler, *Becoming America: The Revolution Before 1776* (2000); Jack P. Greene, *Pursuits of Happiness: The*

Social Development of Early Modern British Colonies and the Formation of American Culture (1988); Woody Holton, *Forced Founders: Indians, Debtors, Slaves, and the Making of the American Revolution in Virginia* (1999); Thomas J. Humphrey, *Land and Liberty: Hudson Valley Riots in the Age of Revolution* (2004); Cathy Matson, *Merchants and Empire: Trading in Colonial New York* (1998); Brendan McConville, *These Daring Disturbers of the Public Peace: The Struggle for Property and Power in Early New Jersey* (1999); Gary B. Nash, *The Urban Crucible: Social Change, Political Consciousness, and the Origins of the American Revolution* (1979); and Gregory H. Nobles, *Divisions Throughout the Whole: Politics and Society in Hampshire County, Massachusetts, 1740–1775* (1983).

For more on the British empire in North America, see: Fred Anderson, *A People's Army: Massachusetts Soldiers and Society in the Seven Years' War* (1984); Fred Anderson, *Crucible of War: The Seven Years' War and the Fate of Empire in British North America, 1754–1766* (2000); Francis Jennings, *Empire of Fortune: Crown, Colonies, and Tribes in the Seven Years' War* (1988); Timothy J. Shannon, *Indians and Colonists at the Crossroads of Empire: The Albany Congress of 1754* (1999); and Richard White, *The Middle Ground: Indians, Empires, and Republics in the Great Lakes Region, 1650–1815* (1991).

For more on elite and popular protest against British rule, see: Bernard Bailyn, *The Ideological Origins of the American Revolution* (1967); Richard D. Brown, *Revolutionary Politics in Massachusetts: The Boston Committee of Correspondence and the Towns, 1772–1774* (1970); Edward Countryman, *A People in Revolution: The American Revolution and Political Society in New York, 1760–1790* (1981); Philip Deloria, *Playing Indian* (1998); Dirk Hoerder, *Crowd Action in Revolutionary Massachusetts* (1977); Ronald Hoffman and Peter J. Albert, eds., *The Transforming Hand of Revolution: Reconsidering the American Revolution as a Social Movement* (1996); Rhys Isaac, *The Transformation of Virginia, 1740–1790* (1982); Pauline Maier, *From Resistance to Revolution: Colonial Radicals and the Development of American Opposition to Britain, 1765–1776* (1972); Jerrilyn Greene Marston, *King and Congress: The Transfer of Political Legitimacy, 1774–1776* (1987); Mary Beth Norton, *Liberty's Daughters: The Revolutionary Experience of American Women, 1750–1800* (1980); Ray Raphael, *A People's History of the American Revolution: How Common People Shaped the Fight for American Independence* (2001); Richard Alan Ryerson, *The Revolution Is Now Begun: The Radical Committees of Philadelphia, 1765–1776* (1978); Joseph S. Tiedemann, *Reluctant Revolutionaries: New York City and the Road to Independence, 1763–1776* (1997); Richard Walsh, *Charleston's Sons of Liberty* (1959); Alfred F. Young, ed., *The American Revolution: Explorations in the History of Ameri-*

can Radicalism (1976); and Alfred F. Young, *The Shoemaker and the Tea Party: Memory and the American Revolution* (1999).

For more on the American Revolution, see: Edward Countryman, *The American Revolution* (1985); Eric Foner, *Tom Paine and Revolutionary America* (1976); Robert Gross, *The Minutemen and Their World* (1976); Pauline Maier, *American Scripture: The Making of the Declaration of Independence* (1997); and Gordon S. Wood, *The Radicalism of the American Revolution* (1992).

5

Revolution, Constitution, and the People

1776–1815

The American Rattle Snake

The British political artist James Gillray's 1782 cartoon commented on the military situation the king's delegates faced at the start of peace negotiations with the United States. British forces commanded by Generals Burgoyne and Cornwallis are shown trapped within the snake's coils, while its rattle carries a placard stating, "An Apartment to Lett for Military Gentlemen." James Gillray, etching, London, April 12, 1782 — Prints and Photographs Division, Library of Congress.

AS WAR ERUPTED between the American colonies and Britain and the colonies declared independence, many working men and women joined the Patriot cause. Six hard years passed between the war's first shots and a decisive American victory in 1781; two more passed before Britain signed the Treaty of Paris, recognizing American independence. For the first time, overseas colonies of a European power had achieved political independence from their mother country and had gained the opportunity to set up their own form of society.

Ordinary people not only helped to achieve the military successes that secured independence, but also questioned older hierarchical assumptions and claimed for themselves a stake in political sovereignty. The Boston shoemaker George Hewes, who served as a seaman aboard Massachusetts warships, recalled an incident that illustrated his new sense of equality. One day in the street, he met an officer from the ship on which he had enlisted, who ordered Hewes to remove his hat to him. Hewes, who "refused to do [this] for any man," signed onto another vessel instead. For Hewes and for many others, the Revolution meant rejecting the deferential habits of colonial days and becoming citizens in the new republic.

Americans had to decide how to govern themselves, who would get a say in public affairs, and how they should use the vast territory over which they now claimed control. Large groups were excluded from the aspiration for equality. Economic conditions ensured that inequalities would persist. Many among the nation's elites disagreed with popular conceptions of republican society, and their views shaped the U.S. Constitution that would be drafted and ratified in the late 1780s. Yet America was changed by the

Revolution, and new social and political attitudes ensured that the colonial world would not be re-created.

The Course of the War

From the British evacuation of Boston in 1776 to their surrender at Yorktown in 1781, armies campaigned in New York, New Jersey and Pennsylvania, and the South, with numerous secondary actions on the coasts and the frontier. Although the war had started in New England, its center shifted southward as the British increased their forces in an effort to recapture the colonies. Americans were able to win a notable victory in 1777 at Saratoga, New York, when they trapped a British army marching down from Canada and captured over 5,000 soldiers. This victory removed the threat of invasion from the north and convinced the French government that American success in the war was possible. France joined the war on the American side and was soon contributing military and naval assistance. Later, Spain and then Holland also declared war on Britain, forcing it to confront three of Europe's most significant powers as well as the American revolutionaries.

Surrender of the British Army
A French print depicted the 1781 victory of American and French armies over the British in Yorktown, Virginia. As shown here, French ships blocked the entrance of Chesapeake Bay, preventing British ships from resupplying their troops on the shore. But having no knowledge of the locale, the French artist rendered Yorktown as a European walled city. Mondhare, *Reddition de l' Armée Angloises Commandée par Mylord Comte de Cornwallis*, etching with watercolor, Paris, 1781 — Chicago Historical Society.

Reddition de l'Armée Angloises Commandée par Mylord Comte de Cornwallis aux Armées Combinées des Etats unis de l'Amérique et de France aux ordres des Generaux Washington et de Rochambeau à Yorck town et Glocester dans la Virginie le 19 Octobre 1781. Il s'est trouvé dans ces deux postes 8000 hommes de troupes reglées Angloises ou Hessoises et 22 Drapeaux 1800 Matelots 119 Canons de tout Calibre dont 75 de Fonte 8 Mortiers 40 Bâtiments dont un Vaisseau de 50 Canons qui a été Brûle 20 Voiles Bas: Ce jour à jamais memorables pour les Etats unis où ce qui assura definitivement leurs independences.

A. Yorck Town   C. Armée Angloise sortant de la place   E. Armée Française   G. Armée nard de France aux Ordres du Comte de Grace   I. Rivière d'Yorck
B. Glocester   D. Les armées des ennemis passé en Vaisseaux   F. Armée Américaine   H. Baye de Chesapeack

French help would prove critical in bringing the fighting to a close. In 1781, George Washington's Continentals, together with a French army, trapped a British force in the fortress at Yorktown, Virginia. At a crucial juncture, a French fleet evaded a British naval blockade, crossed the Atlantic, and prevented British supply ships from relieving Yorktown. Faced with starvation, the 9,500 British troops surrendered, giving the Americans a decisive victory.

Waging War, North and South   Prior to Yorktown, dramatic military gains had been rare for the Americans. An attempt in late 1775 to invade Canada and capture Quebec ended in disaster. American success often depended less on winning battles than on avoiding losing them — on keeping armies intact and scoring minor victories when opportunity arose. Regrouping after their withdrawal from Boston, British forces returned in strength in the summer of 1776, capturing Long Island and then New York City, which remained their main base until 1783. Defeated on Long Island, Washington (aided by East River fishermen) escaped with the remains of his army and retreated, eventually crossing the Hudson River into New Jersey. The people of eastern New York and New Jersey included many Loyalists, and the British used the area to obtain supplies. By late 1776, they had driven Washington's army into Pennsylvania. Yet Washington's men avoided being crushed. After months of dodging defeat, they won small victories at Trenton and Princeton in the winter of 1776–1777, causing the British to withdraw from much of New Jersey. The following summer, however, the British attacked again and, brushing Washington aside, captured Philadelphia, which they held until the following year.

Yet the British found that they could not control New Jersey and Pennsylvania. Although they held New York City and they occupied Philadelphia for a period, they could not conquer the countryside, where the majority of the population lived. Warfare imposed a great burden on the people. As armies moved to and fro, families fled their homes for safer areas. One woman recalled "so much suffering . . . that it has always been painful for me to dwell upon." British depredations and the continued presence of an American army in the Mid-Atlantic states restrained the further growth of support for the Loyalist cause there and helped to keep the region on the revolutionary side.

Accordingly, in the late 1770s, the British embarked on a campaign in the South, aiming to use the support of the many Loyalists in the backcountry to help restore royal authority there. They captured Savannah and Charleston; defeated a Patriot army at Camden, South Carolina; and went some way toward restoring control over Georgia and South Carolina. But British efforts sparked a civil war between Patriots and Loyalists, whose armed militias waged a grim guerrilla-style struggle across the countryside.

YANKEE - DOODLE, or the American SATAN.

Yankee Doodle, or the American Satan

This print, by an American-born engraver living in London, may have mocked British characterizations of the Patriot enemy by portraying the "evil" archetypal American as a plainly dressed, serious-looking young man. After British soldiers started losing battles, their favorite song deriding colonists, "Yankee Doodle," was proudly appropriated by American forces. Joseph Wright, *Yankee Doodle, or the American Satan*, engraving, c. 1778 — Chicago Historical Society.

In October 1780 at King's Mountain, North Carolina, Patriot fighters won a battle in which almost all the participants on both sides were Americans. The following January, a Patriot force defeated a British detachment at Cowpens, South Carolina. Resentments ran high. More than one Loyalist militia leader, captured by Patriots, was seized by vigilantes and murdered. South Carolina's David Ramsay would remark that few people in his state "did not partake of the general distress."

Fighting Forces   The American war effort relied on two distinct kinds of military force. Each province (or, after Independence, state) raised its own militia from among its citizens, often for short enlistments. Congress raised the Continental Army for longer-term service. In all, about 200,000 men served at one time or another.

The militias comprised the majority of soldiers. At first, the kinds of men who had started the fighting in Massachusetts in 1775 filled the militia

The Home Front

A detail from an English printed handkerchief presented the contributions of three American sisters to the struggle for independence: while their husbands fought, they ran the farm — milking, baking, and, shown here, plowing. Concord Museum, Concord, Massachusetts. www.concordmuseum.org.

units. Farmers, artisans, their sons, and apprentices, with a scattering of merchants, lawyers, and clergymen, dropped their work to fight off the invaders of their countryside. Six thousand or so militiamen rallied to help defeat the British at Saratoga. But the early enthusiasm of these units waned. Militiamen became harder to recruit, and they were reluctant to serve for extended periods or far from their homes. In a rural society, particularly outside plantation regions with their slave labor, young and able-bodied men were essential for raising crops. As a North Carolinian noted, "a soldier made is a farmer lost," and without labor available for farming, the country would have starved. Farm labor was scarce, even so. A Connecticut woman recalled that "so many [men] were gone" in the fall of 1776 "that she, her aged Father in Law . . . and such little children as could be had, dug the potatoes and husked the corn."

The Continental Army and militias began to recruit from more marginal segments of society: the young and the poor. Most Continental soldiers were young men. Jeremiah Greenman of Rhode Island was seventeen when he marched to take part in the siege of Boston in 1775. Without a trade or land to inherit, he decided to enlist in the Continental service. Captured twice and wounded three times, he was an officer by the time he left the army in 1783.

Some men, like Greenman, enlisted voluntarily; some were draftees; others served as paid substitutes for richer men. Some African Americans, such as the Connecticut slave Gad Asher, who was wounded and lost his sight at Bunker Hill, fought in place of their masters. Many other slaves, in both North and South, ran away to enlist, expecting to gain their freedom by fighting. After the British surrender at Saratoga, revolutionary leaders even tried to recruit prisoners of war. Thousands of women, too, traveled with the armies. Many were "on the ration" as cooks, nurses, laundresses, orderlies, or gravediggers. Their work was essential to the war effort. They endured all the hardships of soldiers except that of battle itself. A few women, usually disguised as men, did in fact fight.

Continentals and militia often faced worse conditions than the British soldiers they were confronting as acute shortages of supplies added to the discomforts and dangers of war. During the winter of 1777–1778, when the British occupied Philadelphia and were well supplied, Washington's army endured severe privations encamped at Valley Forge only twenty miles away. At Morristown, New Jersey, two winters later, on one-eighth rations and with pay five months in arrears, the army faced even worse

"I Heard the Roar of the Artillery": Sarah Osborn Travels with the Continental Army

In 1780, Sarah Matthews Read was a servant in the household of a blacksmith in Albany, New York, when she met and married Aaron Osborn, a blacksmith and Revolutionary War veteran. Without Sarah's knowledge, Aaron reenlisted in the Continental Army and insisted that his wife travel with him. Sarah ultimately agreed to "volunteer" for the duration of the war, working as a washerwoman and cook. This account comes from a deposition she filed in 1837, at the age of eighty-one, as part of a claim under the first pension act for Revolutionary War veterans and their widows.

In about one day, we reached the place of encampment about one mile from Yorktown. I was on foot as were the other females. My attention was arrested by the appearance of a large plain between us and Yorktown and an entrenchment thrown up. I saw a number of dead Negroes lying round, whom I was told the British had driven out of the town and left to starve, or were first starved and then thrown out. I took my stand just back of the American tents, say about a mile from the town, and busied myself washing, mending, and cooking for the soldiers, in which I was assisted by the other females; some men washed their own clothing. I heard the roar of the artillery for a number of days, and the last night the Americans threw up entrenchments; it was a misty, foggy night, rather wet but not rainy. Every soldier [built] for himself, and I afterwards went into the entrenchments. My husband was there throwing up entrenchments, and I cooked and carried in beef, and bread, and coffee (in a gallon pot) to the soldiers in the entrenchment.

———————

Record Group 15, Records of the Veterans Administration, National Archives, Washington, D.C.

---

conditions. When Jeremiah Greenman's unit was finally issued clothing, he wrote that it "altered their Condition they being almost naked for nigh two Months."

Morale almost broke. A private, Joseph Plumb Martin, wrote in 1780 that soldiers cursed themselves for their "imbecility in staying there and starving . . . for an ungrateful people." At Morristown, two Connecticut regiments "paraded under arms" to demand better conditions, but Pennsylvania troops dispersed them. The next January, the Pennsylvanians themselves mutinied; 1,500 marched off toward Philadelphia to protest to Congress. Even after Yorktown, the agony continued. The Continental Army remained at Newburgh, New York, for nearly two years awaiting payment of its wages,

"We Should Suffer Every Thing for Their Benefit": Winter at Valley Forge

Albigence Waldo, a surgeon serving with the Continental Army, wrote this graphic description of conditions at the encampment at Valley Forge, Pennsylvania, in his diary entry for December 14, 1777. Winters on campaign meant particular hardships for soldiers.

December 14. Prisoners and deserters are continually coming in. The army, which has been surprisingly healthy hitherto, now begins to grow sickly from the continued fatigues they have suffered this campaign. Yet they still show a spirit of alacrity and contentment not to be expected from so young troops. I am sick—discontented—and out of humour. Poor food—hard lodging—cold weather—fatigue—nasty cloathes—nasty cookery—vomit half my time—smoked out of my senses—the Devil's in't—I can't endure it—Why are we sent here to starve and freeze?—What sweet felicities have I left at home: A charming wife—pretty children—good bed—good food—good cooking—all agreeable—all harmonious! Here all confusion—smoke and cold—hunger and filthyness—a pox on my bad luck! People who live at home in luxury and ease, quietly possessing their habitations, enjoying their wives and families in peace, have but a very faint idea of the unpleasing sensations and continual anxiety the man endures who is in a camp, and is the husband and parent of an agreeable family. These same people are willing we should suffer every thing for their benefit and advantage and yet are the first to condemn us for not doing more!!

Alden Vaughan, ed., *Eyewitness Accounts of the American Revolution*.

and soldiers disbanded with only a token settlement of what they were owed.

Throughout the war, Washington knew that his task was to keep the Continental Army together, however much suffering it faced. With the mix of poor whites, slaves, foreigners, and women who composed or supported the army, he achieved this aim. Without them, the British would have triumphed. At its largest, the Continental Army numbered fewer than 20,000. But it was more than a military force; it symbolized the new American nation, and its preservation offered a political guarantee of independence. The state militias also served a vital political role. Particularly in the former Middle Colonies and the South, where many Loyalists entered the action when British armies came nearby, Patriot militias often violently restored American authority once the British had gone again.

The endurance of American forces was sufficient to prevent Britain from reconquering its colonies despite its great military and naval strength. As other European nations joined the war against them, the British had to defend other parts of their empire and guard against a French invasion of England itself. As these pressures mounted and as serious riots in London in 1780 added the fear of domestic insurrection, the British government lost the will to fight in America. The surrender at Yorktown convinced many British officials that the war was lost and soon led to peace negotiations.

The War and Slavery "In every human Breast," wrote the African-born Boston slave Phillis Wheatley in 1774, "God has planted a principle which we call love of Freedom. It is impatient of Oppression, and pants for Deliverance." The inspiration of revolution and the confusion of war led thousands of slaves to seek freedom. To some white Americans, including Quakers and evangelicals, some southerners among them, slavery seemed a travesty of the principles for which Patriots were fighting. To most slaves, it was an abomination.

Many slaves ran away when opportunity arose. Runaways were often young men without family ties, but women also fled, some taking children with them. A considerable number of runaways headed for Philadelphia, where antislavery sentiment was becoming prominent.

Some slaves sought liberty by fighting for the British. In 1775, Lord Dunmore, Virginia's last royal governor, promised freedom to those who rallied to the king, and many—including several of George Washington's own slaves—escaped to serve in British or Loyalist units. A New Jersey slave named Titus became "Colonel Tye," leader of an irregular Black Brigade that harassed Patriots. Between 1779 and 1781, some 12,000 slaves escaped in South Carolina alone. One was a man called Boston, who ran from a plantation at Tranquil Hill to the British lines around Charleston in 1779.

Several thousand other slaves sought freedom by fighting with the American forces. Seeing "liberty poles and the people all engaged for the support of freedom," the New England slave Jehu Grant fled his master and enlisted in the Continental Army. A few states, especially Rhode Island, solved their military recruitment problems by promising freedom to slaves who would enlist. But in the South, slaveholders opposed recruiting slaves even when military necessity seemed to compel it.

Often enough, both British and Americans kept the promises of emancipation made to slaves who enlisted. When the British evacuated New York City in 1783, over 3,000 African Americans sailed with them to resettle in Nova Scotia. Boston from South Carolina was among them; he had married another runaway and renamed himself Boston King after his new sovereign. But some promises were broken. Besieged at Yorktown, the British expelled African Americans from the fort, leaving them to the mercy of the Ameri-

Wishful Thinking
A British caricature portrayed the American soldier as disheveled and maladroit, in contrast to the reputed disciplined and orderly appearance of the British military man. Metropolitan Museum of Art.

Phillis Wheatley

Born in 1754 in Africa, Wheatley was enslaved and transported to America, where she became the house servant of a Boston tailor. At the age of fourteen, she began to write poetry, and in 1773 she published a collection of her work in England. A year later, she was freed. *Memoir and Poems of Phillis Wheatley, A Native African and a Slave* (Boston 1835) — Chicago Historical Society.

cans camped outside. Recaptured slaves faced violent punishment and the risk of being sold away. George Washington and other planters negotiated the return of their escaped slaves from the British who had harbored them.

Native Americans and War on the Frontier The war was not confined to contests over settled regions. Colonists' desire for frontier land had been one of the underlying sources of antagonism to British policy. Britain's purpose in establishing the unpopular Proclamation Line of 1763 had been to moderate trans-Appalachian settlement and settler-native conflict (see Chapter 4). When war broke out in 1775, fighting rapidly began in the West, as

"A Natural and Inalienable Right to . . . Freedom": Slaves Petition the Massachusetts Legislature

This petition to the Massachusetts legislature was drafted by Prince Hall, a free African American who fought at the Battle of Bunker Hill, on behalf of the state's enslaved people. Throughout the revolutionary era, scores of slaves signed petitions that linked their demands for freedom with the cause of American independence.

To the honorable Counsel and House of Representatives for the State of Massachusetts in General Court Assembled, January 13, 1777:

The petition of a great number of blacks detained in a state of slavery in the bowels of a free and Christian country humbly show that your petitioners [state] that they have in common with all other men a natural and inalienable right to that freedom which the Great Parent of the heavens has bestowed equally on all mankind and which they have never forfeited by any compact or agreement whatever. They were unjustly dragged by the hand of cruel power from their dearest friends and some of them even torn from the embraces of their tender parents—from a populous, pleasant, and plentiful country, and in violation of laws of nature and of nations, and in defiance of all the tender feelings of humanity brought here to be sold like beasts of burden and like them condemned to slavery for life. . . .

Every principle from which America has acted in the course of their unhappy difficulties with Great Britain pleads stronger than a thousand arguments in favor of your petitioners, and they, therefore, humbly request that your honors give this petition its due weight and consideration and cause an act of the Legislature to be passed whereby they may be restored to the enjoyments of that which is the natural right of all men—and their children who were born in this land of liberty—not to be held as slaves.

Collections of the Massachusetts Historical Society, 5th Series, III (Boston, 1877), 436–37.

Patriots sought to dislodge British frontier garrisons and seize land to which they had been denied access. Armed settlers and militia pushed into fresh territory, and both British and American combatants did what they had done in previous wars: they sought supporting alliances with Indians.

Indians, too, pursued familiar strategies, though under new circumstances. With the removal of the French in the early 1760s, the Iroquois had negotiated with the British to protect their lands from colonial incursions, and in the Revolutionary War, most continued to support Britain as the most likely protector against invasion. A few other tribes chose instead to ally with the revolutionaries in the hope that this could spare them from the worst depredations of white settlers. Still others sought to remain neutral, but the toll of conflict and murder drove them to resistance.

"A Determined Resolution to Get Liberty . . .": Slaves Respond to Lord Dunmore

After Virginia's royal governor, Lord Dunmore, promised freedom to slaves who would escape and serve in the British forces, newspapers printed numerous advertisements for runaways whose owners suspected them of responding to Dunmore's proclamation.

Stafford County, Aquia, Nov 3, 1775.

Run off last night from the subscriber, a negro man named CHARLES, who is a very shrewd sensible fellow, and can both read and write; and as he has always waited upon me, he must be well known through most parts of Virginia and Maryland. He is very black, has a large nose, and is about 5 feet 8 or 10 inches high. He took a variety of clothes, which I cannot well particularise, stole several of my shirts, a pair of new saddle bags, and two mares, one a darkish, the other a light bay, with a blaze and white feet, and about 3 years old. From many circumstances, there is reason to believe he intends an attempt to get to lord Dunmore; and as I have reason to believe his design of going off was long premeditated, and that he has gone off with some accomplice, I am apprehensive he may prove daring and resolute, if endeavoured to be taken. His elopement was from no cause of complaint, or dread of a whipping (for he has always been remarkably indulged, indeed too much so) but from a determined resolution to get liberty, as he conceived, by flying to lord Dunmore. I will give 5l. to any person who secures him, and the mares, so that I get them again.

Robert Brent.

Virginia Gazette (Dixon and Hunter), February 3, 1776.

Patriots attacked Indian settlements along the frontier, scattering inhabitants, destroying crops, and spreading disease. William Henry Drayton urged South Carolinians to "cut up every Indian cornfield and burn every Indian town and every Indian taken shall be the slave and property of the taker." Natives retaliated. In Kentucky, Cherokee warriors resisted an illegal land purchase by attacking settlers until white counterattacks dispersed them and destroyed their villages. Southern Patriot militias attacked Cherokees and Creeks to prevent them from assisting the British. After enduring for three centuries, the Iroquois Confederacy broke apart. Many followed the Mohawk leader Thayendanegea (Joseph Brant) in supporting the British, but a smaller number allied with the Americans, so at the battle of Oriskany in 1777, there were Iroquois fighters on both sides. Britain's Iroquois allies faced repeated attacks. In 1779, Patriot troops under General John Sullivan burned forty Iroquois settlements in western New York, destroying crops and driving the population away. Starvation and disease ravaged the refugees.

The Bucks of America

This flag was carried by Boston's black militia unit, one of three African American companies that served in the Continental Army. Massachusetts Historical Society.

But Patriots attacked even Indian allies whom they wanted to clear from the land. After occupying Kentucky, American forces pressed on into the Ohio country. In 1781, they raided their Delaware and Shawnee allies near Coshocton on the Muskingum River, and the next year, they attacked

"We Are for Peace": The Oneida Indians Declare Neutrality

Just as colonists had to choose sides between the Patriot cause and loyalty to Britain, so too did Indian groups as military conflict became imminent. In this 1776 address to Connecticut Governor Jonathan Trumbull, the Oneida declare their neutrality and urge New England officials not to seek alliances with other Indian groups. The Oneida later allied with the American colonists against the British.

BROTHERS—We have heard of the unhappy differences and great contention between you and Old England. We wonder greatly, and are troubled in our minds.

BROTHERS—Possess your minds in peace respecting us Indians. We cannot intermeddle in this dispute between two brothers. The quarrel seems to be unnatural. You are two brothers of one blood. We are unwilling to join on either side in such a contest, for we bear an equal affection to both you Old and New England. Should the great King of England apply to us for aid, we shall deny him; if the colonies apply, we shall refuse. The present situation of you two brothers is new and strange to us. We Indians cannot find, nor recollect in the traditions of our ancestors, the like case, or a similar instance.

BROTHERS—For these reasons possess your minds in peace, and take no umbrage that we Indians refuse joining in the contest. We are for peace.

BROTHERS—As we have declared for peace, we desire you will not apply to our Indian brethren in New-England for their assistance. Let us Indians be all of one mind, and live with one another; and you white people settle your own disputes between yourselves.

Three Rivers, http://www.threerivershms.com/borderwarsch3.htm.

Thayendanegea

Guy Johnson, who succeeded his father-in-law Sir William Johnson as British superintendent of Indian affairs, was the ostensible subject of Benjamin West's painting, but it was the shadowy figure of Thayendanegea, or Joseph Brant, that characterized the picture. This Mohawk chief, educated at New Hampshire's Indian School (later Dartmouth College), saw the war as an opportunity to gain Indian independence; he sided with the British in exchange for specific concessions. After a brief visit to Great Britain in 1775–1776 (where this picture was painted), Thayendanegea returned to the colonies. Throughout the war, he led Iroquois raids on New York frontier settlements. Benjamin West, *Colonel Guy Johnson*, 1776, oil on canvas, 79 3/4 × 54 1/2 inches — National Gallery of Art, Washington, D.C.

a settlement of Moravian converts at Gnadenhütten, killing 96 and sending many survivors fleeing to Canada. Such attacks prompted natives to form alliances of their own against American incursions as the war drew to a close. The Shawnees and others launched counterattacks and laid the ground for further resistance in subsequent decades.

Building a Republic

Even as fighting flared across eastern North America, Americans were forging a republican ideology of revolution. They were trying not just to free themselves from British rule, but also to build a new political order.

Affirming that "all men" were "created equal" and had "unalienable rights" to "life, liberty and the pursuit of happiness," the Declaration of

Independence suggested that proper government rested on universal truths that were apparent not just to an educated political elite, but to the common sense of all. This was not merely an abstract statement of principle; it was an instrument designed to forge unity across the revolutionary political coalition of farmers, artisans, laborers, slaveholders, merchants, and professional men. It indicated that common folk as well as the wealthy and powerful could claim a role in their own government. Conflict between elite and popular influences had been evident during the protests of the 1760s and in the period from 1774 to 1776, when the Patriot cause was in the hands of extralegal committees (see Chapter 4). These divisions persisted as the new states moved to establish their own permanent governments and constitutions. Debates about price regulation and markets, state finances and taxation, were charged by the inflation, indebtedness, and serious economic hardships many people faced. In Massachusetts these difficulties would provoke armed rebellion in 1786. The formation of new governments both opened and closed democratic possibilities. For many white men political participation offered hopeful prospects, but women and slaves gained little from the revolution's rhetoric of liberty and equality.

The Movement for a People's Government   Most supporters of the revolution agreed that new American governments should be republican, resting not on the sovereign authority of a monarch but on "the consent of the governed." But Americans differed over how democratic their republics should be and how broadly or directly ordinary people should participate in political affairs.

In Philadelphia's radical atmosphere early in 1776, Thomas Paine's pamphlet *Common Sense* sketched a vision of democratic government for the new nation. Confident that people could govern themselves without the artificial distinctions of monarchy or aristocracy, Paine advocated a simple direct democracy. Each state, and the nation as a whole, would be governed by an annually elected assembly and headed by a president. Paine's popularity among the artisans and farmers whom the revolution had aroused ensured that his pamphlet would remain a symbol of this popular democracy. When Jeremiah Greenman's Rhode Island regiment celebrated the Fourth of July in 1783, its thirteen toasts included "the Congress of 1776 and Common Sense." Paine's was the clearest argument that, as another pamphleteer put it, "the people" would make "the best governors."

The men who came to power in Pennsylvania in 1776 fashioned a state constitution that drew on Paine's ideas. They created a state legislature with a single chamber, elected annually by all taxpaying adult males, with no property requirements for officeholders. They lodged executive power not in a "governor"—connoting arbitrary, royal power—but in a president and council who served the legislature. Except on "occasions of special neces-

The Rights of Man: or Tommy Paine, the Little American Taylor, Taking the Measure of the Crown, for a New Pair of Revolution Breeches.

British conservatives had little love for the author of *Common Sense* — especially after he returned to England in 1787 and pressed for radical republican goals in the land of his birth. Caricaturist James Gillray lampooned Paine in this 1791 cartoon, which appeared soon after the publication of Paine's *The Rights of Man*. But the British establishment took Paine more seriously; within the year, he fled to revolutionary France to avoid imprisonment. James Gillray, engraving, 1791, 13 13/16 × 9 3/4 inches — American Philosophical Society Library.

sity," bills that came before the legislature would be "printed for the consideration of the people" before becoming law. Paine helped to inspire Patriots who were radical both in their support for independence and in their desire to form a democratic, egalitarian political system. From 1776 to 1790, Pennsylvanians governed themselves on these principles, designed to keep government under the close scrutiny of the people.

Elsewhere, too, people felt exhilarated by the notion of abandoning old ways. The Green Mountain Boys spearheaded their own local revolution, declaring independence from New York in 1777 and establishing Vermont as a separate republic. Their constitution, inspired by Pennsylvania's, set up a direct democracy that continued to operate after Vermont joined the United States in 1791. Georgia also established a single-chamber legislature, while Delaware, New Hampshire, and South Carolina adopted the democratic

"Common Sense and a Plain Understanding": Drafting Pennsylvania's Constitution

Radical patriot leader James Cannon addressed the following broadside to the members of the Philadelphia militia, setting forth the qualities— including "common Sense and a plain Understanding"—that he thought delegates to Pennsylvania's convention to frame a state constitution should possess.

A government made for the common Good should be framed by Men who can have no Interest besides the common Interest of Mankind. It is the Happiness of America that there is no Rank above that of Freeman existing in it; and much of our future welfare and Tranquillity will depend on its remaining so forever; for this Reason, great and overgrown rich Men will be improper to be trusted, they will be too apt to be framing Distinctions in Society, because they will reap the Benefits of all such Distinctions. . . . Honesty, common Sense, and a plain Understanding, when unbiased by sinister Motives, are fully equal to the Task—Men of like Passions and Interests with ourselves are most likely to frame us a good Constitution. . . . Some who have been very backward in declaring you a free People, will be very forward in offering themselves to frame your Constitution; but trust them not, however well recommended.

Eric Foner, *Tom Paine and Revolutionary America* (1976).

title "president" for their chief executives. Farmers and tradesmen replaced some wealthy men in the legislatures (Figure 5.1). Before 1775, only one-sixth of New Hampshire, New Jersey, and New York assemblymen were of modest means; by the 1780s, over three-fifths of them were. Even the Virginia legislature was, according to an observer, "composed of men not quite so well dressed, nor so politely educated, nor so highly born as . . . formerly."

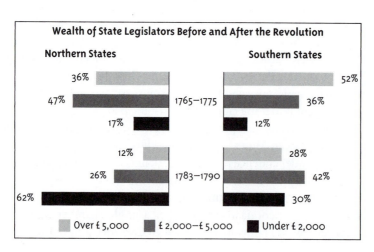

Wealth of State Legislators Before and After the Revolution

Northern States — Southern States

1765–1775
- 36% / 52%
- 47% / 36%
- 17% / 12%

1783–1790
- 12% / 28%
- 26% / 42%
- 62% / 30%

Over £5,000   £2,000–£5,000   Under £2,000

FIGURE 5.1 Legislatures Become More Democratic, 1765–1790

State legislatures after the Revolution were considerably less dominated by men of wealth than the colonial assemblies had been in the decade before war with Britain began. In the North, the rise in the proportion of legislators with less than 2,000 pounds' worth of property was particularly striking. From James A. Henretta et al., *America's History*, 2nd ed., vol. 1 (New York: Worth Publishers, 1993); adapted from Jackson Turner Main, "Government by the People: The American Revolution and the Democratization of the Legislatures," *William and Mary Quarterly*, 3rd ser., vol. 23 (1966).

The Limits to Democratization   But there were limits to this democratic thrust. Some Americans feared the possibilities of democracy. John Adams of Massachusetts was as keen as Paine for independence, but his vision of government was more conservative. Published in 1776 as a counter to Paine's *Common Sense*, Adams's *Thoughts on Government* argued that it was impossible to govern without "balanced" institutions that gave elites a voice alongside that of the people. Legislatures should have two chambers, not one, so that the elite members of the upper house could counter the influence of the citizenry represented in the lower. The issue was social as much as political. Who should rule: the "better sort," who had long held sway, or the artisans, farmers, and small traders for whom Paine had spoken? Adams was a republican, but he envisaged a republican society based on hierarchy and order.

Virginia, Maryland, New York, and Massachusetts formed governments that were closer to Adams's conception than to Paine's. The Virginia gentry adopted a constitution that preserved their political control. Maryland's planter class, frightened by the revolution's democratic implications, fashioned a constitution that put as much distance as possible between ordinary people and their rulers. It prescribed stiff property requirements for voting, stiffer ones for holding office, and long intervals between elections. The New York constitution created a state senate that was intended to represent property, not people, and a strong governor who was independent of the legislature, not its servant. Massachusetts followed suit.

The Articles of Confederation   During the war and its aftermath, the states remained substantially independent of one another. Each sent representatives to the Continental Congress, which oversaw the war's conduct and constructed a rudimentary government for the new United States. In 1777, Congress put forward a framework for a national government: the Articles of Confederation. Many states accepted this quickly, but others were skeptical of signing away powers to a distant government. There was disagreement on whether western lands should be assigned to the federal government. Only reluctantly did some states with land claims across the Appalachian Mountains begin to give them up. As a result, it was 1781 before the Articles went into effect.

The Articles preserved the sovereignty of the states and held a tight rein on federal government. The states' annually elected delegations to Congress varied in size, but each state had only a single vote. Congress could create executive departments, but these remained under its direct control. To become law, its decisions required the support of a majority of states, but amendments to the Articles had to be unanimous. Above all, Congress had no independent power to levy taxes. For its expenditures—including financing the war—it had to rely on requisitions from the states, which might or might not provide them. To many Americans, these provisions gave assurance that no federal government could exercise a tyranny of the sort that they had feared from Britain and that power would lie with the states and their people. To some, however, the Articles of Confederation seemed weak and ineffectual, and advocates of stronger national government soon challenged them.

Regulated Prices or Free Markets?   In addition to debating how democratic government should be, the revolutionary coalition was also divided over economic problems. Wartime inflation, shortages, property damage, loss of life, and the disruption of farming, trade, and manufacturing created severe difficulties. The war's end brought depression and glut, as goods that people could not afford went unsold. Production declined sharply. It would be a quarter of a century before America's output per head of population regained its pre-Revolutionary level. Circumstances trapped many of the poor and middling in conditions that they could do little to influence.

Congress and most state governments had financed their war contributions by printing ever-larger quantities of paper money. The result was the worst inflation America had ever known. Many people turned to traditional concepts of social responsibility and justice, arguing that in a good society, public interest should come before private gain. If supplies were scarce, they suspected "hoarders" of holding them back for profit. If prices rose, they blamed "speculators." Crowds, often made up of women, used the rituals of

"We Cannot Live Without Bread": Revolutionary Food Shortages

In December 1778, a Philadelphia resident, styling himself "Mobility," wrote the following letter to a local newspaper, attacking monopolizers and calling, in no uncertain terms, for strong measures by crowds to guarantee the distribution of bread, "the Staff of Life."

This country has been reduced to the brink of ruin by the infamous practices of Monopolizers and Forestallers. Not satisfied with monopolizing European and West-Indian goods, they have lately monopolized the Staff of Life. Hence, the universal cry of the scarcity and high price of Flour. It has been found in Britain and France, that the People have always done themselves justice when the scarcity of bread has arisen from the avarice of forestallers. They have broken open magazines [warehouses] — appropriated stores to their own use without paying for them — and in some instances have hung up the culprits who have created their distress, without judge or jury. Hear this and tremble, ye enemies to the freedom and happiness of your country. We can live without sugar, molasses, and rum — but we cannot live without bread. Hunger will break through stone walls, and the resentment excited by it may end in your destruction.

Eric Foner, *Tom Paine and Revolutionary America* (1976).

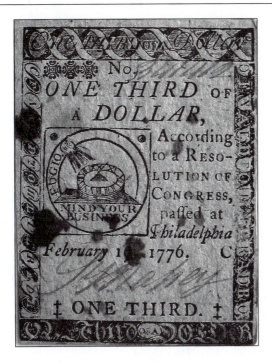

Not Worth a Continental

Taxation to finance the war effort was a limited option for the Continental Congress. Instead, it authorized the printing of paper money in 1775; state governments did so as well. These notes were known as "Continentals" and would be redeemable when the colonies achieved independence. As more money was printed, amounting to $450,000,000 between the state and continental governments, its purchasing power plummeted for consumers. In January 1777, $105 in Continentals equaled $100 in gold and silver; by April 1780, it took $4,000 worth of Continentals to equal the same amount of gold and silver. Faced with this hyperinflation, farmers balked at selling their produce to the army, and women seized overpriced goods from merchants. One-third dollar, 1776 — Smithsonian Institution.

popular price setting to fight wartime inflation. In Fishkill, New York, in August 1776, a group of women formed a committee to confront a prominent merchant who was refusing to sell from his stock of tea. Appointing a "clerk" and a "weigher," the women measured out the tea, announced that they would pay "the continental price" for it, and then gave the money to the local county committee. By the late 1770s, inflation was so severe that people revived their revolutionary committees. When the price of bread rose in Philadelphia during the winter of 1778–1779, an advocate of crowd action to regulate prices warned merchants and bakers that "Hunger will break through stone walls, and the resentment excited by it may end in your destruction."

Not everyone favored price regulation by committee. In 1776, the Scottish political economist Adam Smith had published *The Wealth of Nations*, his famous argument in favor of free markets. By 1779, American critics of regulation, including Thomas Paine himself, suggested that free markets could be liberating and need not lead to the rich trampling the poor. The city's tanners attacked the committee revival and declared that trade ought to be "as free as air, uninterrupted as the tide." At the height of the crisis in Philadelphia, a militia armed by merchants faced down crowds seeking price controls and broke the power of their movement. Knowing that to get what they wanted, they would need to be organized as a political force, Philadelphia merchants and artisans began to gather into a "Republican society" to oppose the state's radical constitution and promote free trade.

At first, advocates of free markets accomplished little, because many states followed policies dictated by popular wishes: issuing paper currency, making it legal tender for the payment of taxes and private debts, and giving debtors relief from lawsuits by their creditors. New York also confiscated the estates of Loyalists and redistributed them. Even Maryland's elite, which virtually monopolized political office, recognized "the wisdom of sacrifice" and gave in to popular demands.

Shays's Rebellion   In Massachusetts, however, the advocates of hard currency, free trade, and balanced political institutions held sway, with disastrous results for farmers in the interior who faced heavy debts. It took the state until 1780 to adopt its constitution, and commercial men then dominated the government. They ensured that Massachusetts adopted strict policies on money and debt. Paper currency was not acknowledged as legal tender, and debtors received no protection from their creditors, regardless of whether these were Patriots, Loyalists, or British.

When the former colonies made peace with Britain in 1783, American ports reopened to British commerce, unleashing a burst of consumption as people with money craved goods that had been unavailable during the war. But this boom soon reversed, into a trading slump that lasted for three years. British creditors called in debts from American merchants, who in turn demanded payment from cash-poor rural traders and customers. In most states, the law would have given debtors some protection, but not in Massachusetts. There, farmers, artisans, and small traders were expected to pay both their debts and their taxes in cash, which they did not have. They believed that the public good was being sacrificed to privilege. As the people of Dracut, Massachusetts, protested, "Money . . . seems to have . . . hid itself in the secret confines of those who have a greater love to their own Interest than they have to that of their Neighbours." As in the past, the fear that they would lose their property and be reduced to the status of tenants or hired laborers haunted them. When creditors brought lawsuits and defendants began to crowd the courts and debtors' prisons, popular fears became real.

People again took traditional steps to relieve their burden, producing an uprising in interior Massachusetts in 1786 that became known as Shays's Rebellion, after one of its leaders, Daniel Shays, a former captain in the Continental Army. Having formed committees and conventions to oppose the government's policies, farmers gathered under arms to close the courts and prevent lawsuits being heard. In concert with Boston radicals such as Samuel Adams, they had done the same in 1774 in response to the Coercive Acts. Now they found themselves pitted against some of these same radicals, including Adams, who controlled the state government in alliance with conservative merchants. Adams defended the law and the courts as agents of a constitution adopted by the people and as necessary to preserve commerce.

To disperse the rebels and restore the courts, the Boston government sent General Benjamin Lincoln and a well-organized militia force to the west. When Shays and his armed farmers mounted an ill-coordinated assault on the federal armory at Springfield, the local militia scattered them. Lincoln's army then chased the rebels into the hills and captured many in a surprise attack. Shays and others fled into exile in neighboring states. Four rebel leaders were captured, tried, and condemned to death for treason. The government mounted a theatrical display of judicial terror. At the trial, Chief Justice William Cushing berated the rebels for trying "to overturn all government and order, to shake off all restraints, human and divine." Just as they were about to be hanged, the governor reprieved them in a public show of mercy. These methods worked as intended. Individuals and whole towns begged forgiveness for rebelling. "'Tis true that I have been a committee-man," wrote one, but "I am sincerely sorry . . . and hope it will be overlooked and pardoned."

This defeat at the hands of men who had been their revolutionary allies taught Shaysites and their sympathizers a lesson about the politics of the new republic. The old notion that small communities could defend themselves against outsiders no longer applied when the government itself was theoretically of the people. To overturn policies that they resented, people with common interests would have to organize themselves and formally enter the political arena. Almost immediately, Massachusetts farmers did just that. In the 1787 state elections, they unseated the hard-money governor James Bowdoin and replaced him with the popular John Hancock. New men, many from western towns that for years had not bothered to send

Shays's Rebellion

The portraits of Daniel Shays and Job Shattuck, leaders of the Massachusetts Regulators, appeared on the cover of *Bickerstaff's Boston Almanack* in 1787. *Bickerstaff's Boston Almanack of 1787* (c. 1787) — National Portrait Gallery, Smithsonian Institution.

delegates, flooded into the legislature. Symbolically, at least, the elite made concessions to ordinary peoples' demands. Never again would the state's government allow debtors to be hounded with the ruthlessness that had been evident in the mid-1780s.

The Limits and Possibilities of the Revolution   The revolution raised more questions about equality and human rights than it answered. Prominent among these was the issue of slavery. White colonists had proudly borne the status of "freeborn Englishmen" that distinguished them from slaves, and the Patriots' chief grievance against Britain was that the crown seemed bent on reducing them to political slavery. To many of them, there was no contradiction between the Patriot cause and ownership of slaves; having other human beings as property was simply a fact of life. But British and Loyalist commentators were quick to condemn American revolutionaries who complained of enslavement but were complicit in slavery itself. For some slave owners, including Washington and Jefferson, slavery was a problem they agonized over but could not resolve. When Jefferson included in an early draft of the Declaration of Independence a clause condemning the king for conducting the slave trade, other members of Congress struck it out as an embarrassing hypocrisy.

Nevertheless, the Revolution did alter American slavery. In the North, an increasing number of people opposed slavery on principle. The Vermont constitution outlawed it. One New Yorker condemned slavery as "cruelty in the extreme" and "the severest reproach" to the new nation. Notables such as Alexander Hamilton manumitted (released) slaves they had acquired and helped to found organizations such as the New York Manumission Society to promote the abandonment of slavery. In Massachusetts, several slaves brought lawsuits, and the case of Quok Walker struck a heavy blow against slavery. Walker had declared his own freedom in 1781 and then sued his master for wages and for damages for the assault and imprisonment he had endured when the man recaptured and beat him. Chief Justice Cushing, the judge who would later condemn the Shays rebels, ruled in 1783 that Walker's enslavement violated the declaration of Massachusetts's new constitution that "all men are born free and equal." This effectively abolished slavery in the state. New Hampshire soon followed suit.

However, abolition was embraced only where economic circumstances permitted. Although declining, slavery did remain important in other northern states and was dismantled only slowly. Starting with Pennsylvania in 1780 and ending with New Jersey in 1804, these states passed abolition laws that bound the children of existing slaves to labor until they were adults. In the resulting "gradual" abolition, New Jersey's last slave was not freed until 1846, and Pennsylvania's was not freed not until 1847. After the

Revolution, the number of slaves throughout the North fell from the 50,000 who had lived there in 1775; but in 1810, there were still 27,000 northern slaves working in craft occupations, as laborers, or as domestic servants (Map 5.1).

In the Upper South, a shift from tobacco to grain cultivation reduced the demand for plantation slave labor, and the number of manumissions rose. In Virginia, about 10,000 slaves obtained freedom in the decade after 1782. Some owners freed their slaves on principle because slavery violated "the inalienable rights of mankind" or was "contrary to the command of

MAP 5.1 Slavery after the American Revolution: Emancipation and Expansion

This map illustrates the emerging contrasts between northern and southern states. Whereas the South continued to permit slavery and carried the system into new territories in the Southwest, northern states took steps to ban slavery or gradually phase it out. *Source:* Arwin D. Smallwood, *Atlas of African-American History and Politics* (1998).

FRONTISPIECE.

Published at Philad.ᵃ Dec.ʳ 1.ˢᵗ 1792.

Opportunities and Limitations
In the frontispiece from a 1792 Philadelphia publication (left), *The Lady's Magazine and Repository of Entertaining Knowledge*, Columbia was presented with a petition for the "Rights of Woman." In contrast, an engraving published sometime after 1785 (right) offered the homily that "a virtuous woman is a Crown to her Husband" and prescribed the limits beyond which no respectable woman's aspirations should go. *The Lady's Magazine and Repository of Entertaining Knowledge* (December 1, 1792) — Library Company of Philadelphia. *Keep Within Compass*, c. 1785–1805, sepia engraving, 9 5/16 × 7 1/8 inches — Henry Francis duPont Winterthur Museum.

Christ." But many slaves had to purchase their freedom with their own earnings or those of relatives. Graham Bell of Petersburg, Virginia, obtained his liberty in 1792 and then spent the next thirteen years working to buy the freedom of another nine slaves. Before independence, free blacks were rare in Virginia, but by 1820, their numbers exceeded 200,000. Where plantation agriculture remained strong, however, freedom was hardest to achieve. In the Lower South, only 4 percent of African Americans were free by 1810, compared with 10 percent in the Upper South.

For women, too, the rhetoric of revolution seemed to raise new possibilities for freedom. A Rhode Island woman declared that "The Women of

this State are Animated with the Liveliest Sentiments of Liberty." Women had been heavily involved in the war effort; had run farms, shops, and businesses when men went to fight or were killed; and had undertaken extra manufacturing work that helped America to achieve a degree of economic autonomy. In protest movements and food riots, women carried forward the campaigns for price regulation that dominated wartime politics. For perhaps the first time, women had formed public organizations, to raise funds for soldiers and similar purposes. "America will not wear chains," wrote Abigail Adams, "while her daughters are virtuous."

Revolutionary ideals led some women to question the subordination that their mothers and grandmothers had taken for granted. Elite women discussed politics and called for improved education. In parts of the North, the proportion of women who could read and write rose toward the high level already attained by men. A small number of women used more liberal divorce statutes to free themselves from oppressive marriages. In 1788, Abigail Strong of Connecticut noted in her divorce petition that if "even Kings may forfeit . . . the allegiance of their subjects," husbands could not command unconditional control over their wives.

In practice, however, the Revolution little altered women's social position. Many people regarded women's proper role in the new republic as raising and educating good republican citizens. Abigail Adams could urge her husband and his colleagues to "remember the ladies" in their political deliberations (see p. 201), but men were not prepared to overturn institutions that served their interests. "We know better," John Adams replied to his wife, "than to repeal our masculine systems." In only one state, New Jersey, did any women achieve political rights. Free, propertied women could vote in local elections there in the 1780s, and a 1790 state election law referred to voters as "he or she." These rights would soon be abolished, however.

Nevertheless, although the actual opportunities available to them were often restricted, the Revolution encouraged many people—men and women; rich, middling, and poor; black and white—to think it possible to take greater control of their circumstances. Merchants and some farmers gained greater access to commercial markets. The confiscation of Loyalists' property and the opening of vast new western territories gave more farmers access to land. This vision of taking control further undermined older colonial concepts of deference. In 1788, an elderly New Hampshire congressman complained that now "young and old all mix together, & talk & joke alike so that you cannot discover any distinction made or any respect shewn to one more than to another." Some Americans saw the possibility of taking control of their societies, even at the risk of conflict with those whose interests differed from their own.

Creating a National Government

Members of the elite saw too much democracy as dangerous. In 1787, only months after the suppression of Shays's Rebellion, a group of delegates drawn from the elites of the thirteen states met in a special convention at Philadelphia. Its ostensible purpose was to revise the Articles of Confederation, but it quickly resolved to scrap them altogether and to draw up a new framework for government. After vigorous argument and numerous compromises over such issues as the balance of federal and state power and the nature of representation, the result was the U.S. Constitution, which sought to put a conservative curb on America's political development. The decision to ratify this framework for a new, stronger national government was hotly debated, and in several states ratification was contingent on the addition of amendments that would specify the rights guaranteed to citizens. After special conventions in nine states had ratified it, this Constitution went into effect in 1788, and the remaining four states joined the union within two years. The adoption of the Constitution marked the completion of the political revolution and took a step away from the Revolution's most radical possibilities.

The Constitution's Framers Most members of the Philadelphia convention were merchants, lawyers, landholders, or southern planters. They included Robert Morris of Philadelphia, the "financier" of the Revolution, whose land speculations would soon make him America's richest man; New York's Alexander Hamilton, who had risen from obscurity to be George Washington's aide-de-camp, marry into the New York landed elite, and wield influence as a lawyer, essayist, and politician; and James Madison of Virginia, who had already written a private essay on "The Vices of the Political System of the United States," which outlined many of the changes that the Constitution would make. George Washington himself chaired the convention.

The Looking Glass for 1787
New Haven engraver Amos Doolittle's 1787 print commented on the political situation preceding the Constitutional Convention. While a wagon labeled "Connecticut" sinks in a mud pit, nationalists (left) and localists (right) are too divided to cooperate in its rescue. Prints and Photographs Division, Library of Congress.

Delegates had been at the Revolution's center, as army officers, traders and suppliers, members of Congress, or ambassadors. They had experienced the difficulties of organizing the war, been repeatedly embarrassed by America's inability to deal straightforwardly with foreign nations, and watched states ignore provisions in the peace treaty, such as its promise to end the harassment of Loyalists. They had protested in vain when states passed laws that they saw as heedless of the interests of creditors and damaging to the international reputation of American traders and had been horrified at the threat posed by Shays's Rebellion in the one state that had refused to pass such laws.

The radical democratic possibilities of the Revolution subverted what these men considered to be good government. They were republicans, believing that government must rest on the people's consent, but had little faith that ordinary people could run society well. Most held that government should be conducted by "the best men"—those fitted by birth, education, and sober political principle to govern wisely. Since 1782, Hamilton and others who called themselves "nationalists" had been arguing for a strong central government run by men "whose principles are not of the leveling sort." In New York, Hamilton had forged an alliance of landlords and merchants to end the political dominance of a coalition of farmers and artisans.

The Constitution's Compromises   The Constitution that emerged from the Philadelphia convention strengthened national government and the position of propertied elites. However, it also reflected compromises between conflicting elite interests and between the elite views of government and the popular demands for participation that the revolutionary process had generated.

The convention was seeking a new understanding of republicanism, because in eighteenth-century thinking, the American effort to establish republics seemed unpromising. The examples of classical Greece and Rome suggested that republics could succeed only in special circumstances: when they were small in size and population, were bound by a single economic interest, and were populated by virtuous people who would put the common good above private interests. Most republics had, in fact, collapsed or turned into tyrannies. Now Americans were establishing republican governments in large, varied societies that seemed the very opposite of ideal for the purpose. The rebellion in Massachusetts seemed to confirm to the men who met in Philadelphia that republicanism in America might prove another failure.

But some of them took a new point of departure, which James Madison expressed in the tenth and fifty-first of the *Federalist* papers that he, Hamilton, and the New Yorker John Jay published in 1788, during the campaign to ratify the Constitution. Instead of a small republic, Madison saw the potential of a large one; instead of a single, virtuous public interest, he envisaged the jostling and competing of many private interests. If the arena were large enough, he argued, no single interest would become so powerful as to oppress the others. "Extend the sphere," he wrote, "and you take in a greater variety of parties and interests; you make it less probable that a majority . . . will have a common motive to invade the rights of other citizens." This breakthrough in political thought guided the Philadelphia convention to its first solution to the American situation: create a large republic that would dwarf any previous attempt to live without a monarch.

The second solution was to establish a stronger government than had existed under the Articles of Confederation. The Confederation had succeeded in winning the war and negotiating a favorable peace, but it could not pay its debts, enforce the terms of the peace treaty, or resolve disputes between states. Lacking the power to tax, an executive to do its will, or courts to enforce laws and treaties, federal government relied entirely on the will of the states.

Although many Americans regarded these circumstances as acceptable, even essential, in a republic, the delegates at Philadelphia saw them as weaknesses and designed the new Constitution to rectify them. They erected a set of balances and compromises that would enable a new federal government to be built on top of the existing social and political institutions in the various states. One compromise was to leave the states themselves intact. Hamilton and Madison would have gladly reduced states to simple administrative units, but the system of "dual federalism" that emerged made both federal and state governments the legal creatures of the people, who were the real sovereign power. Resolving what Madison regarded as the greatest difficulty, that of representation, the convention adopted the proposal that Congress's single chamber be replaced by two houses: a Senate, in which all states would be equally represented, and a House of Representatives, in which representation would be based proportionally on population.

But vexing questions remained concerning the relationships between the central government, the separate states, and American society as a whole. These issues arose in several forms at the convention; it resolved, for instance, that entitlement to vote in federal elections would be governed by the laws of individual states rather than by nationwide rules. Nothing was more difficult than the differences that emerged between northern and southern states over slavery. Though some southerners, including Washington, had qualms about slavery, most planters did not question its legitimacy or the concept of human property. Still, the fact that slaves were both people and chattels presented unavoidable problems.

Should slaves be counted as part of the southern states' populations for the purpose of deciding the size of delegations to the House of Representatives? Southern delegates, including Madison, wanted to have it both ways. Slaves would not, of course, be entitled to vote, but counting them into the population would significantly increase southern political influence. Northerners saw through this ploy. Gouverneur Morris of Pennsylvania pointed out that slavery was just one special interest and that if it won representation, other special interests should as well. Other delegates agreed. The outcome was a compromise, the first of many between North and South. Slaves would be counted for political representation — but not fully; by the "three-fifths clause," five enslaved persons would count as three free persons.

Other compromises followed. While the convention was sitting, the Continental Congress passed the Northwest Ordinance, containing a clause that banned slavery from the western territories north of the Ohio River. But the Constitution embodied two further concessions to southerners: a clause that Congress could not consider a ban on the international slave trade before 1808 and a clause that obliged states to return fugitive slaves to their owners. Although it did not use the word *slavery*, the Constitution gave slavery legal standing at a time when many Americans were questioning its legitimacy.

As the Constitution bowed to the requirements of southern planters, it also suited the needs of northern commerce. It created a vast common market, regarding uniform laws and the needs of long-distance trade as more important than local custom or the needs of particular communities. States would be restricted from erecting trade barriers against each others' goods. In addition to certain powers to tax, Congress would be able to regulate interstate and foreign commerce, establish a uniform bankruptcy law, mint coins, regulate money, "fix the standard of Weights and Measures," register patents and copyrights, and create a postal service. Each state would be obliged to give "full faith and credit" to court decisions made in other states. States were forbidden to "emit Bills of Credit, make anything but Gold or Silver Coin a Tender in Payment of Debts" or "pass any . . . Law impairing the obligation of Contracts." The framers of the Constitution would not allow the problems of the mid-1780s, when many states protected insolvent debtors against their creditors, to recur.

The Fight for Ratification   The Constitution was written by elites to address their own interests, but it also proved to have popular appeal, largely because it was grounded in the sovereignty of the people. Popular support for the Constitution was essential. It would go into effect only when elected conventions in nine states ratified it, so the election of enough delegates who favored it was necessary for its success. There was powerful opposition. Two states refused to ratify the Constitution, and in four others, the contest was extremely close. State politicians who feared loss of influence joined many popular radicals, who distrusted the schemes of those who had met in Philadelphia, in an effort to prevent ratification. As the Constitution's advocates started to call themselves "Federalists," their opponents became known as Anti-Federalists.

The New York Anti-Federalist leader Melancton Smith feared that the Constitution would create a government of "the few and the great" and exclude "those of the middling class of life" whom the revolution had brought into politics. Farmers in the interior, notably from areas with a history of rural unrest, voiced the strongest opposition. In some states, only clever political maneuvering overrode their influence. Pennsylvania leaders called that state's ratification convention at short notice, preventing the backcountry from organizing its opposition. In the New York convention, Anti-Federalists won a massive majority, but strong support from New York City Federalists and their threat that the city would secede and ratify the Constitution on its own persuaded the rest of the state to consent (Map 5.2).

Citizens in the major towns overwhelmingly supported the Constitution. Working people, especially artisans, saw in strong national government their best chance for regular employment and markets for their products. They had little hand in drafting the Constitution, but in Pennsylvania and Massachusetts as well as in New York, they played a key role in getting it ratified.

In Massachusetts, the fight over ratification was critical, for failure to ratify there might defeat the Constitution altogether. When the ratifying convention met in January 1788, the state was still deeply divided after Shays's Rebellion. Delegates from the Massachusetts interior, aware that the

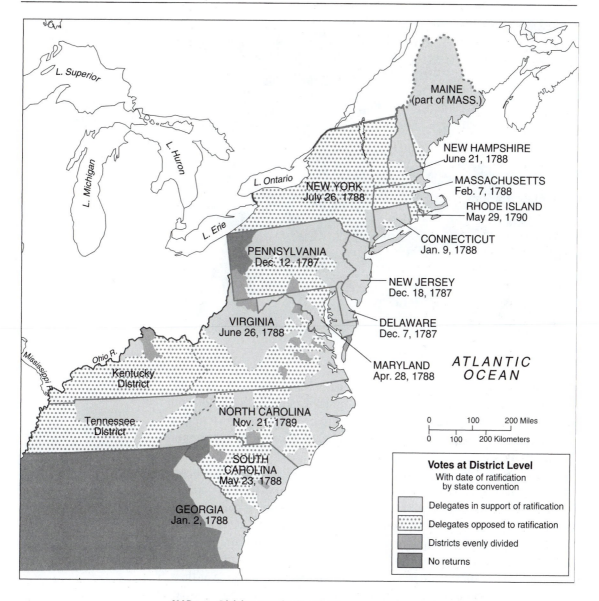

MAP 5.2 Division over the Constitution

In several of the most important states, there was sharp division between the supporters and opponents of ratifying the U.S. Constitution. This map, which plots votes in state ratifying conventions, reflects the broad support for the Constitution in seaboard regions and strong opposition in the backcountry. Note, for example, the small areas of support in Massachusetts and New York and the split between the coast and the interior in South Carolina — a legacy of the Regulator movement of the 1760s.

Solid and Pure

This flag was carried by master, journeymen, and apprentice pewterers in the July 1788 parade in New York City celebrating ratification of the Constitution. Many artisan groups constructed floats and carried banners in this parade, with slogans and mottos that revealed their reasons for supporting a stronger federal government. New-York Historical Society.

Constitution would threaten the power of community solidarity on which their rebellion had been based, strongly opposed ratification. But Boston artisans wanted the Constitution. Paul Revere presided over a meeting of 400 of them who gathered to persuade the other delegates to vote in favor of ratification, and the convention did so.

In what a newspaper called "an exhibition to which America has never witnessed an equal," Boston artisans celebrated the news with a parade in which forty different groups of tradesmen marched. Similar parades were held in other states as they too voted to ratify. The biggest, in Philadelphia on July 4, 1788, included eighty-six units in its line of march and reflected the coalition of elites and working men that had achieved ratification in Pennsylvania. Elaborate floats carried men and women working at their trades and symbols of what artisans thought the Revolution had achieved. One depicted the "New Roof" or "Grand Federal Edifice" that the Constitution would erect over the states and was followed by members of the city's construction trades. Another, the Federal Ship Union, with a crew of twenty-five, was followed by pilots, boatbuilders, sailmakers, ship carpenters, ropemakers, merchants, and traders. Beneath the motto "By Hammer and Hand All Arts Do Stand," blacksmiths beat swords into sickles and plowshares, symbolically demonstrating that the skills of peace had superseded those of war.

"They Will Swallow Up All Us Little Folks": The Massachusetts Ratifying Convention

In the debates at the convention held in Massachusetts in 1788 to consider how the state should vote on constitutional ratification, Amos Singletary, a farmer from the interior who claimed never to have had a day of schooling in his life, expressed his fears. They were shared by many rural Americans who opposed the ratification of the Constitution, contending that the new federal government would be controlled by "aristocrats" and wealthy men.

Hon. Mr. Singletary: Mr. President, I should not have troubled the Convention again, if some gentlemen had not called on them that were on the stage in the beginning of our troubles, in the year 1775. I was one of them. I have had the honor to be a member of the court all the time, Mr. President, and I say that, if any body had proposed such a Constitution as this in that day, it would have been thrown away at once. It would not have been looked at. We contended with Great Britain, some said for a threepenny duty on tea; but it was not that; it was because they claimed a right to tax us and bind us in all cases whatever. And does not this Constitution do the same? Does it not take away all we have—all our property? Does it not lay all taxes, duties, imposts [import fees], and excises? And what more have we to give? They tell us Congress won't lay dry taxes upon us, but collect all the money they want by impost. . . . They won't be able to raise money enough by impost, and then they will lay it on the land, and take all we have got. These lawyers, and men of learning, and moneyed men, that talk so finely, and gloss over matters so smoothly, to make us poor illiterate people swallow down the pill, expect to get into Congress themselves; they expect to be the managers of this Constitution, and get all the power and all the money into their own hands, and then they will swallow up all us little folks, like the great Leviathan, Mr. President; yes, just as the whale swallowed up Jonah.

Massachusetts Gazette, January 25, 1788.

Securing a Bill of Rights   Although urban and elite support ratified the Constitution, the margin of victory was narrow. At the Philadelphia convention, George Mason of Virginia had called for a Bill of Rights as a check against the creation of an excessively powerful federal government, but most of the framers had thought it unnecessary, and delegates from every state voted against him. In state ratifying conventions, however, Anti-Federalists exerted strong pressure for a Bill of Rights, and ratification in five states (including Massachusetts, New York, and Virginia) occurred on the understanding that a Bill of Rights would quickly follow. Federalist leaders acceded to popular demand. Under Madison's leadership, Congress drafted constitutional amendments suggested by the state conventions. Ten of these, known as the Bill of Rights, were finally ratified and appended to the Constitution late in 1791.

The Bill of Rights addressed issues that had been raised in the 1760s resistance to Britain and in the experience of revolution. The first amendment guaranteed freedom of speech, the press, religion, and assembly. Other amendments guaranteed the right to petition government for redress of grievances, to trial by jury, and to the "due process of law" and protected citizens from unwarranted searches and seizures or "cruel or unusual" punishments. To establish local militias and so avoid the need for a standing army, the Second Amendment guaranteed the right to bear arms. These were weak versions of the protections that Anti-Federalists wanted against strong government. In practice, the Bill of Rights played little part in American politics for decades to come. It did not settle the perpetual issue of the relationship between federal and state governments. Its provisions, moreover, concerned property as well as people. Indeed, the new constitutional arrangements fulfilled a double-edged purpose. They protected individuals, but they also protected privileges—such as the ownership of slaves—that accompanied wealth.

American Society: Competing Visions

The adoption of the Constitution and the Bill of Rights did not end the debates about who should rule and who should benefit from the new social and political order. The tension between elite presumptions and popular pressure that had marked the revolutionary struggle continued to shape the politics of the early American republic.

To northern merchants and traders, the Constitution was a necessary underpinning for commercial wealth and their own class advantage. For southern planters, it became a bulwark for the perpetuation of slavery. For urban artisans, the powers of the new federal government could encourage their crafts to flourish. Even small farmers, initially opposed to the Constitution, soon learned that the federal system made possible a society in which people could organize around their own common interests.

The first federal administration, with George Washington as president, took office in 1789, assuming that consensus over the Constitution could achieve political unity. Washington had been chosen by acclamation, and despite Madison's theoretical endorsement of competition between conflicting interests, most Americans still believed that republican government was best secured by political harmony that factional or party divisions would undermine. But congressmen, like most state legislators, were elected by the people, and senators were appointed by state legislatures. It was inevitable that such choices would come to be contested.

Political Tumult in the Early Republic   The 1790s saw increasing factional strife. Washington's administration was divided between men such as Jefferson and Madison, who were suspicious of strong central power, and those such as Hamilton, who favored it. Differences over commercial policy and foreign affairs became focused on France and on the French Revolution that had begun in 1789 and moved in an increasingly radical direction until 1794. Hamilton and commercial elites, who continued to identify themselves as Federalists, rejected France's radical democracy and instead advocated trading agreements with Britain. Jefferson, with support among planters, small farmers, and urban workingmen, stood at the center of a political opposition to the Federalists that had started to organize in "Democratic-Republican" clubs and advocated alliance with France against Britain. Among the Jeffersonians' supporters were many who, as Anti-Federalists, had once opposed the ratification of the Constitution in the first place.

Although the emerging political parties each drew supporters from across society, Federalists argued for rule by the "best men" and Democratic-Republicans for a more popular democracy. This division produced great drama and paranoia after war broke out between Britain and France in 1793. The United States declared its neutrality in the war, and its merchants and ship owners profited greatly by trading with both sides. But America's relative military and naval weakness made it vulnerable to pressure, or even the risk of attack, by one of the European powers. To Federalists in government, the presence of a political opposition seemed a threat to the republic's continued existence.

Divisions over foreign policy accompanied domestic conflict. The parties divided particularly over financial policy. As secretary of the treasury, Hamilton produced plans to resolve the financial problems that remained from the Revolution and tie the nation's wealthy elites more tightly to the new political system. The federal government would assume the debts of the states and would pay its debts at the full face value of the paper notes that had been issued to pay for war supplies or soldiers' wages. The policy would mean levying federal taxes and import duties. However, Hamilton's plan was not to pay off the debts. By retaining a national debt, he would encourage those with means to invest in federal bonds and notes on which interest would be paid. The Federalist administration also organized a Bank of the United States to handle the government's transactions and so help to influence the financial system.

Jeffersonians scorned the "large monied interest" that this funding scheme and the Bank of the United States would create, condemning Hamilton's measures as socially unjust and an excessive extension of federal power. Thousands of Revolutionary soldiers who had been paid in paper money or land certificates had been forced by necessity to sell them at heavily discounted prices, often to wealthy speculators. Under Hamilton's plan, the government would pay the speculators the full value of the paper, using the tax revenues collected from ordinary Americans.

Disputes over taxation also provoked protest in rural regions. A federal liquor tax provoked riots by armed farmers in western Pennsylvania who had not forgotten their opposition to ratifying the Constitution. Protesters attacked revenue officers, and a crowd of 7,000 people set fire to the then-new town of Pittsburgh. In 1794, Washington dispatched an army of 15,000 men under Hamilton's command to hunt down these "Whiskey Rebels," but they had dispersed and could not be found. Another small uprising in Pennsylvania in 1798, provoked by a direct federal tax on houses and other property, added to a sense of panic in the administration of John Adams, who had served as vice president under Washington and was elected president in 1796. Federalists so feared opposition that when a naval war broke out with France in that year, they used their majority in Congress to pass the Alien and Sedition Acts, severely curtailing free political expression. Critics of the government were prosecuted for seditious speech or writings, but their trials mainly exposed the Federalists themselves to ridicule. The republican congressman Matthew Lyon of Vermont, imprisoned for accusing the administration of incompetence, got the satisfaction of being reelected while he was in jail. The Federalists' attempts at repression hastened the turning of the political tide against them and led to a sound defeat in the 1800 elections that secured Jefferson the presidency.

GENERAL GEORGE WASHINGTON.
Reviewing the Western army at Fort Cumberland the 18th of October 1794

Washington Suppresses a Rebellion

Faced with a primitive transportation system, western Pennsylvania farmers distilled whiskey from grain as the best means to get their produce to eastern markets. In 1794, after a new federal liquor tax disrupted their livelihood, the farmers rebelled. In this painting, President Washington is shown at Fort Cumberland, Maryland, reviewing the vanguard of the 15,000 troops he dispatched to suppress the Whiskey Rebellion. Frederick Kemmelmeyer, *General Washington, Reviewing the Western Army at Fort Cumberland the 18th of October, 1794*, c. 1794, oil on paper backed with linen, 18 1/8 × 23 1/8 inches — Henry Francis duPont Winterthur Museum.

A Republic of Citizens   The election of 1800 marked another step in the erosion of social deference that had begun in the 1760s during the protests against British rule. Jefferson saw his election as a victory in the battle between "the advocates of republican and those of kingly government." Colonists had been subjects of a monarch who sat at the apex of a social hierarchy. Because of the Revolution, working people could see themselves as equal participants in a social order in which they were sovereign. Americans were increasingly reluctant to view the wealthy or well-born as their social betters or as entitled to power or influence. No man, declared a Massachusetts farmer, deserves "any degree or spark of . . . a right of dominion, government, and jurisdiction over [an]other."

Participating in Fourth of July celebrations every year, farmers, artisans, and other workingmen could mark both their identities as members of a trade and their positions as equal citizens of the republic. In New York, Patriotic contingents paraded behind the banner of the General Society of Mechanics and Tradesmen. Like similar groups in Boston, Albany, Providence, Portsmouth, Charleston, and Savannah, New York's General Society was composed mainly of master craftsmen but sought to promote the common interest of all artisans and to foster "a general harmony . . . throughout the whole manufacturing interest of the country." Masters claimed responsibility for the journeymen and apprentices in their workshops, who, they assumed, could in time become masters themselves. Artisans and others claimed equal rights with the elites who dominated politics. Fourth of July speakers emphasized civic equality. As a Pennsylvanian put it, "no man has greater claim of special privilege for his hundred thousand dollars than I have for my five dollars."

Opportunity for Some, Exclusion for Others   Even so, republican theory did not accord full citizenship and access to politics to everyone. It reserved them for those who were deemed personally "independent," capable of acting without reliance on others, and whose "disinterestedness" could guarantee the republic against corrupt manipulation. Most states restricted the right to vote to white men with property or taxable income, so the great majority of people — some 80 percent in the 1780s — were excluded from public life. Most poor laboring men could not vote, because lack of property or status as servants disqualified them. Most women and people of color were excluded because of their gender, race, or status as wives or slaves. All were said to be "dependents," unable to exercise their own judgment. For these groups, the revolutionary era raised possibilities of freedom that were only inadequately fulfilled.

Democratic-Republicans' attacks on Federalist privilege did continue the Revolution's democratizing tendencies into the nineteenth century. The Jefferson administration abolished federal direct taxes and opened up access to western land. After 1800, many states abolished property qualifications for voting, opening the franchise to all adult white men; by 1830, all but three had done so. Participation in elections soared. But including all white men in politics still meant excluding others. The law of 1807 that abolished New Jersey's property qualification also abolished the limited voting rights of the state's women.

For many African Americans, the Revolution produced only limited or temporary hope of liberty. The Constitution represented a major blow to slaves' and many free blacks' hopes of freedom. It did nothing to interfere with state rules that disenfranchised most free blacks on grounds of color or poverty. The three-fifths clause, the guarantee of property rights, and the

"Certain Information of a Conspiracy": Charleston Slave Owners Fear Revolution

News of the revolution in Saint-Domingue was an inspiration for American slaves but a source of severe anxiety for their owners. The arrival of refugees from Saint-Domingue—black, white, and mulatto—in American port cities, including Charleston, increased slave owners' fear that the black revolution would spread to the United States. Slave owners cracked down, nervously interpreting every transgression as an uprising in the making. This article appeared in the Charleston State Gazette *in 1797; it was reprinted in the* Philadelphia Gazette.

On Tuesday, the 14th inst. the Intendant received certain information of a Conspiracy of several French negroes to fire the city, and to act here as they had formerly done at S. Domingo—as the discovery did not implicate more than ten or fifteen persons, and as the information first given was not so complete as to charge all the ringleaders, the Intendant delayed taking any measures for their apprehension until the plan should be more matured, and their guilt more closely ascertained; but the plot having been communicated to persons, on whose secrecy the city magistrates could not depend, they found themselves obliged on Saturday last to apprehend a number of negroes, and among others the following, charged (together with another not yet taken) as the ring-leaders, viz.—Figaro, the property of Mr. Robinett; Jean Louis, the property of Mr. Langstaff; Figaro the younger, the property of Mr. Delaire; and Capelle. . . .

On examination they all at first positively denied their knowledge or concern in the plot; but the younger Figaro, after some time, made a partial confession, and was admitted in evidence on the part of the state. The others were on Monday brought to trial, in the City Hall, before as respectable a court and jury as we ever remember to have been convened. A number of witnesses were examined, and fully proved the guilt of the prisoners; and the court, on mature consideration, unanimously condemned Figaro, Sen. and Jean Louis, to be hung, and Capelle and Figaro the younger to be transported. The rest who were apprehended are under confinement, for further examination.

After the condemnation of Jean Louis, he turned to the two Figaros and said, "I do not blame the whites, though I suffer, they have done right, but it is you who have brought me to this trouble."

Figaro and Jean Louis were yesterday executed in pursuance of their sentence.

The Pennsylvania Gazette, December 13, 1797.

fugitive-slave law lent renewed legitimacy to slavery. The protections of the Bill of Rights offered nothing to slaves, who were not regarded as citizens in the first place. Although the Revolution enabled some to emancipate themselves, it also paved the way for economic developments that would enslave many more.

Toussaint L'Ouverture

This portrait of the leader of the Saint-Domingue revolution was published in a contemporary British history book. Marcus Rainsford, *An Historical Account of the Black Empire of Hayti* (1805) — New-York Historical Society.

Nevertheless, the revolutionary period provided ideological markers for African Americans and their supporters as they struggled for emancipation. The possibility of revolution, itself a new ingredient, was especially charged by events in Saint-Domingue (now Haiti) in 1791, when slaves rebelled, toppled the French colonial government, seized power, and defended their new republic against repeated efforts to destroy it. The insurrection in Saint-Domingue struck fear into the hearts of slaveholders across the New World and may have emboldened some American slaves to attempt rebellion. In 1800, a slave and blacksmith named Gabriel organized an insurrection in an attempt to seize the city. Gabriel and his followers, who were reported to number nearly one thousand, were apparently prepared to kill all whites in their path except those few who were deemed friendly: Quakers, Methodists, and Frenchmen. The insurrectionists planned to march under a banner proclaiming "Death or Liberty," a slogan that fellow Virginian, and slave owner, Patrick Henry would surely have recognized. Two African Americans, however, revealed the plot to white authorities. The Virginia militia put down the revolt before it began, and Gabriel was executed, along with thirty-five others. At his trial, Gabriel was alleged to have declared that "we have as good a right to be free from your oppression, as you had to be free from the tyranny of the King of England."

A renewed evangelical movement that would become known as the Second Great Awakening emphasized the equal brotherhood of believers. Yet this was tempered by growing white racism. Churches that, in the late colonial period, had included white and black members, began in the 1790s to erect racial barriers. Black Methodists in Philadelphia, for example, withdrew from a church they had just helped to rebuild in 1792 when the elders insisted that they occupy segregated seating. Such episodes reinforced the efforts of African Americans, both slave and free, to organize institutions of their own. In northern towns, freedpeople built families and neighborhoods, created their own styles of dress and deportment, founded their own churches and schools, and formed voluntary associations such as the African Union Society of Newport, Rhode Island, and the Free African Society of Philadelphia.

Even for whites who had the benefits of citizenship, the Revolution's legacy was mixed. Inequalities of wealth widened during the Revolution, and even the economic revival of the 1790s distributed the benefits of prosperity unevenly. Of Philadelphia's journeymen shoemakers, only about half were able to set up as masters with shops of their own during the decade; among tailors, the proportion was just one in ten. A young woman, Polly Nugent, had been a servant of the city's wealthy Drinker family before she married a blacksmith. By 1796, her husband was facing hard times, and Polly had to turn to her old employers for financial assistance. Revolution may have unleashed opportunity for many, but it also meant disappointment for others.

Post-Revolutionary America in the World

Yet creating an independent United States out of a disparate group of British colonies and erecting a federal system of republican governments based on popular sovereignty were in themselves massive changes. The Revolution also altered the balance of power on the North American continent, profoundly affecting the peoples in the territory to the west of the United States and in the Americas in general. An independent United States had, furthermore, to negotiate its standing as a trading nation and diplomatic entity among the European powers, which continued their struggles with one another and their efforts to exercise influence over the new American republic. American governments turned their attention both to the west— where the Louisiana Purchase of 1803 nearly doubled the territory under U.S. control, and where ever greater tracts of land were wrested from Native Americans, often in the face of sharp resistance—and to the Atlantic and international trade. Wars in Europe and tensions over maritime policies would eventually provoke a further conflict with Britain in the War of 1812.

Crisis in the Spanish Empire   The Revolutionary War and creation of the United States brought more sweeping and permanent change to North America than any previous war had done. American independence curbed British power on the continent but did not extinguish it. Now, however, a people with material interest in the remainder of America were rooted in the continent itself, so U.S. influence over the continent would be stronger than that of any previous power.

Spanish lands still girdled North America's southern and western margins after 1763, from Louisiana to Texas and New Mexico, and Florida would return to Spanish control twenty years later. Political reforms in Spain produced new efforts to regulate its New World colonies; one consequence was the decision in 1768 to occupy present-day California, partly to counter Russian activity on the Pacific coast.

Spanish California, formed by the building of missions as well as military and civil institutions, developed characteristics similar to those of earlier conquests. California's natives, who lived mainly in small, decentralized

Lith. de Langlumé r de l'Abbaye N.4.   *Lith par V.Adam d'après Choris*

Vue du Presidio s^n Francisco.

The Presidio of San Francisco

In 1776, the Spanish government used Indian labor to build a *presidio*, or military post, on a high cliff overlooking the mouth of San Francisco Bay to defend its colony from Russian and other foreign rivals. When artist Louis Choris visited California in 1816 as part of a Russian military expedition, he depicted Spanish soldiers leading captured Indians for forced agricultural labor toward the Presidio. Victor Adam (after Louis Choris), Vue de Presidio Sn. Francisco, *Voyage pittoresque autour du monde* (1822): 71, hand-colored acquatint — I. N. Phelps Stokes Collection, Miriam and Ira D. Wallach Division of Art, Prints and Photographs, New York Public Library, Astor, Lenox and Tilden Foundations.

groups that were unused to war, were in a poor position to resist Spanish encroachments. But the invaders' efforts to extract labor, punishments for infractions, and the rape of Indian women sparked retaliation. In 1775, local Ipais attacked and burned the mission at San Diego, killing its priest. Other rebellions followed. Even the Spanish governor declared the condition of Indians at the missions to be "worse than that of slaves." Like previous peoples subject to invasion, California's Indians fell victim to European diseases. The coastal region's population of about 60,000 in 1769 had been reduced to 35,000 by 1800. Meanwhile, there had been no great rush of Hispanic settlers to California, with fewer than 1,000 in 1790 and about 1,800 ten years later.

The uneasy balance between Hispanic and Indian societies in New Mexico, established after the conflicts of the seventeenth century, continued. Florida settlements remained small and interfered little with native groups in the interior. Altogether, Spanish society in North America's borderlands remained marginal to the larger interests of Spain and its empire. This was evident after 1800, when it became known that Spain had secretly traded back to France the territory of Louisiana and its vast land holdings in the Mississippi valley. Control of the great river could have made Louisiana the nucleus of a North American commercial empire; instead, Spain found the region an encumbrance.

The United States soon benefited from Spain's decision to relinquish Louisiana. France was now in no position to exploit the territory. The revolution in Saint-Domingue had shaken France's hold on the Caribbean, and disease had ravaged a large army sent to reconquer the island. The French ruler Napoleon, fighting wars in Europe and the Middle East, no longer had use for Louisiana, and in 1803, he sold the whole territory to the American government for fifteen million dollars. With the Louisiana Purchase, the United States in a single stroke acquired a claim to land from the Mississippi River to the Rocky Mountains, roughly doubling its land area (Map 5.3).

External events and internal rebellions soon crippled Spain's American empire. Many factors fed aspirations for Latin American political independence: long-standing tensions between colonial-born *criollos* and Spanish-born *peninsulares*, administrative reforms, tax revolts, warfare, and the example of a successful rebellion in North America. In 1808, Napoleon sent French armies to conquer Spain itself. As the empire's center tottered, uprisings erupted from Mexico to Argentina, setting off protracted revolutionary

MAP 5.3   The United States After 1803

The Louisiana Purchase of 1803 doubled U.S. land territory and helped to confirm that the new nation's orientation in the nineteenth century would be westward, across the continent. Within a few years, revolutions across the Spanish empire would weaken Spain's grip on the American South and West.

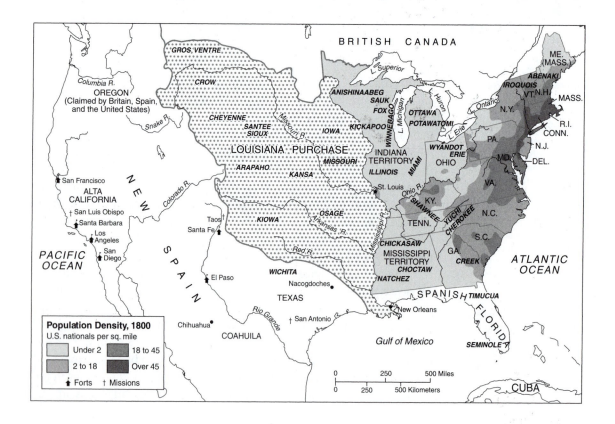

struggles between nationalists and royalists. In consequence, most of mainland Spanish America seized independence from Spain in the years around 1820, forming a chain of new postcolonial republics.

North Americans welcomed this advance of republicanism against monarchy. But their intentions were not wholly benign. In 1819, after American settlers and fighters had entered Florida, the United States took advantage of the chaos in the Spanish empire to annex it. When Mexico gained its independence in 1821, assuming control of Spanish territories in California, Texas, and the Southwest, some Americans saw this as another opportunity to gain more land for themselves. Struggles over Mexico's North American territories would dominate American politics in the 1830s and 1840s.

Westward Expansion and Indian Resistance   Meanwhile, between the Appalachians and the Mississippi, the American Revolution had begun to make Indians strangers in their own land. Native Americans were largely missing from the new constitutional provisions, state or federal, in the United States. Unlike most indigenous peoples in Central and South America, who were regarded as subjects of Spain and then citizens of newly independent republics, native North Americans were excluded from U.S. citizenship, and their tribes were treated as separate foreign nations.

The 1783 peace with Britain opened up access to lands across the Appalachians that settlers had been seeking for decades. The American government quickly assumed control of land distribution in the West. Congressional negotiations with states that claimed western land under their original colonial charters led to these claims being surrendered to federal control. In 1785 and 1787, land ordinances laid the basis for the creation of new states and the surveying of land for settlement. Providing for newly settled regions to be admitted to the United States on an equal basis with existing states, the ordinances encouraged white settlement and underlined the exclusion of Indians from the new arrangements. The Louisiana Purchase brought yet more territory in line for similar treatment.

The Northwest Ordinance of 1787 stated that Indians' land should not be taken without consent, but treaties and legal procedures frequently veiled fraud, extortion, and theft. Implicit, too, was a notion that would frame more than a century of western expansion: although individuals and groups of pioneers carried out the settlement process, federal and state governments assisted it.

Wartime destruction, population growth, contempt for Indians and their ways of life, and European concepts of absolute property ownership all meant that Indians were the immediate losers in post-Revolutionary

America. The alliances and understandings of previous decades collapsed under pressure from a white invasion of the West. Indians were either divided and demoralized by this new onslaught or driven to attempt a concerted resistance.

The Iroquois's location and their wartime alliance with the British both contributed to the fragmentation of their society. War and white settlement shattered their confederation and its strategy for resisting European incursion. Some Mohawks, led by Joseph Brant, moved to Canada. Other Iroquois retreated westward to preserve their way of life. Those who remained, largely in upstate New York, exchanged most of their land for guaranteed settlements in reservations. This averted their removal but did not prevent social collapse. At the end of the 1790s, however, among Seneca Iroquois settled in new reservations, there arose a spiritual revival led by a former warrior, Sganyadai:yo, or Handsome Lake, to whom visions had appeared calling for a strict moral reform of Seneca society. Preaching the rejection of white notions of individualism, Handsome Lake sought to restore Iroquois society's communal traditions and persuaded many Indians to give up whiskey, gambling, and other evils associated with whites. Yet he also encouraged accommodation to "American" customs, welcoming Christian missionaries and seeking the transformation of Iroquois hunters into farmers and female farmers into housewives. He was particularly critical of women who rejected demands to give up their traditional power and authority.

Indians farther west resisted white settlers more vigorously. American migrants in southern Ohio encountered resistance from the Algonquian-speaking Shawnees, who forged a confederacy of tribes to block American settlement and turn back U.S. military efforts to dislodge them. In 1791, members of nine tribes killed, wounded, or captured 900 soldiers out of an American force of 1,500 sent against them. But at length, the Shawnees were outnumbered. In 1794, 3,000 U.S. soldiers defeated them at the Battle of Fallen Timbers, and by treaty the next year, the Shawnees ceded most of their land east of the Mississippi. What was left was soon invaded by whites, and the Shawnees were driven close to starvation. Officials solemnly advised the Shawnees to take up agriculture instead of hunting and to sell more land for cash.

From Ohio westward, the federal government wrested land cessions from tribes, often with the help of pliant "government chiefs" whose conduct drove young warriors into rebellion. Among the Shawnees, social disintegration, growing dependence on trade with whites, and mounting frustration drove many to alcohol. Again demoralization sparked a spiritual awakening, which, spreading from the Shawnees to other northwestern

Medals for Peace and War
Like the British, the new Americans bestowed medals on cooperating Indian leaders. Made by Philadelphia silversmith Joseph Richardson, Jr., this medal was decorated with images that heralded peaceful relations between the new nation's leaders and Native Americans. President George Washington holds out his hand in peace while an Indian leader extends a peace pipe and casts off a tomahawk. But the medal also sent a warning: Washington was shown in his military uniform, a reminder to Indians of American military power, and in the background, America's vision of the future was indicated by a "civilized" Indian farmer plowing a field. Joseph Richardson, Jr., Peace Medal, 1793 — American Numismatic Society, ANS 1915.138.4.

tribes between 1805 and 1808, galvanized them to resist once more. Inspired by a prophet known as Tenskwatawa, or the Open Door, who promised to show his people the entrance to a paradise where spirits could follow the life they were once used to, the movement demanded self-discipline, the renunciation of liquor, and avoidance of goods or techniques acquired from whites. In 1808, Tenskwatawa declared an intention to disconnect Indian and white societies entirely and to forge the unity among tribes that could defend Indians' separation.

Leadership shifted from Tenskwatawa toward his warrior brother Tecumseh. To stop the whites' invasion of their lands, Tecumseh announced, "all the red men [should] unite in claiming a common and equal right in the land . . . ; for it never was divided, but belongs to all, for the use of each." But the northwestern Indians' success turned out to require more advanced military technology and greater political unity than were compatible with the traditions they were striving to defend. The United States again threw heavy military force against them. In November 1811, territorial governor William Henry Harrison advanced with a thousand troops on the Shawnee headquarters at Prophetstown (in what later became Indiana). Several hundred warriors attacked Harrison's encampment on the Tippecanoe River but were beaten back. The setback weakened Tenskwatawa's efforts at tribal unification. A further defeat in 1813 at the Thames River in Canada caused Tecumseh's death and ended Shawnee armed resistance to white settlement.

This collapse paved the way for the cession by the 1830s of most Indian land in Ohio, southern Indiana, Michigan, and Illinois. Farther south, Cherokees, Creeks, Choctaws, and other tribes also used various strategies to avoid being overrun. They, too, mounted armed resistance or voluntarily withdrew westward. However, many Cherokees and others became agriculturalists, turning their societies into miniature republics that claimed equal standing with whites on whites' own terms. But they still faced defeat and forced removal in the 1830s. Land-hungry settlers and planters brushed them aside with little compunction. Even sympathetic whites came to regard Indian cultures as doomed and their decline and removal as inevitable. Indian leaders rejected the white view that they were "savages" obstructing "civilization." A Chickasaw chief, Shullushoma, wrote in 1824, "it has been a great many years since our white brothers came across the big waters and a great many of them has not got civilized yet."

American Societies and the Atlantic World   Americans' conquest of territory in the West intersected with the commercial competition and international rivalries of the Atlantic and the implications these had for the

Vente des deserts du Scioto par des Anglo-americains

Sale of the Deserts of Scioto by the Anglo-Americans
As this 1799 French engraving demonstrates, Americans were selling land to the French as well as purchasing it. The Scioto Company was one of many land companies that bought property from the federal government to resell at great profit to speculators and prospective settlers in the United States and abroad. Often the value of the land was not what the companies claimed. "Better to ensnare dupes," this print's caption commented, "they draw up geographical maps, convert the rocky wastes into fertile plains, show roads cut through impassable cliffs, and offer shares in lands which do not belong to them." The Scioto Company went bankrupt, but not before it had relieved many French investors of their francs. Chicago Historical Society.

future development of the United States. Trade, agricultural exports, and the coastal port cities had boomed in the 1790s when the United States could trade as a neutral with warring European nations. But the renewal of war between Britain and France after 1803 jeopardized American shipping and seamen, as each of the combatant nations tried to stop neutrals from dealing with the other. Britain seized ships and cargoes that it suspected of involvement in trade with France, and when the French followed suit, President Jefferson tried to put pressure on both sides by declaring an embargo in 1807, preventing trade with either power. For two years, until the embargo was lifted, men and women working in American ports suffered much hardship as ships lay idle and available work diminished.

The resumption of trade during the administration of Jefferson's successor, his ally James Madison, not only renewed tension with Europe, but also provoked fierce political divisions between Americans. American sailors fell foul of the British navy's practice of searching neutral vessels for alleged deserters and forcibly impressing them into service aboard their warships. Farmers and planters in the South and West were angered by the depressing effect of a British naval blockade on agricultural prices and by Britain's support for Indians hostile to white settlers. Pressure from these groups persuaded Madison to declare war on Britain in 1812, but merchants and traders from New England and the Mid-Atlantic coast vigorously disputed the decision, fearing the destruction of maritime trade. The divisions over the war accentuated regional differences that would shape U.S. society and politics in the decades to come. At an 1814 convention in Hartford, Connecticut, some Federalists proposed that New England should secede from the Union.

Advocates of the war badly underestimated America's vulnerability to superior British military and naval forces, which staved off an American invasion of Canada and sustained a naval blockade of the East Coast. Britain mounted an invasion of its own that culminated in the capture and burning of Washington, D.C., before its troops were repulsed. The United States was rescued largely by the defeat of Napoleon's armies in Europe and Britain's desire to end two decades of warfare with peace on all fronts. The United States signed a peace treaty at Ghent in 1814, but before word of this arrived in America, an army commanded by General Andrew Jackson, a Tennessee slave owner, crushed a British effort to capture the port of New Orleans. Although Jackson's force consisted mainly of regular troops and a contingent of French-speaking black soldiers, the success at New Orleans became celebrated as a symbol of the determination of frontier fighters. It also marked the ability of the United States to sustain its political independence.

Conclusion: Legacies of the Revolution

Achieving independence and new forms of republican government, the Revolution created fresh arenas in which Americans would seek to realize their aspirations and also come into conflict with each other. It unleashed a long period of economic expansion, which entailed both the invasion and settlement of the trans-Appalachian West and the growth and development of established rural and urban societies in the seaboard states, processes that were assisted by the renewed growth of Atlantic commerce after 1815 and by the collapse of Spanish influence in North America. But formal political equality for white men did not translate into economic equality. Development would lead to sharper conflict between rich and poor, master and journeyman, planter and small farmer. Barriers of gender and race also became firmer in the early nineteenth century, but the visions of emancipation conjured up by the Revolution continued to shape events.

Above all, the different regional patterns that had been established in colonial America continued to influence the development of the United States. Distinctions widened between northern societies based on family and wage labor and southern societies shaped by slavery. The growth of plantation slavery and its territorial expansion came into conflict with the development of wage labor in the North and the emergence there of an industrial society.

The Years in Review

1775

- Ipai Indians attack and burn the mission at San Diego in response to Spanish expansion in California.

1776

- British troops evacuate Boston but then capture New York City and Long Island, which they hold until 1783.

- Radicals come to power in Philadelphia and establish a democratic, egalitarian form of government that is inspired by the ideas of Thomas Paine.

- Seeking to counter Paine's *Common Sense*, John Adams publishes *Thoughts on Government*, which offers a more conservative vision of republican government.

1777

- George Washington and his 11,000 troops spend the winter in Valley Forge, Pennsylvania.

- British troops capture Philadelphia.

- The Continental Congress adopts the Articles of Confederation, which go into effect in 1781.

- The American victory at Saratoga, New York, convinces the French government to join the war against the British.

1779

- Patriot forces attack and burn forty Iroquois settlements in western New York.

- In response to rising bread prices, working people in Philadelphia revive their revolution committees to seek price controls; merchants arm a militia, which faces down protesting crowds and breaks their movement.

1780

- Pennsylvania passes law providing for gradual abolition of slavery, as do Rhode Island and Connecticut in 1784; a court decision ends slavery in Massachusetts in 1783.

1781

- The British surrender at Yorktown, Virginia.

1783

- The Revolutionary War is officially ended by Treaty of Paris, by which Britain recognizes American independence.

1786

- In Shays's Rebellion, indebted farmers from central and western Massachusetts close the local courts to prevent lawsuits being heard and attempt to seize the U.S. armory at Springfield, Massachusetts.

1787

- The Constitutional Convention meets in Philadelphia, adopting the U.S. Constitution on September 17.

- The Northwest Ordinance lays the basis for the creation of new states, encourages white settlement, and excludes American Indians from the new political arrangements.

1788

- James Madison, Alexander Hamilton, and John Jay write and publish eighty-five essays, known as the *Federalist Papers,* arguing for the ideas embodied in the new Constitution adopted in Philadelphia.

- New Hampshire becomes the ninth state to ratify Constitution and, by doing so, officially puts it in effect as of March 4, 1789.

1789

- The first federal administration, with George Washington as president, takes office.

1791

- The Bill of Rights (the first ten amendments to the U.S. Constitution) is ratified.

- Toussaint L'Ouverture leads a slave revolt to secure Saint-Domingue's (Haiti's) independence from France and strikes fear into the hearts of slave owners in the New World.

- The Federalist administration of President George Washington establishes the Bank of the United States (devised by Alexander Hamilton) to handle the government's transactions and influence the nation's financial system.

- Members of a confederation of Shawnee tribes kill, wound, or capture 900 soldiers out of an American force of 1,500 sent to dislodge them from southern Ohio.

1792

- Washington wins reelection for second term as president in a unanimous vote of the Electoral College; the only contest is for the office of vice president, which John Adams wins.

- Construction of the White House and Capitol begins.

- Black Methodists in Philadelphia withdraw from a church when the elders insist on segregated seating, part of a trend toward separate black churches.

1793
- War breaks out between Britain and France; the United States declares its neutrality, and American merchants and ship owners profit greatly by trading with both sides.

1794
- Federal liquor tax leads to the Whiskey Rebellion in western Pennsylvania.
- English writer Mary Wollstonecraft publishes *Vindication of the Rights of Women*, which attacks the oppression of women and proves influential in the United States.

1795
- Having been defeated by U.S. troops at the Battle of Fallen Timbers the previous year, the Shawnees sign the Treaty of Grenville and cede most of their land east of the Mississippi River to the U.S. government.

1796
- Federalist John Adams defeats Democratic-Republican Thomas Jefferson in first contested presidential race.

1798
- Congress passes the Alien and Sedition Acts, severely curtailing rights to free political expression.

1800
- Thomas Jefferson defeats Federalist John Adams in a bitter campaign for the presidency. Federalists whisper that Jefferson had fathered a child with his slave Sally Hemings. The results of DNA tests in 1998 suggest that this was indeed the case.

1803
- The United States makes the Louisiana Purchase (of territory between the Mississippi River and the Rocky Mountains) from France and roughly doubles its land area.

1805
- Tenskwatawa leads a religious awakening among Northwest Indian tribes.

1807
- New Jersey abolishes the property qualification for voting, one of many states to do so in this period, but also ends the limited voting rights of women.

- The Jefferson administration imposes a trade embargo on the warring Britain and France.

1811
- William Henry Harrison, governor of the Northwest Territories, defeats Shawnee troops at their headquarters at Prophetstown, helping to end Shawnee armed resistance to white settlement. By the 1830s, Indians will have reluctantly ceded most of their land in Ohio, southern Indiana, Michigan, and Illinois.

1812
- The United States declares war on Britain.

1814
- U.S. troops, commanded by General Andrew Jackson, defeat British troops in the Battle of New Orleans; both sides are unaware that the United States and Britain had already signed the Treaty of Ghent, ending their war.

Additional Readings

For more on the Revolutionary War, see: Edward Countryman, *A People in Revolution: The American Revolution and Political Society in New York, 1760–1790* (1981); John C. Dann, ed., *The Revolution Remembered: Eyewitness Accounts of the War for Independence* (1980); Ronald Hoffman and Peter J. Albert, eds., *Arms and Independence: The Military Character of the American Revolution* (1984); Ronald Hoffman, Thad W. Tate, and Peter J. Albert, eds., *An Uncivil War: The Southern Backcountry During the American Revolution* (1985); Jean B. Lee, *The Price of Nationhood: The American Revolution in Charles County* (1994); Charles Royster, *A Revolutionary People at War: The Continental Army and American Character, 1775–1783* (1979); and John Shy, *A People Numerous and Armed: Reflections on the Military Struggle for Independence*, revised edition (1990).

For more on Indian groups and the American Revolution, see: Celia Barnes, *Native American Power in the United States, 1783–1795* (2003); Colin G. Calloway, *The American Revolution in Indian Country: Crisis and Diversity in Native American Communities* (1995); Gregory Evans Dowd, *A Spirited Resistance: The North American Indian Struggle for Unity, 1745–1815* (1992); R. David Edmunds, *The Shawnee Prophet* (1983); R. David Edmunds, *Tecumseh and the Quest for Indian Leadership* (1984); Richard White, *The Middle Ground: Indians, Empires, and Republics in the Great Lakes Region, 1650–1815* (1991); and Greg O'Brien, *Choctaws in a Revolutionary Age, 1750–1830* (2002).

For more on African Americans and the American Revolution, see: Ira Berlin, *Many Thousands Gone: The First Two Centuries of Slavery in North America* (1998); Ira Berlin and Ronald Hoffman, eds., *Slavery and Freedom in the Age of the American Revolution* (1983); W. Jeffrey Bolster, *Black Jacks: African American Seamen in the Age of Sail* (1997); Sylvia R. Frey, *Water from the Rock: Black Resistance in a Revolutionary Age* (1991); Gary B. Nash, *Forging Freedom: The Making of Philadelphia's Black Community, 1720–1840* (1988); and Shane White, *Somewhat More Independent: The End of Slavery in New York City, 1770–1810* (1991).

For more on the various meanings of radicalism in the American Revolution, see: Michael Durey, *Transatlantic Radicals and the Early American Republic* (1997); Lester D. Langley, *The Americas in the Age of Revolution, 1750–1850* (1995); Edmund S. Morgan, *Inventing the People: The Rise of Popular Sovereignty in England and America* (1988); Steven Rosswurm, *Arms, Country, and Class: The Philadelphia Militia and the "Lower Sort" During the American Revolution* (1987); Billy G. Smith, *The "Lower Sort": Philadelphia's Laboring People, 1750–1800* (1990); Charles G. Steffen, *The Mechanics of Baltimore: Workers and Politics in the Age of Revolution, 1763–1812* (1984); Gordon S. Wood, *The Creation of the American Republic, 1776–1787* (1969); Gordon S. Wood, *The Radicalism of the American Revolution* (1992); and Alfred F. Young, *Beyond the American Revolution: Studies in the History of American Radicalism* (1993).

For more on women and the American Revolution, see: Carol Berkin, *Revolutionary Mothers: Women in the Struggle for America's Independence* (2005); Susan Juster, *Disorderly Women: Sexual Politics and Evangelicalism in Revolutionary New England* (1994); Linda K. Kerber, *Women of the Republic: Intellect and Ideology in Revolutionary America* (1980); and Mary Beth Norton, *Liberty's Daughters: The Revolutionary Experience of American Women, 1750–1800* (1980).

For more on the ratification of the Constitution, see: Richard R. Beeman, Stephen Botein, and Edward C. Carter II, eds., *Beyond Confederation: Origins of the Constitution and American National Identity* (1987); John Ferling, *A Leap in the Dark: The Struggle to Create the American Republic* (2003); Robert A. Gross, ed., *In Debt to Shays: The Bicentennial of an Agrarian Rebellion* (1993); and Herbert J. Storing, *The Antifederalists* (1985).

For more on the early republic period, see: Ronald Hoffman and Peter J. Albert, eds., *Launching the "Extended Republic": The Federalist Era* (1996); Susan Dunn, *Jefferson's Second Revolution: The Election Crisis of 1800 and the*

Triumph of Republicanism (2004); Thomas P. Slaughter, *The Whiskey Rebellion: Frontier Epilogue to the American Revolution* (1986); Larry E. Tise, *The American Counterrevolution: A Retreat from Liberty, 1783–1800* (1998); David Waldstreicher, *In the Midst of Perpetual Fetes: The Making of American Nationalism, 1776–1820* (1997); David J. Weber, *The Spanish Frontier in North America* (1992); Alfred F. Young, *The Democratic-Republicans of New York* (1967); Alfred F. Young and Terry J. Fife, with Mary E. Janzen, *We the People: Voices and Images of the New Nation* (1993).

Part Two

Free Labor and Slavery

1790–1850

ETWEEN ROUGHLY 1790 AND 1850, America was transformed from a small agrarian society along the Atlantic coastline into a wealthy, economically diverse country that stretched across the continent to the Pacific. Eighteen new states joined the original thirteen, and the nation's population swelled from four million to over twenty-three million. These numbers included slaves and free blacks as well as native-born and immigrant whites. In 1850, the figure also included those American Indians who did not live on government reservations. With increases in slavery and immigration during the early nineteenth century, the nation's population grew more heterogeneous as it grew larger. One result was that this period of unparalleled growth and prosperity deepened divisions of class, race, gender, and nationality. The most divisive issue — whether America would be a society based on free labor or on slavery — repeatedly sparked crises that, in each case, were settled by legislative compromises. But over the course of sixty years, no long-term solution was reached.

In 1790, however, the issue of slavery seemed of minor importance to most Americans of European descent. The new nation was confidently launching an unprecedented experiment in national republican government, backed by a seemingly limitless supply of land and natural resources. Most white Americans were optimistic about the nation's future. Even African Americans had some reason for hope as substantial numbers gained freedom and organized churches and mutual aid societies in the decade following the Revolution.

In the North, a market economy and a new system of industrial production took root. Here, revolutions in transportation, communication, and manufacturing undermined the old systems of local craft production and family farming. By the 1830s and 1840s, New England capitalists had brought workers — either women or entire families — together in the nation's first factories to weave cloth. Other workers labored in their homes to make shoes and clothing for market. An expanding network of roads, canals, and, later, railroads carried consumer goods from the Northeast to the new settlements in Ohio, Indiana, and Illinois and brought raw materials and foodstuffs produced in the west to the east.

The South remained predominantly agricultural, but there, too, Americans felt the profound changes wrought by an international industrial revolution. Aided by the invention of the cotton gin, Southern landowners replaced tobacco with cotton as their principal cash crop, and large quantities of the raw fiber fueled industrial development in England and New England. As a result, the plantation economy burgeoned, spreading from the Upper South to Alabama, Mississippi, Louisiana, and, by the 1840s, to Texas. As large planters increasingly dominated the South's economy and government, they wielded kinship, religion, and racism to strengthen bonds with the majority of southern whites who owned a few slaves or no slaves at all. Yet economic differences led to growing tensions, particularly between those who lived in areas where slavery flourished and those who lived in areas where it was in decline.

Tensions among whites did not, however, limit the brutality of the plantation system for African Americans. If the bonds of slavery had loosened briefly in the Revolutionary era, they now tightened with renewed vigor. To keep pace with the demand for cotton, the slave labor force expanded both numerically and geographically. For vast numbers of African Americans, these changes worsened working conditions and tore families apart.

American Indians and Mexicans also faced hardships because of whites' insatiable desire for land. As they had during European colonization, many Indian tribes confronted either extermination or migration further westward. Some were forced out of their communities in the Southeast and onto reservations in the Indian Territory of present-day Oklahoma. Many Mexicans were also pushed out of their homes to make way for U.S. settlers in Texas and California. And in the aftermath of Texas statehood in 1845 and the Mexican War of 1846–1848, hundreds of thousands of Mexicans came under U.S. jurisdiction.

The economic growth that drove geographic expansion also dramatically altered the lives of working Americans. By midcentury, millions of Americans — including artisans, factory hands, domestic servants, day laborers, and even some slaves — had been drawn into a market economy in which they sold their labor or their products. In the process, the ideal of the self-sufficient, independent farm or artisan family was undermined as increasing numbers of women and men became dependent on wages. At several points in this era, wage workers (by now, two out of every five American workers) experienced the full impact of that dependency as manufacturing ground to a halt and tens of thousands were suddenly jobless.

Despite periodic recessions and depressions in the early nineteenth century, northern employers were more concerned about a shortage of labor than an oversupply. That concern lessened when, beginning in the 1840s, a massive wave of immigrants from Northern and Western Europe entered the United States, willing to work for all kinds of manufacturing and agricultural enterprises. Most of these new immigrants — many of whom came to escape economic, social, and political injustices at home — became wage laborers, contributing to the formation of a growing and distinctly multinational working class. They also intensified the effects of the Industrial Revolution: the growth of cities, a new urban culture, and transformations in family structures and gender roles. In addition, some immigrants introduced radical theories and practices, including socialism, to American politics and broadened the base of American religion.

The contributions of immigrants were not always welcomed, however. In the 1840s and 1850s, many native-born Americans blamed new immigrants for the wrenching changes that resulted from industrial and urban development. Some joined anti-immigrant political movements; others initiated moral reform campaigns aimed at controlling the behavior of working-class immigrants; and still others physically attacked immigrants. Although free blacks were also subject to attacks by native-born whites, they rarely made common cause with immigrants. Instead, the two groups clashed with each other as they competed for jobs and housing.

Industrialization and the demographic and cultural changes that accompanied it profoundly affected the nation's political life. Americans engaged in intense debates over what kind of society they were creating. The commercial and industrial elite embraced a liberal capitalist interpretation of the revolutionary legacy, emphasizing the role of self-interest and the marketplace in governing social and economic relations. Many working people, especially those who did well in the new order, were attracted to the idea that liberty meant individual freedom to better themselves and improve their living standards. Others, including many of the working people who were dislocated by industrialization, criticized the emerging order as a betrayal of revolutionary ideals and celebrated instead republican traditions of independence, mutuality, and citizen participation derived from the French and other European revolutions as well as the American Revolution.

Working Americans—men, women, and children; free-born, slave, and emancipated; native-born and immigrant—resisted the dependent status that came with industrial and agricultural development. They insisted that the United States had not been created to make a few men rich and powerful at the expense of all others. They attacked the "tyranny" of their employers and masters, condemning them as "Tories in disguise," in the words of women textile workers in the 1830s. Others argued for liberty and equality as they embraced new religious principles espoused by evangelical, Quaker, and Moravian sects. Poor whites, African Americans, and women were especially keen to claim their spiritual equality and to translate it into practical demands for divinely sanctioned rights whenever they could. Working people defended their interests in a variety of other ways as well, through local workingmen's parties, trade unions, cooperative workshops, utopian communities, strikes (engaged in by free and enslaved workers), and outright rebellion, most notably among slaves. Some working women demanded rights for their sex, as did their middle-class counterparts. Growing numbers of women and men also denounced alcohol and prostitution and demanded the abolition of slavery.

Of all the diverse claims for social justice that were raised in these years, one—the end of slavery—became the central political issue of the day. Over the decades, the country divided between Americans who desired a nation of free labor, as in the North, and Americans who believed that only a system based on slave labor, as in the South, could guarantee social order. A basic question, one that shaped American politics, moral values, and the economy, thus emerged as the United States expanded westward and new territories sought statehood: should these new states be free or slave? Several political compromises from 1820 onward maintained an uneasy peace between the two systems. By 1850, however, the acquisition of new territories as a result of the U.S. war with Mexico intensified debates and steered the young nation toward civil war.

6

The Consolidation of Slavery in the South

1790–1836

"Five Generations on Smith's Plantation, Beaufort, South Carolina"

This African American family was photographed in 1862. Despite the depredations of the internal slave trade, enslaved African Americans maintained a strong sense of family and kinship through naming practices and other methods of remembrance. Prints and Photographs Division, Library of Congress.

THE WAR OF 1812 wreaked havoc along the northern and western borders of the United States, transforming the lives of all who settled on the frontier: whites, Indians, and African Americans. Disruptions of a different kind shaped the experiences of those who resided in long-settled regions such as the agrarian communities of eastern Virginia. There, the annual round of births, deaths, and marriages redrew family ties for blacks as well as whites. In the midst of the war, Fanny, a slave whose owner had recently died, was sold with two of her children to an up-and-coming young planter, John Cowper Cohoon, Jr. Fanny was forced to leave behind several other children (the records are not clear on how many) and probably a husband and other relatives as well. She was sent to Cedar Vale plantation in Nansemond County, Virginia, located some fifty miles from the lower Chesapeake Bay. The slave community at Cedar Vale included thirty-eight men, women, and children acquired from at least a dozen different owners. Like Fanny, many of the Cedar Vale slaves had been separated from family and friends so that Cohoon and his young bride could stake their own claim to independence.

Cohoon's power over his property set the boundaries of his slaves' lives. Fanny, whether by choice or by force, set up house with another slave, Jacob, whom Cohoon purchased around 1815. Over the next twenty years, Fanny worked in the fields and gave birth to at least seven more children. And although Cohoon apparently never separated a husband and wife by sale when he owned them both, he did sell slaves, including Fanny's daughter Lucy. Cohoon also gave slaves as gifts to his sons; seventeen slaves in all were

sent away to help younger Cohoons make their fortunes on newly established plantations. When Fanny died in 1857, at age 68, Cohoon noted, "She
was a good and faithful servant, leaving many children and grandchildren
to mourn her loss." Yet good and faithful as she was, Fanny could not make
even the most fundamental decisions about her life: where she lived, whom
she married, what kind of work she performed, and what happened to her
children.

John Cowper Cohoon, Jr., and thousands like him grew rich by using
slaves such as Fanny and her offspring. Slave labor provided the raw materials, especially cotton, for burgeoning industries in the North and in
Europe and grew the food needed to feed the rapidly expanding urban populations in America and abroad. By 1830, a cotton kingdom had been established across the South, with millions of enslaved men, women, and
children laboring to produce that crop. Most lived in a broad area in the
Deep South that stretched westward like a belt from coastal South Carolina
inland through central Georgia, Alabama, and Mississippi and then bent
southward down the lower Mississippi Valley to New Orleans. The creation
of this cotton belt and the consolidation and defense of slavery needed to
support it reshaped the lives of all southerners. Whites and blacks, slaves
and free people, men and women, wealthy planters, small farmers, and landless whites alike found themselves living in a new era that revolved around
slavery and cotton cultivation. Western expansion also put whites on a collision course with indigenous peoples, forcing American Indians off their
lands and shattering their economies and cultures. Over time, the great
profits to be made in the slave trade and in cotton pushed up the price of
slaves; retarded the growth of southern industry, towns, and cities; and
shaped all other aspects of economic life in the South.

Cotton and the Expansion of Slavery

The invention of the cotton gin led to the expansion and consolidation of
slavery in the South. This, in turn, encouraged the acquisition of new territories and the establishment of new states and fueled the birth of industry
in England and the northern United States. These developments sparked
the first major sectional controversy over slavery in the nineteenth century,
resulting in the Missouri Compromise of 1821. Cotton's success also led to
the forced removal of American Indians from southern soil, to make more
room for plantations, and the sale of African Americans from the Upper
South to the Lower South.

The Invention of the Cotton Gin In the 1780s, the future of slavery had
seemed uncertain as profits from traditional crops—especially tobacco and
indigo—declined. As many white southerners began moving west to find

new opportunities, New England–born Eli Whitney, living on a Georgia plantation, revived the southern economy when he invented the cotton gin in 1793. This simple device transformed southern agriculture. Long-staple cotton, with its resistance to rot and characteristic long fibers and smooth seeds, was already profitable in the Sea Islands of the Carolinas and Georgia. By 1791, planters there, responding to demands from British factory owners, had produced some two million pounds. But long-staple cotton could be grown only in the mineral-rich alluvial soils of the southern coast. Short-staple cotton could be grown much more widely, but slaves required substantial time and effort to pluck out its sticky seeds by hand, limiting the crop's profitability.

Whitney solved this problem by constructing a wooden box filled with a series of combs attached to a handle. As a worker (usually a slave) cranked the handle, the combs separated seeds from fiber. Using even the most primitive gin (short for engine), a worker could clean ten times more than was possible when plucking seeds by hand. By the early 1800s, cotton could be produced profitably almost anywhere south of Virginia, Kentucky, and Missouri (Map 6.1). It was produced not only on large plantations by bound labor, but also on small farms where white families, sometimes assisted by one or two slaves, could hope to turn a profit.

The spread of short-staple cotton generated by the invention of the cotton gin coincided with two other developments that guaranteed "King Cotton" would rule throughout the region. The first happened just after 1750, when a population explosion in Europe created an enormous demand for

MAP 6.1 The Westward Spread of Cotton Production, 1820–1860

In 1793, the invention of the cotton gin made it profitable to grow short-staple cotton in many parts of the South. Between 1820 and 1860, the most important areas of cotton production shifted from the Carolinas and Georgia into Alabama, Mississippi, Louisiana, and Texas. This also meant a massive shift in the slave labor force and the painful disruptions of slave life caused by an expanded internal slave trade.

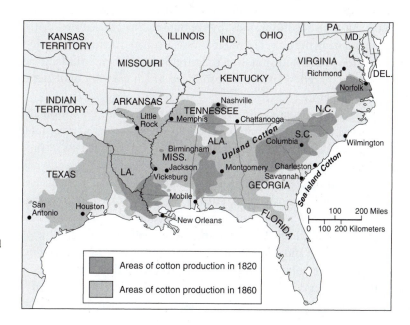

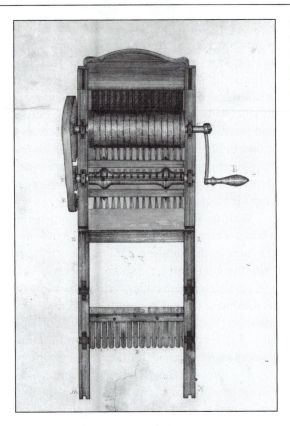

Cotton Gin
This sketch was submitted by Eli Whitney in 1793 when he applied for a patent for his new invention. Eli Whitney Papers, Yale University Library.

food, clothing, and shelter. Technological innovations further fueled the booming market, enabling English textile factories to increase production and lower the price of cotton goods. By the mid-eighteenth century, British craftsmen, utilizing the power of water and steam, had developed machines to drive textile looms and spin thread. Entrepreneurs then built factories where workers, paced by machines, produced much greater quantities of cloth than ever before.

In the early nineteenth century, the domestic demand for cotton also began to grow. While the Embargo Act of 1807 (see Chapter 5) devastated the economy of the nation's young seaports, crippled the business of merchants, and threw sailors and dockworkers out of work, New England's nascent textile manufacturers benefited. Entrepreneurs had managed to replicate some of the most important British inventions and now, for a short time at least, had access to cheap southern cotton and protection from the flood of English cloth. This combination helped to create a domestic market in raw cotton and manufactured cloth. Cotton soon became not just the South's but the nation's leading export, ensuring that a vast army of enslaved workers and huge expanses of fertile soil would be harnessed to produce cotton. Realizing that the importation of slaves would come to an

King Cotton
The South's staple, packed into bales and awaiting transport up the Mississippi River, filled a New Orleans wharf. Prints and Photographs Division, Library of Congress.

end in 1808 (as allowed by the U.S. Constitution), planters undertook frenzied purchases of Africans and then participated in an expanding internal slave trade. By the 1810s, that internal slave trade stretched across the Deep South into the Mississippi Territory and the southern portions of the Louisiana Territory. The invention of the cotton gin, then, transformed the South and the nation and even helped to fuel industrial growth internationally. It also inspired resistance and rebellion among the growing population of slaves, posed new challenges for nonslaveholding whites, and fed antislavery sentiments among wary whites, North and South. As the new republic grew, it was influenced at every turn by the profits and problems associated with slavery and cotton.

Territorial Expansion Throughout the early 1800s, the United States acquired vast tracts of new territory through purchase, the repayment of debts, and military conquest. The Louisiana Purchase of 1803 was the most important in opening land to small farmers and large planters (Map 6.2). It also set the stage for the national government to play a new role, as land that was deemed the "frontier" by those living along the eastern seaboard was turned into "property" that could be legally owned by whites. Throughout the 1810s and 1820s, the president and Congress supported explorations of western territories, such as the groundbreaking journey of Meriwether Lewis and William Clark in 1804, as well as land surveys and the establishment of legal land titles. They also debated whether the U.S. government should fund internal improvements, such as roads, bridges, canals, and other forms of transportation, to assist settlement in these new territories. They argued as well over whether and how to remove American Indians who lived in regions that white planters and farmers now desired.

In the long run, geographical expansion ensured political conflict as slavery became more entrenched in the South and free labor grew dominant in the North. In 1790, the populations of the North and South were about equal, and so was their representation in Congress. But the North's population grew faster, and the balance of power in Congress shifted accordingly. By 1820, the states that relied on slave labor found themselves with just 42 percent of the votes in the House of Representatives; only in the U.S. Senate was North-South parity maintained.

During these years of declining southern political power, many white southerners left the Piedmont region of the Carolinas and Georgia. More

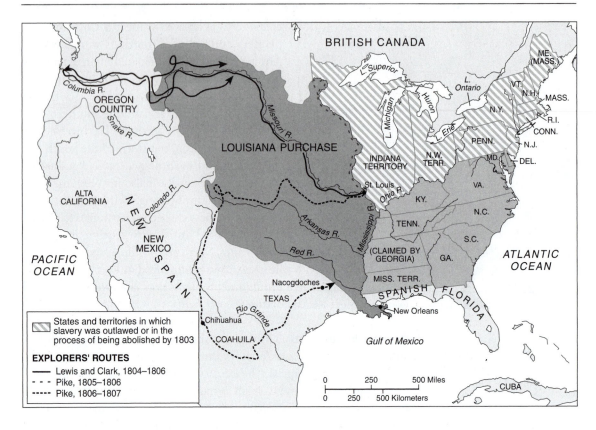

MAP 6.2   The Louisiana Purchase

The Louisiana Purchase doubled the territory of the young United States, providing opportunities for many, mainly white, Americans to seek their fortunes on the new frontier. At the same time, the expansion of settlement into this region over the next forty years sparked conflicts with a number of Indian societies and intensified debates over the place of slavery in a democratic republic.

than 100,000 headed west to Kentucky and Tennessee as early as 1790. Beginning then and increasing throughout the early 1800s, state governments chartered private companies that invested in internal improvements. Most of the charters granted these companies the power of eminent domain, a legal device that allowed them to force owners to sell land at "a reasonable price," thereby allowing states to gain land along the rights-of-way for bridges, roads, and canals. Although eminent domain was challenged by small farmers and others whose land was taken, state courts upheld it on numerous occasions, judges agreeing that "progress for great numbers" of Americans should prevail over the lesser rights of individual property owners.

A number of Democratic-Republican leaders, including James Madison and James Monroe of Virginia and Henry Clay of Kentucky, argued that the federal government should promote internal improvements that benefited more than one state. Clay followed the economic nationalist logic of Federalist Alexander Hamilton, but he proposed an "American System" that would aid the common man as well as planters and merchants by funding roads that linked new western settlements to eastern ports and markets. But President James Monroe's 1817 veto of the Bonus Bill, which

A Regular Row in the Backwoods

The 1841 issue of the *Crockett Almanac*, named after the Tennessee backwoodsman made famous by his self-serving tall tales, portrayed a rough rural "sport." Inexpensive comic almanacs combined illustrated jokes on topical subjects with astrological and weather predictions. *Crockett Almanac* (1841) — Prints and Photographs Division, Library of Congress.

would have established a national fund for roads and other internal improvements, left the states in charge of internal improvements. Most states continued to charter private companies to perform the actual work of building and improving the nation's transportation system.

New Opportunities As these debates continued, western migration accelerated. The network of roads expanded, and the steamboat was invented and improved. Furnace-heated boilers powered steam engines that allowed these boats to travel as quickly upstream as downstream. Despite early problems with fires, explosions, and sinkings, steamboats greatly increased the speed and ease of transporting goods and people. In 1817, the port of New Orleans welcomed some seventeen steamboats, loaded with migrants and freight. Just three decades later, more than five hundred steamboats arrived and departed each year. A large proportion of the early migrants were single men, seeking adventure as well as economic opportunity. Often as practiced at drinking, gambling, and fighting as at farming, they embraced frontier life.

The level of violence that characterized everyday existence in the region shocked many Americans. Eye-gouging contests, ear biting and teeth bashing, stabbings, and knifings all reflected the rough-and-tumble quality of life on the southern frontier. The stories of Davy Crockett and other legendary figures, who were said to have killed bears or Indian warriors with their bare hands, epitomized the raw virility that defined and dominated much of frontier culture.

The earliest migrants, whether they moved out to the Louisiana Territory or closer to home in western Georgia, Tennessee, or Kentucky, often chose to "squat" on land rather than to buy it. Squatters simply staked claims to what they considered empty acreage by selecting a spot, settling on it, and implementing "improvements": building a rough cabin, clearing the land, and planting crops. In most newly opened frontier areas, squatters were as prevalent as owners. Over time, however, state and federal agents, land speculators, and planters sought to regularize land ownership, demanding land titles and payments to ensure continued occupancy.

The state of Georgia, which claimed lands reaching to the Mississippi River, instituted a lottery to distribute land in the sparsely settled western part of the state. Most winners, however, took cash for their land certificates from speculators, who then resold the land to small farmers. The federal government also sold western land on credit. In 1800 and 1804, Congress hoped to assist cash-poor migrants by lowering both the

Politics on the Tennessee Frontier: The Autobiography of Davy Crockett

Davy Crockett (1786–1836) was a frontiersman, soldier, and politician who used his autobiography to help create an image of himself as a larger-than-life American hero. The description of frontier politics presented here is based on his campaign for a seat in the Tennessee legislature in 1821. He suggests that humor, hunting skills, and male camaraderie were as important to electoral success as a clear stance on the issues of the day.

I . . . set out electioneering, which was a bran-fire new business to me. It now became necessary that I should tell the people something about the government, and an eternal sight of other things that I knowed nothing more about than I did about Latin, and law, and such things as that. . . .

I went first into Heckman country to see what I could do among the people as a candidate. Here they told me that they wanted to move their town nearer to the centre of the county, and I must come out in favour of it. There's no devil if I knowed what this meant, or how the town was to be moved; and so I kept dark, going on the identical same plan that I now find is called "non-committal." About this time there was a great squirrel hunt on Duck river, which was among my people. They were to hunt two days: then to meet and count the scalps, and have a big barbecue, and what might be called a tip-top country frolic. The dinner, and a general treat, was all to be paid for by the party having taken the fewest scalps. I joined one side, taking the place of one of the hunters, and got a gun ready for the hunt. I killed a great many squirrels, and when we counted scalps, my party was victorious.

The company had every thing to eat and drink that could be furnished in so new a country, and much fun and good humor prevailed. But before the regular frolic commenced, I mean the dancing, I was called on to make a speech as a candidate. . . .

The thought of having to make a speech made my knees feel mighty weak, and set my heart to fluttering almost as bad as my first love scrape with the Quaker's niece. But as good luck would have it, these big candidates spoke nearly all day, and when they quit, the people were worn out with fatigue, which afforded me a good apology for not discussing the government. But I listened mighty close to them, and was learning pretty fast about political matters. When they were all done, I got up and told some laughable story, and quit. I found I was safe in those parts, and so I went home, and didn't go back again till after the election was over. But to cut this matter short, I was elected, doubling my competitor, and nine votes over.

David Crockett, *A Narrative of the Life of David Crockett of the State of Tennessee* (1973).

minimum acreage for purchases and the price per acre. Again, however, most land ended up in the hands of speculators rather than of individual owners.

By the 1810s, improved transportation facilitated the movement of people and products between the East and the new Northwest settlements in Ohio, Indiana, and Illinois. With the aid of the steamboat, northwesterners could market their surplus grain and livestock in the new South, just as new planters in Louisiana, Mississippi, Arkansas, and Tennessee could sell some sugar, rice, and cotton in the Northwest. Towns and cities along steamboat routes—including Pittsburgh and Cincinnati on the Ohio River and New Orleans and St. Louis on the Mississippi—flourished. In this manner, these newly settled western areas, north and south, became temporarily linked in an economic partnership. Representatives from these areas were among the strongest supporters of federal funds for internal improvements and government removal of American Indians to lands farther west.

Unlike small farmers who lived in the cotton belt, those on the frontier were less likely to raise crops demanded by the export economy. For most, staking everything on cotton was too risky; a sudden drop in prices could land them in debt, even strip them of their land. Ferdinand Steel farmed a small plot with his brother in Mississippi in the 1830s. He noted in his diary, "I do not think it is a good plan to depend so much on cotton; it takes up all our time. . . . raise corn and keep out of debt and we will have no necessity of raising cotton." Farm families like the Steels concentrated on fishing, hunting, and raising grain to produce the food, tools, and clothing they needed to survive. If they produced more than they needed, they could sell or exchange the surplus locally for such necessities as coffee, molasses, nails, needles, and cooking utensils. Corn was the preferred crop because it was useful regardless of its market price; it could be eaten by family members and by livestock, and it could easily be bartered for other goods. Fishing was another important source of food and income.

For frontier residents, family labor and local exchange networks were the keys to success. Trade among neighbors led to the formation of social as well as economic ties and created communities out of scattered households. In this context, the marriage market was as important as the cotton or produce market for those seeking a larger stake. Landless men hoped to marry the daughters of settled farmers, and farmers sought to marry the daughters of neighbors as a way of increasing their holdings. Wives and daughters enhanced a family's standing by selling domestic manufactures for cash or raising chickens, churning butter, and working in the fields. Expansion, then, shaped not only economic opportunities and choices, but also family and community relations.

The Missouri Compromise in 1820–1821 and the Westward Expansion of Slavery Although these frontier communities seemed far removed from events in the nation's capital, they were in fact deeply affected by both domestic and foreign politics. Small farmers were particularly concerned about the acquisition of territory and the building of roads into the trans-Appalachian region. Threats from Indians, on whose lands white settlers repeatedly trespassed, led to frequent demands that the government provide protection to settlers. The War of 1812 heightened tensions between migrants and local Indians who had hoped that alliances with the British would end white encroachment. Instead, western expansion after the war widened sectional fissures over slavery and sparked heated political conflicts.

The War of 1812 had inspired intense opposition from many merchants and politicians in the Northeast because of its devastating effect on maritime trade (see Chapter 5). Farmers in the South and West, however, enthusiastically supported the war. They hoped that victory would reopen the British cotton market and lessen Indians' ability to thwart white settlement. Indeed, the federal government did open new lands for settlement after 1815, thereby expanding opportunities available to landless sons and daughters, small farmers, and large planters. The U.S. government also rewarded War of 1812 veterans with land warrants, increasing pressure on western territories. In 1820, Congress lowered the price per acre, from $2.00 to $1.25, to make settlement even more appealing. International developments provided the opportunity for further expansion. In 1817, on the heels of a military incursion into Florida led by U.S. General Andrew Jackson, Spain agreed to sell the territory to the United States. According to the terms of the 1819 Adams-Onís Treaty, Spain gave Florida to the United States along with its lands in the Northwest, and the United States gave up its claims to Texas.

That same year, one long-term implication of the U.S. expansion became clear. In 1819, the Missouri Territory applied for admission to the Union as a slave state and touched off a fierce debate over the place of slave and free labor in the nation. Confirming planters' fears that the North would apply its political power to weaken the institution of slavery, New York congressman James Tallmadge, Jr., proposed as a condition of Missouri statehood that no additional slaves be admitted within its borders and that all slave children born following statehood be emancipated at age twenty-five. Such gradualist approaches to emancipation were popular among northern whites. Despite the limited form of manumission in Talmadge's proposal, it triggered a sectional battle. Most northern congressmen, 87 of 101, voted for the proposal; the vast majority of southerners opposed it. The U.S. Senate, where slave owners exercised more power, voted to impose no restrictions on slavery in Missouri. But the Senate alone could not admit a state into the Union.

MAP 6.3   The Missouri Compromise

The Missouri Compromise, which provided for the nearly simultaneous admission to statehood of Maine and Missouri, established a pattern that would be followed for the next thirty years. To maintain equal representation of free and slave states in the U.S. Senate, each admission of a free state necessitated the admission of a slave state and vice versa. Although, in the end, the Missouri Compromise did not resolve the debates over slavery in western lands, it did produce a temporary truce that ensured further expansion.

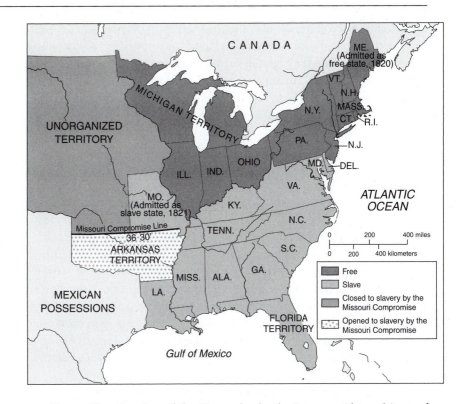

Henry Clay, Speaker of the House, broke the impasse. The architect of the American System, Clay was committed to putting national interests first, politically as well as economically. When Maine applied for statehood in 1820, Clay engineered a compromise that a majority of northern and southern congressmen could support. According to this Missouri Compromise, Missouri would be admitted with no restrictions on slavery. At the same time, Missouri's southern border (see Map 6.3) would be extended westward through the rest of the Louisiana Purchase. Henceforth, no territory north of that line would be admitted to the Union as a slave state. The Missouri Compromise also opened the way for statehood for Maine, which had been blocked in the U.S. Senate until the Missouri issue was resolved

Many northerners bitterly denounced the 1820 compromise as a slaveholder victory. But planters were unhappy, too; the entire affair confirmed their suspicions about the North's attitude toward their labor system. Congress's freewheeling debate over the Missouri Compromise had made public views that southerners considered subversive. Worse, free blacks living in the capital had filled the House galleries during the debates and listened intently to the antislavery speeches. Who knew how far these words might travel and what their effect might be?

Still, the conflicts that were engendered by territorial expansion did not stop southerners from seeking lands farther west. As early as the beginning of the century, some American whites had settled in the Mexican province of Coahuila-Texas. Despite the terms of the Adams-Onís Treaty, systematic colonization of the area began in earnest during the 1820s, organized by Virginia-born Stephen Austin. Even after Mexico, now independent from Spanish control, outlawed slavery in 1829, southerners continued to move into the region. In 1830, about 1,000 slaves, owned by U.S. citizens, also lived in the province. Austin had secured a special provincial law permitting slavery to operate under a different name: "permanent indentured servitude."

Planters also moved in great numbers into the rich and fertile U.S.-controlled lands along the Mississippi Delta and the Gulf of Mexico. The mixed population of poor whites, small farmers, free blacks, and Indians that had earlier characterized the lower Mississippi was supplanted in the 1820s and 1830s by a vast plantation society in which small numbers of whites controlled the labor of thousands of slaves. Over time, differences in access to land, slaves, and wealth would increase antagonism among southern whites of different classes. In addition, planters increased profits through the massive importation of slaves and more brutal work regimens, prompting growing fears of slave rebellions. These problems would not surface in their most acute forms for another generation, however. In the early 1800s, Indians provided the greatest resistance to white Americans' plans for westward expansion.

American Indians: Resistance and Retreat King Cotton set white settlers on a collision course with Indians. In 1790, Indians occupied villages throughout the twenty-five million acres of what would become the cotton-growing states. During the early 1800s, many were herded onto reservations. Others moved west, voluntarily or not. Still others tried to survive by adopting the ways of white missionaries and farmers. Some tribal members shifted property ownership from women to men, adapted to plows and spinning wheels, and sent their children to English-language schools and Christian churches. Cherokees welcomed Moravian missionaries in 1799, for instance, because they offered to open a school. Some Indian farmers even adopted slavery. Such efforts at integration ultimately failed, however.

Among the largest tribes in the Southeast were the Cherokees, Creeks, Choctaws, Chickasaws, and Seminoles (Map 6.4). Despite the fierce resistance offered by the Seminoles to white invaders in Florida, these Indian nations became known among white Americans as the Five Civilized Tribes because they adopted many of the institutions of the surrounding white settlers. For many American Indians, conversion to Christianity seemed to offer one of the best hopes for peaceful coexistence with whites. Moravians, Quakers, Baptists, Methodists, Presbyterians, and Congregationalists all sent missionaries into southeastern Indian societies in the late eighteenth and early nineteenth centuries, with limited success. Even where missionaries enjoyed success, however, many Indian converts continued to practice traditional burial and marriage rituals.

MAP 6.4   Indian Cessions, 1790–1820

Between the end of the American Revolution and 1820, most Indian tribes living east of the Mississippi River were forced to cede their lands to the U.S. government. Battles between the U.S. Army and various confederations of Indians in the 1790s and 1810s ensured U.S. control of most Indian territories that could not be obtained by purchase or treaties. Still, Cherokees and Seminoles continued to fight their removal from the Southeast to the Indian Territory in present-day Oklahoma into the 1830s.

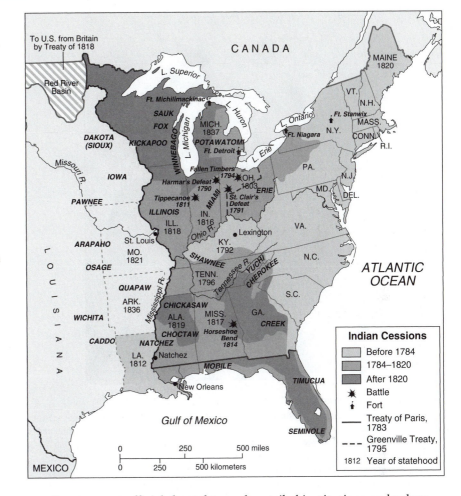

Government officials hoped to replace tribal institutions and values with those more appropriate to a market-oriented society and specifically targeted communal land ownership. A U.S. commissioner of Indian affairs argued, "Common property and civilization cannot coexist." Yet replacing communal land ownership meant weakening the ties connecting the individual Indian to the community and binding the community as a whole to its land. Dividing tribal land into private plots made it easier for whites to acquire legal title to that land. One method was already tried and true: merchants drew Indians into debt, often through questionable bookkeeping, and then accepted land in payment of that debt.

As a result of government policy, missionary intervention, and trade relations, by the early 1800s, a new class of American Indians (many of mixed Indian and white parentage) embraced Euro-American ways of life. Because clan membership passed through the mother's line in many of these tribes, the sons of white men and Indian women could claim seats on tribal councils. The children of such marriages were often bilingual and

"Saving the Indian from Oblivion"

The lawyer-turned-Indian-portraitist George Catlin trekked across the Great Plains in the 1830s to record the faces and customs of the Assiniboines (a tribe in present-day North Dakota) and other American Indians before they passed into "oblivion." In this dual portrait painted in the late 1830s, Catlin depicted the Indian leader Pigeon's Egg Head, or Wi-Jun-Jon, as a victim of progress. Shown first striking a noble pose before leaving his community, Pigeon's Egg Head is tragically transformed in the second half of the painting; his return from white civilization reveals a foppish figure armed with an umbrella and a fan, a whiskey bottle peeking out of his rear pocket. George Catlin, *Pigeon's Egg Head (The Light) Going to and Returning from Washington*, 1837–39, oil, 29 × 24 inches — Smithsonian American Art Museum, Gift of Mrs. Joseph Harrison, Jr.

familiar with both white American and Indian ways. With white backing, these men acquired growing political power within tribal councils and used it to promote the transformation of Indian society into an approximation of white male-dominated America. Indeed, many sought to deprive women of traditional property and tribal membership inheritance rights that were rooted in matrilineal descent.

The decision to embrace white ways spurred resistance within many tribes. For instance, some young Creek warriors became increasingly estranged from Creek elders, who favored accommodating to U.S. authority. In 1813, a bloody war erupted, pitting these young "Red Sticks," as they were known, against thousands of white southern militiamen, as well as against Creek, Cherokee, Choctaw, and Chickasaw warriors who hoped for

"The Craving Desires of the White Man": Creek Leaders Petition Congress

In this 1832 petition to Congress, leaders of the Creek nation protested their forcible expulsion from the Gulf coast region onto lands beyond the Mississippi River, in present-day Oklahoma. Their arguments and questions reflect a keen understanding of how unreliable the government's assurances often proved.

It has been . . . with alarm and consternation that we find ourselves assailed in these our last retreats. Though our possessions have shrunk to a narrow compass, they contain all that endears itself to our heart. Beneath the soil which we inhabit, lie the frail remnants of what heretofore composed the bodies of our fathers and of our children, our wives and our kindred. . . . Yet we are now menaced with being driven from these narrow limits, and compelled to seek an asylum from the craving desires of the white man, beyond the great river. If the alternative offered us—if the lands offered us be, as we are told, of greater value than those which we derived from our ancestors, and they from God, we freely relinquish all the advantages which they possess, and will be satisfied with that which we already have. If they are inferior in value, we submit it to the justice of our white brethren, whether they will compel us to a disadvantageous exchange. If there be any particular inducements either to individuals or communities which render our lands particularly valuable, why should not we, the rightful proprietors, be suffered to enjoy them? Can any adventitious value enhance them more in the eyes of the white man, than the solemn associations to which we have adverted, do in our own?

We are assured that, beyond the Mississippi, we shall be exempted from further exaction; that no State authority can there reach us; that we shall be secure and happy in these distant abodes. Can we obtain, or can our white brethren give assurances more distinct and positive, than those we have already received and trusted? Can their power exempt us from intrusion in our promised borders, if they are incompetent to our protection where we are? Can we feel secure when farther removed from our father's [the president's] eye than now, when he hears our remonstrances and listens to our complaints? We have heretofore received every assurance and every guarantee that our imperfect knowledge could desire; we confided in it as ample for all our purposes; and we know not what to require which would obviate further embarrassments.

House Document 102, 22nd Cong., 1st Sess. (1832).

greater leniency from whites in exchange for this alliance. The fierce but unequal combat ended in March 1814 at the battle of Horseshoe Bend, where more than 1,000 Indians died. White Americans considered Andrew Jackson, then commanding the Tennessee militia, the hero of this engagement.

Among the losers were those Creeks who allied with Jackson. The Treaty of Fort Jackson, which ended the fighting, transferred fourteen million acres (more than half the land in Alabama) from Creek to U.S. control. Moreover, the Indian defeat at Horseshoe Bend opened the floodgates to southern white migrants. By 1826, the Creek Indians of Georgia had been driven westward, setting a precedent that would eventually unseat almost the entire population of the Five Civilized Tribes. Throughout the 1820s, white southerners repeatedly sought to secure lands owned by Indians, setting off jurisdictional disputes not only between sovereign tribes and state courts, but also between state courts and federal authorities. Georgia led the way, forcing the Creeks to cede land to the state in 1825 and 1827 and claiming in 1828 that the Cherokee was not an independent nation but simply a collection of individuals subject to state laws.

American Indians Seek Justice but Face Removal

In response to these threats of removal, some southeastern Indians turned to U.S. courts. Over the course of the early nineteenth century, Indian tribes—although technically recognized as independent nations—were increasingly subject to federal and state laws. They now hoped to use those laws, along with existing treaties, to save themselves from eradication. In 1827, the Cherokees adopted a formal constitution modeled on that of the United States. Whites, however, were less interested in transforming the Indians than in removing them from the region altogether. When it became clear that removal was the ultimate goal of southern whites, a majority of Cherokees opposed further concessions and fought their removal right up to the U.S. Supreme Court.

Led by Chief Justice John Marshall, who had shaped the federal judiciary since his appointment in 1801, the U.S. Supreme Court held responsibility for adjudicating cases between states and foreign governments. Marshall had been involved in many landmark decisions, including *Marbury v. Madison* (1803), which established the court's right to review the constitutionality of acts of Congress and of state legislatures. He was an ardent defender of the authority of the national government. In *McCulloch v. Maryland* (1819), the Supreme Court ruled that the establishment of the Bank of the United States was constitutional, and Marshall declared: "The government of the Union, though limited in its powers, is supreme within its sphere of action." In *Cherokee Nation v. Georgia* (1831), Marshall once again reinforced the power of the central government, this time at the expense of Indian tribes as well as states. The plaintiffs argued that their tribe was a sovereign, thereby "foreign," nation, requiring the protection of the federal courts. Sympathetic to the Indians' claims but unwilling to grant them independent political authority, the Court ruled that Indian tribes had a special but still dependent status within the nation. Marshall used the analogy of "a ward to his guardian" to express this special status and, on that basis, argued that the Cherokee tribe had no standing before the U.S. Supreme Court. Still,

"Our Cause Is Your Own": Chief John Ross Protests the Treaty of New Etocha

Chief John Ross was the principal chief of the Cherokee in Georgia; in this 1836 letter addressed to "the Senate and House of Representatives," Ross protested the Treaty of New Etocha that forced the Cherokee out of Georgia, calling it fraudulent, and emphasized the similarities between the Cherokee and white Americans. In 1838, federal troops forcibly displaced the last of the Cherokee from their homes; their trip to Indian Territory (Oklahoma) became known as the Trail of Tears.

. . . By the stipulations of this [treaty] . . . We are stripped of every attribute of freedom and eligibility for legal self-defence. Our property may be plundered before our eyes; violence may be committed on our persons; even our lives may be taken away, and there is none to regard our complaints. We are denationalized; we are disfranchised. We are deprived of membership in the human family! We have neither land nor home, nor resting place that can be called our own. And this is effected by the provisions of a compact which assumes the venerated, the sacred appellation of treaty. . . .

The instrument in question is not the act of our Nation; we are not parties to its covenants; it has not received the sanction of our people. The makers of it sustain no office nor appointment in our Nation . . . we cannot but contemplate the enforcement of the stipulations of this instrument on us, against our consent, as an act of injustice and oppression . . . nor can we believe it to be the design of these honorable and highminded individuals, who stand at the head of the Govt., to bind a whole Nation, by the acts of a few unauthorized individuals. . . .

In truth, our cause is your own; it is the cause of liberty and of justice; it is based upon your own principles, which we have learned from yourselves; for we have gloried to count your [George] Washington and your [Thomas] Jefferson our great teachers; we have read their communications to us with veneration; we have practised their precepts with success. And the result is manifest. The wildness of the forest has given place to comfortable dwellings and cultivated fields, stocked with the various domestic animals. Mental culture, industrious habits, and domestic enjoyments, have succeeded the rudeness of the savage state.

We have learned your religion also. We have read your Sacred books. Hundreds of our people have embraced their doctrines, practised the virtues they teach, cherished the hopes they awaken, and rejoiced in the consolations which they afford. To the spirit of your institutions, and your religion, which has been imbibed by our community, is mainly to be ascribed that patient endurance which has characterized the conduct of our people, under the laceration of their keenest woes. . . . On your kindness, on your humanity, on your compassion, on your benevolence, we rest our hopes. . . . Spare our people! Spare the wreck of our prosperity! Let not our deserted homes become the monuments of our desolation! . . .

John Ross, *Letter from John Ross, Principal Chief of the Cherokee Nation of Indians, in Answer to Inquires from a Friend Regarding the Cherokee Affairs with the United States* (Washington, D.C., 1836), 22–24.

he viewed Indians as federal, not state, wards.

Just a year later, in *Worcester v. Georgia* (1832), the Marshall Court strengthened federal authority over American Indians while also strengthening tribal sovereignty. The Court determined that Indians were members of "domestic dependent nations" with a right to their own land and "distinct political communities" with exclusive authority within their territorial boundaries. Upholding his earlier commitment to federal authority, the Chief Justice concluded that only the federal government, not the states, could regulate commerce with tribes.

The Court's rulings proved largely meaningless, however. Andrew Jackson, who was elected president in 1828, had pushed through an Indian Removal Act in 1830, offering Indians reservations west of the Mississippi in exchange for their current lands. Despite some opposition from northern religious groups and a massive antiremoval petition initiated by northern women, Indian removal had substantial popular support among whites, especially among southern planters and backcountry settlers. Under pressure from federal agents and threat of military intervention, many tribes, or at least tribal leaders, signed away most of their eastern territory. The federal government quickly set out to relocate all southeastern tribes. Twenty-three thousand Choctaws and some Cherokees were pressured into moving west in 1831–1832. Most of the Seminole Nation was removed between 1832 and 1835. Others were transported by force: the Alabama Creeks in 1836 and the Chickasaws the next year. In 1838, those Cherokees who had refused the government's offer of land in the West were uprooted by federal troops. The troops herded some 15,000 members of the tribe across the 800-mile "Trail of Tears" to present-day Oklahoma. One in four Cherokees died on the way (Map 6.5).

Cherokee Phoenix

The *Cherokee Phoenix*, the first Native American newspaper in the United States, was published in English and in the Cherokee "syllabary" devised by Sequoyah in the 1820s. The General Council of the Cherokee Nation established a printing office in New Echota, Georgia, in the 1820s as part of their effort to further integrate into American society. When Georgia and other states sought instead to remove the Cherokees, the newspaper was started as a tool to elicit public support and unify the Cherokee nation. Prints and Photographs Division, Library of Congress.

Southern Slave Experiences

The removal of the Five Civilized Tribes from lands that could be profitably cultivated in cotton and sugar opened the door to an expanded plantation economy based on slave labor. In the two decades before the 1808 stoppage

MAP 6.5   Removal of American Indians

Those American Indians who retained control of eastern lands after 1820 were forced to move to reservations west of the Mississippi River during the 1830s. The most famous of these compulsory migrations is that of the Cherokees along the Trail of Tears in 1838. Although many Cherokees and other members of the so-called Five Civilized Tribes adopted Anglo-American language, religion, and customs, southern planters still insisted that they be removed west to open their lands for white settlement.

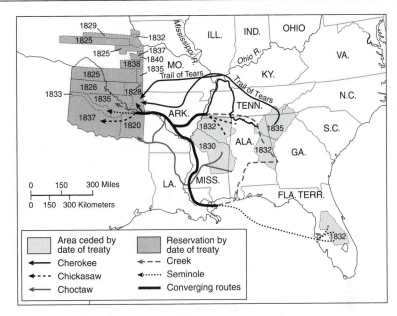

of slave importation, planters purchased some quarter of a million Africans, doubling the number who had been imported in the previous two centuries. In the following years, natural reproduction and the internal slave trade would replace importation from Africa in meeting the demand for workers.

The need for labor was motivated in large part by the rapid expansion of cotton production. "To sell cotton in order to buy negroes," one Mississippian

From Dawn to Dusk

An unknown photographer captured this scene of men, women, and children picking cotton under the watchful eye of an overseer. Prints and Photographs Division, Library of Congress.

noted, "to make more cotton to buy more negroes, ad infinitum, is the aim and direct tendency of all the operations of the thoroughgoing cotton planter." Yet cotton was not the only source of profit for slaveholders. Rice and sugar also underwrote the expansion of slave labor and, in the case of sugar, the movement westward as well. Following the fate of the Indians, tens of thousands of enslaved black workers from the Chesapeake and the Carolinas were forced to move to new homes and adapt to new work regimens. For slaves, those work regimes were shaped most significantly by the size of the farm or plantation and the particular crops being cultivated: cotton, tobacco, sugar, or rice.

Slavery on Small Farms and Large Plantations   The growing number of slaves who were trapped in bondage labored under a variety of conditions. In 1830, a significant portion of slaves still worked on small farms, where a laborer might cook one day and hoe cotton the next. Here, patterns of labor varied from season to season as owners tried to ensure profits and, at the same time, cultivate enough food and raw materials to sustain their own families. In such situations, slaves had more direct interaction with owners and could hope that a successful owner might purchase nearby family members. But African Americans who lived on small holdings also had less chance of developing kin and community ties within their own quarters, and they faced a greater danger that one bad season could cause them to be transferred as payment for debts.

"We Weren't Allowed to Sit Down": Memories of a Slave Childhood

As young female slaves grew old enough, most went to work in the fields. But some became personal servants to their owners, an experience that one of them later recalled in a 1930s interview.

When I was nine years old, they took me from my mother and sold me. Massa Tinsley made me the house girl. I had to make the beds, clean the house, and other things. After I finished my regular work, I would go to the mistress's room, bow to her, and stand there till she noticed me. Then she would say, "Martha, are you through with your work?" I'd say, "Yes, mam." She'd say, "No you ain't; you haven't lowered the shades." I'd then lower the shades, fill the water pitcher, arrange the towels on the washstand, and anything else mistress wanted me to do. Then she'd tell me that was about all to do in there. Then I would go to the other rooms in the house and do the same things. We weren't allowed to sit down. We had to be doing something all day. Whenever we were in the presence of any of the white folks, we had to stand up.

Interview of Martha Showvely, May 19, 1937. WPA Life History Collection, Library of Virginia.

Ration Day

A master distributed provisions in an illustration from a weekly newspaper report on the operations of a plantation around 1860. The engraving suggested that this planter provided his slaves with a varied and nutritious diet, which was not typically the case. It failed to show the gardens and other methods slaves used to supplement often meager or boring fare. *Harper's Weekly* — American Social History Project.

On large plantations, the demands on laborers differed from place to place, from crop to crop, and from job to job. For instance, house slaves lived under quite different conditions from those of field hands. Frederick Douglass remembered that domestic slaves "constituted a sort of black aristocracy" who "resembled the field hands in nothing except their color." Yet house slaves, although privileged in certain ways, still worked hard. Moreover, female domestics lived in closer proximity to whites and were thus more vulnerable to sexual exploitation and abuse. Black women washed clothes, cleaned, and cooked, tasks that involved heavy and tedious labor in the early nineteenth century.

Fugitive slave James Curry recalled the burdens his mother faced as a cook on a North Carolina plantation. "My mother's labor was very hard." She milked fourteen cows early each morning, started preparing the bread for breakfast, and churned the cream. After feeding and "clearing away the family breakfast, she got breakfast for the slaves. . . ." Once she had completed chores around the house, she cooked the family dinner, simple or fancy, depending on whether there were guests. She was still working in the kitchen at eight to nine o'clock at night, when the "slaves' dinner was to be ready," and then she milked the cows again. "She would not get to her log cabin until nine or ten o'clock at night. She would then be so tired that she could scarcely stand," so she would sit by the fire and sew and darn clothes for her children until she fell asleep.

James Curry's mother was also responsible for watching the youngest children of the mothers who worked in the field. Although the specific demands on field hands varied from crop to crop, the general conditions of agricultural labor were harsh indeed. From planting time through harvest season, dawn signaled the start of a working day that often extended far into the night. Most fieldwork ended at dusk, but there might be cotton to gin, sugar to mill, corn to grind, or any number of other jobs that could be done indoors by the light of a lantern. Even in winter, there were miscellaneous chores: fences to build and mend, hogs to slaughter, and wood to chop, haul, and stack. Slaves also performed the carpentry and blacksmithing that kept a plantation productive and in good repair.

Whatever the season, after laboring for the white master, slaves needed to prepare their own meals; feed and wash their children and put them to bed; clean their cabins; wash and mend their clothes; and do all the other chores of daily life. If slaves were fortunate enough to have their own gardens or access to hunting or fishing, late nights and early mornings were almost the only times they could take advantage of these opportunities to improve their diet.

The work that women and men performed in the slave quarters was essential to their survival, since most owners spent as little as they could on food, shelter, and clothing for their slaves. Even generous owners supplied slaves with inferior and inadequate clothing, shelter, and food. Planters typically supplied a weekly food ration of only three and a half pounds of salt pork or bacon and a quarter-bushel of cornmeal. Although high in the calories needed for heavy labor, that diet had serious nutritional deficiencies.

Rice Cultivation and the Task Labor System   Slaves on rice plantations worked according to a task system that allowed many of them more time to take care of their own needs. Still, rice cultivation—of major importance in the South Carolina and Georgia low country and in Louisiana—required highly skilled but backbreaking labor. Women generally were responsible for March plantings. Unlike cotton, corn, or wheat, rice could not be scattered about a plowed field; each grain had to be carefully placed in a single row along the deep trenches that had been plowed and shaped earlier. Over the next five months, the fields had to be alternately flooded, left to dry in the sun, and hoed. Delay in any of these steps could ruin an entire crop. Beginning in August, the harvest kept every able-bodied slave in the fields until October. Men cut the rice plants with sickles while women followed, bundling the plants. Later, the plants had to be flailed by hand to separate the grain from the stalk. Rice cultivation involved intricate systems of dams and dikes to flood and drain the land; these were usually built or repaired by slaves after the harvest and before the spring planting.

Much of the work on rice plantations was organized according to the task system, in which each slave was assigned a particular task each day. Those who worked slowly might find themselves working long hours, but if the task was completed early, the rest of the day was free. This arrangement was intended to encourage slaves to do their work quickly even without close supervision. It also shifted some of the responsibility for feeding the slaves onto themselves. Former slave George Gould remembered that his

Technology in the Fields

Cultivating rice involved a multitude of backbreaking tasks. Even before the planting and cultivation of the crop (see the rice field at the center), an elaborate system for controlling the waters had to be completed. This 1867 engraving of a plantation near Savannah, Georgia, shows completed dikes and flood gates and cleared fields. Many scholars believe that much of the technology involved in rice cultivation originated in West Africa's rice-producing regions and was brought by slaves across the Atlantic. Alfred R. Waud, *Harper's Weekly*, January 5, 1867 — American Social History Project.

master "used to come in the field, and tell the overseers not to balk [us], if we got done soon to let us alone and do our own work as we pleased." For some slaves, the task system permitted a degree of personal autonomy and even modest economic well-being. Those who finished their tasks early might spend their free time producing or acquiring fish, game, handicrafts, crops, or even livestock for personal use, barter, and sale.

But rice cultivation also involved special perils. Work in the fields exposed slaves to malaria, pneumonia, and tuberculosis. One visitor attributed the high number of deaths among slaves to the "constant moisture and heat of the atmosphere, together with the alternate floodings and dryings of the fields, on which the negroes are perpetually at work, often ankle-deep in mud, with their bare heads exposed to the fierce rays of the sun. . . . At such seasons every white man leaves the spot, as a matter of course, and proceeds inland to the high grounds; or, if he can afford it, he travels northward to the springs of Saratoga, or the lakes of Canada."

Tobacco, Sugar, Cotton, and the Gang Labor System

Unlike rice cultivation, tobacco plantations relied primarily on gangs of slaves performing the largely unskilled work. Plowing began in April. In May, the tobacco plants that had been growing indoors since March were transplanted to the fields. For the next several months, gangs periodically worked in the fields, weeding, hoeing, and pruning the lower leaves of the tobacco plants. The plants were harvested in August and September and hung to dry. Slaves then

MAP 6.6 Rice, Cotton, Tobacco, and Sugar Production in the 1830s

Although cotton was considered the king of southern agricultural products by 1830, several other crops competed with cotton for labor and profits. Tobacco, rice, and sugar, although they could not be grown in as many parts of the South as cotton, were highly profitable in those sections where the climate and soil were favorable. These crops demanded different kinds of labor and were characterized by different growing seasons and cycles, which contributed to the distinct experiences of slaves on rice, tobacco, cotton, and sugar plantations.

stripped the stalks and prepared the leaves for export or manufacturing. Charles Ball, a slave who worked both rice and tobacco, recalled that in the winter, there was "some sort of respite from the toils of the year," as he and other slaves "repaired fences, split rails for new fences, slaughtered hogs, cleared new land, [and] raised tobacco plants for the next planting."

Large gangs also cultivated sugar and cotton, and planters could profit from the labor of the entire slave family—men, women, and children (Map 6.6). In the interest of profit, cotton planters emphasized supervision and discipline, dividing most jobs by age and sex. In general, men plowed and women hoed, working side by side with members of their own sex. As schoolteacher Emily Burke observed, "During the greater part of the winter season, the negro women are busy in picking, ginning and packing cotton for market," while men repaired buildings and cleared land.

During the harvest season, men and women worked together as they swept across one field after another, picking at an unrelenting pace. Solomon Northup, a free black man from New York, was kidnapped and sold to a Louisiana cotton planter. He recalled that the fastest worker took "the lead row," and anyone who fell behind or was "a moment idle [was]

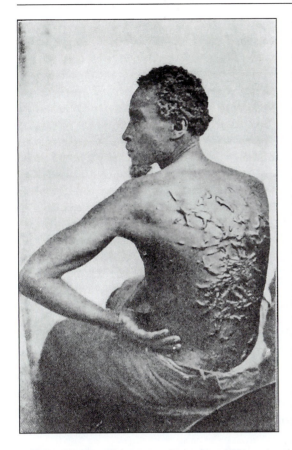

A Map of Servitude
The back of a Louisiana slave named Gordon, photographed in 1863 after he escaped to the Union forces. Whipping was one method of punishment suffered by plantation slaves. Prints and Photographs Division, Library of Congress.

whipped." Through the heat of August, September, and October, all able-bodied men and women picked the cotton, stooping as they walked, pulling the bolls from the prickly pods, which cut their hands. This unrelenting labor kept them in the fields from sunrise until it was, Northup wrote, "too dark to see, and when the moon is full, they oftentimes labor till the middle of the night." No one stopped "until the order to halt" was heard. Each day ended at the scales, where an overseer weighed the cotton each slave had picked. Those who fell short of their quota were whipped.

Punishment was used more often than reward to induce slaves to work harder, and whipping was the most common means. In the South Carolina rice-growing region, according to former slave Hagar Brown, "Don't do your task, driver wave that whip, put you over a barrel, beat you so blood run down." On the Louisiana cotton plantation of Bennett Barrow, some three-quarters of the incidents that led to physical punishments were work-related: "for not picking as well as he can," for picking "very trashy cotton," "for not bringing her cotton up," and so forth. On average, Barrow whipped one of his slaves every four days. Others were imprisoned, chained, beaten, shot, or maimed in other ways. And with all this, his biographer tells us, Barrow treated slaves better than did many of his neighbors.

The Internal Slave Trade The growing importance of slavery to southern agriculture was accompanied by rising prices for slaves. In the seventeenth and eighteenth centuries, competition from Caribbean sugar planters had begun to bid up slave prices. Congress's 1808 prohibition against the importation of Africans further constricted the supply, boosting prices even higher. These high prices led early-nineteenth-century owners to place a premium on the survival and natural reproduction of the slaves they already owned, sometimes limiting their cruelty and even inspiring them to more generous food and housing allotments. Yet the value of slaves and the movement of plantation agriculture into new areas also ensured the expansion of the internal slave trade. Perhaps nothing symbolized the human cost of bondage as vividly as the wholesale destruction of slave families through this trade—the key to success for some masters, especially in the Chesapeake. Plantation owners there managed to adapt to the declining profits of

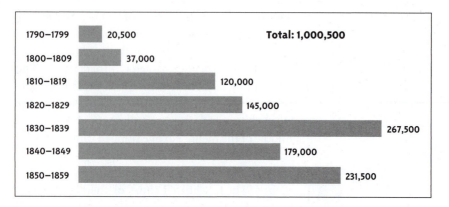

Period	Number
1790–1799	20,500
1800–1809	37,000
1810–1819	120,000
1820–1829	145,000
1830–1839	267,500
1840–1849	179,000
1850–1859	231,500

Total: 1,000,500

FIGURE 6.1 Movement of Slaves from Upper South to Lower South, 1790–1860
The invention of the cotton gin, the forced removal of American Indians from their lands, and the 1808 federal ban on the importation of slaves all contributed to a boom in cotton cultivation and a concurrent increase in the trade of slaves within the United States. This dramatic increase in the internal slave trade ruptured slave families and communities starting in the early nineteenth century, sending nearly 800,000 slaves from the settled areas of the Upper South to the new plantations of the Lower South and Southwest. From James A. Henretta et al., *America's History*, 6th ed., vol. 1 (Boston: Bedford/St. Martin's, 2008). Based on data in Robert William Fogel and Stanley L. Engerman, *Time on the Cross* (Boston: Little, Brown, 1974); and Michael Tadman, *Speculators and Slaves: Masters, Traders, and Slaves in the Old South* (Madison: University of Wisconsin Press, 1996).

tobacco production by turning to the sale of surplus slave labor (Figure 6.1). When sold to an Alabama cotton planter, a Louisiana sugar baron, or a Car-olina rice grower, a slave born and raised in Maryland or Virginia fetched his or her master a handsome return on his investment, often thousands of dollars.

Although some planters tried to sell slave families intact or at least to keep mothers and their children together, this practice declined over time. Increasingly, buyers sought younger and less expensive slaves, and sellers ultimately complied with the demands of the market. Of course, some white owners never recognized the existence of slave families at all. Of those who did, many felt no obligation to maintain kin connections when high prices promised otherwise unobtainable profits.

Particularly from the 1820s on, the market in slaves wreaked havoc on the

"Sold to Tennessee"
Lewis Miller, a sometime artist and carpenter whose work often took him to Virginia, observed this "cottle" of slaves en route to new owners in Tennessee. Miller sketched the scene and transcribed the words of the slaves' song. Lewis Miller, *Virginia Sketchbook* — Abby Aldrich Rockefeller Folk Art Center, Williamsburg, Virginia.

"The Bargain Was Agreed Upon": A View of the Slave Market

In 1841, Solomon Northup, a free African American living in New York, was kidnapped while visiting Washington, D.C., and sold into slavery. He spent the next twelve years working on plantations in Louisiana, finally attaining freedom in 1853. His book, Twelve Years a Slave, *presented a stark, detailed account of day-to-day slave life, including this depiction of a sale run by a slave dealer named Freeman.*

Next day many customers called to examine Freeman's 'new lot.' The latter gentleman was very loquacious, dwelling at much length upon our several good points and qualities. He would make us hold up our heads, walk briskly back and forth, while customers would feel of our hands and arms and bodies, turn us about, ask us what we could do, make us open our mouths and show our teeth, precisely as a jockey examines a horse which he is about to barter for or purchase. Sometimes a man or woman was taken back to the small house in the yard, stripped, and inspected more minutely. Scars upon a slave's back were considered evidence of a rebellious or unruly spirit, and hurt his sale. . . .

During the day, however, a number of sales were made. David and Caroline were purchased together by a Natchez planter. They left us, grinning broadly, and in a most happy state of mind, caused by the fact of their not being separated. Sethe was sold to a planter of Baton Rouge, her eyes flashing with anger as she was led away.

The same man also purchased Randall. The little fellow was made to jump, and run across the floor, and perform many other feats exhibiting his activity and condition. All the time the trade was going on, Eliza was crying aloud, and wringing her hands. She besought the man not to buy him, unless he also bought herself and Emily. She promised, in that case, to be the most faithful slave that ever lived. The man answered that he could not afford it, and then Eliza burst into a paroxysm of grief, weeping plaintively. Freeman turned round to her, savagely, with his whip in his uplifted hand, ordering her to stop her noise, or . . . he would take her to the yard and give her a hundred lashes. . . . Eliza shrunk before him, and tried to wipe away her tears, but it was all in vain. She wanted to be with her children, she said, the little time she had to live.

All the frowns and threats of Freeman could not wholly silence the afflicted mother. She kept on begging and beseeching them, most piteously, not to separate the three. Over and over again she told them how she loved her boy. A great many times she repeated her former promises—how very faithful and obedient she would be; how hard she would labor day and night, to the last moment of her life; if he would only buy them all together. But it was of no avail; the man could not afford it. The bargain was agreed upon, and Randall must go alone. Then Eliza ran to him; embraced him passionately; kissed him again and again; told him to remember her—all the while her tears falling in the boy's face like rain. . . .

> The planter from Baton Rouge, with his new purchase, was ready to depart.
>
> 'Don't cry, mama. I will be a good boy. Don't cry,' said Randall, looking back, as they passed out the door.
>
> ———————
>
> Solomon Northrup, *Twelve Years a Slave* (1853).

families of African Americans, causing them enormous anguish. In March 1829, a Virginia resident wrote to the *Genius of Universal Emancipation*, an antislavery paper, describing "a most tragic occurrence . . . occasioned by those monsters who traffic in HUMAN FLESH." A planter in the town of Hillsborough had sold a group of slaves to a trader, who held the chattel in a room overnight. In the morning, a middle-aged woman among those sold was found dead, "choosing death rather than be dragged off by these tyrants." Henry Watson, another Virginia slave, recalled his agony when, as a small child, his mother was sold away. An older woman tried to comfort him, but Watson was inconsolable. "Every exertion was made on my part to find her, or hear some tidings of her, but all my efforts were unsuccessful; and from that day, I have never seen or heard from her."

The Slave Auction

Slavery, and particularly slave auctions, left an indelible impression on many visitors to the antebellum South. One of them was a British artist, Eyre Crowe, who sketched a Richmond slave sale in 1853. During the Civil War, he painted a series of pictures based on his earlier drawings and notes that delineated the auction and subsequent separation of slave families. Eyre Crowe, 1862, oil on canvas, 13 ×21 inches — Kennedy Galleries, Inc., New York.

Slave families were also broken apart by the death of owners, which led to the division of estates for inheritance or payment of debts. Slave families might be broken up through the marriage of white planters, which were often accompanied by "gifts" of young slaves to the new couple. Or a slave owner moving from one county to another might take his chattel with him, thereby severing connections between slave husbands and wives who lived on neighboring plantations. Slaves, then, were dependent on their owners not just for food, clothing, and shelter, but for the very existence of their families.

Southern White Experiences

Although the lives of all whites in the South were affected by the spread of slavery, they did not all have the same relationship to that institution. Wealthier whites, who obtained larger and larger numbers of slaves, formed an elite planter class that controlled much of the economic and political power in the region. Small farmers often became dependent on neighboring planters for the transportation and sale of their cotton, yet they also challenged planters' right to fence off property, dam rivers, and in other ways encroach on the customary privileges of local residents. Poorer whites generally lived short and brutal lives. The most fortunate hired themselves out to planters and farmers or headed west in hopes of finding cheaper land and new opportunities.

The planter class was a powerful group economically and politically, but they were not united on every issue. They differed in their ideas about slave management, in the roles played by women in their families, and in their ideas about the future of slavery. These differences were shaped in part by the size of their holdings in land and slaves. Nonslaveholding whites also differed in their wealth, ideas about slavery, and attitudes toward those above and below them in the southern social order. Successful farmers might hope to rise into the planter class one day, while those barely scratching out a living often resented the wealth and power wielded by local and regional elites. During the 1820s and early 1830s, the future of slavery, at least in Upper South states such as Virginia, hinged not only on relations between blacks and whites, but also on relations between planters and nonslaveholding whites.

The Planter Class   Planters were, of course, dependent on their slaves. Slavery was first and foremost a way of controlling the labor that produced profits from the commercial production of cotton, sugar, rice, and tobacco. Yet planters responded in different ways to the black workers who served as the foundation of their world. Some planters were incredibly cruel, frequently employing the lash and the branding iron. Others, particularly those with close ties to the church, believed in a more benevolent style of authority. They might teach a few slaves to read, allow them to attend church, and provide lighter workloads for pregnant and nursing women. At the same time, many planters who embraced evangelical teachings used religion to defend slavery as an institution and assert their authority over slaves.

Plantation mistresses as well as masters varied in their responses to slaves. Most mistresses were responsible for directing the house slaves and for organizing clothing, food, and health care for field hands. While many mistresses complained about these responsibilities, few thought that slavery should be eliminated. At most, they sought to improve slaves' living conditions and to diminish harsh punishments. But some were as likely as their husbands to inflict the whip or the branding iron. Plantation mistress Lucilla McCorkle, angry at "some disobedience, much idleness, sulleness and slovenliness" among the slaves on her plantation, "Used the rod." Others, like Sophia Smede, reminded her daughters that slaves "are not machines, they are just like you, made from the same flesh and blood."

The ranks of slave owners expanded steadily in the early nineteenth century. By 1830, some 225,000 white Southerners owned slaves. Because slave labor yielded slaveholders their wealth, power, and leisure, successful planters felt compelled to accumulate more slaves. Although the absolute number of slave owners grew, the total white population grew faster. Slaves were becoming more expensive, and a shrinking proportion of all southern whites could afford to own them. The 36 percent of white families who owned slaves in 1830 shrank to 31 percent in 1850 and to 26 percent by 1860. Nonetheless, it was this slave-owning segment of the white population that controlled the great bulk of the region's wealth and wielded most of its political power.

Of course, not all slaveholders were wealthy planters. The elite among plantation owners were those who held fifty or more slaves and owned enough land to make such an investment in labor profitable. Next were the more numerous but less wealthy middling planters who owned between fifteen and fifty slaves. Even more numerous were the small farmers who owned five or six slaves and land valued at about $3,000. Even that much property made the small southern slave owner many times wealthier than the average northerner. But dependence on the export economy left the southern farmer vulnerable to sharp decreases in crop prices or increases

Family Amalgamation Among the Man-Stealers

An illustration from an 1834 antislavery tract depicted an unlikely domestic scene in a plantation household, with slave children joining their owners at the dinner table. Some antislavery advocates viewed the potential for intimacy between whites and blacks as one of the demoralizing effects of the "peculiar institution." George Bourne, *Pictures of Slavery in the United States of America* (1834) — Prints and Photographs Division, Library of Congress.

The Old Plantation Home

This lithograph by the popular firm of Currier and Ives portrayed the slave quarters as a carefree world, basking in the glow of the planter's benevolence. The plantation as the perfect extended family was a common theme of proslavery prints before the Civil War — and after. Currier and Ives, 1872, lithograph, 9 × 12 1/2 inches — Prints and Photographs Division, Library of Congress.

in the cost of land, transport, and, most significantly, slaves. Debt and economic uncertainty affected such people much more than they did the planter aristocracy. And as eastern lands became depleted, some elite planter families were compelled to uproot themselves, join the southwestern migration, and submit to the ruder life on the cotton frontier.

We know the planter elite best from its self-descriptions and later from novels and films that romanticized their life as elegant, cultured, and removed from the hectic pace and pressures of commerce or industry. Planters liked to see themselves in the role of stern but loving fathers guiding the lives of their plantation families—especially their slave "children"—with paternal wisdom and justice. But the story of slave masters and mistresses seated on the porches of grand mansions sipping mint juleps and ordering others benevolently to do their bidding was largely fictive and had little to do with life on most plantations in the 1820s and 1830s. Instead, many planters along the coast and on the frontier built modest homes on their country estates. When Pierce Butler brought his new wife, British actress Fanny Kemble, to his South Carolina Sea Islands rice plantation in 1834, she considered herself "on the outer bounds of civilized creation." The house, she noted in despair, "consists of three small rooms . . . a wooden recess by way of a pantry, and a kitchen detached from the dwelling."

At least through the 1830s, the expansion of planters' power was visible mainly in cities and towns rather than in the more remote agricultural hinterlands where their wealth was produced. Urban centers offered the chance to inhabit fancier living quarters, participate in the best social and political circles, join in courting rituals and marriage arrangements with other planter families, buy new furniture and the latest fashions, and keep up with news on national and international markets and prices.

On election and court days, held in county seats and major cities, planters could mingle with nonslaveholding whites, small farmers, and lesser masters to cement ties of credit, kinship, and political clout. Meanwhile militia musters, market days, and slave auctions in cities and towns provided regular opportunities for elite whites to demonstrate their mastery, authority, and largesse. The wives of wealthy planters did their part by assisting the sick and poor and planning church and social events. Such functions were particularly important in the first three decades of the nineteenth century, when unstable markets, slave rebellions, antislavery campaigns, evangelical revivals, and the pressure for westward expansion buffeted the planter elite.

Still, despite the uncertainties of the early nineteenth century, the planter class was increasingly in control of the South's economy and politics. Southern elites controlled political offices in their home states and maintained a powerful presence in the nation's capital. In towns and cities across the South, they established a strong political, religious, and economic presence. These elites stood on the cusp of a new era, in which cotton was king and the plantation owner its favored subject.

Poor Whites and Small Farmers Confront a Slave Society

After about 1820, opportunities began to narrow for the South's small farmers, known as yeomen. The frontier no longer offered them the chance to start a better life, as large planters took over the most fertile areas. The removal of Indians, however, provided access to new lands in the Georgia upcountry, the western Carolinas, and northern sections of Louisiana and Mississippi. Here, many independent farm families managed to secure a comfortable livelihood, while others at least succeeded in owning their own home and land.

The South's small farmers were never completely isolated from the plantation economy. But from the 1820s on, they became more enmeshed in its web as cotton, rice, and sugar became more central to the region's economy. Small farmers often depended on planters for credit in hard times, and members of yeoman families might be employed on plantations as overseers or skilled laborers. In addition, the extensive family networks that character-

Woodcutter's Cabin on the Mississippi

French artist August Hervieu sketched a poor white family in 1827. The drawing later appeared as an illustration in British author Frances Trollope's acerbic and very popular account of a stay in the United States, *Domestic Manners of the Americans*, published in 1832. (August Hervieu) Frances Trollope, *Domestic Manners of the Americans* (1832) — Rare Books and Manuscripts Division, New York Public Library, Astor, Lenox and Tilden Foundations.

ized southern life ensured that some small farmers and even poor whites might claim kinship with their more well-to-do slaveholding neighbors.

Despite their ties to the planter elite, yeomen farmers did not always side with planters in their defense of slavery. By the 1820s and 1830s, throughout the Upper South—in Missouri and Kentucky as well as Maryland and Virginia—residents questioned the financial profitability of slavery. Many farmers turned from tobacco to other crops, such as wheat, that did not require year-round labor. In 1831–1832, the Virginia state legislature considered resolutions that supported the gradual emancipation of slaves or their shipment to Africa. Representatives from the western part of the state (what is today West Virginia), where yeomen rather than planters dominated the population, supported most of these resolutions. The resolutions received a substantial number of votes but failed to pass. This debate and the defeat of the resolutions was the result, in part, of timing, for in 1831 a major slave rebellion (see pages 311–312), led by Nat Turner, erupted in Virginia. Nonetheless, the existence of such a debate suggests the problems Upper South planters faced in sustaining the institution of slavery.

In states such as North Carolina and Georgia that had strong plantation economies in their coastal counties, residents who lived in more mountainous regions often questioned the wisdom of expanding slavery. Small farm families in the South also objected to the ways in which wealthy planters usurped their rights and privileges as landowners. In the post-Revolutionary era, southern legislators had expanded the voting rights of white men and the representation from newly settled western counties. Wielding their increased political clout, yeomen petitioned for better fence laws, payment for wartime damages, and fishing rights. In Georgia and the Carolinas in the early 1800s, upcountry farmers found their access to shad, a source of cheap and abundant food, severely curtailed by plantation owners who built dams and millraces downriver, thereby diminishing the fish supply upriver. Arguing that "the allmity [sic] intended" the fish "for all man kind," petitioners complained, "We are rogued out of a part of our rights." These non-slave-owning yeomen may have accepted slavery as an institution, but they continued to protest when planters trampled on rights they held dear.

Poor whites, who owned neither land nor slaves, were largely at the mercy of planters and yeomen for their sustenance. In frontier areas, they might survive by hunting, fishing, and trapping, but in established regions, poor white women and men generally sold their labor to more well-to-do neighbors. Some moved to southern seaport cities, seeking work along the docks or as seamstresses or day laborers, but there they had to compete with free black as well as slave labor, making steady employment unlikely. Although some managed to remain in the same community for years, others drifted from place to place, seeking opportunities wherever they might be.

By the 1830s, then, poor whites and small farmers across the South found themselves simultaneously pushed to the margins and enmeshed in a slave-based market economy. The plantation economy rewarded single-crop agriculture and reinforced a clear social hierarchy. Of course, being white and male promised some measure of status and protection against dependency. But increasingly, it was large slaveholders who ruled the South, politically, socially, and economically.

Religion, Resistance, and Rebellion

As slavery grew and spread into new areas of the South, African Americans sought new sources of support and honed older forms of resistance. The evangelical church provided one of the few arenas in which more harmonious relations between the races could develop in the eighteenth century. By the early 1800s, however, white churches had become more deeply involved in sustaining slavery even as growing numbers of blacks embraced evangelical Protestant beliefs. All-black congregations offered one means of resisting white domination, but most were located in cities. For the vast majority of African Americans enslaved in rural areas, more direct means of resistance were necessary.

On plantations and small farms, slave women and men employed a variety of methods to slow the pace of work, subvert the owners' authority, and create a sense of identity and community distinct from whites. A small number of slaves chose open rebellion over everyday resistance. Although none of these uprisings succeeded in toppling the institution of slavery, or even doing significant damage to it, each sent a shock wave of fear through the white South. Along with a small but growing movement opposed to slavery in the North, southern blacks' embrace of religion, resistance, and rebellion made clear that the institution of slavery could be maintained only by physical force and a strong political will.

Blacks Embrace Evangelical Religion   In the early 1800s, evangelical Protestantism had questioned the sense of hierarchy favored by most large planters, but by the 1820s, this challenge had begun to fade. Nationwide, churches that embraced the new evangelical creed—Methodists, Baptists, and Presbyterians—saw their combined formal membership multiply more than thirteen times between 1800 and 1860. African Americans made up nearly one-third of Baptist membership and perhaps one-quarter of Methodists. Yet a vision of a Christian community united across race and class lines did not materialize.

In the 1820s, southern evangelical churches still housed diverse congregations, but increasingly, such mixed bodies of worshippers reinforced rather than subverted social and political hierarchies. Although poor whites

"The Meeting Continued All Night, Both by the White & Black People"

Camp meetings such as this one, held near Sparta, Georgia, in 1807, were a manifestation of the nationwide Second Great Awakening of the early nineteenth century. Like the first Great Awakening of the eighteenth century, the Second Great Awakening was notably egalitarian, with men, women, blacks, and poor whites mingling together in worship.

The Methodists have lately had a Camp Meeting in Hancock County, about three miles south of Sparta in Georgia. The meeting began on Tuesday, 28th July, at 12 o'clock, and ended on Saturday following. We counted thirty-seven Methodist preachers at the meeting; and with the assistance of a friend I took an account of the Tents, and there were one hundred and seventy-six of them, and many of them were very large. From the number of people who attended preaching at the rising of the sun, I concluded that there were about 3000 persons, white and black together, that lodged on the ground at night. I think the largest congregation was about 4000 hearers.

We fixed the plan to preach four times a day-at sunrise, 10 o'clock, 3 o'clock and at night; and in general we had an exhortation after the sermon.

. . . The first day of the meeting, we had a gentle and comfortable moving of the spirit of the Lord among us; and at night it was much more powerful than before, and the meeting was kept up all night without intermission however, before day the white people retired, and the meeting was continued by the black people.

On Wednesday at 10 o'clock the meeting was remarkably lively, and many souls were deeply wrought upon; and at the close of the sermon there was a general cry for mercy; and before night there were a good many persons who professed to get converted. That night the meeting continued all night, both by the white & black people, and many souls were converted before day. . . .

Friday was the greatest day of all. We had the Lord's Supper at night, by candlelight, where several hundred communicants attended; and such a solemn time I have seldom seen on the like occasion; three of the preachers fell helpless within the altar; and one lay a considerable time before he came to himself. From that the work of convictions and conversion spread, and a large number were converted during the night, and there was no intermission until the breake of day at that time many stout hearted sinners were conquered.

Farmer's Gazette (Sparta, GA), Aug. 8, 1807, signed Jesse Lee, reprinted U. B. Phillips, *A Documentary History of American Industrial Society: Plantation and Frontier* vol. 2 (Cleveland: A. H. Clark, 1910), 284–286.

and slaves might pray alongside yeomen farmers and large planters, the minister to whom they listened was beholden to the wealthier parishioners. The denominations and ministers who continued to preach a more radically egalitarian message—the Quakers and Wesleyan Methodists, for instance—found themselves marginalized in the South, even silenced. Religion still provided solace for the less fortunate, but at least among southern whites, it no longer provided a powerful vehicle for resistance against planter domination.

From its emergence in the late 1700s, evangelical religion held a strong appeal for blacks as well as whites. Many African Americans sought to combine traditional African beliefs with elements of Christianity introduced by white preachers or by their owners. Although owners often used Christian beliefs to support the institution of slavery, claiming that it was God's will that Africans were in bondage and whites were free, slaves still found solace in religion. By accepting Christianity, slaves could claim membership in the same spiritual world as whites. Indeed, one unnamed black man, probably a slave of the Reverend John Fort, challenged a white preacher to include slaves equally in his ministries. "If God sent you to preach to sinners," the man asked, "did he direct you to keep your face to the white folks constantly or is it because these give you money[?]" The money might be "handed to you by our master," he noted, but "we are the very persons who labor for this money."

Some Protestant denominations allowed independent black congregations to form in the early 1800s. They were often linked to free black denominations in the North, such as the African Methodist Episcopal Church. Although frequently sponsored and supervised by whites, these churches were the first and only community-wide institutions that allowed slaves membership. Their deacons and preachers (commonly free blacks) were some of the only African Americans whom whites permitted to play any kind of leadership role among slaves. Some black ministers even attracted a white following.

Missionary Society

The iconography on the certificate of the Methodist Episcopal Church's Missionary Society espoused the church's evangelical creed but obscured growing division among its members over the issue of slavery. Smithsonian Institution.

Plantation Burial

Funerals were sad occasions in the slave quarters, but they gave African Americans a chance to confirm their community identity. They were often held at night, so that friends and family members from neighboring farms could attend. John Antrobus, 1860, oil on canvas, 53 × 81 1/2 inches (1960.46) — The Historic New Orleans Collection.

In rural and frontier areas, ordained black ministers and established black or mixed-race congregations were harder to find. There, charismatic individuals gathered groups of believers around them, opening leadership roles to slaves and to African American women, who were largely excluded from the ordained ministry. A traveler in the Georgia backcountry in the 1830s witnessed a group of some two hundred slaves attending an open-air funeral service under the direction of a "preacher" from the local slave community.

Black women were especially active in the evangelical movement. Evangelical practices could replace traditional African birth rituals as protection for their children. Evangelicalism could also be wielded as a weapon against sexual abuse, as when women called on church authorities to discipline owners, employers, and even ministers who exploited them. Women made up well over half of black evangelical converts throughout the early 1800s, and some women drew on African customs that recognized women as spiritual leaders. Clarinda, a self-appointed preacher in Beaufort, South Carolina, attracted unrelenting hostility from white and black church leaders but also welcomed a steady stream of followers to attend weekly meetings in her home.

Relying on African American forms of evangelical Protestantism, slaves and free blacks were able to formulate their own standards of proper behavior. They used these to judge their treatment by whites and to clarify mutual rights and obligations among themselves. For instance, the all-black Gillfield Baptist Church in Petersburg, Virginia, expelled a man named David for adultery and for slandering "every Sister in the Church." Through such means, southern blacks strengthened their sense of group identity and their ties to one another. At the same time, they asserted an increased (if still very restricted) degree of self-regulation and self-rule.

A Battle of Wills: Daily Resistance and Open Rebellion

Although some African Americans accommodated themselves to their owners' wishes in order to avoid sale, brutal beatings, or other forms of punishment, others demonstrated their opposition to bondage through everyday acts of resistance. Using whites' own prejudices about the laziness and irresponsibility of black labor, slaves broke tools, worked at a slow pace, damaged property, feigned illness or pregnancy, and engaged in other forms of sabotage. Slave cooks might spoil meals or spit in the soup before serving it. A few even poisoned their owners. Suspicious fires were also common on plantations. Slaves might use them to distract masters from other crimes, such as the theft of meat or other goods. Many enslaved men and women also ran away, hiding out for days or weeks at a time. Some of them, mostly men, found their way to freedom in the North.

Despite nearly impossible odds, a small number of slaves chose open revolt over daily resistance. These revolts revealed the deep feelings and aspirations that slaves normally had to conceal from their masters. Although such open rebellions were rare, they were greatly feared by white southerners of all classes, and their outbreak often resonated across the region no matter how limited the actual event was.

In these direct challenges to planter authority, enslaved African Americans often wielded the values, language, and symbols of evangelical Protestantism that were regularly invoked by the whites who held them captive. Free African Americans who supported such rebellions made use of the nation's revolutionary and republican heritage to express their views. Certainly, the events

Discipline
During the Civil War, Wilson Chinn, a former Louisiana slave, exhibited instruments of punishment devised by masters. Difficult to discern here, as well as in the original photograph, the initials of Chinn's master were branded on his forehead. Prints and Photographs Division, Library of Congress.

in Sainte-Domingue and the slave Gabriel's planned revolt in Richmond (see Chapter 5) worried southern planters. Most slaveholders were unaware of day-to-day resistance on their own plantations, both because it was concealed by the slaves' skilled performance and because their own social blindness led them to regard their slaves as docile, shiftless, or clumsy. Nonetheless, the image of the contented slave never fully managed to calm the slaveholders' deep-seated fear that, given the right circumstances, their slaves might rise up and cut their masters' throats. As Virginia Congressman John Randolph reported, "the night bell never tolls for fire in Richmond, that the [white] mother does not hug the infant more closely to her bosom."

In 1822, Denmark Vesey, a free black carpenter living in Charleston, South Carolina, was charged with organizing one of the broadest and best-planned insurrectionary conspiracies in southern history. Vesey, a merchant seaman, traveled widely, read antislavery literature, and quoted antislavery speeches and the Bible to convince other blacks of the possibility of emancipation. The white authorities believed that he had organized an insurrection that might involve as many as 9,000 slaves. Despite questionable evidence of an actual conspiracy, white authorities quickly arrested 131 Charleston blacks. Whatever the actual extent of Vesey's activities, he had managed to terrify local whites. In the summer of 1822, as a brutal warning to other would-be rebels, Vesey and thirty-six others were hanged.

Open rebellion against white domination did not end in 1822, however. Free blacks and skilled slaves, inspired by evangelical religion and whites' own debates over the place of slavery in the nation, would continue to play central roles in slave rebellions until the Civil War. Yet by 1830, it was clear that armed resistance was unlikely to overcome white hunger for bound labor, just as American Indian resistance was unable to thwart white hunger for land. With the power of government regulation and military force behind them, southern whites seemed destined to defeat all who stood in their way.

Emancipation by Any Means In the aftermath of the American Revolution, many white southerners, particularly in the Upper South, had imagined that slavery would one day end. After all, George Washington had left instructions in his will to free his slaves on his widow's death, and Thomas Jefferson had worried about sustaining the institution of bondage in a republic. In this context, ideas circulated regarding systems of gradual emancipation in which planters would be repaid for their investment in human flesh. Some, such as the wealthy white southerners who helped to found the American Colonization Society in 1816, planned for that day by raising funds to ship African Americans back to their "homeland." The organization received funds from private donors in the North and the South, evangelical churches, the U.S. Congress, and the Virginia and Maryland state legislatures and did manage to send several boatloads of African Americans out of the country. In 1830, the Society established the nation of Liberia on the west coast of Africa to receive those it bought out of bondage.

Southern antislavery societies, usually dominated by Quakers, Methodists, or Baptists, also continued to exist during the first third of the nineteenth century, especially in the Upper South. Some white craft workers and farmers may have supported them. There were certainly instances in which white workers and tenant farmers encouraged and even helped individual slaves to escape from their masters.

Yet during the early 1800s, the total number of slaves who were freed by colonization or antislavery societies was tiny in comparison to the rapid growth in the slave population. With the profits promised by cotton, sugar, and rice, the entrenchment of slavery was assured. More and more opponents of human bondage, South and North, abandoned hopes for the peaceful and gradual disappearance of slavery, which was increasingly considered a "peculiar institution" within American society.

By the mid-1820s, some northern states had abolished slavery, and others had passed laws to ensure its eventual demise. New York was the last northern state to end slavery. In 1810, more than 60 percent of white households in Flatbush, on western Long Island (in what is today Brooklyn), con-

---

"Let No Man of Us Budge One Step": David Walker Demands Freedom

In a work that soon came to be known as David Walker's Appeal, *David Walker in 1829 demanded the complete and immediate emancipation of slaves in the United States, challenging the prevailing beliefs among most white critics of slavery that emancipation should come gradually and that free blacks should be sent abroad to distant colonies.*

Will any of us leave our homes and go to Africa? I hope not. Let them commence their attack upon us as they did on our brethren in Ohio, driving and beating us from our country, and my soul for theirs, they will have enough of it. Let no man of us budge one step, and let slaveholders come to beat us from our country. America is more our country, than it is the whites' — we have enriched it with our blood and tears. The greatest riches in all America have arisen from our blood and tears: — and will they drive us from our property and homes, which we have earned with our blood?

. . . Throw away your fears and prejudices then, and enlighten us and treat us like men, and we will like you more than we do now hate you; and tell us now no more about colonization, for America is as much our country, as it is yours. — Treat us like men, and there is no danger but we will all live in peace and happiness together. For we are not like you, hardhearted, unmerciful, and unforgiving. What a happy country this will be, if the whites will listen.

David Walker, *David Walker's Appeal: To the Coloured Citizens of the World* (1829).

The Scenes which the above Plate is designed to represent, are—Fig. 1, a Mother intreating for the lives of her children.—2, Mr. Travis, cruelly murdered by his own Slaves.—3. Mr. Barrow, who bravely defended himself until his wife escaped.—4. A comp. of mounted Dragoons in pursuit of the Blacks.

Turner Rebellion

This woodcut was published in an 1831 account of the slave uprising. Samuel Warner, *Authentic and impartial narrative of the tragical scene which was witnessed in Southampton County (Virginia) . . .* (New York, 1831) — Prints and Photographs Division, Library of Congress.

tained slaves. Owners of vast estates in New York's Hudson River Valley also held large numbers of slaves. Under New York's 1817 abolition act, children who were born into slavery before July 4, 1827, would have to serve as indentured servants until the age of twenty-eight if male and twenty-five if female. Most blacks throughout the North and Midwest were still denied voting rights, the right to testify in court, equal access to public accommodations and public schools, and entrance into an array of occupations. They were confined to menial and low-paying jobs and were subject to racist abuse and physical attacks. Still, more and more were technically free, and they founded an array of churches, schools, and mutual aid and literary societies to improve the quality of their lives.

Northern free blacks expressed their horror of slavery in a variety of ways. In 1826, members of the Massachusetts General Colored Association advocated both abolition and the advancement of free blacks. One especially compelling spokesperson was David Walker, the free-born son of a slave father. Walker had left his native North Carolina for Boston as a youth and there earned a living by selling clothing. He soon became a leading figure in the city's growing free black community and an agent and writer for the New York–based *Freedom's Journal*, the nation's first newspaper published by African Americans.

In 1829, Walker published *Appeal to the Coloured Citizens of the World*, a pamphlet that caused a sensation. Its militant tone and call to action by the slaves marked a fundamental breach with earlier antislavery arguments. "Brethren," Walker urged, "arise, arise! Strike for your lives and liberties. Now is the day and the hour." When he did address white readers, Walker quoted their own revolutionary principles: "ALL MEN ARE CREATED EQUAL, that they are endowed by their Creator with certain inalienable rights; that among these are life, liberty, and the pursuit of happiness." Walker claimed for slaves the rights proclaimed "in this Republican Land of Liberty."

On an oppressively hot August night in 1831, Walker's demands were written in blood in an uprising in Southampton County, Virginia. Nat Turner, a religious leader and self-styled Baptist minister, was also a skilled slave who had been forced into field work and then sold away from his wife. Turner had received a vision while working in the fields, and he believed that God had assigned him a mission. Although he was polite and respectful when in the company of whites, he plotted with a close circle of friends and family to overthrow their masters. On the night of August 21, 1831, Turner and a group of supporters killed all the members of the Travis family, his owners, beginning a bloody insurrection and a desperate, ultimately unsuccessful, bid for freedom that would end in the deaths of some 60 white men, women, and children.

Turner and all his coconspirators were captured and tried, but Turner refused to acknowledge that he had done anything wrong. In prison, the rebellious prophet continued to draw strength from his Christian faith. "Was not Christ crucified?" he proclaimed. Although Turner and sixteen of his compatriots were executed, the uprising continued to haunt southern whites. A letter published in the *Richmond Whig* a month after Turner's capture placed responsibility for his religious zealotry squarely in the hands of white evangelical preachers and their "canting about equality." It was they, or perhaps the master's son who had taught Turner to read, who had infected "an imagination like Nat's" with "the possibility of freeing himself and his race from bondage."

Slaves paid dearly in the aftermath of the rebellion. Many were randomly killed all over Southampton County; some were beheaded and their heads posted along roads to serve as a warning to others. In nearby Richmond, the Virginia legislature defeated the proposal that would have instituted gradual emancipation and colonization. Instead, southern planters now tightened their grip on blacks, free and enslaved, and on anyone else who challenged their right to hold humans in bondage.

These hard-nosed planter tactics allowed northern abolitionists to gain a more sympathetic audience for their cause. Labor leader George Henry Evans openly defended Turner's insurrection in his New York City abolitionist paper, the *Daily Sentinel*. Regretting the bloodshed, Evans noted that the rebels

> no doubt thought that their only hope . . . was to put to death, indiscriminately the whole race of those who held them in bondage. If such were their impressions, were they not justifiable in doing so? Undoubtedly they were, if freedom is the birthright of man, as the declaration of independence tells us. . . . Those who kept them in slavery and ignorance alone are answerable for their conduct.

In the year of Turner's uprising, important new voices arose in the slaves' defense. William Lloyd Garrison, a white journalist and reformer living in Boston, invoked evangelical and republican principles to demand the "immediate abolition" of slavery. Noting that the U.S. Constitution failed to abolish the institution of slavery, he called it "a covenant with death, an agreement with Hell." He insisted that slave owners should receive no compensation for slaves who were liberated through abolition, since the owners had already received the profits of the slaves' labor. Such demands, however, only hardened resistance to the antislavery message among the planter class.

The Planter Class Consolidates Power

Faced with resistance by slaves and a small but growing critique of human bondage by whites, southern planters worked to shore up the institution of slavery. They did so by further limiting the rights of slaves and free blacks in the South and by reinforcing their economic supremacy through political dominance. They depended as well on the support of northern whites, whose financial success was tied to the spread of plantation agriculture, especially cotton. Still, fearing that these efforts were not sufficient to protect the system of slavery, southern Congressman tried to silence discussions of abolition in Congress. They also argued with growing vehemence that the rights of states to determine their own economic and social policies had to be defended against unconstitutional assertions of federal authority.

Planters Tighten Their Grip   Only a small minority of northerners ever signed an antislavery petition or subscribed to abolitionist newspapers, yet those who did represented a serious threat to white southerners. Legislators in Virginia and North Carolina, fearing the influence of antislavery literature, made it illegal to teach slaves to read. Other states outlawed black-controlled worship services. James Henry Hammond, a South Carolina planter, informed his journal in 1831, "Intend to break up negro preaching and negro churches. . . . [And] ordered night [prayer] meetings on the plantation to be discontinued."

Increasingly, the only preaching that planters allowed was that which bound slaves more tightly to their masters. Slaves were clear about the effects of this shift in attitudes. "Talk not about kind and Christian master," James W. C. Pennington, a Maryland-born slave, wrote after his escape. "They are not masters of the system. The system is master of them." One of the last hopes for racial cooperation in the South, the evangelical church with a mixed-race congregation, was lost.

By 1830, the growth of the free black population in the South had slowed considerably. Those who managed to avoid the chains of enslavement and to remain in the region lived predominantly in urban areas, such as Baltimore, the District of Columbia, Savannah, and New Orleans. They supported themselves as manual laborers, domestics, petty traders, artisans, or small shopkeepers. Within these free black communities, women generally outnumbered men, making it difficult to form and sustain intact free

"The Colored Man Has No Redress": Free African Americans Struggle in the South

Uneasy about the existence of a free black population in the South, lawmakers passed strict measures restricting the rights of nonslave African Americans in their states, as described by a black Kentuckian named Washington Spaulding.

Our Principal Difficulty here grows out of the police laws, which are very stringent. For instance, a police officer may go [to] a house at night, without any search warrant, and, if the door is not opened when he knocks, force it in, and ransack the house, and the colored man has no redress. At other times, they come and say they are hunting for stolen goods or runaway slaves, and, some of them being great scoundrels, if they see a piece of goods, which may have been purchased, they will take it and carry it off. If I go out of the state, I cannot come back to it again. The penalty is imprisonment in the penitentiary. . . . If a freeman comes here (perhaps he may have been born free), he cannot get free papers, and if the police find out that he has got no free papers, they snap him up, and put him in jail. Sometimes they remain in jail three, four, and five months before they are brought to trial. My children are just tied down here. If they go to Louisiana, there is no chance for them, unless I can get some white man to go to New Orleans and swear they belong to him, and claim them as his slaves. . . . There are many cases of assault and battery in which we can have no redress. I have known a case here where a man bought himself three times. The last time, he was chained on board a boat, to be sent South, when a gentleman who now lives in New York saw him, and bought him, and gave him his free papers.

American Freedmen's Inquiry Commission Interviews, Samuel G. Howe, in John W. Blassingame, *Slave Testimony* (Baton Rouge, LA, 1977), 385–386.

black families. The children of free mothers, especially when a father was not present, were subject to apprenticeship laws that placed them in virtual bondage to white employers. To survive in this setting, free blacks in the South formed support networks among themselves, founded their own churches and clubs, and demonstrated, at least in public, deference to the whites who paid their wages, bought their goods and services, and tolerated their presence.

Yet in the aftermath of Nat Turner's rebellion, whites assumed that the freedom of any blacks could stimulate dangerous notions among slaves. An 1831 petition to Virginia's legislature explained whites' fears. Once "indulged with the hope of freedom," otherwise "submissive and easily controlled" slaves "reject restraint and become almost wholly unmanageable." The Virginia legislature immediately passed new restrictions on the activities of free blacks, denying them the right to own firearms, be ordained as ministers, or meet for worship without the permission of local white officials. By the 1830s, free blacks in every southern state found their rights limited, their movements restricted, and their very presence assailed and sometimes banned. The mere presence of free blacks in a society built on racial slavery marked a powerful contradiction, one that white elites worked hard to contain.

Having further restricted the rights and movements of slaves and free blacks, state and local governments in the South also suppressed nearly all opposition to, and even doubts about, chattel slavery. They banned antislavery messages in books, newspapers, schools, politics, or any other public forum. And they fought back directly against northern abolitionists. Georgia offered a $5,000 reward for the trial and conviction "under the laws of this state" of abolitionist editor William Lloyd Garrison. A reward of $1,000 was offered for the delivery of David Walker's corpse and $10,000 if he was captured and returned to the South alive.

The Political Dimensions of Planter Control

Southern planters were relieved that as the battles over slavery escalated, they could count on the support of the nation's highest authority, the president of the United States. Andrew Jackson, a Tennessee slave owner, Indian fighter, and celebrated military leader, had captured the White House in 1828 with widespread support from southern and western voters (see Chapter 7).

In most cases, Jackson rewarded his southern constituency by supporting their goals, particularly when it came to slavery. In his annual message to Congress in 1835, the president called for legislation to prohibit, "under

New Method of Assorting the Mail, as Practised by Southern Slave-Holders

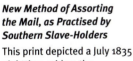

This print depicted a July 1835 nighttime raid on the Charleston, South Carolina, Post Office. An antiabolitionist crowd broke into the building, removed antislavery mail, and burned it in the street. Library Company of Philadelphia.

Nullification

An anonymous contemporary cartoon provided a simple diagram of the tariff issue from the southern perspective. Northern industry is represented by the corpulent figure on the right, thriving thanks to the tariff's protection from foreign competition. Meanwhile, his conjoined twin, a skeletal South, staggers beneath his economic burden in front of a foreclosed farmhouse and an idle ship. General Collections, Library of Congress.

severe penalties, the circulation in the Southern States, through the mail, of incendiary publications intended to instigate the slaves to insurrection." Recognizing their support in the White House, in May 1836, southern congressmen succeeded in instituting a gag rule in the House of Representatives so that all antislavery petitions were rejected without consideration.

However, aware of the dangers posed by antislavery advocates, by the North's greater representation in the U.S. Congress, and by the nation's commercial and industrial development, southern planters could not depend on federal power alone, even with a sympathetic president in the White House. They needed as well to reassert the power of the states to control their own destinies. Therefore, they argued with renewed force that the U.S. Constitution had given only certain powers to the federal government; the rest were reserved for the states. This reassertion of states' rights drove a wedge between President Jackson and southern political leaders.

Determined to assert the primacy of states' rights, South Carolina seized the political initiative in the early 1830s. The tariff of 1832 provided the pretext. In 1828, Congress had increased tariffs on a range of manufactured goods, passing a bill known to southern critics as the "tariff of abominations." Before the northern and southern economies had begun to diverge sharply, slave owners such as South Carolina Senator John C. Calhoun had supported protectionism. As cotton prices plunged from 1819 on, however, high tariffs on manufactured goods created a crisis. Although the Tariff of 1832, signed into law by President Jackson, moderated some high rates, it did not lower rates on cloth or iron products. Moreover, southern politicians had now come to despise tariffs on imported, manufactured goods as an arbitrary tax levied by the industrializing North on the agricultural South. Because of their emphasis on growing cotton and other crops for export, Southern planters wanted to lower the price of manufactured goods, most of which they had to purchase at tariff-inflated prices. This way, they could keep their profits from flowing into the pockets of northern merchants. In November 1832, South Carolina's leadership met in special convention and declared the tariffs of 1828 and 1832 "null, void, no law, nor binding upon this state, its officers or citizens." Sounding surprisingly like the Cherokee Nation in declaring its sovereignty, South Carolina forbade the collection of the tariff by federal agents and refused to enforce it within state boundaries.

This stance was backed by stronger sentiments and deeper calculations than those connected simply with the tariff. By nullifying this federal law, South Carolina meant to serve notice that it would not allow the federal government to impose any laws harmful to planter interests. Thus, even as government agents and troops were welcomed in Georgia and the Carolinas to help in the removal of Indians, planters were asserting their freedom from unwanted federal interference. As Robert Turnbull, a South Carolina planter, explained of his opposition to the tariffs: "[G]reat as is this evil, it is perhaps the least of the evils which attend an abandonment of one iota of the principle of controversy. Our dispute involves questions of the most fearful import to the institutions and tranquility of South Carolina."

Although sympathetic toward his fellow planters, President Jackson considered Carolinians' fears exaggerated and responded angrily to their attacks on the federal government, of which he was, after all, the chief executive. He promptly reinforced the federal fort in Charleston Harbor and obtained a "force bill" from Congress authorizing the use of the military to implement federal law. Henry Clay, his opponent in the presidential race, joined with other congressmen to fashion a compromise. Congress agreed to reduce tariffs over the next nine years, and in early 1833, South Carolina repealed its nullification act. But to demonstrate its continued belief in the right of states to veto federal law, South Carolina also nullified Jackson's force bill. The defiant gesture kept the states' rights claim alive, but it could not conceal the defeat of the nullification strategy at this stage.

Conclusion: The Challenges of a Slave Society

Despite southern planters' attempts to isolate themselves from northern antislavery advocates and unpopular federal mandates, the expansion of agricultural production continued to link them with merchants, manufacturers, cotton factors (entrepreneurs involved in the cotton trade), and industrial and maritime workers in the North and in England. Although other goods were important in the South's economy, cotton was the one that formed the strongest ties to those outside the region. It also served as the main thread that connected poor whites, small farmers, and slaves with plantation owners. Within the web of southern labor and economic relations, growing distinctions appeared between blacks and whites, between free people and slaves, and between wealthy planters and yeoman farmers. By the mid-1830s, as the plantation system expanded and consolidated, differences among these diverse groups crystallized, and social movement became more and more difficult. Yet one consequence of the growing differentiation among southerners was the increasing dependence of slaves, free blacks, and yeomen on the resources and largesse of large planters. Plantation owners considered the growing classes of dependents as evidence of their success. Those lower down the ladder chafed at the restrictions placed on them, but few could seriously contest the new order.

At the same time, planters themselves were caught up in a larger web of regional, national, and global connections in which they found themselves dependent on others for their own success. In fact, protecting the plantation system depended in part on the planters' ability to ensure that the strength of a cotton economy would bind together whites of all classes across the South as well as affluent whites across the nation and across the sea who served as the planters' trading partners.

Moreover, even as northern states gradually abolished slavery within their own borders, residents of those areas continued to rely on the products and profits of slave labor to support the industry and commerce that fueled their economic growth. Manufacturers who supplied the South with textiles, shoes, plows, and other finished products were deeply committed to the cotton economy. Such economic ties ensured that, even as those in the free states saw themselves as increasingly distinct from their southern neighbors, they were still intimately connected to the success of slavery. In this sense, King Cotton spun a web that encompassed the entire nation.

The Years in Review

1793

- Eli Whitney invents the cotton gin, a machine that removes seed from cotton bolls, significantly reducing the labor required to harvest large amounts of cotton.

- Congress passes the Fugitive Slave Act, making it a federal crime to assist an escaping slave, even in "free" states.

1800

- A Virginia slave and blacksmith named Gabriel organizes an insurrection aimed at seizing Richmond; white authorities discover the widespread conspiracy, and Gabriel and thirty-five others are hanged.

1803

- The French government sells the Louisiana Territory to the United States; Meriwether Lewis and William Clark set out to map it the next year.

1804

- Thomas Jefferson is reelected president of the United States over Federalist Charles C. Pinckney.
- After a decade of violent struggle against Spanish and French colonial rulers, Haiti declares itself an independent republic; these developments inspire free African Americans and slaves and alarm southern slave owners.

1807

- To protest British and French interference with U.S. shipping during the Napoleonic wars, Congress passes the Embargo Act, which forbids U.S. ships to sail for any foreign ports.

1808

- Congress enacts the ban on slave importation recommended in the U.S. Constitution, leading to growth in the internal slave trade.
- Republican James Madison defeats Federalist Charles C. Pinckney for the presidency; Madison is reelected four years later.

1812

- The United States declares war on Great Britain.

1814

- The Battle of Horseshoe Bend ends more than a year of violent resistance by young Creek warriors (known as Red Sticks), who were defeated by white southern militiamen and their Indian allies; the Treaty of Fort Jackson transfers fourteen million acres of Creek territory to U.S. control.

1816

- James Monroe is elected president in a landslide; four years later, he is reelected without organized opposition.

1817

- The American Colonization Society is founded with the goal of eventually freeing slaves and resettling all African Americans in Africa.
- New York is the last northern state to abolish slavery, enacting a gradual abolition act that phases out slavery over more than two decades.
- President Monroe vetoes the "Bonus Bill," which would have established a national fund for constructing roads and other internal improvements, thus leaving such efforts to the states.

1819

- Secretary of State John Quincy Adams negotiates the Adams-Onís Treaty, whereby the United States purchases the territory of Florida from Spain for $5 million, Spain gives up all claims on the Oregon territory, and the United States gives up its claims to Texas.

1820

- Congress breaks a stalemate over admitting Missouri to the union as a slave state by devising the Missouri Compromise: Missouri is admitted with no restrictions on slavery, Maine is admitted as a free state, and the line of Missouri's southern border is extended westward with the provision that no territory north of that line will be admitted to the union as a slave state.

1822

- Free black carpenter Denmark Vesey allegedly organizes an insurrectionary conspiracy in Charleston, South Carolina; 131 free and enslaved African Americans are arrested, and 37 are hanged.
- The American Colonization Society establishes Liberia on the west coast of Africa to resettle African Americans.

1824

- No candidate receives the majority in the presidential election; the House of Representatives selects John Quincy Adams over Andrew Jackson, who had received the largest number of popular and electoral votes.

1827

- The Cherokees adopt a formal constitution modeled on that of the United States.

1828

- Congress passes a new tariff law imposing taxes on imported manufactured goods; southern critics label it the "Tariff of Abominations," and four years later, South Carolina declares it "null" and "void."
- Andrew Jackson is elected president over John Quincy Adams in a dirty campaign.

1829

- Mexico outlaws slavery in Texas, but southerners, led by Stephen Austin, continue to settle there in defiance of the terms of the Adams-Onís Treaty.
- David Walker publishes his *Appeal to the Coloured Citizens of the World*, a seventy-six-page pamphlet that calls on slaves to "Strike for your lives and liberties."

1830

- President Andrew Jackson promotes and Congress passes the Indian Removal Act, which offers Indians land west of the Mississippi River in exchange for their current territorial holdings; under pressure and threats, many tribes sign away land; tens of thousands are pressured to move west.

1831

- In the case *Cherokee Nation v. Georgia*, the U.S. Supreme Court rules that Cherokees, who are trying to fight removal, do not have independent political authority.
- Religious leader Nat Turner leads a slave insurrection in Virginia; Turner and sixteen of his allies are caught, tried, and executed.

1832

- Andrew Jackson wins reelection to the presidency over Henry Clay.
- A state convention in South Carolina declares the federal tariff null and void and threatens to secede if the federal government tries to enforce its collection; a year later, South Carolina repeals this nullification act after Congress agrees to reduce tariffs over the next nine years.

1836

- The U.S. House of Representatives institutes a gag rule that automatically prevents debate on all future antislavery petitions.

1838

- Fifteen thousand Cherokees who had earlier refused the U.S. government's offer of land in the West are uprooted by federal troops and led across the 800-mile Trail of Tears to present-day Oklahoma; 4,000 die from starvation and exposure to the cold.

Additional Readings

For more on American Indians in the early nineteenth century, see:
Colin G. Calloway, *One Vast Winter Count: The Native American West Before Lewis and Clark* (2003); Robbie Ethridge, *Creek Country: The Creek Indians and Their World* (2003); Theda Perdue, *Cherokee Women: Gender and Culture Change, 1700–1835* (1998); Anthony F. C. Wallace, *Jefferson and the Indians: The Tragic Fate of the First Americans* (1999); and Richard White, *The Roots of Dependency: Subsistence, Environment and Social Change among the Choctaws, Pawnees, and Navajos* (1983).

For more on the experiences of American slaves, see: Frederick Douglass, *The Life and Times of Frederick Douglass* (1969); Barbara Jeanne Fields, *Slavery and Freedom on the Middle Ground: Maryland During the Nineteenth Century* (1985); Charles Joyner, *Down By the Riverside: A South Carolina Slave Community* (1984); August Meier and Elliott Rudwick, *From Plantation to Ghetto*, 3rd ed. (1976); Gilbert Osofsky, ed., *Puttin' On Ole Massa: The Slave Narratives of Henry Bibb, William Wells Brown, and Solomon Northrup* (1969); Dylan C. Penningroth, *The Claims of Kinfolk: African American Property and Community in the Nineteenth-Century South* (2003); Willie Lee Rose, ed., *A Documentary History of Slavery in North America* (1976); Marie Jenkins Schwartz, *Born in Bondage: Growing Up Enslaved in the Antebellum South* (2000); Brenda E. Stevenson, *Life in Black and White: Family and Community in the Slave South* (1996); and Deborah Gray White, *Ar'n't I a Woman? Female Slaves in the Plantation South* (1985).

For more on planters and nonslaveholding whites, see: Charles Bolton, *Poor Whites of the Antebellum South: Tenants and Laborers in Central North Carolina and Northeastern Mississippi* (1994); Frances Anne Kemble, *Journal of a Residence on a Georgia Plantation, 1838–1839*, edited with an introduction by John A. Scott (1984); Stephanie McCurry, *Masters of Small Worlds: Yeomen Households, Gender Relations, and the Political Culture of the Antebellum South Carolina Low Country* (1995); and James Oakes, *The Ruling Race: A History of American Slaveholders* (1982).

For more on free African Americans, see: Ira Berlin, *Slaves Without Masters: The Free Negro in the Antebellum South* (1974); Leonard P. Curry, *The Free Black in American Society, 1800–1850* (1981); Virginia Meacham Gould, ed., *Chained to the Rock of Adversity: To Be Free, Black and Female in the Old South* (1998); and Benjamin Quarles, *Black Abolitionists* (1969).

For more on religion and resistance among slaves, see: Sylvia Frey and Betty Wood, *Come Shouting to Zion: African American Protestantism in the American South and the British Caribbean to 1830* (1998); Donald Matthews, *Religion in the Old South* (1977); Gerald W. Mullin, *Flight and Rebellion: Slave Resistance in Eighteenth-Century Virginia* (1972); Stephen B. Oates, *The Fires of Jubilee: Nat Turner's Fierce Rebellion* (1975); and Albert J. Raboteau, *Slave Religion: The "Invisible Institution" in the Antebellum South* (1978).

For more on the economic effects of slavery, see: Stuart Bruchey, ed., *Cotton and the Growth of the American Economy, 1790–1860* (1967); Eugene

D. Genovese, *The Political Economy of Slavery: Studies in the Economy and Society of the Slave South* (1965); Steven Hahn, and Jonathan Prude, eds., *The Countryside in the Age of Capitalist Transformation: Essays in the Social History of Rural America* (1985); Allan Kulikoff, *The Agrarian Origins of American Capitalism* (1992); Joseph P. Reidy, *From Slavery to Agrarian Capitalism in the Cotton Plantation South* (1992); and Mark V. Tushnet, *The American Law of Slavery* (1981).

7

Northern Society and the Growth of Wage Labor

1790–1837

L IKE ONE IN THREE Massachusetts women of her generation, Abigail McIntire was pregnant when she married in 1788. Her husband, Mayo Greenleaf Patch, owned no property, so the couple lived in a small house built by Abigail's father, earning money by shoemaking. A decade and six children later, the Patches were struggling to make a living from rented farms and shoemakers' shops in various places and getting deeper into debt. In 1807, they moved to Pawtucket, Rhode Island, where spinning mills turned slave-grown cotton from the South into yarn for making cloth. Abigail and the children worked at home, cleaning cotton and weaving cloth for the mills. Mayo took to drink, stole Abigail's and the children's wages, and in 1812 walked out on them. Six years later, after he had been imprisoned for counterfeiting, Abigail divorced him. She and her children continued to support themselves by working for wages in Pawtucket. One of the sons, Sam, later obtained notoriety as a daredevil jumper. Poverty and wage labor, the growth of manufacturing and the factory system, women's labor in early factories and domestic outwork, the connections between northern industry and the slave economy of the South—all these facets of Abigail's life also had broad significance for the transformation of the North in the early nineteenth century.

New Hampshire Textile Mill Workers

Framed portraits of workers of the Amoskeag Manufacturing Company in Manchester, New Hampshire, c. 1854. Manchester Historic Association.

The Early-Nineteenth-Century North

The Patches' story illustrates the struggle of thousands of northern families to sustain their economic independence in the years after the American Revolution. Many faced scarce resources in settled rural regions such as eastern

Massachusetts and were obliged to move or change their occupations. Many would leave for the newly opening West, hoping to establish successful farms on frontier land. Others went to sea or to the growing port cities. The Patches were among the first to become wageworkers in the North's new manufacturing industries. Men and women who remained in the country-side also became increasingly involved in producing goods for sale or in working for wages (Map 7.1).

Many Northerners hoped that economic prosperity would guarantee their material independence. Whereas in the plantation South, the expansion of slavery created a growing propertyless and dependent workforce, it seemed possible that the North, where slavery was disappearing, would become a society of independent proprietors. Instead, northern towns, industries, and farms came to rely increasingly on the labor of wageworkers. In 1800, about 12 percent of the U.S. labor force worked for wages. By 1860, the proportion was around 40 percent, and the majority of wage employees were concentrated in the North. This change signaled a growing divergence between northern and southern societies and called into question the republican vision of property-owning independence for most Americans. It also gave rise to a working people's movement. By the 1830s, wage earners were defending their economic position and asserting their right to equal respect with their more prosperous fellow citizens.

Republican Ideology   One legacy of the American Revolution was the belief that the republic would best be preserved if voters were politically "independent," not subject to coercion by others. At first, this seemed best assured if voters were economically "independent," too. They should own property, which would give them a stake in society and free them from the influence of people with some hold over them. Those without property— women, children, the poor, servants, and slaves—were regarded as "dependent" on others and so to be excluded from voting, officeholding, or public political debate. Women were assigned the role of "republican mothers," expected to raise their children to be virtuous citizens but not themselves to obtain the full benefits of citizenship.

These "republican" assumptions were widely shared, North and South. An overwhelming majority of Americans were engaged in agriculture, many on small freehold farms, and a significant proportion of men owned land. Indeed, most people expected the United States to have an agrarian future, and this expectation was to some extent borne out. Rural society expanded rapidly. By 1840, over 80 percent of people in the North still lived in rural areas; in the South, the proportion was over 90 percent. Most continued to work in agriculture, and agricultural goods such as cotton, grain, and lumber were among the United States' most important products.

MAP 7.1 The United States at the Beginning of the Nineteenth Century

While migration to the frontier pushed the settled areas of the United States westward and southward, the northeastern states were already emerging as a region of denser population, larger urban centers, and better roads than in the rest of the nation. D. W. Meinig, *The Shaping of America: A Geographical Perspective on 500 Years of History*, vol. 2, *Continental America, 1800–1867* (1993).

Belief in the virtues of rural life was deeply ingrained. Suspicious of cities with their crowds and potential disorder, Thomas Jefferson wrote in 1785 that farmers were "the chosen people of God" and implied that urban growth would threaten the republic's future. When he arranged the Louisiana Purchase of 1803, doubling the territory of the United States, Jefferson hailed the acquisition of a vast reserve of land that could ensure the future of a property-owning republic; the United States would grow crops to feed its population and export abroad, exchanging them for manufactures produced in more socially unequal countries such as Britain. As late as 1810, Treasury Secretary Albert Gallatin claimed that "the superior attractions of agricultural pursuits, the abundance of land compared with the population, the high price of labor, and the want of sufficient capital" would inhibit the growth of American manufacturing.

"Venerate the Plough"
The independent farmer plowed the path to prosperity for the Republic on this seal of the Philadelphia Society for Promoting Agriculture. "The Plan of a Farm Yard," *Columbian Magazine*, October 1786 — American Philosophical Society Library.

Other circumstances also appeared to favor an agrarian future. The cotton gin boosted cotton exports from the South, and wars in Europe following the French Revolution of 1789 fostered American trade with markets in Western Europe and the Mediterranean. Northern merchants established new trade links with Asia. All expanded the overseas commerce that could supply America's need for manufactures.

Jefferson and others who extolled rural America's republican virtues did not suggest that all rural people were fit to exercise political leadership. Beneath the partisan strife of the 1790s and 1800s between the Federalists and Democratic-Republicans lay shared expectations about who should rule. Federalists were explicitly elitist. "The best men," whose birth, education, or wealth guaranteed their virtue and independence, should govern; lesser property owners should defer to these leaders and accept their authority. Democratic-Republicans attacked the most hierarchical of these assumptions, but leaders such as Jefferson also assumed that power would be exercised by a "natural aristocracy" whose talents best suited them for government.

Yet the success of the Revolution, the opening of the continent, and the establishment of new state and federal governments sowed the seeds of economic change and new political traditions. During the early nineteenth century, political culture was transformed, turning republicanism in a more democratic direction, although restricting participation to white males only. It also became clear that the United States would not remain simply an agrarian society. Particularly in the North, economic development altered the republican vision. By 1840, an industrial revolution was under way in the Northeast. Cities were growing rapidly in size and influence. Population growth and commercial expansion were creating new divisions, both between North and South and within northern society itself.

Rural Society in the North Though North and South were both mainly rural in 1800, they differed greatly. Southern planters used a large enslaved workforce to produce exportable commodities. Most northern whites, in contrast, lived in small-farm regions that consumed much of what they produced. Family farming, supported by cooperation between neighbors, sustained a republican notion of economic independence that contemporaries often referred to as a "modest competence."

Typical northern farms were modestly sized, between 40 and 120 acres, and worked by the families that owned them. Employment as a laborer or tenant was often a stepping-stone to acquiring one's own farm. Even so,

---

"There Is No Want of Meat and Drink Here": An Immigrant Writes Home

In the following letter, written in August 1818 from Germantown, Pennsylvania, Alice Barlow describes in detail the bounty of available food and drink. Letters such as this helped to lure other Northern Europeans to migrate to America in the decades that followed.

Dear Mother:

I write to say we are all in good health, and hope this will find you so. . . . Tell my brother John I think he would do very well here; my husband can go out and catch a bucket of fish in a few minutes; and John brings as many apples as he can carry, when he comes from school; also cherries, grapes, and peaches, we get as much bread as we can all eat in a day for seven pence; altho' it is now called dear [expensive]. Dear mother, I wish you were all as well off as we now are: there is no want of meat and drink here. We have a gallon of spirits every week; and I have a bottle of porter per day myself, in short I have everything I could wish. . . . Tell little Adam, if he was here, he would get puddings and pies every day. Tell my old friends I shall be looking for them next spring; and also tell my brother John and sister Ann, if they were here, they would know nothing of poverty. I live like an Indian Queen. . . .

Your affectionate daughter,
Alice Barlow

Edith Abott, ed., *Historical Aspects of the Immigration Problem* (1926).

The Residence of David Twining, 1787

Edward Hicks, a Quaker painter of coaches and signs, completed this painting in the late 1840s. Hicks's idealized representation of a "well-ordered" eighteenth-century farm was based on memories of his childhood with the Twining family in Bucks County, Pennsylvania. Edward Hicks, 1845–1848 — Abby Aldrich Rockefeller Folk Art Center, Williamsburg, Virginia.

inequality was widespread. Tenancy blighted parts of New York and other states, and some farmers still held slaves who were not yet freed under gradual emancipation laws. Landless farm laborers could be found everywhere, and a majority of free blacks in the rural North owned little or no land. Still, the ideal of land ownership remained within reach for many. Journeying through New York and New England, the Reverend Timothy Dwight was convinced that "[n]o man here begins life with the expectation of being a mere laborer. All intend to possess, and almost all actually possess, a comfortable degree of prosperity and independence." For white farmers at least, landownership conferred the right to be treated by others as an equal.

Economic independence required the labor of all family members. Husbands and sons, by and large, worked the fields. Most other tasks, including manufacturing household goods, fell to wives and daughters. One farm journal reported that women's work amounted to half of all farm labor:

> Women . . . picked their own wool, . . . spun their own yarn, drove their own looms, made and mended their own chairs, braided their own baskets, wove their own carpets, quilts, and coverlets, . . . milked their own cows, [and] fed their own calves.

On their Maine farm in the 1790s, Martha Ballard and her daughters produced cloth, raised garden produce, preserved vegetables, and did household chores, and Ballard served as a midwife in her neighborhood. Women raised children, nursed the sick, and cared for the elderly. Men celebrated an economic independence that rested heavily on the skills and exertions of their sisters, wives, and daughters.

Farm families were often linked by ties of kinship, religion, and ethnicity. Most settlements included a church, a general store, and a few artisans, such as carpenters and blacksmiths, who might ply their trades only part-time. Proper schoolhouses, doctors, and lawyers were scarce. Families exchanged work and goods, sharing tools or lending a hand when harvesting or barn raising required extra help.

Beyond these local ties, rural independence also rested on links to outside markets, most significant in grain-exporting regions such as Pennsylvania but essential everywhere for the assurance of even minimal comfort. Salt, sugar, molasses, coffee, tea, tobacco, gunpowder, guns, knives, and axes could not be produced at home, and farm families exchanged crops or home manufactures to pay for them. Yet as late as 1820, only one-fifth of the North's farm output found its way beyond local communities into urban markets. Farm families also purchased modestly. About two-thirds of the clothing rural Americans wore between 1810 and 1820 was homemade, mostly by women. Poor transportation hindered inland trade, protecting those producing for local markets from distant competitors. With few rivers and poor roads connecting coast and hinterland, a ton of goods cost as much to ship 30 miles overland as to be brought by sea from Europe.

Towns and Commerce   In 1800, the northern merchant elite conducted business largely in the cities and smaller port towns of the coast. Unlike southern planters, they were not generally directly concerned with production but obtained their wealth from trade. Urban markets were small; fewer than one in twelve Americans lived in places with populations of 2,500 or more. The biggest mercantile profits went to traders in oceangoing commerce between the Americas and Europe. American neutrality in the European wars of the 1790s and early 1800s gave merchants from the Northeast dominance of trade routes that were largely closed to other nations. Trade with China, first established in the mid-1780s by merchants in Philadelphia and Salem, Massachusetts, offered substantial profits from the sale of the tea, silks, porcelain, lacquerware, and other exotic goods brought back to the United States.

Mercantile success brought great wealth to some Americans and provided employment to many others, especially smaller merchants and the sailmakers, ropemakers, carpenters, caulkers, and barrel makers whose crafts were connected with shipping. But the benefits were not equally shared. After farmers, the nation's largest group of workers were seamen, who labored for modest wages in dangerous conditions, often on long voyages. Large numbers of women in the port towns struggled for livelihoods while their husbands were absent: Lydia Almy of Salem wove cloth, tanned leather, made cider, looked after livestock, worked in the fields, carted wood, and cooked for boarders at her house. Boston mariners' wives worked for the city's ropemakers and other employers. Many were poor. In every port lived widows and families of men who never returned from the sea.

Maritime trade did not substantially improve the North's position in world production. "The brilliant prospects held out by commerce," wrote Adam Seybert, a Philadelphia congressman, "caused our citizens to neglect the mechanical and manufacturing branches of industry." Between 1795 and 1815, the United States ran up a large trade deficit, spending $350 million more for foreign goods than it received for exports. Indeed, nearly half of U.S. exports were really re-exports—goods produced abroad, purchased by American merchants, and resold to other countries. Although this kind of trade amassed profits, it did not directly stimulate the growth of domestic commercial agriculture or industry.

A Transformation Begins

Pressure for change came from several directions. Immigration from Europe, especially to the Middle Atlantic region, increased the supply of urban labor. European warfare in the early nineteenth century encouraged many merchants to redirect their attention from overseas to domestic investment. Transportation improvements, linking coastal areas to the interior, fostered the emergence of regional and national markets for goods. Faced with population growth and inequalities, farm families in rural areas migrated or sought fresh sources of income. All these developments contributed to the expansion of manufacturing in many parts of the North and to the emergence of new patterns of labor and social division.

Population Pressure and Westward Movements   This pressure for change arose partly within rural society. For some farmers, maintaining independence required accumulating wealth, but for most, it meant achieving a "competency": cultivating enough land to feed a family, to acquire necessities that could not be made at home, and to obtain land on which grown sons could establish their own farms. Population growth and land scarcity in older regions made these things difficult to achieve. Many southern New England farms were too small to support all the offspring of large families and ran short of essentials, such as wood for fuel. One son might be given a farm of his own on coming of age, but dividing a homestead among several sons would create small, unprofitable holdings. According to their means, farmers took various steps to avoid this. They turned to the market-

Harriet Noble's Life on the Michigan Frontier

Harriet Noble and her family took the northernmost of the major migration routes west, crossing upstate New York and Lake Erie to reach Detroit. While helping her husband to complete their cabin on their isolated farm, Harriet, like many women on the frontier, lamented the absence of neighbors and social institutions.

There was one house here, Judge Dexter's; he was building a sawmill, and had a number of men at work at the time; besides these there was not a white family west of Ann Arbor in Michigan territory. . . . I helped to raise the rafters and put on the roof [of their log house], but it was the last of November before our roof was completed. We were obliged to wait for the mill to run in order to get boards for making it. The doorway I had no means of closing except by hanging up a blanket, and frequently when I would raise it to step out, there would be two or three of our dusky neighbors peeping in to see what was there. It would always give me such a start, I could not suppress a scream, to which they would reply with "Ugh!" and a hearty laugh. They knew I was afraid, and liked to torment me. Sometimes they would throng the house and stay two or three hours. If I was alone they would help themselves to what they liked. . . . At last we got a door. The next thing wanted was a chimney; winter was close at hand and the stone was not drawn. I said to my husband, "I think I can drive the oxen and draw the stones, while you dig them from the ground and load them." He thought I could not, but consented to let me try. . . . My husband and myself were four days building [our chimney]. I suppose most of my lady friends would think a woman quite out of "her legitimate sphere" in turning mason, but I was not at all particular what kind of labor I performed, so we were only comfortable and provided with the necessaries of life. . . . The roads had been so bad all the fall that . . . I think it was December when my husband went to Detroit for supplies. Fifteen days were consumed in going and coming. We had been without flour for three weeks or more, and it was hard to manage with young children thus. After being without bread three or four days, my little boy, two years old, looked me in the face and said, "Ma, why don't you make bread; don't you like it? I do." His innocent complaint brought forth the first tears I had shed in Michigan on account of any privations I had to suffer, and they were about the last. I am not of a desponding disposition, nor often low-spirited, and having left New York to make Michigan my home, I had no idea of going back, or being very unhappy. Yet the want of society, of church privileges, and in fact almost every thing that makes life desirable, would often make me sad in spite of all effort to the contrary. . . .

Elizabeth F. Ellet, *Pioneer Women of the West* (New York: Charles Scribner's Sons, 1852), 388–395.

place to raise the cash (at least $600 in the 1830s) to buy new farms for their sons. They tried new crops and raised more livestock for sale. In some regions, farm women increased their output of dairy produce.

In search of more land, many people migrated westward. Starting in the 1780s but in increasing numbers after 1815, families moved from older farming districts in New England, New York, and Pennsylvania to "new" land in western New York, the Ohio Valley, and the Great Lakes region. Expansion led to the destruction of Native American groups such as the Shawnees and the Wyandots, the seizure of their lands, and the removal of their populations. By 1800, the white population of Ohio had reached 45,000; twenty years later, it was 581,000. Though many new settlers found renewed prosperity by moving west and encouraged others to follow them, some advised caution. John Stillman Wright sold his New York farm in 1818 and went to Ohio but later published *Letters from the West*, warning of "the cruel disappointment and vain regret, which so many thousands are now enduring."

Instead of migrating, some sons (as well as daughters) without land or other means stayed in the East but moved to the towns, tried new occupations, or became laborers. With new immigrants from Europe, they swelled urban populations, turning small market centers into bustling towns and large ports such as New York, Philadelphia, and Baltimore into metropolises. Both in the countryside and in towns, more people engaged in manufacturing and formed America's first industrial workforce.

Improvements in Transportation and Communication   Wealthy merchants reinforced these changes as they turned their attention from international trade to the American continent. Some speculated in urban property or western land; a handful invested directly in manufacturing. But most early-nineteenth-century investors concentrated on improving internal commerce and transportation, financing the construction of roads, bridges, and canals and later of steamboats and railroads. State and local governments encouraged such investments. By 1812, Massachusetts had authorized the building of 105 turnpike roads, and New York had authorized more than 50. Labor for local road building was recruited from farm families, but larger projects required greater numbers of workers. Some states poured public funds directly into transport improvements. Others rewarded investors with tax exemptions, banking and lottery franchises, and corporate charters conferring lucrative monopoly privileges.

Expenditures increased steadily, producing great improvements in travel. New York State's Erie Canal had the most remarkable effects. Built at public expense between 1817 and 1825 by thousands of laborers, both local recruits and immigrants, the canal stretched 364 miles from Albany to Buffalo, linking the Great Lakes region with New York City and transatlantic trade. Freight rates fell sharply as a result. In 1817, it cost 19 cents a mile to

CORRECT LIKENESSES,
TAKEN WITH ELEGANCE AND DESPATCH BY
RUFUS PORTER.

Prices as follows—
Common Profile's cut double, - - $.0 20
Side views painted in full colours, - - 00
Front views, - - - - - - - 3 00
Miniatures painted on Ivory, - - - 8 00
☞ *Those who request it will be waited on, at
their respective places of residence.*

Correct Likenesses, c. 1820
Itinerant portrait artists offered rural people reasonably priced portraits, using simplified techniques to render enough of a "correct likeness" to satisfy a client. Portraitists and other traveling tradesmen served as scouts for capital, introducing attractive goods and services to the countryside. American Antiquarian Society.

move a ton of goods from New York to Buffalo; by the 1830s, it cost less than one-tenth of that. Other states sought to emulate the Erie's success by building their own canals. Railroad developments soon followed. Baltimore promoters started a railroad line to the Ohio River in 1828, although it took a quarter-century to complete. By 1840, shorter railroads connected Boston and other cities with manufacturing and commercial centers in the hinterlands.

Speedier travel was only one dimension of a broader improvement in the circulation of information. Literacy rates were high in the North, and the printing and distribution of published materials flourished. Aided by improvements in printing, such as the development of the steam press, books, periodicals, and inexpensive newspapers multiplied and flowed from a growing number of local and regional centers. By 1836, nearly one in four New York City residents purchased newspapers daily. "These papers," noted one observer, "are to be found in every street, lane, alley, in every hotel, tavern, and counting house. . . . Almost every porter and drayman, while not engaging in his occupation, may be seen with a paper in his hands." Women's magazines, the labor press, African American papers, and antislavery journals were all initiated during the 1820s and early 1830s.

Better communications helped to knit together regional and national markets and steadily reduced household manufacture for home use. Upstate New York farm households made an average of more than ten yards of cloth per person in 1825, but this output dropped to less than half a yard thirty years later as people switched to buying factory-made cloth. Falling freight costs made internal trade more profitable for merchants and made store-bought items of decent quality available to rural families at declining prices. Between 1809 and 1836, the prices of soap and candles fell by about one-third, and glassware, cotton mattresses, buttons, pins, and many other goods also became cheaper. "Formerly," noted a Pennsylvanian in 1836, "no man thought of going to a tailor for a sheet. Now everybody goes to one even for a handkerchief."

Needing cash to buy these goods, farm families devoted more of their time to raising crops and other produce for market. Instead of providing much of their own food, they purchased foodstuffs from others. Some farmers flourished as commercial producers, adding to their property, hiring less-fortunate neighbors as laborers and servants, and supporting

Building the Erie Canal
A contemporary lithograph by Anthony Imbert shows the excavation at Lockport, New York. Excavating the canal took heavy physical labor involving more than 3,000 workers. Accidents and disease took their toll on the canal workmen; during the summer of 1819, hundreds of laborers digging in the marshes adjacent to Syracuse, New York, came down with fevers, leading to many fatalities. Cadwallader Colden, *Memoir on the Celebration of the Completion of the New York Canals* (1825) — Metropolitan Museum of Art.

measures to increase commerce. "Our sons," said the *New England Farmer* in 1835, "from the very cradle, breathe the air of independence — and we teach them to owe no man. It is to gratify this love of independence that they rake the ocean and the earth for money."

But farmers who lost out in the new competition often found their independence threatened by debt or poverty. Caught between rising costs and dwindling incomes, farm families faced ruin if they could no longer produce much of their own food and clothing. They mortgaged property to stay afloat, but unless they used the loans to increase output, the debt became just another burden. By 1832, one farmer claimed, "[t]his business of mortgage has already dispossessed a large portion of the best farmers in New England, and it constantly increases." He feared that "the independent yeomanry of our country" would soon "give place to wretched tenantry" and that "a very few rich men . . . will own the whole soil." Another voiced the fears of many: "We are willing to work, our wives are willing to work — but spare us . . . the humiliation of performing the servile offices and living in the kitchens of our more fortunate neighbors."

Competition from the West also challenged eastern farmers. With improved transport, produce from newly cultivated lands competed in the market with crops grown on rocky, nearly exhausted New England soils. Commerce through the Erie Canal reduced wheat production in the East and put pressure on hog and cattle raising, too. Even so, western expansion also fostered eastern commerce and manufacturing. Although little merchandise had moved westward from the seaports in 1810, by 1835, the annual value of goods westbound on the Erie Canal alone approached $10 million. Located on newly bustling trade routes, cities such as Buffalo, Pittsburgh, and Cincinnati boomed. By the 1830s, Cincinnati was the leading center of pork packing, and the foundations were being laid for industries that would later dominate the Midwest: grain milling, meatpacking, distilling and brewing, lumbering, iron smelting, and the production of farm equipment and consumer goods.

The Start of an Industrial Revolution   Manufacturing first began to develop in the East, however. Before 1850, three-quarters of America's industrial employment was concentrated in New England and the Mid-Atlantic states. Many Easterners sought new occupations to supplement or replace their reliance on the land. Growing urban populations and immigrants from Europe provided the workforce that was needed to sustain an industrial revolution.

Dividing Labor

Well before mechanization, the division of labor within the workshop made possible the production of more products at cheaper prices. This trade card for William Buttre's Fancy Chair Manufactory shows the way in which production was subdivided; in the lower panel, for example, one man turns chair legs on a lathe while in the background, a younger man "seats" a chair. After 1800, fancy chairs could be found in the homes of all classes of Americans because of their attractive "classical" style and inexpensive price. Trade Card, William Buttre's Fancy Chair Manufactory, c. 1813, New York City — Winterthur Library: Joseph Downs Collection of Manuscripts and Printed Ephemera.

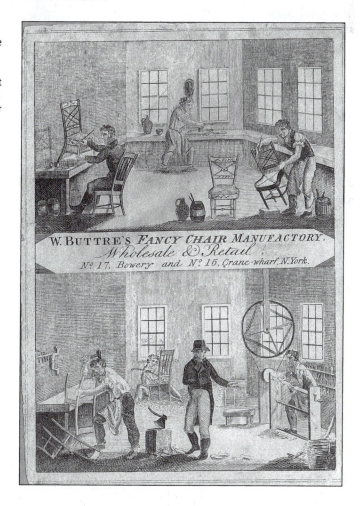

Advocates of an agrarian America opposed large-scale industry, urging that the expansion of manufactures take place at the household level: "Domestic manufacture," wrote one, "is the object contemplated[,] instead of establishments under the sole control of capitalists." Apart from shipbuilding and ironworking, most early manufacturing was performed in households. From the late eighteenth century onward, rural artisans and farmers complemented their work on the land with seasonal manufacturing, making tools, wagons, barrels, and other items for sale. Families supplemented meager farm earnings by making goods at home; women worked on shoes, wove straw hats, and sewed shirts for merchants who paid them by the piece. Urban artisans ran shops at their homes, assisted by live-in apprentices. Those who expanded their businesses to meet demand often did so by putting work out to other local households.

Soon, however, growing demand and investment were moving some manufactures from households into larger workshops and factories. In skilled crafts such as clothing and hat making, shoemaking, leatherworking, furniture making, printing, and bookmaking, masters took on extra apprentices or journeymen and so increased the numbers of urban wageworkers. They also divided skilled tasks into separate stages, for which they could employ cheaper labor. In Connecticut, master clockmakers such as Eli Terry and Seth Thomas organized farmers and artisans to make different parts of the wooden clock movements and cases that were then assembled in their workshops.

Most yarn, cloth, and thread production also moved from homes into factories. Merchants began investing profits from overseas trade in textile operations that employed machinery that had been developed in eighteenth-century Europe. "The time spent in a factory," explained a Massachusetts observer, "will produce at least ten times as much as it will in household manufactures." In 1790, Samuel Slater, an immigrant with experience of the English textile industry, set up the first water-powered spinning machines in the United States in an old clothier's shop at Pawtucket Falls, Rhode Island. Slater's capital came from the Brown family, wealthy Providence merchants, and his success encouraged the firm of Almy, Brown, and Slater to erect the country's first substantial textile factory in 1793. This modest, two-and-a-half-story spinning mill depended largely on children to run its machines. Adults, often the parents of child employees, were paid to weave the yarn into cloth in their own homes. It was for Slater's mills that Abigail Patch and her children worked from 1807 onward. By 1815, southern New England boasted several yarn-spinning factories based on the Rhode Island model, and by 1840, they were common across Rhode Island, south-

A New Form of Clock

Eli Terry's invention of a new box or shelf clock (only twenty inches tall) around 1816 transformed the clock industry and the very notion of a clock. The small and affordable shelf clock became the standard nineteenth-century timepiece, sold throughout the United States by a network of peddlers. Before Terry's innovation, clocks were large and expensive objects made of imported brass. The box clock used less expensive wooden parts that were interchangeable — and it even came in its own case! Eli Terry, Box Clock, c. 1814–1816 — National Museum of American History, Smithsonian Institution.

"No. 5 & 7 Looms Stopped — No Weavers": A Mill Manager's Diary

Finding and disciplining an adequate supply of competent weavers plagued early textile mill managers such as N. B. Gordon, who managed a small woolen mill in rural Massachusetts. The daily entries in his 1829 diary reveal recurring problems of absenteeism, unpredictable natural conditions, and poor production standards.

January

5: One weaver sick, four looms stopped. Water wheel froze up this morning. Took until 8 o'clock to start it.

6: One weaver still sick. Four looms stopped. Water failed some about 4 o'clock.

8: Last night and yesterday warm, which gave plenty of water this day for all hands. One weaver sick. Four looms stopped.

13: 6 weavers—2 looms stopped. One weaver sick. Sally and Mary Ann Leonard out 3/4 of the day by permission.

14: Looms all in operation.

16: Fine warm day. Almira Lowell absent this day and also to be tomorrow, to bury her grandmother. P.M. went to Mr. Carver's to get harness made.

March

23: No. 4 weaver absent 1/2 day. No 5 and 6—1/4 day each. Extreme cold. Lovell's children did not get in until 1/2 past 7 a.m. on account of water on the road.

24: Mr. Thayer's party last night broke up 3 o'clock. Morning hands in consequence come in late, and one, No. 6 weaver, not until noon. H. Kingman commenced repairing the old looms.

April

18: No. 6 loom stopped, no weaver. No. 5 weaver quit.

19: Went to Norton after weavers.

21: No. 5 & 7 looms stopped—no weavers. New spinning badly tended.

Gary Kulik, Roger Parks, and Theodore Z. Penn, eds., *The New England Mill Village, 1790–1860* (1982). Reprinted with permission of MIT Press.

ern Massachusetts, and eastern Connecticut. Baltimore and Philadelphia merchants also invested in mills, and the latter city and nearby river valleys emerged as another important industrial region.

During the War of 1812, Boston merchants established another textile factory system in eastern Massachusetts, first with a mill at Waltham and during the 1820s with additional mills at a site on the Merrimack River that became the town of Lowell. The Waltham system differed from the Rhode Island system, involving a greater financial investment and operating on a

View of Lowell, Massachusetts
In this illustration, which was printed in a Merrimack Company folder containing fabric samples, the Lowell mills nestled peacefully in the countryside. American Textile History Museum.

larger scale. The first Waltham factory cost $400,000, over ten times as much as the average Rhode Island mill. Incorporating powered weaving as well as spinning, the system mechanized each stage of cloth production. While many smaller mills were run by their owners, the Waltham and Lowell mills were managed by agents hired by the merchant proprietors. To obtain the labor they needed, they had to recruit a different kind of workforce. Most workers were young, single women from rural New England, who were attracted to the mills as household textile production declined and were called "operatives" because they worked powered machinery. Because factory work drew them away from their families' homes, the companies constructed special boarding houses for workers, calculating that good wages and strict discipline would make them a reliable labor force.

All these developments marked a shift away from household-based production. By 1830, a decreasing number of workers lived in their employers' households. Factory workers inhabited their own rented accommodation or—as in Waltham or Lowell—lived with fellow operatives in company boarding houses. Even when the scale of production remained small, residential separation of workers and bosses became common. Most New York City artisans had workshops attached to their homes in 1790, but by 1840, two-thirds of them lived and worked in separate places. In Rochester, New York, by 1827, fewer than one journeyman in four lived in an employer's household. This residential separation was just part of a trend toward greater social division.

Industrialization and Social Stratification   Many people born around 1800 found greater prosperity than their parents had. For some, the growth of manufacturing brought economic success. Chauncey Jerome, son of a Connecticut blacksmith and nailmaker who died when Chauncey was eleven, started work making clock dials for Eli Terry but then built his own business. By 1840, he owned one of America's largest clock-manufacturing firms. Another Connecticut-born artisan, Thomas Rogers, began as a house carpenter, moved to Paterson, New Jersey, and was a loom builder and machinist before helping to establish, in 1831, what would become one of the nation's largest locomotive builders. Successful manufacturers such as Jerome and Rogers viewed themselves as beneficiaries of the republican ideal of a property-owning citizenry, and Rogers named his factory the Jefferson Works to commemorate this ideal's political hero. For them, industrialization brought opportunities for independence.

But amid prosperity, there was also poverty and insecurity. Trade and manufacture were increasingly competitive, there was greater reliance on wageworkers, and disparities between rich and poor grew. Periodic economic slumps created hardship and uncertainty. The first severe downturn, in 1819, ended the import boom that followed the War of 1812, putting many people into debt and out of work. Other slumps would follow, particularly in the late 1830s. Industrial growth created larger numbers of people whose labor was essential but whose access to property and wealth was limited or precarious.

Urban growth widened the disparities between rich and poor. By 1840, 38 percent of the Massachusetts population lived in settlements of over 2,500 inhabitants. Although much manufacturing took place in small towns, large industrial centers also developed, of which Philadelphia and New York City were the biggest. New York's population, over 312,000 in 1840, had almost tripled in two decades, and its manufacturing workforce — already over 25,000 strong — would more than triple in the next ten years. Migration from the countryside and from Europe provided much of this growth. Poorer workers arriving in the cities were often obliged to take low-paid unskilled or casual labor for incomes that were only a fraction of those of urban elites.

Conditions for the urban poor were often bleak. Thousands of women labored in the clothing and millinery trades for extremely low wages. An 1830 report noted needlewomen earning as little as $55 a year and having to pay $26 for rent alone. A missionary described visiting many homes whose "entire furnishings" were "one bed, one chair, . . . one table, one candlestick, one cup, an old pot, and a piece of a frying pan." Some middle-class reformers protested these conditions. Fearing that poverty would cause prostitution, crime, or disorder, they urged folk to stay in the countryside and called on employers to be kinder. But they had no practical solutions to propose. Poorer workers sought better pay or working conditions, but circumstances were often against them.

Wage Labor and Resistance

The early expansion of industry involved different types of labor and economic organization, as well as people of different social and national backgrounds. The changing organization of work and growing numbers of wage earners challenged the ideal of a republic of property owners. During the 1820s and 1830s, working people began to act together to defend the principles of equality in a divided society. They resisted changes in the work process, organized labor unions to secure better pay or working hours, or campaigned for legal measures that might secure their rights in a harsh economy.

Artisans and Outworkers   Two important wage-earning groups were artisans (skilled craftsmen and occasionally women) and outworkers, people who were paid by the piece to perform manufacturing tasks in their homes. Traditional craft production centered on master artisans, their journeymen, and apprentice helpers, who worked together in small shops. Apprentices were boys who were contracted to work during their youth in return for instruction in the master's trade. Journeymen were trained workers who earned wages by the day. Although their relationship with the master was not an equal one, most apprentices and journeymen could hope to become masters in their own right once they had acquired skill and capital.

Commercial growth and transportation improvements increased competition between artisans and undermined their independence. Enlarged markets encouraged larger-scale output of ready-made goods, instead of custom-made production of a few items. Boston, New York, Newark, and Philadelphia shoemakers, for example, competed not only with one another, but also with Lynn, Massachusetts, the nation's rising center of shoe production. By 1820, especially in trades that supplied goods to southern and other nonlocal markets — where quantity and price, rather than quality, counted — workshops had grown in size, and tasks were subdivided into less skilled segments of work. Some New York shoe manufacturers each employed from twenty to thirty-five men and women.

Many artisans prospered in these new conditions, but more were obliged to migrate to more promising areas or face debt and eventual dispossession of their shops and perhaps even their tools. Deprived of independent means, they became employees, working up materials supplied by merchants or working in a master's shop for wages. Many urban shoemakers, tailors, hatters, and others were reduced to living on low pay in cramped, squalid conditions.

Working patterns in many trades were irregular. On one hand, this relieved the monotony of the job. New Jersey ironworkers left work to take in the harvest, go hunting, get drunk, or go to the beach. When one iron-

Urban Crafts Under Siege

Tailoring was one of the crafts most affected by changes in the organization of production. As late as 1874, when Boston lithographer Louis Prang published a series of views of the occupations for use in public schools, the nonmechanized urban workshop remained small in scale, but a rigid hierarchy among workers had long been established. In this print, the skilled cutter works in his shirtsleeves but is otherwise well dressed, while across the room, younger and less skilled male workers sew by the window, and a woman operates a sewing machine. Through the door, a master tailor or clothier measures a customer in the separate retail establishment. "Prang's Aids for Object Teaching: Trades and Occupations — Tailor," lithograph, 1874 — Prints and Photographs Division, Library of Congress.

master threatened fines for bringing liquor to work, he was told that a worker had "got drunk on cheese." On the other hand, many workers faced periods of idleness. A skilled workman might in theory make $600 a year but could have difficulty earning half this amount because there were days or seasons when there was no work to do.

Master craftsmen faced a dilemma. Some remained loyal to tradition and to their journeymen and apprentices, resisting pressure for change. In 1830, a New York master refused to divide the work in his shop according to skill because this would violate republican principles: "this Sir is a free country[;] we want no one person over another which would be the case if you

Job Visited by a Master Tailor from Broadway

An illustration from the 1841 novel *The Career of Puffer Hopkins* caricatured the growing distinction between masters and journeymen. The master tailor's prosperous outfit, stance, and fancy business address (New York's Broadway) sharply contrasted with the journeyman's wretched appearance and workshop-home. Cornelius Mathews, *The Career of Puffer Hopkins* (1841) — American Social History Project.

"No One Ever Hurried During 'Cake-time'": Traditional Patterns of Work

Here, a ship carpenter recalls the frequent breaks for food and drink that punctuated a typical day in an early-nineteenth-century New York shipyard. In the early nineteenth century, traditional work patterns still limited the pace and intensity of labor in many industries. Employers increasingly came to regard such practices as intolerable obstacles to efficiency and profit.

In our yard, at half-past eight a.m., Aunt Arlie McVane, a clever kind-hearted woman but awfully uncouth . . . would make her welcome appearance in the yard with her two great baskets, stowed and checked off with crullers, doughnuts, ginger-bread, turnovers, pies, and a variety of sweet cookies and cakes; and from the time Aunt Arlie's baskets came in sight until every man and boy, bosses and all, in the yard, had been supplied, always at one cent a piece for any article on the cargo, the pie, cake, and cookie trade was a brisk one. Aunt Arlie would usually make the rounds of the yard and supply all the hands in about an hour, bringing the forenoon up to half-past nine, and giving us from ten to fifteen minutes' "breathing spell" during lunch; no one ever hurried during "cake-time."

After this was over we would fall to [work] again, until interrupted by Johnnie Gogean, the English candyman, who came in always at half-past ten, with his great board, the size of a medium extension dining table, slung before him, covered with all sorts of "stick," and several of sticky candy, in one-cent lots. Bosses, boys, and men—all hands, everybody—invested one to three cents in Johnnie's sweet wares, and another ten to fifteen minutes is spent in consuming it. Johnnie usually sailed out with a bare board until eleven o'clock, at which time there was a general sailing out of the yard and into convenient grog-ships after whiskey. . . .

In the afternoon, about half-past three, we had a cake-lunch, supplied by Uncle Jack Gridder, an old, crippled, superannuated ship carpenter. No one else was ever allowed to come in competition with our caterers. Let a foreign candyboard or cake basket make their appearance inside the gates of the yard, and they would get shipped out of that directly.

At about five o'clock p.m., always Johnnie used to put in his second appearance; and then, having expended money in another stick or two of candy, and ten minutes in its consumption, we were ready to drive away again until sundown; then home to supper.

Herbert G. Gutman, *Work, Culture and Society in Industrializing America* (1976), 34–35.

divided the labour." But this stance usually led to economic ruin. Other masters pressed their employees to produce more. As their shops grew in size, some hired agents or foremen to supervise and discipline workers. When Thomas Babcock became foreman of a New Haven, Connecticut, printing office in 1825, he was expected to set working hours, oversee production, "keep . . . [workmen] . . . still, sober and peaceable, and attentive to their business," and hire and fire workers as needed. "Capitalists," objected the *New York State Mechanic* in 1842, "have taken to bossing all the mechanical trades, while the practical mechanic has become a journeyman, subject to be discharged at every pretended 'miff' of his purse-proud employer."

Workers resisted what they saw as encroachments on their rights. When the owners of a Catskill, New York, machine works installed a bell in 1836 to signal the beginning and end of the workday, their twenty-eight employees threatened to strike. There was a compromise: workers retained the right to determine their working hours but promised in return to work steadily and cease drinking and storytelling on the job. Such agreements, though, did not stem the tide of changes sweeping over many craft industries.

Changes in shoe production in Lynn, Massachusetts, illustrate a general pattern. In the eighteenth century, most shoemakers worked in their own homes or small workshops (called ten-footers), cutting and sewing leather pieces and joining soles and uppers. There was minimal division of labor. Masters had a journeyman or two and a couple of apprentices and trained them in all the tasks of production. Around the turn of the nineteenth century, however, demand for cheap shoes for the expanding southern slave population altered the way in which shoemaking was conducted. Shops multiplied, the division of labor increased, and some masters established large central shops, where they concentrated on cutting the leather, leaving other tasks to journeymen. In time, the job of cutting was delegated to workers, and masters became bosses (supervising others' labor) or merchants (selling finished shoes). Journeymen resented masters' changing attitudes toward them. "They seem to think it is a disgrace to labor," complained one, "that the laborer is not as good as other people. These little stuck-up, self-conceited individuals. . . . You must do as they wish . . . or you are off their books; they have no more employment for you."

As the new system took root, tasks were further subdivided, making it possible to replace skilled journeymen with less fully trained workers, including women and children. Journeymen's wives and daughters often took on the work of binding—stitching together shoe uppers and linings—leaving journeymen only the tasks of lasting (fitting the uppers over a shaped wooden last) and bottoming (attaching uppers to the soles). Dividing tasks and reducing skill worsened most journeymen's prospects. Few now became masters. Apprenticeship declined. Journeymen protested the

"The Natural Tie Between Master and Apprentice Has Been Rent Asunder"

The American Revolution, with its rampant egalitarianism, dissolved much of the paternalistic control that had once been wielded by fathers, masters, and other authority figures, as the anonymous author "An Old Apprentice" made clear in this 1826 letter to the New York Observer. *In addition, employers began dividing up manufacturing tasks, and semiskilled and unskilled women and children performed this labor rather than apprentices or other workingmen of the traditional artisanal system. A loss of reciprocity and responsibility occurred on both sides.*

. . . It is generally admitted, that intemperance among mechanics, and among the boys employed by them, has alarmingly increased of late; and it is, I conceive, a natural consequence of the present loose system of taking boys. In the course of my inquiries I saw four or five boys, from ten to fourteen years of age, romping at their work; and upon asking, "Are not these boys apprenticed?" was answered, "Oh no! they are little journeymen; they are received upon the same footing, are paid their wages regularly, and know and feel that they are freemen; and of course soon discover it by their conduct. If one of them should dislike a word of reproof, he will call for his wages and quit me instantly; and there are employers enough who will receive them, and care nothing for their moral character, or their steadiness, or constancy at their work." There are too large a portion of mechanics who prefer the present system, as they look not beyond their own immediate wants. . . . These men prefer that the boys should not be bound as in that case there is nothing binding upon them. If the boy is taken sick or is guilty of misconduct, he can be turned adrift upon the public or his friends, and no responsibility attached to the employer.

There is one important view of the subject, which this class of men seem entirely to have overlooked, viz. that they are contributing, by their practice, to form and to perpetuate the insubordinate characters of which they complain. Masters will tell you that their journeymen repeatedly leave them, with no word of explanation, for several days together; and it is proverbial that during the Spring races, troops of them invariably drop the paint brush or the saw, for the race-course; and the whole family is thus left in confusion till the races are past and the workmen are sobered. . . .

Now, I ask, what is the cause of all these complaints? . . . Is it not because the natural tie between master and apprentice, has been rent asunder? As there is now no community of interest, so there is no community of feeling between them. The master no longer lives among his apprentices, watches over their moral as well as mechanical improvement, accompanies them on Sunday to a place of public worship, counsels them when in trouble, keeps them and comforts them in sickness, and when he is able, gives them, with their good name, some assistance to begin the world for themselves. . . .

New York Observer (New York, New York), October 7, 14, and 28, 1826.

"anti-republican" distinctions that were emerging between them and masters, which they likened to "those existing between the aristocracy and the laboring classes in Europe."

Shoe bosses scoured New England for new workers. Part-time rural craft workers competed for journeymen's work, enabling employers to hold down wages and lengthen working hours. Yet families facing hard times came forward eagerly. Thousands of farmers and fishermen supplemented their incomes by lasting and bottoming shoes at home, and increasing numbers of women took up shoe binding as outwork, at one-third to one-half the wages paid to male shoemakers in the central shops.

From the 1820s on, more and more manufacturing tasks were "put out" to rural families or the urban poor, who worked for merchants for piece-rate wages. Counting outworkers, almost half of all manufacturing workers,

Killers

As master artisans' supervision of their journeymen and apprentices dwindled, their former charges were freer to choose how to spend time away from the workshop. Some, like these two "Killers," joined proliferating urban gangs. This is the cover of an 1850 novel that was based on the violent activities of a notorious Philadelphia gang of journeymen, laborers, and apprentices. George Lippard, *The Killers. A Narrative of Real Life in Philadelphia . . .* (1850) — Historical Society of Pennsylvania.

THE KILLERS.

A NARRATIVE

OF

REAL LIFE IN PHILADELPHIA,

In which the deeds of the Killers, and the great Riot of election night, October 10, 1849, are minutely described. Also, the adventures of three notorious individuals, who took part in that Riot, to wit:

CROMWELL D. Z. HICKS, *the Leader of the Killers,*

DON JORGE, *one of the Leaders of the Cuban Expedition, and*

"THE BULGINE," *the celebrated Negro Desperado of Moyamensing.*

BY A MEMBER OF THE PHILADELPHIA BAR.

PHILADELPHIA:
PUBLISHED BY HANKINSON AND BARTHOLOMEW.
1850.

and about two-thirds of those in New England, were women. Eighteen thousand Massachusetts women braided straw hats at home in the 1830s; others made buttons, socks, mittens, suspenders, and palm-leaf hats. Rural outwork was initially a strategy for household independence adopted by families with daughters who would previously have undertaken home textile production. As wage rates fell, however, outwork was taken up by poorer families — often by women with young children who did it in gaps left by other tasks. Homeworking also became a staple for the urban poor. In 1831, Mathew Carey estimated that in America's four largest cities, 12,000 or 13,000 women worked at home making paper boxes, shirts, collars, artificial flowers, and similar goods.

Urban trades underwent changes similar to those in shoemaking. Until the early 1800s, the New York clothing trade was dominated by male tailors who catered to upper-class demand for custom-made garments and by female dressmakers and seamstresses who worked on dresses, children's clothing, shirts, and mending. But under the federal protective tariff of 1816, the U.S. clothing trades expanded. City merchants, using cheap cloth from the new textile mills, captured from England the market in clothing for southern slaves. Later, these merchants added clothing for plantation owners, and the opening of the Erie Canal gave them new western markets. New York merchants' profits were handsome. In the early 1830s, ready-made clothing sold for five times what it cost to produce. By the middle of the decade, there were several clothing firms with over 300 employees each.

Profits rested on low wages and low overhead costs. The outwork system allowed manufacturers to replace skilled tailors with less-skilled women homeworkers. Some were the wives and daughters of laborers, but most women clothing workers headed their own households. Many had been widowed or abandoned and had children to support. Swelling numbers of poor women and families, including immigrants, increased competition for work, further depressing piece rates and lengthening the hours of work required to earn an income. Isolated at home, outworkers had difficulty banding together to defend common interests. Frequently, they could not afford for themselves the clothing they made for others.

Manual Laborers and Factory Operatives

Demand for manual laborers also grew. The building of roads, canals, and railroads and construction in burgeoning towns and cities furnished employment to thousands of men. Commerce required the labor of carters, warehousemen, dockworkers, and

Scenes and Occupations Characteristic of New England Life
This engraving in a popular 1850s magazine heralded the centrality of rural women in antebellum work. While a variety of men such as a farmer, a drover, and a lumberman are shown at work, the illustration features three working women: a "factory girl," a woman picking hops, and — in the center — a palm-leaf hat braider. Thousands of rural women made palm-leaf hats in their homes, adding valuable cash to their family's income, all part of a vast rural outwork system organized by rural merchants. *Ballou's Pictorial Drawing-room Companion*, June 16, 1855 — General Research Division, New York Public Library, Astor, Lenox and Tilden Foundations.

sailors, who loaded, transported, unloaded, and stored the commodities that created rising mercantile fortunes. Within a year of its opening, for example, some 8,000 men were employed in moving the goods that traveled along the Erie Canal.

All these tasks were considered unskilled; in an age before power-driven machinery they involved heavy exertion, often under harsh conditions. Canal construction, for instance, entailed winter work in water and ice and summers of digging through leech- and mosquito-infested swamps. Living conditions were wretched. Workers shared tents or rough shanties—"more like dog-kennels than the habitations of men," one observer wrote—poorly built, scantily furnished, and offering little protection from harsh weather.

After 1820, manual laborers' wage rates rose about 12 percent each decade in real terms, but for many reasons, this rise often failed to produce incomes much above bare subsistence. Migrants from the countryside and from Europe fed the pool of available workers. Wage payments were often irregular or were made in the form of credit at an overpriced company store. Many jobs were intermittent or seasonal; the average day laborer found work only two hundred days a year. Large construction projects were handled by contractors who bid for jobs "as low as labor and capital can afford" and hired workers for as little as they could. Not infrequently, contractors went bankrupt and fled without paying workers the wages they had earned.

Laborers' low earnings placed a premium on enhancing family incomes. Wives and children worked to help fulfill everyday needs. Many women took in outwork or boarders. Children worked in factories or in casual jobs. Daughters hired out as live-in servants for money wages averaging a dollar a week or less besides room and board.

Factories grew in number and size, becoming a major source of wage work. Large mills, such as those of the Waltham-Lowell system, recruited workers in sizable numbers. Many of Lowell's first women workers were the daughters of farmers. Rural economic change both pushed them out of their parents' homes and attracted them to factory work, typically for periods from a few months to a few years; sisters often followed one another to

Starting for Lowell

An illustration from T. S. Arthur's reform tract *Illustrated Temperance Tales* presented a young woman leaving her farm family to work in a cotton mill. This picture was accurate in showing that New England farm families often had to rely on income from factory labor. But reformers blamed economic hardship on personal weaknesses — in the case of Arthur's story, the father's alcoholism. Timothy Shay Arthur, "The Factory Girl," *Illustrated Temperance Tales* (1850) — American Social History Project.

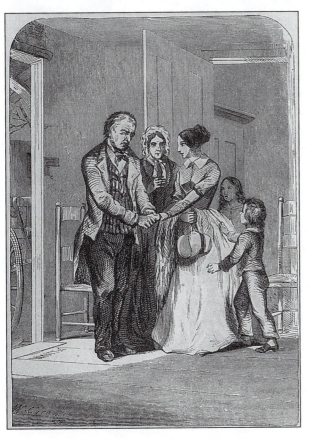

Spinning

This picture depicts the spinning of yarn, part of the process of cotton production chronicled in a series of twelve prints published from 1835 to 1840, called *The Progress of Cotton*. The woman on the left is repairing broken threads while a child crouching below the threads (a "scavenger") cleans the machine. J. R. Barfoot, lithograph, c. 1840 — Mabel Brady Garvan Collection, Yale University Art Gallery.

work in the mills. By the 1830s, most were from northern New England, where farm households were hardest pressed. The Fowler family owned a small farm in Boscawen, New Hampshire; four of their five daughters worked in a Lowell mill at different times between 1831 and 1842.

Women hoped that factory work would give them cultural opportunities and the chance to earn a dowry, which impoverished farm life denied them. Although early wages for the young, unmarried Yankee women who came to Lowell's mills and boardinghouses were lower than those for male laborers, they were better than the wages that were otherwise available to women. Mary Paul of Barnard, Vermont, worked in her early teens as a domestic servant before seeking her father's permission to work in Lowell. "I think it would be better for me than to stay out here," she wrote him. "I am in need of clothes which I cannot get about here and for that reason I want to go to Lowell or some other place." Some young women saw factory work as a chance for some independence. Sally Rice found being a farm worker isolating and exhausting. Telling her parents that she wanted to find work in a textile mill, she wrote, "I am most 19 years old. I must of course have something of my own before many more years have passed over my head. And where is that something coming from if I go home and earn nothing?"

Work in the mills, never easy, grew harder over time. In the 1820s, the average Lowell operative worked twelve hours a day, six days a week, with brief holidays only for July Fourth, Thanksgiving, and the first day of spring. Still, the companies needed to provide tolerable working and living conditions if they were to induce women to stay at work for several years. But increasing competition in the textile industry cut profits, and by the 1830s, operatives found wages cut, boardinghouse rents raised, or workloads increased. Twice, in 1834 and again in 1836, women took strike action to resist these changes.

The Workingmen's Movement   From the mid-1820s to the late 1830s, there was a tide of protest by working men and women who resisted their subordination to bosses and asserted their equal rights under circumstances in which economic power was unequally distributed. New political parties, labor journals and newspapers, trade unions, and spontaneous actions by workers all campaigned against the emerging division between capital and labor. The Revolution's vision of equality served as a reference point for working people asserting their rights.

A workingmen's party first arose in Philadelphia around 1827 out of a short-lived union of mechanics' associations. The idea spread quickly.

"No More Grinding the POOR — But Liberty and the Rights of Man"
An engraving printed around 1830 depicted the forces of monopoly attempting to undermine the workingman's vote. While the devil offered an aristocrat the support of his "favourite" newspapers "to grind the WORKIES," a mechanic placed his faith in suffrage. Kilroe Collection, Butler Library, Columbia University.

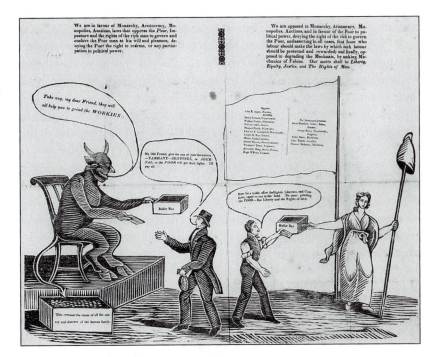

"Throughout this vast republic," declared the *Albany Advocate*, "the farmers, mechanics, and workingmen are assembling . . . to impart to its laws and administration those principles of liberty and equality unfolded in the Declaration of our Independence." Thomas Skidmore, a self-educated New York City machinist, wrote a radical prescription for a workingmen's policy. In *The Rights of Man to Property* (1829), he argued that the poor should win control of government and redistribute property equally among all adults, including women and slaves, and abolish inheritance to maintain equality over generations. Society would have "no lenders, no borrowers; no landlords, no tenants; no masters, no journeymen; no Wealth, no Want," and independent self-employment would become general.

Actual workingmen's parties adopted more modest proposals, including the abolition of paper money, a homestead law to provide free land in the West, and some of the earliest calls for publicly funded schooling. By the early 1830s, their candidates also pledged to enable mechanics to enforce payment for their work, to abolish compulsory militia duty and imprisonment for debt, and to curb the power of banks and corporations. Their electoral success, though modest, was sufficient to jolt the major parties into adopting many of their policies. Unable to withstand this competition, most of the workingmen's parties dissolved during the 1830s, many of their leaders affiliating with the Democrats and a few with the Whig Party. But the end of their electoral challenge did not erase the issues that had given rise to it.

Strikes and Protests   In 1838, journeymen carriage makers from small Massachusetts workshops protested a proposal to incorporate a large carriage-building firm, arguing that this would block their aspirations to

A Militia Drill Thirty Years Ago
Congress authorized universal military duty for all males, but inequalities in the system led to calls for reform. The Workingmen's Party in Pennsylvania and New York attacked privately organized elite units whose members' costly uniforms and elaborate ceremonies displayed their wealth and connections. The aristocratic pretensions of "private" units contrasted with the ragtag appearance of "public," neighborhood militias (remembered here in an 1862 lithograph). Public militia service was a financial burden: members lost wages to attend drills and risked fines if they were absent or violated dress codes. David Claypool Johnston, 1862, lithograph 10 7/8 × 16 inches — American Antiquarian Society.

"This Monopoly Should Be Broken Up": Workingmen Protest Inequality

Like the Philadelphia Workingmen's Committee that published this report in 1830, many workingmen's political parties condemned the inequality between the education available to those who could afford it, and the lack of provision for the poor. They advocated the adoption of free public schooling in their states, as a means of promoting "general and equal education" and "equal knowledge" as a step toward achieving "equal liberty."

The original element of despotism is a monopoly of talent, which consigns the multitude to comparative ignorance, and secures the balance of knowledge on the side of the rich and the rulers. If then the healthy existence of a free government be, as the committee believe, rooted in the will of the American people, it follows as a necessary consequence, of a government based upon that will, that this monopoly should be broken up, and that the means of equal knowledge (the only security for equal liberty) should be rendered, by legal provision, the common property of all classes. . . .

It appears, therefore, to the committee that there can be no real liberty without a wide diffusion of real intelligence; that the members of a republic should all be alike instructed in the nature and character of their equal rights and duties, as human beings and as citizens; and that education, instead of being limited, as in our public poor schools, to a simple acquaintance with words and cyphers, should tend, as far as possible, to the production of a just disposition, virtuous habits, and a rational self-governing character.

When the committee contemplate their own condition, and that of the great mass of their fellow laborers, when they look around on the glaring inequality of society, they are constrained to believe that until the means of equal instruction shall be equally secured to all, liberty is but an unmeaning word, and equality an empty shadow, whose substance to be realized must first be planted by an equal education and proper training in the minds, in the habits, in the manners, and in the feelings of the community.

Working Men's Advocate, March 6, 1830.

---

become proprietors in their own right. Although they currently worked for others, "We . . . do look forward with anticipation to a time when we shall be able to conduct the business upon our own responsibility and receive the profits of our labor, which we now relinquish to others." Large incorporated businesses, they argued, would destroy the republican ideal: "we believe that incorporated bodies tend to crush all feeble enterprise and compel us to work out our days in the Service of others."

As a growing number of wageworkers had little chance of achieving propertied independence, the benefits of republican citizenship came to depend on reasonable wages and working conditions. Philadelphia journeymen house carpenters noted that "in this favored nation we enjoy the inestimable blessing of 'universal suffrage,' and constituting, as we everywhere do, a very great majority, we have the power to choose our own legislators." However, "this blessing . . . can be of no further benefit to us" unless "we possess sufficient knowledge to make proper use of it." To acquire knowledge, workers needed more time to read, think, and discuss and less time chained to the workbench. In 1827, they struck in support of a demand that their working day be shortened from twelve hours to ten. Antagonism between masters and journeymen and between employers and employees continued to deepen during the 1830s, causing an unprecedented mobilization of trade unions and labor protest.

The issue of working hours sparked heated conflict. In 1824, Pawtucket mill owners tried to extend the workday and lowered piece rates. Led by women weavers and supported by townsfolk, workers went on strike to resist the changes. When, in 1828 and 1829, it was rumored that New York employers were about to extend the workday from ten hours to eleven, mass meetings of journeymen and their supporters denounced the proposal as a selfish assault on republican citizens' rights. Several thousand workers threatened to strike against any boss who insisted on more than ten hours, and the employers backed down.

Wages were a more frequent source of friction and often a basis on which labor unions could organize. Despite their relative isolation in the outwork system, 1,600 women joined the New York Tailoresses' Society, founded in 1831, to fight a series of wage cuts by merchants. In 1833, journeymen carpenters in the city struck for higher wages, winning a month-long campaign. The New York carpenters obtained the support of organizations in fifteen other trades, and the printers' union president John Finch noted the "necessity of combined efforts for the purpose of self-protection." Finch's union issued a call for all organized trades to unite in a citywide federation of craft unions. Representatives of nine trades attended the first convention of New York's General Trades Union (GTU). In 1834, a GTU parade stretched for a mile and a half. The GTU aided strikes over wages or

Bells, Bells, Bells

The mill workers' day in 1853, as dictated by the managers of the Lowell Mills. American Textile History Museum.

conditions among bakers, hatters, ropemakers, sailmakers, weavers, and leatherworkers in New York, Newark, Poughkeepsie, Boston, and Philadelphia.

Radical printer and former Workingmen's Party leader George Henry Evans urged that such mutual support should become general, so that "[t]he rights of each individual would then be sustained by every workingman in the country, whose aggregate wealth and power would be able to resist the most formidable oppression." An August 1834 convention formed the National Trades Union (NTU), with delegates representing over 25,000 workers. A labor upsurge in the next few years spawned at least sixty new unions and called more than a hundred strikes.

Organizing across trades and regions was accomplished mostly by skilled craftsmen, but other groups, including women, could be equally militant. When Lowell mill owners cut wages in 1834, women operatives struck, in a "turn-out" that involved one-sixth of the Lowell workforce. Their action failed. Companies recruited other women to tend machines, and within a week, most mills were operating near capacity. But two years later, the Lowell employers raised rents in their boardinghouses, provoking a more widespread and better-organized response from women operatives, who stayed out on strike until the rent increases were canceled or reduced.

Almost two decades before the birth of a formal women's rights movement, female strikers asserted the right of women to defend their interests in a society that denied them political participation or a public voice. New York Tailoresses' leader Sarah Monroe asked, "if it is unfashionable for the men to bear oppression in silence, why should it not also become unfashionable with the women?" In 1833, women shoebinders from Lynn and neighboring towns formed their own protective organization. They drew on the Declaration of Independence and the Constitution to proclaim that "Women as well as men have certain inalienable rights, among which is the right at all times of 'peaceably assembling to consult upon the common good.'" Lowell strikers warned that the mill owners' "oppressive hand of avarice would enslave us" and, rebuffing the employers' suggestion that those in need could turn to charity, proclaimed, "We prefer to have the disposing of our charities in our own hands; and as we are free, we would remain in possession of what kind Providence has bestowed upon us; and remain daughters of freemen still."

Some male unions supported campaigns by women workers, but the labor movement was generally hostile to women. According to the NTU's committee on female labor, "the physical organization, the natural responsibilities, and the moral sensibility of women prove conclusively that their labors should be only of a domestic nature." Most men regarded women's employment as an attack on their own independence or dignity as providers, as taking women away from their proper domestic roles, and as threatening to undercut their own wage rates.

"I Cannot Be a Slave": Remembering the 1836 Lowell Mill Strike

Harriet Hanson Robinson began work in Lowell at the age of ten, later becoming an author and advocate of women's suffrage. In 1898, she published a memoir of her Lowell experiences. In the following excerpt, she recounts the strike of 1836.

One of the girls stood on a pump, and gave vent to the feelings of her companions in a neat speech, declaring that it was their duty to resist all attempts at cutting down the wages. This was the first time a woman had spoken in public in Lowell, and the event caused surprise and consternation among her audience.

Cutting down the wages was not their only grievance, nor the only cause of this strike. Hitherto the corporations had paid twenty-five cents a week towards the board of each operative, and now it was their purpose to have the girls pay the sum; and this, in addition to the cut in the wages, would make a difference of at least one dollar a week. It was estimated that as many as twelve or fifteen hundred girls turned out, and walked in procession through the streets. They had neither flags nor music, but sang songs, a favorite (but rather inappropriate) one being a parody on "I won't be a nun."

> "Oh! isn't it a pity, such a pretty girl as I
> Should be sent to the factory to pine away and die?
> Oh! I cannot be a slave,
> I will not be a slave,
> For I'm so fond of liberty
> That I cannot be a slave."

My own recollection of this first strike (or "turn out" as it was called) is very vivid. I worked in a lower room, where I had heard the proposed strike fully, if not vehemently, discussed; I had been an ardent listener to what was said against this attempt at "oppression" on the part of the corporation, and naturally I took sides with the strikers. When the day came on which the girls were to turn out, those in the upper rooms started first, and so many of them left that our mill was at once shut down. Then, when the girls in my room stood irresolute, uncertain what to do, asking each other, "Would you?" or "Shall we turn out?" and not one of them having the courage to lead off, I, who began to think they would not go out, after all their talk, became impatient, and started on ahead, saying, with childish bravado, "I don't care what you do, I am going to turn out, whether any one else does or not"; and I marched out, and was followed by the others.

As I looked back at the long line that followed me, I was more proud than I have ever been since.

Harriet Hanson Robinson, *Loom and Spindle or Life Among the Early Mill Girls* (New York, T. Y. Crowell, 1898), 83–86.

Like women, unskilled workmen were initially disdained by the skilled craft unions but organized on their own behalf. Dockers and maritime workers in New York stopped work in 1828 and again in 1834 to protest layoffs and wage cuts. Canal laborers struck on at least four occasions in the 1820s and another fourteen times in the 1830s. On the Chesapeake & Ohio and other canals, Irish laborers formed secret societies to protect wages and conditions, fighting off men who refused to join or who were hired by the companies to break the societies' influence. One pitched battle on the C & O Canal in January 1834 was suppressed by federal troops. But four years later, when the company failed to pay wages and laborers destroyed the work they had not been paid for, militiamen who were called out to quell them refused to march, declaring their sympathy with the workers.

By the mid-1830s, some urban labor activists were pursuing collaboration between the skilled and the unskilled and even talked of a general strike of all organized workers to improve conditions. Philadelphia coalheavers accomplished the first such strike in American history when they walked off the docks in 1835 to demand shorter hours and were joined by shoemakers and other craftsmen. The strike spread to other trades, including textile workers and outworkers, before employers conceded shorter hours and a wage increase, and a city ordinance made ten hours the legal working day on public projects. Cooperation between skilled and unskilled workers continued, and in 1836, the Philadelphia General Trades Union voted to allow laborers into its ranks—the first time skilled workers reached across the gap that had separated them from the unskilled.

"By Hammer and Hand All Arts Do Stand"

The artisan's symbol adorned an announcement in New York's General Trades' Union newspaper, *The Union*, calling for a demonstration to support union tailors convicted of conspiracy in 1836. *The Union*, June 14, 1836 — Rare Books and Manuscript Division, New York Public Library, Astor, Lenox and Tilden Foundations.

A Voice from the People!

Two Outlooks: Morality or the Market?

In a republic, the NTU insisted, a citizen's conduct and the "value of all social institutions" should be guided by standards of "moral justice" rather than those of profitability; the private pursuit of profit jeopardized "the social, civil, and intellectual condition of the laboring classes" and resulted in "the most unequal and unjustifiable distribution of the wealth of society in the hands of a few individuals." Labor organizations and their activities defended working people against "a humiliating, servile dependency, incompatible with . . . natural equality" and "subversive of the rights of man."

Many merchants and employers, outraged by strikes, held an alternative view that identified republican order with the free play of the market—a market in which labor was a commodity like any other. "The true regulator of prices," held the New York *Journal of Commerce*, "whether of labor, goods, real estate, or anything else, is demand." Certainly, the editor agreed, "we wish to see all men, mechanics as well as others, receive an adequate compensation for their labor." But collective action was "at war with the order of things which the Creator has established for the general good." In trade unions and strikes, he advised, the best workingmen—"whose wages would go up . . . if they would but go on their own merits"—suffered needlessly because they aided in "lifting up the unworthy, [even] though they sink themselves."

These outlooks—one demanding that economic life conform to republican principles, the other insisting that life in the republic be regulated by the marketplace—clashed in New York in 1836. For two years previously, rapid price inflation had driven shoemakers, carpenters, cabinetmakers, weavers, and others to strike for higher wages. Now New York employers sought to make an example of the journeymen tailors' association, one of the city's strongest unions. Early in the year, masters and merchant tailors repudiated a negotiated pay scale and agreed with each other not to hire union members. Journeymen picketed the masters' shops to discourage other journeymen from taking their places. A grand jury, however, labeled this conduct "conspiracy"—a criminal offense under a state law of 1829 prohibiting collective action "to commit any act injurious to public morals or to trade and commerce."

At trial in May, twenty tailors were found guilty, fined heavily, and lectured by Judge Ogden Edwards on the error of their ways. Echoing the city's employers and antilabor newspapers, Edwards told them that in this "favored land of law and liberty, the road to advancement is open to all, and the journeymen may by their skill and industry and moral worth soon become flourishing master mechanics." Unions, he claimed, were alien to

"The Rich Against the Poor!": A Strikers' Handbill

Shortly after New York's striking tailors were convicted in 1836, a placard appeared in various parts of the city. Its text was printed within the outline of a coffin, signifying the "coffin of equality." Following are excerpts from that text. The Common Council promptly offered a reward for the apprehension of the anonymous author of this "Coffin Handbill."

The rich against the Poor! Judge Edwards, the tool of the Aristocracy, against the People! Mechanics and Workingmen! A deadly blow has been struck at your Liberty! The prize for which your fathers fought has been robbed from you! The Freemen of the North are now on a level with the Slaves of the South! with no other privileges than laboring that drones may fatten on your lifeblood! Twenty of your brethren have been found guilty for presuming to resist a reduction of their wages! and Judge Edwards has charged an American jury, and agreeably to that charge, they have established the precedent, that workingmen have no right to regulate the price of labor! or, in other words, the Rich are the only judges of the wants of the Poor Man!

New York Courier and Enquirer, June 8, 1836.

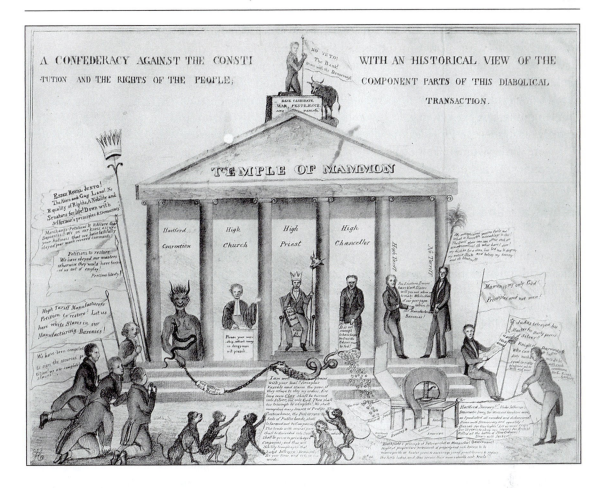

A Confederacy Against the Constitution and the Rights of the People

A typically busy 1830s cartoon denounced monopoly and privilege. On the right side of the "Temple of Mammon" (named after the New Testament false god of wealth and avarice), a northern manufacturer conspired with a southern planter: "You Southern Barons have black Slaves; will you not allow us to make white Slaves of our poor population in our Manufacturing Baronies?" Anonymous, 1833, lithograph — The Library Company of Philadelphia.

American society "and . . . mainly upheld by foreigners." The trial verdict and Edwards's attack on the right to organize and strike provoked massive protest. Twenty-seven thousand people — over a tenth of New York City's population — attended a rally that burned Judge Edwards in effigy and branded the trial "a concerted plan of the aristocracy to take from them that Liberty which was bequeathed to them as a sacred inheritance by their revolutionary sires." While Edwards claimed that workers in a republic were free to advance themselves, workers argued that only their freedom to organize could restore republican rights that had been undermined by class division and social inequality.

This conception of labor's rights, however, was increasingly confined to white men. There was a small, prosperous black middle class in the Northeast, but most African Americans faced segregation and job discrimination that kept them in relative poverty. By the 1820s, they were excluded from many occupations, even those with long traditions of black participation. In Philadelphia, the number of black artisans fell by more than one-quarter between 1832 and 1837 alone. An observer claimed that there were no black workmen in many New York City trades and that Boston had only a handful. Whites hostile to black workers rioted in Providence in 1831 and in Philadelphia in 1834, driving many African Americans out of their homes. Black workers of both sexes were increasingly confined to service or heavy laboring jobs, but even domestic servants were displaced by European immigrant women. In Philadelphia, over half of black women workers by 1837 were washerwomen. Few black workmen joined labor organizations because they rarely worked in organized trades and often met with hostility.

Democracy and Class in Jacksonian Society

The changes of the early nineteenth century transformed America's political landscape, introducing greater participation—at least for white men. The expansion of commerce, industry, and wage labor fostered a growing middle class, anchored by women's work at home, and new patterns of division between proprietors and workers. While social division did call forth political and religious movements that aimed to bridge growing class distinctions, it also prompted political rivalries and pressures for reform and would be deepened by economic crises at the end of the 1830s.

Politics and the Second Party System   Under pressure, the conception that republican citizenship should be based on possession of property gave way to reform. State after state modified its electoral rules to reduce or abolish property qualifications for voting. In the North, by the 1820s, all states but Rhode Island had granted the vote effectively to all adult white males. However, no state permitted women to vote, and many barred African American men from voting on grounds of race. Only white men could share in the privileges of political "independence."

Increased participation promoted new, more democratic political styles. Astute politicians grasped that genteel methods appropriate to government by "natural aristocracy" were inadequate to channel the votes of an expanding electorate. In New York State in the 1820s, the Democratic Party led by Martin Van Buren pioneered local organizing and campaigning tactics—making skillful use of newspapers—that emphasized popular inclusiveness, tactics that would spread across the nation. Committees drummed up local support, and elections were dominated by public meetings, picnics, and parades that became part of the fabric of social life. A new breed of professional politicians, such as Van Buren, built their careers on appeals to voters and the ability to dispense state or federal government patronage. Government jobs became rewards for favors and political support from outside the elite. Campaign speeches, banners, and handbills effused loyalty

Penny Pictures

Expanded political participation was aided by and contributed to the rise of new, inexpensive newspapers that trafficked in scandal and sensation. The *New York Herald*, more than any other of the so-called penny newspapers, published topical pictures. Most of the time, the pictures were simple maps or crude portraits of people in the news. Occasionally, special events received greater pictorial coverage. But when the *Herald* published five detailed pictures on its cover showing New York's 1845 funeral procession honoring Andrew Jackson — the first full-page cover devoted to pictures ever to appear in a daily newspaper — rival newspapers charged that the same engravings had been used to illustrate Queen Victoria's coronation, William Henry Harrison's funeral, and the celebration of the opening of the Croton reservoir. The *Herald* discontinued illustrating the news after 1850, leaving that task to the weekly illustrated press. Prints and Photographs Division, Library of Congress.

to "the working man" and "the producing classes." In practice, working people were divided in their political allegiances.

For a brief period after the War of 1812, commentators had celebrated an "era of good feelings" in which it appeared that party differences had dissolved. Advocates of federal involvement in the economy had secured broad support in 1816 for the chartering of a Second Bank of the United States to help stabilize the financial system. Henry Clay of Kentucky, a politician with followers both North and South, became the leading advocate of a program of federal sponsorship of transportation improvements and other measures aimed at fostering both national expansion and economic development. But the upheavals of the panic of 1819 and the growth of white men's political participation helped to obstruct Clay's ambitions and sow the seeds of new party divisions.

Epitomizing the new political culture was the figure of Andrew Jackson, who, having lost the 1824 presidential election in controversial circumstances, won the presidency four years later as a symbol of popular democracy. The first president not to come from the Virginia gentry or from New England, Jackson attacked "privilege" and the apparent threat of "aristocracy" arising from government power. "The first principle of our system," he told Congress, "[is] that the majority is to govern." His Democratic Party aimed to minimize government's ability to grant "special privileges and monopolies" that the wealthy could exploit to their own advantage. In the early 1830s, Jackson vetoed the rechartering of the Second Bank of the United States and condemned "the undue aggregation of capital in the hands of a . . . few" that threatened to rob the people of "the enjoyment of the fruits of their labor." Democrats believed that corporations concentrated "large masses of property" and impeded "the natural tendency of capital to an equal distribution among the people." They resisted bankruptcy statutes, which they suspected of sheltering the rich from their poorer creditors. Above all, they attacked federal expenditure for internal improvements such as roads and canals and attempted to break what they saw as "aristocratic" monopolies allegedly sought by a national elite.

Jackson's Democrats drew support from rural planters and proprietors, particularly in the South and Southwest, and from the urban poor, some craftsmen, and some businessmen in the North. By the mid-1830s, opponents of Jackson, comprising some Southerners but mostly northern commercial farmers, financiers, and industrial craftsmen and proprietors, joined to create the new Whig Party. Using campaigning and organizing methods similar to those of the Democrats, the Whigs' emergence signaled the creation of what historians have called the "second American party system." Both parties sought a broad appeal among the mainly white electorate and, above all, sought to avoid making slavery, with its potential for dividing the nation on sectional lines, into a contentious issue. Their different positions on "privilege" and federal power divided their appeal to workingmen.

The Democrats acted in the name of equality. Yet avoiding the use of government to create privilege did not always benefit working people. Since 1816, the federal government had enacted protective import tariffs to encourage manufacturing. By the 1830s, under pressure from southern members of the party, many Democrats were criticizing tariffs and working for their reduction, despite northern workers' support for them. Democrats' preference for leaving the economy unregulated also made it hard for workers to obtain laws that could protect them from long hours and poor working conditions. Meanwhile, the Whigs became strongly associated with a middle-class ideal rooted in the interests of urban and rural property holders that also proved appealing to some wageworkers and craft workers.

Gender, Domesticity, and the Emergence of a "Middling Class" Commercial prosperity and industrial development swelled the ranks of property-owning farmers, merchants, professionals, and master manufacturers. During the 1820s and 1830s, many such people came to view themselves as members of a "middling class" whose interests, as Boston publisher Joseph T. Buckingham wrote, were distinct from those of the "unprofitable poor and the unproductive rich."

The decline of household manufacturing, the separation of home and business, and the increased availability of consumer goods altered the lives of these people. Around them, writers and moralists constructed a new ideal of family life, centered on a home that was sheltered from the anxieties of work and business, in which age and gender roles were subtly altered from the patriarchal and hierarchical assumptions of an earlier period. In such families, fathers increasingly conducted business in offices, shops, and factories separate from their homes. Their wives remained at home, now excluded from most income-earning activities. In the workshops of master craftsmen, the labor of employees replaced that of family members. In shoemaking, for example, the responsibility for stitching shoe uppers shifted from the master's wife to the daughters of poorer families, employed as outworkers.

The American Woman's Home

These were the frontispiece and title page of a popular 1869 guide to the "formation and Maintenance of Economical, Healthful, Beautiful, and Christian Homes." Intended to instruct young women on their proper role in the middle-class home, this book was continually expanded and reprinted after its first publication in 1841. Its lessons about "domestic science" ranged from the correct way to raise children to the appropriate type of picture to hang in the parlor. Catherine E. Beecher and Harriet Beecher Stowe, *The American Woman's Home or, Principles of Domestic Science . . .* (1869) — American Social History Project.

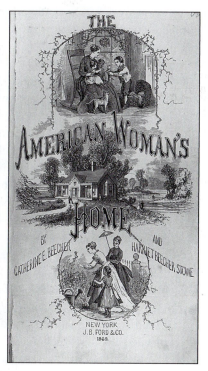

Mose and Lize on the Third Avenue, New York

This 1848 print showed the exuberant style of dress and behavior favored by many young working-class women. Although Lize (like her boyfriend, Mose) was a fictional character, her popularity in the press and theater suggested that the principles of domestic science did not represent the ideal for all young women. James Baillie, 1848, lithograph — New-York Historical Society.

Middle-class women contributed to the family economy by performing household work and shrewdly planning purchases. The availability of stoves and, in some cities, a public water supply began to ease some burdens of housework. Women who could afford to hired domestic servants, whose numbers since 1800 had grown twice as fast as the number of white families and whose ranks in northeastern cities by the 1830s were becoming dominated by immigrant women, particularly from Ireland. Servants, typically working for sixteen to eighteen hours a day, relieved middle-class women of strenuous or unpleasant household tasks. In 1841, the writer Lydia Maria Child claimed that genteel women no longer washed or dressed their children, made clothing, laid fires, scrubbed floors, or emptied slops.

Writers idealized home life as a refuge from the economic pressures and personal frictions of a man's working life. Sarah Josepha Hale, editor of *Godey's Lady's Book*, one of the 1830s' most popular magazines, told her middle-class female readers, "Our men are sufficiently money-making; let us keep our women and children free from the contagion as long as possible." Women's role, in this view, was to make the home a domestic haven and to instill in their children the standards of behavior deemed essential to republican government and prosperity: hard work, perseverance, and diligence; frugality and saving; self-discipline, emotional restraint, and steady, temperate habits.

Child rearing came to rely less on physical punishment and more on affection and patient instruction. Children were now expected not simply to bend to authority but to understand and internalize their parents' values.

Machinist Morton Poole encouraged his sister to cultivate in her son "the liberties which are essential to the formation of a free and independent spirit," relying on "superior understanding" instead of fear. "A child that is afraid of its parents," he wrote, "can never feel that confidence which is necessary to the receiving of information in conversations with its parents."

But this new concept of women's role as homemaker and teacher of values did not challenge husbands' power over their wives and households or bring women into political life. They performed their domestic roles at their husbands' pleasure. An 1840 book addressed to "the American mechanic" explained that the proper wife would be "patient, resolute, [and] love . . . her home," and her place would be "eminently at the fireside." Wives, Sarah Josepha Hale advised, should be "pure, pious, domestic, and submissive."

Shielded from the public sphere, the mother-supervised home became equated with proper Christian values. Indeed, middle-class women now assumed greater responsibility for overseeing the morals not only of their own households, but also, by extension, of society as a whole, by becoming active in their churches and setting examples for others. While men saw to the nation's material needs, women would see to its spiritual ones. Yet this very formula proved a means by which some women would gain a new degree of influence in the public sphere.

The Second Great Awakening   Middle-class, domestic ideals were shaped by, and helped to reinforce, a strong resurgence of evangelical Protestantism across early-nineteenth-century America. Beginning in the South with events such as the great "camp meeting" at Cane Ridge, Kentucky in 1801, this "Second Great Awakening" swept northward during the 1820s and 1830s to take root in new farming regions such as upstate New York and among the middle classes of the cities and smaller commercial towns. Evangelical revivals drew strength from many sources—from democratic thought and economic development, as well as from changes in family life. As the enthusiasm spread, more Americans than ever before entered active religious life.

The emotional scenes that marked southern revival meetings were repeated across the North. Western New York was dubbed the "Burned-Over District" because of the repeated fiery revivals there. The movement embraced many, often opposing, doctrines but affirmed that anyone who experienced a religious conversion and lived an upright Christian life could avoid eternal damnation. Like Charles Grandison Finney, who became the most famous and influential of revivalist preachers, most believed that this salvation was an act of free will, not—as Calvinists had maintained—predestined by God. Individuals had the power to choose for themselves the path to eternal life. Self-discipline and self-control could save them after death as well as gaining them material comfort and prosperity on Earth. The confidence that, with self-discipline and effort, people could influence

Revivalist Meeting

A camp meeting in the woods painted by Pennsylvania artist Jeremiah Paul. Jeremiah Paul, c. 1815, oil on board, 18¾ × 28 inches — Billy Graham Center Museum, Wheaton College.

their afterlives complemented their belief in personal initiative, hard work, and individual advancement.

The evangelical movement sought to bridge widening social divisions, and it embraced people from every social class. Though merchants, masters, and journeymen now lived and worked separately, they might still worship together. Everywhere, women formed a majority of church members and congregations, and in one sense, evangelicalism endorsed women's separation from business and their moral authority as teachers and exemplars. However, their importance in the churches gave them a new semipublic role and enabled many evangelical women to develop wider social influence.

Evangelicals believed in changing society by reforming ("perfecting") the individuals who composed it. "To the universal reformation of the world [we] stand committed," wrote Finney. Through personal example and by spreading the word of Christ, evangelicals would reform society. Most saw the causes of social ills in "the ungoverned appetites, bad habits, and vices" of individuals, not in the workings of society itself. Their activism generated an impressive network of voluntary organizations pledged to fight alcohol and prostitution, enforce a strict Sabbath, and encourage public and religious education. Men usually headed these organizations, but women composed much of the membership and were prominent as organizers and activists.

The revivals were an important spur to the antislavery movement, which grew rapidly in many northern towns and agricultural districts in the 1830s and would sharpen the distinctions and antagonism between North

and South in the decades that followed. The American Anti-Slavery Society—founded by Arthur Tappan, William Lloyd Garrison, and others in
1833—employed techniques that were already being used by revivalist
organizations: itinerant lecturers, emotional oratory, and printed periodicals and tracts that condemned slavery as a sin and spurred the campaign
for emancipation.

Although evangelicals sought social inclusiveness, they by no means
gained universal support. Even many Christians rejected their efforts to
become "their brothers' keepers." Class distinctions, especially, shaped evangelical activism. Families of successful master craftsmen, merchants, and
farmers who had adapted to the new, competitive economy were among the
strongest supporters of reformist revivalism, which also became closely
associated with the Whig Party in politics. Although commercial and industrial change brought them prosperity, businessmen worried about the
threats to order that change produced. Reform often meant converting the
poor to evangelical ideas about proper family life and personal behavior.
Drinking alcoholic beverages, the Presbyterian minister Albert Barnes
argued, "produces idleness and loss of property. . . . [T]he man who will not
work . . . is the enemy of his country." Other Whig evangelicals warned
against "the ascendancy of the rabble, . . . the filth and offscouring of all
things," and advocated the influence of "the mass of intelligence and property of the country."

Evangelicalism offered reformers a means to convert others—including their own employees—to their values. Hoping to secure docile workers,
employers such as Samuel Slater and the owners of the Waltham-Lowell
mills encouraged church attendance by their operatives to foster regularity
and discipline. Mill owners were also among the sponsors of evangelical
churches built in the Rockdale district of Pennsylvania in the 1830s.

But workers' religious attachments were not just imposed on them by
employers. Itinerant preachers—working men and women themselves—
evangelized in factory villages, and young workers found spiritual and social
companionship in church activities. Nor did piety necessarily make them
more docile. Camp meetings and prolonged revivals sometimes disrupted
work, causing frustrated manufacturers to combat local churches or evan-
gelists. In one Massachusetts textile district, revivals were followed by
increased labor turnover in the mills.

Radically minded working people also identified with evangelicalism
because it stressed spiritual equality and sincere belief over elitism and for-
mality. They sought a religion that would help workers to defend and extend
their rights. They endorsed the emphasis on self-discipline, viewing alcohol,
gambling, and prostitution as snares set by a corrupt society to trap people
or distract them from exercising their liberties. Although evangelicalism
fostered acceptance of the wage system, it also promoted self-assurance and

a strong sense of equal rights. As it grew in importance during the 1830s, evangelicalism helped to fuel, as much as diminish, the determination of labor leaders and activists to secure justice for working people.

Depression and Crisis in Northern Society   However, a serious economic depression, starting with a financial crisis in 1837, wiped out much of the organized labor movement and marked a deep crisis in the North's emerging wage labor economy. A fall in the price of cotton in Europe, driven by rising output from the slave South, bankrupted some brokerage firms. The Bank of England called in American loans, sparking a panic in New York and other eastern cities. Banks collapsed, and thousands of businesses and individuals were ruined. Whigs blamed the Jackson and Van Buren administrations' policy of removing federal funds from the Bank of the United States to favored state-chartered "pet banks" for exacerbating the crisis.

Recovery proved difficult. Commerce and transportation declined, most construction ceased, and goods went unsold. Countless businesses folded, including many manufacturing operations, large and small, scattered across the rural and urban Northeast. Most of New York City's large clothing firms and many of its metal foundries were wiped out. Even firms whose products were in high demand, such as the printing press manufacturer R. Hoe and Company, were caught out by the financial disruption, failed, and laid off their employees. In all the main centers of industry and commerce, many workers found themselves without work or income.

In Lynn, Massachusetts, thousands of shoemakers were jobless, and the wages of those still employed were cut in half. The poor in Philadelphia were reported to be "dying of want." A committee of Boston citizens sought to drive unemployed people out of the city. In New York City, more than one-third of the total labor force was thrown out of work, and a similar proportion were reduced to working part-time or at drastically cut wages. When a notice appeared offering rural employment for 20 laborers at one-quarter of the usual wage, 500 men applied. Growing numbers of the poor were forced to live in cramped buildings, as one report put it, "crowded beneath mouldering, water-rotted roofs, or burrowed among rats in clammy cellars." More than 7,000 people were living in New York City cellars by 1842, and their numbers were rising.

The labor movement plunged into crisis. In contrast to their resistance in 1834 and 1836, Lowell factory women organized no protests against wage cuts between 1837 and 1843. With so many jobs lost and people desperate for work at any pay, strike threats lost their effect, and most unions dissolved. For employers, this was the depression's silver lining. A hat manufacturer boasted that his workers were now free of "the moral gangrene of Trades Union principles" and "the inconveniences" of "regular combina-

THE TIMES.

The Times

The ravages of the depression were catalogued and blamed on the Jackson administration in this 1837 lithograph by a Whig printmaker. In the foreground, a family descended into alcoholism, a mother and child begged for charity, and unemployed workers stood about. In the background, citizens lined up outside of a pawnbroker's establishment while others made a run on a bank. Signs all around announced the devaluation of currency and lack of credit. Above the dismal scene shone Andrew Jackson's well-known beaver hat, spectacles, and clay pipe. Henry R. Robinson (after a drawing by Edward W. Clay), 1837, lithograph, 19 × 12 inches — J. Clarence Davies Collection, Museum of the City of New York.

tions and periodical strikes." The editor of the *Journal of Commerce* urged proprietors to "employ no men who do not forever abjure the unions." The opportunity had now arrived to eradicate labor organizations, and "it should be done thoroughly."

But hardship also fanned the flames of antibusiness sentiment. In 1837, a flour riot in New York reflected popular conceptions of justice handed down from the Revolutionary period. A meeting of 4,000 to 5,000 hungry people heard speakers denounce landlords and high rents, along with merchants holding back food from starving neighbors. One speaker announced that the firm of Hart and Co. had thousands of barrels of flour at their store and suggested that the crowd "go and offer . . . eight dollars a barrel for it" — a figure below the market rate, but deemed just by the public. As crowds had done in the eighteenth century, the New Yorkers went to extract economic justice from an individual who was more powerful than they.

Rioters were met at the store by police and by the mayor with an appeal to disperse, but they chased the authorities away, broke into the store, and seized the flour. After the police returned with state militia and made arrests, the crowd regrouped to rescue the prisoners. They were eventually broken up, but rioters had made their point: a depression might undermine labor organizations, but it would not reconcile working people to the absolute rule of the marketplace. Alternative conceptions of popular rights and community justice retained their strength.

Conclusion: A Divided Republic

"Whoever looks at the world as it is now," Thomas Skidmore had written in 1829, "will see it divided into two distinct classes: proprietors, and non-proprietors; those who own the world, and those who own no part of it." Growth in commerce, productivity, and total output seemed only to deepen the chasm between rich and poor and further erode values of mutual assistance and community rights. Depression and the hardship to which it led further undermined working peoples' ability to share in the products of their own labor. "No one can observe the signs of the times with much care," wrote Bostonian Orestes Brownson, "without perceiving that a crisis as to the relation of wealth and labor is approaching."

The social conflict Brownson anticipated was attributable to the "system of labor at wages." If America were truly to become a society grounded in equality, he argued, "there must be no class of our fellow men doomed to toil through life as mere workmen at wages." The North in the 1820s and 1830s had witnessed a crucial modification of the republican conception of personal "independence" and its political significance. Laboring men continued to claim the respect due independent citizens, but had rejected the old idea that political participation should be restricted to those with property. As supporters of workingmen's parties or the mainstream parties, they asserted the dignity of labor and condemned the notion that power should belong to an "aristocracy" of wealthy or professional men. Some laboring women in the 1830s claimed the same rights to respect and independence that laboring men did. As union members and as strikers, they asserted their right as poor laborers to live in dignity. Criticism of "aristocracy" led some working people to become suspicious of slave society in the South, where a planter class lived off the labor of unfree men and women. Yet white males continued to assert the priority of manhood and race over women and people of color, whom they sought to exclude.

The Years in Review

1793
- The first U.S. textile factory, modest in size and equipped only to spin yarn, is built in Pawtucket Falls, Rhode Island, by the firm of Almy, Brown, and Slater.

1801

- A "camp meeting" in Cane Ridge, Kentucky, helps to begin the Second Great Awakening, an evangelical movement emphasizing the need to perfect the individual that sweeps the nation and involves people from every social class.

1812

- Congress declares war against the British on June 14.

1814

- Boston Associates build a textile mill in Waltham, Massachusetts, that is much larger than "Rhode Island system" mills and mechanizes all stages of cloth production.

1815

- The Treaty of Ghent ends the war with the British.

1816

- Congress charters the Second Bank of the United States in an attempt to standardize state and local banking practices.

1817–1825

- Construction of the 364-mile Erie Canal links the Great Lakes and Ohio Valley to the Hudson River, New York City, and transatlantic trade.

1818

- The president's residence reopens after being burned out by the British in 1814; it is now called "White House" because of a new coat of white paint.

1819

- Second Bank of the United States tightens the availability of credit, sparking similar restrictions by state and local banks and resulting in the nation's first financial panic; economic growth slows, and unemployment increases.

1821

- Troy Female Seminary begins higher education for women in the United States.

1823

- President Monroe says that the United States will not tolerate European interference in the internal affairs of the Western Hemisphere—what comes to be called the "Monroe Doctrine."

1824

- Pawtucket weavers strike to resist a reduction of piece rates and an extension of their workday.

- Robert Owen creates a cooperative community in New Harmony, Indiana, which influences the many communitarian experiments of the period.
- John Quincy Adams is elected president by the House of Representatives after neither he nor his opponent, Andrew Jackson, receives a majority of votes in the election (although Jackson earns the largest number of popular and electoral votes).

1827
- A movement to create workingmen's parties spreads from Philadelphia to other major cities as well as small towns and rural districts.
- Philadelphia journeymen house carpenters strike in support of a demand that their workday be shortened from twelve hours to ten.

1828
- Construction of the Baltimore & Ohio Railroad begins.
- Democrat Andrew Jackson is elected president.

1829
- The inauguration of Andrew Jackson as president includes thousands of his supporters tramping through the White House—an action that is symbolic of the era of the "common man."
- Sam Patch (the Evel Knievel of his day) dies in an attempt to leap over Genesee Falls. He had previously made many successful jumps over cliffs, gorges, and bridges.

1830
- The steam press is invented, eventually leading to a drastic reduction in the cost of printing.
- Robert Dale Owen publishes the first American book on birth control.
- *Godey's Lady's Book* is the first U.S. magazine directed at women.

1831
- The New York Tailoresses' Society is founded.

1832
- Believing that the federal bank's power threatens democratic government, President Jackson vetoes rechartering of the Second Bank of the United States and removes federal deposits from the bank.

1833
- New York journeymen carpenters strike for higher wages and gain the support of fifteen other trade organizations.
- The American Anti-Slavery Society is founded.

1834

- Lowell, Massachusetts, workers strike to protest worsening working conditions; they strike again in 1836.
- The National Trades Union representing 25,000 workers is founded.
- A strike by Chesapeake & Ohio Canal workers is suppressed by federal troops.
- The U.S. Senate censures President Jackson for removing deposits from the Bank of the United States—the only censure of a president in U.S. history.

1836

- Democrat Martin Van Buren is elected president over candidates of the new Whig Party.
- Twenty journeymen tailors on strike are convicted of conspiracy by a New York state judge, who denies them the legal right to organize and strike; 27,000 New Yorkers attend a rally to protest the verdict.
- The Philadelphia General Trades Union votes to allow laborers into its ranks.

1837

- A nationwide financial crisis spurs widespread and severe economic depression and unemployment.
- Angry New Yorkers protest high rents and food prices by storming a local firm and offering what they considered a fair price for the barrels of flour there; police and state militia break up this "flour riot."

1838

- Oberlin becomes the first coeducational college in the nation.
- Chesapeake & Ohio Canal workers protest nonpayment of wages; militiamen called to suppress the protest refuse to do so out of sympathy with the workers.

Additional Readings

For more on changes in the agricultural economy and rural life, see:
Christopher Clark, *The Roots of Rural Capitalism: Western Massachusetts, 1780–1860* (1990); John Mack Faragher, *Sugar Creek: Life on the Illinois Prairie* (1986); Paul E. Johnson, *Sam Patch, the Famous Jumper* (2003); Jonathan Prude, *The Coming of Industrial Order: Town and Factory Life in Rural Massachusetts, 1810–1860* (1983); Mary Ryan, *Cradle of the Middle Class: The Family in Oneida County, New York, 1790–1865* (1981); Alan Taylor, *William Cooper's Town: Power and Persuasion on the Frontier of the Early*

American Republic (1995); and Anthony F. C. Wallace, *Rockdale: The Growth of an American Village in the Early Industrial Revolution* (1978).

For more on Jacksonian era economic and political change, see: Joyce Appleby, ed., *Recollections of the Early Republic: Selected Autobiographies* (1997); Charles Sellers, *The Market Revolution: Jacksonian America, 1815–1846* (1991); Carol Sheriff, *The Artificial River: The Erie Canal and the Paradox of Progress, 1817–1862* (1996); Harry L. Watson, *Liberty and Power: The Politics of Jacksonian America* (1990); Peter Way, *Common Labour: Workers and the Digging of North American Canals, 1780–1860* (1993); and Sean Wilentz, *The Rise of American Democracy: Jefferson to Lincoln* (2005).

For more on the transformation of artisan and industrial work, see: Mary P. Blewett, *Men, Women, and Work: Class, Gender, and Protest in the New England Shoe Industry, 1780–1910* (1988); Paul Gilje and Howard B. Rock, eds., *Keepers of the Revolution: New Yorkers at Work in the Early Republic* (1992); Herbert G. Gutman, *Work, Culture and Society in Industrializing America: Essays in American Working-Class and Social History* (1976); Bruce Laurie, *Artisans into Workers: Labor in Nineteenth-Century America*, rev. ed. (1997); Walter Licht, *Industrializing America: The Nineteenth Century* (1995); Howard B. Rock, Paul A. Gilje, and Robert Asher, eds., *American Artisans: Crafting Social Identity, 1750–1850* (1995); Ronald Schultz, *The Republic of Labor: Philadelphia Artisans and the Politics of Class, 1720–1830* (1993); Cynthia Shelton, *The Mills of Manayunk: Industrialization and Social Conflict in the Philadelphia Region, 1787–1837* (1986); and Michael Zakim, *Ready-Made Democracy: A History of Men's Dress in the American Republic, 1760–1860* (2003).

For more on women's labor, see: Jeanne Boydston, *Home and Work: Housework, Wages, and Ideology in the Early Republic* (1990); Thomas Dublin, ed., *Farm to Factory: Women's Letters, 1830–1860* (1981); Thomas Dublin, *Transforming Women's Work: New England Lives in the Industrial Revolution* (1994); Thomas Dublin, *Women and Work: The Transformation of Work and Community in Lowell, Massachusetts, 1826–1860* (1979); Nancy A. Hewitt, *Women's Activism and Social Change: Rochester, New York, 1822–1872* (1984); Joan M. Jensen, *Loosening the Bonds: Mid-Atlantic Farm Women, 1750–1850* (1986); Catherine E. Kelly, *In the New England Fashion: Reshaping Women's Lives in the Nineteenth Century* (1999); Marla R. Miller, *The Needle's Eye: Women and Work in the Age of Revolution* (2006); Nancy Grey Osterud, *Bonds of Community: The Lives of Farm Women in Nineteenth-Century New York* (1991); and Laurel Thatcher Ulrich, *A Midwife's Tale: The Life of Martha Ballard, Based on Her Diary, 1785–1812* (1991).

For more on urbanization and class stratification, see: Edwin Burroughs and Mike Wallace, *Gotham: A History of New York City to 1898* (1999); Alan Dawley, *Class and Community: The Industrial Revolution in Lynn*, rev. ed. (2000); Karen Halttunen, *Confidence Men and Painted Women: A Study of Middle-Class Culture in America, 1830–1870* (1982); Edward Pessen, *Riches, Class and Power: America before the Civil War* (1990); Steven J. Ross, *Workers on the Edge: Work, Leisure, and Politics in Industrializing Cincinnati, 1788–1890* (1985); Christine Stansell, *City of Women: Sex and Class in New York, 1789–1860* (1986); and Sean Wilentz, *Chants Democratic: New York City and the Rise of the American Working Class, 1788–1850* (1984).

For more on the Second Great Awakening, see: Jon Butler, *Awash in a Sea of Faith: Christianizing the American People* (1990); Richard Carwardine, *Evangelicals and Politics in Antebellum America* (1993); Paul Johnson, *A Shopkeeper's Millennium: Society and Revivals in Rochester, New York, 1815–1837* (1978); Jama Lazerow, *Religion and the Working Class in Antebellum America* (1995); and William R. Sutton, *Journeymen for Jesus: Evangelical Artisans Confront Capitalism in Jacksonian Baltimore* (1998).

8

Immigration, Urban Life, and Social Reform in the Free-Labor North

1838–1860

Sunshine and Shadow
Regular mid-nineteenth-century publications presented the East's industrializing cities — New York, Philadelphia, and Baltimore — as fractured societies. According to articles, novels, and city guides, each was really two cities: one orderly, prosperous, and bathed in "sunlight" and the other menacing, poor, and steeped in "darkness" (or "gaslight"). In this frontispiece from the 1868 *Sunshine and Shadow in New York*, the symbolic extremes of day and night were represented by a Fifth Avenue mansion and the Old Brewery, an infamous "thieves' den." Matthew Hale Smith, *Sunshine and Shadow in New York* (1868) — American Social History Project.

EARLY IN 1849, two Irish travelers, Bridget Murphy and Patrick Kennedy, landed in Boston Harbor after a storm-tossed Atlantic crossing. They had met on the ship bringing them to America, and they married a few months after their arrival. Both were fleeing the potato blight that had devastated Irish agriculture and had left millions of men, women, and children in a state of starvation. The young couple settled into a corrugated metal shack on Noddle's Island in Boston Harbor. They had few resources, but they were willing to work hard, which meant a good deal in a country that was eager for labor. Patrick found a job as a cooper, crafting wooden barrels and Conestoga wagon wheels. Like many newly arrived Irish women, Bridget may have sewed or performed domestic work to help build a nest egg.

The Irish seeking refuge from the famine constituted the young nation's first large-scale wave of immigration, and the Boston Irish formed the first immigrant ghetto in the United States. They coped with overcrowded and dilapidated housing, epidemics of cholera and consumption, inadequate water supplies and abundant raw sewage, and the suspicion and prejudice that New England's more prosperous Protestant majority heaped on impoverished Catholic newcomers.

A decade after their arrival, Patrick's skill as a cooper sustained them economically, and Bridget was pregnant with their first child. Then catastrophe struck. Shortly after his son P. J. was born in 1858, Patrick Kennedy, then in his early thirties, died, probably of cholera or consumption. In 1860, the widowed Bridget was eking out a living for herself and P. J. by running a notions shop.

Although P. J. Kennedy would eventually become the patriarch of a wealthy and powerful political clan that, two generations later, would produce a president of the United States, his humble origins reflected the circumstances of millions of immigrants in the mid-nineteenth century. Forming a massive movement from Western and Northern Europe, these immigrants were pushed out of their homelands by famine, political upheaval, and economic crisis. They were drawn to the United States by the availability of land, the promise of a better life, and the high demand for labor.

That demand for labor was fueled by the growth of American cities, new technologies and western settlements, a boom in commerce and industry, and rapid increases in agricultural production. Daniel Webster, the senator from Massachusetts, declared, "It is an extraordinary era in which we live, remarkable for scientific research into the heavens, the earth, and what is beneath the earth" and its application "to the pursuits of life." But the economic and technological transformations that Webster exulted required a radical reorganization of the relations between labor and capital. A smaller and smaller percentage of people were able to rise from common laborers to skilled artisans to master craftsmen or from agricultural workers to landowners. Instead, more and more American workers, whether immigrant or native-born, spent their lives earning a wage.

The term *free labor* was used in this period to distinguish workers in the North from the brutalities of legalized slave labor in the South. Still, free laborers were no longer independent in the sense that Thomas Jefferson or even Alexander Hamilton had intended when the nation was new. Free labor still included independent farmers, shopkeepers, and artisans but also growing numbers of people who contracted with employers to work for wages. In prosperous times, such as the late 1840s, jobs were relatively plentiful and wages were generally sufficient to support a family. But in periods of economic crisis, such as the depressions that hit in the 1830s and the 1850s, unemployment skyrocketed, wages plummeted, workers struggled to survive, and once-affluent businessmen went bankrupt. Some merchants, industrialists, professionals, and commercial farmers, however, were able to turn depressions to their advantage, buying land, labor, and goods at low prices, then consolidating their capital until good times returned. Such shrewd business deals spawned a widening gap between rich and poor in American society, a gap that was exacerbated by the massive influx of impoverished immigrants.

Immigration transformed the meaning of race as well as class in the United States. Some native-born white Protestants viewed Irish Catholics in particular as racially inferior and religiously threatening. Lumping Irish Catholics together with African Americans at the bottom of the social hierarchy and suspicious of their loyalty to the Catholic Church and the Pope in

Rome, they forged nativist societies to defend the white, Protestant world they valued. Some employers took similar measures. Relegated to the least skilled jobs and the least desirable neighborhoods, many Irish immigrants found themselves in fierce competition with African Americans.

The growth of cities and industry, the periodic upheavals created by financial panics, and the development of immigrant and poor communities challenged old values and ways of life. For many Americans, the transformations of the 1830s and 1840s fostered a moral crisis. The North was characterized not only by changes in the relations between workers and employers, blacks and whites, and native-born and immigrant residents, but also by increases in poverty and crime; resistance to religious and familial authority; and the spread of prostitution, alcohol use, and disease.

Many Americans, including some who were moved by the spiritual revivals of the Second Great Awakening and members of the growing middle class, believed that these social ills had to be addressed and joined charitable and missionary efforts. By the 1840s, smaller groups of Americans advocated more dramatic changes in society, such as land reform, utopian communities, racial equality, and the rights of workers and women. These movements for social change brought new groups of Americans into the public sphere and reshaped the meaning and structure of politics.

The Transformation of the American Labor Force

When prosperity returned in the early 1840s, technological advances in transportation, communication, and agriculture fueled the nation's rapid urban and industrial growth. Opportunities existed for people even of modest means to enjoy the fruits of this transformation, which created such midlevel occupations as insurance agents, railroad dispatchers, and telegraphers. These were workers who were paid in wages or commissions, but they had hopes of rising to positions as managers or independent entrepreneurs. While many farmers left agriculture for more stable wage labor, some who remained benefited from the expansion of commerce and the growth in wholesale and retail establishments. Aside from two economic slumps in the 1850s, commerce and industry expanded at an unprecedented rate.

As the northern United States became an increasingly market-oriented and industrial society, greater economic competition, urban growth, and westward migration transformed working people's lives. The influx of hundreds of thousands of immigrants from Ireland and Germany in the 1830s, 1840s, and 1850s offered a reliable and often cheap solution to the labor shortage created by urban and industrial demands. However, these immigrant workers, as well as native-born white women and free African Americans, found their opportunities for work dictated by their ethnicity, race, and gender. And neither the wage-earning, free-labor North nor the increasingly distinct slave-labor South conformed to the ideal of a nation of independent landowners.

A Changing World for Northern Working People   Technology led to impressive gains in productivity in both agriculture and industry. Compared to a worker in 1800, a worker in 1860 could produce twice as much wheat, twice as much pig iron, and more than four times as much cotton cloth. New power-driven machines — reapers, looms, sewing machines, lathes, and steam boilers — fueled this soaring productivity. Refinements in production processes contributed too, each worker now completing smaller and more simplified tasks. Combined with a growing population, increased productivity led to a staggering increase in national wealth. For instance, between 1840 and 1860 alone, the nation's agricultural output more than doubled in value, and that of its construction, mining, and manufacturing industries grew four times or more.

New means of transportation also transformed the economic landscape (Map 8.1). As the canal era gave way to the railroad age, the region beyond the Appalachian Mountains was accessible to easterners and European immigrants as never before. Ten thousand miles of railroad track laid in the 1850s helped to link western farmers to older railroad lines — the New York Central, the Pennsylvania, and the Baltimore & Ohio — and to eastern markets. People and goods now moved at far lower cost, as freight rates dropped by about 95 percent between 1820 and 1860. And the speed of travel increased almost as dramatically. In 1817, the fastest freight shipments from New York to Cincinnati took almost two months. By the early 1850s, shipping freight by railroad between these two cities took only about a week.

At the same time, technological advances allowed Americans to communicate with each other more readily, even across great distances. During the 1840s, the telegraph made it possible for the first time to send information (including commodity prices and election results) instantaneously across the country. Cheap newspapers, made possible by the steam press, and itinerant lecturers traveling by railroad spread new ideas that sparked ongoing debates throughout the free states. The pleasures and dangers of city life were broadcast to small towns and farming communities. The benefits of frontier life; the possibilities for industrial jobs; the horrors of racial, sexual, and wage slavery; the threat of mass immigration; the saving grace of evangelical conversion or utopian lifestyles — all were proclaimed far and wide across the United States.

The improvements in communication and transportation pulled local markets and scattered communities into regional and interregional networks. As canals and then railroads replaced rivers as the primary link between regions in the 1840s and 1850s, the Northwest exchanged more goods and people with the Northeast than it did with the South. Particularly

MAP 8.1 The Mobility of Goods and People, 1800–1857

Advances in technology made the movement of goods and people across the United States faster and more reliable. In 1800, a traveler from New York City required a full week to reach western New York, an area that was still largely settled by American Indians. By the late 1850s, western New York cities such as Buffalo served as hubs for the transhipment of goods and people between the eastern seaboard and the western frontier of white settlement. It took only one day to reach Buffalo from Chicago and another day to travel on to New York City.

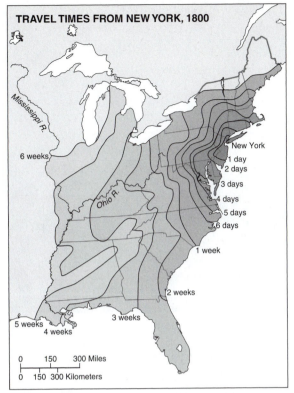

TRAVEL TIMES FROM NEW YORK, 1800

Mississippi R.

6 weeks

Ohio R.

New York
1 day
2 days
3 days
4 days
5 days
6 days
1 week

2 weeks

3 weeks

5 weeks
4 weeks

0   150   300 Miles
0   150 300 Kilometers

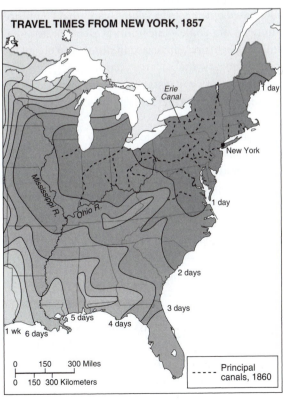

TRAVEL TIMES FROM NEW YORK, 1857

Erie Canal

Mississippi R.

Ohio R.

1 day

New York

1 day

2 days

3 days

5 days
4 days

1 wk 6 days

0   150   300 Miles
0   150 300 Kilometers

- - - - Principal canals, 1860

The Lackawanna Valley
George Inness's panoramic painting, commissioned by the Delaware, Lackawanna, and Western Railroad in 1855, placed the symbol of industrialization in a bucolic setting. The railroad's president paid Inness $75 to paint a scene showing three locomotives. The artist gave him only one train but obliged the president's zeal for advertising by painting three tracks leading into the new Scranton, Pennsylvania, roundhouse instead of the one that actually existed. George Inness, oil on canvas, 1855, 33 7/8 × 50 1/4 inches — Gift of Mrs. Huttleston Rogers, National Gallery of Art, Washington, D.C.

in cities, the general store gave way to specialty shops that offered wider selections of specific goods—hardware, dry goods, groceries, and so on. Owners, relying on state incorporation laws passed in the 1830s, moved from individual and family-based businesses to selling shares that combined the resources of a larger number of people while limiting each investor's liability. Banks, although still risky ventures, increased in number to create the credit required by merchants who now traded large quantities of goods over long distances. A growing number of capitalists also turned from investing in trade to investing in factories to feed Americans' voracious demand for manufactured goods.

These economic and technological changes led as well to the emergence of a new category of professionals and managers, many of whom were willing to forgo the ownership of land or businesses for the relative security of a salary. The members of this group, who embraced the values and ideals of the emerging middle class, sought to stave off the risks associated with boom-and-bust cycles by investing their savings in new financial institutions such as state banks. At the same time, they bought a growing number of mass-produced consumer products—pianos, chairs, rugs, glass mirrors, silverware, and carriages—to show off their newfound wealth and status.

Wageworkers also hoped to mute the effects of economic downturns. But during hard times, they had to rely primarily on good luck and extensive family and friendship networks. Both were risky supports in bad times. Moreover, workers who were hit by economic recession could no longer hope to eke out survival by relying on goods produced in their local communities. A consumer society was emerging in which workers increasingly

Dumping Ground at the Foot of Beach Street

According to a *Harper's Weekly* editor, this engraving of people scavenging on garbage barges — searching for coal, rags, and other discarded items that might be used or sold to junk dealers — showed how some people in New York were forced to "live upon the refuse of respectable folk." Stanley Fox, *Harper's Weekly*, September 26, 1866 — American Social History Project.

exchanged their wages for the goods they required in order to live. This entailed a further decline in the local self-sufficiency that had characterized rural areas and small towns until the early nineteenth century.

The Shift Away from Agriculture   Throughout the nineteenth century, the absolute size of the nation's farm population continued to grow steadily, but the number of people working outside of agriculture grew considerably faster. Moreover, rural as well as urban workers were caught up in the new cash economy. By the 1840s and 1850s, steadily declining prices for manufactured goods allowed farmers to buy more and more items, including stoves, kitchenware, and harnesses. To get the cash needed to purchase these goods, farm families devoted more of their time to producing marketable crops that would command high prices in expanding urban markets. As a result, farmers were soon buying large quantities of food themselves. Ironically, then, the northern farmer, like the northern factory worker, was becoming more dependent on others for basic needs. Rural sellers had to fight to maintain their market position, and competition began to replace cooperation, pitting farmer against farmer. The *New England Farmer* warned

> The cultivator who does not keep pace with his neighbors as regards agricultural improvements and information will soon find himself the poorer in consequence of the prosperity that surrounds him. . . . He will be like a stunted oak in the forest, which is deprived of light and air, by its "towering neighbors."

Farmers were also competing with others far away. Improved transportation brought produce from the West into competition with crops grown on rocky and nearly exhausted New England soil. During 1840, only ten thousand bushels of grain and flour left Chicago for the East; twenty years later, over fifty million bushels followed that route. Much of this increased yield went to feed the people of New England and the Middle Atlantic states, but some went to feed the South, Ireland, and other parts of Europe.

As the center of northern agriculture moved West, so too did the farming population. By 1860, fully one-third of all those born in Connecticut and New Hampshire and four of every ten Vermonters had left their home states in search of a second chance, mostly out West. There were other attractions to western migration. Gold, discovered in California in 1848, provided one powerful magnet. So did a boom in western construction and manufacturing, especially mining (lead, copper, iron) and smelting, lumbering, farm equipment, and food processing (milling, meatpacking, distilling, and brewing). The demand for labor thus drew industrial workers as well as farmers to the West.

The surge in commerce and industry also swelled the number and size of cities (Map 8.2). In 1790, the entire country claimed only twenty-four towns or cities, defined as locations with populations greater than 2,500, and there were none larger than 50,000. But by 1860, there were nearly four hundred towns and cities, and more than one-third of all northeasterners lived in them. In addition to the many small cities and towns, there were several major metropolises. In the East, New York City and Philadelphia became the dominant manufacturing cities in the nation. Located at key points along the now-bustling East-West trade routes, western urban centers such as Rochester, Buffalo, Pittsburgh, and Chicago also boomed.

Immigrants Swell the Wage Labor Ranks   The greatest number of immigrants came to the United States between 1840 and 1859, when over four million arrived. By 1860, nearly one-third of adult white men in the free states were immigrants. A few were well-to-do merchants, manufacturers, and professionals or landowning farmers. A far larger number, many from impoverished rural areas, ended up working as unskilled or low-skilled laborers in industry, construction, or the maritime trades or as domestic servants or casual workers paid by the day (Figure 8.1, p. 386).

Drought, famine, revolution, and political persecution in Europe all contributed to this massive wave of emigrants to the United States. England, for example, had worked for centuries to concentrate land, wealth, religious authority, and political power in the hands of Ireland's pro-English Protestant minority at the expense of the Catholic majority. In pursuit of increased revenue, the largely Protestant landlord class steadily squeezed the

MAP 8.2 The Nation's Major Cities in 1840

In 1840, the eastern seaboard was still the site of the nation's largest cities, including New York, Boston, Philadelphia, and Baltimore. New urban areas were developing, however, to the west and south. These included industrial centers such as Rochester, Pittsburgh, Cincinnati, and Richmond and regional centers such as Petersburg, Virginia; St. Louis, Missouri; and Louisville, Kentucky. Port cities such as Norfolk, Charleston, Savannah, and New Orleans were also growing rapidly in the early 1800s.

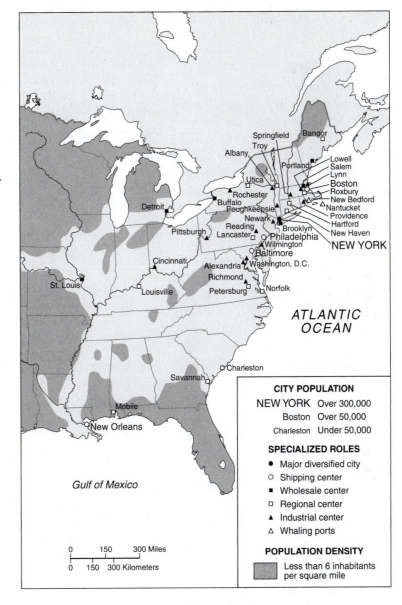

CITY POPULATION

NEW YORK Over 300,000
Boston Over 50,000
Charleston Under 50,000

SPECIALIZED ROLES

● Major diversified city
○ Shipping center
■ Wholesale center
□ Regional center
▲ Industrial center
△ Whaling ports

POPULATION DENSITY

Less than 6 inhabitants per square mile

already impoverished Catholic tenants and landless laborers. Then, in 1845, a potato blight hit Ireland, causing hundreds of acres of the island's most basic foodstuff to blacken and die. The blight continued for five years. Men, women, and children starved to death; the faces of the young were "bloated yet wrinkled and of a pale greenish hue." In the midst of the potato famine, corn, cattle, and dairy products were all produced in Ireland, but landlords sold them abroad for profit rather than giving them to the starving people at home. "God sent the blight," went an Irish saying, "but the English landlords sent the famine!"

Landlords evicted over a half-million tenant farmers who could no longer pay their rent. At the same time, Ireland's traditional small industries declined under the weight of English competition. People who were lucky found their way onboard ships whose bottom decks were crammed with their countrymen. Although about one in ten died on the journey, nearly 1,700,000 Irish arrived on American shores between 1840 and 1860. Although thousands of Irish immigrants had settled in the United States in previous decades, this massive influx increased prejudice against the Irish among native-born Americans.

Arriving in the same period were more than 1,350,000 Germans. German peasants, too, faced the devastation of the potato blight,

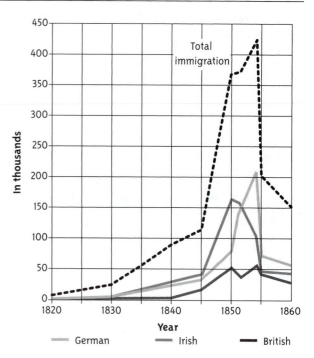

FIGURE 8.1 Immigration to the United States, 1820–1860
The most dramatic increase in immigration to the United States occurred between 1845 and 1855. In that decade, hundreds of thousands of people left Ireland, Germany, and other parts of Northern Europe in hopes of finding a better life in America. With improved economic conditions in Ireland and Germany and the onset of depression and then the Civil War in the United States, immigration declined significantly in the late 1850s and early 1860s. U.S. Bureau of the Census, *Historical Statistics of the United States, Colonial Times to 1970* (1975).

agricultural depression, and competition from English goods. At the same time, shoemakers, furniture makers, and other artisans faced the deskilling of their crafts as mass production broke the manufacturing process into discrete tasks, each of which required less and less skill to perform. Economic stagnation was reinforced by political upheaval, as the short-lived revolution of 1848 failed to overturn Prussian rule. In its aftermath, those who had supported the revolution fled their homeland.

Other countries experienced similar exoduses. The English government attacked workers who advocated such democratic reforms as universal manhood suffrage, annual meetings of Parliament, and the secret ballot. This repression led many to seek asylum in the United States. Italian radicals, who were defeated in their attempt to win independence from Austria in 1849, also sought asylum. Scandinavians, too, faced agricultural stagnation and repressive landlords; many came to the United States and settled on America's vast western farmlands. Chinese migrants began arriving as well. Almost all of them were men seeking employment in the cities and mines of the West (Figure 8.2).

The largest concentration of immigrants arrived in the Northeast and settled in seacoast and inland cities in that region. Three-quarters entered the United States through the Port of New York. Although most of these immigrants eventually moved on, those who stayed drove the population of Manhattan from 313,000 to 814,000 between 1840 and 1860 and that of Brooklyn from 11,000 to 267,000 in the same period.

FIGURE 8.2 Sources of Immigration, 1840–1860

The largest group of immigrants to arrive in the United States between 1840 and 1860 came from Ireland, followed by those from Germany and England. Most were driven out by famine, political upheaval, and religious persecution and drawn to America by democratic promises and economic opportunities. Immigrants provided a critical source of skilled and unskilled labor to fuel industrial, commercial, and agricultural development in the northern and western United States.

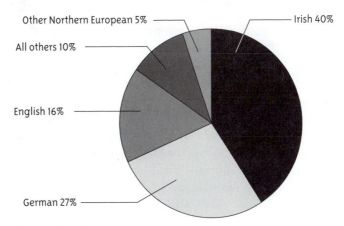

Sources of Immigration, 1840–1860

- Other Northern European 5%
- All others 10%
- English 16%
- German 27%
- Irish 40%

The Irish Harvest

"In many districts of Ireland," says the caption accompanying this 1852 illustration in a Boston weekly, "there are scenes like this which give unmistakable evidence of prosperity, notwithstanding the reports that are constantly reaching us of want and misery in that unfortunate land." Although the British press depicted the ravages of the Irish potato famine, American publications seemed reluctant to unsettle their readers with disturbing images. *Gleason's Pictorial and Drawing-room Companion,* December 11, 1852 — American Social History Project.

"Wretched Indeed": A Novelist Describes Transatlantic Steerage

Herman Melville, the author of Moby Dick, *was a cabin boy on a packet ship sailing between New York and Liverpool, England, in the 1830s. In his novel* Redburn, *Melville describes the conditions of work and life on board the sailing ship* Highlander. *The following selection describes the horrifying conditions and effects of an outbreak of fever on Irish immigrants traveling below decks in steerage.*

The sight that greeted us, upon entering [steerage], was wretched indeed. It was like entering a crowded jail. From the rows of rude bunks, hundreds of meager, begrimed faces were turned upon us; while seated upon the chests were scores of unshaven men, smoking tea-leaves, and creating a suffocating vapor. But this vapor was better than the native air of the place, which from almost unbelievable causes, was fetid in the extreme. In every corner, the females were huddled together, weeping and lamenting; children were asking bread from their mothers, who had none to give. . . .

About four o'clock that morning, the first four died. They were all men; and the scenes which ensued were frantic in the extreme. . . . By their own countrymen, they were torn from the clasp of their wives, rolled in their own bedding, with ballast-stones, and with hurried rites, were dropped into the ocean.

At this time, ten more men had caught the disease. . . .

However this narrative of the circumstances attending the fever among the emigrants on the Highlander may appear . . . the only account you obtain of such events, is generally contained in a newspaper paragraph, under the shipping-head. There is the obituary of the destitute dead, who die on the sea. They die, like the billows that break on the shore, and no more are heard or seen. . . . What a world of life and death, what a world of humanity and its woes, lies shrunk into a three-worded sentence!

Herman Melville, *Redburn* (1849).

Immigrants changed the economic landscape of the North. The lower wages they were paid increased profits for employers and contributed greatly to economic growth. At the same time, having so many workers from different cultures speaking different languages made it hard for labor to organize collectively on its own behalf. Some immigrants, particularly exiled German revolutionaries, held more radical views than did their American counterparts. Others hoped for little more than a steady job and a bare-subsistence lifestyle when they first arrived. Native-born white workers often resented the competition for work from immigrants. While employers sought cheap labor, many also embraced popular prejudices against immigrants. These attitudes ensured that ethnicity would join race as a critical division in American society.

National Origins and American Jobs   As both the kinds of work to be done and the kinds of workers seeking jobs multiplied, employers created a more elaborate division of labor. The vast majority of wageworkers before 1840 were native-born white men who were ranked primarily by their skills: artisans, outworkers, laborers, and factory operatives. White women, who entered textile mills in the 1820s, and African Americans, who most often worked as domestic servants or manual laborers, occupied their own well-defined niches near the bottom of this occupational hierarchy. After about 1840, however, the kind of jobs a person could obtain was dictated by national origin as well as by skill, sex, and race. This transformed the face of America's labor force and further complicated the ability of workers to unite around common grievances.

In general, the only work in the United States that was open to Irish men was unskilled and temporary. After the mid-1840s, Irish immigrants dominated day labor in most coastal towns and cities and formed the majority of workers on canals, railroads, and other construction projects. A visiting Irish journalist remarked in 1860, "There are several sorts of power working at the fabric of this Republic: water-power, steam-power, horse-power, Irish-power. The last works hardest of all."

Young Irish women did their share of heavy work. Some families in Ireland kept their sons at home to eke out a living on the land and sent their daughters to America to create a foothold there. With more Irish women than men arriving in the United States and most families impoverished, few Irish women could afford the luxury of leisure. The largest number labored as domestic servants. Beginning in the 1830s and throughout the next two decades, prosperous urban families hired Irish women in swiftly rising numbers. Most families employed only one woman to do all the chores. It was her responsibility to cook, clean, prepare and serve meals, care for the children, mend the family's clothing, and haul all the wood, coal, and water that were needed.

New England textile factories also recruited significant numbers of Irish women. In 1836, fewer than 4 percent of the workers in a typical Lowell factory were foreign-born. But that proportion rose to nearly 40 percent by 1850; most of these were women. By then, the workload of the average Lowell spinner and weaver—immigrant and native born alike—had more than doubled. The heavy work and low wages that had been initially reserved for immigrants became the standard for all textile operatives.

Economic hardship was widespread among Irish immigrants. The real wages—that is, wages adjusted for inflation—for unskilled day laborers rose about 12 percent per decade between 1820 and 1860. Yet most unskilled jobs lasted only a few weeks, sometimes only a day or two, and competition from a growing pool of unemployed laborers made finding work difficult. As a

"They Were Desperate Men and Would Have Work or Food": Day Laborers Protest

This Buffalo, New York, newspaper account describes a protest by 1,000 Irish day laborers at the Welland Canal in August, 1842. The laborers had come in response to the canal company's handbill promising jobs, but when they appeared, they found no jobs were to be had. As in the New York City flour riots that took place five years earlier, a sense of the workers' goals, determination, and concept of justice emerges from this report.

The laborers assembled in immense masses with banners bearing various devices and inscriptions and proceeded to supply their wants with the strong hand. All efforts to arrest their proceedings were unavailing. The Catholic priest resident there informed the authorities that all his efforts to restrain them had proven useless and they were desperate men and would have work or food. The town was completely given up to them, none daring to make any resistance. Several stores and mills were plundered of goods and flour, and an American schooner . . . boarded and plundered of the pork which formed her cargo. We have not heard that any lives were lost, but our informant says it was a terrible thing to see so many hundreds of men frenzied with passion and hunger with no restrain upon the impulses of their wild natures.

Buffalo Commercial Advertiser, August 27, 1842.

result, the average day laborer worked only about two hundred days a year. Because the wages of the unskilled in 1820 were so low, subsequent increases failed to pull the incomes of many Irish immigrants much above bare subsistence. Under these circumstances, temporary unemployment, illness, or the death of a wage earner could quickly lead to economic crisis for a family.

Irish families lived in crowded and decaying neighborhoods. Cholera and other infectious diseases thrived in such neighborhoods, and according to the Boston physician Josiah Curtis, mortality rates there equaled "anything we have been able to discover in European cities." Yet for many Irish in the United States, however difficult their plight, they stood a better chance of survival than did their friends and relatives back home. Irish immigrants, such as Patrick Dunny of Philadelphia, praised America's more democratic atmosphere. He wrote to family and friends back in Ireland that

> People that cuts a great dash at home, when they come here they think it strange for the humble class of people to get as much respect as themselves. For when they come here it won't do to say I had such-and-such and was such-and-such back at home. But strangers here they must gain respect by their conduct and not by their tongue.

"Let the Public Look at These Plague-Spots"

An illustration from an 1860 edition of the *New York Illustrated News* showed a reporter and artist working on a story about the Glennan family, residents of a shanty district near the city's East River called Dutch Hill. Although newspapers and magazines failed to recognize the causes of urban poverty, by midcentury, editors consistently dispatched reporters to cover the "dark background of our civilization." *New York Illustrated News*, February 11, 1860 — American Social History Project.

For Irish Catholics, the growth of the Catholic Church in the United States was also something to applaud. The church provided immigrants with spiritual, social, economic, educational, and charitable services and offered solace in the face of hard work, homesickness, and discrimination.

In some ways, Germany's emigration resembled Ireland's. In Germany, too, crop failures forced many tenants and small landholders off their land and onto ships bound for America. Both peasants and artisans chafed at the tax burdens, social restrictions, and political repression imposed by the German nobility. But the German experience differed from the Irish in several important respects. For one thing, skilled craft workers made up a larger proportion of those leaving Germany. For another, Germany's national crisis produced full-scale revolution in 1848–1849. Craft workers provided much of the driving force and popular following for the revolution. They demanded limits on the length of the working day, free universal education, producers' and consumers' cooperatives, and a guaranteed right to employment. Although they represented only a small percentage of immigrants to the United States, these exiled revolutionaries made their voices heard through German mutual aid societies, newspapers, and labor organizations.

By the 1850s, one-third of German immigrants lived in New York, Pennsylvania, and New Jersey, the three states favored by the Irish. Even more Germans ventured into Ohio, Indiana, Illinois, Missouri, Michigan, Iowa, and Wisconsin. Germans were more likely than the Irish to become farmers, shopkeepers, and skilled tradesmen. Given the higher wages earned by German men, a far smaller percentage of German than Irish women worked for wages.

Large numbers of German immigrants entered the traditional skilled crafts as well as jobs tied to the expansion of new consumer industries. Germans excelled in piano and furniture making, the printing trades, cigar making, baking, brewing, and butchering. German-Jewish bakers provided their landsmen with matzohs, bagels, and other specialty foods. Brewers such as Adolph Busch transformed American tastes by offering a more highly carbonated, lighter, and less intoxicating beer—lager—that kept better and longer than English ales, porters, and stouts. Heinrich Steinwig and his sons opened a piano factory in New York City that employed 300 workers by 1860. In deference to middle-class Americans' preference for

A German Beer Garden on Sunday Evening

Although German immigrants did not mix politics and liquor, reformers were disconcerted by the atmosphere of their social establishments. Unlike the bars in Irish neighborhoods, beer gardens catered to whole families. As this 1859 engraving shows, public drinking was only one attraction at a beer garden; but to reformers, the presence of women and children suggested immorality. *Harper's Weekly*, October 15, 1858 — American Social History Project.

English pianos over German and Austrian ones, the Steinwegs Anglicized their name to Steinway and called the company Steinway and Sons. German printers produced cigar labels and other early forms of advertising for U.S. companies and German-language newspapers for their fellow Germans and Austrians in the United States. German entrepreneurs also opened beer gardens, which provided music, food, and drinks for the whole family and kept alive memories of their German language and culture.

Of course, most German immigrants in urban areas ended up as employees rather than owners of these industries, and the pay and working conditions continually declined. Still, the entrance of a significant segment of German immigrants into skilled crafts, farming, and the professions ensured that they, far more than their Irish counterparts, would be accepted as fully "white" by Anglo-Americans, despite the differences in their language and culture. Indeed, a racist editor at the Chicago *Daily Tribune* was delighted to find that "our German population" was "fitted to do the cheap and ingenious labor of the country." They "will live as cheaply and work infinitely more intelligently than the negro," he concluded.

From Europe's northern tier, nearly 40,000 Swedes and Norwegians made their way to the United States in the 1840s and 1850s. Like other Europeans, Scandinavia's small farmers, tenants, and laborers were plagued by agrarian crisis, semifeudal class relations, and political inequality. The downtrodden groups were soon driven to religious dissent, mass protest movements, and emigrant fever.

In the United States, most Scandinavians first settled in Illinois and Wisconsin, then spread into northern Iowa, the Minnesota Territory, and Kansas. About half became farmers, a proportion three times that of the Irish and twice that of the Germans. Other Scandinavian immigrants gravitated toward agriculture-related industries such as lumbering, furniture making, and the manufacture of farm implements. Many women became domestic servants in rural or small town areas.

English, Scottish, and Welsh settlers also found opportunity in America. The British government actively encouraged the expansion and mechanization of industry at the expense of both farmers and traditional craftspeople. These policies fueled mass protest movements and large-scale migration across the Atlantic. Once in the United States, about one-fourth became farmers, and many others became industrial workers. British workers brought with them more skills and greater experience with modern machinery than any other national group. They were also more at home with U.S. language and customs. These two factors helped them to move quickly into some of the most desirable manufacturing jobs.

More than 100,000 people also migrated from Canada to the United States between 1840 and 1860. Some were refugees, fleeing the aftermath of unsuccessful nationalist revolts in the provinces during 1837–1838. Others were victims of British trade policies in the lumber, shipbuilding, and provisioning industries of the Maritime Provinces. Especially numerous were French Canadian farmers fleeing from land speculation and British repression. Some sought farms in Illinois, Michigan, and Wisconsin. Others obtained wage labor in New England or northern New York State, commonly in textile mills and brickyards or as lumberjacks and farmhands.

Whatever the particular circumstances that drove English, Scottish, Canadian, and Scandinavian peoples to the United States, they were generally more skilled, better educated, and more culturally assimilable than were the Irish or German immigrants and were assumed to share the values and characteristics of native-born whites. This assured many of them entry into better jobs and better schools and provided them with the political influence that would enhance their position in the future.

African Americans in the Free-Labor North   No group of native-born workers in the North was more affected by the mass immigration of the mid-nineteenth century than African Americans. Although gradually freed from slavery in the late eighteenth and early nineteenth centuries by state legislative action in the Northeast, blacks still suffered enormous disadvantages and discriminations. In most northern states, African Americans had to meet higher standards of residency and property qualifications than did whites in order to vote. Educational facilities were often segregated, and schools for blacks were more crowded and less well funded. Theaters, public conveyances, and even most white-controlled churches forced African Americans to sit in separate and inferior sections. African Americans were also forced to live in the most dilapidated housing in the least desirable sections of a city.

In addition, white trade unions excluded black workers from their ranks; white employers refused to hire them for any but the most unskilled and lowest-paying jobs; and newly arrived immigrants pushed them out of the few more lucrative occupations—construction, the maritime trades, and carpentry—where they had earlier gained a foothold. Most African Americans, then, worked as day laborers, as domestics, or in the lowest ranks of maritime and construction jobs.

A Black Joke
A racist cartoon from an 1854 edition of the humor magazine *Yankee Notions* inadvertently illustrates the everyday harassment and cruelty to which free African Americans were subjected in the North. At a performance of a play based on Harriet Beecher Stowe's antislavery novel, *Uncle Tom's Cabin*, some white members alter a seat reservation card and, to the derisive laughter of the rest of the audience, pin it on a black woman's shawl. *Yankee Notions* (September 1854) — American Social History Project.

Despite the many obstacles they faced, African Americans fought to improve their status within the United States. When whites advocated colonization, a plan to resettle blacks in lands outside the United States, African Americans vigorously objected. In meeting after meeting, they asserted, "This is our home, and this is our country. Beneath its sod lie the bones of our fathers; for it, some of them fought, bled, and died. Here we were born, and here we will die."

Whether denouncing colonization or organizing to obtain better jobs and schools, African Americans often gathered in churches founded earlier in the century. Churches formed the centerpiece of community life for many northern African Americans, and black ministers often served as political as well as spiritual leaders. Men such as Samuel Cornish, Amos Beman, Henry Highland Garnet, Samuel R. Ward, and J. W. C. Pennington combined religious and educational uplift with campaigns against colonization and slavery. In the 1830s, Reverend Cornish served as editor of the *Colored American*, one of the era's most widely circulated black newspapers. Reverend Beman, who presided over New Haven's African Congregational Church, helped to build a network of free black organizations in his city and state, including a benevolent association, a library club, a temperance society, an employment office, and schools. Not all black ministers were as reform-minded as these, however. Some saw their role as helping parishioners to accept discrimination in this life by focusing on the joys of the next. But despite the different approaches of their ministers, most black churches in the mid-nineteenth-century North offered solace, hope, and a place for community engagement outside the control of whites.

The small number of African Americans who had achieved success in business and the professions also served as spokespersons for their communities. Several, including editor Frederick Douglass, sailmaker James Forten, and teacher Sarah Douglass, were in the forefront of public efforts to improve the lives of freed blacks and to eradicate the institution of slavery. Yet they, too, were subject to discrimination and humiliation at the hands of whites. Douglass, for instance, was a skilled caulker when he escaped slavery. But on reaching the North and freedom, he was refused employment in his trade because his presence would drive white workers away. He struggled as a common laborer, a coachman, and a waiter until, in 1847, he had collected enough funds to establish himself as an abolitionist editor in Rochester, New York. Even as a leading light of the antislavery cause, he often depended for funds on white supporters and audiences, although many viewed him as an aberration from rather than a model for his race. Such prejudices were deeply rooted in native-born white Americans and were quickly embraced by many immigrants.

Wage-Earning Women Expand Their Sphere But Not Their Rights   All wage-earning women in the mid-nineteenth century faced a small circle of options, most of them low paying and of low status. In 1840, women (including outworkers) held almost half of all manufacturing jobs in the nation and about two-thirds of those in New England. Because manufacturing expanded rapidly in this period, the numbers of both immigrant and native-born women working in factories grew. The irregular employment and low wages of men put a premium on increasing the family income through the labors of women and children.

Racial and gender discrimination put African American women in a double bind when seeking employment. Teaching and selling homemade goods remained almost the only means by which black women could achieve a modicum of economic independence. Their opportunities in industry were far more restricted than those available to immigrant or native-born white women. Moreover, in the 1840s, as Irish immigrants entered domestic service in growing numbers, the demand for black servants declined markedly, further limiting one of the few occupations available to African American women.

Technological advances sometimes improved the opportunities available to workers, but the invention of the sewing machine in 1846 did not work to women's advantage. The machine did reduce the labor required to make each garment, but employers reaped the benefits. They dropped the rates paid for each completed piece so low that women often worked fifteen to eighteen hours a day on the new machines just to sustain themselves. Furthermore, their social subordination as women, their isolation from one

Lowell Offering
During the 1840s, the *Lowell Offering* published writing by women who worked in the Lowell mills. Contributions to the publication, which was supported by the city's textile companies, promoted the morality and industry of mill women, carped occasionally about working conditions, but avoided any harsh criticism of employers. On the *Offering* cover, a pure textile maiden, book in hand, stood adjacent to a beehive (representing industriousness). By the middle of the decade, the *Offering*'s perspective was challenged by *The Voice of Industry* and other labor reform publications. *Lowell Offering*, December 1845 — American Textile History Museum.

another, and their poverty made these women easy victims of other abuses, such as sexual harassment and the arbitrary withholding of wages.

Female outworkers in large urban areas found themselves in the most destitute circumstances. In 1845, the *New York Daily Tribune* described housing conditions among these workers. Most rented "a single room, perhaps two small rooms, in the upper story of some poor, ill-constructed, unventilated house in a filthy street. . . . In these rooms all the processes of cooking, eating, sleeping, washing, and living are indiscriminately performed." These women, the *Tribune* reported, spent "every cent" of their wages on necessities but still often lacked cash to "buy any other food than a scanty supply of potatoes and Indian meal and molasses for the family." The winter cold brought freezing temperatures to their garrets, yet few could afford warm clothes or fuel.

Some female clothing workers were the wives and daughters of poor day laborers, declining craftsmen, and men seeking work in the West, but many headed their own households and had children to support. Thou-

"Who Shall Practice Virtue Under Circumstances Like These?": Working Women in Philadelphia

In 1829, Robert Dale Owen, son of utopian social reformer Robert Owen, cofounded and coedited the Free Enquirer *weekly newspaper. In this editorial, he commented on a report detailing the deplorable status of working women in the city of Philadelphia.*

The first and obvious conclusion to be deduced from the Philadelphia report is that several kinds of labor are, in that city, most inadequately rewarded; so inadequately that incessant and skillful industry from females engaged in these branches [of industry] is insufficient to procure them an honest support. . . .

I [wish] I could find terms to express the extreme importance which I attach to this subject. Not as it regards alone the poor, destitute victims to whom the report more immediately refers; but as it involves the interests of all the working and all the commercial classes of our country. . . .

I pray our readers' undivided attention to the facts now presented to them. In Philadelphia, women who are willing to work, and who do work, at tedious, sedentary employments, early and late, day after day, obtain for food and clothing SIXTEEN DOLLARS per annum: that is to say, *if* they be expert, and *if* they be constantly employed. . . . Is there, then, a possiblity for women so employed honestly to maintain themselves?

This is not a tempting, it is a constraining to vice. IT IS A CONDEMNING TO PROFLIGACY UNDER PENALTY OF STARVATION. It is very easy to talk of character and of virtue in a drawing room; but who shall practice virtue under circumstances like these?

Philadelphia *Free Enquirer*, May 6, 1829.

sands labored for Brooks Brothers and other big companies or for contractors and subcontractors. Supplying their own work space, fuel, light, needles, and thread, they received orders and cloth from a merchant or tailor and returned the completed work to him. Fierce competition lowered pitifully low piece rates even further, while isolation in cramped apartments made it difficult for outworkers to band together to defend their common interests.

Isolation also affected the lives of domestic servants. In the 1850s, more than half of all female wage earners were domestics whose wages averaged just over a dollar a week, plus room and board. These women were often on call twenty-four hours a day, six days a week, and under the constant surveillance of their employers. Most found themselves stuck in attics or cellars with little heat or light, eating cold leftovers. Moreover, these women might find themselves subject to sexual advances by male employers or their sons,

The Intelligence Office
This 1849 painting depicted an interview in an employment agency for domestic servants. Although these agencies were ostensibly organized to shield young women from exploitation, they operated more as a reference service to prospective employers to insure against the hiring of women who were deemed unreliable or criminal. William Henry Burr, 1849, oil on canvas, 22 × 27 inches — New-York Historical Society.

with little recourse short of leaving their position. Servants were a mobile lot, but few situations offered more than minimal benefits, and most white servants left the occupation after a few years.

Teaching was one of the few occupations that offered women some real economic independence, yet it, too, was underpaid. As northern states began to require public education at the elementary level, local officials saw the advantage of hiring women at one-third to one-half the salary demanded by men. This was a profession that was open to black as well as white women, although black women were hired only to teach black children and so generally worked under more difficult conditions and for less pay than their white counterparts. Women teachers were constrained by a variety of rules and regulations: they generally had to remain single; attend church regularly; provide their own wood, water, and school supplies; and avoid even the hint of scandal. Still, they were the lucky ones—women who earned wages and respect at the same time.

Urban Mayhem and Middle-Class Reform

New forms of leisure activity offered respite from hard work and social upheaval for women and men from a wide range of ethnic and racial groups. Yet these activities both accompanied and fueled increases in noise, crime, drink, and disorder in urban areas. No doubt middle-class critics found these boisterous entertainments particularly galling because they often took place right under their noses. The city was only just beginning to divide into distinct neighborhoods defined by income, and in older cities, this change would be very gradual. As late as 1863, according to one resident, New York's fashionable Washington Square area still encompassed lives of "every variety from luxury to poverty, and almost every branch of industry is represented."

Disorderly public conduct, whether on the streets, in saloons and theaters, or at sporting events, deeply affronted affluent urbanites. They increasingly prized dignity, decorum, and strict self-control. To watch a city's public spaces being dominated by the unruly behavior of workers, immigrants, and the poor repelled them and challenged their right to dictate society's moral standards. Consequently, in city after city, taxpayers and the officials they elected decided that it was time to curb such disruptions by investing in a paid police force. Boston established a police force in 1837, and New York established one in 1844, both in response to the riots, strikes, intemperance, crime, and prostitution that now plagued large cities. Responses to perceived urban disorder took other, more far-reaching, forms as well. Native-born members of both the middle and working classes engaged in a range of moral reform campaigns, nativist political organizing, and even violence aimed at immigrants.

Leisure Activities and Class Conflict Men joined militias, volunteer fire companies, and fraternal associations and formed other organizations that brought structure and regularity to leisure activities, such as team sports and choral singing. Immigrants founded societies to preserve their distinctive cultural and political traditions in an unfamiliar setting. Other leisure time activities (such as boxing matches and plays) brought people together from diverse ethnic backgrounds or different social classes. Theater, for instance, once the province of the wealthy, was now open to working people, too. Reduced ticket prices made this possible. In the late 1700s, tickets at New York's Park Theater had cost $2.00 for the boxes, $1.50 in the pit, and $1.00 in the gallery. By the 1830s, these prices had fallen to 75¢, 50¢, and 37¢, respectively. Another popular form of entertainment was P. T. Barnum's American Museum, which offered visitors dwarfs, wax figures, jugglers, snake charmers, bearded ladies, and fortune tellers. In the 1840s, racetracks opened; and in the 1850s, baseball parks and music halls welcomed spectators.

The evolution of the theater reveals the main forces shaping popular leisure and culture in this period. Theaters grew in size and attracted a more diverse audience. Less self-consciously highbrow, theaters now offered many kinds of dramas (including temperance plays such as *The Drunkard* and so-called equestrian dramas featuring horses onstage) as well as comedies, musical revues, and specialty acts. Black-face minstrel shows (in which white actors crudely portrayed African Americans) mixed antitemperance, anticapitalist, and racist themes and were especially popular with white audiences. But Shakespeare also drew large audiences, owing to Americans' great love of melodramas with strong moral themes and larger-than-life heroes who took their fate into their own hands.

Democratic and patriotic themes especially pleased the working-class crowds. Most popular were those plays in which a rough-and-ready American told off (and often knocked down) a pompous aristocratic Englishman. Audiences cheered such confrontations enthusiastically, and Irish immigrants eagerly joined in. "When a patriotic fit seized them," British observer Frances Trollope noted, "and Yankee Doodle was called for, every man seemed to think his reputation as a citizen depended on the noise he made." Thus, working people clamored to see the American actor Edwin Forrest, while elite theatergoers favored the English actor William Macready. When Macready performed at the Astor Place Opera House in May 1849, a mob attacked the theater. In the melee that resulted after the police and the Seventh Regiment were called out, at least 22 members of the crowd were killed, and more than 140 were wounded. As one reporter wrote, the riot revealed "an opposition of classes— . . . a feeling that there is now in our country, what every good patriot hitherto has considered it his duty to deny—a high and a low class."

Clashes between advocates of "high" and "low" culture reinforced growing divisions in the audiences for popular entertainments. Baseball and horse racing, for instance, offered respectable gentlemen a chance to enjoy the sporting life, whereas boxing matches and cockfights attracted working-class crowds. The middle classes praised the sentimental ballads of Swedish singer Jenny Lind; spontaneous outbursts at neighborhood saloons or the racist tunes offered at minstrel shows were more common fare among the poor. This does not mean that workers might not have enjoyed the chance to hear Jenny Lind or that respectable gentlemen were averse to "slumming" in working-class taverns. Rather, the differences in access to various forms of social life were, like access to jobs, determined by class and often by sex and race or ethnicity as well.

Working people also clashed with each other. Boxing matches, for instance, often pitted Irish pugilists against African American or native-born white fighters, feeding ethnic and racial rivalries among the crowds of

The Soaplocks, or Bowery Boys
This 1847 watercolor depicted the young men who habituated New York's working-class entertainment area: the Bowery. They wore the fashionable long sideburns that gave them the nickname. Around them, posters advertised some of the Bowery attractions the "B'hoys" attended after their workday ended. Nicolino Calyo, c. 1847, watercolor on paper, 10 7/16 × 14 7/8 inches — New-York Historical Society.

Barnum on Broadway

Opening on New York's bustling lower Broadway in 1841, P. T. Barnum's American Museum soon became, as one contemporary observed, "the most visited place in America." Offering a cornucopia of education and entertainment, from archaeological antiquities to human "oddities" (actual and invented), Barnum's was the first institution to encompass the aspirations and predilections of an increasingly diverse urban public. As the chaotic street scene in this 1855 lithograph shows, Barnum's attractions included the building exterior, which featured a band of musicians that was said to play so badly that it drove people *into* the museum. Thomas Benecke, *Sleighing in New York*, 1855. Lithograph — Old York Library.

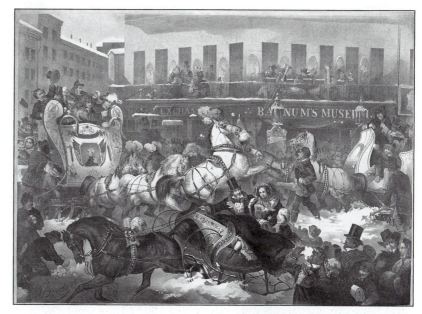

men in attendance. During the 1830s, 1840s, and 1850s, Philadelphia mummers—bands of youths who were often mockingly made up as women or blacks—marched through the city at Christmastime, assaulted members of various ethnic or racial groups, and filled the air with fireworks, gunfire, and loud music. These events clearly reflected real hostilities between groups of working people, but they also ridiculed, annoyed, and harassed individuals higher up the social ladder. In 1843, a newspaper decried the "riotous spirit raging" among the mummers that had turned Philadelphia into a "theater of disorders which practically nullify civil government." In cities throughout

Young Democracy at the Theater

As this 1852 lithograph indicated, it was often hard to tell where the performance really was situated in popular urban theaters. The raucous audience in this print included an aggressively critical German immigrant (in the center wearing a hat) and a tough Bowery "B'hoy" preoccupied with a hasty meal (on the left). *The Old Soldier* (1852) — American Antiquarian Society.

the North, raucous public celebrations of New Year's, July Fourth, and other holidays—replete with boxing matches, cock fights, bull and bear matches, and other violent entertainments—elicited similar expressions of outrage.

Urban Disorder and Family Crises   In the late 1840s, New York's chief of police cited another "deplorable and growing evil, the constantly increasing number of vagrant, idle, and vicious children . . . who infest our public thoroughfares." To most middle-class journalists and reformers, these children roamed the streets because their parents were morally bankrupt. An agent of the New York City Children's Aid Society described one mother of such roaming children, saying, "In such a woman there is little confidence to be put." The agent assumed that she had indulged "some cursed vice" that had reduced her to poverty in the first place and that "if her children be not separated from her, she will drag them down, too."

In fact, these children were a byproduct of the social changes and the enormous pressures their impoverished parents faced. Rural American and immigrant families flowed into cities, filling them with children. Although some hard-pressed parents did neglect or abandon their children, most needed their children's help to survive. Sons and daughters might do household chores, run errands, look after younger sisters and brothers—even beg and scavenge for food, wood, and coal or for items that could be sold to junk dealers. Boys as young as eight or nine years of age earned money by peddling hot corn, sweet potatoes, string, pins, or newspapers. Girls worked alongside mothers doing outwork or helped out in more affluent households for a few pennies. The death of one parent (or both) while their children were still young resulted in even more dire economic circumstances and forced many children into the streets to survive as best they could.

These street children seemed to fuel the growing incidence of crime and prostitution, which was reported in lurid detail in the mass-circulation "penny press." Such urban disorders aroused concern among many Americans. Prostitution was the danger most closely associated with impoverished women. In 1832, John McDowall, agent for New York City's evangelical Magdalen Society, proclaimed, "We have satisfactorily ascertained the fact that the number of females in this city, who abandon themselves to prostitution is not less than TEN THOUSAND!!!!!" Although accurate statistics on the incidence of prostitution in the nineteenth century are nearly impossible to obtain, some two hundred "official" brothels, recognized by the police and listed in visitors' guides, existed in New York City in the 1830s. It is likely that the numbers of brothels and prostitutes rose steadily as cities grew.

Like so many other aspects of working-class life in the 1840s and 1850s, prostitution was a product of changing economic relations. With more women needing to earn a living and few chances for them to find full-time, year-round work at a living wage, women fell into prostitution during times

Hooking a Victim
This lithograph printed around 1850 depicted three prostitutes soliciting on a gas-lit city street. Some women chose prostitution as an alternative to (or to supplement) low-wage domestic or sewing work. Reformers and artists alike alternately sentimentalized and demonized prostitutes, viewing them either as betrayed innocents, victimized by poverty or deceitful seducers, or as "abandoned women" who craved sex and liquor. Serrell and Perkins, *New York by Gas-Light. Hooking a Victim*, c. 1850, lithograph — Museum of the City of New York.

of economic crisis. Some turned to it only temporarily or episodically, but others became trapped in this life. Many may have decided that prostitution was not the worst choice a workingwoman could make, offering better wages and hours than the more respectable jobs available to them.

As prostitution increased, certain urban areas gained reputations based on the quality of both their prostitutes and their clientele. In New York, for example, the notorious Five Points district was inhabited, according to the New York *Evening Post*, "by a race of beings of all colours, ages, sexes, and nations." A center of poor black and poor Irish settlement, it was home to numerous bars, gambling dens, and brothels.

Guides printed in such papers as *The Whip* helped more genteel visitors and locals find a better class of brothel. In the early 1840s, they ranked "Princess Julia's" house, located at 55 Leonard Street, as one of the best in New York. A full-time police officer lived across the street, an opera house was down the block, and a former mayor, Edward P. Livingston, lived nearby, on the other side of the Zion Methodist Church, whose black congregants included some of the city's most respectable families. Yet such locations made clear that prostitution was no longer confined to poor neighborhoods. Instead, social investigator William Sanger claimed, it "boldly strikes through our most thronged and elegant thoroughfares." But this elegance did not save prostitutes from disease, assaults, or the inevitable decline in wages that occurred with age.

Middle-Class Efforts at Moral Reform Prostitution became a growing concern among middle-class Americans in cities across the country. In Rochester, New York, a canal town of fewer than 15,000 in 1836, the wives of upwardly mobile bankers, merchants, and professionals formed a local Female Moral Reform Society and discussed such questions as "Ought licentious men be exposed?" Throughout the late 1830s and early 1840s, they prayed for the salvation of prostitutes, condemned the men who bought their services, and circulated religious tracts and periodicals. In 1849, they institutionalized their rescue efforts by founding a Home for Friendless and Virtuous Females to offer refuge to young women who were at risk of becoming prostitutes (although not to those already fallen). Many of these reform-minded women were also active in the city's temperance society;

several helped to found the Rochester Orphan Asylum; and dozens signed petitions on behalf of the abolition of slavery.

Earlier reformers had often argued that social ills were the fault of individuals rather than society. Female moral reformers, however, took a different tack, blaming men, usually well-to-do and native-born, for ruining young women and driving them into a life of prostitution. These reformers believed that disseminating middle-class Protestant values could save society. In the 1850s, for instance, the New York's Children's Aid Society placed poor urban (often Catholic) youngsters with rural Protestant foster parents as the best means of "saving" them from dangerous influences. At times, they "rescued" such young people without their parents' approval. The society's industrial schools and lodging houses also taught street girls that "nothing was so honorable as industrious house-work," thereby preparing them for the kind of domestic service jobs that made the lives of middle-class housewives easier.

Moral reform campaigns appealed not just to well-to-do women, but also to people of lesser means who had high hopes for themselves. The promise of advancement for those who lived right and worked hard spoke to the dreams of many small shopkeepers, farmers, and craftsmen. Among this group, many disapproved of the growing ranks of propertyless laborers below them, with their irreverent and unruly behavior. This disapproval mounted in the 1840s and 1850s as more and more Irish and German immigrants flowed into low-income occupations. In this case, however, many reform-minded Americans blamed the poor for their poverty and provided support to nativist movements.

Nativist Attacks on Immigrants, African Americans, and Workers

Native-born whites had often disparaged immigrant laborers, claiming that the newcomers belonged in the low-paying jobs they held. Massachusetts educator and politician Edward Everett, for example, argued that the Irish should be welcomed to America because "their inferiority as a race compels them to go to the bottom" of the occupational scale, "and the consequence is that we are all, all of us, the higher lifted because they are here." Even before the influx of Irish famine refugees, anti-Catholic sentiment flourished. In 1834, a group of Protestant workingmen, prompted by the rumor that the nuns in Boston's Ursuline convent school were forcing their primarily Protestant students to convert to Catholicism, burned the convent to the ground. State authorities failed to intervene on the sisters' behalf.

By the 1840s, such prejudices had spawned a national movement. An army of anti-immigrant writers, educators, ministers, and politicians overlooked the contributions of immigrant laborers and argued that most of the

House of Refuge

Reformers blamed poverty on the moral failure of working-class households. Giving up on adults, many "missionaries" focused on the children of the poor. This emblem of the Philadelphia House of Refuge declared the reformers' belief in their capacity to convert children into model citizens. C. G. Childs, Philadelphia House of Refuge — Print Collection, Miriam and Ira Wallach Division of Art, Prints, and Photographs, New York Public Library, Astor, Lenox and Tilden Foundations.

"Can This Be the Sabbath?": Protestant Reform

*In the House of Indus-
try's 1857* Monthly
Record, *a shocked
Protestant missionary,
Louis M. Pease, describes
the Sunday activity in
the Five Points, a work-
ing-class immigrant
neighborhood in New
York City. Troubled by
evidence of extreme
poverty in the nation's
industrializing cities,
many Protestant reform-
ers set up mission houses
in poor, immigrant
neighborhoods to minis-
ter to the needs of the
largely Catholic resi-
dents. But a cultural
abyss divided reformers
from the people they
wanted to help.*

"Can this be the Sabbath—God's holy day?" I involuntarily exclaimed,
as I stood for a moment at the entrance of one of the avenues leading
to the Five Points, and beheld the crowd of people pressing up and
down Chatham street, while the heavily laden cars passed by, crowded
with pleasure-seekers bound for the country, on their weekly holiday
excursion. And then, as I walked slowly up Baxter street, to see the
rum-shops, the junk-shops, the pawn-shops, the groceries, and the low
Jewish clothing-stalls all open, the side-walks lined with apple-stands,
and juvenile traffickers in papers and peanuts, while here and there
were groups of night-thieves, vagabond boys, and loathsome, shame-
less girls prematurely ripened into infamous womanhood. Oh! who
would suppose that this was the sabbath of the Metropolis of this great
and Heaven-blessed country!

_____

Five Points Monthly Record, May 1857.

nation's ills were the result of the newcomers' rejection of "American" work
habits, culture, and religion. Immigrants' consumption of liquor and beer
deeply offended these pious nativists, who linked temperance to morality.
Even temperate and devout immigrants angered nativists if the immigrants
were Catholic. In addition, nativists believed that the votes of immigrant
men could be easily bought with promises of drink or employment.

Immigration bolstered the number of Roman Catholics in the United
States in the 1840s and 1850s. Their ideals and beliefs contrasted sharply with
those of evangelical Protestants. Where evangelicals pursued human perfection, Catholics adhered to an older and more lenient point of view: human
beings were conceived in sin and were incapable of perfection on Earth.
Although the church demanded moral conduct from Catholics, it granted
that human frailty would inevitably, and repeatedly, lead them astray. The
way back from sin could be found not in a single conversion, but in regular
confession, repentance, and priestly absolution. Many Protestants also

The Voting-Place
Evangelical reformers objected to the undisciplined and some-times violent atmosphere of working-class saloons. But, as indicated in this 1858 engraving of a bar in the Irish "Five Points" section of New York, reformers' concern involved more than the excesses of public drinking. The saloons were the organizing centers for the reformers' rivals, urban political machines like New York's Tammany Hall.
Harper's Weekly, November 13, 1858 — American Social History Project.

mistakenly believed that the Catholic Church required a kind of loyalty from its congregants that undermined democratic political practices.

In 1850, scattered clusters of secret anti-immigrant and anti-Catholic societies banded together into a national organization, and a year later, they formed a new political party. Officially named the American Party, its followers were popularly labeled "Know-Nothings" because when questioned by outsiders, members often responded, "I know nothing." The Know-Nothings sought to disfranchise immigrant voters through literacy tests and to unite northern and southern whites against the "alien menace." They believed that a Catholic conspiracy was threatening America's republican institutions. One important goal, which they shared with some antislavery advocates, was keeping the West open for free settlement, although in this case, they explicitly meant native-born white settlement.

In some cases, nativists clashed violently with immigrants. In May 1844, shots emanating from an Irish firehouse scattered participants in a nativist rally in Philadelphia. Three nativists were killed in the opening skirmish, and ten more along with one Irishman were slain as the hostilities dragged on. The following night, a full-scale riot erupted as nativist residents went on the attack, burning and looting Irish establishments and homes and attacking churches and other community institutions. A decade later, in Brooklyn, immigrants and Know-Nothings clashed during the fall elections. Know-Nothings challenged the citizenship papers of Irish voters, inspiring an Irish mob to beat to death an election official. The mob also drove off the nine deputies who were sent to protect the polls. Some women threw stones

Defenders of the True Faith

The popular political cartoonist David Claypool Johnston, who converted to Catholicism, condemned the nativist rioters who burned down the Ursuline Convent in Charlestown, Massachusetts, on August 11, 1834. *Scraps* (1835) — Boston Athenaeum.

Defenders of the True Faith

and flatirons, and a Mrs. Murphy urged the crowd to "kill them bloody Know-Nothings."

Competition for jobs provided another volatile arena for native-born and foreign-born groups. Many native-born workers found more desirable positions in these years, but many others were displaced by lower-paid immigrants. Some stayed in their old jobs, resenting their new foreign-born coworkers. Employers frequently encouraged nativist attitudes, partly out of genuine conviction, partly to deflect workers' anger away from themselves, and partly to undermine their employees' capacity to organize across ethnic lines. During the 1840s and 1850s, bloody brawls repeatedly broke out as groups of workers of different origins pitted themselves against one another.

The most brutal battles occurred between newly arrived immigrants and native-born blacks. Irish immigrants had been forced to the bottom of the occupational hierarchy by native-born whites, and there they vied for jobs with African Americans. Some employers, who preferred what they perceived as "docile Negroes" to "rowdy Irish," encouraged such conflict. An ad in the *New York Herald* in the 1840s read, "Wanted, A Cook, Washer, and Ironer; who perfectly understands her business; any color or country except

Nativist and Immigrant Arguments in the 1840s

Nativist—anti-immigrant—appeals to American-born workers and merchants were common throughout the 1840s and 1850s. This election circular, printed in the New York Daily Plebeian on April 20, 1844, conveys a sense of how fear of immigrants was manipulated by politicians in search of votes and by business-men looking to further divide the urban working class. Immigrants re-sponded to such nativist attacks in various ways. In this 1847 letter to the New York Champion of American Labor, one foreign-born worker warned of the effects of nativism on mutual sup-port between American- and foreign-born work-ers in the United States.

"Look at the Hordes of Dutch and Irish Thieves and Vagabonds": A Nativist Election Appeal

Look at the hordes of Dutch and Irish thieves and vagabonds, roaming about our streets, picking up rags and bones, pilfering sugar and coffee along our wharves and slips, and whatever our native citizens happen to leave in their way. Look at the English and Scotch pick-pockets and burglars, crowding our places of amusement, steam-boat landings, and hotels. Look at the Italian and French mountebanks, roaming the streets of every city in the Union with their dancing monkeys and hand-organs, all as an excuse for the purpose of robbing us of our property the first favorable opportunity. Look at the wandering Jews, crowding our business streets with their shops as receptacles for stolen goods, encouraging thievery and dishonesty among our citizens. Look at the Irish and Dutch grocers and rum-sellers monopolizing the busi-ness which properly belongs to our own native and true-born citizens.

New York Daily Plebeian, April 20, 1844.

"We Are Strong and Getting Stronger": Immigrants Challenge Nativist Beliefs

You intend to shut out the foreigners or naturalized citizens of this country from any benefit that will arise from your plans to get better wages. . . . You use the word American very often and nothing at all is said about naturalized citizens, but if you think to succeed without the aid of foreigners you will find yourself mistaken; for we are strong and are getting stronger every day, and though we feel the effects of compe-tition from these men who are sent here from the poorhouses of Europe, yet if you don't include us to get better wages by shutting off such men, why, you needn't expect our help.

Champion of American Labor, April 17, 1847.

Irish." In response to such prejudice, Irish immigrants often laid claim to the "wages of whiteness," ridiculing, demeaning, and attacking the African Americans with whom they competed. In 1842, Irish coal miners in Penn-sylvania attacked blacks who competed for their jobs; in 1853, armed African Americans replaced striking Irishmen on the Erie Railroad; and in 1855, Irish and black dockworkers battled along the New York City water-

The Day We Celebrate

Harper's Weekly cartoonist Thomas Nast portrayed a riot on St. Patrick's Day as a violent urban "sport." Nast's portrayal of the Irish, baring their teeth along with other weaponry, was typical of nineteenth-century cartoonists, who tended to give each immigrant working-class group the physical traits that were supposedly characteristic of its "race" and place in a social hierarchy. *Harper's Weekly,* April 6, 1867 — American Social History Project.

front. Over and over again, those on the bottom rungs of the economic ladder struggled to keep one step above the nearest competition.

Although nativists embraced conservative values, many viewed themselves as part of broader reform movements of the era. Most advocated temperance, condemned prostitution, and supported colonization. Some even advocated the end of slavery, joining with those abolitionists who believed that African Americans were inferior to whites, just as immigrants were inferior to native-born Americans.

Radical Reform

Evangelical Protestantism was a driving force among both conservative nativists and progressive advocates of reform. Even some radicals emerged among evangelicals, but they usually joined with activists who embraced other religious traditions or who rejected religion altogether as a basis for social change. Radicals were drawn to many of the same reform campaigns as their moderate counterparts, but they approached these issues in a distinctive spirit. Whereas moderate reformers hoped that public schools would help to tame the lower classes and create more conscientious and disciplined wives and workers, radicals wanted the schools to help working people learn and defend their rights as citizens and producers. The same point of view influenced radicals to advocate for land reform and to form separate groups such as the Washingtonian Temperance Society, through which reformed drunkards worked to uplift themselves and convert other

"Industry Without Drudgery": Planning for Brook Farm

In 1840, Unitarian minister George Ripley wrote to the Transcendentalist author Ralph Waldo Emerson in an (unsuccessful) effort to convince him to join, or at least invest in, Ripley's planned utopian community. Brook Farm began operations in 1841 in West Roxbury, Massachusetts; its members lived and dined communally and divided their time between farm work and artistic and scholarly pursuits. Although other utopian communities, such as Oneida in upstate New York and Amana in Iowa, achieved self-sufficiency, Brook Farm ultimately failed. The community never recovered from a devastating fire in 1846, and it closed its doors in 1847.

My Dear Sir,—

. . . Our objects, as you know, are to insure a more natural union between intellectual and manual labor than now exists; to combine the thinker and the worker, as far as possible, in the same individual; to guarantee the highest mental freedom, by providing all with labor, adapted to their tastes and talents, and securing to them the fruits of their industry; to do away the necessity of menial services, by opening the benefits of education and the profits of labor to all; and thus to prepare a society of liberal, intelligent, and cultivated persons, whose relations with each other would permit a more simple and wholesome life, than can be led amidst the pressure of our competitive institutions.

To accomplish these objects, we propose to take a small tract of land, which, under skillful husbandry, uniting the garden and the farm, will be adequate to the subsistence of the families; and to connect with this a school or college, in which the most complete instruction shall be given, from the first rudiments to the highest culture. Our farm would be a place for improving the race of men that lived on it; . . . we should have industry without drudgery, and true equality without its vulgarity. . . .

George Ripley

P. S. . . . let me suggest the inquiry, whether our Association should not be composed of various classes of men? . . . I think we should be content to join with others . . . whose gifts and abilities would make their services important. For instance, I should like to have a good washer-woman in my parish admitted into the plot. She is certainly not a Minerva or a Venus; but we might educate her two children to wisdom and varied accomplishments, who otherwise will be doomed to drudge through life. The same is true of some farmers and mechanics, whom we should like with us.

George Ripley to Ralph Waldo Emerson, November 9, 1840, in O. B. Frothingham, *George Ripley* (Boston: Houghton Mifflin Company, 1882), 307–312.

workingmen to their cause. The result was a tug-of-war between radical and moderate reformers, with one side stressing popular participation and democratic rights and the other emphasizing social order.

Faced with more urban disorder than their counterparts from the 1820s and 1830s, some radical reformers established utopian communities in the hopes of creating new models for social harmony. Others focused on mak-

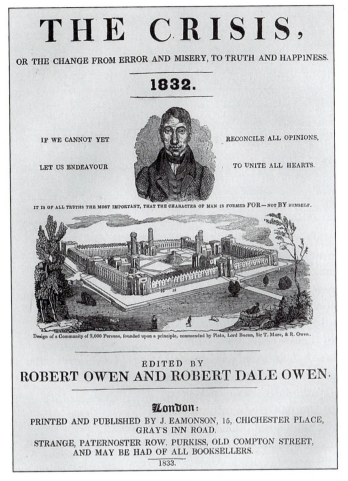

THE CRISIS,

OR THE CHANGE FROM ERROR AND MISERY, TO TRUTH AND HAPPINESS.

1832.

IF WE CANNOT YET   RECONCILE ALL OPINIONS,

LET US ENDEAVOUR   TO UNITE ALL HEARTS.

IT IS OF ALL TRUTHS THE MOST IMPORTANT, THAT THE CHARACTER OF MAN IS FORMED FOR—NOT BY HIMSELF.

Design of a Community of 2,000 Persons, founded upon a principle, commended by Plato, Lord Bacon, Sir T. More, & R. Owen.

EDITED BY

ROBERT OWEN AND ROBERT DALE OWEN.

London:

PRINTED AND PUBLISHED BY J. EAMONSON, 15, CHICHESTER PLACE, GRAY'S INN ROAD.

STRANGE, PATERNOSTER ROW. PURKISS, OLD COMPTON STREET, AND MAY BE HAD OF ALL BOOKSELLERS.

1833.

"The Change from Error and Misery, to Truth and Happiness"
Robert Owen and the design of his New Harmony utopian community in Indiana appeared on the title page of *The Crisis*, written by Owen and his son in 1833. Robert Owen and Robert Dale Owen, *The Crisis, or the Change from Error and Misery, to Truth and Happiness* (1833) — Rare Books and Manuscripts Division, New York Public Library, Astor, Lenox and Tilden Foundations.

ing land available to all. Women came together in an attempt to advance their own rights as well as those of enslaved African Americans. The abolition of slavery became the primary goal of a number of northern reformers. These efforts brought together women and men, blacks and whites, working-class and middle-class activists, and native-born and immigrant Americans. Most believed, as labor journalist William Young proclaimed in 1845, that God intended that humanity "should be bound together by nature's golden chain . . . into one harmonious whole — no slaves — no servants — no masters — no oppressed and no oppressors — but in the language of Christ — 'For one is your master, and all ye are brethren.'"

Communal Experiments and Cooperative Enterprises

One of the most radical movements of the nineteenth century involved establishing entirely new communities based on collective ownership of property and infused with the spirit of cooperation instead of competition. European immigrants had first erected such utopian societies in North America in the eighteenth century. The largest of these was created by a religious movement called the Shakers. By the 1830s, several Shaker communities in New York and Massachusetts housed more than 6,000 members.

Other founders of utopian communities drew their ideas from more secular sources. In the 1820s, the Irish-born industrialist Robert Owen applied ideas that he had developed about social reform in Scotland to communities in the United States. In Owen's New Harmony, Indiana, community, there would be "no personal inequality, or gradation of rank and station; all will be equal in their condition."

In the late 1830s and 1840s, utopian communities multiplied. Some, such as Brook Farm in Massachusetts, founded in 1841, expressed Christian disenchantment with commercializing and industrializing America. More, however, followed the lead of Robert Owen, Charles Fourier, and other European socialists and sought economic equality among their residents.

Whether religious or secular, most of the communities that were founded in this period were closely tied to other social movements, especially peace, abolition, and woman's rights movements.

The most famous, and controversial, of these nineteenth-century utopian societies was founded at Oneida, New York, by John Humphrey Noyes in 1848. Following the same economic plan as New Harmony and Brook Farm, women and men at Oneida shared labor and were paid equal wages for equal work. But Noyes also advocated sexual reform. Oneida residents practiced something called "complex marriage," in which women and men could divorce and remarry, children were raised communally, and reproduction was planned. The system of sex and marriage, which was intended to free women from the burdens of male domination and frequent childbearing, was highly regulated. The community had to approve marital unions, for example, and men were required to control their sexual urges. Women, however, gained little authority over their work or their sexual relations and lost authority over their children. Still, Oneida thrived for four decades despite the popular outrage provoked by the community's sexual practices.

The greatest obstacle to the dozens of utopian communities that emerged in the 1830s and 1840s was economic failure, not public outrage. Most began with only limited financial resources, which made it difficult to match the enticements offered by the competitive world outside. Moreover, even modest economic setbacks could spell disaster for communities that were already operating close to the margin. Critics cited failed communities as proof that the whole experiment was futile. Yet many utopian residents felt differently. Mary Paul, a former Lowell textile worker who lived in a utopian community in Red Bank, New Jersey, in 1853–1854, wrote her father about the benefits of her new life. In just one year, Paul reported, I have "already seen enough to convince me that [this] is the true life. And although all the attempts that have ever yet been made towards it [a society built on Fourier's principles] have been failures . . . my faith in the principle is as strong as ever, stronger if possible."

Movements for Land Reform

Land reform offered another means of improving the plight of working-class Americans. The promise of abundant land had lured millions across the Atlantic. It still beckoned in the 1840s and 1850s. The federal government owned huge tracts of unimproved soil in the West, but most was given in subsidy to private railroad companies or sold in

Nashoba, April 19, 1828
Influenced by Robert Owen and New Harmony, Frances Wright established an interracial utopian community, Nashoba, near Memphis, Tennessee. Its white and black residents (including slaves purchased by Wright) worked and lived together. Believing that racism could be defeated only by the "amalgamation of the races," Wright permitted interracial sexual relationships in the Nashoba community. Even abolitionists condemned the experiment. This is a sketch by Charles-Alexandre Lesueur, a French artist-naturalist who spent ten years at New Harmony. Charles-Alexandre Lesueur, April 19, 1828, pencil drawing — No. 43122, Musée d'Histoire Naturelle du Havre.

"The Money-power Must Be Superseded by the Man-power": Workers' Cooperatives

In 1845, the Boston Mechanics' and Laborers' Association founded a cooperative society. A committee of that association drafted the statement excerpted here to explain the purpose and methods of cooperation.

. . . Here, as [in Europe], the soil, motive power, and machinery are monopolized by the idle few; all the sources of wealth, all the instrumentalities of life, and even the right and privilege of industry are taken away from the people. Monopoly has laid its ruthless hands upon labor itself, and forced the sale of the muscles and skill of the toiling many, and under the specious name 'wages' is robbing them of the fruits of their industry. . . .

The remedy lies in a radical change of principle and policy. Our isolated position and interests, and our antisocial habits, must be abandoned. The Money-power must be superseded by the Man-power. Universal Monopoly must give place to Societary ownership, occupancy, and use. . . . The direction and profits of industry must be kept in the hands of the producers. Laborers must own their own shops and factories, work their own stock, sell their own merchandise, and enjoy the fruits of their own toil. Our Lowells must be owned by the artisans who build them, and [by] the operatives who run the machinery and do all the work. And the dividend, instead of being given to the idle parasites of a distant city, should be shared among those who perform the labor. Our Lynns must give the fortunes made by the [shoe] dealer and employer, to those who use the awl and use the material.

The Awl, January 18, 1845.

large tracts on the open market. Big land companies, banks, and wealthy individual speculators bought up enormous quantities of public land. By 1860, speculators owned over twenty million acres in Illinois and Iowa alone—nearly a quarter of the land in those states. They then jacked up prices and resold the land in smaller plots to homesteaders. Those who could not afford land on these terms became laborers or tenants of large landowners. Those who did buy their own farms frequently went into debt to do so. Later, unable to meet their payments, many lost both their homesteads and their life savings.

Reformers protested these government land policies, demanding that public lands be distributed to the needy, which would slow the growth of wage labor and tenancy. The most energetic land reformer in the 1830s and 1840s was George Henry Evans, a Welsh-born printer and a leader of the Workingmen's Party. Evans insisted, "If any man has a right . . . to live, he has a right to land enough for his subsistence. Deprive anyone of these rights, and you place him at the mercy of those who possess them." Public land must be made available free of charge to those who would actually settle and till it.

The National Trades Union, which was organized as a labor union in 1834, also linked "the interests and independence of the laboring class" to the land question. Its members believed that if "public lands were left open to actual settlers," surplus workers would be "drained off" from the cities into agriculture, relieving unemployment and job competition. The Massachusetts labor newspaper *Voice of Industry*, warmly endorsed demands for "free soil," as did Lynn's shoe workers. As one shoemaker demanded, "Where shall we go but on to the land? Deprive us of this and you reduce us to the condition of the serfs of Europe." Many German immigrants agreed, hoping that wider access to land would lessen job competition and thus undermine nativism.

Women Reformers Seek Rights for Themselves   Women were active in many of the reform and radical movements of the 1830s and 1840s. In this period, most women lacked the right to keep their wages, retain custody over their children, or protect their bodies from assault. Free black and immigrant women were especially limited in their occupational options, yet many had to support their families and face harassment and assaults by white employers. Although few of these women joined the formal women's rights movement in this period, many recognized the need for wider opportunities and collective action.

In 1825, New York seamstresses had organized the first all-women's strike in the United States. By 1831, striking tailoress Sarah Monroe claimed, "It needs no small courage from us . . . to come before the public in the defence of our own rights, but . . . if it is unfashionable for the *men* to bear oppression in silence, why is it not also become unfashionable with the women?" Lowell mill girls organized themselves for better wages and working conditions throughout the 1830s and 1840s (see chapter 7). In 1845, members of the Ladies Industrial Association in New York City who sought similar goals declared, "The boon we ask is founded upon RIGHT alone." For these women, the most important issues involved rights to good jobs and fair wages.

Middle-class women did not expect to work for wages, and they generally viewed their lives as superior to those of the poor and working class. Few recognized or supported these women's claims for rights of their own. Elizabeth Cady Stanton, one of the founders of the women's rights movement in the United States, did claim that the condition of Irish women in her hometown of Seneca Falls, New York, helped to inspire her interest in the cause. Yet she viewed her Irish neighbors as passive victims of male domination, expressing both concern and condescension for their plight:

"The Amazonian Convention"
The proceedings of a women's rights meeting were disrupted by hecklers in an 1859 cartoon published in *Harper's Weekly*. J. M'Nevin, *Harper's Weekly*, June 11, 1859 — American Social History Project.

Yᵉ MAY SESSION OF Yᵉ WOMAN'S RIGHTS CONVENTION—Yᵉ ORATOR OF Yᵉ DAY DENOUNCING Yᵉ LORDS OF CREATION.

Alas! Alas! who can measure the mountains of sorrow and suffering endured in unwelcome motherhood in the abodes of ignorance, poverty, and vice, where terror-stricken women and children are the victims of strong men frenzied with passion and intoxicating drink?

Most woman's rights advocates in the 1840s and 1850s were prompted to analyze the position of women in society because of their involvement in other social causes, most notably the abolition of slavery. As abolitionist Angelina Grimké noted, "The investigation of the rights of the slave has led me to a better understanding of my own." It was members of the Society of Friends, known as Quakers, who provided the core of the movement for women's rights in the mid-nineteenth century. Led by Lucretia Mott of Philadelphia, Mary Ann McClintock of Waterloo, New York, and Amy Post of Rochester, these women claimed a decade of experience as advocates of abolition, Indian rights, land reform, and other causes. The campaign for equality of the sexes was important as part of this larger effort to achieve racial and economic justice.

Four Quaker activists joined Elizabeth Cady Stanton in organizing the first women's rights convention in the United States, held in July 1848 at Seneca Falls, New York. Attended by some 200 to 300 people, the convention celebrated the achievements of women past and present but noted the many burdens placed on them on account of their sex. One hundred participants signed a manifesto modeled on the Declaration of Independence, declaring "all men and women are created equal." Demands for greater social and

"Repeated Injuries and Usurpations": The Seneca Falls Convention

The resolutions passed at the first women's rights convention, at Seneca Falls in 1848, parts of which are presented here, demanded that women be given their full political and civil rights as citizens of the United States.

The history of mankind is a history of repeated injuries and usurpations on the part of man toward woman, having in direct object the establishment of a absolute tyranny over her. To prove this, let facts be submitted to a candid world:

He has never permitted her to exercise her inalienable right to the elective franchise.

He has compelled her to submit to laws, in the formation of which she had no voice.

He has made her, if married, in the eye of the law, civilly dead.

He has taken from her all right in property, even to the wages she earns.

. . . In the covenant of marriage, she is compelled to promise obedience to her husband, he becoming, to all intents and purposes, her master — the law giving him power to deprive her of her liberty, and to administer chastisement.

He has monopolized nearly all the profitable employments, and from those she is permitted to follow, she receives but a scanty remuneration. He closes against her all the avenues to wealth and distinction which he considers most honorable to himself. As a teacher of theology, medicine, or law, she is not known.

He has created a false public sentiment by giving to the world a different code of morals for men and women, by which moral delinquencies which exclude women from society, are not only tolerated, but deemed of little account in man.

He has endeavored, in every way that he could, to destroy her confidence in her own powers, to lessen her self-respect, and to make her willing to lead a dependent and abject life.

Philip S. Foner, ed., *We the Other People* (1976).

economic rights for American women had been voiced before this. But only now did an organized movement arise, led by women and dedicated to winning for women a wider sphere and equal rights. For a few leaders, including Stanton, the most crucial demand to ensure women's first-class citizenship was the right to vote. Supported by Frederick Douglass, who was deeply concerned with votes for free blacks, the suffrage resolution passed, though not unanimously, as the other resolutions did.

For most women's rights advocates, however, an enlarged sphere of action for women in the home, the church, education, and work was as

"Am I Not a Woman and a Sister?"

This 1837 engraving was a variation on the standard American abolitionist symbol of the supplicant male slave. The symbol, accompanied by the motto "Am I not a man and a brother?," was adopted from the seal of the British Society for the Abolition of Slavery, created by the English abolitionist and potter Josiah Wedgwood in 1787. George Bourne, *Slavery Illustrated in Its Effects upon Women* (1837) — Prints and Photographs Division, Library of Congress.

important as political rights. For many women, equal education was considered the most important right. Individuals such as Elizabeth Blackwell, the first woman in the United States to receive an M.D. degree, from Geneva Medical College in central New York in 1849, showed what women could do if given the chance. Many women with far fewer opportunities than Blackwell, including immigrant, African American, and working-class women, recognized the value of greater access to education, decent wages, and legal rights. A few woman's rights advocates recognized these connections and joined their working-class sisters in forming Working Women's Protective Unions. Most also remained ardent abolitionists.

Abolitionists Fight Slavery and Each Other   For many reform-minded women and men, the eradication of slavery was the most important movement of the day. Led by advocates of immediate emancipation such as William Lloyd Garrison, Frederick Douglass, and Abby Kelley, radical abolitionists argued that other forms of bondage—wage slavery and prostitution, for instance—paled in comparison with the millions who were held in servitude by southern planters. Seeking to create a movement that reflected democratic and egalitarian ideals, radical abolitionists demanded that antislavery groups, including the American Anti-Slavery Society (AASS), be open to women as well as to men and to African Americans as well as to whites.

The commitment of radical abolitionists to principles of both racial and sexual equality ensured that some who agreed with the abolition of slavery would disagree over the means to achieve emancipation. By the late 1830s and 1840s, the result was factionalism and infighting among abolitionists. But such disagreements also multiplied the number and range of antislavery movements, forcing more and more of those who lived in the free-labor North to confront their complicity with slavery in the South.

In 1837, tensions among antislavery advocates mounted in response to a controversial lecture tour by Sarah and Angelina Grimké. Southern-born daughters of a slaveholder, the Grimkés rejected the values of their family and region, moved to Philadelphia, and joined the Society of Friends. On speaking tours, they noted, among other issues, the links between the plight of slaves and their own plight as women, and they were condemned by the Congregational ministers of New England. Although the Grimkés were supported by the AASS, some in the organization were not eager to embrace their pioneering call for women's rights, fearing that it would undermine the power of the antislavery message.

In 1840, all of these issues came to a head at the AASS's annual meeting. After a bitter fight over Abby Kelley's election to the executive committee, more moderate abolitionists walked out. One politically oriented group formed the Liberty Party, hoping to achieve through the electoral system what seemed impossible by using merely the power of moral persuasion. Another evangelically oriented faction, led by Lewis Tappan, founded the American and Foreign Anti-Slavery Society, which urged participants to work within Protestant churches.

Those who remained in the AASS formed an even more tightly knit and radical group than before. Quaker women and free blacks played prominent roles in the organization, which attacked churches and the government as props of southern slavery. Among this contingent, many opposed war and capital punishment, refused to buy slave-produced products, embraced health reforms such as high-fiber diets and water cures, rejected traditional forms of religious worship, participated in utopian experiments, and campaigned for women's rights, Indian rights, and land reform. Most free black and some white radical abolitionists also provided assistance to fugitive slaves, fought segregation in northern schools and jobs, and advocated black voting rights.

Throughout the 1840s and early 1850s, the battle to abolish slavery moved along several tracks at once. Political abolitionists followed an important new path by seeking to end slavery through Congressional intervention. This politically oriented segment of the antislavery movement entered electoral contests just as the influx of immigrants was beginning to change the face of American politics. Together, these two new forces would redraw the political system in the United States.

The Abolition of Slavery and Party Politics   Most Garrisonian abolitionists viewed electoral politics as corrupt and the U.S. Constitution as a proslavery document. But beginning with the founding of the Liberty Party in 1840, a growing number argued that the political system and the national government were simply too powerful to ignore. Although working within the existing electoral system, they offered a radical alternative to the political status quo by forming third parties dedicated to ending slavery.

They were inspired in part by the reluctance of either the Whigs or the Democrats to address the problem of slavery. The Whigs, building on Henry Clay's American System, sought to expand the federal government, encouraging industrial and commercial development and promoting temperance and education that would ensure a sober and intelligent working class. They appealed especially to substantial merchants and manufacturers in the North, wealthy planters in the South (who sought to strengthen their ties with northern commercial interests), and successful farmers in the West who needed government-funded roads, canals, and railroads. The Democrats were convinced that they could defeat the Whigs by appealing to the rapidly increasing wage-earning and immigrant populations. They favored the use of state power to expand economic opportunities, but they opposed great wealth and industrial and commercial monopolies in favor of western expansion, which they believed would help small farmers and workers.

Whereas evangelical Protestants generally favored Whig policies, the Democrats were far more successful in attracting Irish and German immigrants, including Catholics, to their banner. In 1840, the Whigs won the White House, but when the newly elected president William Henry Harrison died in office after just one month, they were left with ex-Democrat John Tyler in his place. Although Tyler had brought the party much-needed southern votes, he was not a successful advocate of the Whig platform. By 1844, Tyler and other conservative southern Whigs were ready to rejoin the Democratic Party.

By 1844, the Democrats had built powerful political machines in several cities with large immigrant populations. They nominated James K. Polk for president, and he ran on a strongly expansionist platform. Seeking to secure Texas and the disputed Oregon Territory for the United States, Polk won a significant victory, although he outpolled the Whig candidate Henry Clay by fewer than forty thousand popular votes. The Liberty Party, funded in large part by wealthy abolitionist Gerrit Smith, ran James G. Birney. Birney had once been a wealthy Alabama planter, but on a trip North in the 1830s, he denounced slavery. He was declared a traitor by his home state, and his property, including slaves, was seized. Birney never returned to Alabama but instead became an abolitionist lecturer in the North. He and the Liberty Party had a single goal: the abolition of slavery through legislation. This single-issue approach proved too narrow, however, to attract a significant number of voters. Still, Birney received sixty-two thousand votes, including many from disaffected antislavery Whigs who might otherwise have voted for Clay.

Over the following four years, Polk succeeded in implementing his expansionist program, but in doing so, he alienated a substantial number of northern Democrats. It was in this context that a new political party was formed in 1848. The Free-Soil Party drew heavily on former Liberty Party supporters, including free black abolitionists, and the new party attracted disaffected antislavery Whigs and northern Democrats as well. In 1848, Free-Soilers nominated former Democrat Martin Van Buren as president and former Whig Charles Francis Adams, the son of John Quincy Adams, as his running mate. This party was less radical in its goals than the Liberty Party and thus could appeal to many more voters.

The Free-Soil Party focused less on the moral and political rights of blacks and instead sought to defeat the "Slave Power" conspiracy. Free-Soilers claimed that the "Slave Power" endangered the rights of free speech and free press as well as free labor. The critical issue, they argued, was the exclusion of slavery from newly opened western territories. By 1848, then, the goals of political abolitionism had shifted dramatically away from

MARRIAGE OF THE FREE SOIL AND LIBERTY PARTIES.

ending slavery in the South and toward promoting the settlement of free men, particularly free white men, in the West.

The Free-Soil campaign angered many people. Radical abolitionists such as Garrison denounced the party platform, and many saw the nomination of Van Buren, who had earlier allied with slaveholders, as a travesty. Yet slave owners, too, were infuriated by the emergence of Free-Soilers, who threatened to undermine the two major political parties and the federal union. Northern business and political leaders likewise feared that this third party might dangerously polarize the nation.

Considered too moderate by Garrisonians and too radical by traditional Whigs and Democrats, the Free-Soil platform nonetheless attracted widespread support. Van Buren received almost three hundred thousand votes in the 1848 election. This represented nearly one in every seven ballots cast in the free states, nearly five times as many as Liberty Party candidate James G. Birney had received four years earlier. Especially successful among small farmers, the Free-Soil Party also found support among some industrial workers, including shoemakers in Lynn, Massachusetts.

Despite the critiques of Garrisonians, the Free-Soil Party gained the support of many ardent abolitionists, including women and African Amer-

Marriage of the Free Soil and Liberty Parties

This 1848 lithograph cartoon commented on the formation of the Free-Soil Party in 1848. Free-Soil presidential candidate Martin Van Buren, whose political career included alliances with slaveholding interests, was shown entering a "marriage of convenience" with the forces of the antislavery Liberty Party. The racial stereotypes were typical of the visual representation of African Americans in the antebellum period. National Museum of American History, Smithsonian Institution.

icans. In the Midwest, antislavery women formed dozens of societies to support the Free-Soil campaign. Perhaps even more significantly, black abolitionists such as Frederick Douglass, Samuel R. Ward, Henry Highland Garnet, Charles Remond, and Henry Bibb embraced the Free-Soil platform, despite the antiblack sentiments of some party leaders. "It is nothing against the actors in this new movement," wrote Douglass later, "that they did not see the end from the beginning—that they did not at first take the high ground that further on in the conflict their successors felt themselves called upon to take." Douglass and other black abolitionists viewed the party as an opening wedge in the larger fight against slavery and believed that future events would force Free-Soilers to reexamine their prejudices.

The Free-Soil Party was not strong enough in 1848 to transform the existing two-party system. Whigs and Democrats both avoided the most divisive issues, particularly slavery. The Whigs won the 1848 election, but they did so by running a presidential candidate, General Zachary Taylor, who had gained his national stature by serving as a leader in Polk's efforts to conquer new western territories. The Democrats ran Lewis Cass, a northerner who embraced the South's position on slavery. Taylor's lackluster reputation among abolitionists and Cass's failure to gain a victory made it likely that in the next election, the Free-Soil Party could pick up even more votes from disaffected members of the two major parties.

Conclusion: The Free-Labor North Faces an Uncertain Future

At midcentury, economic and technological change, massive immigration, urban growth, and the rise of religious and reform movements had transformed the United States in myriad ways. Conflicts over class, race, and gender relations disrupted the traditional social hierarchies, and reformers offered diverse solutions to the young nation's problems. Evangelical churches, nativist organizations, utopian communities, and advocates of land reform, woman's rights, and abolition all debated how to create a nation that combined opportunity with order.

The political scene, too, was in flux. The Whigs were in decline, and the Democrats disagreed about how to grow without antagonizing their northern or southern constituency. The Free-Soilers were a growing but as yet small force on the national scene, while another small segment, nativists, looked backward to a nation of Anglo-American farmers and small-town Protestants. In the 1840s, it seemed that none of these parties was powerful enough to shape the agenda of the United States in its image.

The assistance that abolitionists needed to strengthen their hand would come from an unlikely source: southerners. At the same time that northerners were struggling to adjust to an expanded commercial, capitalist, and industrial society, southerners were confronting economic and political challenges of their own. The contradictions posed by slave labor in a supposedly democratic society led more and more northerners—white as well as black—to see in the South a threat to all that they held dear. But only when those contradictions began to create conflicts between wealthy slaveholders and poorer southern whites did the institution of slavery become precarious enough to be abolished.

The Years in Review

1837

- The Panic of 1837 lasts five years and devastates the nation.
- Boston establishes a regular police force in response to riots, strikes, and increased crime; New York City does the same seven years later.

1840

- The American Anti-Slavery Society's annual convention is split over the issue of women's rights; some moderate abolitionists leave the group to found the politically oriented Liberty Party and the religiously focused American and Foreign Anti-Slavery Society.
- Whig William Henry Harrison is elected president over Democrat Martin Van Buren, but Harrison dies one month after taking office and is replaced by ex-Democrat John Tyler.

1841

- Unitarian minister George Ripley founds Brook Farm, a cooperative community, in Massachusetts.

1844

- A bloody riot in Philadelphia reflects growing tensions between nativists and Catholic immigrants.
- Democrat James K. Polk defeats Whig Henry Clay on a strongly expansionist platform; the Liberty Party runs slaveowner-turned-abolitionist James G. Birney as its candidate.

1845

- A potato fungus sets off the Irish famine, ultimately resulting in the deaths of an estimated one million Irish and the emigration to the United States or Canada of another one to two million.
- New York women employed in the needle trades form the Female Industry Association (also known as the Ladies Industrial Association) to fight wage cuts; the organization quickly disappears after an unsuccessful strike.

1846

- The invention of the sewing machine reduces the amount of labor it takes to make garments, but employers reap the benefits by dropping the rates they pay.

1847
- Escaped slave Frederick Douglass establishes himself as an abolitionist editor in Rochester, New York.

1848
- An unsuccessful German revolution leads many Germans to emigrate to the United States.
- Gold is discovered in California and lures people westward.
- The first American women's rights convention is held in Seneca Falls, New York; resolutions declare that all people are equal and that women should have the right to vote.
- Mexican War hero General Zachary Taylor, a Whig, defeats Democratic candidate General Lewis Cass for the presidency.
- The Free-Soil Party is formed, drawing supporters from the former Liberty Party and other antislavery voters; its candidate, former president Martin Van Buren, aids in Taylor's victory by capturing Democratic votes.
- The Associated Press is established to take advantage of the telegraph's ability to transmit news across the country.
- Spiritualism, a religion based on the ability to communicate with the spirits of the dead, gains a popular following, especially among advocates of abolition, women's rights, and utopian communities.

1849
- Thousands of angry New Yorkers riot outside of Astor Place Opera House to protest a performance by English actor William Macready; the riot reflects class conflict over the burgeoning urban culture.
- Elizabeth Blackwell, the first woman doctor in the United States, graduates at the head of her class at Geneva Medical College in New York, where she was shunned by male students.

1850
- Anti-immigrant and anti-Catholic societies come together as the American Party, usually called the Know-Nothings.
- Swedish singer Jenny Lind tours the United States, playing to packed halls—part of the emergent popular culture.
- President Zachary Taylor dies (apparently from an illness brought on by cherries and ice milk he consumed at the laying of the cornerstone for the Washington Monument); Millard Fillmore becomes president.

1852
- Democrat Franklin Pierce is elected president in an election that marks the death of the Whig Party.

1853

- German immigrant Heinrich Steinwig founds Steinway and Sons piano-manufacturing company, anglicizing his family name in deference to American tastes.

1855

- Irish and black dockworkers battle on the New York City waterfront—one of many conflicts between Irish and African Americans over jobs.

1857

- Failure of the Ohio Life Insurance and Trust Company sparks an economic panic and slump.

Additional Readings

For more on the changes experienced by northern working people in the antebellum decades, see: Hal S. Barron, *Who Stayed Behind: Rural Society in Nineteenth-Century New England* (1984); Christopher Clark, *The Roots of Rural Capitalism: Western Massachusetts, 1780–1860* (1990); David A. Hounshell, *From the American System to Mass Production, 1800–1932: The Development of Manufacturing Technology in the United States* (1984); Paul Johnson, *Sam Patch: The Famous Jumper* (2003); Bruce Laurie, *The Working People of Philadelphia, 1800–1850* (1980); Steven J. Ross, *Workers on the Edge: Work, Leisure, and Politics in Industrializing Cincinnati, 1788–1890* (1985); Charles Sellers, *The Market Revolution: Jacksonian America, 1815–1846* (1991); Carol Sheriff, *The Artificial River: The Erie Canal and the Paradox of Progress, 1917–1862* (1996); Peter Way, *Common Labor: Workers and the Digging of North American Canals, 1780–1860* (1993) and Sean Wilentz, *Chants Democratic: New York City and the Rise of the American Working Class, 1788–1850* (1984).

For more on mid-nineteenth-century immigration, see: Kathleen Conzen, *Immigrant Milwaukee, 1836–1860: Accommodation and Community in a Frontier City* (1976); Hasia Diner, *Erin's Daughters in America: Irish Immigrant Women in the Nineteenth Century* (1983); Jay P. Dolan, *The Immigrant Church: New York's German and Irish Catholics, 1815–1865* (1975); Maurice Lee Hansen, *The Atlantic Migration, 1607–1860* (1961); Bruce Levine, *The Spirit of 1848: German Immigrants, Labor Conflict, and the Coming of the Civil War* (1992); Kirby A. Miller, *Emigrants and Exiles: Ireland and the Irish Exodus to North America* (1985); and Gerald Rosenblum, *Immigrant Workers: Their Impact on American Labor Radicalism* (1973).

For more on urban life and culture, see: Edwin Burroughs and Mike Wallace, *Gotham: A History of New York City to 1898* (1999); Patricia Cline

Cohen, *The Murder of Helen Jewett: The Life and Death of a Prostitute in Nineteenth-Century New York* (1998); Susan G. Davis, *Parades and Power: Street Theatre in Nineteenth-Century Philadelphia* (1986); Bruce Dorsey, *Reforming Men and Women: Gender in the Antebellum City* (2002); Ann Fabian, *The Unvarnished Truth: Personal Narratives in Nineteenth-Century American* (2000); David Grimsted, *American Mobbing, 1828–1861* (1998); David Grimsted, *Melodrama Unveiled: American Theatre and Culture, 1800–1850* (1968); Karen Halttunen, *Murder Most Foul: The Killer and the American Gothic Imagination* (1998); David M. Henkin, *City Reading: Written Words and Public Spaces in Antebellum New York* (1998); Helen Lefkowitz Horowitz, *Rereading Sex: Battles over Sexual Knowledge and Suppression in Nineteenth-Century America* (2002); Lawrence Levine, *Highbrow/Lowbrow: The Emergence of Cultural Hierarchy in America* (1988); Roy Rosenzweig and Elizabeth Blackmar, *The Park and the People: A History of Central Park* (1992).

For more on free African Americans in the antebellum North, see:

William L. Andrews, *To Tell a Free Story: The First Century of Afro-American Autobiography, 1760–1865* (1986); James Oliver Horton and Lois Horton, *Black Bostonians: Family Life and Community Struggle in the Antebellum North* (1979); Leon Litwack, *North of Slavery: The Negro in the Free States, 1790–1860* (1961); Nell Painter, *Sojourner Truth: A Life, A Symbol* (1996); Patrick Rael, *Black Identity and Black Protest in the Antebellum North* (2002); Dorothy Sterling, ed., *We Are Your Sisters: Black Women in the Nineteenth Century* (1984); James B. Stewart, *Holy Warriors: The Abolitionists and American Slavery* (1997); and Albert J. Von Frank, *The Trials of Anthony Burns: Freedom and Slavery in Emerson's Boston* (1998).

For more on women's work and reform activism, see:

Norma Basch, *In the Eyes of the Law: Women, Marriage, and Property in Nineteenth Century New York* (1982); Jeanne Boydston, *Home and Work: Housework, Wages and the Ideology of Labor in the Early Republic* (1990); Ann Boylan, *The Origins of Women's Activism: New York and Boston, 1797–1840* (2002); Nancy Cott, *The Bonds of Womanhood: "Woman's Sphere" in New England, 1780–1835* (1977); Thomas Dublin, *Transforming Women's Work: New England Lives in the Industrial Revolution* (1994); Faye Dudden, *Serving Women: Household Service in Nineteenth-Century America* (1983); Lori D. Ginzberg, *Women in Antebellum Reform* (2000); Julie Roy Jeffrey, *The Great Silent Army of Abolitionism: Ordinary Women in the Antislavery Movement* (1998); Christine Stansell, *City of Women: Sex and Class in New York, 1789–1860* (1986); and Judith Wellman, *The Road to Seneca Falls: Elizabeth Cady Stanton and the First Woman's Rights Convention* (2004).

9

The Spread of Slavery and the Crisis of Southern Society

1836–1848

THE LAND OF LIBERTY.

RECOMMENDED TO THE CONSIDERATION OF "BROTHER JONATHAN."

IN THE 1830S, Charleston, South Carolina, was home to many wealthy whites who owned slaves. In one such slave-owning family, the wife was a deeply religious woman. She regularly assembled her children for family prayer and was known in the community for her charity and her work among the poor. Yet the young African American woman who worked for her as a seamstress and maid experienced little of this kindness. Perhaps it was because she was a mulatto (raising fears in her mistress that the master was sexually exploiting slave women), or perhaps it was because the young woman maintained an independent spirit despite having been enslaved for all of her eighteen years. She ran away several times and, when captured, was sent to the Charleston workhouse to be whipped. When the brutal whippings, which left finger-deep scars along her back, did not deter the woman's desire for freedom, her owners placed a heavy iron collar around her neck. Three prongs projected from it to hold the collar tight. Her owners also yanked out her front tooth to make it easier for them to describe her in case she ran again. The supposedly charitable mistress watched the seamstress work, with her deeply lacerated back, her mutilated mouth, and her bowed neck, but could never be sure that she had shackled the young African American's heart and soul as well as her body.

Although the seamstress may have persisted in her resistance to bondage longer than most slaves did and labored under closer scrutiny within an urban household, she was certainly not alone in challenging planters' authority. A black field hand from South Carolina, looking back on his days in bondage, claimed that when slaves gazed on southern soil, they saw "land that is rich with the sweat of our faces and the blood of our back." When planters noted the richness of that same land, they focused on the

Actions Speak Louder Than Words

"The Land of Liberty" was the ironic title of this cartoon published in an 1847 edition of the British satirical weekly *Punch*. *Punch* (1847) — American Social History Project.

wealth it produced for them. As the number of African Americans held in slavery grew, this irrepressible conflict between slaves and masters generated repeated crises in plantation society during the 1830s and 1840s. The resulting upheavals affected not only masters and slaves, but a range of other residents as well. Some were nonslaveholding white farmers who envied the profits made on plantations as they supported their own families on marginal land without the benefit of bound labor. Others were landless whites, who struggled to sustain body, soul, and family as they moved from place to place and from job to job. They competed with free blacks for jobs, housing, and the patronage of well-to-do whites but also shared their disparagement of wealthy whites. These groups vied with each other for respect, authority, and some degree of independence throughout the early nineteenth century.

The conflicts that were generated by southerners' competing economic, social, and political visions escalated in the years between the establishment of Texas as an independent republic in 1836 and the end of the U.S. war against Mexico in 1848. The planters' two goals — to consolidate power and to expand the lands under their control — often worked at cross-purposes, because the extension of slavery raised new conflicts and controversies both within and outside the South. During these years, planters became ever more dependent on slave labor. As one South Carolina plantation owner bluntly explained, "Slavery with us is no abstraction but a great and vital fact. Without it our every comfort would be taken from us. Our wives, our children made unhappy . . . all, all lost and our people ruined forever." In the 1840s, however, the consequences of extending slave labor into new western territories became clearer as expansion promoted regional, racial, and class conflicts that shattered party alignments and presaged the Civil War. During this decade, planters were driven to defend the institution of slavery more aggressively. Yet their proslavery arguments only heightened northern fears that human bondage threatened free labor and defied moral logic.

Planters, who had long been masters of their domain, found themselves facing challenges from both inside and outside the South. In the years preceding the final confrontations over slavery — from roughly 1836 to 1848 — African Americans and poorer whites forced planters to recognize limits on their authority. Although the planters certainly retained their power, they had to make concessions, especially to nonslaveholding whites, to ensure continued control.

The Master's Precarious Domain

Throughout the 1830s and 1840s, planters successfully fended off challenges to their personal, political, and economic authority from southerners who received fewer benefits from a slave-based economy. Enslaved and free blacks, American Indians, and nonslaveholding whites resisted the spread of the "peculiar institution," as slavery was euphemistically called. Even some plantation mistresses criticized (if only in their private diaries) the effects of slavery on their families. White plantation employees, too, found fault with the planters who hired them. In response, slave owners were forced to develop new strategies to maintain their control and consolidate their authority in the household, the community, and the region.

The Consolidation of Planters' Power   For many southern planters, Texas came to symbolize their ability to expand slavery and consolidate their power. Slave owners such as Moses Austin began settling the fertile lands in eastern Texas in the 1820s, when Texas was one of the outlying provinces of the Republic of Mexico. With only about 2,000 Spanish-speaking residents, or *tejanos*, and a much larger number of Comanche Indians in the region, the Mexican government initially encouraged American settlement. Then, in 1829, the Republic of Mexico outlawed slavery, but thousands of Americans continued to bring enslaved blacks into Texas. By the early 1830s, a new government in Mexico, led by General Antonio López de Santa Anna, sought to stem the tide of U.S. migrants by imposing greater control over Texas. When U.S. migrants and planters failed to recognize Santa Anna's authority, he sought to drive the Americans out.

Skirmishes between Mexican troops and U.S. settlers began in 1835, and by March 2, 1836, Americans led by Moses Austin's son Stephen declared independence from Mexico. Four days later, 4,000 Mexican troops attacked the Alamo, an abandoned mission near San Antonio. When the 187 Americans who were defending the outpost, including Davy Crockett, refused to surrender, they were killed by Mexican soldiers. Soon afterward, more than 300 American rebels were killed at Goliad even after they had agreed to surrender. By April, however, the tide had turned as eager volunteers from the United States joined their countrymen already in Texas to defend American interests. Commanded by Sam Houston, U.S. forces routed the Mexican army at the battle of San Jacinto on April 21 and captured Santa Anna himself. As a result, Santa Anna signed a treaty in May 1836 granting independence to the Republic of Texas. Although conflicts continued for more than a decade between Mexicans and Texans and between Texans and Comanches, southern slave owners viewed the triumph of U.S. forces in Texas as a victory for slavery.

The heady economic dreams that followed Texas independence from Mexico in 1836 were delayed, but not destroyed, by the onset of depression the following year. The Panic of 1837 destroyed the fortunes of plantation owners across the South as prices fell by almost half between 1837 and 1843 (Map 9.1). Yet those who survived the crash were rewarded when British and U.S. banks began extending credit on more favorable terms in the early

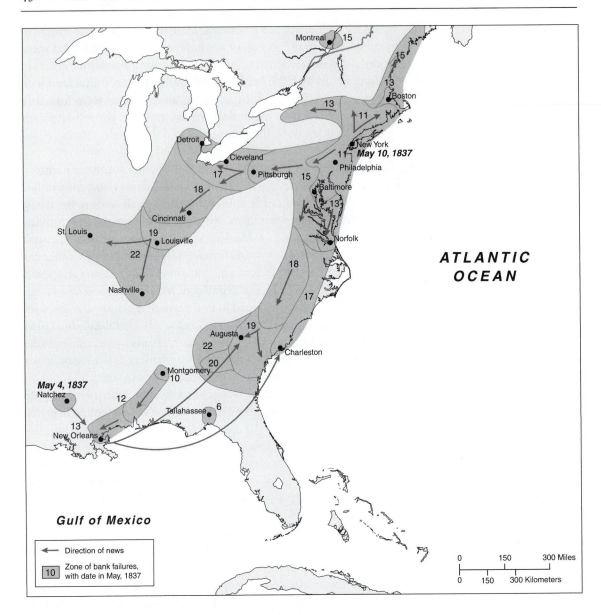

Montreal 15

15

13

Boston

13

11

Detroit

Cleveland

New York

May 10, 1837

11

Pittsburgh

Philadelphia

17

15

Baltimore

18

13

Cincinnati

Norfolk

St. Louis

19

Louisville

22

18

Nashville

17

19

Augusta

22

Charleston

20

Montgomery

10

May 4, 1837

Natchez

12

Tallahassee 6

13

New Orleans

ATLANTIC OCEAN

Gulf of Mexico

← Direction of news

[10] Zone of bank failures, with date in May, 1837

0   150   300 Miles

0   150   300 Kilometers

MAP 9.1   Anatomy of a Panic: Bank Suspensions in May 1837

Although New York City served as the financial center of the United States, the Panic of 1837 began in the South. Bank failures in Natchez, Mississippi, and Tallahassee, Florida, produced the first alarms on May 4 and 6, 1837. By May 22, northeastern financial centers as well as key western and southern cities were engulfed in the Panic.

A "Model" Plantation

This pictorial survey of Oak Lawn, a large Louisiana sugar plantation on the Bayou Teche, includes a view of its slave quarters, consisting of forty-two cabins. C. E. H. Bonwill, *Frank Leslie's Illustrated Newspaper*, February 6, 1864 — American Social History Project.

1840s. By that time, the failure of farms and businesses had lessened competition, and the demand for many goods, including cotton, once again rose. In fact, pent-up demand ensured a steady market for both agricultural and manufactured items for the next several years.

Like some northern merchants and speculators, the most successful southern gentlemen took advantage of the devastation the panic wreaked on more vulnerable neighbors to expand their holdings. The percentage of white families who owned large plantations shrank, but their power was growing along with their desire to make their wealth and status more visible. As cotton prices rose, these affluent planters began to replace their rough and unpretentious farmhouses with newer, more ostentatious mansions. Across the South, but especially in Alabama, Louisiana, and the Mississippi Delta — the areas along the Gulf Coast into which slavery was expanding — the new plantation houses were decorated with expensive, often imported, furnishings and filled with fine wines, fancy clothes, numerous guests, and a domestic labor force large enough to care for the new amenities.

This new aristocracy with its opulent lifestyle was typified in Mississippi by the Natchez "nabobs," a group composed of the region's forty wealthiest families, who had begun to buy up land in the 1820s. During the Panic of 1837, members of this elite circle added both slaves and acreage at depression era prices and then took advantage of rising cotton prices in the mid-1840s to complete their climb to the top. Nabob Stephen Duncan, for instance, was a Pennsylvania-born physician who had moved to Mississippi in 1808. In the early 1830s, he was a successful planter and banker with close ties to the Whig Party and the American Colonization Society. Two decades later, Duncan owned six cotton plantations and two sugar cane plantations spread across three counties in two states, along with more than 1,000 slaves, 23 of whom labored as domestic servants at Auburn, his Natchez mansion.

Duncan and his fellow nabobs threw elaborate parties and balls, traveled extensively, bred and raced horses, and planted English-style boxed gardens. William Johnson, a free black barber in Natchez, detailed the comings and goings of local aristocrats in his diary. In 1840, in the midst of the depression, Johnson commented on the marriage of nabob Louis Bingaman, Duncan's brother-in-law, to a New York socialite. "The N.P. [newspaper] speaks of the wedding Dress Costing $2000. And of the marriage Contract or Settlement $100,000—Not bad to take," he concluded.

Marriage played a critical role in the economic strategies of southern planters. Stephen Duncan's wealth, for instance, was built not only on his medical practice, shrewd land speculation, and effective slave management practices, but also on two well-placed marriages (after the death of his socially prominent first wife, he married into another wealthy family). For men, a good marriage required obtaining both a large financial settlement and a wife who understood her place. Planter society celebrated strongly patriarchal families. The father supervised the plantation's production of the staple crop and the financial transactions that were directly linked to it, including the purchase and sale of slaves. His wife was assigned the domestic sphere and was denied access to most aspects of public life. "The proper place for a woman is at home," declared the *Southern Quarterly Review*. "One of her highest privileges [is] to be politically merged in the existence of her husband."

But a wealthy southerner's business dealings often took him away from home, requiring his wife to assume many duties in running the plantation. This created enormous strains. Catherine Hammond, wife of prominent South Carolina planter and politician James Henry Hammond, found herself in charge of affairs at Silver Bluff plantation during her husband's frequent travels. Catherine had inherited Silver Bluff at age eleven, when her father died. Six years later, in 1831, Hammond, a dashing young lawyer of twenty-three, married the shy teenage heiress despite her family's misgivings. In the summer of 1840, Catherine was pregnant for the seventh time in nine years. Yet she was suddenly forced to preside over the plantation when James decided that he needed "to go somewhere" to recover from the strain of his ongoing campaign for the governorship.

James spent the next six weeks in New York City, purchasing silver, linens, and furniture for a newly constructed residence in Columbia, while Catherine endured the hot and humid weather at Silver Bluff, overseeing the crops and slaves and entertaining a full house of family members and guests. Hammond returned to the plantation in September, just three days before Catherine gave birth. Women such as Catherine Hammond, although enjoying all the benefits of wealth and position that planter society had to offer, led lives that were restricted by the masculine authority that prevailed in the planter class.

The Price of Blood
Thomas Satterwhite Noble's painting reflected on the ways in which property overwhelmed any ties of affection in the plantation "family." His 1868 picture portrayed the sale of a plantation master's mulatto son to a slave trader. 1868, oil, 39 1/4 × 49 1/2 inches — The Morris Museum of Art, Augusta, Georgia.

Southern society's dependence on slaves strengthened traditional beliefs in the sanctity of social order and the strict subordination of the members of one (supposedly inferior) social group to those of another (supposedly superior). Planters viewed their children, wives, poorer neighbors, white employees, and slaves as being, to one degree or another, inferior to themselves in social standing and personal rights. The master's power over his slaves was merely an extension of his power over his wife and children. "Do you say that the slave is held to involuntary service?" one spokesman asked rhetorically, before offering his justification. "So is the wife. Her relation to her husband, in the immense majority of cases, is made for her, not by her." This linking of slavery with white family relations did not prevent the forcible breakup of slave families or keep planters from enslaving or selling children whom they conceived with female slaves. It did, however, reinforce the patriarch's supremacy within his own home and emphasize still more than in the North the wife's subordinate position.

Household Discord and Challenges from Below   Although planters asserted their authority over their families, tensions often lurked just beneath the surface. First and foremost, the planter's sexual access to female slaves strained marital bonds and undermined the mistress's self-respect and moral authority on the plantation. A proper lady would, of course, try to ignore evidence of sexual indiscretion. Mary Boykin Chesnut, in an oft-quoted passage from her diary, observed that "the Mulattoes one sees in every family exactly resemble the white children—and every lady tells you who is the father of all the Mulatto children in everybody's household, but those in her own she seems to think drop from the clouds or pretends so to think."

Sometimes the evidence was so overwhelming that it could not be ignored. Catherine Hammond left her husband over his sexual relationship with the slave Louisa but only after having overlooked earlier liaisons with Louisa's mother and with four of Catherine's own nieces. The absence of testimony from Louisa, her mother, or the nieces about the agonies they experienced as a result of this abuse makes it impossible to understand the full horror of the man's actions. However, his flagrant infidelity, which eventually forced Catherine to leave him to save her own reputation, illuminates the dark underside of domestic relations that was often concealed to preserve the family honor. That Catherine eventually reconciled with her husband suggests the limited options available to even the best-positioned southern women. Moreover, that Catherine apparently did nothing to stop the sexual exploitation of slave women or her own nieces also indicates the ease with which plantation mistresses became accomplices in the abusive system.

Prevailing attitudes not only minimized the private "indiscretions" of masters, they also denied the master's wife most public credit for the plantation's upkeep. Yet the wife's domestic sphere could be huge. She supervised a broad range of essential tasks not only in her family's living quarters (often known as the Big House), but also in the separate kitchen, dairy, smokehouse, and storehouse. Managing the household budget and negotiating with local merchants might also fall within her sphere. If the husband was deceased or temporarily absent, she usually administered the plantation alone or with the aid of an overseer. But chattel slavery discredited menial labor, associating those who performed it with the slave's lowly status. Unlike industrious northern businessmen, planters generally prided themselves on being men of leisure and culture, freed from hard work and financial concerns. The popular image of the plantation mistress reflected those values, rendering her the very embodiment of grace, gentility, and refinement. Strict adherence to these ideals placed the plantation mistress in the contradictory position of having to appear to be a delicate woman of leisure while performing hard work on a daily basis.

Plantation mistresses, like northern women, were encouraged to find solace in religion, but they discovered fewer opportunities there for self-expression and social initiative. In the late eighteenth and early nineteenth centuries, southern women, at least in more densely settled areas, had formed prayer, missionary, and benevolent associations. A scattering of temperance societies flourished in southern cities beginning in the 1820s.

Soon, however, northern women's increasing visibility in antislavery agitation, much of it linked to religious awakenings, triggered a backlash in the South that curbed women's participation there in voluntary associations, whether church-based or secular. While such restrictions severely limited women's ability to launch collective and public protests against the abuses linked to male domination, they may have nurtured a more intimate form of guerrilla warfare in southern households when wives believed that their planter husbands had overstepped the boundaries of patriarchal authority.

Other individuals on the plantation also challenged planters' ideal of total control. Overseers were the most important paid laborers on most large plantations—and often the most problematic. They were expected to keep slaves working to their utmost capacity, keep them healthy and relatively content, and expend a minimum of funds on their care. Owners were demanding, but so too were the slaves, who recognized overseers as a potentially weak link in the chain of command and withheld their labor power from them or protested to owners against especially brutal overseers.

Many planters hired a new overseer every year, hoping to find one with the perfect mix of agricultural expertise, personal authority, and managerial integrity. In the diaries and letters of planters, problems with overseers loomed large: they were too harsh or too lenient; they were more interested in sexual exploitation than agricultural production; they were unhappy with their wages or housing or chances for becoming a planter themselves; they had gained too much control in the absence of the owner; they were out of control. This catalogue of complaints penned by slave owners certainly must have had its counterpart among discontented overseers, although few had the leisure time or the education to leave a written record. Occupying a difficult middle ground between black laborers and their white owners, overseers provided a constant reminder that planters' authority was limited in numerous ways.

The Ties That Bind?: Religion and Slavery   Planters used various means to reinforce their control over family members, subordinates, and slaves. Religion offered one vehicle for creating bonds among diverse groups in southern society. Evangelical Protestantism had inspired opposition to slavery among some poor whites and fueled resistance by free blacks and slaves in the early 1800s. By the 1830s, however, slaveholding elites had gained more power within evangelical churches, and church leaders generally welcomed the approval and sponsorship of the planters and all the benefits their wealth and influence brought to the church.

Planters tried to use religion to bind slaves more tightly to the southern system, and owners increasingly controlled their slaves' attendance at church. During his years as a slave, Frederick Douglass was frustrated by the "many good, religious colored people who were under the delusion that

Family Worship in a Plantation in South Carolina

An engraving from a British illustrated weekly depicted the scene in a "rude chapel" of a Port Royal, South Carolina, plantation, where the master and mistress were "engaged in Divine worship, surrounded by [their] slaves, in a state of almost patriarchal simplicity." Frank Vizetelly, *Illustrated London News*, December 5, 1863 — American Social History Project.

God required them to submit to slavery and to wear their chains in meekness and humility."

Other blacks, however, resisted this message of servility. Robert Ryland, a white pastor in Virginia, began preaching in Richmond's First African Baptist Church in the 1840s. A defender of slavery, he claimed, as one free black man recalled, "that God had given all this continent to the white man, and that it was our duty to submit." Yet groups of African Americans lingered after Ryland's services to listen to blacks preach. Ryland himself admitted that one of these black preachers "was heard with far more interest than I was." Another witness noticed that at these informal services the "most active were those who had slept during [Ryland's] sermon."

In a few cities, independent black churches thrived. Membership in Baltimore's African Methodist Episcopal conference more than doubled between 1836 and 1856, and other southern cities experienced a similar upsurge in religious enthusiasm. In rural districts, however, separate black churches were rare, and slaves were forced to convene secret "night meetings," which continued despite being prohibited. Moreover, slaves might pick up dangerous ideas even from preachers who were sanctioned by whites. Many white southerners worried that prayers, songs, and sermons intended for their ears (and so filled with references to human freedom and universal brotherhood) might be "misinterpreted" by slaves and free blacks. Given the different meanings of salvation to blacks and whites, Christian appeals to blacks and the development of uniquely African American forms of Christianity remained sources of conflict for decades.

"Shout and Pray All Night": Slave Religion in Secret

Interviewed in 1937, former slave Charles Grandy recalled the difference between religious services supervised by whites and those that slaves conducted in secrecy.

In the church the white folks was on one side an' the colored on the other. The preacher was a white man. He preached in a way like, 'Obey your master an' missus' an' tell us don't steal from your master an' missus.' 'Course we knowed it was wrong to steal, but the niggers had to steal to get somethin' to eat. I know I did. . . .

Whites in our section used to have a service for us slaves every fourth Sunday, but it wasn't enough for them who wanted to talk with Jesus. Used to go across the fields nights to a old tobacco barn on the side of a hill. . . . Had a old pot hid there to catch the sound. Sometimes would stick your head down in the pot if you got to shout awful loud. I remember ole Sister Millie Jeffries. Would stick her head in the pot and shout and pray all night while the others was bustin' to take their turn. Sometimes the slaves would have to pull her head out of the pot so's the others could shout.

Charles L. Perdue, Thomas E. Barden, and Robert K. Phillips, eds., *Weevils in the Wheat: Interviews with Virginia Ex-Slaves* (University Press of Virginia, 1976), 116, 119.

Growing concerns over slavery among northern Christians also tested the alliance between southern evangelicals and planters. In the mid-1840s, northern Methodists and Baptists tried to convince their southern counterparts to oppose slavery on Christian grounds. The struggle intensified when slavery extended into new territories, which heightened northern opposition to the institution and prompted many northern churches finally to take a stand on issues they had long tried to ignore.

When southern congregations resisted northern entreaties, the national organizations of these denominations split. The most important schisms occurred among Methodists in 1844 and the Baptists in 1845 as both churches split along regional lines. Southern whites, particularly planters, found the antislavery stand of northern ministers treasonous. While planters overemphasized the abolitionist beliefs of mainstream northern ministers, the division between northern and southern churches no doubt reinforced the belief among slaves that southern white preachers did not have the final say on the Bible's meaning.

Native and African American Resistance on the Frontier As white men and women debated the proper role of the church in free and slave societies, many southern blacks continued to find solace in religion. Slaves who excelled at preaching, singing, and playing instruments provided role models for those with whom they shared their bondage and inspired some to resist their enslavement. Yet after Nat Turner's rebellion in 1831, open revolts were extremely rare. Moreover, the rapid settlement of whites in new areas of the South in the 1830s and 1840s deprived potential black insurrectionists of a safe refuge where they might escape capture. African Americans in the South therefore continued to depend on the forms of resistance developed earlier—feigning illness, destroying tools, injuring livestock, petty theft, arson, and running away—to survive within the confines of bondage (see Chapter 6).

Some Africans sought to escape the brutalities of slavery by rising up against their captors while being transported to the Americas. The United States had outlawed the international slave trade in 1808, but other nations still participated in the trade between Africa and the West Indies. In July 1839, captive West Africans under the leadership of Joseph Cinqué revolted and took control of the Spanish slave ship *Amistad*. They ordered the owners to return them to Africa, but after a meandering course through the Atlantic Ocean, they were waylaid by a U.S. Navy brig. The Africans were charged with the murder of the *Amistad*'s captain and jailed in New Haven, Connecticut. Abolitionists came to their support, however, and former president John Quincy Adams represented them in court. After a long legal battle, the U.S. Supreme Court freed the "mutineers" in 1841. They returned to Africa the following year.

For blacks who were already enslaved in the United States, frontier regions remained one of the few areas where open revolt against bondage was still possible. During the 1830s, one of the most successful and sustained battles against the white majority took place in Florida, which had long served as a haven for runaway slaves (known as maroons). Here, the swampy terrain provided protection for isolated groups of fugitives, the rich lands provided food and shelter, and the Seminole Indian nation provided allies.

Although some Seminoles held African Americans as slaves, Seminole society was not rigidly racist. Here, bondage resembled the traditional slavery of Africa more than it did the commercially oriented institution fashioned by European settlers and their descendants. Slaves often lived on small farms with their own families and enjoyed many of the rights and liberties of full members of the tribe. Many married into the tribe, creating a mixed-race culture that drew on African, American, and Seminole traditions.

Escape

This icon, or symbol, appeared on notices about fugitive slaves in the classified section of the Mobile, Alabama, *Commercial Register* in the 1830s. Richard Brough, *Commercial Register,* June 16, 1832 — Prints and Photographs Division, Library of Congress.

Joseph Cinqué
One of the most famous anti-slavery visual documents was a painting commissioned by the influential black abolitionist Robert Purvis to champion the cause of the *Amistad* captives. While awaiting the U.S. Supreme Court decision, Purvis hired the New Haven painter and abolitionist Nathaniel Jocelyn to celebrate the *Amistad* revolt's leader. Dressed in a toga and grasping a staff, which linked Joseph Cinqué to classical republicanism and religious prophecy, the portrait showed a man who boldly contradicted contemporary notions of African savagery and also challenged the standard abolitionist symbol, the supplicant slave. The *Amistad* defense committee disseminated prints of this painting across the country, and the portrait inspired at least one other act of resistance: the successful 1841 takeover of the *Creole*, a slave ship bound for New Orleans. 1839, oil on canvas, 30 1/4 × 25 1/2 inches — New Haven Colony Historical Society. Gift of Dr. Charles B. Purvis, 1898.

The Seminoles and the maroons who lived among them fought two wars against the United States. The First Seminole War broke out in 1812 when U.S. marines invaded Florida, hoping to wrest control of the region from Spain. The Seminoles and maroons repelled the invaders, the black fugitives resisting most fiercely. Andrew Jackson again led U.S. troops against Spanish and Seminole settlements in Florida in 1818, and Spain ceded Florida to the United States the next year. A decade later, the U.S. government sought to remove Seminoles from the region. Between 1832 and 1835, most of the Seminole nation was resettled in Oklahoma and other western territories. A minority, however, refused to leave. Under the direction of a militant and charismatic leader named Osceola, they fought a successful seven-year guerrilla action against the U.S. Army.

The Second Seminole War, which began in 1835, was expected to last only a few months. Instead, it lasted years and cost the lives of some 1,600 U.S. troops as well as $30 million to $40 million. It erupted partly because of federal efforts to drive all southeastern Indian tribes beyond the Mississippi, but slave traders, slave owners, and would-be slave owners who hoped to get their hands on fugitive slaves also supported the war. Osceola counted many maroons and mixed-race warriors among his supporters. According to a contemporary account, "The negroes, from the commencement of the Florida war, have, for their numbers, been the most formidable foe, more bloodthirsty, active, and revengeful than the Indian." Even more alarming to whites was the fact that hundreds of slaves escaped from nearby white-owned plantations and joined the Seminole ranks. American General Thomas Sidney Jessup wrote in late 1836, "This, you may be assured, is a negro, not an Indian war."

Finally stalemated, General Jessup hoped to separate the mixed-race fighters from the full-blooded Seminoles. He offered to send those with African American blood to the Indian (Oklahoma) Territory while allowing the Seminoles to remain in southern Florida. "Separating the negroes from the Indians," he wrote in 1838, would "weaken the latter more than they would be weakened by the loss of the same number of their own people." Other white military feared that black warriors, having tasted comparative freedom and proven themselves in battle, would prove more dangerous than ever if reenslaved. "Ten resolute negroes," warned one officer, "with a knowledge of the country, are sufficient to desolate the frontier, from one extent to the other."

Ultimately, the Second Seminole War ended in a U.S. victory but only after Osceola was lured into the U.S. Army camp by false promises of a treaty. The Army took him captive, devastating the exhausted Seminole and maroon forces. Even then, however, the victors were forced to allow the fugitive slaves among the Seminoles to accompany the Indians westward rather than being returned to their former white owners.

The fierce resistance by the former slaves and the Seminole warriors speaks eloquently of the courage, determination, and military capacity that existed among blacks and Indians in this area of the South, where a strong alliance between them was possible. Unfortunately for slaves, such allies were extremely rare. Even other Indian groups, such as the Cherokee, practiced a form of slavery from the 1830s on that was closer to that of whites than of Seminoles.

In the Indian Territory of Oklahoma, where the Five Civilized Tribes were resettled in the 1830s, slaves held by Cherokee, Creek, Chickasaw, and Choctaw masters fled to the Seminoles, just as those owned by Georgia whites had done decades before. Others fled north to find freedom. The slave Henry Bibb, for instance, escaped to Michigan and published his story, *The Life and Adventures of Henry Bibb*, which was widely read among northerners. Mexico, too, though a great distance from most plantations, offered a safe haven much like that provided by Florida in the early nineteenth century. In 1842, two dozen slaves in the Cherokee settlement attempted a mass escape, fleeing southward in hopes of reaching Mexico. Slaves among the Creeks joined the group, which later liberated eight more blacks held by Choctaw slave catchers. Eventually, however, Cherokee militiamen overtook the fugitives, only two of whom escaped.

Free Blacks Threaten Planters' Control

Free blacks as well as slaves threatened planters' authority. In fact, by the 1830s, free blacks were often seen as a more serious threat to white supremacy than were rebellious slaves. The mere existence of free blacks in the South challenged any simple connection between race and enslavement.

Fearing the influence that free blacks exerted on slaves, the Virginia General Assembly in 1837 reaffirmed an 1806 statute that allowed county courts to determine whether free blacks would be allowed to remain in residence permanently. To stay in Virginia, the petitioner had to demonstrate

Methought the souls of all that I had murder'd came to my tent. Act. 5 Sc. 3.

RICHARD III.

Richard III

Andrew Jackson's role in the First Seminole War was resurrected in this anti-Democrat cartoon published during the 1828 presidential campaign. Whig caricaturist David Claypool Johnston fashioned the Democratic candidate's head and shoulders out of a military tent, cannons, swords, and the bodies of dead Indians. The cartoon was captioned with a line from Shakespeare's play about the treacherous, despotic king of England: "Methought the souls of all that I had murder'd came to my tent." David Claypool Johnston, 1828, engraving with stipple, 6 1/8 × 4 3/8 inches — American Antiquarian Society.

Seminoles

George Catlin's 1838 sketch showed 7 of the 250 Seminoles imprisoned at Fort Moultrie, Charleston, South Carolina. They were captured with Seminole leader Osceola near St. Augustine, Florida, after U.S. troops violated a truce agreement. George Catlin, *Seminolee,* 1838, pencil drawing — New-York Historical Society.

that he or she was "of good character, peaceable, orderly and industrious, and not addicted to drunkenness, gaming or other vice." African American men had a more difficult time than women persuading courts to let them remain in the state as free persons. It was hard for them to be industrious without being viewed as competitors with white workingmen, and they were more likely to be considered disorderly by their mere presence in the population.

Free black women posed less of a threat because their most marketable skills were in areas—laundry, domestic work, petty trades, and sewing—that were largely reserved for their sex and race. Harriet Cook, a washerwoman in Leesburg, Virginia, worked for twelve years after her 1838 emancipation to build an impressive and supportive clientele among that city's white residents. When she petitioned to gain permanent residence status, leading citizens swore that "It would be a serious inconvenience to a number of the citizens of Leesburg to be deprived of her services as a washerwoman and in other capacities in which in consequence of her gentility, trustworthiness, and skill, she is exceedingly useful." Her petition was granted.

The larger numbers of women who were emancipated, the job opportunities afforded them in cities, and the greater leniency of courts and

A Free Man of Color

A form issued by a Virginia county court in 1858 to Richard Cogbill certified his claim to be a free-born African American. Mary O'H. Williamson Collection, Prints and Photographs Department, Moorland-Spingarn Research Center, Howard University.

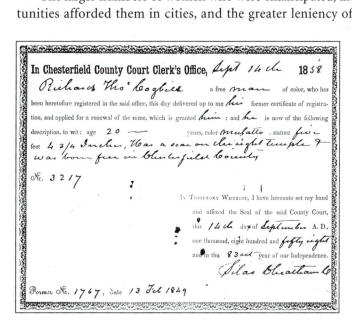

legislatures in granting them permanent residency resulted in a skewed sex ratio in the South's urban areas. As a result, free black women often had to support themselves and their families and to fend off economic and sexual exploitation by whites without the assistance of husbands, fathers, or brothers. Nonetheless, they were able to build and sustain communities in many southern cities.

The number of free blacks in the South remained small throughout the mid-nineteenth century, and most of them lived in towns and cities rather than plantation areas. Yet their presence still created considerable anxiety among whites. By 1840, the state of Mississippi had passed laws expressly prohibiting free blacks from testifying against whites, serving in the militia, voting, or holding office. A year later, a group of Natchez whites called a meeting at City Hall to consider "imposing a fine on the owners of slaves who permit them to go at large and hire their time; and also . . . requiring free persons of color to remove from [Mississippi] and to prevent their emigration into the state."

Like planters, nonslaveholding whites often opposed the presence of free blacks in the South. They tended to see free black workers as unwanted competition for jobs. In the North, immigrants from Ireland, Germany, and elsewhere reshaped the labor force and created tensions among whites as well as between whites and blacks. With smaller cities and less industry, the South attracted far fewer immigrants, leaving free blacks as the major source of economic competition. Still, a minority of southern whites believed that exemplary free blacks should be allowed to reside in southern communities, and some supported the petitions of free blacks who sought to remain in the region. Most of the whites who supported the presence of free blacks lived in small towns and rural areas of the upper South. Many belonged to small religious denominations, such as German Moravians and Quakers. In Loudoun County, Virginia, for instance, some three dozen citizens, mostly Quakers and Germans, argued in 1843 that "every man [sic], not convicted of a crime, has a natural right, to reside in the community where he was born." Although such sentiments were expressed more and more rarely after 1840, they did not entirely disappear.

In cities, however, where white workers competed directly with free black laborers, tensions between the two groups often ran high. There, many whites wanted to ensure that restrictive laws were enforced. Throughout the 1830s, 1840s, and 1850s, southern white workers strove to force blacks, slave and free, out of their neighborhoods and out of their occupations. Frederick Douglass remembered a white ship's carpenter named Thomas Lanman who had murdered two slaves. Regularly boasting of the crime, Lanman added that "when others would do as much as he had done, they would be rid of the d——d niggers." Douglass himself experienced this attitude more directly in 1836. When he was hired out by his owner as a

"So Cheapened the White Man's Labor": Conflict Between Black and White Workers

Far from viewing black workers as allies, most southern white workers saw them as competitors and hoped to exclude them from their trades. In this 1838 open letter to a local newspaper, a white Georgia artisan complains about whites hiring cheaper slave tradesmen over white men struggling for economic survival. He also lays out his case for the superiority of white tradesmen and their role in maintaining the slave system.

Gentlemen:

. . . I am aware that most of you have [such a] strong antipathy to encouraging the masonry and carpentry trades of your poor white brothers, that your predilections for giving employment in your line of business to ebony workers have either so cheapened the white man's labor, or expatriated hence with but a few solitary exceptions, all the white masons and carpenters of this town.

The white man is the only real, legal, moral, and civil proprietor of this country and state. . . . By white men alone was this continent discovered; by the prowess of white men alone (though not always properly or humanely exercised), were the fierce and active Indians driven occidentally: and if swarms and hordes of infuriated red men pour down from the Northwest, like the wintry blast thereof, the white men alone, aye, those to whom you decline to give money for bread and clothes, for their famishing families . . . would bare their breasts to the keen and whizzing shafts of the savage crusaders—defending negroes too in the bargain, for if left to themselves without our aid, the Indians would or can sweep the negroes hence, "as dewdrops are shaken from the lion's mane."

The right, then, gentlemen, you will no doubt candidly admit, of the white man to employment in preference to negroes, who must defer to us since they live well enough on plantations, cannot be considered impeachable by contractors. . . . As masters of the polls in a majority, carrying all before them, I am surprised the poor do not elect faithful members to the Legislature, who will make it penal to prefer negro mechanic labor to white men's. . . .

Yours respectfully,
J. J. Flournoy

Athens (Georgia) *Southern Banner*, January 13, 1838.

caulker in a Baltimore shipyard, white workers severely beat Douglass. Such scare tactics occasionally achieved limited results. Douglass's master pulled him out of the shipyard just as the white workers wanted.

White workers largely depended on legislation to remove free blacks from the region and from the labor force. Some politicians expressed sympathy for demands to limit certain occupations to whites only. But to write such provisions into law and enforce them would have limited the freedom of the planters to make use of the blacks they held in bondage in whatever way they saw fit. No southern legislature was prepared to do that. Angered by such legislative failures but unwilling to champion emancipation, white workers generally blamed their woes on the helpless black population.

New Frontiers and New Challenges for Southern Slavery

Many southern whites hoped that the opening of western lands to white settlement would ease conflicts created by differences of wealth. The availability of lands once occupied by American Indians or controlled by Mexico provided a temporary safety valve, especially for white yeomen who hoped to join the plantation elite. There were other western areas, most notably the Appalachian foothills and highlands that ran from northwestern Virginia through Georgia, where slavery would never be profitable. These regions offered nonslaveholding whites the chance to carve out a living with only tenuous ties to the economic, political, and social system that was built on slave labor.

Yet as white southerners pushed farther west, the planter elite faced new challenges. Both slaveholders and nonslaveholders in frontier areas demanded political representation and legislation that threatened the authority of planters back east. At the same time, the spread of plantations westward expanded the internal slave trade and fueled growing criticisms from northern abolitionists. In response, slave owners developed an elaborate proslavery ideology to justify their "peculiar institution." Some wealthy southerners, anxious about the difficulties of sustaining a slave society, sought to diversify the South's economy. However, this, too, was viewed as a threat to planters' political and economic power. Thus, the expansion of slavery westward provided opportunities but also presented new problems.

Southern Whites Move Westward and Demand Rights   The vast majority of southern white workers and farmers betrayed no sympathy for slaves. Most of those who lived on the margins of the rich plantation lands were closely tied to external cotton markets and large planters. Their counterparts who settled in the foothills and highlands, however, relied on diversified farming and benefited little from policies that enhanced the power of the big slave owners. Yet most wanted simply to be left to their own devices, and many still believed that slavery was the best way to maintain proper order in a society populated by both whites and blacks. Meanwhile, white workers in the state's urban areas, particularly those along the coast, benefited from the slave-produced cotton boom because it improved the general business climate.

Throughout the 1840s, the South continued to expand in both population and areas settled. In the mid-1840s, a rise in cotton prices increased the optimism and the profits of small farmers, rural merchants, and large planters alike. Between 1840 and 1860, the South's total population grew by half (from seven million to eleven million). In the wake of the removal of the Cherokee and other Indian nations during the 1830s, whites flooded into former Indian lands, and the railroad soon followed. The cotton kingdom, which in 1845 already extended from the Carolinas southwestward to Texas and from Tennessee down to Florida, now pushed into new areas. Frontier settlements in western Missouri and Arkansas, which contained but a tiny number of settlers in 1840, experienced the most rapid growth (Table 9.1).

Life on the frontier was difficult, and for whites who had become used to living in more settled eastern regions, the move westward often required substantial adjustments. Small farmers had to carve fields out of forests without the aid of slaves, and well-to-do planters were forced to subject their families to the ruder life on the cotton frontier. Having moved from North Carolina to Alabama with her slaveholder husband, May Drake expressed her discontent in letters to her family: "To a female who has once been blest with every comfort, and even every luxury, blest with the society of a large and respectable circle of relations and friends . . . to such people Mississippi and Alabama are but a dreary waste." Another wrote, "The farmers in this country [Alabama] live in a miserable manner. They think only of making money, and their houses are hardly fit to live in." Although some planters, like the Natchez nabobs, tried to bring luxury and refinement to the frontier, many relocating white families found themselves struggling to rebuild homes, communities, and social networks.

Yet even in these new territories where everyone faced some hardships, settlers of moderate means developed resentments against wealthy planters. For instance, the *Mississippi Free Trader*, published in Natchez, editorialized

TABLE 9.1 Geographic and Economic Mobility of Poor Household Heads in North Carolina and Mississippi, 1840–1860

Poor whites moved frequently in search of better opportunities. As the southern frontier pushed westward, so did poor whites, and at least some acquired land in these frontier areas. Nonetheless, the vast majority remained landless, whether they stayed in one place or resettled farther west. This chart illustrates the geographic mobility and the difficulties in obtaining land for poor whites in Davidson County in central North Carolina from 1840 to 1860 and in the newly opened settlements of Pontotoc County and Tishomingo County in northeast Mississippi from 1850 to 1860. Charles C. Bolton, *Poor Whites of the Antebellum South: Tenants and Laborers in Central North Carolina and Northeast Mississippi* (1994).

	Davidson Co. 1840–1850[*]	Davidson Co. 1850–1860[*]	Pontotoc Co. 1850–1860[*]	Tishomingo Co. 1850–1860[*]
Left the county[†]	86 (48%)	116 (64%)	143 (80%)	134 (75%)
Stayed in the same county and acquired land	51 (28%)	18 (11%)	20 (11%)	22 (12%)
Stayed in the same county and remained landless	44 (24%)	47 (26%)	15 (8%)	22 (12%)
Total number of household heads	181	181	178	178

[*]Source: Tax Lists, 1840, Davidson County Records, NCDAH; 1840 Federal Census for Davidson County, Schedule 1; 1850 and 1860 Federal Censuses for Davidson County, Schedules I and IV. 1850 and 1860 Federal Censuses for Pontotoc and Tishomingo counties, Schedules I and IV. A determination of household heads for Davidson County in 1840 was made by matching people from Tax Lists with the household heads listed on the 1840 Federal Census.
[†]Includes individuals who died during the period.

"They Had Given Me the Best They Had": A Traveler Describes the Rural South

This account was written by a traveler in the interior areas of Georgia in 1849, who prevailed upon local families for hospitality. His description conveys one family's poverty; later in the same account, he describes the household of an alcoholic, illiterate owner of forty slaves in even less flattering terms.

Being anxious to see how the poorest class of people lived in the interior, at night I stopped at the door-way of a very small and rudely-constructed hut, and inquired if I could 'get stay' for the night. At first I was refused; but upon representing myself a stranger in the country, and fearing to go farther, as there were 'forks in the road' and 'creeks to cross' before reaching another house, they finally consented to my staying.

The cabin contained but one room, with no windows; the chimney, built of mud and stones, was, as is usual in the South, outside the house. The furniture of the house was scanty in the extreme; a roughly-constructed frame, on which was laid a corn-shuck mattress, a pine table, and a few shuck-bottomed 'cha'rs.'

I had not been long in this place, before preparations for supper commenced. An iron vessel . . . was brought and set over the fire; in this dish was roasted some coffee; afterward, in the same dish, a 'corn cake' was baked, and still again some rank old ham was fried, and the corn-cake laid in the ashes to have it 'piping hot.' This constituted our supper. . . . A pet deer stalked in through the open door-way, and helped himself from the table without molestation.

Bed-time coming, one by one the family retired to the corner, and all lay together on the cornshucks. . . . Morning came, and . . . I asked the hostess for a wash, and the vessel which had served for roasting, baking and frying the evening previous was now brought; and . . . I washed myself in the dish out of which twelve hours before I had eaten a hearty supper. I paid them well, and thanked them kindly, for they had given me the best they had.

"Interior Georgia Life and Scenery by a Southern Traveler," *Knickerbocker Magazine,* August 1849, 113–118; reprinted in William E. Gienapp, ed., *The Civil War and Reconstruction: A Documentary Collection* (W. W. Norton, 2001), 17–18.

in April 1842 on the relative value of small farmers and larger planters to the city's economy. The small farmers, it noted,

would crowd our streets with fresh and healthy supplies of home productions, and the proceeds would be expended here among our merchants, grocers, and artisans. The large planters . . . for the most part, sell their cotton in Liverpool; buy their wines in London or Havre; their negro clothing in Boston; their plantation implements and supplies in Cincinnati; and their groceries and fancy articles in New Orleans.

Conflicts among southern whites centered on several issues, including political representation, taxation, debt, and common rights to land and waterways. Planters, for instance, successfully supported legislation that put a ceiling on the taxation of slaves. This meant fewer state funds available for projects—such as roads, railroads, and canals—that might benefit the citizens at large. Nonslaveholding whites had a difficult time changing such laws because many southern states continued to use property qualifications to restrict voting rights and holding office. In the seaboard states, the eastern counties where large planters held sway were accorded much greater representation than were the western counties, which initially had been sparsely settled. As those western counties became more populated, the planter-dominated legislatures failed to reapportion representation.

In addition, the property limits on voting lessened the electoral leverage of small farmers and working-class whites throughout each state. In North Carolina, which had some of the most restrictive requirements in the South into the 1850s, only adult white males who owned at least fifty acres could cast a ballot in the state senate election. This requirement disenfranchised about one-half of the state's potential voters. To run for the state senate, a man had to own at least three hundred acres, and election to the state's House of Commons required a one-hundred-acre holding. The governor was required to own land worth $2,000 and was not chosen by popular election until after 1850.

Not all southern states imposed such severe restrictions on political participation. Mississippi, for instance, eliminated property qualifications for office much earlier than elsewhere in the South. Still, the vast majority of those who held office were planters, slave owners, or prosperous nonslaveholding yeomen. This was in part because party leaders were prominent and privileged men, such as the Natchez nabobs, and they set the agenda as well as the election slates for local, county, and state elections. In addition, elections were public events, presided over by local planters or merchants. The secret ballot was not yet utilized, ensuring that most nonslaveholding whites, who depended on their economic superiors for credit, employment, or other forms of assistance, would support the planter candidate.

Yet nonslaveholding whites did not simply defer to the planter elite. Despite their limited electoral power, they made demands on legislators and through the courts. During the 1840s and 1850s, property qualifications for voting were eliminated in nearly all the southern states, and the number and proportion of representatives from western regions in state legislatures were increased. Like their counterparts in the early nineteenth century, less well-to-do whites continued to protest the confiscation of property for debts, the construction of dams that interfered with fishing rights, and the fencing of supposedly communal lands by individual farmers and planters. Sometimes the protests were orderly affairs, involving petitions to legislatures and claims made at court. At other times, near riots erupted as mobs of dispossessed or indebted whites railed against their treatment at the hands of wealthier neighbors or high-handed judges.

There were, however, significant barriers to sustaining opposition to planter policies among nonslaveholding whites. First, many poor and working-class whites were as deeply racist as their elite counterparts. When planters claimed that challenges to their authority would increase the chances of slave uprisings or an expansion of free black rights, most southern whites toned down their grievances. Just as important, nonslaveholding whites were themselves a varied group. Yeomen farmers who owned land and made a good living joined planters in confiscating the goods of indebted landless whites. Even those at the very bottom of white society did not always feel that they had a common cause. Some couples lived as man and wife without benefit of marriage and found their only allies among petty criminals, free blacks, and other marginal groups. These were ostracized by their more respectable counterparts who, although landless, maintained steady work habits, stable families, and a proper distance from blacks and criminals.

Probably numbering some 30 to 50 percent of all whites in the South in the mid-nineteenth century, landless whites comprised a large and diverse population at the bottom of the white social hierarchy. It was these very differences among the South's nonslaveholding residents that limited their ability and desire to forge a meaningful opposition to planter control. Yet various groups outside the planter class continued to assert their own rights and interests, thereby complicating the lives of planters who hoped to achieve absolute authority over their inferiors, white as well as black.

The Ravages of the Internal Slave Trade Until about 1850, as slavery expanded southward and westward, declining profits characterized older areas of cultivation, such as Virginia, Maryland, and North Carolina. The resulting losses were offset in part by monies made on the internal slave trade. Planters in the Upper South could reap a significant return on early investments by selling the best field hands and most fertile mothers among their slaves to planters in South Carolina, Georgia, Alabama, and lands west (Map 9.2). But without new slaves coming into the Upper South, the prospects for future income were limited, and the ability to leave one's heirs a planter lifestyle was subverted.

The internal slave trade was one of the cruelest aspects of a harsh system. Although slaves had always been subject to sale, the possibility of being

MAP 9.2 The Spread of Cotton, 1820–1860

In 1820, cotton production was centered in the eastern seaboard states. Its spread to the South and West in the 1830s, 1840s, and 1850s ensured that the internal slave trade would also expand throughout this period. The sale of slaves from the Upper South to the Lower South provided profits for slave owners in both regions but resulted in painful separations for African American families and harsher working conditions for those African Americans who were sold into the Deep South.

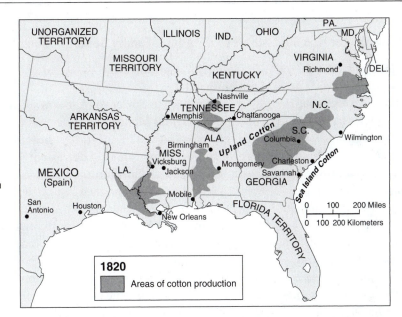

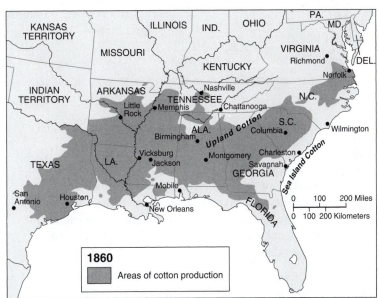

sold to a plantation hundreds of miles from one's family increased dramatically in the 1840s with the extension of slavery into Alabama, Louisiana, Mississippi, Missouri, Arkansas, and Texas. Because the slaves who were in greatest demand were between the ages of twenty and fifty years, a high percentage of those sold left spouses and children behind. As slavery's heartland moved southwestward, the forced migration of hundreds of thousands of African Americans caused the massive destruction of families. Fannie

"My Master Has Sold Albert to a Trader": Family Separation in Slavery

Maria and Richard Perkins were owned by different masters, one in Charlottesville and the other in Staunton, Virginia. In 1852, a frantic Maria wrote to Richard about the sale of their children and the possibility of being sold herself. Most slaves did not know how to read and write, and this letter, in Mrs. Perkins's own handwriting, is unusual.

Charlottesville, Oct. 8th, 1852

Dear Husband

I write you a letter to let you know my distress. My master has sold Albert to a trader on Monday court day and myself and [our] other child is for sale also and I want [to] . . . hear from you very soon before next court [day] if you can. . . . I don't want you to wait till Christmas. I want you to tell Dr. Hamelton and your master if either will buy me they can attend to it now and then I can go afterwards. I don't want a trader to get me. They asked me if I had got any person to buy me and I told them no. They took me to the courthouse too [but] they never put me up [for sale]. A man [by] the name of Brady bought Albert and [he] is gone. I don't know where. They say he lives in Scottesville. My things is in several places some is in Staunton and if I should be sold I don't know what will become of them. I don't expect to meet with the luck to get that way till I am quite heartsick. Nothing more.

I am and ever will be your kind wife,
Maria Perkins.

Ulrich B. Phillips, ed., *Life and Labor in the Old South* (1929).

Berry, a former Virginia slave who was interviewed in 1937, recalled a day when

> There was a great crying and carrying on among the slaves who had been sold. Two or three of them gals had young babies they were taking with them. . . . As soon as they got on the train this ol' new master had the train stopped and made them poor gal mothers take babies off and laid them precious things on the ground and left them to live or die.

At other times, it was the mothers who were left behind and the children who were sold away. Whether adults or children, slaves sold into the Deep South faced even hotter and less hospitable climates, more demanding work schedules, and harsher punishments than those they had experienced in the Upper South.

The internal slave trade also created problems for whites who resided in what had once been profitable plantation regions. The sale of slaves to other regions increased owners' fears that slaves would retaliate against slaveholders and their families and sometimes ensured that those left behind would be more recalcitrant and resistant than ever. In certain areas of Virginia and

"I Will Come Back"

Having purchased his freedom, an Alabama ex-slave named Peter Still bade farewell to his enslaved wife, Vina. Still's self-purchased manumission in 1850 — an opportunity few masters offered their slaves — had no effect on his wife, who was owned by a different individual. Kate E. R. Pickard, *The Kidnapped and the Ransomed, Being the Personal Recollection of Peter Still and His Wife "Vina," After Forty Years of Slavery* (1856) — American Social History Project.

Maryland, the sale of large numbers of slaves increased the relative proportion of free blacks in the population. This development raised further anxieties about free blacks' influence on those left in bondage and their competition for jobs with poor whites, more of whom were now forced to seek work in urban areas. Some whites in the Upper South wondered whether slavery's advantages still outweighed its costs.

The Proslavery Movement During the 1830s and 1840s, revolts and escapes by slaves, the growth of the free black community, demands by nonslaveholding whites, and conflicts with overseers and wives all challenged the power of planters. The British abolition of West Indian slavery in 1833, the Panic of 1837, and the emancipation of slaves in the French West Indies in 1848 intensified slave owners' concerns over the future of the South's increasingly peculiar institution. Attacks from northern opponents—a growing abolitionist movement, the defection of the Grimké sisters and fugitive slaves, the condemnation of church leaders, and massive petition campaigns—heightened slave owners' concerns as well.

The defenders of slavery did not retreat, however. Believing that expansion into western lands presaged a new day for planters, they developed an aggressive defense of their way of life and further restricted possibilities for change. Previously referred to apologetically as a necessary but temporary evil, black bondage was now described as the natural order of things. In the words of South Carolina Senator John C. Calhoun, slavery was "a positive good," an institution that was beneficial to planters, slaves, and all other social groups.

Calhoun held up slave labor as in all respects superior to wage labor. The sharpening of social conflicts in the North, he claimed, testified to the superiority of outright bondage. "There is and has always been, in an advanced stage of wealth and civilization," Calhoun told the U.S. Senate, "a conflict between labor and capital. The condition of society in the South exempts us from the disorders and dangers resulting from this conflict." This fact, he asserted, demonstrates "how vastly more favorable our condition of society is to that of other sections for free and stable institutions." According to Calhoun and like-minded planters, the food, shelter, and clothing provided to slaves were superior to those available to free laborers of the North, and planters did not cut loose their slaves when sick or aged.

Thomas Dew, a young professor at the College of William and Mary in Virginia, crafted the first significant proslavery document. His *Review of the Debates in the Virginia Legislature of 1831 and 1832* offered an argument on behalf of slavery in the guise of commentaries on the legislature's debates. Drawing on historical examples from ancient civilizations and on biblical justifications from the Old and New Testaments, Dew claimed that slavery was best both for the South and for the slaves. Planters, in this scenario, were both the instruments of God and the upholders of classical traditions and values. Indeed, biblical support for slavery may have been the most widely cited rationale for maintaining the institution, because scripture offered the most effective response to northern abolitionists and ministers who claimed to have right and righteousness on their side.

South Carolina Governor George Duffie was one of many politicians who embraced biblical justifications for slavery. Speaking before his state legislature in 1835, he clearly distinguished between the character and rights of whites and of blacks, justifying slavery only for those of African ancestry. Blacks, he proclaimed, were "destined by providence" for bondage. They were "in all respects, physical, moral, and political, inferior to millions of the human race" and therefore "unfit for self-government of any kind."

During the next twenty-five years, proslavery politicians, professors, physicians, and publicists dutifully elaborated the racist argument, offering a stream of scientific as well as religious evidence in slavery's defense. The culmination of these arguments appeared in the 1850s in two books written by Virginian George Fitzhugh. In *Sociology for the South* and *Cannibals All*, Fitzhugh claimed that the reckless individualism fostered by "free labor" in the North was far more exploitative than was the paternal guardianship that characterized slavery. In his view, African Americans were a childlike race that required lifetime care and control.

Such racist doctrine was scientific nonsense, but it served three important purposes for the slave owners. First, it justified the bondage of African Americans by ruling out all arguments based on universal human rights. Second, it undermined the status and claims of free blacks. Third, it accomplished both of these objectives without explicitly threatening the rights of poor southern whites, whose support (or at least toleration) the slaveholders required.

The development of the proslavery argument both reflected and reinforced an increasingly rigid southern political and social structure at precisely the moment when reform and innovation were most necessary. The expansion of plantations into new geographical areas turned labor abundance into labor scarcity for many planters and exacerbated their financial dependence on single-crop, export-driven agriculture. As the Panic of 1837 had shown, dependence on a single crop and on foreign

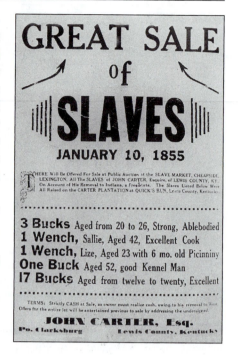

Slaves for Sale

The 23 slaves to be sold belonged to a Kentucky planter, John Carter, who decided to "liquidate his assets" before moving to the free state of Indiana. *Picaninny* was a derogatory term commonly used by whites to refer to a black child. John Winston Coleman, *Slavery Times in Kentucky* (1940).

"Guarded from Want, from Beggary Secure": A Southern Defense of Slavery

The following poem, written in 1856 by William J. Grayson, a South Carolina planter, lawyer, and congressman who opposed secession but supported slavery, argues that slavery not only guaranteed a stable labor force, but also benefited blacks by providing them with a secure life. The poem is entitled "The Hireling and the Slave."

Taught by the master's efforts, by his care
Fed, clothed, protected many a patient year,
From trivial numbers now to millions grown,
With all the white man's useful arts their own,
Industrious, docile, skilled in wood and field,
To guide the plow, the sturdy axe to wield,
The Negroes schooled by slavery embrace
The highest portion of the Negro race;
And none the savage native will compare,
Of barbarous Guinea, with its offspring here.

If bound to daily labor while he lives,
His is the daily bread that labor gives;
Guarded from want, from beggary secure,
He never feels what hireling crowds endure,
Nor know, like them, in hopeless want to crave,
For wife and child, the comforts of the slave,
Or the sad thought that, when about to die,
He leaves them to the cold world's charity,
And sees them slowly seek the poor-house door—
The last, vile, hated refuge of the poor. . . .

The master's lighter rule insures
More order than the sternest code secures;
No mobs of factious workmen gather here,
No strikes we dread, no lawless riots fear; . . .

Seditious schemes in bloody tumults end,
Parsons incite, and senators defend,
But not where slaves their easy labors ply,
Safe from the snare, beneath a master's eye;
In useful tasks engaged, employed their time,
Untempted by the demagogue to crime,
Secure they toil, uncursed their peaceful life,
With labor's hungry broils and wasteful strife.
No want to good, no faction to deplore,
The slaves escape the perils of the poor.

William J. Grayson, *The Hireling and the Slave, Chicora, and Other Poems* (1856), 21–45.

THE NEGRO AS HE WAS.

THE NEGRO AS HE IS.

THE NORTHERN LABORER.

THE SOUTHERN LABORER.

markets made white southerners vulnerable to economic developments over which they had little control. The spread of slavery also intensified challenges from northerners who opposed the system on moral, political, and economic grounds; from slaves whose family and community networks were shattered by the internal slave trade; and from southern whites who feared competition from blacks or resented the tyranny of planters.

The Benefits of Slavery

Two pages from a proslavery tract published around 1860 presented the contrasting fates of unfree and free labor: while fortunate slaves were civilized and, in old age, cared for by benevolent masters, the northern wageworker faced only exhaustion and destitution. From the private collection of Larry E. Tise.

Resistance to Industrialization and the Limits of Economic Diversification   Although few planters questioned the institution of slavery itself, some began considering the advantages of economic diversification in the South. But during the mid-1840s, despite serious fluctuations in the prices paid for cotton, tobacco, and rice, the profitability of plantation agriculture allowed those who supported the status quo to gain the upper hand. Advo-

Free Negroes in the North

Apologists for slavery often constructed a grotesque picture of free blacks in the North. According to this etching published during the Civil War, without the supervision of benevolent masters, northern African Americans descended into violence and degradation. V. Blada (A. J. Volck), *Sketches from the Civil War in North America, 1861, '62, '63* (1863) — Print Collection, Miriam and Ira Wallach Division of Art, Prints, and Photographs, New York Public Library, Astor, Lenox and Tilden Foundations.

cates of diversification found it difficult to gain adherents when both agricultural production and the demand for plantation crops were on the increase. With the wealthiest residents of the South investing larger and larger sums in land and slaves, nonstaple food crops remained marginal to the region's economy.

Some investors, particularly in the cities and towns of the Southeast, did begin to diversify by investing in industry. In the 1840s, William Gregg's textile factory in Graniteville, South Carolina, and Joseph Reid Anderson's Tredegar Iron Works in Richmond, Virginia, were among the most profitable southern industrial ventures. Whereas the textile labor force was composed primarily of poor white women and children, the iron industry recruited African Americans, enslaved and free, in large numbers. Although these employment patterns demonstrated the capacity of women and blacks for industrial labor, they limited the potential for industrial growth. Only the poorest white women could work for wages without damaging their family's reputation; the increased employment of free blacks raised anxieties among skilled white men; and slaves were generally more valuable in agriculture than in industry. Factories, then, could flourish only on the periphery of plantation society.

Although industrialization was marginal to the southern economy, some planters still saw it as a threat to the institution of slavery. Any work off the plantation brought a slave into close contact with free laborers and with new ideas about life and liberty. That exposure encouraged and assisted attempts to escape slavery. Frederick Douglass's experiences provide a good example. Hostile southern white workers had once forced Douglass to return to his plantation from the docks of Baltimore. Later, however, he found himself hired out on the docks again in friendlier surroundings. There, according to Douglass, two Irish longshoremen "expressed the deepest sympathy for me, and the most dedicated hatred of slavery. They went so far as to tell me that I ought to run away and go to the North, that I should find friends there, and that I should then be as free as anybody." Douglass "remembered their words and their advice" and, a few years later, escaped to the North by passing as a free black sailor, an impersonation that was aided by his experience in the shipyard and the assistance of real free blacks. Other slaves simply took advantage of the relative anonymity that large cities provided and disappeared into the South's urban free black population.

Old Virginia Labor-saving Machine

A cartoon in an 1857 edition of the northern *Harper's New Monthly Magazine* satirized the planting techniques espoused by "Squire Broadacre," a Virginia farmer. With access to slave labor, many southern planters resisted technical innovations, mechanical and otherwise, that would improve agricultural output. "A Winter in the South," *Harper's New Monthly Magazine* (September 1857) — American Social History Project.

It was urban life more than industrial labor that led to Douglass's escape. In fact, in some areas, such as Richmond and Lynchburg, Virginia, slaves worked in factories without any weakening of the system of bondage. Moreover, industrial slavery was one way to breathe new life into the southern economy without challenging the basic racial and labor relations of the region. Still, many planters assumed that industry and urbanization were synonymous and that both threatened the southern way of life.

For the cities' detractors, slave flight was by no means the only problem. The greater freedom (especially freedom of movement) that generally accompanied urban employment tended to erode the slave owners' power and ability to demand unquestioned deference from blacks. "The ties which bound together the master and the slave," the New Orleans *Daily Picayune* complained, were being "gradually severed" in that city, as slave workers "become intemperate, disorderly, and lose the respect which the servant should entertain for the master." The behavior of free blacks, fugitives, and resistant slaves in cities was considered "contagious upon those who do not possess these dangerous privileges."

Most slave owners, then, feared and despised the possibility of increased industrialization and the growth of cities in the South. "We have no cities. We don't want them," exclaimed one white Alabaman, who no doubt expressed the feelings of many of his neighbors. "We want no manufactures; we desire no trading, no mechanical or manufacturing classes. As long as we have our rice, our sugar, our tobacco, and our cotton, we can command wealth to purchase all we want."

Above all, slave owners worried that free wage earners and their employers would seek first to limit the use of slave labor and eventually collide with the whole slave-labor system. The small circle of southern leaders who advocated economic development and diversification agreed. One of their leading spokesmen, Senator George Mason of Virginia, complained that "slavery discourages arts and manufactures. The poor despise labor when performed by slaves." To distinguish white from black urban workers, white artisans demanded preferential hiring and voting rights based on their race, justifying planters' fears that industrialization and urbanization were the beginning of a slippery slope that would disrupt their traditional power and privilege.

Even more frightening to slave owners, however, was the idea that white and black workers might make common cause, a situation that was more likely to occur in the few cities with high rates of immigration from Europe. In Baltimore, New Orleans, Charleston, and Richmond, for example, the urban working-class population increasingly included immigrants, who seemed to have little loyalty to or even respect for the region's deeply rooted system of chattel slavery. A Richmond newspaper assured its white subscribers that a major advantage of slave labor was its tendency to exclude "a populace made up of the dregs of Europe." But some African Americans viewed those "dregs" as potential allies and tried to assist them. For instance, in 1847, the members of Richmond's First African American Baptist Church sent $40 to Ireland to help victims of the famine. Later, they donated smaller sums to assist the Irish poor in Richmond. The *Charleston Standard* no doubt spoke for many slave owners when it branded foreign-born workers as "a curse rather than a blessing to our peculiar institution."

The South might have sustained a plantation system based on slavery and staple-crop agriculture and, simultaneously, developed an extensive industrial base by encouraging immigrants to settle in the region. In fact, many southerners who advocated economic diversification insisted that commerce and manufacturing would complement, not threaten, agriculture. James D. B. DeBow, who was inspired by the Memphis commercial convention of 1845, established a journal, the *Commercial Review of the South and the West*, that proclaimed in print, "Commerce is King." DeBow was also an ardent proslavery advocate who believed that only by creating southern commercial and industrial enterprises could the region maintain its existing traditions and institutions. This approach was rendered impossible, however, by planters' fears of foreign workers and their refusal to recognize manufacturing or wage labor as more than unworthy stepchildren in the southern economy. Indeed, planters tended to regard free labor as subversive and actively disruptive of the benefits of bound labor.

By the time DeBow's *Review* gained a significant readership at midcentury, the opportunity to reshape the South's economic structure had passed. Although complaints about planters' dependency on northern capital and commerce persisted, when it came to practical action, most planters chose to invest in land and slaves. By the late 1840s, as prices and profits for cotton, rice, sugar, and tobacco rose, ventures that would extend the geographical boundaries of plantation slavery generated more interest than those that would diversify the economy.

Extending the Empire for Slavery

Southern whites had long dreamed of extending their dominion into tropical climates. Congressmen and presidents cast greedy glances at Cuba and
Central America throughout the early and mid-nineteenth century. In New
Orleans, the large number of French, free blacks, and slaves who arrived
from Sainte-Domingue (present-day Haiti) after the revolution there in the
1790s gave the city a Caribbean flair that made planters in the area think of
the possibilities of exploiting the West Indies. Proslavery adventurers actually mounted invasions of Mexico, Cuba, and Nicaragua in this period. And
the successful settlement and "emancipation" of Texas in the 1830s revitalized dreams of a slave empire that stretched into Mexico and the Caribbean
(Map 9.3).

Yet opening new lands to slavery created perils as well as opportunities.
Territories acquired by the United States in the 1830s and 1840s inspired
increasingly heated debates over the boundaries of slave society. When war
erupted with Mexico in 1846, the criticisms from abolitionists intensified. In
its aftermath, Whigs and Democrats were faced with difficult choices as
some Americans who were adamantly opposed to the extension of slavery
began to take a stand in the partisan political arena.

The Lure of New Territories to the South and West   After Texas, Cuba
was perhaps the most appealing prospect for annexation. In 1823, Secretary
of State John Quincy Adams claimed, "There are laws of political as well as
physical gravitation, and if an apple, severed by a tempest from its native
tree, cannot choose but fall to the ground, Cuba, forcibly disjoined from its
own unnatural connection with Spain, and incapable of self-support, can
gravitate only towards the North American Union." In 1848, President James
K. Polk tried unsuccessfully to help this "natural" gravitation along by offering Spain $100 million for the island. Similar offers, supported by circles of
Cubans who were dissatisfied with Spanish rule, were made several more
times over the next decade, although without success.

Southern planters also investigated economic possibilities in California during the 1840s. To encourage larger numbers of U.S. residents to
settle the region, Anglo-American immigrants to the West Coast described
the rich lands of the Sacramento and San Joaquin valleys and the docile
population of Indian workers. Initially, these pioneers cared little about the
origins of the new settlers, as long as the United States gained control of the
region from Mexico. But planters, such as Richard Fulton of Missouri,
wanted to know, "Is California a slave state and could our citizens bring
their slaves with them?"

Those who were already established in the area tried to reassure potential southern émigrés. Rancher John Marsh, who had gained significant

MAP 9.3   The Lure of Caribbean Territories

After the United States acquired the Louisiana Territory and Florida, wealthy white South-erners began looking for new areas in which to expand their plantation economy. Some set their sights on the Caribbean. Easily accessible from Florida and with a long history of slave-produced sugar, rum, tobacco, and coffee, Cuba seemed particularly attractive. Even Sainte-Domingue (Haiti), the site of a successful slave rebellion led by Toussaint L'Ouverture in 1791, was considered a possibility for future development of the plantation system. Although plans to add Caribbean islands to the United States did not progress much in the mid-nineteenth century, Cuba and Puerto Rico were the first areas to come under U.S. control when the United States engaged in its first imperial adventures in the 1890s. Louis A. Pérez, Jr., *Cuba and the U.S.: Ties of Singular Intimacy* (1994).

experience in Indian affairs, admitted that Mexico did have laws against slavery, but he assured prospective migrants that the native peoples were willing workers. He even claimed that they submitted to "flagellation with more humility than negroes." Pierson B. Reading, a former New Orleans cotton broker who resettled in California, wrote to a friend back home in 1844, "The Indians of California make as obedient and humble slaves as the negroes in the south," and "for a mere trifle, you can secure their services for life." Although the indigenous peoples proved more resistant than these descriptions suggest, southern whites, encouraged by increased demand for agricultural products, eagerly envisioned plantations stretching from the Atlantic to the Pacific, worked by dark-skinned slaves.

The dreams of westward expansion had fueled political conflicts within and between the North and the South since the 1810s (see Chapter 8). The Lone Star Republic of Texas generated intensive debates in the 1830s and 1840s. It had sought U.S. statehood from the moment it achieved independence in 1836, but northern hostility to admitting this immense slaveholding territory into the Union had postponed action for several years. In 1844, however, the Democratic Party platform tied support for Texas statehood to the demand—popular among northern farmers—for the annexation of all of Oregon (a region that was claimed by both England and the United States). Farmers from the Old Northwest had been eyeing Oregon's Willamette Valley for years. By 1843, thousands of wagons were already following the Oregon Trail west from Missouri. Southern planters and politicians began to believe that the North's appetite for new lands might at last provide the basis for Texas statehood. The election the following year turned on the issue of admitting Texas and annexing Oregon.

As was noted earlier, the Democrats chose James K. Polk as their party standard-bearer, overlooking both President Tyler, who was considered ineffective, and Martin Van Buren, who was less enthusiastic about the admission of Texas. Andrew Jackson was a great fan of Polk who, like Jackson, was a Tennessee Democrat with a vision of America as an expansive nation. The Whigs nominated Henry Clay, but the party was divided over the wisdom of westward growth. Southern Whigs were particularly angered at Clay's failure to support the admission of Texas, whereas northern Whigs were annoyed that Clay even considered taking such a stand.

Polk's election was viewed as a mandate for expansion. The new administration did not annex all of Oregon, however. Instead, it agreed with Britain to define the forty-ninth parallel as the northern boundary of the United States, simply extending the eastern border with Canada westward. But even before this boundary dispute was settled, the U.S. Congress approved the annexation of Texas in December 1845.

The War with Mexico President Polk had even grander plans for expansion. During his one term in office, he oversaw the acquisition of more territory by the United States than any other president. His predecessor, President John Tyler, completed the annexation of Texas, but Polk presided over the settlement of the disputed Oregon Territory and then turned his attention to wresting more land from Mexico. Knowing that this plan would necessitate war, Polk sent U.S. troops across the Nueces River in Texas in January 1846 and into territory claimed by Mexico (Map 9.4). News that Mexican troops had crossed the Rio Grande River in April and attacked American soldiers then led Polk to demand war with Mexico. Whigs, however, thought that Polk had provoked the conflict, and a majority voted

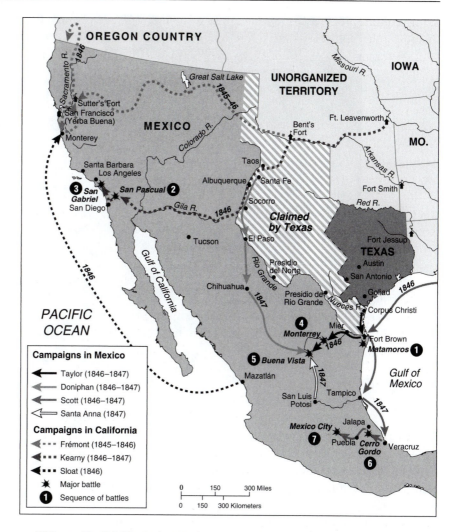

MAP 9.4 The U.S. War Against Mexico, 1846–1848

During the war with Mexico, U.S. troops seized the northern sections of Mexico, and John C. Frémont led an uprising of U.S. settlers in present-day California. At the same time, under the leadership of generals Winfield Scott and Zachary Taylor, the U.S. Army repulsed Mexican troops led by General Santa Anna. Defeated on all fronts, Mexico surrendered vast territories to the United States, comprising all or parts of present-day Texas, Arizona, New Mexico, Colorado, Utah, Nevada, and Wyoming. California became an independent republic but was soon annexed by the United States as well.

against the declaration of war. The newly elected Whig representative from Illinois, Abraham Lincoln, even demanded evidence about the precise spot where Mexicans had supposedly shed American blood.

Still, the Democratic majority carried the day. "As war exists," the president then told Congress, "we are called upon by every consideration of duty and patriotism to vindicate with decision the honor, the rights, and the

War News from Mexico
In Richard Caton Woodville's 1848 painting, guests at the "American Hotel" (who represented a cross-section of the nation's white citizenry) demonstratively reacted to news about the Mexican War. Their almost comical behavior was in marked contrast to the subdued response of the black man and child in the picture's foreground. 1848, oil on canvas, 27 × 24 3/4 inches — National Academy of Design.

interests of our country." Many, probably most, Americans, North and South, agreed. Another Illinois representative, for instance, Democrat Stephen A. Douglas, was a fervent champion of westward expansion. He helped to boost the war spirit in Congress and branded critics such as Lincoln "traitors."

Despite the arid lands that made up most of northern Mexico, many slaveholders eagerly looked forward to creating new slave states from these hoped-for territories. "Every battle fought in Mexico," cheered the Charleston, South Carolina, *Courier*, "and every dollar spent there, but insures the acquisition of territory which must widen the field of Southern enterprise and power in the future. And the final result will be to readjust the power of the [Southern] confederacy, so as to give us control over the operation of government in all time to come."

For proslavery forces, the chance to acquire additional lands in the Southwest offered numerous benefits. The spread of slavery would aid planters in the Upper South by creating an even greater demand and higher price for their excess slaves. Small farmers who owned no slaves (a group that would constitute three-fourths of southern white families by 1860)

"We Are Engaged in a War of Conquest": Opposition to the War Against Mexico

These excerpts from a lecture by Charles C. Shackford, a Unitarian Universalist minister in Lynn, Massachusetts, criticize the premises and results of the U.S. war against Mexico and the lack of vocal opposition to it by northern citizens and politicians.

We are engaged in a war of conquest. All the resources of our nation for to-day and many days to come, are applied to inflict the horrors of war upon a neighboring people. We are recorded in the book of history, as the murderers of thousands whose only crime was living upon their native soil. . . . Truly is this matter the question of to-day; and the question not of politicians merely, but of every individual who has heart, or thought, or conscience. . . .

With the cancer of slavery feeding upon our system, this war was inevitable. . . . The North, with a fatal spirit of acquiescence, has submitted to one encroachment after another upon the spirit of freedom; and now, floated upon the surface, it is borne along to share the retribution. There remains but one way of escape. Slavery, that hydra, which but gains in strength from every act of feeble opposition and tame submission, must be slain. . . . At every new victory of the accursed system, some feeble cry is raised, 'that this encroaching evil must be opposed henceforth,' and then all is still. . . . A war in [our country's] defence, however iniquitous, a measure however wrong, has but to be entered upon, and then they pronounce it right to aid in its completion. . . .

Glorious government! which can spend millions . . . to subdue a weak, divided, miserable country, while a deaf ear is turned to a whole people of noble-hearted workmen dying for bread. . . . No money for charity, none for justice, none for the payment of claims long due our citizens, none for internal commerce, for science, for the promotion of the means of human comfort; all must be taken to pay the hirelings in this war of slavery! Such is the glory that encircles our nation's brow!

Charles C. Shackford, *Citizen's Appeal in Regard to the War with Mexico. A Lecture* (Andrews & Prentiss, 1848).

could hope for a better chance on the new western lands, thereby alleviating the pressures on the planter class to respond to their needs by redistributing existing wealth. Finally, the rapid growth of a nonslaveholding and increasingly antislavery North endangered the political autonomy of the slaveholding South. Geographical expansion would help to ensure that planters had increased representation in the Senate through the admission of new slave states. This would prevent the North from using the federal government to block the interests of slaveholders.

In some parts of the country, however, the enthusiasm of slaveholders for war and their vision of a slave confederacy inspired vigorous opposition. Despite the passage of a resolution supporting the president's declaration of war, a majority in the House of Representatives also voted in favor of a Whig proposal that declared that the war had been "unnecessarily and unconstitutionally begun by the President of the United States." And while a prowar demonstration on May 20, 1846, occupied one part of New York's City Hall Park, George Henry Evans and John Commerford addressed an antiwar rally in another. Having "great reason to believe" that the Mexican War was the work of Texans and their business allies, the rally organizers urged "the Commander in Chief of the army to withdraw his forces, now on the Rio Grande, to some undisputed land belonging to the United States." And if war proved finally unavoidable, then the American sponsors of prowar meetings and messages "ought to be the first to volunteer, and the first to leave for the seat of war."

Opposition to the war was strong among northern farmers as well as some businessmen. The Massachusetts state legislature denounced the war and its "triple object of extending slavery, of strengthening the 'Slave Power,' and of obtaining control of the Free States" by gaining a slave-state majority in the Senate. The Cleveland *Plain Dealer* carried a speech by an Ohio

Genl Wool's Staff
Calle Real to South

Dimly Viewed
Popular fervor for the Mexican War was fanned by visual reporting that promoted patriotic and nationalistic sentiments. Printmakers strove to satisfy the public's desire for news from the front. In the field, daguerreotypists struggled with a cumbersome and fragile new technology, trying to capture the world's first photographs of war. In this rare outdoor scene, Brigadier General John E. Wool and his mounted troops paused for a photographer in Saltillo's Calle Real, halting in the middle of the road to accommodate the long time required to expose a photographic plate. Daguerreotype, c. 1847 — Yale Collection of Western Americana, Beinecke Rare Book and Manuscript Library.

Uncle Sam's Taylorifics

A beardless Uncle Sam sliced and booted Mexico across the Rio Grande in this bellicose 1846 lithograph cartoon. Henry R. Robinson (after a drawing by Edward W. Clay), 1846, lithograph — New-York Historical Society.

UNCLE SAM'S TAYLORIFICS

Democrat who argued that the administration's willingness to compromise with Britain on the Oregon boundary while going to war with Mexico over the Texas boundary demonstrated that "the administration is Southern! Southern! Southern! . . . Since the South have [sic] fixed boundaries for free territory, let the North fix boundaries for slave territories." And Connecticut Congressman Gideon Welles probably spoke for a majority of his constituents when he declared, we must "satisfy the northern people . . . that we are not to extend the institution of slavery as a result of this war."

Abolitionists helped to foment and then reinforce northern fears that the war was a planter conspiracy to ensure southern control over the nation. During the 1830s, nearly every acquisition of territory in the South inspired abolitionist outcries against the extension of slavery. Announcement of the outbreak of war with Mexico was received at the 1846 meeting of the American Anti-Slavery Society by means of the new magnetic telegraph. Abby Kelley, an abolitionist who had not planned to speak at the New York gathering, impulsively rose in indignation to express her opposition to the war. "Our fathers were successful in the Revolution, because they were engaged in a holy cause, and had right on their side. But in this case we have not. This nation is doomed," she proclaimed. She prayed for defeat but envisioned instead a U.S. victory followed by the day of reckoning, when southern slaves would join forces with western Indians, "who are only waiting to plant their tomahawks in the white man's skull."

As abolitionists engaged in acts of civil disobedience to protest the war, pacifists sometimes joined them. A young Henry David Thoreau refused to pay his taxes in protest against the war and was jailed in July 1846. The brief imprisonment inspired his classic essay "Resistance to Civil Government" (republished in 1866 under the title "Civil Disobedience"). Other antislavery advocates, however, followed Abby Kelley in taking a more belligerent pro-Mexico stance. Abolitionists across the country signed antiwar pledges and advocated military victory for Mexico. William Lloyd Garrison spoke for many abolitionists when he declared,

> I desire to see human life at all times held sacred; but in a struggle like this, so horribly unjust and offensive on our part, so purely of self-defence against lawless invaders on the part of the Mexicans, I feel as a matter of justice, to desire the overwhelming defeat of the American troops, and the success of the injured Mexicans.

The abolitionist campaign bolstered opposition to the war among some Americans, but popular enthusiasm was inspired by the rapid advancement of U.S. troops into Mexico.

Although the war lasted eighteen months, U.S. troops dominated the fighting. General Zachary Taylor captured northeastern Mexico, including Monterrey, in September 1846. Colonel Stephen Kearney captured Santa Fe that same fall and then joined the ongoing battle in California, where Mexican forces were quickly defeated. When Mexico refused to surrender, Polk sent General Winfield Scott to march troops north from Veracruz, on Mexico's Gulf Coast. Scott's army seized Mexico City in September 1847, forcing the Mexican government to negotiate the Treaty of Guadalupe-Hidalgo soon thereafter.

The success of the U.S. Army ensured the dismemberment of Mexico. In March 1848, the Senate approved the Treaty of Guadalupe-Hidalgo, granting the United States control over the provinces of California and New Mexico and moving the Texas-Mexican border southward from the Nueces River to the Rio Grande. The United States thus acquired vast new lands that offered seemingly limitless opportunities for economic advancement. But who would benefit most from these opportunities: southern planters, small farmers, or northern laborers? This question moved center stage in the nation's political debates.

Manifest Destiny and the Conflict over Slavery in the New Territories

Most white Americans, and certainly most Whigs, were not opposed to expansion. They might oppose expansion by force of arms or in the interest of slave owners, but even antiwar northerners generally agreed that the conquest of western lands benefited the nation. Journalist John L. O'Sullivan rallied support for westward expansion; in 1845, he claimed that

WANTED!
3,000 LABORERS
On the 12th Division of the
ILLINOIS CENTRAL RAILROAD
Wages, $1.25 per Day.

Fare, from New-York, only - - $4 ¾

By Railroad and Steamboat, to the work in the
State of Illinois.

Constant employment for two years or more given. Good board can be obtained at two dollars per week.

This is a rare chance for persons to go West, being sure of permanent employment in a healthy climate, where land can be bought cheap, and for fertility is not surpassed in any part of the Union.

Men with families preferred.

For further information in regard to it, call at the Central Railroad Office,

173 BROADWAY,
CORNER OF COURTLANDT ST.
NEW-YORK.
R. B. MASON, Chief Engineer.
H. PHELPS, Agent,

JULY, 1853.

Go West, Young Man!

This Illinois Central Railroad advertisement, probably directed to immigrants, was posted in New York City in 1853. American Museum of Immigration, National Park Service, U.S. Department of the Interior.

it was Americans' "manifest destiny to overspread the continent allotted by Providence for the free development of our yearly multiplying millions." Although O'Sullivan's New York colleague Horace Greeley cautioned that a "nation cannot simultaneously devote its energies to the absorption of others' territories and the improvement of its own," settlers in the disputed western territories were enthusiastic about expansion and relatively unconcerned about contradictions between American principles and practice.

In California, John C. Frémont, who worked with the U.S. Army's topographical corps there, was happy to oblige when Polk indicated that the U.S. naval fleet in the Pacific would support a settler uprising along the West Coast. In 1846, Frémont helped to organize a rebellion among U.S. citizens living in California, and the "Bear Republic" soon declared its independence from Mexico. Frémont was certain that annexation would soon follow, counting on his father-in-law, Senator Thomas Hart Benton of Missouri, to carry the banner of California statehood in Congress.

With war underway and further expansion seeming inevitable, politicians turned their attention to the fate of slavery in the territories that were now sure to be acquired. Congressman David Wilmot, a Pennsylvania Democrat, opened the debate almost immediately. In 1846, at Wilmot's initiative, the House of Representatives voted to prohibit slavery in any territory that was acquired through the war with Mexico. Although defeated in the Senate, the Wilmot Proviso had received the endorsement of all but one northern state legislature by 1849.

Wilmot never considered his proposal a move "designed especially for the benefit of the black race." Nevertheless, it won fervent support among people in the free states who opposed slavery. This sentiment was strongest in New England, where clergymen, followers of Garrison, Liberty Party adherents, and free blacks were among the numerous contingents of anti-slavery advocates by the late 1840s. In 1846, a convention of working people protested the fact that "there are at the present time three millions of our brethren and sisters groaning in chains on the Southern plantations." Delegates to the convention declared their refusal to do anything "to keep three millions of our brethren and sisters in bondage" and called on other labor groups "to speak out in thunder tones" to secure for "all others those rights and privileges for which we are contending for ourselves."

But the majority of working people in the North were more cautious about abolishing slavery throughout the nation. Some no doubt recognized

"I Plead the Cause of White Freemen": Representative Wilmot's Proviso

In 1847, Representative David Wilmot of Pennsylvania proposed a legislative amendment (which came to be known as the Wilmot Proviso) that would ban slavery from any territory acquired as a result of the war with Mexico. In this speech to his fellow members of the House, Wilmot makes clear that he cares only for the prospects of free white workers and not at all for enslaved African Americans.

I make no war upon the South nor upon slavery in the South. I have no squeamish sensitiveness upon the subject of slavery, nor morbid sympathy for the slave. I plead the cause of the rights of white freemen. I would preserve for free white labor a fair country, a rich inheritance, where the sons of toil, of my own race and own color, can live without the disgrace which association with negro slavery brings upon free labor. I stand for the inviolability of free territory. It shall remain free, so far as my voice or vote can aid in the preservation of its character.

. . . O, for the honor of the North—for the fair fame of our green hills and valleys, be firm in this crisis—be true to your country and your race. The white laborer of the North claims your service; he demands that you stand firm to his interests and his rights; that you preserve the future homes of his children, on the distant shores of the Pacific, from the degradation and dishonor of negro servitude. Where the negro slave labors, the free white man cannot labor by his side without sharing in his degradation and disgrace.

Congressional Globe, 29th Congress, 2d sess., 1847, Appendix, 317. Reprinted in William E. Gienapp, ed., *The Civil War and Reconstruction: A Documentary Collection* (W. W. Norton, 2001), 17–18.

the economic contradictions highlighted in the Richmond, Virginia, *Enquirer*'s attack on working-class abolitionists. Referring to shoemakers in Lynn, Massachusetts, an editorial noted that they are "a people working all day on brogan shoes for the negroes at the South" but "who go to Abolition prayer meetings at night." Others feared that concerns over abolition were taking attention away from the needs of free white workers. George Henry Evans, once an outspoken enemy of slavery, became convinced that the fight for the emancipation of blacks must be postponed until the war against the exploitation of wage labor was won.

Still, if most northerners were wary about the effects of abolishing slavery, they also hotly opposed its extension beyond what then constituted the borders of the South. Northern farmers wanted western lands held free for settlement as homesteads, not as slave plantations. Many urban workers and small producers also hoped eventually to populate the West's towns and cities or have them kept free for their children and grandchildren. Immigrants, too, saw the West as a land of opportunity, and many eastern residents hoped that immigrants would settle there and thus alleviate competition for industrial and commercial employment in the East. Finally, free blacks in the North were appalled at the thought that slavery would spread beyond its present borders. They rightly feared that their own liberties would be jeopardized by such an expansion.

None of these groups wanted to live among slaves and slave owners or to compete with slave labor. They believed that slavery had imposed multiple indignities, political restrictions, depressed wages, and harsh conditions on free workers in the South, and at the same time, it had encouraged industrial stagnation. To all these people, slavery signified the death of everything they cherished or aspired to: personal independence, mutual respect, political equality, the right to enjoy the fruits of their own labor. In attacks on their employers, Lynn shoemakers, Lowell mill operatives, and many other workers compared factory owners with slave owners and proclaimed the degrading conditions of their own labor by calling themselves "wage slaves." By accusing their employers of treating them like blacks, they hoped to horrify other white Americans and thereby gain their support.

With so negative a view of slavery, northern workers, farmers, merchants, and manufacturers could hardly relish having the institution gain new vigor by spreading farther west. Only a minority of them were abolitionists; most simply wanted slavery to remain restricted to the South. The vast majority of northern whites, including a number of abolitionists, believed that blacks were innately inferior and therefore supported state laws that limited the economic, social, and political rights of free African Americans. They envisioned the western territories as a place where free white men could gain access to cheap and abundant land. Even though far more free whites were now wage laborers than independent farmers or artisans, they were proud that they could sell their labor as free persons. Although in the midst of strikes and protests, they might wield the rhetoric of wage slavery, most would have agreed with the abolitionist who distinguished between slaves and free workers by saying, "Does he not own himself?" Moreover, whatever their circumstances at that point, many northern workers still hoped one day to own their own home, land, or business, a hope that the image of wide-open spaces and new opportunities in the West kept alive.

This antipathy to slavery, and in many cases to African Americans, explains why the Wilmot Proviso was so appealing to northern whites. In addition, free-soil clubs, which opposed the spread of slavery, sprang up quickly in cities and towns throughout the Northeast and upper Midwest at the start of the war with Mexico. By joining these clubs, workers, farmers, and shopkeepers—native-born and immigrant alike—announced that they would not tolerate chattel slavery in the territories acquired from Mexico.

Territorial Expansion and Political Turmoil The dispute over the spread of slavery became more and more important in American politics as the war

Union on the Battle Field

Mexican War hero Zachary Taylor rode popular enthusiasm for American conquest to victory in the presidential election of 1848. In this earliest-known presidential campaign poster, the names of Taylor's victorious battles wind down columns entitled Justice and Peace, while a sunlit dove of peace descends toward the unlabeled candidate (Taylor's fame making the mention of his name superfluous). Borrowing the style of large, colorful circus posters, this campaign poster promoted the election as another grand-scale public spectacle of the time. Thomas W. Strong. *Union*, woodcut printed in colors on paper, 1848 — Prints and Photographs Division, Library of Congress.

with Mexico ended. This issue would remain central for the next decade and a half, splintering the two main political parties, the Whigs and Democrats. Even before 1848, abolitionists had run for political office under the auspices of the Liberty Party. But when former president Martin Van Buren bolted from Democratic ranks to become the candidate of the new Free-Soil Party in 1848, the tension mounted. Although not an abolitionist, Van Buren ran on a platform that coupled opposition to the westward spread of slavery with support for "the free grant [of land] to actual settlers."

In 1848, the Free-Soil Party was not strong enough to oust the Whigs or Democrats from national power, in part because it inspired fierce opposition in the North and the South. William Lloyd Garrison and many other radical abolitionists dismissed the Free-Soilers for supporting "whitemanism" (that is, keeping the West open to white men only). Most of the northern economic elite also denounced the Free-Soil Party. Although in most cases, they morally opposed slavery, they opposed even more strongly the organized antislavery movement. Their reasons were many: A mass campaign against slavery would dangerously polarize the nation. It would infuriate slave owners, whom the northern elite counted on as business and political partners. It would undermine the two major political parties and threaten the federal union itself. For instance, Whig leader and financier Philip Hone denounced Free-Soilers as "firebrands" who were ready to tear down the edifice of government to erect "altars for the worship of their own idols." And southern slaveholders were adamant in their opposition. As a result, Free-Soil candidate Van Buren lost his bid for a second chance as president, and Zachary Taylor, the Whig candidate, was elected.

Conclusion: Western Expansion and the Path to War

Despite this defeat, the issues that the Free-Soil Party had raised did not die. Instead, debates over land and labor grew more heated after 1848. Between 1845 and 1848, the United States had acquired 1.2 million square miles of territory. The victory over Mexico transferred California and the vast New Mexico territory to the United States and ensured that the Rio Grande would be recognized as the Texas border. Nearly 80,000 Spanish-speaking people, mostly of mixed Mexican-Indian descent, lived in the annexed areas. These people would perform much of the low-paid labor that was needed to make agriculture, ranching, mining, and industry profitable in the region. In addition, there were other racial and ethnic groups already settled in the western territories: Indians who had long inhabited the West, slaves taken there by their owners, immigrants and free blacks migrating westward to gain land and a better chance for an independent livelihood, and Chinese arriving in increasing numbers to work on railroads and in mining camps. These various groups increased the labor force, the competition for land, and the difficulties of resolving questions about the nation's social, racial, economic, and political order.

In 1848, however, Anglo-Americans focused more on their victory over Mexico than on the problems it spawned. Such vast territorial expansion in such a short time exhilarated many Americans. Didn't the war demonstrate the country's growing military prowess and finally seal its "manifest destiny" to dominate the continent from sea to sea? Certainly, southern planters felt confident that expansion had given new life to the system of plantation slavery.

During the 1830s and 1840s, southern planters had expanded their reach westward, removed most American Indians to Oklahoma Territory, developed an elaborate proslavery ideology, and consolidated their political and economic power in the region. Yet they could not rest easy. The acquisition of new territory and the expansion of a brutal internal slave trade inspired resistance among enslaved women and men, outcries from free blacks and fugitive slaves, and growing criticisms of slavery from nonslaveholding southern whites and northern abolitionists. Tensions emerged even within the two major political parties over the best means for handling the increasingly volatile issues raised by slavery's spread westward. Indeed, winning the war against Mexico greatly sharpened the internal conflict in the United States. The debate over what to do with the new land—specifically, whether to permit slavery there—aroused emotions that ultimately exploded in the Civil War.

The Years in Review

1812
- The First Seminole War occurs, in which U.S. Marines invade Florida to recapture runaway slaves and meet resistance from black fugitives and Seminole Indians.

1832
- The majority of Seminole Indians leave Florida.
- College of William and Mary professor Thomas Dew crafts an influential proslavery document, which claims that slavery is best both for the South and for the slaves.

1833
- The British government abolishes the slave trade in the West Indies.

1835
- The Second Seminole War occurs, in which fugitive slaves (known as maroons) join Seminole Indians in their fight against the United States. The peace agreement in 1842 forces the Seminoles to leave Florida but allows maroons to accompany them to Oklahoma rather than returning to their masters.

1836
- The Republic of Texas declares its independence from Mexico; outnumbered Texans lose at the Battle of the Alamo and are all killed, but Texans defeat Mexicans six weeks later at the Battle of San Jacinto, crying "Remember the Alamo!"

1837
- The Panic of 1837 lasts five years and devastates the nation.
- The Virginia General Assembly reaffirms the 1806 statute that allows individual counties to determine whether free blacks could remain in residence.
- The First Anti-Slavery Convention of American Women meets in Philadelphia.

1840
- The Liberty Party is founded by abolitionists.

1841
- The Supreme Court rules that Joseph Cinqué and other slave mutineers on the Spanish ship *Amistad* should be free because international slave trading is illegal.

1844
- Democrat James K. Polk defeats Whig Henry Clay in the presidential election on a strongly expansionist platform.
- The Methodist Episcopal Church splits into northern and southern branches over slavery; the Baptists split the following year.

1845
- Congress approves the annexation of the Lone Star Republic (Texas).
- Newspaper editor John L. O'Sullivan proclaims Americans' "manifest destiny to overspread the continent."

1846
- A compromise with Britain establishes the northwestern border of the United States at the forty-ninth parallel despite expansionists' cries of "54°40′ or Fight!"
- The United States declares war against Mexico; many northern farmers, businessmen, and abolitionists oppose it as a scheme to expand slavery into the West.
- Henry David Thoreau is jailed for refusing to pay taxes in protest of the Mexican war; his subsequent essay, "Resistance to Civil Government" (later published under the title "Civil Disobedience"), will later influence Mohandas (Mahatma) Gandhi and Martin Luther King, Jr.
- The Wilmot Proviso prohibiting slavery in any territory acquired through the Mexican War is passed by the House of Representatives but defeated in the Senate.
- Colonel John C. Frémont organizes U.S. citizens living in California in a rebellion against the Mexican government, declares the "Bear Republic" independent from Mexican rule, and anticipates annexation by the United States.

1847
- The U.S. Army under General Winfield Scott seizes Mexico City.

1848
- President Polk tries unsuccessfully to buy Cuba from Spain for $100 million.

- The Treaty of Guadalupe-Hidalgo ends the Mexican War, gives California and New Mexico to the United States, and moves the Texas-Mexico border south to the Rio Grande.

- The Free-Soil Party, formed to oppose slavery in the West, runs ex-Democrat Martin Van Buren for president; however, Whig Zachary Taylor wins the presidency.

- The Seneca Indians write their own constitution.

- The minié ball (a bullet with a conical head and hollow base that expands when fired) is perfected; it will prove extremely deadly in the Civil War.

- France abolishes slavery in its West Indies colonies.

Additional Readings

For more on slave-owning whites and the nature of plantation communities, see: Carol Bleser, ed., *Secret and Sacred: The Diaries of James Henry Hammond, a Southern Slaveholder* (1988); Catherine Clinton, *The Plantation Mistress: Woman's World in the Old South* (1982); William J. Cooper, Jr., and Thomas E. Terrill, *The American South: A History* (1990); Drew Faust, *A Sacred Circle: The Dilemma of the Intellectual in the Old South, 1840–1860* (1977); Sally G. McMillen, *Southern Women: Black and White in the Old South* (1992); James Oakes, *The Ruling Race: A History of American Slaveholders* (1982); William Kauffman Scarborough, *Masters of the Big House: Elite Slaveholders of the Mid-Nineteenth-Century South* (2003); Brenda Stevenson, *Life in Black and White: Family and Community in the Slave South* (1996); and Bertram Wyatt-Brown, *Southern Honor: Ethics and Behavior in the Old South* (1982).

For more on non-slave-owning whites, see: Charles Bolton and Scott P. Culclasure, eds., *The Confessions of Edward Isham: A Poor White Life of the Old South* (1998); and Steven Hahn, *The Roots of Southern Populism: Yeoman Farmers and the Transformation of the Georgia Upcountry, 1850–1890* (1983).

For more on free African Americans in a slave society, see: Ira Berlin, *Slaves Without Masters: The Free Negro in the Antebellum South* (1974); John Hope Franklin and Alfred J. Moss, Jr., *From Slavery to Freedom: A History of Negro Americans*, 7th ed. (1994); Virginia Meacham Gould, *Chained to the Rock of Adversity: To Be Free, Black and Female in the Old South* (1998); Harriet A. Jacobs, *Incidents in the Life of a Slave Girl* (1861); and Dorothy Sterling, ed., *We Are Your Sisters: Black Women in the Nineteenth Century* (1984).

For more on the internal slave trade, see: Robert H. Gudmestad, *A Troublesome Commerce: The Transformation of the Interstate Slave Trade* (2003); Walter Johnson, *Soul by Soul: Life Inside the Antebellum Slave Market* (1999); and Charles L. Perdue, Jr., Thomas E. Barden, and Robert K. Phillips, eds., *Weevils in the Wheat: Interviews with Virginia's Ex-Slaves* (1976).

For more on western expansion and political tensions over slavery, see: Eric Foner, *Free Soil, Free Labor, Free Men: The Ideology of the Republican Party Before the Civil War* (1970); Paul Foos, *A Short, Offhand, Killing Affair: Soldiers and Social Conflict During the Mexican-American War* (2002); Lawrence Friedman, *Gregarious Saints: Self and Community in American Abolitionism, 1830–1870* (1982); and Archie P. McDonald, ed., *The Mexican War: Crisis for Democracy* (1969).

Part Three

War, Reconstruction, and Labor

1848–1877

ETWEEN 1848 AND 1860, societal changes created by immigration, industrialization, western expansion, and the growth of slavery led to repeated confrontations between political leaders as well as among ordinary Americans. Political compromises, such as the Compromise of 1850 and the Kansas-Nebraska Act, resolved the most bitter issues for a time. But it was not until the North defeated the South in the Civil War that the most volatile issue—slavery—was finally settled and the future development of the United States under industrial capitalism was assured. The dramatic and bloody events surrounding the Civil War constituted a second American revolution, which formed the centerpiece of this era.

This second revolution resulted not only in emancipation, but also in a fundamental expansion of legal guarantees of citizenship and political equality. In this way, it paralleled the first American Revolution, when colonists gained both independence from Great Britain and the liberties that are guaranteed in the Bill of Rights. Still, like the first revolution, the Civil War and its aftermath demonstrated that differences of class, race, and sex still limited the practical implementation of constitutional claims for equality.

From the end of the Mexican War in 1848 through the 1870s, women and men—including African Americans, Mexican Americans, Indians, Chinese and European immigrants, and native-born whites—continued to build the expanded territory that was America. They constructed towns and railroads, managed farms, and extracted minerals in the West; furthered industrial and commercial growth in the North; and contributed mightily to agricultural production in the South and Midwest. Members of the laboring classes also engaged in the era's increasingly heated debates over immigration, westward expansion, and women's rights, even as they banded together to advance social and political causes. They joined both antislavery and antiabolitionist groups; formed unions and staged strikes; and participated in political rallies, electoral campaigns, and the founding of the Republican Party. Large numbers of working-class men eventually took up arms to further one cause or another: the defeat of Mexico, battles in Indian territory, and Confederate independence or the salvation of the Union.

Although few Americans believed, even in the 1850s, that the struggle over slavery would erupt in a civil war, when war finally broke out in April

1861, nearly all Americans' lives were affected in profound ways. The South seceded from the Union to maintain the system of racial slavery on which the region's very identity was based. Northern whites went to war, for the most part, not to free the slaves, but to limit slavery's expansion westward and to maintain the Union. Still, during the South's departure from the federal Congress, legislators from the free states reshaped western development by funding the transcontinental railroad and passing the Homestead Act. This legislation would gradually transform western society, further limiting the ability of American Indians to maintain traditional lifeways. The war also transformed women's lives. As men were drawn into the military, their wives, sisters, and daughters took over jobs in fields and factories, managed businesses and plantations, entered new occupations as clerks and nurses, and formed organizations to aid soldiers and newly freed slaves.

Over time, the purpose of the war changed, especially for the Union. As the North faced unexpected military defeats and the unanticipated actions of slaves, more and more northerners embraced emancipation as a critical goal of the war. African Americans escaped from slavery in huge numbers. Many of them, along with northern free blacks, demanded the right to fight for the Union; ultimately, nearly 200,000 African Americans served in the Union Army. They helped to turn the tide in the war's final two years and convinced northerners to fight for the end of slavery as well as the preservation of the Union.

Neither side in this conflict was completely united. Clashes erupted within the South and the North over the war's personal, economic, and political costs. In the North, however, a broad coalition — farmers, workers (including recent immigrants), businessmen, and politicians — emerged to support the Republican Party's policy of massive military action against the South. This wartime coalition then formed the core of support for Republican policies toward the South after the war.

The Confederacy's defeat raised as many questions as it answered. Slavery was now destroyed, but what kind of labor system would replace it? African Americans were now free, but what would they do with their new freedom? How would their former masters react? Who would lead the new South now? The policies of the period called Reconstruction attempted to answer these questions.

The freedpeople knew exactly how they wanted those questions answered. To them, emancipation meant the right to speak and act as free people, to reunite their families, and to end their automatic deference toward whites. And freed men and women acted decisively to guarantee these freedoms. Their claims of individual rights quickly grew into collective demands for education, the ownership of land, and full political participation.

Southern whites had a very different notion of what Reconstruction should mean. Former slave owners wanted a rapid return to stability and a continuation of their rule in spite of emancipation. Few of them could abide the freedpeople's demands for political and social equality. White farmers and workers did not want to face economic or political competition from millions of former slaves.

Most of the North's white workers, though they did not want to compete with African Americans for jobs or consider them as equals, were unwilling to accept the continued domination of slave owners over the freedpeople. Most industrialists were committed to rebuilding the ravaged South as quickly as possible on free-labor principles, transforming slaves into wage laborers. And Republican Party leaders, intent on blunting the political power of the Democrats and former slaveholders, needed the votes of newly enfranchised African Americans to build their party in the South.

The diverse objectives of blacks and whites, North and South, resulted in sharp conflict and a growing sense of crisis. No group won all of its demands — least of all the freedpeople. For most, their quest for land of their own remained unfulfilled, although they did win important victories, especially citizenship and black male suffrage. Even these gains engendered intense opposition among southern whites. So, too, did the increasingly radical policies of the Republican Party and the efforts of some in the party to impeach President Andrew Johnson, the Tennessee politician who rose to power when President Abraham Lincoln was assassinated in April 1865.

Some whites came to believe that only terror could ensure white supremacy in the South. The rise of the Ku Klux Klan after 1867 and the use of violence to subvert constitutional guarantees soon halted the freedpeople's progress. Within a decade, the southern elite had reestablished its control, thanks in part to tacit support from moderate Republicans, who came to dominate the northern party after 1870. Reconstruction ended tragically for the freedpeople, who saw their former masters returned to power through the combined force of vigilante violence and political compromise.

Meanwhile, the North and West were being transformed by technological change and the massive influx of migrants from the eastern United States and immigrants from abroad. Developments that began in the midst of the war accelerated after 1865. A transcontinental railroad system soon linked northern cities to western towns, mines, and farms. Industrial manufacturing multiplied as access to raw materials increased. Unprecedented numbers of immigrants filled the growing ranks of America's postwar industrial working class. Economic growth and immigration further fueled westward expansion, creating new problems as well as increased conflict between settlers and Indians, Mexican Americans, and native-born whites and among various native societies.

The wartime coalition that had joined farmers, workers, and businessmen in the North broke apart in the face of these changes. Even as transportation and communication networks drew Americans across the continent closer together, differences of race and economic opportunity sharpened political divisions. The severe industrial depression that began in 1873 forced Americans to realize that their nation, too, was suffering the wrenching dislocations and class divisions that were already evident in Europe; increasingly, great wealth and opulence coexisted with grinding poverty and human misery. This widening gulf helped to revive the labor movement.

Many Americans sought to ignore this gulf during the celebration of the nation's centennial in 1876, yet in the following year, America experienced its first nationwide industrial rebellion when hundreds of thousands of railroad strikers and their supporters brought the nation to a standstill. The end of Reconstruction and the nationwide railroad strike in 1877 closed out an era. Decades of conflict over slavery had ended, but the drama that pitted capital against labor continued, as did the struggles over the place of women and men, whites, blacks, and Indians, and native-born Americans and immigrants in the society, economy, and polity.

10

The Settlement of the West and the Conflict over Slave Labor

1848–1860

Police Conveying Sims to the Vessel

Thomas Sims escaped slavery in Georgia, but in April 1851, he was arrested in Boston and, under the Fugitive Slave Law, returned to his owner. The city's abolitionist movement agitated for his release, and large crowds surrounded the courthouse in which Sims was incarcerated. But these efforts, which included plans to forcibly free the prisoner, did not succeed. This picture from a Boston illustrated weekly shows how Sims was conducted by 300 armed police and marshals to a Navy ship that carried him back to slavery. On his return south, Sims was sold to a new master in Mississippi. He escaped again in 1863. *Gleason's Pictorial Drawing-room Companion*, May 10, 1851 — American Social History Project.

IN FALL 1850, HENRY BUSH, a forty-five-year-old stove maker from Rochester, New York, headed to California. He left behind his pregnant wife Abigail, aged forty, their three young children, and two older children from his first marriage. Friends and fellow abolitionists in the Western New York Anti-Slavery Society bid him good-bye, doubting that they would ever see him again. Although Henry had been among those who opposed the Mexican War in 1846 because of its threat to expand slave territories, he now hoped that new lands in the West would offer him economic opportunity. Having lost his business in the Panic of 1837 and having struggled since then to support his growing family, Bush was lured to California by the promise of gold.

Many Americans hoped that the gold and other resources to be found in the 1.2 million square miles that had been added to the United States through President James Polk's expansionist policies would provide them with a new start. Shopkeepers and craftsmen such as Henry Bush valued the greater economic independence and security that the West promised. Speculators, merchants, and manufacturers also enthused over business prospects there. Yeoman farmers from both the North and the South hoped to expand their holdings and their profits by moving to the more fertile lands of the Great Plains and the Far West. And slaveholders envisioned the region as the salvation of plantation agriculture by opening up fresh land for cotton and sugar cultivation. The discovery of gold in California added to the jubilation among Americans, gave a boost to the U.S. economy, and swelled the already high tide of westward migration.

Whether they imagined the West as a refuge for slavery or a haven for free labor, most Americans back East considered it a vast and largely empty space. In reality, the region was filled with diverse inhabitants with whom newcomers had to compete for resources. After 1848, American Indians, Mexicans, and Spaniards with deep roots in the region were joined by massive numbers of immigrants from Latin America, Europe, and the eastern United States; slaves taken west by their owners; free blacks seeking greater independence; and Chinese immigrants, who arrived in growing numbers to work in mining camps and on railroads. Although individuals from many backgrounds thrived in this setting, differences of race, nationality, and class created greater opportunities for some than for others.

The convergence of these diverse groups in a single region increased not only the competition for wealth and land, but also the difficulties of resolving questions about the nation's racial, economic, and political order. Men like Henry Bush did not leave their abolitionist principles back East, nor did slaveholders intend to give up their human chattel when resettling in the West. To southern planters, western expansion was slavery's salvation. As one Georgia politician told Congress in the 1850s, "There is not a slaveholder in this House or out of it, but who knows perfectly well that whenever slavery is confined within certain specified limits, its future existence is doomed." For northern businessmen and politicians, the West offered a different kind of safety valve, one that would alleviate the economic pressures caused by the growing number of propertyless workers and the massive wave of immigrants from Germany, Ireland, and other European countries. Many workers and immigrants also viewed the West as a beacon of opportunity. Although industrial laborers and skilled artisans reinvigorated efforts to organize unions in the North, most workers remained unorganized at midcentury. To these men and women, the West offered a second chance. Some envisioned rich farmlands; others hoped for steady employment on railroads, in construction, or as shopkeepers; and still others dreamed of quick riches panning for gold.

Debates over free versus slave labor shaped the dreams and the experiences of western settlers. These debates had first arisen at the Constitutional Convention of 1787 and led to a political crisis in 1819–1820 that was finally resolved by the Missouri Compromise. After the U.S. victory in the Mexican War, however, much more serious conflicts over the spread of slavery erupted. These included battles over the admission of California to statehood in 1850, the status of Kansas and Nebraska territories in 1854, the Supreme Court ruling on Dred Scott's freedom in 1857, and the armed attack on the federal arsenal at Harpers Ferry, Virginia, in 1859. Although the best-known leaders of the proslavery and antislavery forces lived in the East, these conflicts deeply affected residents of the West, who held their own opinions about what was best for their territory or state.

The Transformation of the West

People who were native to the western territories had suffered significant changes well before the United States defeated Mexico. The pace of change quickened, however, after the United States acquired the vast lands won from Mexico and especially after gold was discovered in California in 1848. Then, the influx of people, rapid growth of towns and cities, expansion of roads and railroads, increased demand for land and labor, and battles over economic and political control transformed nearly every aspect of western life (Map 10.1). For Indian societies, mining, urbanization, and railroad construction devastated local habitats and intensified conflicts among tribes and with U.S. citizens and soldiers. As U.S. citizens gained political control of the region, they passed laws to limit the rights of longtime Indian, Mexican, and Spanish residents. Even U.S. residents who moved West found themselves competing for rights and resources.

Despite increased opportunities for some, inequalities of class, race, and gender were largely reproduced in the western territories of the United States. The status of African Americans was uncertain in many parts of the

MAP 10.1 Settlement of the Trans-Missouri West, 1840s

The Oregon and Santa Fe trails opened up the western plains, the Rocky Mountains, and the Pacific Coast to thousands of pioneers and settlers from the eastern and midwestern United States. In 1842, the first party of over 100 people left Independence, Missouri, and headed across the Oregon Trail. Over the next eighteen years, some 350,000 men, women, and children traveled this overland route to the Pacific Coast. Nearly one-tenth died along the way. One of the largest groups of migrants were the Mormons. Driven out of western New York in the 1830s and out of Illinois in the early 1840s by mobs who protested the Mormon practice of polygamy, the Mormons built an agrarian empire in the Great Salt Lake basin in present-day Utah.

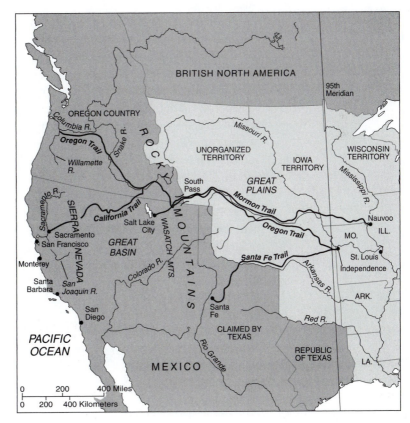

Contrasting Views of Oregon Territory

In 1847, the Illinois Journal, *a newspaper based in Springfield, Illinois, decided to publish letters from former Illinoisans who had been tempted by the promise of Oregon and had emigrated there. Readers who were curious about what life was like in the wild, northern territory got a mixed bag of reviews. Two of the letter excerpts follow.*

Mr. Isaac Statts, in a letter to a friend, dated "Polk County, Oregon, April 8, 1847," says—

"I am highly pleased with this country, and so far as I can now say, shall spend the remainder of my days in it. It has assuredly the most healthy climate in the world. . . . Grass has been very fine and abundant for the last six weeks. When wheat is well put in, you can safely count on 30 bushels an acre. Hemp, tobacco and flax do well here. It is a good country for sheep. There is sufficient water power to carry on manufacturing to any extent. I have built my house in a commanding situation, and have a fine view of the country for ten miles around, and it is quite refreshing on a warm summer's day to feel the invigorating breeze from the Cascade mountains. . . . I am convinced that this is as fine a country as can be found. Any man disposed to be industrious and who would be satisfied any where, would be satisfied in this country."

Mr. Hezekiah Packingham, formerly of Putnam County, in this State, thus writes to his brother under date of "Willamette Valley, March 1, 1847:"

"I arrived in the Wallamette [Willamette] Valley on the 30th of September, and my calculations are all defeated about Oregon. I found it a mean, dried up, and drowned country. . . . I can give Oregon credit for only one or two things, and these are, good health and plenty of salmon, and Indians; as for the farming country there is none here—wheat grows about the same as in Illinois; corn, potatoes, and garden vegetables cannot grow here without watering. The nights are too cold here in summer. The soil is not as good as in Illinois—the face of the country is hilly, and high mountains covered with snow all summer, and small valleys. . . . Oregon is rapidly filling up with young men, (but no girls,) of whom two-thirds are dissatisfied, and many would return to the States if they were able, but the road is long and tedious, and it is hard for families to get back . . . We were uninjured by the Indians, though they were very saucy—they have no manners; they worship idols, and I saw one of their gods at the mouth of the river. There is no society here . . . I shall return to the States next spring. Don't believe all that is said about Oregon, as many falsehoods are uttered respecting the country."

Illinois Journal (Springfield, Illinois), November 11, 1847.

West. Southern whites transported slaves into newly acquired lands, and free blacks suffered discrimination in the new territories much as they had back east. Many white men found their opportunities limited when gold mines failed to produce the riches for which they had hoped and they were forced to return to wage labor to survive. Women's status also differed by nationality and race. Some women benefited from the scarcity of women in the West at midcentury, but these temporary opportunities rarely offset the economic, political, and legal disadvantages of their sex.

American Indians Face New Obstacles   Between the time of the first Spanish settlements in California in 1769 and the Gold Rush of 1849, disease, death, and labor exploitation devastated the native population. The availability of horses and guns, which spread across the West in this same period, made nomadic tribes more mobile, settled villages more vulnerable, big game hunting more wasteful, and conflicts among neighboring groups more deadly. Intertribal conflict on the Plains increased as well under the pressure of forced tribal movement. The Chippewas, for example, pushed the Sioux out of the Minnesota territory in the 1830s, and by midcentury, the Sioux had themselves seized land from the Poncas, Pawnees, Hidatsas, Assiniboines, Crows, Mandans, Arikaras, and Iowas. In the 1840s and 1850s, once they possessed guns, the Navajos, who were skilled horsemen, staged more destructive attacks not only against U.S. soldiers and settlers, but also against their traditional enemies, the Utes and Pueblos.

In the late 1840s, when the United States took possession of the western Plains, California, and Oregon, some 360,000 Indians occupied the West (Map 10.2). There were probably some 75,000 native peoples on the Great Plains, including the Cheyennes, Blackfeet, and Sioux. These buffalo-hunting and warring tribes fed European and American stereotypes of teepees, painted warriors, and chiefs in headdresses. Close to 85,000 Creeks, Cherokees, and other Southeastern Indians also inhabited western lands. Another 25,000, mostly Comanches and Apaches, resided in Texas. The Mexican Cession brought another 150,000 Indians into the United States, swelling the Navajo and Apache populations and placing a number of small California tribes under Anglo-American laws and customs. Finally, some 25,000 Nez Perce, Yakimas, Walla Wallas, and Coeur d'Alenes occupied the Oregon territory, which came under U.S. control in 1846.

Some Indians quickly recognized the significance of the arrival of large numbers of Americans. In 1846, as thousands of U.S. soldiers swarmed into the West on their way to wage war with Mexico, Cheyenne leader Yellow Wolf noted the "diminishing numbers of his people, and the decrease of the once abundant buffalo" and asserted that Indians would "have to adopt the habits of the white people." Although many Indians would have agreed with their aging Cheyenne brother, others, especially the younger ones, were

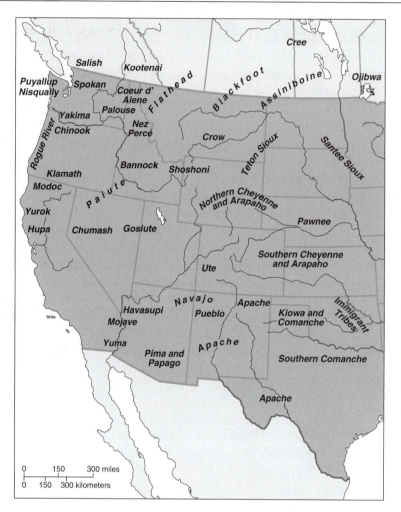

MAP 10.2   Major Indian Tribes in the American West in 1850

Before the arrival of vast numbers of Europeans and white Americans in the West, hundreds of Indian tribes coexisted on the land. The abundance of land, game, and edible plants compared to the relatively small size of the population ensured that these diverse tribes could survive despite differences in political and economic systems, military capabilities, and religious beliefs. Though conflicts among some native peoples had always existed, the conflicts increased substantially when the native groups were forced by the pressure of white settlement to share ever-smaller territories. By 1850, these intertribal conflicts were exacerbated by growing tensions between the various Indian tribes and the large numbers of white Americans arriving from the eastern United States. Robert Utley, *The Indian Frontier of the American West, 1846–1890* (1984).

not yet ready to make further concessions. Resistance by Plains Indians ended only after decades of bloody warfare, which greatly decimated their numbers. Yellow Wolf himself was killed in a massacre by U.S. soldiers in 1864 at Sand Creek in the Colorado territory.

In California, the small size of existing Indian societies and the outbreak of deadly epidemics limited native resistance (Table 10.1). In the early 1840s, men such as U.S. Army Captain John Sutter, stationed in California, confiscated tribal lands in the central part of the state, a process that was made easier by a smallpox epidemic that claimed thousands of native lives in the 1830s. Sutter recruited and coerced the Nisenan people who lived in the area to work his land, alternating material incentives with corporal punishment to control them. When California declared independence from Mexico in 1846, the U.S. government began playing a more important role

TABLE 10.1 California's Indian Population, 1852

Though California Indians had confronted Spanish and American soldiers and settlers for nearly eighty years before the discovery of gold, the rapid influx of non-Indians to the area after 1848 disrupted their ways of life in new and profound ways. By 1852, in the northern and central districts of California where mining was most important, the percentage of Indians in the total population had dropped precipitously. Only on the southern edge of the main mining districts, in Mariposa and Tulare counties, did Indians still constitute a significant portion of the population.
Albert L. Hurtado, *Indian Survival on the California Frontier* (1988).

Domesticated Indians in California by Mining District and County in 1852

County	Non-Indians	Indians	Indians as Percentage of Total Population
Northern District			
Klamath	523	0	0
Shasta	3,855	73	1.8
Siskiyou	2,214	26	1.2
Trinity	1,933	4	0.2
Subtotal	8,525	103	1.2
Central District			
Butte	8,542	30	0.3
Calaveras	28,936	1,982	6.4
El Dorado*	40,000	---	---
Nevada	18,139	3,226	15.1
Placer	10,867	730	6.3
Sierra	4,808	0	0
Tuolumne	25,730	590	2.2
Yuba	20,593	120	0.6
Subtotal	157,615	6,678	4.1
Subtotal w/o El Dorado	117,615	6,678	5.4
Southern District			
Mariposa	4,231	4,533	51.7
Tulare	175	8,407	98.0
Subtotal	4,406	12,940	74.6
TOTAL	170,546	19,721	10.4
TOTAL w/o El Dorado	130,546	19,721	13.1

* El Dorado County returned a population estimate of 40,000 that was not broken down by age, race, or sex.
Source: 1852 California Special Census, California State Archives.

in the region, and Sutter became the local Indian agent, in charge of land grants, labor contracts, and the distribution of supplies. At the same time, more and more Americans began moving into California, most coming south from Oregon or across the Plains from the east. Soon, the discovery of gold near Sutter's Mill unleashed a floodtide of migration, creating even more difficult conditions for Indians in the region.

The Gold Rush   On January 24, 1848, James Marshall discovered gold in a millrace along the American River. Word of the event quickly circulated through the local area. In May, the San Francisco *Californian* reported that "the whole country from San Francisco to Los Angeles, and from the sea shore to the base of the Sierra Nevada, resounds with the sordid cry of 'gold, GOLD, GOLD!' while the field is left half planted, the house half built, and everything neglected but the manufacture of shovels and pickaxes." By year's end, the news had spread across the nation.

The 700 or so new settlers who had arrived in California in 1848 were joined by thousands and then tens of thousands of others in 1849 and 1850. These later pioneers, known as Forty-Niners, cared little about farming, trading, or building settlements. They came to stake a claim. Gold fever drew Irish, Scottish, French, and German miners to California along with Chileans, Mexicans, Peruvians, and Americans. In 1849 alone, some 80,000 gold-hungry adventurers—most of them men—poured into the area (Map 10.3). In the rush to control the most promising sites, armed Americans assaulted foreign-born competitors, especially Chinese, Chilean, Peruvian, Mexican, and French miners, often driving them off their claims. In one case, U.S. miners drove out a group of 60 Chinese immigrants who had been hired by a British mining company. Whites knew that amid the general violence and lawlessness that characterized life along the mother lode, assaults on Asians or Hispanics—even deadly assaults—were unlikely to lead to arrest, much less conviction.

Yellow Wolf

This 1846 sketch of the Cheyenne chief by Lt. J. W. Abert was included in the officer's official report. "Report of Lieutenant J. W. Abert, of His Examination of New Mexico, in the Years 1846-'47," Senate Executive Documents, 30th Congress, 1st session, no. 23 (1848) — Western History Collections, University of Oklahoma Library.

Despite the violence, mining camps turned into boomtowns literally overnight. A typical mining camp, Nevada City emerged at the intersection of two creeks in the Sierra foothills in the fall of 1849. A few cabins, a general store, and hundreds of tents appeared along the creek beds during the winter. In the spring, thousands of men streamed into the area seeking their fortunes. A few decided to pursue wealth not by panning for gold, but by providing the necessities of life for those who did. Stores and saloons sprang up on the small flat along Deer Creek. New roads, carved out to ensure a steady supply of goods, brought more merchants and miners into the town. In spring 1850, miner William Swain described the area's astonishing growth:

> The speculators, traders, gamblers, women and thieves keep their eyes on the mines and when miners move, they all move. This spring there was but one house in Nevada City, now there is said to be 17,000 men in and about it. . . . Everything is in a state of fermentation, rolling and tumbling about.

The fermentation that Swain observed created new problems for the region's American Indians, such as the Nisenan. The miners and others rushing in razed the forests to make way for camps, towns, and roads. They used timber for sluices, dams, houses, shops, and fuel. The miners imported food from afar, since they considered nutritionally inadequate the seeds and

MAP 10.3   The California Gold Rush

Beginning in 1849, hundreds of thousands of people from the eastern United States, Canada, Mexico, South America, and other parts of the world converged on California. Because of the rapid rise in population and because so many of the newcomers were young men seeking gold rather than farmers, merchants, or manufacturers, an enormous demand for food, clothing, equipment, and housing was created. San Francisco, the main port of entry for those who arrived by sea, became a booming metropolis, and smaller trading outposts such as Sacramento and Stockton were transformed into important commercial centers. Agricultural production increased in the rich interior river valleys, and new jobs were created by miners' demands for clean clothes, home-cooked meals, and adequate housing.

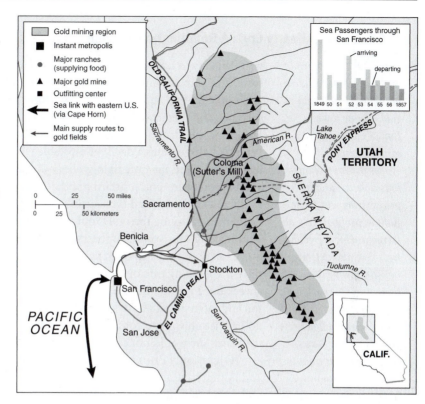

acorns that the Nisenan harvested. The new settlers killed off deer and other animals and destroyed fish habitats, while devastating fires swept the Sierra mining towns and water remained in short supply. The Nisenan nearly disappeared along with their homes and food supplies.

Over the next decade, the mining camps spread. New methods, such as hydraulic mining, made the process of mining more profitable for a few, but most Forty-Niners eventually worked for wages, just as they had back east. These changes were even more detrimental to the land and to native communities. The experience of the Nisenan was echoed in every area where miners settled, shattering the fragile ecosystems that had supported many California Indian communities. Meanwhile, Spaniards and Mexicans found themselves exploited in the same ways in which they had once mistreated the Indians: the newcomers expropriated their land, imposed new forms of labor, and sexually abused local women. In California during the 1850s, the Indian population plummeted to between 30,000 and 35,000. Even native peoples who had served the American cause — fighting with U.S. troops against Mexico in 1846 or aiding American forces in putting down a rebellion led by the Cupeno tribe in 1851 — were denied the rights to citizenship, suffrage, and property that were guaranteed to whites.

"I Often Have a Hearty Cry": A Boardinghouse Keeper in the California Gold Rush

Mary Ballou and her husband ran a boarding-house in a California gold mining town. Ballou's letter to her son, written in 1852, evokes the rough hous-ing, violence, and high prices (from which the Ballous profited) in Cali-fornia during the gold rush. She also describes how the few women there provided each other with companionship and consolation. Ballou's ref-erences to "the States" suggest how far from home California must have felt, since California had been a state for two years when she wrote this letter.

well I will try to tell you what my work is here in this muddy Place. . . . somtimes I am washing and Ironing somtimes I am making mince pie and Apple pie and squash pies. . . . Sometimes I am making gruel for the sick now and then cooking oisters sometimes making coffee for the French people strong enough for any man to walk on that has Faith as Peter had. three times a day I set my Table which is about thirty feet in length and do all the little fixings about it such as filling pepper boxes and vinegar cruits and mustard pots and Butter cups. sometimes I am feeding my chickens and then again I am scareing the Hogs out of my kitchen and Driving the mules out of my Dining room. . . . Somtimes I am making soups and cramberry tarts and Baking chicken that cost four Dollars a head and cooking Eggs at three Dollars a Dozen. . . .som-times I am taking care of Babies and nursing at the rate of Fifty Dollars a week but I would not advise any Lady to come out here and suffer the toil and fatigue that I have suffered for the sake of a little gold neither do I advise any one to come. Clarks Simmon wife says if she was safe in the States she would not care if she had not one cent. . . .

[O]ccasionly I run in and have a chat with Jane and Mrs Durphy and I often have a hearty cry. no one but my maker knows my feelings. and then I run into my little cellar which is about four feet square as I have no other place to run that is cool. . . . [today] I have been to church to hear a methodist sermon. his Text was let us lay aside every weight and the sin that doth so easely beset us. I was the only Lady that was present and about forty gentleman. So you see that I go to church when I can.

Mary B. Ballou, *"I Hear the Hogs in My Kitchen": A Woman's View of the Gold Rush*, ed. Archibald Hanna (New Haven: Yale University Press, 1962), reprinted in Christiane Fischer, ed., *Let Them Speak for Themselves: Women in the American West, 1849–1900* (New York: E. P. Dutton, 1977), 42–46.

Work and Race   Life on the western mining frontier was difficult even for white workers, who had the privileges accorded their race. Most did not strike it rich, and after using up their original stake searching for gold, they had nothing with which to purchase land, tools, or supplies. Many were thus forced to become wage laborers in mines or railroads or to find jobs as sea-sonal workers or tenants on large farms owned by wealthy whites. Others moved to the region's widely scattered cities, seeking jobs on the docks in San Francisco or in Sacramento's food-processing plants. Many found

Washing Away the Landscape

In 1853, hydraulic mining was introduced in the California gold fields, harnessing the power of water forced through a system of hoses to cut away tons of rock and dirt to extract the gold hidden beneath. "Thus," rejoiced one local newspaper, "banks of earth that would have kept a hundred men employed for months in their removal will now be removed by three or four men in two weeks." But as this cartoon from the *Sacramento Bee* indicated, the new process worsened erosion that had already been caused by excessive timber cutting, clogging rivers with the runoff that flooded and devastated rural settlements. "What Hydraulic Mining Is Doing for the Country," Sacramento Archives and Museum Collection Center, The Eleanor McClatchy Collection/ 82.04(MC8:14)/G.F. Keller/n.d./dl.

themselves working shoulder to shoulder with the Chinese, Mexicans, and African Americans they had hoped to rise above.

Still, to most white Americans, California remained a land of promise, and a few achieved the success they sought, though not necessarily in the way they had imagined. Henry Bush, for instance, who failed to strike it rich in the mines, bought a plot of land north of San Francisco, started a vineyard there, and made his fortune in grapes rather than gold. Continuing dreams of economic opportunity led many workers who faced miserable conditions and low wages to ignore the benefits of class solidarity. Instead, in an effort to keep California's wealth for whites only, white employees often cooperated with employers to exclude those they defined as "intruders": Indians, African Americans, Mexicans, Spaniards, and Asians.

The obstacles that white workers and employers created were reinforced by the passage of laws that taxed "foreigners" working in mining areas, including Mexicans who had lived in the region longer than many of the lawmakers. Another series of California regulations restricted the rights of residents who were considered to be nonwhite. African Americans, although free, were denied the right to vote, claim a homestead, hold public office, serve on a jury, or attend school with white children. In San Francisco in the 1850s, it was even illegal for blacks to ride streetcars. In addition, "no black or mulatto person or Indian" was "permitted to give evidence in favor of or against a white person" in court. In 1854, the state Supreme Court affirmed, in the case of *People v. George Hall*, that Indians could not testify against whites in court and — incredibly — that Asians were Indians. Therefore, Chinese also were prohibited from giving testimony in court.

In 1855, the court clarified its stance, arguing that the Chinese were "a race of people whom nature has marked as inferior . . . incapable of progress or intellectual development beyond a certain point." Still, the Chinese population in California increased—numbering some 25,000 by the mid-1850s—and spread into other western states, such as Nevada and Idaho. Though these immigrants performed critical services for mine owners and other miners—cooking, cleaning, and doing the most arduous manual labor—they were never accepted as part of the new western working class.

Pioneer Women's Work and Rights   When native-born white women began moving west in large numbers in the 1850s, they harbored popular but distorted images of Indians, Mexicans, and other "foreigners." White women's initial scarcity in the West and their growing numbers after 1850 created challenges and opportunities for all women in the region.

Susan Magoffin, the wife of a trader, was one of the first U.S.-born women to travel in the "New" Mexico territory, in 1846. In her diary, she noted with shock that Mexican women wore loose blouses, flowing skirts, and no corsets, which to her suggested that they had loose sexual morals. Yet she also appreciated their personal warmth and hospitality. Magoffin was surprised to discover that Mexican law granted married women property rights that were denied women under U.S. law. When the region was annexed by the United States in 1848, Mexican women lost not only the right to control their own property after marriage, but also the right to custody of their children and the right to sue in court without the consent of fathers or husbands. Still, Spanish and Mexican legal traditions did mitigate some of the worst features of Anglo-American law in the West. For instance, married women in the West held greater rights over family property than did their counterparts back East.

Despite some legal benefits accorded to western women, pioneer wives generally had to accede to their husbands' wishes, including the man's desire to uproot his household and head to the frontier. Of course, some women eagerly embraced the opportunity and adventure that the frontier offered, but those who did not had little choice but to acquiesce. In spring of 1853, for example, Abigail Bush, whose husband Henry had left for California three years earlier, finally followed him west. With her "wee daughter" and three sons, she traveled to New York City and then set sail for the long voyage around South America to California. Despite the desire to reunite her family, Abigail lamented those forced to "leav[e] Home, its Comforts and Endearments" only to be "Doomed to Disappointment, Sorrow, & a Grave" far from family and friends. Although Abigail Bush had been the first

Sam Pit
Pit was one of the many Californian Indians who labored in the gold fields. California State Library, Sacramento.

"We Are Not the Degraded Race You Would Make Us": Protesting Anti-Chinese Sentiment in California

In 1852, Norman Asing, a restaurant owner and leader in San Francisco's Chinese community, wrote this open letter to California Governor John Bigler, who had called for a restriction on Chinese immigration. California had experienced a dramatic upsurge in Chinese immigration, from a few thousand Chinese immigrants in 1850 to 20,000 in 1852, when they constituted almost one-quarter of California's workforce. Bigler cited the inability of the Chinese to assimilate as European immigrants had before them; Asing assails the governor for his anti-Chinese stance while making his own distinctions about the superiority of some racial groups over others.

Sir: I am a Chinaman, a republican, and a lover of free institutions; am much attached to the principles of the government of the United States, and therefore take the liberty of addressing you as the chief of the government of this State. . . .

[S]o far as the history of our race in California goes, it stamps with the test of truth the fact that we are not the degraded race you would make us. We came amongst you as mechanics or traders, and following every honorable business of life. You do not find us pursuing occupations of degrading character, except you consider labor degrading, which I am sure you do not; and if our countrymen save the proceeds of their industry from the tavern and the gambling house to spend it on farms or town lots or on their families, surely you will admit that even these are virtues. . . .

Your Excellency will discover, however, that we are as much allied to the African race and the red man as you are yourself, and that as far as the aristocracy of skin is concerned, ours might compare with many of the European races; nor do we consider that your Excellency, as a Democrat, will make us believe that the framers of your declaration of rights ever suggested the propriety of establishing an aristocracy of skin. I am a naturalized citizen, your Excellency, of Charleston, South Carolina, and a Christian, too; and so hope you will stand corrected in your assertion "that none of the Asiatic class" as you are pleased to term them, have applied for benefits under our naturalization act. I could point out to you numbers of citizens, all over the whole continent, who have taken advantage of your hospitality and citizenship, and I defy you to say that our race have ever abused that hospitality. . . . You find us peculiarly peaceable and orderly. It does not cost your state much for our criminal prosecution. We apply less to your courts for redress, and so far as I know, there are none who are a charge upon the state, as paupers.

"To His Excellency Gov. Bigler," *Daily Alta California* (San Francisco, California), May 5, 1852.

American woman to preside over a woman's rights convention (see Chapter 8), she could not refuse her husband's decision to move to California.

Many women shared Abigail Bush's dilemma, but few traveled by sea to California. In the years after the Gold Rush, most migrants journeyed in family groups on the overland trails by wagon train. These trains included many recently married couples with young children, infants, or babies on the way. During the long and difficult journey, families were often forced to abandon some of their possessions to lighten the wagons, family heirlooms and other items of "merely sentimental" value being the first to go. Women and children typically gathered fuel and hauled water, tasks that could be incredibly burdensome on the Plains, where both water and trees were scarce. Frontier families often cooked over "buffalo chips," that is, dried dung, gathered along the edges of the trail. In addition, whether pregnant, ill, or exhausted, women still performed the necessary domestic chores of washing clothes, preparing meals, and caring for children amid the chaos of constant movement.

During the crises that all too frequently confronted these pioneers, women might also take on men's roles, such as driving the wagons, caring for the horses, or burying the dead. Catherine Haun and her husband traveled west from Iowa in spring 1849. She later recalled that one man "was bitten on the ankle by a venomous snake," and "his limb had to be amputated with the aid of a common handsaw. Fortunately, for him, he had a good, brave wife who helped and cheered him into health and usefulness." Still, "the woman had to do a man's work as they were alone," that is, they had no other family with them on the trail.

Elizabeth Smith, who traveled the Oregon Trail two years earlier, might have offered sympathy and advice. Her husband fell ill in November 1847, after nearly six months on the trail. Elizabeth had to take charge of the wagons and seven children, including her baby daughter. After reaching Portland, Oregon, Mrs. Smith found shelter; cared for her husband and children through the cold, wet winter; and sold what goods they had to buy food. On February 2, 1848, the final tragedy hit. "Today we buried my earthly companion," she wrote in her diary. "Now I know what none but widows know; that is, how comfortless is that of a widow's life, especially when left in a strange land, without money or friends, and the care of seven children."

Forty-Niner

With the aid of a shoulder pole, which derived from his homeland, a Chinese immigrant carried one of the prospector's essential tools: a rocker box, also known as a cradle. While a sluice box was used in streams to retrieve gold, the rocker box was designed for dry places. Miners poured a small amount of water into the box and then rocked it from side to side until dirt and other materials sifted through its perforated bottom, leaving the heavier gold behind. Bancroft Library, University of California at Berkeley.

Lightening the Load on the Overland Trail

Traveling on the overland trail meant giving up cherished family possessions and familiar domestic conveniences. A woman might be able to bring along only an iron cooking pot, a kettle, and a coffee pot to prepare meals for her family on the journey west — and things might not get much better for a while after arrival at their new frontier home. Iron cooking pot, mid-1800s, 88.227.2 — Autry National Center.

As the Smiths' experience suggests, when families settled in mining camps or farm villages, life could be even more difficult than it was along the trail. Houses were sometimes widely separated, leaving women with little social contact or domestic help beyond their immediate family. Men's employment was often erratic, and work for women, though plentiful, rarely paid well. Moreover, many of the opportunities for female employment — in the dance halls and brothels that sprouted in mining towns, for instance — were not considered appropriate for respectable married women. Mrs. Smith sent her two oldest sons to work in the mines while they were still quite young, and she did laundry and cooking for others to make ends meet. A year and a half after her husband's death, she married a widower who had ten children of his own and finally found the economic security that had driven her husband to move west in the first place.

Even those whose families survived the westward journey intact, staked a homestead, and started a farm faced hardship. Enormous labor was required to build a house, construct basic furnishings, break the ground, plant the first crops, keep a cow and chickens, do the milking, collect the eggs, churn the butter, make the clothes and bedding, complete the harvest, haul the water, chop the wood, and keep the household clean and the family fed. Although men, women, and children all did their share, women's work was particularly taxing. For young wives, childbearing and caring for infants added to the physical burdens of frontier life. Women had far fewer opportunities than their husbands and sons to travel to nearby farms, trading posts, or towns; as a result many suffered from isolation and depression. Churches were few and far between, and doctors and midwives were often too far away to attend births or provide assistance in emergencies. This placed the major burden of caring for the family's physical and spiritual needs on women.

Despite these burdens, some white women benefited from moving west. Because of the scarcity of white women on the frontier, those who made the trip were often highly prized as wives and mothers. Single women could marry into established families, and widows such as Elizabeth Smith usually found new husbands quickly. Those who chose to remain single and had the skills to farm could gain access to homesteads. Other women used their skills at sewing, cooking, laundry, shopkeeping, or writing to launch successful business ventures. By the late nineteenth century, pioneer women would build on the importance of their labor to achieve political rights and professional status that were not available to women back east.

Pioneers on the western frontier led lives that were filled with work and family. Even after the invention of the telegraph and the construction of railroads, many households remained isolated and did not receive regular mail deliveries or newspaper reports. Western political leaders, however, were often eager to gain access to federal support, and most hoped one day to apply for statehood for their territories. When statehood was at stake, western residents quickly became swept up in the political dramas that were unfolding back East. The most important issue in many cases was whether a territory would gain admission as a free state or a slave state. The outcome of these debates was significant for all westerners, but particularly for the African Americans who had moved or been forced to travel west.

Slavery Expands West   Slavery existed in many of the western territories, though of the newly settled lands, it flourished only in Texas and Oklahoma. Still, however circumscribed, the expansion of the plantation system exacerbated the brutality of slavery. On the frontier, slaves were increasingly subject to abuses as a consequence of absentee ownership. Black women, denied the minimal protections that were offered by extended families, suffered increased sexual abuse in frontier regions, where men once again dominated the population. There, too, it was difficult to supply slaves with sufficient food, clothing, and housing because the expansion of settlement outstripped the extension of railroads, banks, and other agents of commercial development.

Slavery was legal only in the Utah territory, Texas, and Oklahoma in the mid-nineteenth-century West, and the number of slaves in the Far West remained small throughout the period. The vast majority of African Americans living west of the Mississippi River worked as slaves in Texas, where they made up 30 percent of the population in 1860, and Oklahoma, where they made up nearly 15 percent and were held in bondage by Cherokee, Creek, and other Indians. Yet officials in other territories generally ignored the existence of slaves within their borders rather than challenge their white owners, who were seen as valuable settlers. Black laborers thus suffered oppressive conditions whether legally enslaved or technically free.

Brutal work conditions, harsh discipline, and scorching temperatures affected growing numbers of enslaved African Americans as the planter frontier pushed west. There was little division of labor by sex or age; everybody was needed to pull stumps; dig ditches; cut cane; plant cotton; and build houses, slave quarters, barns, and roads. One Texas slave recalled years later that the workday lasted from "can see to can't see." Throughout the Southwest, moreover, enslaved African Americans were captured and killed in raids by Comanches and other Indian groups that were trying to stop the influx of white settlers. Slaves who escaped still faced capture by Indians as well as vast stretches of arid land.

Life on the frontier could be particularly harsh for isolated slave women, whether on the Oklahoma and Texas frontier or in older settlements such as Missouri. Celia, a thirteen-year-old African American, learned the horrors of isolation as soon as her new master, Robert Newsom, picked her up in his wagon. On the trip to his Missouri farm, Newsom, a widower, raped the girl. Once she was settled on the farm, he repeated his sexual assaults whenever he chose. When Celia sought protection by taking up with one of the two male slaves on Newsom's farm, her owner ignored her pleas to be left alone. Celia refused to accept her fate and set a trap for her master. She killed Newsom with a hatchet on the night of June 23, 1855, after he had assaulted her. She then cut up and burned his body in her fireplace. Celia was eventually charged with murder and found some sympathy among whites who were appalled by her tale of abuse. Unfortunately for Celia, her case came to trial in the midst of renewed conflicts over slavery, most notably in the neighboring Kansas territory. In this context, acts of open defiance by a slave could not go unpunished. An all-white jury found Celia guilty, and she was hanged.

Uneasy Compromises over Slavery

The expansion of slavery as the nation pushed west inspired growing opposition in the free states. Although the majority of whites, North and South, accepted slavery where it already existed, more and more opposed its extension into new territories. Of course, many people were more concerned with saving western lands for whites than with limiting the abuse of blacks. Nonetheless, these converts to free-soil principles began to swell the antislavery ranks. Between 1849 and 1854, those who opposed slavery and/or its expansion clashed head to head with southern planters and their supporters. The most severe conflicts erupted over the admission to statehood first of California and then of Kansas. Although a resolution was reached in each case, the battles heightened suspicions on both sides, and the compromises themselves laid the foundation for future conflicts.

For instance, the Compromise of 1850, by which California was admitted to the union, included a new and expanded Fugitive Slave Law that ignited outrage in the free states and attracted new recruits to the antislavery cause.

The Compromise of 1850   In California, the number of U.S. residents had grown so rapidly that in 1849, political leaders sought statehood without having ever applied for territorial status. This made California the focal point of debates over slave labor and free labor that continued to dominate eastern political life. Just before California applied for statehood, northerners who wanted the West left open for settlement by free men founded the Free-Soil Party (see Chapter 8). Seeking to alleviate the pressures that were created by immigration and provide a fresh start for families who were unable to find prosperity in increasingly crowded eastern cities, Free-Soilers advocated a nonslave West but did not advocate abolition. They were will-ing to leave slavery alone where it already existed, thereby hoping to assuage the concerns of southerners.

The events unfolding around California tested the strengths and limits of free-soil sentiment. Zachary Taylor, a Whig slave owner, had been elected president in 1848 (see Chapter 8). He encouraged California's application for statehood as a means of strengthening the Whig Party nationally. Here, thought Taylor, was an opportunity to defuse Free-Soil Party support by demonstrating that a southern Whig could oversee the entrance of free states to the Union. Taylor's success in this endeavor depended on his abil-ity to convince other southern Whigs that slavery could be protected in the South without expanding the institution into every western territory.

Taylor's plan ran into several obstacles. Congressional Democrats, Whigs, and Free-Soilers all wanted reassurances that the interests of their constituents would be protected. And no one seemed convinced that the simple admission of California as a free state could ensure those interests. After lengthy and contentious arguments, Congress rejected the idea of either allowing or forbidding slavery in the West by federal law and instead stitched together a compromise.

The construction and passage of this compromise involved some of the most charismatic figures and some of the most dramatic oratory in the his-tory of the U.S. Senate. Henry Clay, architect of the Missouri Compromise thirty years earlier, spearheaded this effort at national reconciliation even though he was old and ill. His bill called for passage of five measures: (1) California would be admitted as a free state; (2) territorial governments would be formed without restrictions on slavery in the rest of the land acquired from Mexico; (3) the federal government would assume Texas's public debt in exchange for Texas yielding in its border dispute with New Mexico; (4) the slave trade, but not slavery itself, would be abolished in Washington, D.C.; and (5) a new and more effective fugitive slave law would go into effect. But despite his appeals to shared national principles, Clay could not get the bill passed.

Among his most forceful opponents was John C. Calhoun, sixty-six years old and in worse health than Clay. Because Calhoun was unable to rise from his seat, a colleague read his speech. Calhoun demanded that the South be granted equal rights in the territories, that the North obey all fugi-tive slave laws, and that the North cease its attacks on the institution of slav-ery. He even suggested that the country be ruled by two presidents, one representing the North and one the South, each with veto power. Though he claimed that he, like Clay, wanted to save the Union, his blueprint for sec-tional reconciliation required the North to acquiesce to the South.

Massachusetts' elder statesman, Senator Daniel Webster, reassured the North that this would not happen. Older than Calhoun by two years but still healthy, and hopeful of gaining the White House one day, Webster rallied support to Clay's cause. In a brilliant speech, he urged calm, advocated idealism, and praised patriotism. But even Webster could not convince a majority of his colleagues to vote for Clay's compromise bill. He was perhaps glad when his appointment as secretary of state removed him from the Senate and the acrimonious debate. Death removed Calhoun, in July 1850. And although Clay remained in the Senate until his death two years later, he retreated from its leadership.

After six months of debate, then, the California issue remained unsettled. At this point, a younger and more pragmatic group of Senators took over the negotiations. These men — including William H. Seward of New York, Jefferson Davis of Mississippi, and Stephen A. Douglas of Illinois — initially seemed even less willing to compromise. Seward adamantly opposed Clay's bill; Davis just as adamantly favored slavery and its expansion; and Douglas staunchly favored western growth and development. Yet the three managed to move the legislation forward. Douglas provided the critical breakthrough when he broke Clay's bill apart, allowing senators to vote for the sections they favored without accepting the sections they opposed.

Ultimately, the Compromise of 1850 consisted of a series of separate bills passed by different, and sometimes competing, coalitions. Northeasterners and midwesterners, for instance, nearly all supported the admission of California as a free state and the abolition of the slave trade in the District of Columbia. Southerners, on the other hand, voted overwhelmingly for the new Fugitive Slave Law, which denied jury trials to accused runaway slaves and empowered any marshal pursuing them to force local citizens to join the hunt. On each issue, just enough party loyalists crossed sectional lines to ensure passage. In addition, the sudden death of President Taylor in July 1850, who, despite his support for California's admission, had threatened to veto the larger compromise of which it was a part, paved the way for the bill's passage. The new president, Millard Fillmore, not only supported the compromise, but used his powers as president to convince northern Whigs to support it as well.

Leaders of both major parties congratulated themselves on the 1850 compromise. "Much . . . may be effected by a conciliatory temper and discreet measures," declared Whig Philip Hone. "All praise to the defenders of the Union!" Former Democratic presidential candidate Lewis Cass declared confidently, "I do not believe any party could now be built in relation to this question of slavery. I think the question is settled in the public mind." Political and business leaders organized rallies in New York, Philadelphia, Boston, Pittsburgh, and Cincinnati, in support of the compromise.

Many workers and farmers also approved the new agreement in hopes that it would prevent disruption of the Union and improve their chances for upward mobility. Large numbers of working people saw slavery as synonymous with degradation, and cries of "wage slavery" condemned capitalists who oppressed their employees. But equating wage labor with slavery did not lead to sympathy for slaves themselves. Native-born and immigrant white workers were equally likely to define their own status as free men by distinguishing themselves from slaves. In addition, many white workers harbored racist attitudes not only toward slaves, but toward free blacks as well. They often viewed with suspicion fugitive slaves who had escaped to the North, seeing them as competition for scarce jobs and as diminishing, by their race alone, the wages and status of free white workers. This led once again to a desire to keep slavery and African Americans out of the western territories, where white workers assumed that African Americans would necessarily undermine the value of free labor.

Still, although Douglas, Seward, and Davis could take credit for completing the work Clay had begun, they failed to embrace the elder statesman's concern about national reconciliation. Achieving compromise only through the appeasement of separate and antagonistic interests did not solve the nation's racial crisis. Instead it soon revitalized sectional hostilities. The most controversial section of the 1850 Compromise—the Fugitive Slave Law—served as the next lightning rod.

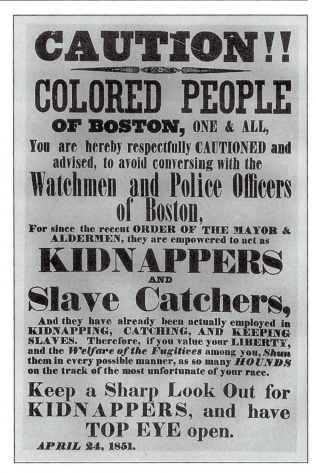

The Fugitive Slave Law

A notice posted by Boston abolitionist Theodore Parker in 1851. Boston Public Library.

The Fugitive Slave Law   One of the Fugitive Slave Law's major targets was the "underground railroad," a network of thousands of free blacks and white sympathizers who concealed, sheltered, clothed, and guided runaway slaves in the course of their northward flight. The best known of the "conductors" who served this railroad was Harriet Tubman, who escaped from slavery in Maryland in 1849. Over the next decade, Tubman returned to the South nineteen times, repeatedly risking capture and death to liberate more than 300 others. In the North, local vigilance committees—composed largely of free blacks and white Quakers—kept the railroad going. Free blacks provided most of the labor and funds required by the cause, despite their long hours of work and limited economic opportunities. African American members of the New York support committee were able to pledge only fifty

Freedom or Death

Soon after passage of the Fugitive Slave Law, Margaret Garner fled from her Kentucky master with her four children. Slave patrollers followed her to Ohio. Faced with capture, Garner killed two of her children rather than see them be returned to slavery. The surviving children were taken from her, and on the return trip to Kentucky Garner drowned herself in the Ohio River. Her story inspired an acclaimed nineteenth-century painting by Thomas S. Noble (on which this engraving was based) and Toni Morrison's Pulitzer Prize–winning novel *Beloved*. *Harper's Weekly,* May 18, 1867 — American Social History Project.

cents a month; those in Philadelphia contributed even less. Fortunately, a few wealthy families, such as the Fortens (free blacks) and the Motts (white Quakers), were also deeply committed to keeping the railroad running.

During the 1840s, slave owners grew more anxious about the underground railroad, even though the number of successful slave escapes may not have increased. Escapes affected far more than the few thousand slaves who actually fled. News traveled through the slaves' "grapevine telegraph," emboldening many who were still in bondage. At the same time, successful fugitives such as Frederick Douglass and William and Ellen Craft, who had escaped from Georgia in December 1848, became powerful and effective antislavery speakers in the United States and Britain. The proponents of the Fugitive Slave Law hoped that it would not only reduce the number of escapes, but also drive earlier runaways such as Tubman, Douglass, and the Crafts back into hiding.

Instead, the new law had the opposite effect, reinvigorating protests against slavery and against slave owners, who were viewed as abusing federal power. A law that forced them to assist slave owners in returning fugitives to bondage enraged long-time abolitionists and their new allies. They held mass meetings throughout the North and Midwest. At one gathering in Allegheny City, near Pittsburgh, land reformer John Ferral, a veteran of the workingmen's movement of the 1820s and 1830s, attacked the Fugitive Slave Law and proposed a state constitutional amendment that gave black males the right to vote. The meeting approved his proposal at a time when only five northern states enfranchised African Americans on an equal basis with whites. A number of antislavery Whigs captured seats in northern

"What a Disgrace to a City Calling Itself Free": Harriet Jacobs on the Fugitive Slave Law

Harriet A. Jacobs's Incidents in the Life of a Slave Girl, published in 1861, was one of the few narratives of slavery written by a woman. Having escaped from her master in 1845, Jacobs—along with other fugitive slaves—found herself once more imperiled when Congress passed the Fugitive Slave Law. Here, she describes the impact of the 1850 law on the African American community of New York City.

About the time that I reentered the Bruce family, an event occurred of disastrous import to the colored people. The slave Hamlin [James Hamlet], the first fugitive that came under the new law, was given up by the bloodhounds of the north to the bloodhounds of the south. It was the beginning of a reign of terror to the colored population. The great city rushed on in its whirl of excitement, taking no note of the "short and simple annals of the poor." But while fashionables were listening to the thrilling voice of Jenny Lind in Metropolitan Hall, the thrilling voices of poor hunted colored people went up, in an agony of supplication, to the Lord, from Zion's church. Many families, who had lived in the city for twenty years, fled from it now. Many a poor washerwoman, who, by hard labor, had made herself a comfortable home, was obliged to sacrifice her furniture, bid a hurried farewell to friends, and seek her fortune among strangers in Canada. Many a wife discovered a secret she had never known before—that her husband was a fugitive, and must leave her to insure his own safety. Worse still, many a husband discovered that his wife had fled from slavery years ago, and as "the child follows the condition of its mother," the children of his love were liable to be seized and carried to slavery. Everywhere, in those humble homes, there was consternation and anguish. But what cared the legislators of the "dominant race" for the blood they were crushing out of trampled hearts?

. . . I was subject to it; and so were hundreds of intelligent and industrious people all around us. I seldom ventured into the streets; and when it was necessary to do an errand for Mrs. Bruce, or any of the family, I went as much as possible through back streets and by-ways. What a disgrace to a city calling itself free, that inhabitants, guiltless of offence, and seeking to perform their duties conscientiously, should be condemned to live in such incessant fear, and have nowhere to turn for protection! This state of things, of course, gave rise to many impromptu vigilance committees. Every colored person, and every friend of their persecuted race, kept their eyes wide open.

Harriet A. Jacobs, *Incidents in the Life of a Slave Girl* (1861).

A Bold Stroke for Freedom
On Christmas Eve, 1855, patrol-lers finally caught up with a group of teenaged slaves who had escaped by wagon from Loudon County, Virginia. But the posse was driven off when Ann Wood, leader of the group, brandished weapons and dared the pursuers to fire. The fugitives continued on to Philadelphia. William Still, *The Underground Rail Road* (1872) — American Social History Project.

congressional elections in fall 1850 as a result of this popular reaction to the Fugitive Slave Law.

Other dissenters took direct action. In Boston, Philadelphia, Syracuse, Chicago, and elsewhere, black and white opponents of slavery used force to protect fugitives from their hunters, sometimes attacking and even killing the pursuers. In October 1850, Boston abolitionists helped two slaves to escape to freedom and drove from town the Georgia slave catcher who was pursuing them. A year later, in Syracuse, New York, a crowd of 2,000 broke into the courthouse to free a fugitive slave. That same fall, a group of free blacks and fugitive slaves in the Quaker community of Christiana, Pennsylvania, armed themselves with guns against a group of slave catchers, killed a Maryland slave owner, and severely wounded his son. In this case, despite the willingness of federal officials to intervene on the slave owners' behalf, public outrage forced the government to drop charges against those who had defied the Fugitive Slave Act by force of arms.

The 1852 publication of *Uncle Tom's Cabin,* a tragic tale of slavery and slave hunters, enhanced popular opposition to the Fugitive Slave Law. Harriet Beecher Stowe first published the story in serial form in the *National Era,* an abolitionist newspaper. When published in book form, it sold three hundred thousand copies in one year, electrified northern readers, and infused opposition to the Fugitive Slave Law with a powerful emotional appeal.

Against this background, the Free-Soil Party expanded its ranks. Contradicting some politicians' claims that the Compromise of 1850 would forestall the growth of parties focused on slavery, the legislation created stronger bonds between established antislavery forces and free-soil advocates. In addition, the Free-Soil Party gained support from some immigrant groups, including German émigrés who had been politicized by their experience in European revolutions in 1848–1849. These immigrants focused first on issues of class inequality. "The rich and distinguished here stand higher above the law than in any country," exclaimed one German-born Pittsburgher. In America, he went on, "in the land that boasts of its humanity, that claims to be at the very top of civilization . . . the laboring classes are treated in as shameful a manner as in Europe, with all its ancient prejudices." The passage of the Fugitive Slave Act reinforced the sense among many immigrants that the fight for free soil and against slavery must be won if the move to America was truly going to improve their lives.

Contrary to the hopes of its sponsors, then, the Compromise of 1850 inflamed antislavery feeling in the North. As long as slavery seemed geographically contained and remote, free-state residents could try to ignore it, considering it someone else's worry and someone else's sin. But by refusing to outlaw slavery in the West and then welcoming slave hunters into the free states and requiring all citizens to aid them, the new law put an end to those illusions. Like the Mexican War, the Fugitive Slave Law seemed to bear out the abolitionist claim that chattel slavery endangered freedom everywhere, not merely in the South.

Unveiled
After passage of the Fugitive Slave Law, escaped slave women living in the North sometimes wore veils when they appeared in public to avoid identification by slave catchers. William Still, *The Underground Rail Road* (1872) — American Social History Project.

Broken Covenant: The Kansas-Nebraska Act of 1854

Before the battles over the Fugitive Slave Law could ebb, struggles over slavery erupted in the Great Plains. The focal point of this battle was the Kansas-Nebraska bill, submitted to Congress in January 1854 by Democratic Senator Stephen A. Douglas of Illinois. Douglas had speculated heavily in western lands and hoped that by attracting settlers to the region he could persuade Congress to route a planned transcontinental railroad through the area. Because many southern senators preferred a more southern route, Douglas offered them an incentive to vote for his bill: he included a clause that allowed residents of the territory to decide by popular vote whether or not they would permit slavery. Because the Nebraska territory lay north of the 30° 30' line set by the Missouri Compromise, allowing residents there to vote on whether to become a slave state or a free state would effectively remove all federal barriers to the spread of slavery throughout the West.

In its final version, Douglas's bill not only explicitly annulled the terms of the Missouri Compromise, which in the more than three decades since its passage had become nearly sacrosanct as the final statement on the boundary between free and slave territory. It also divided the Great Plains into two territories — Kansas and Nebraska — to assuage the concerns of free-state Iowans and slave-state Missourians (Map 10.4). New antislavery and proslavery forces could each hope to win control over one of the new territories. Then, to replace the Missouri Compromise line, Douglas proposed a doctrine that he called "popular sovereignty." This doctrine left the future of

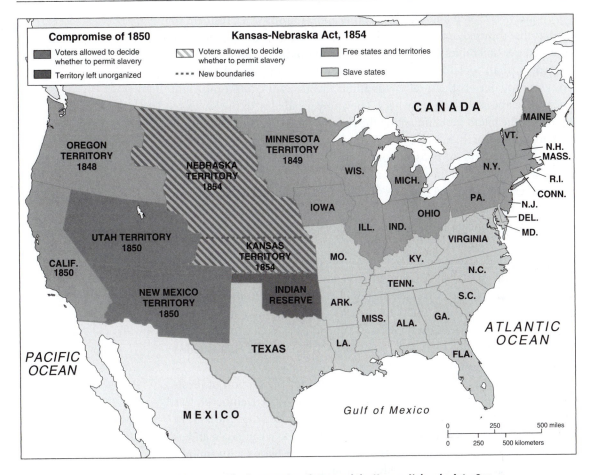

MAP 10.4   The Compromise of 1850 and the Kansas-Nebraska Act, 1854

By the early 1850s, vast new lands in the West had come under U.S. control. The desire of both northerners and southerners to settle those lands renewed the conflict between the advocates of free- and slave-labor systems. In the Compromise of 1850 and the Kansas-Nebraska Act, politicians attempted to settle these disputes through legislative action. However, leaving the final decision on slavery in large parts of the West to popular sovereignty ensured that the battle over slave and free labor would only intensify in coming years.

slavery to be decided by registered voters in each territory that sought admission as a state.

Reaction was almost instantaneous. A group of antislavery congressmen issued an impassioned and widely circulated manifesto calling the new law "a criminal betrayal of precious rights." In the West, they said, "it has been expected, freedom-loving emigrants from Europe, and energetic and intelligent laborers from our own land, will find homes of comfort and fields of useful enterprise." But Douglas's law would turn this great expanse "into a dreary region of despotism, inhabited by masters and slaves."

Widely reprinted and translated, this appeal aroused a firestorm of protest that dwarfed opposition to the Fugitive Slave Law. More than three hundred free-soil rallies in the North and West mobilized tens of thousands of people of all social backgrounds. Some were leading merchants and bankers in major northern cities, longtime advocates of compromise and friendly relations with slave owners. They now pleaded with the South to withdraw the bill to avoid inflaming the already dangerous antislavery sentiment in the North. Whig leader Amos Lawrence, a Boston merchant, begged southerners to "pause before they proceed further to disturb the peace which we hoped the Compromise of 1850 would have made perpetual." Others who opposed Douglas's bill were staunchly against slavery on principle. They denounced the bill not for causing bad sectional feelings, but because (as one group declared) it "authorizes the further extension of slavery."

Despite these strong objections, the Senate passed the Kansas-Nebraska Act on March 3, 1854. The majority that favored the legislation included many southern senators, who viewed "popular sovereignty" as the best hope for expanding slavery into the West. To achieve victory, these southerners combined with northern Democrats who hoped that this bill would provide the basis for expanding their party's support. On May 22, the House added its assent by a narrow margin.

Advocates in both houses of Congress had gained the support of President Franklin Pierce. Pierce, an obscure New Hampshire Democrat, was elected in 1852 when the Whig Party suffered deep divisions over the issue of slavery. Pierce attempted to avoid the issue of slavery as a candidate and as president. But his election just a year after the Fugitive Slave Law went into effect made such a stance impossible. Instead, Pierce chose to send federal troops into northern cities, such as Boston, when abolitionists stormed courthouses and attempted to free recaptured slaves. In 1854, Pierce came out in support of the Kansas-Nebraska Bill, helping to win over enough northern Democratic congressmen to assure its passage. He signed it into law in May 1854.

In elections that fall, candidates of the so-called Know-Nothing Party (see Chapter 8), who claimed that they, too, wanted to protect the white race, gained ground in local and state contests. They temporarily controlled the governments of Massachusetts and Pennsylvania. Yet voters in these very same states elected Free-Soilers to office in significant numbers. Clearly, this latest attempt at resolving the slavery controversy had only inflamed the conflict.

Bleeding Kansas During the next two years, political passions burned fiercely in Kansas. Proslavery Missourians poured across the border, hoping to claim the Kansas territory for themselves. But even more settlers

"Come by the Thousands": The Struggle for Kansas

Concluding that Missouri "has done her duty" to populate the Kansas territory with slavery supporters, this "appeal" appeared in DeBow's Review, a journal on agricultural and political subjects for southern plantation owners. It calls on other slavery supporters from throughout the South to do the same by contributing their bodies and their funds to support the struggle over the future of slavery—indeed over the future of the Union itself.

To the People of the South: On the undersigned, managers of the "Lafayette Emigration Society," has devolved the important duty of calling the attention of the people of the slaveholding States, to the absolute necessity of immediate action on their part, in relation to the settlement of Kansas Territory. The crisis is at hand. Prompt and decisive measures must be adopted, or farewell to southern rights and independence. . . .

The great struggle will come off at the next election, in October, 1856, and unless the south can at that time maintain her ground, all will be lost. We repeat it, the crisis has arrived. The time has come for action—bold, determined action; words will no longer do any good; we must have men in Kansas; and that too by tens of thousands. A few will not answer. If we should need ten thousand, and lack one of that number, all will count nothing. Let all then, who can come, do so at once. Those who cannot come, must give their money to help others to come. There are hundreds of thousands of broad acres of rich land, worth from $5 to $20 per acre, open to settlement and pre-emption, at $1.25 per acre. Let, then, the farmer come and bring his slaves with him. There are now one thousand slaves in Kansas, whose presence there strengthens our cause. Shall we allow these rich lands and this beautiful country to be overrun by our abolition enemies? We know of a surety that they have emissaries and spies in almost every town, village and city in the south, watching our movements, and tampering with our slaves. Let us, then, be vigilant and active in the cause; we must maintain our ground. The loss of Kansas to the south will be the death knell of our dear Union.

Missouri has done nobly, thus far, in overcoming the thousands who have been sent out by Abolition Aid Societies; we cannot hold out much longer unless the whole South will come to the rescue. We need men; we need money; send us both, and that quickly. Do not delay; come as individuals, come in companies, come by the thousands.

"Kansas Matters—Appeals to the South," *DeBow's Review*, May 1856.

arrived from the free states. Thousands were aided by abolitionists back east who formed the Kansas Emigrant Aid Society to ensure the territory would remain a haven for free labor. Confronted by a free-soil majority, the proslavery forces quickly resorted to armed intimidation and violence. When antislavery forces responded, undeclared guerrilla war followed.

One especially passionate antagonist in this battle was John Brown. Born in 1800 into a white family of New England stock, Brown was deeply attached to the country's revolutionary traditions and stirred by the great religious awakenings of the age. Over the years, he tried his hand at various occupations to support himself and his growing family. He sometimes achieved modest prosperity, but Brown prized other things above commercial success. "To get a little property together," he once wrote his son, "is really a low mark to be firing at through life." Personal independence, democracy, equal rights, self-discipline, and self-respect—the traditional republican values of the North's small producers—meant more to him. The quickening commercialization of American life disturbed Brown, for he perceived it as a threat both to his world and to his moral code. And the Panic of 1837, which ruined him along with so many others, confirmed his worst fears.

John Brown

This recently discovered daguerreotype portrait of the abolitionist — before he grew his famous beard — was taken in 1847 by African American photographer Augustus Washington. National Portrait Gallery, Smithsonian Institution.

As the years went by, Brown's views about society and its ills grew clearer. Of all society's wrongs, none repelled him as thoroughly as human bondage. Here was truly the "sum of all villainies," the starkest challenge to all the social and religious beliefs that shaped his outlook. From the 1830s on, Brown aided fugitive slaves from his home in northern New York State, and after 1850, he worked with free blacks to resist the Fugitive Slave Law.

In the mid-1850s, five of John Brown's sons joined the antislavery advocates who were moving to Kansas. Encountering armed groups of southerners who were determined to force slavery on the territory, they called on their father for aid, and he soon joined them. In the often brutal fighting that followed in "Bleeding Kansas," Brown earned a reputation for ferocity and an uncompromising hostility to slavery and racism generally. He proclaimed "the manhood of the Negro race" and expressed his antislavery convictions with a vehemence that was alien even to many Free-Soilers.

Confrontations in the West soon found their echo back east. Senator Charles Sumner of Massachusetts, an eloquent spokesman for African American rights, denounced the efforts of Democrats in the White House and Congress to force slavery into a free Kansas. He was particularly vehement in a speech he gave in May 1856, in which he attacked his Senate colleague, Andrew P. Butler of South Carolina, for having taken "the harlot slavery" as his mistress. He called the efforts of proslavery forces to establish their own government in the territory the "Crime Against Kansas." In retaliation for Sumner's inflammatory remarks, a distant cousin of Butler, the young congressman Preston Brooks, attacked Sumner with his walking cane. Brooks beat Sumner unconscious, landing some thirty blows while the senator sat trapped by his heavy desk, unable to defend himself.

SOUTHERN CHIVALRY ─ ARGUMENT versus CLUB'S.

Southern Chivalry

A contemporary print denounced South Carolina congressman Preston S. Brooks's assault on Massachusetts senator Charles Sumner on May 12, 1856. In Southern media, however, Brooks was celebrated as a hero for resisting Northern insults. John L. Magee, *Southern Chivalry — Argument Versus Club's*, lithograph, 1856 — American Social History Project.

In Kansas, such brutality had become commonplace. Hannah Anderson Ropes, a young mother of two, had moved to Lawrence, Kansas, in the fall of 1855 to join her husband. She wrote heart-wrenching letters to her mother back in Brookline, Massachusetts, including one on November 21, in which she described the dangers that surrounded her family:

> How strange it will seem to you to hear that I have loaded pistols and a bowie knife upon my table at night, three of Sharp's rifles, loaded, standing in the room. . . . All the week every preparation has been made for our defense; and everybody is worn with want of sleep.

Her fear, and that of her neighbors, was that proslavery Missourians would cross the border and launch an all-out attack on the abolitionist stronghold of Lawrence.

In the summer of 1856, proslavery forces did attack Lawrence, destroying two newspaper offices, burning buildings, looting stores, and beating residents. Hearing the news, John Brown, accompanied by four sons and two antislavery supporters, sought revenge against a small settlement of proslavery families along Pottawatomie Creek. Using broadswords, Brown and his followers rousted five families out of their beds in the middle of the night, murdered and mutilated five of the men, and left their wives and children to spread the tale of terror. The attack on Lawrence and the so-called Pottawatomie Massacre provoked a guerrilla war that raged in Kansas for months and cost some 200 lives.

Despite the passage of the Kansas-Nebraska Act and its support by proslavery Democrats, residents of Kansas finally established a free state government in mid-1858. That victory, however, ended neither the broader dispute over slavery nor John Brown's role in it. The battle in Kansas, in fact,

Rescued
In 1859, the Kansas abolitionist Dr. John Doy, called a slave-stealer by his enemies for his forays into Missouri to free slaves, was kidnapped by proslavery partisans and imprisoned in Missouri. This photograph showed Doy surrounded by the friends who subsequently rescued him. Kansas State Historical Society.

only stoked the flames of national conflict and convinced Brown that a final reckoning was near. If it was only violence that had kept Kansas free, he asked, how could peaceful methods alone secure the same ends throughout the country? When his brother Jeremiah urged moderation, John replied "that he knew that he was in the line of his duty, and he must pursue it, though it should destroy him and his family. He . . . was satisfied that he was the chosen instrument in the hands of God to war against slavery."

Birth of the Republican Party   Many Americans now agreed with Brown that a peaceful end to slavery no longer seemed likely. For decades, the concerted efforts of politicians North and South had staved off a direct confrontation between the slave-labor and wage-labor systems. But in "Bleeding Kansas," the systems met head to head. As Congressman Abraham Lincoln wrote to a Kentucky friend a year before the bloody conflicts in Kansas:

> You spoke [in 1819] of "the peaceful extinction of slavery" and used other expressions to indicate your belief that the thing was, at some time, to have an end. Since then we have had thirty-six years of experience, and this experience has demonstrated, I think, that there is no peaceful extinction of slavery in prospect for us.

The Missouri Compromise line, which had promised so much in 1819, was now gone. With its demise, controversies over slavery multiplied, and the country's two major political parties finally broke apart. The Whigs' disintegration began with the Compromise of 1850. By opposing the Compromise, President Zachary Taylor alienated ardently proslavery voters,

If I Don't Kill Something Else Soon, I'll Spile!

An 1856 drawing commented on Know-Nothing violence in Baltimore. The scene was populated by members of nativist gangs with names such as "Blood-Tubs," "Cut-Throats," and "Plug-Uglies." Maryland Historical Society.

dooming the Whig Party's future prospects in the South. The remaining Whigs were deeply divided; some attempted to overshadow the antislavery movement altogether by combining forces with the nativist American (or Know-Nothing) Party. Anti-immigrant riots in Baltimore and other east coast cities suggested that this strategy might be successful, but after making quick gains, the movement soon collapsed. The slavery question had simply become unavoidable. In mid-1855, the Know-Nothing Party itself split into proslavery and antislavery factions.

Democrats, meanwhile, suffered a series of splits and defections, beginning with the founding of the Free-Soil Party in 1848. By 1854 and 1855, massive numbers of midwestern free-soil Democrats had left the party, alienated by Democratic support for popular sovereignty in Kansas and Nebraska. The formation of a national Republican Party in 1856 cut deeply into northern Democratic support and highlighted the increasingly sectional character of partisan political alignments.

The Republican Party coalesced out of the large but amorphous opposition to the Kansas-Nebraska bill of 1854. In their first party platform, drafted in 1856, Republicans denounced slavery as immoral and insisted on halting its further westward expansion. The new party attracted support from many formerly competing interests, including antislavery Whigs, Democrats, former Free-Soilers, and Know-Nothings. One of its earliest organizers, Alvan Bovay, was a veteran land reformer and former Whig. Labor leader and land reformer John Commerford became a Republican spokesman in New York. But party leaders also included some prosperous northern businessmen, many of them rising manufacturers, often from relatively humble backgrounds, who had been competing against the established mercantile elite for years. Meanwhile, many of the North's largest merchants and manufacturers with important southern ties threw their political support to the Know-Nothings or to northern Democrats. Leading Republicans were more commonly middle-class men (especially lawyers, professional politicians, editors, and journalists) who accepted the values of the North's free-labor industrial system and were ready to fight for it—more so than were many of the elite.

Yet the great majority of those who rallied to the Republican Party's banner during the 1850s were small farmers, small shopkeepers, and skilled urban working people, most of them native-born. Significant numbers of ordinary laborers also voted Republican. And the Republicans gained the support of many reform-minded northerners, including many who were denied the right to vote. Large numbers of free blacks, for instance, who were disfranchised in northern states by literacy, residency, or monetary requirements, supported the Republicans, as they had the Free-Soilers. And many women, white and black, who had earlier formed societies to aid abolition and free-soil efforts, now threw their resources behind the Republican Party.

The election of James Buchanan, the Democratic presidential candidate in 1856, did little to allay fears of sectional conflict. Buchanan had sought the presidential nomination before. He succeeded this time because his party could not afford to renominate the sitting president, Franklin Pierce, who was too closely linked to the bloody events in Kansas. In addition, the Democrats hoped to gain favor among northern voters by nominating a candidate from their region. Buchanan was perfect: a dignified elder statesman from Pennsylvania who had been minister to Great Britain in the years that the Kansas-Nebraska conflict flared. He may have been uninspiring and unimaginative, but Buchanan was also uncontroversial and uncommitted on popular sovereignty and the extension of slavery.

The Republicans chose John C. Frémont, who had gained his reputation as a celebrated army explorer and leader in the conquest of California. He embodied the free-soil vision of America's manifest destiny. Compared with the mere 10 percent of the vote that the Free-Soil candidate, Martin Van Buren, had won just eight years earlier, Frémont's 33 percent of the total votes reflected a major transformation in public thinking. Debates over western territories had inspired this change. Frémont carried eleven of the sixteen free states and 45 percent of all ballots cast in the North. The Republican campaign slogan — "Free soil, free labor, free men" — summarized the goals and ideals that drove millions into its ranks, almost overnight.

Though the Democrats won the 1856 election, the Republican Party's dramatic gains accelerated the drive toward national conflict. Observing the deepening isolation of their political allies in the North, southern planters began to see the majority in the free states as entirely hostile to slavery. To them, it was only a matter of time before Republicans gained control of the national government and used its power to undermine slavery everywhere — first in the West, then in the old South. These specific fears grew out of other, more general worries about southern society and its internal frictions and conflicts. Most immediately, what impact would a Republican national government have on the slave population?

Throughout the South, blacks were paying close attention to national politics, pondering the significance of this new division of the white population, and hoping for liberation through a Republican victory. The 1856 election brought with it stories of plans for slave insurrections in at least six southern states. Though no such uprising occurred in the 1850s, slaves' everyday resistance and attempts to escape to freedom kept planters anxious. The rise of the Republicans only made matters worse. "The recent Presidential canvass has had a deleterious effect on the slave population," reported a Nashville, Tennessee, editor in alarm. "The negroes manifested an unusual interest in the result and attended the political meetings of the whites in large numbers. This is dangerous." A Memphis colleague agreed: "If this eternal agitation of the slavery question does not cease we may expect servile insurrections in dead earnest."

In the meantime, some Republican leaders as well as some writers who supported the new party began courting the nonslaveholding whites of the South. The election of Francis P. Blair, Jr., of St. Louis to Congress in 1856 suggested that Republicans could gain popular support in slave states — at least those on the border. The *National Era*, an antislavery newspaper since the 1840s, responded to Blair's election by declaring, "We no longer stand upon the defensive. We have crossed the line, and are upon slaveholding ground." North Carolinian Hinton Helper's book *The Impending Crisis of the South*, published in 1857, aided Republicans among southern-born residents of the Midwest. Helper argued that slavery was a political and economic curse on the South, driving

"Negro Dogs"

Whether attempting to escape or simply traveling at night to visit friends or family in neighboring plantations, African American slaves were threatened by the slave patrols. These squads, often including nonslaveholders who were required to serve under state law, were notorious for their brutality. Most feared were the dogs that the "pattyrollers" used to track down fugitive slaves. This 1856 advertisement promoted the sale of dogs trained expressly to hunt human beings. Abraham Chapman, comp., *Steal Away: Stories of the Runaway Slaves* (1971).

nonslaveholding whites into poverty, forcing their wives and daughters to labor in the fields, and encouraging many to abandon the South altogether. Although others had made these claims before, here was a "son of the South," as Horace Greeley noted, "who speaks with an authority and a weight which no outsider can have." So impressed were Republicans with Helper's appeal to nonslaveholders in the South that they printed an abridged version of the book in 1859 and circulated it widely in the North.

The immediate impact of Hinton Helper's book in the South was minor. No abolitionist, Helper abhorred the necessity for poor whites to mingle with southern blacks under the plantation system. Nonetheless, planters feared the long-term effects of his work and severely punished those who were caught circulating it. For them, it was another sign of the dangers that the Republican Party posed to slave owners. So it was with growing seriousness that southern politicians threatened to pull their states out of the federal union and beyond the reach of the Republicans to preserve their social power and human property.

The Labor Question in a Time of Rising Tension

Although slavery had emerged as a critical political issue, the enslavement of blacks remained first and foremost a system of labor. Indeed, it was the threatened loss of enslaved workers' labor power and the profits thus generated that led slave owners to fight so vehemently for their "peculiar institution." In this battle, northerners repeatedly touted the superiority of free labor, portraying northern workers as independent and responsible citizens who contributed mightily to both economic prosperity and western expansion. Yet northern workers, especially those who were employed in the burgeoning cities and factory towns along the Atlantic coast and in railroad, maritime, and mining trades throughout the free states, often expressed biting criticisms of the capitalist system. Indeed, those workers who identified themselves as "wage slaves" suggested that their employers were the equivalent of slave drivers. Thus, even as the growing sectional crisis overshadowed the grievances of free workers in national political debates, affluent and working-class northerners clashed with each other in numerous cities and towns. At the same time, conflicts among workers continued to undermine class solidarity as immigrants and the native-born, free blacks and whites, and women and men vied with each other in defining a working-class agenda.

Both Democratic and Republican politicians sought the support of their poor and working-class neighbors. Especially in the North and West, where white workingmen had gained the right to vote in large numbers, elections might turn on who appealed most effectively to their needs. Republicans' use of the slogan "Free soil, free labor, free men" attracted many northern workers to the party. During the 1850s, as elections to national office became crucial in determining the outcome of sectional debates over slavery, some groups of workers renewed their efforts to build powerful labor organizations. Although most were focused on improving wages and working conditions rather than political clout, organized labor had a greater chance of influencing political campaigns than did individual workers.

Workers could not, however, influence the courts. Judges who were sympathetic to slavery had their own responses to questions of citizenship, rights, and race. This was demonstrated most powerfully by the U.S. Supreme Court in its 1857 ruling on a case brought by a slave named Dred Scott.

Defending the Rights of Labor

Throughout the 1840s, efforts to establish unions and other working-class organizations were limited. The prolonged effects of the Panic of 1837, the influx of massive numbers of Irish and German immigrants, the promise of economic opportunity in the West, and highly charged debates over the rights of African Americans and women repeatedly disrupted class-based alliances. Even immigrant workers were divided by language, religious affiliation, and political beliefs. Moreover, some immigrants sought relief from oppressive conditions not through class solidarity, but in neighborhood gangs that pitted one group of young men against another.

By midcentury, however, workers renewed their organizing efforts. As employers repeatedly pitted one group against another, workers gradually learned a hard lesson. Although most white workers still refused to include blacks in their associations and most male organizations continued to exclude women, coalitions among white working-class men developed regionally and nationally. By 1860, some men even supported strikes by women, especially in the shoe and textile industries, in which women formed a large portion of the labor force.

The 1850s thus saw significant advances for the labor movement, including the beginnings of nationwide organization. Such efforts even gained support among free laborers in southern cities such as Baltimore, Richmond, St. Louis, and New Orleans, raising new fears among planters about the rise of Republicanism on their own soil. After 1850, national unions sprang up among hat finishers, cigarmakers, typesetters, plumbers, painters, stonecutters, shoemakers, and iron molders. Some of these unions disappeared almost as fast as they arose, and in most cases, the "national" organizations existed only in the free states.

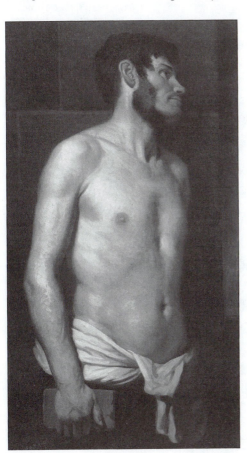

A Dead Rabbit
Also entitled *Study of an Irishman*, George Henry Hall's 1858 painting was rendered shortly after the July 1857 Dead Rabbit–Bowery Boy Riot, a conflict in New York's Five Points between rival Irish working-class street gangs. The painting subtly conveyed a sense of the fear and fascination that poor Irish immigrants provoked in many native-born, middle-class Americans — including, unusually straightforward for the era, a note of homoeroticism. George Henry Hall, 1858, oil on canvas, 32 × 40 1/2 inches — National Academy of Design.

Moreover, the national organizations rarely showed leadership on controversial issues, such as the admission of African American, Mexican, Asian, or women workers to member unions. Nonetheless, in laying the groundwork for later, more successful efforts at labor organizing, these early national unions suggested the power of free workers to develop their own agenda and the need for both northern Republicans and southern slave owners to respond to workers' concerns.

The case of the national union of iron molders—founded largely at the instigation of William H. Sylvis—illustrates the development of national labor organizations. Born in 1828, Sylvis sought training and work as an iron molder in the 1840s, as the iron industry was mushrooming to meet demands for industrial tools and machinery. At first, the few skilled ironworkers earned good wages, but as the number of molders increased, foundry owners reduced wages and imposed harsh working conditions. Simultaneously, a small number of large companies that were able to afford newer and more expensive equipment centralized control over iron production. When Sylvis tried to open his own foundry, the costs drove him out of business, and he was soon trudging Pennsylvania's roads in search of wage work.

Settling in Philadelphia in 1853, he attempted to support his new wife and a growing family on a journeyman molder's meager wages. During the 1830s and 1840s, journeymen molders had formed several local unions around the country, most of which organized to negotiate a single agreement or to call a single strike. The Philadelphia molders were among the first workers to move toward a larger and more permanent organization. Their 1855 constitution declared, "In the present organization of society, laborers single-handed are powerless . . . but combined there is no power of wrong they may not openly defy." Two years later, when some of Sylvis's coworkers struck over a 12 percent wage cut, Sylvis joined the strike as well as the picket committee.

The Philadelphia molders' action failed when an economic depression developed in 1857, but the defeat did not destroy the union. Sylvis, the union secretary, threw himself into the job of strengthening the organization and its ties to other molders' associations. The rise of a national market convinced Sylvis that molders had to organize nationally as well, and he played a central role in founding the National Molders' Union in 1859.

The Great Meeting of Foreigners in the Park

An illustration from an 1855 nativist tract depicted a labor demonstration in New York's City Hall Park demanding relief for the unemployed during the 1854–1855 depression. This wood engraving was one of the few images of organized working-class action published before the Civil War. (Cunnington) J. Wayne Laurens, *The Crisis, or the Enemies of America Unmasked* (Philadelphia, 1855) — American Social History Project.

"An Empty Pocket's the Worst of Crimes!": Supporting the Lynn Shoeworkers

The Hutchinson family was one of the country's most popular singing groups in the nineteenth century. Their successful stage performances combined entertainment with a social reform message; Hutchinson songs often took up the causes of abolitionism and woman suffrage. As natives of Lynn, Massachusetts, the Hutchinsons were particularly aware of the plight of the city's shoeworkers. "The Popular Creed," first sung at shoeworkers' meetings, later became a standard song of the labor movement.

Dimes and dollars! Dollars and dimes!
An empty pocket's the worst of crimes!
If a man's down, give him a thrust!
Trample the beggar into the dust!
Presumptuous poverty, quite appalling!
Knock him over! Kick him for falling!
If a man's up, oh, lift him higher!
Your soul's for sale, and he's the buyer!
Dimes and dollars! Dollars and dimes!
An empty pocket's the worst of crimes!

I know a poor but worthy youth,
Whose hopes are built on a maiden's truth;
But the maiden will break her vow with ease,
For a wooer whose charms are these:
A hollow heart and an empty head,
A face well tinged with the brandy's red,
A soul well trained in villainy's school,
And cash, sweet cash!—he knoweth the rule.
Dimes and dollars! Dollars and dimes!
An empty pocket's the worst of crimes!

I know a bold and honest man,
Who strives to live on the Christian plan.
He struggles against fearful odds—
Who will not bow to the people's gods?
Dimes and dollars! Dollars and dimes!
An empty pocket's the worst of crimes!

So get ye wealth, no matter how!
No question's asked of the rich, I trow!
Steal by night, and steal by day
(Doing it all in a legal way!)
Dimes and dollars! Dollars and dimes!
An empty pocket's the worst of crimes!

The Awl, 1844.

"American Ladies Will Not Be Slaves"
Preceded by the local militia, women shoemakers demonstrated in the streets of Lynn, Massachusetts, on March 7, 1860. In contrast to their failure to cover previous labor actions, illustrated newspapers published a number of images of the 1860 strike. *Frank Leslie's Illustrated Newspaper,* March 17, 1860 — Prints and Photographs Division, Library of Congress.

At the same time, shoemakers in Lynn, Massachusetts, also stepped up their protest activity. Declining wages, repeated layoffs, and disruptions caused by the introduction of the sewing machine finally exploded in 1860 in the largest strike the nation had ever seen. Over 20,000 men and women — more than one-third of all shoe workers in Massachusetts — laid down their tools.

The Lynn strikers said that they were defending individual dignity and freedom. To emphasize that point, they linked their struggle to symbols of national independence, launching the strike on George Washington's birthday, and they defended their rights with the rallying cry "Sink not to the state of a slave." On March 7, 800 women, including strikers and their supporters, marched through the wintry streets of Lynn behind a banner that proclaimed, "American ladies will not be slaves: Give us a fair compensation and we labor cheerfully." The Lynn strikers turned out in huge street demonstrations, fought the use of scab labor, and battled the town marshal when he and his deputies intervened on the side of the bosses. Bolstered by additional police, the employers won the day. Nevertheless, the determined Lynn strikers became a symbol for other laborers who sought better treatment. And their repeated invocation of the slavery theme carried great significance in the context of heightened sectional tensions.

White Southerners Respond to Free Labor's Claims: The *Dred Scott* Decision

Southern planters challenged northern workers' claims that their condition was similar to that of slaves. Many agreed with Virginia planter George Fitzhugh that so-called free labor was more exploitative than slavery (see Chapter 9). Arguing that "the subjection of man to man" occurs in every country and every region of the country, proslavery advocates contrasted the "hunger and cold" and the daily suffering of impoverished "free" laborers with what they considered the humanitarian Christian arrangements of slavery. Using such reasoning in conjunction with older biblical justifications for bondage, more and more southern planters argued that the South must stand firm behind its "peculiar institution."

Indeed, some did more than stand firm. William Walker, a Tennessee-born slaveholder, and 58 mercenaries "invaded" Nicaragua in May 1855. Within six months, Walker succeeded in exploiting civil unrest in the country to declare himself president. His government, which opened Nicaragua to slavery, was recognized by the United States in 1856. But he was overthrown a year later by forces that were financed by his former sponsor, the railroad entrepreneur Cornelius Vanderbilt.

In that same year, 1857, the Supreme Court bolstered planters' commitment to slave labor within the United States when it rejected the claim of a Missouri slave named Dred Scott that he had become free when his master took him out of the South and into a free state (Illinois) and a free territory (Wisconsin). The Court, filled with southerners and Democrats and led by aging Chief Justice Roger B. Taney, a former slaveholder, pronounced unconstitutional all laws restricting the free movement of property, including human property. Indeed, Taney asserted further, Scott had no right to bring suit at all because since the founding of the American republic, no black person in the United States had enjoyed any "rights which the white man was bound to respect." Although Taney had already freed his own slaves, he was committed to defending his beloved South against Republican threats to its time-honored institutions.

Northerners were horrified. They argued that the *Dred Scott* decision, followed to its logical conclusion, could lead to legalizing slave ownership not only in the territories but in the free states as well (Map 10.5). The *New York Tribune* declared the decision was the work of "five slaveholders and two doughfaces," the latter referring to the two northern justices, both Democrats, who supported the majority decision. The "dictum," it claimed, was "entitled to just as much moral weight as would be the judgment of a majority of those congregated in any Washington bar-room." The remedy, according to the *Chicago Tribune*, was "the ballot box" and the election of a Republican president in 1860.

For proslavery firebrands, the *Dred Scott* decision was just the kind of guarantee for slave labor that they sought. Some went so far as to demand the resumption of the Atlantic slave trade. Others called for an automatic veto over all federal legislation affecting southern interests. Southern politicians also tried to limit the rights of the foreign-born in their midst, and southern congressmen blocked homestead legislation that would have made

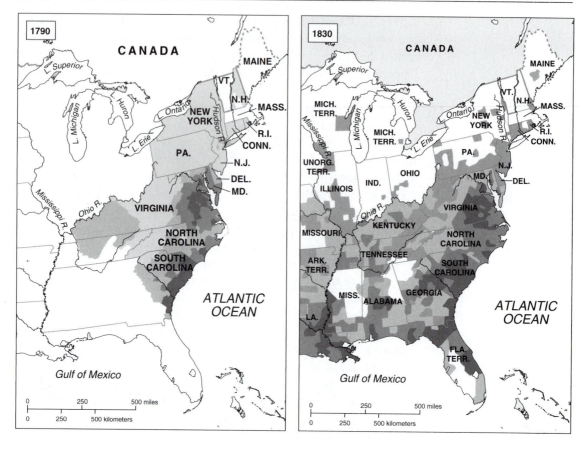

MAP 10.5   The Distribution of Slave Population, 1790–1860

The spread of slavery into the sugar and cotton lands of the lower Mississippi Valley and along the fertile "black belt" that stretched from Georgia through Mississippi increased the profitability of the "peculiar institution" in the first half of the nineteenth century. At the same time, the percentage of the southern population who could afford to own slaves declined, creating the large plantations and wealthy slave owners that have come to dominate our images of southern life in the decades before the Civil War. Life on the western frontier of slavery was anything but bucolic, however, with harsh work discipline, an active slave trade, and the constant threat of disease, debt, and rebellion.

western land more available to small farmers. A law turning western land over to independent farmers rather than reserving it for planters, exclaimed the *Charleston Mercury*, would be "the most dangerous abolition bill which has ever been directly passed by Congress."

In the context of heightened proslavery rhetoric and the *Dred Scott* decision, northern laborers faced new dangers. A Supreme Court that refused Dred Scott's petition for freedom and denied Congress any power to restrict the expansion of slavery was not likely to support the rights of workers. At the same time, they had new opportunities, as the expansion of suf-

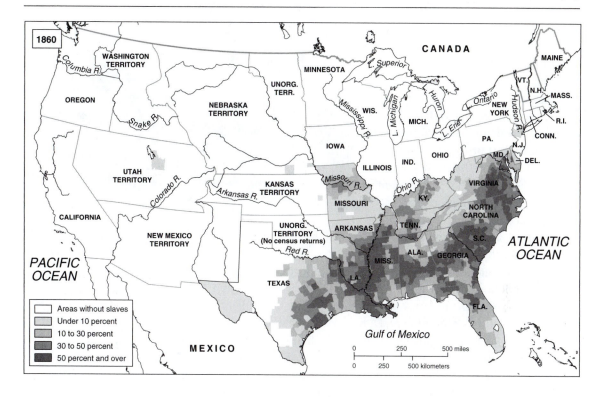

frage to white working-class men in most free states ensured that they would have a critical role to play in political contests for federal power.

Toward a Sectional Showdown

While working-class men and women in the North and West built organizations to defend their rights in the 1850s, most southern slaves had to rely on family and community networks to lessen the brutalities of bondage. Individual acts of resistance continued, but these could only disrupt, not end, the system of slavery. Slaves needed allies, though it is likely that few imagined finding them among white men. Then, in 1859, as the nation lurched toward a final showdown, John Brown reappeared on the national stage and made clear that at least some white men would risk their lives to end the brutal institution. A year later, Abraham Lincoln was elected president of the United States. Although Lincoln was no abolitionist firebrand like Brown, southern planters considered him sufficiently radical that his election heightened fears over the future of slavery.

The Raid on Harpers Ferry   On October 16, 1859, John Brown, three of his sons, and nineteen associates—black and white—launched a raid on the federal arsenal at Harpers Ferry, Virginia. Trained in Kansas, the men planned to seize the arms that were stored at the arsenal, liberate slaves from Virginia plantations, and then retreat into the Allegheny Mountains. There, they hoped to fortify a base from which to encourage, assist, and defend additional insurrections and escapes. The constitution that Brown drafted for this projected haven envisioned a utopian society in which "All captured or confiscated property, and all property [that is] the product of the labor of those belonging to this organization and their families, shall be held as the property of the whole, equally, without distinction."

The Arraignment

Harper's Weekly artist David Hunter Strother sketched John Brown and his coconspirators as they were charged with treason and murder in a Charlestown, Virginia, courtroom. Reporters' access to Brown and the trial was severely restricted because of fears about rescue attempts and local suspicion toward any sympathetic outsiders; indeed, another pictorial reporter was forced to flee Virginia after word spread that he had sold a drawing of John Brown to the antislavery *New York Tribune*. Meanwhile, the Virginia-born Strother was able to cover the trial with little competition, assisted by the presiding judge and the prosecutor who were his close friend and uncle, respectively. David Hunter Strother (Porte Crayon), *Harper's Weekly*, November 12, 1859 — American Social History Project.

Brown had gained substantial financial support from a group of six respected abolitionists, all white, but he could not convince Frederick Douglass or other prominent black abolitionists to join his ranks. Though impressed by Brown's commitment, Douglass was convinced that the project was suicidal. He was right. The plan pitted a handful of poorly armed men against virtually the entire white population of Virginia — and the South — plus the armed forces of the U.S. government. Although Brown and his men did capture the arsenal in the middle of the night, they never managed to free any slaves, and they failed to escape. A detachment of U.S. Marines under Colonel Robert E. Lee and Lieutenant J. E. B. Stuart quickly surrounded the insurgents, subjected them to withering fire, and finally captured most of the survivors. By the afternoon, eight of Brown's men, among them two of his sons, were dead. Three townsmen had also died, and two more raiders were killed in the final battle. Brown was captured; promptly indicted; and tried for treason, murder, and fomenting insurrection. On November 2, he was convicted, and one month later, he was hanged. In one of his last letters, he wrote, "Men cannot imprison, or chain, or hang the soul. I go joyfully in behalf of millions that 'have no rights' that this great and glorious, this Christian republic, 'is bound to respect.'"

Though unsuccessful, the Harpers Ferry raid reverberated through the country. Southern leaders pointed to it as the final proof of the North's violent intentions. Republican moderates such as Abraham Lincoln hastily condemned Brown's deed. Others rejected Brown's tactics but saluted his values and goals. White abolitionists, southern slaves, and free blacks nationwide grieved at Brown's execution and proclaimed him a martyr in the American revolutionary pantheon. Church bells throughout the North pealed in mourning. In December 1859, Baltimore police, concerned about the activities of local African Americans, broke into an annual ball held by

"You Have Been Brave Enough to Reach Out Your Hands": A Letter to John Brown

In the days before his execution, a black woman in Kendalville, Indiana, wrote to John Brown offering her thanks and speculating on the steps America would have to take to erase the "national sin" of slavery. While in prison, Brown received many letters of support from free blacks throughout the North.

Kendalville, Indiana, Nov. 25
Dear Friend:

Although the hands of Slavery throw a barrier between you and me, and it may not be my privilege to see you in your prison-house, Virginia has no bolts or bars [that can stop me from sending you] my sympathy. In the name of the young girl sold from the warm clasp of a mother's arms to the clutches of a libertine or a profligate, in the name of the slave mother, her heart rocked to and fro by the agony of her mournful separations, I thank you, that you have been brave enough to reach out your hands to the crushed and blighted of my race. You have rocked the bloody Bastille; and I hope that from your sad fate great good may arise to the cause of freedom. . . . I would prefer to see Slavery go down peaceably by men breaking off their sins by righteousness and their inequities by showing justice and mercy to the poor; but we cannot tell what the future may bring forth. God writes national judgments upon national sins; and what may be slumbering in the storehouse of divine justice we do not know. We may earnestly hope that your fate will not be a vain lesson, that it will intensify our hatred of Slavery and love of freedom, and that your martyr grave will be a sacred altar upon which men will record their vows of undying hatred to that system which tramples on man and bids defiance to God.

Carter G. Woodson, ed., *The Mind of The Negro as Reflected in Letters Written During the Crisis, 1800–1860* (1926).

free blacks in the city. What they saw no doubt heightened their fears: the hall was draped in banners bearing John Brown's likeness, and a bust of Brown was inscribed "The martyr—God bless him." The struggles that had so long been waged over western territory had finally come home to the South.

A House Divided   In 1860, matters came to a head. The Democratic Party—the last major national bastion of the compromise forces—could not agree on a single platform or candidate. The slavery issue had simply become too explosive. Democrats divided their party and their electoral strength in half as northern Democrats nominated Stephen Douglas while their southern counterparts, desperate to gain federal protection for slavery, chose Buchanan's vice president, John C. Breckenridge of Kentucky. A weak

Undercover

An 1860 anti-Lincoln cartoon portrayed the presidential candidate trying to conceal the antislavery essence of the Republican platform. Currier and Ives, 1860, lithograph, 12 × 11 7/8 inches — Museum of the City of New York.

echo of the old Whig and Know-Nothing forces dubbed itself the Constitutional Union Party and made a futile attempt to delay action on the slavery issue a while longer. Their ticket was composed of John Bell of Tennessee and Edward Everett of Massachusetts.

The Republicans, however, stood united, determined to win and then to resolve the nation's sectional crisis once and for all. Looking past better-known party leaders—such as Senator William Seward of New York and Governor Salmon P. Chase of Ohio—the Republican delegates selected Abraham Lincoln as their presidential candidate. Lincoln had several advantages. He was more moderate on slavery than Seward or Chase; he had demonstrated his skills as a debater during the 1858 Illinois congressional campaign; he had represented small farmers and workers throughout his career; and he lived in an area of the Midwest where voter support was critical to winning the presidency.

Both the North and the West went heavily Republican in the election, with Douglas, supported by northern Democrats, picking up most of the rest of the vote. On national questions, workers had no doubt that their interests lay with the party of Lincoln. The workers of Lynn gave stunning majorities to Republicans at the state level and to Lincoln for president.

In the North, only New Jersey resisted Lincoln's triumphal sweep of the free states. In the South, the small urban vote generally went to the Constitutional Union Party, while the rural majority went heavily to Breckinridge and his proslavery southern Democrats. Lincoln's majority in the North and West proved sufficient to ensure his election as president.

Though he received only 40 percent of the popular vote nationwide, he earned the necessary majority of electoral votes by winning in the most populous states.

Yet this was the first time in American history that a president had been elected without a single southern electoral vote. Clearly, the South was now in a dependent relationship within the national government, and the free states could pass legislation against the interests of the South with the full support of the U.S. president. Lincoln's election opened one of the most important and dramatic chapters in the nation's history. It signaled, as one observer noted, "the beginning of the Second American Revolution."

Conclusion: The Deepening Rift Becomes a Chasm

The Republican victory in 1860 grew out of the social, economic, cultural, and political changes that had taken place in the United States during the preceding half-century. By preserving slave labor, the first American Revolution stopped far short of the Declaration of Independence's stated goal: a society based on the principle that "all men are created equal." For a number of decades, national leaders worked long, hard, and successfully to hold together a nation that was increasingly divided by two distinct labor systems.

But as the slave-labor South and the free-labor North matured, they developed needs, interests, and values that each region found to be ultimately unacceptable in the other. Slave owners and their supporters became more and more committed to chattel slavery, viewing it as the essential prop to their own independence, while to them, the North's vaunted "free society" became an object of fear and loathing. And although northerners hotly disagreed among themselves about the meaning of "free labor," most came to view the expansion of slavery as a direct threat to northerners' own rights, freedoms, and aspirations. The ongoing resistance to slavery and the response that it evoked from slaveholders kept the issue alive and the stakes high.

Disputes over the future of the West manifested and exacerbated the growing sectional clash, destroyed the old two-party system, and gave life to Republicanism. "Bleeding Kansas" and Harpers Ferry revealed how sharp the conflict had become and foreshadowed the way in which it would at last be resolved. John Brown continued to symbolize the powerful currents that drove North and South toward war. In late 1859, Brown died a traitor's death, brought to the gallows by U.S. troops led by Colonel Robert E. Lee. Two short years later, U.S. troops marched into battle against Lee. On their lips was a fighting song that began "John Brown's Body lies a-moldering in the grave," but "his soul goes marching on."

The Years in Review

1846

- California declares its independence from Mexico.

1848

- Gold is discovered in California; about 80,000 people arrive in California the next year.

- Mormon farmers, plowing the shores of the Great Salt Lake, introduce irrigation to U.S. agriculture.

- The nation's first Chinese immigrants arrive in San Francisco; by 1852, an estimated 18,000 Chinese are in the United States.

- The Free-Soil Party is organized; it favors prohibition of slavery in the new territories that were added as result of the Mexican War.

1849

- Harriet Tubman escapes from slavery in Maryland and becomes a "conductor" on the Underground Railway, which got its start about a decade earlier.

1850

- The Compromise of 1850 — a series of bills passed by Congress to appease proslavery and antislavery groups — admits California to the Union as a free state, allows the New Mexico and Utah territories to choose their status, abolishes the slave trade in the District of Columbia, and passes a tough new fugitive slave law.

- German American craftsmen establish General Worker's League, a reflection of the influence of European democratic revolutions of 1848 on American labor activism.

1851

- "Go west, young man," declares John L. B. Soule in an editorial in the *Terre Haute Express* (though Horace Greeley is mistakenly credited with the line); between 1845 and 1869, 1.4 million people follow this advice.

1852

- Harriet Beecher Stowe publishes her antislavery novel *Uncle Tom's Cabin*, which sells 300,000 copies in a year.

1854

- The California Supreme Court rules in *People v. George Hall* that American Indians are prohibited from testifying against whites in court and then defines Asians as "Indians."

- The Kansas-Nebraska Bill, which nullifies the Missouri Compromise and allows each individual territory or state to decide its slave status, becomes law.

- The war along the Kansas and Nebraska border between proslavery and antislavery landowners becomes known as "Bleeding Kansas."

1855
- The Know-Nothing Party splits into proslavery and antislavery factions.

1856
- Antislavery senator Charles Sumner is caned and severely injured by proslavery congressman Preston Brooks on the Senate floor.
- Democrat James Buchanan is elected president over Know-Nothing Millard Fillmore and Republican John C. Frémont; the newly formed Republican Party makes an impressive showing in its first election.

1857
- The U.S. Supreme Court's proslavery decision in *Dred Scott v. Sanford* horrifies northerners.
- The first elevator is installed in New York City.
- North Carolinian Hinton Helper publishes *The Impending Crisis of the South*, which argues that slavery was a political and economic curse on the South.
- Iron molders in Philadelphia strike over a 12 percent wage cut; the strike is unsuccessful but paves the way for later organization of a national molders' union.

1858
- Debates between Republican Abraham Lincoln and Democrat Stephen Douglas during the Illinois Senate race draw national attention to Lincoln.
- Kansas residents vote to establish a free-state government after several years of violent skirmishes between proslavery and antislavery settlers.

1859
- The National Molders' Union is founded; in this decade, national unions also spring up among hat finishers, cigarmakers, and others.
- John Brown leads two dozen people on a raid on the federal arsenal at Harpers Ferry, Virginia, to seize arms and liberate slaves in the area; he is caught after a bloody battle, tried, and hanged.
- Ohio native and blackface minstrel performer Dan Emmett writes "Dixie's Land," which made the word *Dixie* a synonym for the South and later became a battle hymn for the Confederacy; the song is first performed in New York City and first becomes popular in the North.

1860
- Twenty thousand men and women shoe workers go on strike in Massachusetts to protest declining wages and repeated layoffs.

- The Democratic Party divides over the issue of slavery; northerners nominate Stephen Douglas as their presidential candidate; southerners run John C. Breckenridge; Republican Abraham Lincoln defeats both of them and Constitutional Unionist John Bell.

1864
- Cheyenne leader Yellow Wolf dies at the massacre at Sand Creek; decades of bloody warfare have decimated the Plains Indians.

Additional Readings

For more on the transformation of the West, see: John Mack Faragher, *Women and Men on the Overland Trail* (1979); Albert Hurtado, *Intimate Frontiers: Sex, Gender, and Culture in Old California* (1999) and *Indian Survival on the California Frontier* (1988); Patricia Nelson Limerick, *The Legacy of Conquest: The Unbroken Past of the American West* (1987); Hampton Sides, *Blood and Thunder: An Epic of the American West* (2006); Quintard Taylor, *In Search of the Racial Frontier: African Americans in the American West, 1528–1900* (1998); John Kuo Wei Tchen, *The Chinese of America: From Beginning to the Present* (1980); and Robert Utley, *The Indian Frontier of the American West, 1846–1890* (1984).

For more on compromises over slavery, see: Stanley Campbell, *The Slave Catchers* (1970); Merrill Peterson, *The Great Triumvirate: Webster, Clay and Calhoun* (1987); David Potter, *The Impending Crisis: 1848–1861* (1976); and Kenneth Stampp, *The Imperiled Union* (1980).

For more on abolitionist politics in the North, see: Jacqueline Bacon, *The Humblest May Stand Forth: Rhetoric, Empowerment, and Abolition* (2002); W. E. B. DuBois, *John Brown* (1919); Eric Foner, *Free Soil, Free Labor, Free Men* (1970); Leon Litwack, *North of Slavery: The Negro in the Free States, 1790–1860* (1961); John R. McKivigan and Stanley Harrold, eds., *Antislavery Violence: Sectional, Racial and Cultural Conflict in Antebellum America* (1999); Stephen Oates, *To Purge This Land with Blood: A Biography of John Brown* (1970); Michael Pierson, *Free Hearts & Free Homes: Gender and American Antislavery Politics* (2003); Benjamin Quarles, *Allies for Freedom* (1974); C. Peter Ripley et al., eds., *Witness for Freedom: African American Voices on Race, Slavery, and Emancipation* (1993); Richard H. Sewell, *Ballots for Freedom: Antislavery Politics in the United States, 1837–1860* (1976); and Thomas P. Slaughter, *Bloody Dawn: The Christiana Riot and Racial Violence in the Antebellum North* (1991).

For more on the South and slavery, see: Steven Hahn, *A Nation Under Our Feet: Black Political Struggles in the Rural South from Slavery to the Great Migration* (2003); William A. Link, *Roots of Secession: Slavery and Politics in Antebellum Virginia* (2003); Melton McClaurin, *Celia, A Slave* (1991); James McPherson, *The Battle Cry of Freedom: The Civil War Era* (1988); and J. Mills Thorton, *Politics and Power in a Slave Society: Alabama, 1800–1860* (1978).

11

The Civil War: America's Second Revolution

1861–1865

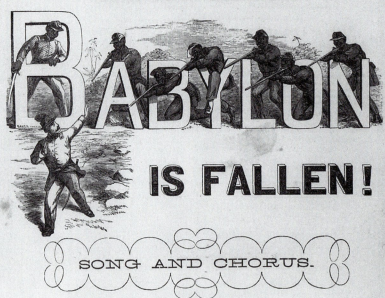

SEQUEL TO
"KINGDOM COMING."

BABYLON

IS FALLEN!

SONG AND CHORUS.

WORDS AND MUSIC BY

HENRY C. WORK.

CHICAGO:
PUBLISHED BY ROOT & CADY, 95 CLARK STREET.

"Babylon Is Fallen!"
An illustrated sheet-music cover published in 1863. An ardent abolitionist whose home was a stop on the Underground Railroad, Henry Clay Work wrote a number of popular Civil War songs. Courtesy of the Lilly Library, Indiana University, Bloomington, IN.

ON APRIL 12, 1861, southern guns opened fire as a U.S. ship tried to deliver supplies to Fort Sumter, South Carolina, and the American Civil War began. Responding to the outbreak of war, antislavery agitator Amy Post proclaimed, "The abolitionists surely have a work to do now in influencing and directing the bloody struggle, that it may end in Emancipation, as the only basis of a true and permanent peace." Her Rochester, New York, neighbor and abolitionist coworker Frederick Douglass agreed. Speaking in June 1861, he declared, "not a slave should be left a slave in the returning footprints of the American army gone to put down this slaveholding rebellion. Sound policy, not less than humanity, demands the instant liberation of every slave in the rebel states."

Throughout the North, African Americans such as Douglass and white allies such as Post quickly came to believe that the war opened a door to emancipation. As one free black newspaper editor argued, "out of strife will come freedom, though the methods are not yet clearly apparent." Yet the path that was so clear to abolitionists was filled with obstacles. When northerners went to war to keep the South in the Union, only a minority of them embraced the radical views held by Amy Post and Frederick Douglass. Most believed that they were fighting to preserve rights that had been won in the American Revolution, but they focused on opportunities for freeborn workers and farmers to attain economic independence. Willing to allow slavery to remain where it already existed, they feared that the institution's spread into western territories would profoundly threaten the free-labor ideal. Not until 1863 would President Abraham Lincoln declare the emancipation of slaves a goal of the war effort; and even then, many northern whites continued

■ 533

The First Flag of Independence Raised in the South, by the Citizens of Savannah, Ga. November 8, 1860

According to this lithograph, the earliest symbol of secession was the "Don't Tread on Me" snake — an image that was familiar to many Americans, having appeared on numerous flags and banners during the American Revolution. R. H. Howell (after Henry Cleenewercke), 1861, lithograph with tint-stone, 13 × 14 inches — Boston Athenaeum.

to believe that African Americans were inferior to whites and unprepared for the rights of full citizens. The Civil War, then, involved not only military battles between North and South, but also social and political struggles within the North to determine the aims and outcomes of the long and bloody conflict that followed the firing on Fort Sumter.

The South, too, faced disagreements within its borders, most notably between slaves and owners, but also among whites in different regions and with different stakes in perpetuating slavery. The distinct interests that dominated particular sections of the South were apparent from the moment of Lincoln's election in November 1860, which forced the hand of the slaveholders. Within three months, slaveholders convinced seven states of the Lower South to secede from the United States. These southern states formed an independent nation, the Confederate States of America. Their secession set off a crisis that rocked America, prompting debates among whites in other slaveholding states over whether to join the Confederacy or remain in the United States. Those who favored secession drew on the symbols and rhetoric of the American Revolution to declare their independence, as an oppressed minority, from the tyranny of Republican rule.

Most white Americans, then, South and North, went to war to defend their version of revolutionary ideals and to maintain, rather than change, the world they knew. Post and Douglass recognized early in the war that this was an epic battle between slavery and freedom, but the vast majority of Americans were unprepared for the brutal ordeal that the Civil War became. Yet as the battles that were fought, soldiers who were killed, and years that were spent embroiled in conflict multiplied, the war did inspire a revolution. White women, North and South, entered the labor force in numbers that had never before been imagined. Working people developed concerns and connections that reached well beyond their local communities. Government extended its reach as well, regulating more and more areas of daily life. Most significant of all, the Civil War emancipated the four million African Americans who were in bondage—enslaved women and men who now claimed the legacy of the Revolution as their own.

The Nation Disintegrates

Neither southern nor northern whites were united in the months leading to war. Despite these uncertainties, South Carolina led the secession movement, declaring its independence from the United States on December 20, 1860, just over a month after Lincoln's election. In the early weeks of 1861, the other Deep South states of Mississippi, Florida, Alabama, Georgia, Louisiana, and Texas, which were most dependent on slavery and farthest from the seat of federal power, followed suit. On February 9, a month before Lincoln took office, representatives from these seven states met in Montgomery, Alabama, to establish the Confederate States of America. They adopted a provisional constitution and elected a Mississippi slave owner and former U.S. senator, Jefferson Davis, as their president.

In response to the establishment of the Confederacy, inhabitants of other southern states had to decide whether to join the secession movement. Their northern counterparts faced an equally critical choice: whether to allow slaveholding states to form an independent nation or go to war to bring them back into the United States.

The Forces Driving Secession   Large slaveholders in the Deep South believed that Lincoln's electoral victory blocked the further growth of slavery and thus placed its future in doubt. As one planter at Alabama's secession convention argued, "Expansion seems to be the law and destiny and necessity of our institutions. To remain healthful and prosperous within . . . it seems essential that we should grow without." Shortly after his election, Lincoln assured a southern acquaintance, Congressman Alexander H. Stephens, that he would not directly or indirectly interfere with slavery where it already existed, but he did plan to keep slavery out of new territories. Lincoln summed up the issue to Stephens: "You think slavery is right and ought to be extended; while we think it is wrong and ought to be restricted. That I suppose is the rub." Not long thereafter, Stephens became vice president of the Confederacy.

There were also grave concerns that the Republican Party would ignore the laws of the land as long as it suited their political interests. From the perspective of southern slaveholders, the federal government had already failed to implement fully both the Fugitive Slave Law of 1850 and the *Dred Scott* decision of 1857. These concerns intensified once southern states began to secede. To keep border states such as Maryland in the United States, President Lincoln put secessionists in jail, arrested state legislators, limited freedom of the press, and suspended the right of habeas corpus, which protects citizens against arbitrary arrest and detention. This last move was necessary, Lincoln believed, so that those who were disloyal to the nation could be easily detained and their cases tried in military rather than civilian courts. Secessionists responded that the formation of an independent nation was the only way to ensure that southern states were not subject to such abuses of federal authority.

Slaveholders had an even more immediate reason for supporting secession: the fear that a Republican government in Washington would lead to a massive uprising of slaves. They remembered John Brown's raid on Harpers Ferry in 1859. One southern newspaper had warned at the time that the region was "slumbering over a volcano, whose smoldering fires may, at any quiet starry midnight, blacken the social sky with the smoke of desolation and death." Some white southerners believed that abolitionists were infiltrating the region and "tampering with our slaves, and furnishing them with arms and poisons to accomplish their hellish designs." The Republican victory in 1860 sparked new fears that "subversive" ideas would "infect" the slave quarters, inciting slaves to revolt. "Now that the black radical Republicans have the power I suppose they will [John] Brown us all," punned one South Carolinian.

Slaveholders' fears and frustrations were compounded by their ongoing concern about the sentiments of white southerners who did not own slaves, a full three-quarters of the southern white population. "I mistrust our own people more than I fear all of the efforts of the Abolitionists," a politician in South Carolina had admitted in 1859. The Republicans, they thought, would highlight the social and economic inequalities among southern whites to recruit nonslaveholders to their party. A southern newspaper warned, "The contest for slavery will no longer be one between the North and the South. It will be in the South between people of the South." Only southern independence, many planters believed, could effectively isolate southern yeomen from their potential Republican allies and thus protect the institution of slavery.

Southerners Consider Secession   The views of southern yeomen, who had long lived on the margins of plantation society, reinforced planters' concern. Most nonslaveholding whites disparaged slaves for what they considered their abject dependency and apparent powerlessness, but they also disliked the haughty pretensions and prerogatives of planters. In the South, as in the North, small farmers and landless whites were drawn to the ideas of free labor and free soil. They resented having the more restrictive policies of planters imposed on them. One farmer from Floyd County, Georgia, expressed this resentment in a letter to the *Rome Weekly Courier*. He and other militiamen had been called to muster one Saturday on the town square as a way of forcing them to listen to a prosecessionist speech by Walter T. Colquitt, a Georgia planter and political leader.

> This [sham muster sort of angered] me that I should be compelled to have the same politics as my general, and I and some of my neighbors are determined more than ever, that we will be for the [Unionists]. . . . I should like to know whether this is a free country, or whether we are to be dragged out from our business to gratify the military men and the political demagogues.

Other southerners also questioned the wisdom of separating from the federal union. In the Upper South, both poor and prosperous whites were less avid for secession than their brethren in the Deep South. The states of Virginia, Arkansas, Missouri, North Carolina, Tennessee, Kentucky, Delaware, and Maryland had a smaller percentage of slaves and slaveholders than did their counterparts who initially formed the Confederate States of America (Map 11.1). Most whites in the Upper South favored a compromise that would maintain both slavery and the nation. The presence of a large number of former Whigs and moderate Democrats made these areas more critical of secessionist principles. The recognition that geography placed them in the path of war and suspicions about the ultimate goals of planters in the Deep South also contributed to unrest in the region. In three Upper South states, no formal discussion of secession occurred before the outbreak of war; in three others, conventions met and rejected secession; and in two, voters rejected the idea of even holding a convention.

Anticipating resistance in the Upper South and among nonslaveholding whites throughout the region, secessionists did not propose a popular vote on the issue. Of the seven states that seceded in early 1861, only Texas allowed voters to speak directly on the question. A delegate to South Carolina's secession convention observed that "the common people" did not understand the issues. "But who ever waited for the common people when a great movement was to be made?" he asked. "We must make the move and force them to follow." Here, the master class's habit of command was wielded over poorer whites as well as blacks to uphold the existing social, economic, and political hierarchy.

Still, most southern yeomen followed their leaders and supported the Confederacy. They did so voluntarily, mainly because of their ties to large planters. Many small farmers had started farming cotton and tobacco in the 1850s and, in the process, grew dependent on large planters for help with

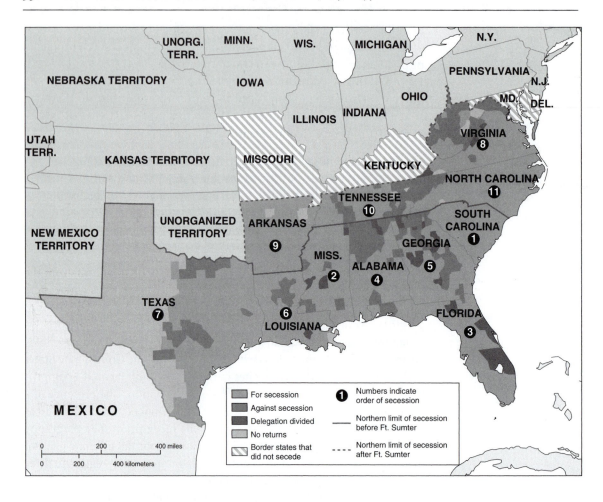

marketing and labor. These close economic ties, reinforced by bonds of kinship and the belief in states' rights and white superiority, led most yeoman farmers to support secession.

Moreover, the vast majority of southern whites, whatever their economic fortunes, defined their own liberty in opposition to black bondage. Fears of racial amalgamation also inspired support for secession among the masses of white Southerners. One Georgia secessionist offered this typical warning to his nonslaveholding neighbors: "Do you love your mother, your wife, your sister, your daughter? If you remain in a nation ruled by Republicans, TEN years or less our CHILDREN will be the slaves of Negroes." With such images in mind, most nonslaveholding whites agreed with the slaveholder who said, "These are desperate means, but then we must recollect that we live in desperate times."

The North Assesses the Price of Peace

Times were desperate in the North as well. Southern secession threatened to throw the nation into a

MAP 11.1 The Process of Secession

The first states to secede from the Union (as noted by the numbers on the map) were those that had the highest concentration of slaves, all of which were located in the Deep South. The states of the Upper South, such as Virginia, Tennessee, and North Carolina, did not secede until after the firing on Fort Sumter. Several border states, that is, states in which slavery was legal but that were geographically closest to the North, remained in the Union throughout the war, although many whites in these areas supported the Confederacy.

financial panic. The cities of the Northeast and the towns along the Ohio River were hardest hit. Stock market prices plummeted, banks shut their doors, factories laid off workers, and unsold goods piled up on docks. Merchants and textile manufacturers worried about the permanent loss of the southern cotton crop, and bankers worried about whether southerners would repay their loans. Many northern businessmen, fearing for their future, called for peace at almost any price.

Some northern working people joined in the call for compromise, concerned that the continuing conflict would lead to mass unemployment. Meeting in Philadelphia on February 22, a group of trade unionists from eight northern and border states denounced the secessionist "traitors" but also called for a peaceful resolution to the conflict. "Our Government never can be sustained by bloodshed," they proclaimed, and opposed "any measures that will evoke civil war."

Yet other working-class citizens feared that compromise would undermine the Republican Party's commitment to free soil. An elaborate compromise, offered by Kentucky Senator John J. Crittenden, suggested they might be right. He proposed that the North accept a return to the principles of the 1820 Missouri Compromise (see Chapter 6). In all western territory then held by the United States, slavery would be prohibited north of 36°30' and permanently protected south of it, including land "hereafter acquired"—an open invitation to the acquisition of more southern territory for slavery. Crittenden also proposed constitutional amendments that would prohibit Congress from abolishing slavery in the District of Columbia, forbid federal interference with the internal slave trade, and provide compensation for any slaveholder who was prevented from recovering escaped slaves in the North.

Northern free blacks and abolitionists as well as working men who were committed to free-soil principles opposed such measures. Frederick Douglass spoke for the opposition when he said, "If the Union can only be maintained by new concessions to the slaveholders, if it can only be stuck together and held together by a new drain on the negro's blood, then . . . let the Union perish." And Lincoln secretly advised Republican congressmen to "entertain no proposition for a compromise in regard to the extension of slavery." In the end, Congress defeated the Crittenden measures and, in doing so, expressed the political commitments of the Republican rank and file: the workers, farmers, and small businessmen who had elected Lincoln president.

The Civil War Begins   Still, when Lincoln took control of the national government, he was not yet prepared to force the South back into the nation by military means. The new president nevertheless needed to demonstrate strength and therefore focused his attention on Fort Sumter in South Carolina's Charleston Harbor. A small federal garrison there was running low on food and medical supplies. Lincoln dispatched reinforcements to Fort

Sumter in April 1861, but he promised to use force only if the Confederates blocked a peaceful effort to send in supplies.

When a U.S. ship set sail for Charleston on April 8, the new Confederate government faced a major dilemma: it could either attack the vessel and bear the responsibility for firing the first shot of the war or allow the supplies to be delivered, thus permitting what it had labeled a foreign power to maintain a fort in one of its key harbors. Jefferson Davis and his advisers chose the more aggressive course, demanding the unconditional surrender of the Fort Sumter garrison. The commanding officer refused, and on April 12, Confederate guns opened fire on the fort. Two days later, Fort Sumter surrendered. The Civil War had begun.

The North and the South faced very different tasks in this war. The South had to defend its own territory and force the North to halt military action. The North had to bring the South to its knees, which in military terms meant invading the South and isolating it from potential allies abroad. Most northern policymakers believed that these ends could be accomplished without challenging the institution of slavery within the South.

But from the first shot, enslaved southerners knew that their future depended on the outcome of the Civil War, and they looked for chances to join the conflict. Their actions, both indi-vidually and collectively, had a profound impact not only on the course of the war, but also on the aims for which it would be fought. The North went to war in April 1861 to preserve the United States and to stop the expansion of slavery, but the actions of African Americans and their abolitionist allies, along with the progress of the war, eventually forced the North to redirect its efforts and abolish the institution of slavery entirely.

The war also transformed the idea of the Union. Initially, a synonym for "the United States," the term *Union* evolved as hostilities erupted. Increasingly, *Union* was used to refer to the free states that opposed the Confederacy. The Confederacy, too, was in transition as several states in the Upper South joined their southern brethren fol-lowing the outbreak of war. Ultimately, *Union* came to mean a nation free of slav-ery, which could be achieved only by the

Secessionist Spectators
Residents of Charleston watched the bombardment of Fort Sumter from the city's rooftops on April 12, 1861. *Harper's Weekly,* May 4, 1861 — American Social History Project.

The March of the Seventh Regiment down Broadway
Newspaper artist Thomas Nast sketched the tumultuous send-off of New York's national guard regiment on April 19, 1861. Eight years later, Nast completed this oil painting of the scene. Thomas Nast, 1869, oil on canvas, 5 feet 6 inches × 8 feet — The Seventh Regiment Fund, Inc.

defeat of the Confederacy, the emancipation of enslaved African Americans, and the reunion of the United States.

The War for the Union and Against Slavery

In the wake of Fort Sumter, northerners lined up behind Lincoln's war policy. The loudest advocates of compromise—manufacturers and merchants, intent on maintaining economic links with the cotton South—now rushed to support Lincoln, hoping that force would succeed where compromise had failed. The outbreak of fighting also galvanized northern workers. William Sylvis—who had earlier advocated that Philadelphia workers endorse the Crittenden compromise—raised an army company among his fellow iron molders. Foreign-born workers joined the patriotic muster. Germans organized ten regiments in New York State alone. New York City's Irish formed a number of regiments, including the Sixty-Ninth, which headed south on April 23, 1861, and played a significant role in the First Battle of Bull Run. Midwestern farmers and farm laborers, the backbone of the free-soil movement, also enlisted in large numbers, making up nearly half the Union Army. The wives and daughters of these volunteers also waxed enthusiastic for the war, believing—as did their menfolk—that the fighting would be short-lived.

Still, despite all the fervor for the Union cause, the goals of the war were not yet clear. It would take efforts by African Americans, diplomatic concerns among Union leaders, prodding by abolitionists, and a year and a half of military engagement to convince a majority of northerners that fighting to unify the nation and stop the expansion of slavery was not enough. Only then would the war to save the Union become also a war to end, rather than merely contain, slavery.

Comparing Military Resources

From a statistical perspective, the Union controlled most of the material resources that were essential to war. The Union states had a considerably larger population than that of the Confederate states, and the Confederacy included several million slaves who were not likely to be armed for combat. The Union also far outstripped the Confederacy in the production of commodities. Although the gap between the two sections was greatest in manufacturing, the North also led the South in the amount of land under cultivation and the quantity and value of agricultural products. The North had far more miles of railroad track, too, ensuring greater facility in moving troops and supplies. And the Union could launch far more ships, a critical advantage in sustaining naval blockades of southern harbors (Figure 11.1).

Yet despite the North's material superiority, the South had many advantages that proved critical early in the war. Three were particularly significant. First, Southerners were fighting on their own ground. This gave them both knowledge of the terrain and a distinct psychological edge, which was often expressed as arrogance about their military superiority. Second, although the Confederate states held only 39 percent of the total population of the United States, black and white, slave labor initially freed a much larger proportion of white working-age men for military service. Third, the military tradition of the slaveholding class took on crucial significance. The Confederacy had the support not only of more than 280 officers who had been trained at West Point, but also of nearly all those trained at Virginia Military Institute, the Citadel, and other southern military academies. Among the officers who had gained their experience on the battlefields of the Mexican War, the best and the brightest (or at least the most daring) joined the Confederate ranks: Pierre G. T. Beauregard, James Longstreet, George Pickett, Albert Sidney Johnston, Joseph E. Johnston, Thomas "Stonewall" Jackson, and Robert E. Lee.

All of the South's advantages were apparent in the first major battle of the Civil War. On July 21, 1861, at Bull Run in northern Virginia, 22,000 Southerners pushed back an attack by 30,000

FIGURE 11.1 Economies of the North and South, 1860
The North entered the war with significant advantages in population, commodity output, farm acreage, factories, and railroad mileage. The advantages were even greater than this chart suggests, since southern commodity production was dominated by farm products, which were less useful in military terms than were manufactured goods. In addition, more southern farm acreage was unimproved, and southern factories were smaller than their northern counterparts.

Comparison of Economics

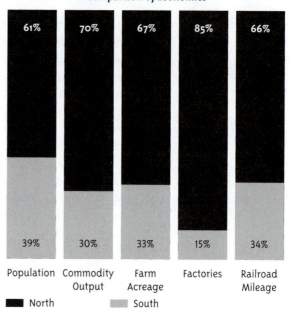

61%	70%	67%	85%	66%
39%	30%	33%	15%	34%
Population	Commodity Output	Farm Acreage	Factories	Railroad Mileage

■ North   South

Source: Stanley Engerman, "Economic Impact of the Civil War," in Robert W. Fogel and Stanley L. Engerman, *The Reinterpretation of American Economic History* (1971).

The Stampede from Bull Run — From a Sketch by Our Special Artist

Northern illustrated newspapers dispatched "special artists" to cover the war. These artists' sketches, engraved on wood blocks and published in *Harper's Weekly, Frank Leslie's Illustrated Newspaper,* and other periodicals, were the North's major source of war imagery. A few short-lived southern illustrated papers appeared, but it was the *Illustrated London News* that most actively portrayed the Confederate point of view. Its "special artist" Frank Vizetelly sketched this rout of Union forces on July 21, 1861. Frank Vizetelly, *Illustrated London News,* August 17, 1861 — American Social History Project.

Union troops. Although only 600 men lost their lives, the battle of Bull Run gave Americans their first taste of the carnage that lay ahead. Northern civilians, who had traveled to the battle site to picnic and witness an afternoon of martial jousting, ended up fleeing for their lives to escape Confederate artillery.

But the Battle of Bull Run was only one of many engagements in the early months of the war. In the others, which included confrontations in the western theater of war and the Union blockade of the South's deep-water ports, northern troops were considerably more successful. This mixture of failure and success on both sides suggested that the war might be a prolonged struggle after all.

African Americans Open the Door to Freedom   The 225,000 African Americans living in the free states initiated another prolonged struggle. One recalled that at the sound of the alarm bell, "Negro waiter, cook, barber, bootblack, groom, porter, and laborer stood ready at the enlisting office." A speaker at an African American recruitment meeting in Cleveland proclaimed, "Today, as in the times of '76, we are ready to go forth and do battle in the common cause of our country." Their country, however, was not yet ready for them. Secretary of War Simon Cameron quickly announced that he had no intention of calling up black soldiers. Local authorities drove his point home by prohibiting African American recruitment meetings as "disorderly gatherings."

Northern optimism contributed in part to this hasty rejection. Although four slave states that had previously opposed secession — Virginia, North Carolina, Arkansas, and Tennessee — joined the Confederacy after Fort Sumter, northern leaders remained confident that the South would be subdued easily. "Jeff Davis and Co. will be swingin' from the battlements at Washington at least by the 4th of July," predicted newspaperman Horace Greeley. "This much-ado-about nothing will end in a month," echoed a Philadelphia newspaper. The rejections were also motivated by a fear that whites would not enlist if blacks were allowed to serve in the Union Army.

But there was a deeper reason. Lincoln and his advisers were wary lest the war for the Union become a war for emancipation. Lincoln, like most Americans, believed that restricting slavery to the states where it already existed would "put slavery on the road to eventual extinction." But it was a significant step from this position to a policy that demanded the immediate emancipation of slaves throughout the nation. Moreover, despite the quick secession of the Upper South once war was declared, four crucial border slave states (Missouri, Kentucky, Maryland, and Delaware) remained in the Union. Any threat to end slavery, rather than merely to confine it, might well drive these states into the Confederacy's waiting arms. Allowing black soldiers to enlist would show that slavery's future in the Union was not secure.

These concerns accounted for Lincoln's reaction to the exceedingly tense situation in Missouri. In August 1861, General John C. Frémont, the famous explorer and former Republican presidential candidate who commanded Union military forces in the West, proclaimed martial law in Missouri and issued an order that freed the slaves of all Confederate sympathizers in the state. Abolitionists hailed Frémont's action as a brilliant military move and a bold step for freedom. Furious Unionist slaveholders, however, called on Lincoln to reverse Frémont's order. Noting that Frémont's move would "alarm our Southern Union friends" and "perhaps ruin our rather fair prospects for Kentucky," the president quickly followed their advice. He insisted to Frémont and the Republican leadership that such a major policy issue must be determined in Washington rather than in the field.

Whatever the intentions of northern politicians, most slaves realized that if Union troops came to the South, they would undermine the authority of slaveholders and make freedom a distinct possibility. African Americans therefore carefully followed the course of the war, using the "grapevine telegraph" to learn about battles and follow Union troop movements. Even in the Deep South, far from the Union Army, slaves were heartened by events. At the outset of the fighting, a white Alabama farmer wrote to Jefferson Davis that slaves in his region "very hiley hope that they will soon be free." Though trying to conceal their hopes from slaveholders, blacks in bondage awaited their chance.

The first of these chances appeared in tidewater Virginia, where the Confederate commander impressed (that is, seized) nearly all the male slaves in the area to build fortifications. Impressment, which became an official and widely used Confederate policy by 1863, allowed the army to take men, food, animals, and other property from farmers. The Confederacy paid farmers for these goods, but the prices were fixed far below market value. Impressment angered slaveholders, who objected to any infringement on what they regarded as their property rights. In response, the slaveholders began "refugeeing" male slaves, sending them out of the area. Knowing that either impressments or removal would mean separation from loved ones, some slaves chose another course: escape.

On the night of May 23, 1861, three escaped slaves paddled up the river to the Union outpost at Fortress Monroe, Virginia, requesting sanctuary

"Contrabands" in Cumberland Landing, Virginia
Union photographer James F. Gibson took this picture of a group of runaway slaves in May 1862. James F. Gibson, May 14, 1862 — United States Army Military History Institute.

from its commanding general, Benjamin Butler. Butler, a Democratic politician from Massachusetts, was no abolitionist, but he realized that the Confederacy would use slaves against the Union. He therefore offered the runaways military protection, refusing the owner's pleas for their return. The slaves, Butler proclaimed, were "contraband" of war, property that rebel slave owners had forfeited by the act of rebellion.

News of Butler's decision spread like wildfire. Two days later, eight runaway slaves arrived at what they called "Freedom Fort." Another 59 African American men and women joined them the next day. Lincoln endorsed Butler's contraband policy as a legitimate tactic of war. The North now possessed a formula that allowed it to strike at the institution of slavery, the linchpin of the southern economy, without proclaiming general abolition and thus alienating the loyal border states. Even African Americans, though offended by the use of *contraband*, a term that related to property, to describe escaped slaves, recognized the significance of Butler's policy. Now they had a new way to demonstrate their importance to the Union cause.

The "Peculiar Institution" Begins to Unravel   In the wake of the Union's shocking defeat at Bull Run, Congress also began to move against slavery. On August 6, 1861, Congress passed its first confiscation act, proclaiming that any slave owner whose bondsmen were used by the Confederate Army would thereafter lose all claim to those slaves. Although it was far from a clear-cut declaration of freedom, this act, in conjunction with Butler's policy, gave slaves and abolitionists a foundation for further action.

In every region that was touched by the war, African American men, women, and children moved quickly to reach the freedom offered by Union camps. In return for protection, they provided labor and knowledge of local terrain and Confederate troop movements. Slave owners also moved quickly, following runaways into the camps and demanding their return. Although no such demands were honored at Fortress Monroe, some Union commanders either returned slaves or simply denied them entrance.

The persistence of the slaves' attempts to gain freedom gradually led many Union officers and ordinary soldiers to help shield escapees from slave catchers. In November 1861, Secretary of War Cameron, who had earlier opposed black enlistment, now publicly supported the radical idea of arming slaves to fight for the Union, labeling as "madness" the policy of leaving the enemy "in peaceful and secure possession of slave property." Lincoln, again acting to calm loyal slaveholders, forced Cameron to back down. Three months later, recognizing that the secretary of war was inept and corrupt, the president removed him from office. Still, with the war dragging on and Union casualties rising, antislavery sentiment was growing in Congress, inside the Union army, and in the North as a whole.

The advocates of abolition, so long scorned by the majority of northern whites, now gained a hearing. In January 1862, Philadelphia abolitionist Mary Grew reflected, "It is hard to believe the wondrous change that has befallen us." Grew had seen an antiabolitionist mob burn Pennsylvania Hall in 1838. Now she responded with glee to the respect accorded her coworkers in the cause. One of them, Wendell Phillips, who had been among the abolitionists attacked in 1861 for supposedly provoking southern secession, was a year later accorded a formal introduction in the U.S. Senate.

At the forefront of those in Congress who applauded Phillips's presence were a handful of abolitionists—the so-called Radical Republicans—who sought to use the war to strike down the "peculiar institution." Although they never represented more than a minority in Congress, the Radical Republicans were able to shape legislation by drawing on the North's growing support for abolition and by emphasizing the military benefits to be gained by striking at the institution of slavery. The Radical Massachusetts senator Charles Sumner explained his strategy for success in November 1861: "You will observe that I propose no crusade for abolition. [Emancipation] is to be presented strictly as a measure of military necessity."

The military argument for emancipation intensified as the war dragged on through 1861 and 1862. The Union Navy began a blockade of southern ports that grew ever more effective, leading to the capture of the major port

Caught in the Middle
An illustration in a May 1862 issue of *Harper's Weekly* depicted one way in which the institution of slavery contributed to the Confederacy's war effort. According to the caption, the northern newspaper artist observed this "struggle between two Negroes and a rebel captain" through a telescope. The captain "insisted upon their loading a cannon within range of [Union] Sharpshooters. . . . [He] succeeded in forcing the Negroes to expose themselves, and they were shot, one after the other." Mead, *Harper's Weekly*, May 10, 1862 — American Social History Project.

of New Orleans in April 1862. Even more significant, in the same month, Union troops commanded by Ulysses S. Grant won a battle at Shiloh in western Tennessee. Shiloh provided a critical victory in the Union's plan to control the Mississippi Valley, but it was a grisly bloodbath, a new kind of battle in which soldiers pushed forward yard by yard under heavy fire. When it was over, nearly 4,000 men lay dead, and more than 16,000 were wounded. Grant's troops were too exhausted to follow up on their victory, but the Confederacy had lost a major battle.

It was in these western campaigns that the diversity of army ranks became visible. At the battles of Pea Ridge on the Arkansas-Missouri border, in the prolonged campaign for Vicksburg, Mississippi, and in the Union capture of Little Rock, Arkansas, the forces that faced each other were not composed simply of native-born whites whose only difference lay in whether they were raised north or south of the Mason-Dixon Line. At Pea Ridge, General Earl van Dorn brought together a force of southern whites, three regiments of Choctaws and Chickasaws, two of Cherokees, and one of Seminoles and Creeks under the leadership of Cherokee General Stand Watie, who hoped that a Confederate victory would provide American Indians with greater autonomy. The Confederate forces were defeated, however, by Union troops that included both native-born white Midwesterners and Franz Sigel's German American regiments. Similarly diverse forces would converge on Vicksburg in July 1863. And in the fighting around Little Rock, also in 1863, African Americans would join native-born whites, immigrant, and Indian soldiers on the Union side against regiments of white and Native American Confederates.

Union advances deep into the cotton belt during and after 1862 gave these diverse companies of Union soldiers a chance to observe slavery firsthand. Few white soldiers were abolitionists, and some believed strongly in the necessity of enslaving African Americans, but many were nonetheless repulsed by what they saw. After visiting several captured plantations near New Orleans and discovering a number of instruments that were used to torture slaves, a Union soldier concluded that he had seen "enough of the horror of slavery to make one an Abolitionist forever." A Union officer wrote from Louisiana, "Since I am here, I have learned what the horrors of slavery was. . . . Never hereafter will I either speak or vote in favor of slavery." Even though the majority of Union troops still questioned the wisdom of complete emancipation, some soldiers

General Stand Watie

Leader of the Southern Cherokee Nation, a splinter group of Cherokees, Degataga ("He Stands Firm") gained fame as one of the most daring and successful Confederate commanders in the western theater of the war. Oklahoma Historical Society.

Harriet Tubman Helps Slaves Flee to Freedom

The following account of South Carolina slaves flocking to meet a regiment of black Union troops is drawn from the testimony of Harriet Tubman, famous for her success in helping hundreds of escaped slaves before the war. Tubman had joined forces with the First South Carolina Volunteers, made up largely of escaped slaves, in raiding plantations and leading slaves to freedom.

"I never saw such a sight," said Harriet; "we laughed, and laughed, and laughed. Here you'd see a women with a pail on her head, rice smoking in it just as if she'd taken it from the fire, young one hanging on behind, one hand hanging around her forehead to hold on, another hand digging into the rice pot, eating with all its might; holding on to her dress two or three more; down her back a bag with a pig in it. One woman brought two pigs, a white one and a black one; we took them all aboard; named the white pig Beauregard, and the black pig Jeff Davis [two prominent Confederate officials]. Sometimes the women would come with twins hanging around their necks; appears like I never seen so many twins in my life; bags on their shoulders, baskets on their heads, and young ones tagging behind, all loaded; pigs squealing, chickens screaming, young ones squalling." And so they came pouring down to the gunboats. When they stood on the shore, and the small boats put out to take them off, they all wanted to get in at once. After the boats were crowded, they would hold onto them so that they could not leave the shore. The oarsmen would beat them on their hands, but they would not let go; they were afraid the gunboats would go off and leave them, and all wanted to make sure [that they were on] one of these arks of refuge. At length Col. Montgomery shouted from the upper deck, above the clamor of appealing tones, "Harriet you'll have to give them a song." Then Harriet lifted up her voice and sang:

> Of all the whole creation in the east or the west,
> The glorious Yankee nation is the greatest and the best.
> Come along! Come along! don't be alarmed,
> Uncle Sam is rich enough to give you all a farm.

John F. Bayliss, Compiler, *Black Slave Narratives* (1970), 125–126.

grew more sympathetic to the plight of runaways and recognized that the Union could gain an advantage by employing African Americans. "The Negroes are our only friends," wrote a Union officer in northern Alabama. "I shall very soon have watchful guards among the slaves on the plantations bordering the river from Bridgeport to Florence, and all who communicate to me valuable information I have promised the protection of my Government."

As fighting continued in 1862, military reversals for the Union set off a panic in the North, which further contributed to antislavery sentiment. In the summer of 1862, Confederate troops led by Thomas "Stonewall" Jackson won a series of stunning victories in Virginia's Shenandoah Valley. The panic in the North increased when Union General George B. McClellan, known for his proslavery views and his vacillating approach to military strategy, ordered a retreat following the crucial Seven Days' campaign at Richmond, Virginia, in June and July. The Confederate Army in Virginia, commanded by Robert E. Lee, now prepared to invade the North itself.

As the war turned against the North, the North turned against slavery. In the spring of 1862, Congress approved a measure to abolish slavery in the District of Columbia, though they tried to mollify more conservative colleagues by appropriating, at the same time, $600,000 to assist in sending former slaves to "colonize" Haiti, Liberia, and Central America. The colonization efforts would collapse over the next year and a half, but the eradication of slavery in the nation's capital stood as a symbol of a new era. That July, Congress passed a second confiscation act, this one declaring that the slaves of anyone who supported the Confederacy should be "forever free of their servitude, and not again held as slaves." Acceding to pleas from free blacks, slaves, and some Union officers, Congress also passed a militia act that allowed "persons of African descent" to be employed in "any military or naval service for which they may be found competent." The first black Union regiment was organized before the end of 1862. And by 1863, African Americans would overcome the objections of whites to their use as front-line soldiers, serving with distinction and contributing directly to key northern victories. Moreover, as Union armies moved south, slaves in ever greater numbers deserted their owners to join the advancing forces. Slave labor was crucial to the South's economy and military effort, and this massive transfer of labor from the Confederacy to the Union had a tremendous impact on the course of the war.

The Bright Side

Harper's Weekly "special artist" Winslow Homer's 1865 painting, based on his wartime sketches, depicted black teamsters relaxing in a Union campsite. While the teamsters were shown resting, the supply wagons and mules in the background reminded the viewer of the crucial role that African Americans played in supplying ammunition and food to northern forces and suggested that their relaxation was well earned. Winslow Homer, 1865, oil on canvas, 13 1/4 × 17 1/2 inches — The Fine Arts Museums of San Francisco, Gift of Mr. and Mrs. John D. Rockefeller 3rd (1979.7.56).

By the end of the summer of 1862, the numbers of African Americans who were employed by the Union Army increased dramatically. Black men built fortifications and roads, chopped wood, carried supplies, and guarded ever-lengthening supply lines. They also worked in more skilled jobs, piloting boats and driving teams. Black women, employed in far smaller numbers, performed essential services as cooks, laundresses, seamstresses, and nurses. The work was often hard and heavy, and although pay was promised, black women and men often received their wages late or not at all. They strongly protested this unfair treatment, since unpaid labor symbolized slavery. But they also believed that their labor played a central role in the struggle for freedom.

Union Officials Consider Emancipation By the fall of 1862, African Americans and abolitionists were no longer alone in advocating emancipation as a necessary outcome of the war. Congress, the larger public, and even President Lincoln began to consider the possibility. Lincoln had to balance several factors, however. He wanted to prevent international recognition of southern independence, keep slaveholding border states in the Union, and unite northern whites behind the war effort.

The question of international recognition was paramount to the Confederacy. Support from European nations could undermine the Union cause and help to persuade the North to accept southern independence. Of more immediate concern, the agricultural South was looking abroad for the manufactured products that were needed in a modern war. Southern attention focused mainly on Britain, the leading market for cotton and a potentially important supplier of goods. Many British political leaders sympathized with the Confederacy, particularly as the Union blockade of southern ports grew more effective, since the blockade had a disastrous effect on the British economy.

Nonetheless, working people throughout England had long maintained a hatred of both slavery and the southern slaveholding aristocracy. During the war, lecture tours in England by American abolitionists such as Sarah Parker Remond, a free black activist from Philadelphia, intensified antislavery sentiments among Britons of all classes. But this powerful group of British abolitionists could not be fully mobilized until the North officially took a strong antislavery position. A firm Union commitment to emancipation might give the North an edge in the battle for British public opinion and prevent Britain's diplomatic recognition of the Confederacy.

In response to these diplomatic considerations, the deteriorating military situation, and the unrelenting pressure from "contrabands," Lincoln decided in the summer of 1862 to issue a proclamation emancipating all slaves in the Confederacy. He withheld its announcement, however, until a Union victory made the proclamation a sign of strength rather than weakness. Confederate troops in the eastern states had won numerous victories in the preceding months. In the Shenandoah Valley, Stonewall Jackson led Confederate troops to five victories against three Union armies. During

Diplomacy

An 1862 cartoon from the northern satirical weekly *Vanity Fair* presented the Confederacy's president trying to gain diplomatic recognition from a skeptical Great Britain. "I hardly think it will wash, Mr. Davis," Britannia commented in the cartoon's caption, "We hear so much about your colors running." Howard, *Vanity Fair*, July 12, 1862 — American Social History Project.

June and July of 1862, General Robert E. Lee, commander of the Army of Northern Virginia, fought McClellan to a standstill in the Seven Days' battles. Lee and Jackson joined forces that August to defeat Union troops at the Second Battle of Bull Run. The chance to claim a victory finally came in the fall of 1862, when Lee led his army north into Maryland. On September 17, in the bloodiest battle yet, Union troops brought Lee's advance to a standstill at Antietam. Nearly 5,000 men lost their lives on that day; another 3,000 would die later of wounds. Although Antietam was the site of the bloodiest single day in American warfare, Lincoln viewed the battle as a victory. Five days later, he announced his preliminary Emancipation Proclamation to the assembled cabinet. Republicans who had come to see the advantages of emancipation spoke on its behalf over the next three months, and white and black abolitionists eagerly awaited the official pronouncement.

On January 1, 1863, Lincoln signed the final edict, proclaiming that slaves in areas that were still in rebellion were "forever free" and inviting them to enlist in the Union Army. In many ways, the proclamation was a conservative document, applying only to slaves who were far beyond the reach of federal power. Its provisions exempted 450,000 slaves in the loyal border states, 275,000 slaves in Union-occupied Tennessee, and tens of thousands more in areas controlled by the Union Army in Louisiana and Virginia. It also justified the abolition of southern slavery on military, not moral, grounds. Despite its limitations, the Emancipation Proclamation prompted joyous "Watch Meetings" on December 31, 1862, as white and black abolitionists met to cheer and give thanks as the edict took effect. Fugitive slaves in Washington, D.C., gathered in celebration and prayer. There was even jubilation among the slaves in loyal border states, who were exempted from the proclamation's provisions. The deepest hopes of antislavery advocates such as Amy Post and Frederick Douglass had finally become part and parcel of the Union cause.

African Americans, slave and free alike, understood, in ways that white Americans only partially did, that the aims of the war had now dramatically changed. The Emancipation Proclamation augured a total transformation of southern society rather than the mere reintegration of the slave states into the nation if the Union proved victorious. Although Lincoln had admonished Congress in 1861 that the war should not

Writing the Emancipation Proclamation

Surrounded by symbols of Satanism and paintings honoring John Brown and slave rebellions, an inebriated Lincoln is shown treading on the Constitution as he drafted the Emancipation Proclamation. This caricature was part of a collection of etchings, *Sketches from the Civil War in North America*, by Baltimore pro-South Democrat Adalbert Johann Volck. V. Blada (A. J. Volck), *Sketches from the Civil War in North America, 1861, '62, '63* (1863) — American Social History Project.

become "a violent and remorseless revolutionary struggle," that is precisely what it had become by 1863.

The Cold Realities of War

For soldiers who were caught in the midst of battle, political pronouncements did little to alleviate the dangers they faced. The Civil War was one of the deadliest wars in history and the deadliest in the United States. Technological innovations in weaponry far outweighed advances in medicine. New forms of ammunition created wounds that could not be healed by existing surgical techniques; amputation saved some lives but ensured the death of others; and diseases ran rampant through army ranks on both the Confederate and Union sides.

Soldiers' Lives   The fighting at Antietam in the summer of 1862 had given Lincoln the victory he needed to issue the Emancipation Proclamation, but it did not mark an overall change in the North's fortunes on the battlefield. The war continued to go poorly for the Union on the eastern front. Against a superior force, Confederate troops won an important victory in December 1862 at Fredericksburg, Virginia, inflicting nearly 13,000 Union casualties while suffering only 5,000 of their own. In the same month, Confederate cavalry cut Union supply lines in the West, preventing a much larger Union force from seizing the strategic river town of Vicksburg, Mississippi. By early 1863, the war had reached a stalemate. Then in May, Lee's army defeated a Union force twice its size at Chancellorsville, Virginia, setting the stage for a Confederate thrust north into Pennsylvania.

The South's victories reflected the Confederacy's advantages of fighting on its own terrain and its officers' greater talents. They also made clear the generally disorganized nature of the Union war effort. Despite having more than twice as many soldiers under their command, northern officers seemed unable to press their advantages in the war's first two years. Early battles, while intense, were separated by long periods of inactivity. Tradition—influenced by impassable roads and the difficulty of providing food, clothing, and shelter—dictated that both armies refrain from fighting during the winter months. Instead, the armies built semipermanent camps to reside in while awaiting the spring thaw. One estimate suggests that in its first two years of operation, the Union's Army of the Potomac spent a total of only one month in actual battle.

The war's casual pace fulfilled the expectations of both northern and southern soldiers. With the exception of the officers who had gained their experience in the Mexican War in the mid-1840s, most soldiers were too young to remember, much less to have experienced, any organized war. Most young men expected war to be conducted in an orderly, even chivalrous

Cavalry Charge at Fairfax Court House, May 31, 1861

Early in the war, artists often drew highly romantic and very inaccurate pictures. Such feats as firing from the saddle were viewed with great amusement by soldiers in the field, who enjoyed seeing illustrations of their exploits almost as much as they enjoyed criticizing their inaccuracies. *Harper's Weekly*, June 15, 1861 — American Social History Project.

Maryland and Pennsylvania Farmers Visiting the Battlefield of Antietam

As the war progressed and artist-reporters experienced battle firsthand, their illustrations often became more realistic. F. H. Schell sketched the carnage after the battle of Antietam and the morbid curiosity of local inhabitants. *Frank Leslie's Illustrated Newspaper*, October 18, 1862 — American Social History Project.

fashion. They were in for a rude shock. A young private wrote home that his idea of combat had been that the soldiers "would all be in line, all standing in a nice level field fighting, a number of ladies taking care of the wounded, etc., etc., but it isn't so."

One reason that this soldier's idea of battle proved wrong had to do with the development of the minié ball, a conical bullet with a hollow end that expanded when fired. This bullet made possible the use of the muzzle-loading rifle, which had extraordinary range and accuracy. These rifles turned early battlefields into scenes of chaos and carnage. Although an individual soldier could fire only a few times a minute, their Enfield and Springfield rifles were murderously effective at great distances.

In early Civil War battles, soldiers marched in tight formation toward an enemy that began killing and wounding them from a quarter of a mile away. These battles thus put a premium on the courage of ordinary soldiers, valuing their willingness to move forward relentlessly under withering fire. In the face of such efficient killing, fixed infantry formations soon gave way to the realities of self-defense and self-protection. By 1863, the nature of battle had changed considerably, relying on heavy fortifications, elaborate trenches, and distant heavy mortar and artillery fire — tactics that resembled those of World War I more than those of the American Revolution or even the Mexican War.

In general, the Civil War proved to be an exhausting, trying experience for the ordinary infantrymen who bore the brunt of the fighting. After a major battle, one Vermont soldier described himself as "so completely worn out that I can't tell how many days . . . in the last two weeks . . . I went without sleeping or eating." The hardships and discomforts that were experienced on both sides extended far beyond the actual fighting. Many soldiers went into battle in ragged uniforms, some without shoes. A Georgia major reported after the battle of Manassas, also known as Bull Run (northerners named battles after local rivers, while southerners named battles after nearby towns), that he "carried into the fight over one hundred men who were barefoot, many of whom left bloody foot-prints among the thorns and briars through which they rushed."

Rations on both sides were sporadic at best; food was often adulterated, and even that was in short supply. Staples of the Union Army diet were bread — actually, an unleavened biscuit called *hardtack* — meat, beans, and coffee, the latter drunk in enormous quantities. Confederate troops got even less, subsisting on cornmeal and fatty meat. Vegetables and fruit were scarce on both sides, making scurvy common. Confederate rations were so short that after some battles, officers sent details of men to gather food from the haversacks of the Union dead. As the war progressed, the Confederate government reduced rations to its soldiers. "I came nearer to starving than I

"I Have Never Conceived of Such Trials": Soldiers' Letters Home

Severe shortages of food, clothing, and medical care plagued soldiers in both the Union and Confederate armies throughout the war. Following are two letters from soldiers to their families, lamenting the travails of army life.

CONFEDERATE SOLDIER AFTER THE LONG MARCH FROM YORKTOWN TO RICHMOND, SEPTEMBER 1862

I have never conceived of such trials as we have passed through. We were for days together without a morsel of food, excepting occasionally a meal of parched corn. . . . The army was kept on the march day and night, and the roads were in some places waist deep in mud. . . . Many of the men became exhausted and some were actually stuck in the mud and had to be pulled out. . . . The men on the march ran through the gardens . . . devouring every particle of vegetables like the army worm, leaving nothing at all standing. Whenever a cow or hog were found it was shot down and soon despatched.

Bell I. Wiley, *The Life of Johnny Reb: The Common Soldier of the Confederacy* (1943), 92.

WOUNDED UNION SOLDIER, BATON ROUGE, JUNE 1863

I never wish to see another such time as the [day I was wounded]. The surgeons used a large Cotton Press for the butchering room and when I was carried into the building and looked about I could not help comparing the surgeons to fiends. It was dark and the building lighted partially with candles; all around on the ground lay the wounded men; some of them were shrieking, some cursing and swearing, and some praying; in the middle of the room was some ten or twelve tables just large enough to lay a man on; these were used as dissecting tables and they were covered with blood. Near and around the tables stood the surgeons with blood all over them and by the sides of the tables was a heap of feet, legs, and arms. On one of these tables I was laid, and being known as a colonel, the Chief Surgeon of the Department was called and he felt of my mouth and then wanted to give me chloroform: this I refused to take and he took a pair of scissors and cut out the pieces of bone in my mouth; then gave me a drink of whiskey and had me laid away.

Bell I. Wiley, *The Life of Billy Yank: The Common Solider of the Union* (1952), 148.

ever did before," noted one soldier in Virginia. The Union soldiers' diet, in contrast, generally improved because of the greater scope and efficiency of the North's supply system.

Ailing in Body and Soul   Disease proved a greater adversary than enemy soldiers did. "There is more dies by sickness than gets killed," a recruit from New York had complained in 1861. His assessment would prove chillingly accurate. For every soldier who died as a result of battle, three died of disease. Measles, dysentery, typhoid, and malaria became major killers, caused or made worse by contaminated water, bad food, and exposure to the elements. One soldier stationed in Louisiana described an outbreak of malaria:

> Two-thirds of the regiment are buried or in hospital. It is woeful to see how nearly destitute of comforts and of attendance the sick are. They cannot be kept in their wretched bunks, but stagger about, jabbering and muttering insanities, till they lie down and die in their ragged, dirty uniforms.

African American troops fared worst of all. The death rate for black Union soldiers from disease was nearly three times greater than that for white Union soldiers, reflecting the generally poorer health of black soldiers at enlistment, their meager food, the hard labor they performed, and the minimal medical care they received while in the field.

Even for white soldiers, medical assistance was primitive. One commentator described military hospitals in the war's early years as "dirty dens of butchery and horror." After the battle of Shiloh in 1862, General Grant's medical director told of "thousands of human beings . . . wounded and lacerated in every conceivable manner, on the ground, under a pelting rain, without shelter, without bedding, without straw to lie upon, and with but little food. . . . The agonies of the wounded were beyond all description." Army doctors on both sides provided little relief. "I believe the Doctors kills more than they cure," wrote an Alabama private. "Doctors haint Got half Sence."

Sick and wounded soldiers were cared for by doctors who had not yet heard of antibiotics or antisepsis, who had no cure for peritonitis or gangrene, and who were perennially short of anesthetics. Union soldiers, however, at least had access to supplies and medical care provided by the U.S. Sanitary Commission. This commission, established by the federal government in 1861, had grown out of the efforts of the Women's Central Association for Relief, a volunteer organization that initially focused on training nurses. By 1862, tens of thousands of women had volunteered through hundreds of local chapters across the North and Midwest, hosting "Sanitary Fairs" to raise money; rolling bandages; shipping food, medicine, clothing, and bedding; and sending nurses to army camps along the battlefront. In

The Effect of a Minié Ball

The catastrophic damage caused by the commonly used cone-shaped bullet is graphically chronicled in this pair of surgical photographs showing the entrance and exit of a minié ball. Prints and Photographs Division, Library of Congress.

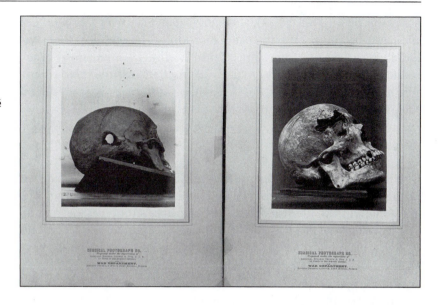

the South, much of the medical care was also voluntary and performed by women. The difference was that without a government-sanctioned body to coordinate efforts and lobby for resources, a Confederate soldier's chances of dying from wounds or disease was even greater than that of his Union counterpart.

The difficulties of camp life and the horrors of battle affected ordinary soldiers' morale. As food, sanitation, and medical care deteriorated and casualties mounted, a large number of soldiers deserted. At Antietam, in the fall of 1862, Confederate general Robert E. Lee estimated that one-third to one-half of his soldiers were "straggling" — that is, absent without leave. Early the next year, Union general Joseph Hooker reported that one in four soldiers under his command was similarly absent. Morale problems in the Union Army during this period were compounded by the fact that the North kept losing battles to seemingly inferior Confederate forces. By 1863, many Union soldiers were openly critical of their leaders. A Massachusetts private concluded that "there is very little zeal or patriotism in the army now; the men have seen so much more of defeat than of victory and so much bloody slaughter that all patriotism is played out."

War Transforms the North

What turned the tide for the Union was not simply improved army leadership and better military tactics, but an improved supply of armaments, food, and clothing to Union troops and of the necessities of life to their families and friends back home as well. The North's economic advantage grew as the war dragged on, but to maintain it required far more Union women than ever before to enter the paid labor force. The sacrifices that were required on the home front were deemed worthy, however, only if Union armies were winning victories on the battlefront. Dissent and protest therefore blossomed in the North until the tide of war turned decisively toward the Union in 1864. By then, African Americans had distinguished themselves in battle, though they continued to struggle against prejudice in the North and for the final eradication of slavery in the South.

The Northern Economic Boom   As the Civil War unfolded, economic change in the North occurred at a quickening pace. Despite military and economic setbacks in 1861 and 1862, the Union grew stronger as the war progressed. Northern factories turned out weapons, ammunition, blankets, clothing, shoes, and other products; and northern shipyards built the fleets that blockaded southern ports. Leading in the production of war materials, the North continued to serve as the center of American industrial development. By 1860, manufacturing establishments in the North outnumbered those in the South six to one, and there were 1.3 million industrial workers in the North, compared with 110,000 in the South.

Initially, however, the effects of the war on northern industry had been little short of disastrous. New England textile production declined precipitously as the flow of raw southern cotton dried up. Shoe factories, which had relied heavily on the orders of southern slaveholders, fell silent. The large seaboard cities of the Northeast, whose very lifeblood was trade, also suffered greatly. By 1863, however, the economic picture had changed dramatically. Coal mining and iron production boomed in Pennsylvania. In New England, woolen manufacturing took up the slack left by the decline of cotton. Merchants dealing in war orders made handsome profits, and industrialists ran their factories at a frenzied pace. The lower wages paid to desperate women and children, recently arrived immigrants, and free blacks seeking entry into new occupations contributed to increases in both profits and the pace of work.

The economic boom of 1863 to 1864 was also linked to a vast expansion in the federal government's activities. Direct orders from the War Office for blankets, firearms, and other goods did much to spark the manufacturing upturn. The government also stimulated the economy by granting large contracts to northern railroads to carry troops and supplies and by making loans and land grants that would finance the railroads' dramatic postwar expansion. Congress instituted a steep tariff on imported manufactured goods, giving American manufacturers protection from competition and encouraging industrial development, policies that northern industrialists had long demanded. With southern Democrats removed from the halls of Congress, Republicans now rushed to meet these demands.

Perhaps the federal government's most significant long-term contribution to the economy was the creation of a national currency and a national banking system. Before the Civil War, private banks (chartered by the states) issued their own banknotes, which were used in most economic transactions; the federal government paid all of its expenses in gold or silver. Various wartime acts of Congress revolutionized this system, giving the federal government the power to create currency, to issue federal charters to banks, and to create a national debt (which totaled $2 billion by the war's end). These developments helped to shape the full flowering of industrial capitalism after the war.

They also had profound short-term effects. To finance the war, the government used its new power to flood the nation with $400 million in treasury bills, commonly called "greenbacks." The federal budget mushroomed—from $63 million in 1860 to nearly $1.3 billion in 1865. By the war's end, the federal bureaucracy had grown to be the nation's largest single employer. These federal actions provided a tremendous stimulus to industry, and northern manufacturers greeted them, on the whole, with enthusiasm.

But industrialists continued to face one daunting problem that government expansion only exacerbated: a shortage of labor. Over half a million workers left their jobs to serve in the Union Army, and others were drawn into jobs with the expanding federal bureaucracy, just as the need for increased production intensified the competition for workers. Employers dealt with the shortage in a variety of ways. Then, as now, mechanization could lessen the need for workers. Reapers and mowers had been developed in the 1850s, but the shortage of labor greatly hastened their adoption by midwestern farmers. "The severe manual toil of mowing, raking, pitching, and cradling is now performed by machinery," noted *Scientific American* in 1863. The war similarly quickened the trend toward mechanization in the manufacture of clothing and shoes.

Northern industrialists also led the way in hiring immigrants to remedy the labor shortage. The industrialists formed organizations such as the Boston Foreign Emigrant Aid Society and were extremely successful in encouraging migration from the European countryside to U.S. factories, mines, and mills. Immigration had fallen off sharply in the first two years of the war, with only about 90,000 immigrants arriving in 1861 and again in 1862—less than half the level of each of the preceding five years. By 1863, the number of immigrants—mostly Irish, German, and British—had again reached the pre-1860 level. The figure climbed to nearly 200,000 in 1864 and exceeded 300,000 in 1865.

Women Expand the Wartime Workforce   The entry of women—immigrant and native-born—into both the agricultural and industrial workforce was a critical factor in easing the wartime labor shortage. On northern farms, women took over much of the work. A popular verse called "The Volunteer's Wife" described the situation:

Take your gun and go, John,
Take your gun and go,
For Ruth can drive the oxen,
And I can use the hoe.

A missionary traveling through Iowa in 1863 reported that he "met more women driving teams on the road and saw more at work in the fields than men." Factories and armories hired women in ever-larger numbers to churn out northern war orders. Most important to the war effort were the thousands of "sewing women," who were mainly poor and working-class women, many of them single or widowed and immigrants. They worked under government contract in their own homes (often in crowded tenements) to make the uniforms that Union soldiers wore. Opportunities for more well-educated native-born white women also opened up in the fields of teaching, government clerical work, and retail sales.

Women's employment in some of the newer industrial jobs was temporary; when the war ended, so did women's employment. But in other areas, such as the nursing profession, women made permanent inroads. Despite strong initial opposition, women eventually obtained work in northern hospitals and Union Army camps. This movement was led by such memorable figures as Clara Barton, Mary Ann "Mother" Bickerdyke, and Dr. Mary Walker, the first woman to be awarded the Medal of Honor. The work these women accomplished created popular support for their entrance into the medical profession. By the end of the war, women had almost entirely replaced men in nursing the sick and wounded.

Industrial Work
Women filled cartridges at the U.S. Arsenal at Watertown, Massachusetts. Winslow Homer, *Harper's Weekly,* July 20, 1861 — American Social History Project.

"And Then I Must Work for Myself": A Northern Workingwoman's Story

The following letter, written by a sewing woman in November 1863 to the New York Sun, *reveals the kinds of jobs and the low wages that were available to northern workingwomen during the Civil War.*

When this rebellion broke out, my brothers joined the Army, and then I must work for myself and help support my mother and my little sister. I would read the advertisements in the paper and go answer them. . . .

A well-known hat manufactory on Broadway wanted five hundred hands. I applied for work. The proprietor . . . promised me 62 cents per dozen. I knew I could not make a dozen per day; but what was I to do? I wanted work, and must get it, or starve. My mother and myself worked from early morning until late a night, but could not make more than $2.50 each per week. . . . Are we nothing but living machines, to be driven at will for the accommodation of a set of heartless, yes, I may say soulless people . . . ? They ought to read the commandment, "Thou shall not kill." But they are murderers that die on feather beds. . . .

Men join the army and leave us with out employers to battle with. I trust that we will have kind friends to aid us; it is a good work. If we were paid better it would save many young girls from worse than poverty. Let us act as one, and I feel sure that with the blessings of God, and assistance of our fellow beings, we will succeed.

E.S.P., A Working Girl

New York Sun, November 17, 1863.

Northern women played an astonishing array of roles over the course of the war. The Woman's National Loyal League gathered some four hundred thousand signatures on petitions calling for a constitutional amendment to end slavery. Women served as spies, couriers, recruiting agents, and even soldiers. Some 400 women, on both sides of the conflict, are known to have disguised themselves as men to join infantry companies; the identities of several were discovered only after they were wounded in battle. Although the financial rewards for such services were small, the efforts of women in wartime helped to transform popular notions of appropriate gender roles and set the stage for new debates in the postwar era over women's rights and responsibilities.

Dissent and Protest in the Union States   Despite an expanding economy, northern working people suffered tremendously during the war years. For those who were not facing enemy fire, the main problem was inflation. As greenbacks flooded the economy and consumer goods fell into short supply, prices climbed rapidly—about 20 percent faster than wages. Skilled

"Nearly Every Article of Consumption Has Doubled": Wartime Inflation

This account, taken from a July 1863 issue of Fincher's Trades Review, *an important labor newspaper of the period, describes the problems of wartime inflation and tainted food that workers faced.*

Two years ago, the man who received $1.50 per day, could satisfy his wants with that sum just as well, if not better, than he can now with $3.00 per day. Nearly every article of consumption has doubled, and if wages are not permitted to keep pace with the cost of necessities, the producer is daily robbed of one-half his earnings. . . . Rents will soon range from 15 to 20 percent higher; and many articles heretofore used by the families of workingmen are now wholly beyond their means.

It will be found, also, that workingmen are subjected to other ills by the fictitious value placed upon the necessaries of life. Flour has become classified into several brands, which plainly indicate impurity in one or more of them, and means something more than the mere color of the wheat; hence, the purchaser of second or third quality is apt to eat his share of worms and other insects, or nauseate his stomach with musty, sour bread. . . . The vegetable and chemical trash mixed up with a small portion of [coffee] is enough to weaken the digestive organs of an ostrich. Tea undergoes the same fraudulent process, and our lady readers cannot be too careful in the selection of the article. These adulterations, in many cases, must result in shattered health, if not premature death.

Fincher's Trades Review, July 1863.

workers, whose labor was in high demand, might be able to keep up. But unskilled workers, especially women, were hit hard by inflation. "We are barely able to sustain life for the prices offered by contractors, who fatten on their contracts by grinding immense profits out of the labor of their operatives," wrote a group of Cincinnati seamstresses to President Lincoln in 1864.

Industrialists garnered huge profits as production boomed. Profits in the woolen industry nearly tripled. Railroad stocks climbed to unheard-of prices. Government contractors made huge gains — sometimes by supplying inferior goods at vastly inflated prices. To working people suffering the ravages of inflation, such extraordinary profits seemed grossly unfair.

Northern workers tried to improve their plight in a variety of ways. From 1863 through 1865, there were dozens of strikes as workers began to form unions to demand higher wages. But wartime strikes could also exacerbate divisions among workers. In a number of cases, such as the long-shoremen's walkout in New York City in June 1863, employers broke strikes staged by largely immigrant workers by hiring African Americans for jobs from which they had traditionally been excluded.

The Irrepressible Conflict

In this cartoon from *Vanity Fair*, an Irish longshoreman told a black worker seeking employment on New York's waterfront: "Well, ye may be a man and a brother, sure enough; but it's little hospitality ye'll get out of yer relations on this dock, me ould buck!" The sharp competition for unskilled jobs contributed to the New York draft riot of 1863. *Vanity Fair*, August 2, 1862 — American Social History Project.

Both black and white workers looked to Lincoln and the federal government for help. The Republicans, after all, had pledged themselves to protect the rights of free labor. But government proved to be a better friend of business. Employers successfully lobbied a number of state legislatures to pass laws prohibiting strikes. They also persuaded the increasingly powerful federal government to help block workers' efforts to organize. When workers at the Parrott arms factory in Cold Spring, New York, struck for higher wages in 1864, the government sent in two companies of troops, declared martial law, and arrested the strike leaders. The army similarly intervened in labor disputes in St. Louis and in the Pennsylvania coalfields. All three strikes were crushed.

Workers who protested federal intervention in strikes raised the hopes of Democrats who were seeking greater political power. The Civil War had deeply divided the Democratic Party in the North. Although some party leaders supported Lincoln and the war effort, many others — whom opponents called Copperheads, after the poisonous snake — rallied behind Ohio politician Clement L. Vallandigham in opposing the war. These antiwar Democrats sought desperately to build support for their position among midwestern farmers and eastern industrial workers. In areas of the Midwest where sympathy for the southern cause and antipathy to African Americans ran deep, both women and men enthusiastically joined the Copperhead campaign.

Democrats enjoyed considerable success in eastern cities as well. There, inflation was running rampant and immigrant workers had long supported Democratic political machines. Racism was the strongest weapon in the party's arsenal. As the Civil War increasingly became a war against slavery, many white workers found an outlet for their racism in supporting the peace wing of the Democratic Party.

The Republican draft law further fueled northern opposition to the war. The Conscription Act of March 1863 provided that draftees would be selected by an impartial lottery. But the act contained a loophole that exempted men who had $300 to spare. A man could pay that $300 to the government in place of serving or to another man who served as the draftee's substitute. This option was unavailable to most workers, who were lucky to earn $300 in an entire year, and they deeply resented the draft law's profound inequality. Others opposed the recent expansion of the North's war aims to include emancipation, as they assumed that freed slaves would join free blacks as competitors for scarce jobs after the war ended.

The simmering resentment of the urban poor reached the boiling point in July 1863, when the new draft law went into effect. Riots broke out in cities across the North. In New York, where war-induced inflation had caused tremendous suffering and where a large immigrant population solidly supported a powerful Democratic machine, implementation of the draft triggered four days of the worst rioting Americans had ever seen. Violence quickly spread through the entire city. Both women and men, many of them poor Irish immigrants, attacked Protestant missionaries, Republican draft officials, and wealthy businessmen. New York City's small free black population became the rioters' main target, however. Enraged immigrants turned on black New Yorkers. One observer reported that he saw "a black man hanged . . . for no offense but his Negritude." Rioters lynched at least a dozen African Americans and looted and burned the city's Colored Orphan Asylum. Leading trade unionists joined middle-class leaders in condemning the riots but to no avail. The violence ended only when Union troops were rushed back from the front to put down the riot by force. At the end, over 100 New Yorkers lay dead.

Buying a Substitute in the North During the War

In his collection of etchings, *Sketches from the Civil War in North America*, A. J. Volck depicted the Union Army as composed of immigrant and native-born deviants and criminals. He was moved less by the inequities of the northern draft law than by his sympathy for the South. V. Blada (A. J. Volck), *Sketches from the Civil War in North America, 1861, '62, '63* (1863) — Print Collection, Miriam and Ira Wallach Division of Art, Prints, and Photographs, New York Public Library, Astor, Lenox and Tilden Foundations.

The New York Draft Riots

The lynching of a black man on Clarkson Street. *Illustrated London News*, August 8, 1863 — American Social History Project.

"A Poor Man, But A Man For All That": New Yorkers Debate the Draft Riots

This exchange between a self-identified participant in the New York City draft riots and the editors of the New York Times *appeared in that newspaper on July 15, 1863, the third day of violent unrest in the streets of New York City.*

You will, no doubt, be hard on us rioters tomorrow morning, but that 300-dollar law has made us nobodies, vagabonds and cast-outs of society, for whom nobody cares when we must go to war and be shot down. We are the poor rabble, and the rich rabble is our enemy by this law. Therefore we will give our enemy battle right here, and ask no quarter. Although we got hard fists, and are dirty without, we have soft hearts, and have clean consciences within, and that's the reason we love our wives and children more than the rich, because we got not much besides them, and we will not go and leave them at home for to starve. Until that draft law is repealed, I for one am willing to knock down more such rum-hole politicians as [Police Superintendent] Kennedy. Why don't they let the nigger kill the slave-driving race and take possession of the South, as it belongs to them.

A Poor Man, But A Man For All That.

[Editors' response]

. . . It may be very hard that a poor man should be compelled to serve his country as a soldier, but he is not asked to do it gratuitously, and every possible precaution is taken to provide for his wife and children. Thousands and hundreds of thousands of such men have volunteered to defend their country now that its existence is in danger, and have never dreamed that they became either "vagabonds" or a "rabble" on that account. It is true that men who have $300 can purchase exemption from this honorable duty—but their $300 goes into the pockets of the poor men who may volunteer to take their places. Money will purchase exemption from a great many of the labors of life, and there always will be a great many men willing to use it for that purpose; and neither laws nor anything else can change this state of things.

But if our correspondent thinks that this justifies him in committing murder and arson, or that he shows his love for his wife and children by plunging the society in which they live into the midst of anarchy and crime, he will live to find out his mistake.

New York Times, July 15, 1863, 4.

Building Consensus Through Military Victory   In the weeks preceding the draft riots, the military situation did not bode well for the Union. Following victories at Fredericksburg and Chancellorsville, Virginia, the Confederate army's premiere general, Robert E. Lee, had led his troops in the first direct invasion of northern territory. By late June 1863, the Confederate army had crossed into Pennsylvania. If Lee won a substantial victory there, European nations might be convinced to recognize the Confederacy, and Peace Democrats might gain substantial support among war-weary Northerners.

But then, as New Yorkers rioted against the draft, the Union won two decisive victories, marking the beginning of its military success. In the eastern theater, Union forces turned back a major Confederate drive at Gettysburg, Pennsylvania (Map 11.2). Neither Lee nor his Union counterpart, General George A. Meade, had set out to wage a major battle in Gettysburg. But Lee was concerned about losing his supply lines if he moved farther north, and Meade was anxious to ensure that the Confederates not gain control of the major roads that crossed in the town. So on July 1, the battle commenced, and three grueling days of fighting followed. Although it appeared at several points that the Confederate Army had the advantage, it failed to gain the victory. The battle of Gettysburg was the bloodiest of the war. Twenty-three thousand Union soldiers were killed, wounded, or listed

MAP 11.2   The Battle of Gettysburg

At the Battle of Gettysburg, Confederate forces threatened for the first time to gain a major victory in the North. Just before moving into Pennsylvania, the Confederate Army had won battles at Fredericksburg and Chancellorsville, Virginia. A victory at Gettysburg could have turned the tide of the war in the South's favor, persuaded Europeans to support the Confederacy, and allowed the Peace Democrats to make a stronger case for ending the war without ending slavery.

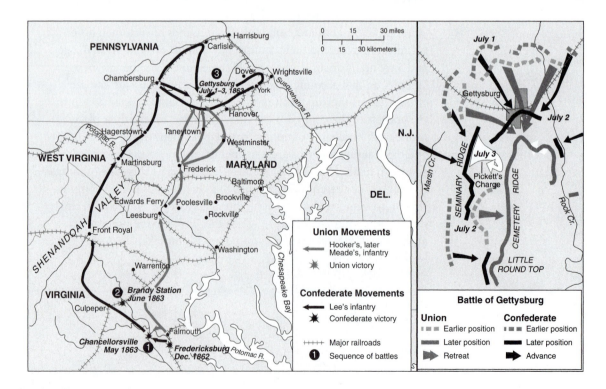

as missing, as were 28,000 Confederate soldiers, more than one-third of Lee's army.

It was probably good that on July 4, as the weary and wounded Confederate troops retreated south, they had no idea of the events that were unfolding in Vicksburg, Mississippi. There, Union troops under Ulysses S. Grant had been pounding entrenched Confederate forces for weeks. In June, Grant had sent his men in a wide arc around the city and attacked from the east, setting the stage for a six-week siege of the city. Exhausted and starving Confederate soldiers finally wrote a letter to their commander, General John C. Pemberton, stating: "If you can't feed us, you had better surrender, horrible as this idea is." On July 4, 30,000 Confederate troops surrendered, giving the Union Army control of the richest plantation region in the South.

The changing Union fortunes helped to turn the tide of northern public opinion, increasing support for Lincoln. At the same time, the heroics of African American soldiers, who in 1863 engaged in direct and often brutal combat against Confederate troops, encouraged wider support for emancipation. In addition, the Union victories at Vicksburg and Gettysburg convinced Great Britain not to recognize the Confederate States of America as an independent government.

The 1864 fall elections tested Northerners' support for Lincoln's wartime policies against the peace platform of the Democrats. The Democrats nominated George B. McClellan, the one-time Union commander, as their candidate for president. McClellan managed to attract many working people who had traditionally supported the Democrats and who now bore

A Harvest of Death, Gettysburg, July 1863

Photographers covered the war, following the Union Army in wagons that served as traveling darkrooms. Their equipment was bulky, and the exposures had to be long, so they could not take photographs during battle. But photography was graphic; this picture taken on the morning of July 4 showed the northern public that dying in battle lacked the gallantry that was often represented in paintings and prints. (Timothy H. O'Sullivan) Alexander Gardner, *Gardner's Photographic Sketch Book of the War,* Vol. 1 (1866) — Prints and Photographs Division, Library of Congress.

the heaviest burden of the war. But whatever hopes for victory these northern Democrats had were crushed when Union General William Tecumseh Sherman captured Atlanta just two months before the presidential election. Lincoln's substantial electoral victory over McClellan gave the president a clear mandate to carry the war to its conclusion. Combined with the military victories at Gettysburg and Vicksburg, Lincoln's reelection raised the curtain on the most important act of the Civil War: the destruction, root and branch, of slavery.

African Americans Battle Confederates and Prejudice   African Americans intervened decisively in the Civil War in two interrelated ways. From January 1863 on, African American soldiers were allowed to serve in the Union Army, and they helped to ensure that nothing short of universal emancipation would be the outcome of the war. In addition, rapid Union advances after 1864 enhanced slaves' opportunities for seizing freedom, further disrupting Confederate war efforts.

When the Union finally began to recruit African Americans into the military, the response was overwhelming. By spring 1865, nearly 200,000 African Americans were serving in the Union Army or Navy, constituting about one-tenth of the total number of men in uniform. Nearly 80 percent of black soldiers had been recruited in the slave states, and these men struck a blow for their own and their people's freedom. As George W. Hatton, a black sergeant with Company C, First Regiment, U.S. Colored Troops, observed in 1864, "though the Government declared that it did not want Negroes in this conflict, I look around me and see hundreds of colored men armed and ready to defend the Government at any moment, and such are my feelings, that I can only say, the fetters have fallen — our bondage is over."

Of course, for many northern whites, recruitment of African Americans into the Union army was not so much a matter of giving blacks a chance to end slavery as it was a practical necessity. As Union manpower needs grew, even outright racists could support black recruitment. "When this war is over and we have summed up the entire loss of life it has imposed on the country," wrote Iowa's governor, Samuel Kirkwood, "I shall not have any regrets if it is found that a part of the dead are niggers and that all are not white men."

Recruitment policies sometimes reflected this racism. In Louisiana and Mississippi, for example, squads from the invading Union Army swept through plantation slave quarters, impressing all able-bodied men into the military. "The Soldiers have taken my husband away . . . and it is against his will,"

To Arms!
This recruiting poster was directed to free African Americans in Pennsylvania, 1863. The Library Company of Philadelphia.

"I Hope to Fall with My Face to the Foe": Lewis Douglass Shows Courage Under Fire

Frederick Douglass's son Lewis was a sergeant in the Massachusetts Fifty-Fourth, a regiment that was made up of free northern blacks and escaped slaves. On July 18, 1863, they unsuccessfully attacked Fort Wagner, the Confederate stronghold that guarded the entrance to South Carolina's strategically vital Charleston Harbor. After the battle, Lewis wrote the following letter to his future wife.

My Dear Amelia:

I have been in two fights, and am unhurt. I am about to go in another, I believe to-night. Our men fought well on both occasions. The last was desperate — we charged that terrible battery on Morris Island known as Fort Wagoner, and were repulsed with a loss of [many] killed and wounded. I escaped unhurt from amidst that perfect hail of shot and shell. It was terrible. . . . Should I fall in the next fight killed or wounded I hope to fall with my face to the foe. . . .

My regiment has established its reputation as a fighting regiment — not a man flinched, though it was a trying time. Men fell all around me. A shell would explode and clear a space of twenty feet, our men would close up again, but it was no use we had to retreat, which was a very hazardous undertaking. How I got out of that fight alive I cannot tell, but I am here. My dear girl, I hope again to see you. I must bid you farewell should I be killed. Remember, if I die, I die in a good cause. I wish we had a hundred thousand colored troops — we would put an end to this war.

Carter G. Woodson, ed., *The Mind of the Negro as Reflected in Letters Written During the Crisis, 1800–1860* (1926).

Assault of the Second Louisiana (Colored) Regiment on the Confederate Works at Port Hudson, May 27, 1863
The bravery of black soldiers was extolled in the pages of *Frank Leslie's Illustrated Newspaper.* F. H. Schell, *Frank Leslie's Illustrated Newspaper,* June 27, 1863 — American Social History Project.

protested one black woman in a letter to the government. African Americans throughout the South condemned these policies, which undermined any real exercise of freedom and tore families apart. In the border states, however, slaves had less mixed feelings about recruitment into the Union Army. Because they had remained in the Union, Delaware, Kentucky, Maryland, and Missouri had been exempted from the Emancipation Proclamation. But slaves in these states who enlisted in the Union Army were granted their freedom. Slaveholders in these loyal states did everything in their power to prevent their slaves from joining the army, including assault, harsh treatment of family members left behind, and even murder. Despite these actions, the proportion of military-age enslaved men in these four states joining the Union Army was staggering, ranging from 25 to 60 percent. By their enlistments, these men delivered slavery in the border states a blow from which it could never recover.

African American soldiers, wherever they were recruited, quickly distinguished themselves in battle. In May 1863, Louisiana black regiments fought with great gallantry and almost reckless disregard for their own lives in the assault on Port Hudson, downriver from Vicksburg. Two weeks later, ex-slaves helped to fight off a Confederate attack at Milliken's Bend in the same region. The valor of African American troops at Port Hudson and Milliken's Bend helped to ensure Grant's victory at Vicksburg the following month.

African American soldiers had to be courageous, for they faced not only death on the battlefield, but also torture and death if they were captured. The Confederate government threatened that any blacks who were taken prisoner would be treated as slaves in rebellion and be subject to execution. This policy was generally not enforced because Lincoln intervened and threatened northern retaliation. In some instances, however, as at Fort Pillow, Tennessee, in April 1864, Confederate troops cold-bloodedly murdered black Union soldiers who had surrendered. By the end of the war, 37,000 black soldiers had given their lives for freedom and the Union.

Northern whites began to acknowledge the courage of the African American soldiers who served with them, helping to undermine the whites' ingrained racism. "The bravery of the blacks in the battle of Milliken's Bend completely revolutionized the sentiment of the army with regard to the employment of negro troops," wrote the assistant secretary of war. Rank-and-file white soldiers, too, were often impressed by the valor of black troops. They gave three cheers to a Tennessee black regiment after one hard-fought battle. "One year ago the regiment was unknown, and it was considered . . . very doubtful whether Negroes would make good soldiers," a white commander noted. "Today the regiment is known throughout the army and is honored."

Nevertheless, African Americans in the army felt the effects of continuing racism. They were segregated in camps, given all the most menial jobs, and treated as inferiors by white recruits and officers. Particularly galling was the early Union policy of paying black soldiers less than whites: $10 versus $13 per month. This inequality outraged African American troops. Black soldiers who openly struggled against this discrimination, like Third South Carolina Volunteers' sergeant William Walker, paid dearly for their courage. Walker, who refused to take orders until given equal pay, was charged with mutiny and executed by firing squad in February 1864.

Despite the execution of William Walker, the protests continued, and in June 1864, the War Department finally equalized wages among black and white recruits. Moreover, the struggle had begun to transform African American soldiers. They now understood that the battle for equality would go on after the war was over and that it would be fought in the North as well as the South. The war had thus not only transformed the North, but also transformed the lives and expectations of African Americans, North and South.

War Transforms the South

The destruction of slavery was the most dramatic, but by no means the only, effect the Civil War had on the South. In the South, as in the North, the war intensified conflict between social classes, altered the role of women, increased the size of cities, and — at least temporarily — launched a small industrial revolution. It also fostered dissent and protest, which were not diminished, as they were in the North, by military victory.

Urbanization and Industrialization   Although Southerners had gone to war to protect an essentially rural society, the war fostered the growth of cities and industry. Before the war, New Orleans had been the only really large southern city. Now Atlanta mushroomed, and Richmond's population more than doubled. Smaller cities also grew tremendously. The population of Mobile, Alabama, for example, climbed from 29,000 people in 1860 to 41,000 five years later.

Several factors encouraged the rapid growth of southern cities. One was the creation of a large governmental and military bureaucracy in Richmond, Virginia. Hundreds of women were recruited to work in government offices in the Confederate capital, such as the Treasury Department, a job that was considered sufficiently genteel to be respectable. Women, along with children and the elderly, also moved to cities during the war in hopes of finding protection from Union troops. These refugees trickled in during the early years of the war, but by 1863 and 1864, they were flooding cities such as Richmond, Atlanta, and Savannah. Perhaps the most important contribution to urban growth was industrialization. By 1863, for example, more than 10,000 people in Selma, Alabama, worked in war industries — industries that had not existed three years earlier.

Military necessity was the spur to industrialization. At the beginning of the war, the South contained only 15 percent of the factories in the United States and produced only 30 percent of the nation's commodities. No longer able to buy industrial goods from the North and handicapped in its trade with Europe by the Union blockade, the South had either to industrialize or die. The 30,000 troops that defended Vicksburg in 1863 depended almost exclusively on clothing and equipment manufactured in Mississippi, some of it by war widows and orphans. Factories in Natchez, Columbus, Jackson, and other southern towns turned out ten thousand garments and eight thousand pairs of shoes a week. At the base of the South's new industries was the huge Tredegar ironworks in Richmond, which, by January 1863, employed over 2,500 men, black and white.

In the end, the South's industrial revolution would be aborted. The victorious Union Army destroyed factories and machinery all across the region as the war drew to a close. Confederates sometimes destroyed their own factories to keep resources from falling into Union hands. More important, even at its height, southern industrialization was a creation of government rather than of an independent class of industrial capitalists. The South remained only a pale reflection of industrial New England. Still, while it lasted, industrialization did trigger wider social change in the South.

One such change was an undermining of traditional gender roles when large numbers of southern women took jobs in the new factories. Women flocked to the mills to make clothing, powder, cartridges, and other armaments. When a roomful of explosives blew up in a Richmond factory in March 1863, most of the 69 workers who were killed were women. Many women became the sole support of their families as fathers, husbands, and brothers in the Confederate Army received inadequate pay, died of injuries or disease, or returned home as invalids.

Industrialization also led to a vast expansion of the region's small urban working class and to a new activism on its part. Led by skilled craftsmen in the war industries, workers formed unions, went on strike, and tried to put political pressure on the Confederate gov-

Richmond in Ruins
In April 1865, facing defeat, retreating Confederate forces set fire to more than nine hundred buildings in the Confederate capital. Prints and Photographs Division, Library of Congress.

ernment. When Virginia legislators introduced a bill in the fall of 1863 to control food prices, a large crowd of Richmond workers expressed their support for price controls and their resentment toward the rich. "From the fact that he consumes all and produces nothing," they proclaimed, "we know that without [our] labor and production the man with money could not exist." Lavish balls hosted by the wives of wealthy industrialists, planters, and politicians only reinforced southern workers' disparaging views of Confederate leaders. Although women such as Mary Chesnut, a planter's wife and prolific diarist, insisted that such events were necessary to maintain morale and demonstrate that the South was far from defeated, the *Richmond Enquirer* argued that they were "shameful displays of indifference to national calamity . . . a mockery of the misery and desolation that covers the land."

Dissent and Protest in the Confederate States Even more pronounced than the growing class antagonisms in the South was the growing dissatisfaction with the war. Popular protests initially emerged when the Confederate Congress introduced a draft in April 1862, a full year before the Union passed its own draft law. Concerned with the weariness of troops in the field and with Grant's successes in the West, Confederate President Jefferson Davis concluded that the war effort required conscription. Other southerners disagreed, maintaining that the very idea of a national (that is, a Confederate) draft undermined the southern tradition of states' rights. Georgia's governor, Joseph E. Brown, for example, attempted to block implementation of the act, arguing that it conflicted with the very principles that had been used to justify secession in the first place. Many ordinary southerners agreed. "I volunteered for six months and I am perfectly willing to serve my time out, and come home and stay awhile and go again," wrote a Georgia soldier to his family. "But I don't want to be forced to go."

As in the North, inequalities in the execution of the draft also incited opposition. A draftee who had money could hire a substitute to serve in his place. Moreover, an October 1862 law exempted any white man who owned 20 or more slaves from service in the army. This special exemption arose in part as a response to the growing unruliness of plantation slaves in the absence of overseers or owners. In practice, however, it meant that large slaveholders, the very ones who had led the South into war, had exempted themselves from dying in it. The point was not lost on the nonslaveholding whites who fought and died for the Confederacy. "All they want is to get you pumpt up and go to fight for their infernal negroes," said one farmer from Alabama, "and after you do their fighting you may kiss their hine parts for all they care."

Impressment, which allowed the Confederate army to take whatever supplies it needed from farmers, planters, and other residents, also caused

"Go Fight for the Negroes of Your Neighbor": A Georgia Soldier Condemns Draft Exemptions for Slaveholders

When the Confederacy passed a draft law in 1862, it contained a provision known as the "twenty Negro law," which required plantations that had 20 or more slaves to retain "one white person" to secure order. In practice, this meant that the male owners of twenty or more slaves were exempt from military service. The law also exempted an additional white person in areas where large plantations existed within five miles of each other. In this letter to an Atlanta newspaper, a Confederate soldier protests the exemption.

But as to the justice of the clause of the Exemption Bill to which you refer, I must say that your ideas of justice and equity are quite different from mine. I cannot for my life see how it is, that because the institution of slavery elevates the social position of the poor man, that therefore the poor should fight the battles of our country, while the rich are allowed to remain at home and to enjoy ease and pleasure. . . . is it just that each conscript, who happens to own ten negroes of certain age should be exempt from military duty? — Why, sir, what say you to the poor white man who has *ten children* all dependent on him for succor and support? Shall he be exempt? No, you answer, "go fight for the negroes of your neighbor, because it elevates you in society." . . .

. . . The poor men who are now in the army are patriots. They deem no sacrifice too great to be made; no privation to severe to be borne for liberty. They leave home and friends for *country's* sake. Let the appeal be made to their patriotism, to the justice of our cause, but for God's sake don't tell the poor soldier who now shivers in a Northern wind while you snooze in a feather bed, that it is *just* and *right* that the men, whom Congress has exempted, should enjoy ease at home, amassing untold riches while *he* must fight, bleed, and even die, for their ten negroes. If we are ever whipped, it will be by violations of our own constitution, infringements of justice and right. When burdens are borne equally, *dangers* must be also.

Atlanta Southern Confederacy, 30 October 1862; reprinted in William E. Gienapp, ed., *The Civil War and Reconstruction: A Documentary Collection* (New York: W. W. Norton & Company, 2001), 133–134.

---

discontent. By 1863, the Confederate Congress had set prices well below market value for the goods that were taken. A group of farmers from Floyd County, Georgia, complained, "These seizures are not impressment, [they] are robbery." Along with a more stringent tax bill that was introduced the same year, impressment placed a heavy burden on the small, food-producing farm families that had the least to gain from a Confederate victory. It brought to crisis proportions a food shortage that had been building for some time in southern cities.

Although overwhelmingly agricultural, the South had built its economy primarily on cotton, tobacco, and other nonedible crops. The absence of a good railroad or canal system in the South, coupled with the Union block-

"Women and Children Are Still Standing in the Streets, Demanding Food": A Woman Witnesses the Richmond Bread Riot

A friend of Sara Rice Pryor, wife of Confederate Army officer Roger A. Pryor, wrote this letter describing the Richmond "bread riot." On April 2, 1863, a large and largely female crowd protested severe wartime food shortages by taking the food they needed from stores in Richmond, the capital of the Confederacy.

The crowd now rapidly increased, and numbered, I am sure, more than a thousand women and children. It grew and grew until it reached the dignity of a mob—a bread riot. They impressed all the light carts they met, and marched along silently and in order. They marched through Cary Street and Main, visiting the stores of the speculators and emptying them of their contents. Governor Letcher sent the mayor to read the Riot Act, and as this had no effect he threatened to fire on the crowd. The city battalion then came up. The women fell back with frightened eyes, but did not obey the order to disperse. The President then appeared, ascended a dray, and addressed them. It is said he was received at first with hisses from the boys, but after he had spoken for some time with great kindness and sympathy, the women quietly moved on, taking their food with them. General Elzey and General Winder wished to call troops from the camps to "suppress the women," but [Secretary of War] Seddon, wise man, declined to issue the order. While I write women and children are still standing in the streets, demanding food, and the government is issuing to them rations of rice.

This is a frightful state of things. I am telling you of it because *not one word* has been said in the newspapers about it. All will be changed, Judge Campbell tells me, if we can win a battle or two (but, oh, at what a price!), and regain the control of our railroads. Your General has been magnificent. He has fed Lee's army all winter—I wish he could feed our starving women and children.

Sara Rice Pryor, *Reminiscences of Peace and War* (New York: Macmillan Company, 1904), pp. 237–239; reprinted in William E. Gienapp, ed., *The Civil War and Reconstruction: A Documentary Collection* (New York: W. W. Norton & Company, 2001), 199–200.

ade of coastal shipping and Union occupation of grain-producing areas in the Confederacy, further hindered distribution of food. As the specter of starvation came to haunt the cities of the South, even people in Richmond, the capital of the Confederacy, went hungry. In March 1863, when government agents began using impressment to take scarce food from city markets to feed the Confederate Army, Richmond's poor channeled their anger into protest.

On April 2, a group of women, including the wives of Richmond ironworkers and Confederate soldiers, marched to the governor's mansion, demanding food. A young woman in the growing throng declared, "We celebrate our right to live. We are starving. As soon as enough of us get together we are going to the bakeries, and each of us will take a loaf of bread. This is little enough for the government to give us after it has taken all our men." The protest soon turned into a major riot, which ended only when Jefferson Davis personally threatened to have troops open fire on the women. Food riots also broke out in cities in Georgia, North Carolina, and Alabama.

Food shortages were closely tied to another problem: inflation. Food shortages forced food prices up, while the blockade and the military focus of southern industry increased the prices of manufactured goods. As the Confederate government issued more and more treasury notes to finance the war, inflation soared. By January 1864, it took twenty-seven Confederate dollars to buy what one dollar had bought in April 1861—an inflation rate of 2,600 percent in less than three years. Urban workers were overwhelmed. In the aftermath of the Richmond bread riots, a woman diarist declared, "I am for a tidal wave of peace—and I am not alone. . . . if we can afford to give $11 for a pound of bacon, $10 for a small dish of green corn, and $10 for a watermelon, we can have a dinner of three courses for four persons. . . . Somebody, somewhere, is mightily to blame for all this business." The culprits, to her mind, were the political leaders who had started the war in the first place.

Small farmers and their families also bore heavy burdens. Despite their loyalty to the Confederacy early in the war, taxation, impressment, inflation, and the inequities of the draft eventually took their toll. To these grievances was added the devastation of war. Since most of the war was fought in the Upper South, small nonslaveholding farmers saw their crops, their animals, and sometimes their very farms destroyed. During the last year of the war, increasing desertion rates and protests by white farmers against the depredation of their property, crops, and homes by Confederate soldiers marked their growing disaffection from a war that would benefit largely the slaveholding elite.

The phrase that had seemed so cynical in 1862—"a rich man's war and a poor man's fight"—had become the rallying cry of the southern peace movement by 1864. The Washington Constitutional Union, a secret peace society with a large following among farmers in Georgia, Alabama, and Tennessee, elected several of its members to the Confederate Congress. The Heroes of America, another secret organization with strength in North Carolina, pro-

Sowing and Reaping
The northern *Frank Leslie's Illustrated Newspaper* presented an unflattering portrait of southern white womanhood in a May 1863 illustration. The depiction contrasted sharply with the view that was promoted by plantation elites of virtuous southern white mothers and wives who obeyed and deferred to men. The panel on the left showed southern women "hounding their men on to Rebellion." The panel on the right depicted them "feeling the effects of Rebellion and creating Bread Riots." *Frank Leslie's Illustrated Newspaper*, May 23, 1863 — American Social History Project.

vided Union forces with information on southern troop movements and encouraged desertion from the Confederate Army. By war's end, more Confederate soldiers had deserted than remained in uniform. In some isolated mountainous regions of the South, such as western North Carolina, draft evaders and deserters formed guerrilla groups that not only killed draft officials but also actively impeded the war effort.

In the eastern part of North Carolina, Indians fueled opposition to the Confederate cause. Native Americans from Robeson County were, like slaves, forced to labor for the Confederate Army. They used the knowledge they gained to mount guerrilla operations and pass information to Union officers. By 1864, Henry Berry Lowry, an Indian and, according to his supporters, the Robin Hood of Robeson County, had organized a band that consisted of his own people plus aggrieved whites and poor blacks to wage a guerrilla war against Confederate troops and the North Carolina Home Guard. Indians also helped to guide Union General William Tecumseh Sherman and his troops — including a number of Oneidas serving with Company F — through the North Carolina swamps, helping to increase the devastation that was wreaked on the area but also to hasten the Union victory.

As the Confederate cause unraveled, many southern white women grew weary of the conflict. Across the South, women had organized aid societies, which provided bandages, blankets, clothing, ammunition, and food to the army. The women also supplied hospitals, raised funds, and supported an increasing number of widows and orphans. Individual women volunteered as nurses, served as couriers and spies, picked up guns in defense of homes and farms, and raised regiments. Among the slaveholding class, many mistresses became "masters," taking over the management of fieldwork and field hands. As one soldier wrote to his wife on a Georgia farm, "You must be a man and woman both while the war lasts." Given the restrictions on women's activities before the war, the changes that the protracted conflict demanded became too much to ask of more and more women. In addition to anxieties about the safety of their men on the front lines of battle, slaveholding southern white women feared the wrath of Yankee soldiers, the antipathy of slaves and free blacks, and the desperation of poor whites. They found obtaining the necessities of life a heavier and heavier burden; and there was no relief, no victory, in sight.

With the military defeats of 1863 and 1864 (Map 11.3), many women who had once supported the Confederate cause began to pray for peace, whatever the price. Some even urged their sons and husbands to abandon the battlefield and return home. Although some women remained ardent supporters of secession, berating generals who ordered retreat or suffered defeat, a growing number agreed with Georgia plantation mistress Gertrude Thomas. In October 1864, she wrote in her diary, "It would be a brilliant thing to recapture Atlanta. And I wish it could be done." But she continued, "Am I willing to give my husband to gain Atlanta for the Confederacy? No, No, No, a thousand times No!"

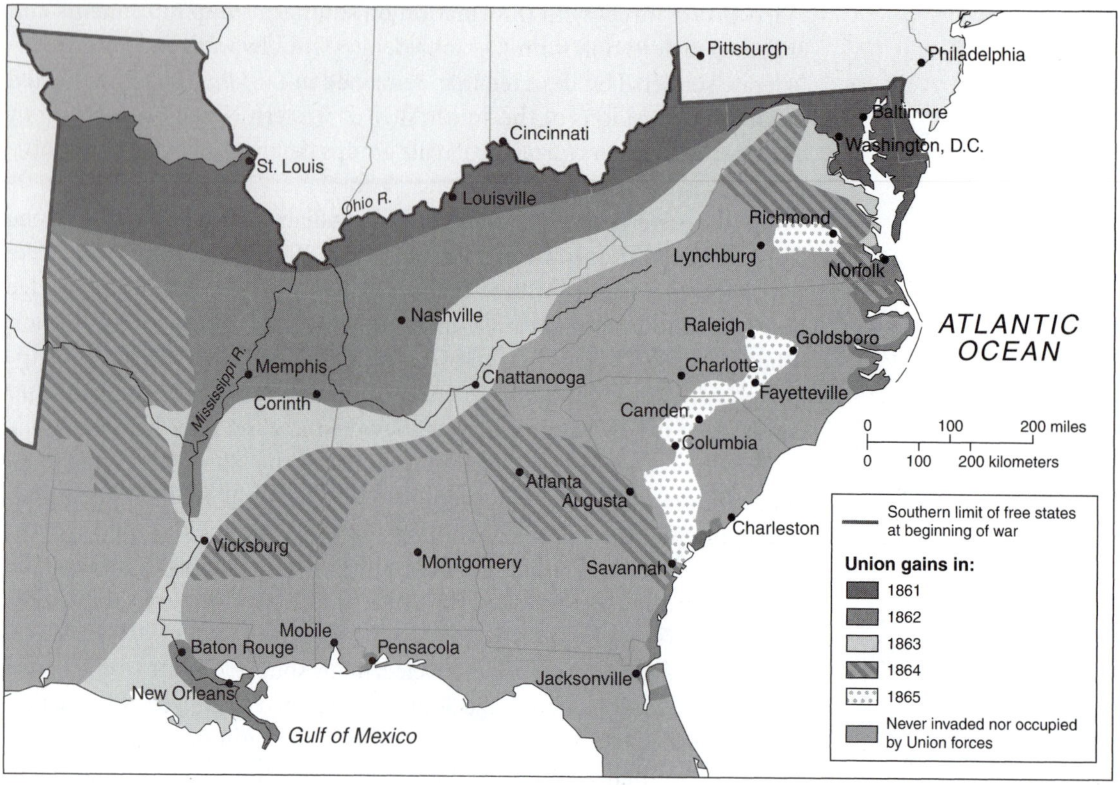

Military Victory Assured

The war had now entered its final months. In March 1864, Lincoln placed General Ulysses S. Grant in charge of all Union forces. In early May, Grant embarked on a strategy that included attacks against military and civilian targets alike and that accepted huge casualties to achieve victory. Grant led his troops overland through the Wilderness, Spotsylvania, Cold Harbor, and Petersburg campaigns in attempts to take Richmond and defeat Lee's Confederate forces. General William Tecumseh Sherman, meanwhile, pushed back the Confederate Army in Tennessee and invaded Georgia. By August 1864, Sherman had forced Confederate General John Bell Hood's army to retreat to Atlanta, one of the most important cities in the South. Early the following month, Sherman's army swept into Atlanta, cutting the South in half. A sense of impending doom spread among those who were loyal to the Confederacy.

MAP 11.3   The Conquest of the South, 1861–1865
Although Confederate forces maintained control over nearly half the area of the South until the end of the war, they did lose control over critical communication and supply lines. As Union forces penetrated the South from the North and the West, strategic railroad, communication, and shipping lines fell into Union hands. At the same time, bloody and prolonged military campaigns in many areas had devastated the Confederate Army, which was recruiting soldiers from a smaller and diminishing pool of men.

MAP 11.4 Sherman's March Through the Confederacy

Sherman's march through Georgia has been memorialized in films and novels as well as in history books. The spectacular, if horrific, burning of Atlanta has gained particular attention. But for Sherman's troops, destroying Atlanta was only the beginning of a seven-month campaign of destruction that brought Union soldiers into the homes, kitchens, barns, and bedrooms of Confederate families from Atlanta, Georgia, through Columbia, South Carolina, and into Bentonville and Raleigh, North Carolina. Moreover, the devastation that Sherman's march wrought was psychological as well as physical, and it drew women, black and white, into the center of the Civil War.

Sherman then began his 300-mile march across Georgia, from Atlanta to the sea, and then up through the Carolinas (Map 11.4). Embracing the concept of "total war," his troops sought to destroy everything in their path. They cut a swath of destruction 50 to 60 miles wide, destroying crops, livestock, and houses before they reached Savannah in late December. Civilians—which often meant women and children—were now official targets of Union military strategists. Sherman's all-white army uprooted thousands of slaves, many of whom tried to attach themselves to the Union forces. In all, nearly 18,000 slaves—men, women, and children—left their plantations to join the victorious Union Army on its march to the sea. To the fleeing slaves' dismay, Sherman's troops turned many away. Marauding Confederate forces subsequently captured many of them, killing some and re-enslaving others.

Sherman's callous actions caused a scandal in Washington. In January 1865, Lincoln dispatched Secretary of War Edwin Stanton to Georgia to investigate the charges. In an extraordinary meeting held in Savannah, Stanton and Sherman met with twenty black ministers to hear their complaints about mistreatment of contrabands and to inquire what, in their opinion, African Americans wanted, now that slavery was ending. The ministers spoke movingly of the war lifting "the yoke of bondage"; freed slaves now "could reap the fruit of their own labor" and, by being given land, could

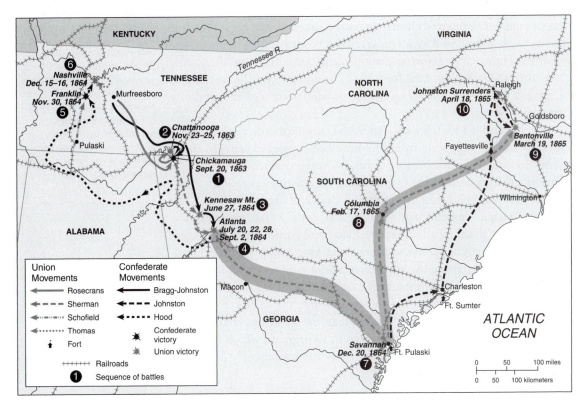

"take care of ourselves, and assist the Government in maintaining our freedom." Four days later, Sherman responded to the ministers' demands and issued his controversial Field Order Number 15, setting aside more than four hundred thousand acres of captured Confederate land to be divided into small plots for the freed slaves. Perhaps as significant as Sherman's order was the fact that a major official of the national government had traveled to Georgia to ask ordinary African Americans what they wanted. The Civil War had truly had revolutionary consequences.

Contrabands Accompanying the Line of Sherman's March Through Georgia
This illustration from a March 1865 *Frank Leslie's Illustrated Newspaper* showed a stereotyped view of the men, women, and children who followed the Union Army's campaign through Georgia. But to northern readers, the engraving's significance may have lain in its unmistakable message about slaves' utter hatred of slavery. "The oft expressed fallacy that they preferred slavery to freedom," ran the picture caption, ". . . [has been] 'crushed to earth,' . . . never to rise again." *Frank Leslie's Illustrated Newspaper,* March 18, 1865 — American Social History Project.

Those consequences were far-reaching. At the end of 1864, as defeat loomed, Confederate leaders themselves began to talk of emancipating the slaves. At almost the same moment that Stanton and Sherman were meeting with African American ministers in Savannah, Jefferson Davis was calling for the general recruitment of slaves into the Confederate Army, their payment to include freedom for themselves and their families. The Confederate Congress ultimately passed such a law in early 1865, but it came too late to allow African Americans actually to enlist in the southern army. The event nonetheless demonstrated a startling fact: the southern planters who had seceded from the Union to protect the institution of slavery were now openly adopting policies that would inevitably destroy it.

As Sherman led his troops north from Georgia and through the Carolinas, Grant's troops were overwhelming Lee's besieged army in Richmond. In one of the war's most dramatic moments, seasoned African American troops under Grant's command led the final assault on Richmond. They marched into the capital of the Confederacy carrying the Stars and Stripes and singing the anthem to John Brown, much to the amazement of Richmond's citizenry, black and white. Finally, in April 1865, with fewer than 30,000 soldiers remaining under his command, Lee surrendered, signing the agreement along with Grant at the home of William McLean in Appomattox Court House, Virginia. Two large Confederate armies continued to engage Union forces in North Carolina and west of the Mississippi and the Confederate government continued on until May, having been reestablished in Georgia, to which Jefferson Davis fled. Still, the Civil War, for all intents and purposes, had come to an end.

Jefferson Davis as an Unprotected Female!

Union troops captured the former president of the Confederacy in May 1865. Whether Davis, who had eluded arrest for over a month, was actually wearing his wife's dress when he was caught is open to question. Nonetheless, the depiction of the captured Davis in woman's clothes was featured in many illustrations and cartoons in the northern press. These images, like earlier pictures of southern women sending their men to war and rioting, questioned the South's claims of courage and chivalry by showing its men and women reversing traditional sex roles. *Harper's Weekly*, May 27, 1865 — American Social History Project.

Conclusion: Revolutionary Consequences and Daunting Questions

The legal abolition of slavery had been initiated in Washington a few months earlier. In 1864, the Republican Party had endorsed a constitutional amendment that would forever end slavery in the United States. On January 31, 1865, Congress finally passed the Thirteenth Amendment to the U.S. Constitution, prohibiting slavery and involuntary servitude anywhere within the jurisdiction of the United States.

Wartime experiences, moreover, had changed the attitudes of many northerners, who had seen firsthand the "peculiar institution" and the suffering it inflicted on African Americans. In some places, new attitudes were translated into law. Ohio, California, and Illinois repealed statutes barring blacks from testifying in court and serving on juries. In May 1865, Massachusetts passed the first comprehensive public accommodations law in U.S. history, ensuring equal treatment for blacks and whites in theaters, stores, schools, and other social spaces. Earlier, San Francisco, Cincinnati, Cleveland, and even New York City had desegregated their streetcars. The logic of a war against the enslavement of southern blacks was now extended to encompass at least limited rights for African Americans in the North.

Still, the task of rebuilding the United States following four years of bitter warfare was daunting. Before it could even begin, a new tragedy engulfed the nation. On April 14, 1865, John Wilkes Booth assassinated President Abraham Lincoln as he sat in a box at Ford's Theatre watching a play. It was just five days after Lee's surrender at Appomattox Court House.

Lincoln's assassination marked the end of an era. Conflict between two social systems—one based on slavery, the other on free labor—had plagued the nation since the American Revolution. More than 600,000 Americans had died in the Civil War, but the issue of slavery was resolved once and for all. In the process, nearly four million Americans who had once been slaves were freed. Now, in the spring of 1865, all Americans had to confront difficult new questions: Who would lead the nation during this difficult time? Would Confederate political and military leaders be punished for their participation in the war? Could the nation prosper, given the devastating impact of the war on southern agriculture? How could the nation address the balance between federal power and states' rights that had fueled secession? Most important, what would be the role of newly freed African Americans in the political and economic reconstruction of the South and the nation?

"A Jubilee of Freedom": Black Charlestonians Celebrate Emancipation

The meaning of freedom for enslaved African Americans can be glimpsed in the following report from Charleston, South Carolina, which was published in the New York Daily Tribune on April 4, 1865—just five days before Lee's surrender. Charleston boasted one of the largest and most important African American communities in the antebellum South. Two months after the Confederate Army fled, the city's black men and women organized a parade to celebrate their emancipation. The parade numbered thousands of marchers and included dramatic tableaux, banners, and songs. Like their white working-class counterparts who had held similar events in the decades before the war, African Americans used such public celebrations to symbolize their deeply held beliefs and feelings.

It was a jubilee of freedom, a hosannah to their deliverers. First came the marshals and their aides, followed by a band of music; then the Twenty-First [U.S. Colored] Regiment; then the clergymen of the different churches, carrying open Bibles; then an open car drawn by four white horses. In this car there were fifteen colored ladies dressed in white—to represent the fifteen recent slave states. A long procession of women followed the car. Then the children—1,800 in line, at least. They sang:

> John Brown's body lies a mould'ring in the grave,
> We go marching on!

This verse, however, was not nearly so popular as one which rapidly supplanted all the others, until along the mile or more of children, marching two abreast, no other sound could be heard than

> We'll hang Jeff Davis on a sour apple tree!
> As we go marching on!

After the children came the various trades. The fisherman, with a banner bearing an emblematical device and the words, "The Fisherman welcome you, [U.S. Army] General [Rufus] Saxton." . . . The carpenters carried their planes, the masons their trowels, the teamsters their whips, the coopers their adzes. The bakers' crackers hung around their necks; the paper-carriers [had] a banner and each a copy of the Charleston Courier; the wheelwrights a large wheel; and the fire companies, ten in number, their foremen with their trumpets.

A large cart, drawn by two dilapidated horses, followed the trades. On this cart was an auctioneer's block and a black man with a bell represented a Negro trader. This man had himself been sold several times, and two women and a child who sat on the block had also been knocked down at auction in Charleston.

As the cart moved along, the mock-auctioneer rang his bell and cried out: "How much am I offered for this good cook? She is an excellent cook, gentlemen. . . . Who bids?"

"Two hundred's bid! Two-fifty. Three hundred."

"Who bids? Who bids?"

Women burst into tears as they saw this tableau and, forgetting that it was a mimic scene, shouted wildly:

"Give me back my children! Give me back my children!"

New York Daily Tribune, April 4, 1865.

The Years in Review

1860

- Republican Abraham Lincoln is elected president.
- South Carolina secedes from the Union on December 20.
- To keep border states such as Maryland in the Union, President Lincoln waives the right of habeas corpus, puts secessionists in jail, arrests state legislators, and limits freedom of the press.

1861

- Mississippi, Florida, Alabama, Georgia, Louisiana, and Texas secede from the United States.
- On February 9, representatives of the seceded southern states establish the Confederate States of America and elect Mississippian Jefferson Davis as president.
- Fort Sumter surrenders to Confederate forces on April 14.
- The Upper South states of Virginia, North Carolina, Arkansas, and Tennessee join the Confederacy.
- At the first battle at Bull Run, in northern Virginia, 22,000 Southerners push back an attack by 30,000 Union troops; civilians bring picnics to the battle site, intending to watch a military spectacle, but have to flee for their lives.
- Federal government establishes the U.S. Sanitary Commission to coordinate efforts of female volunteers providing medical care to Union soldiers.
- In May, General Benjamin Butler declares escaped slaves to be "contraband" of war, property that rebel slave owners had forfeited by the act of rebellion.
- In August, Congress passes its first confiscation act, proclaiming that any slave owner whose bondsmen were used by the Confederate Army would thereafter lose all claim to those slaves.
- Lincoln appeases border state slaveholders by reversing General John C. Frémont's field order freeing all slaves owned by Confederate sympathizers in Missouri.

1862

- The Union Navy captures New Orleans, largely owing to a successful blockade of Confederate ports.
- Union troops commanded by Ulysses S. Grant win a battle at Shiloh in western Tennessee.
- Congress approves the abolition of slavery in the District of Columbia and appropriates $600,000 to assist former slaves in colonizing Haiti, Liberia, and Central America.

- Congress passes a second confiscation bill, which declares the slaves of Confederate supporters to be free.
- The Confederate Congress passes the first conscription act in American history; after a few months, it is modified to exempt from military service owners of 20 or more slaves.
- Union commanders establish "contraband camps" for families of African American soldiers.
- During the summer, Confederate troops led by Thomas "Stonewall" Jackson win a series of stunning victories in Virginia's Shenandoah Valley.
- On September 17, nearly 8,000 soldiers are killed in battle at Antietam, Maryland, as Union troops stop the advance of Confederate troops; Lincoln announces a preliminary Emancipation Proclamation five days later.
- Confederates achieve key military victories at Fredericksburg, Virginia, and Vicksburg, Mississippi.
- The first black Union regiment is organized.
- Robert E. Lee is appointed commander of the Confederate Army.

1863

- On January 1, the Emancipation Proclamation declares the end of slavery in the rebellious states.
- In March, Congress passes a Conscription Act to select military recruits by lottery, but the new law contains a loophole allowing men to pay $300 to the government in lieu of serving or to hire a substitute to serve.
- Richmond women riot over severe food shortages.
- African American soldiers display particular courage in battles at Port Hudson and Milliken's Bend, Louisiana, helping to improve northerners' attitudes toward black soldiers.
- Union soldiers defeat Confederate forces at the Battle of Gettysburg (July 1–3); more than 50,000 combatants die.
- On July 4, 30,000 Confederate troops surrender at Vicksburg, Mississippi, after a six-week Union siege.
- Violent protests against the draft erupt in New York City on July 13–16; 105 people die in bloodiest urban riot in U.S. history.
- Lincoln delivers the Gettysburg Address, declaring "a new birth of freedom" for the nation.

- Low wages and expansion of federal government power drive an economic boom in the North.

1864

- Federal troops crush the Parrott arms factory strike.
- The Democratic Party nominates Union General George B. McClellan for president; he loses to Lincoln.
- In February, African American Union soldier William Walker refuses to take orders until he is given pay equal to that of white soldiers; he is charged with mutiny and executed by firing squad.
- In May, the War Department equalizes pay between black and white recruits.
- Lumbee Indian Henry Berry Lowry organizes a band of Indians, aggrieved whites, and poor blacks, which wages guerrilla war against Confederate troops and the North Carolina Home Guard.
- General William Tecumseh Sherman captures Atlanta and begins a "March to the Sea."

1865

- Sherman issues Field Order Number 15, which sets aside over four hundred thousand acres of captured Confederate land to be divided into small plots for freed slaves.
- The Confederate Congress enacts a law allowing the general recruitment of slaves into the Confederate Army, their payment to include freedom for themselves and their families; the law comes too late for any slaves actually to serve.
- The U.S. Congress passes and states ratify the Thirteenth Amendment to the Constitution, which ends slavery.
- Lee surrenders to Grant at Appomattox Court House.
- John Wilkes Booth shoots President Abraham Lincoln while Lincoln is attending a play at Ford's Theatre; Vice President Andrew Johnson takes office when Lincoln dies the next day.

Additional Readings

For more on politics and society in the Union, see: Iver C. Bernstein, *The New York City Draft Riots* (1990); David Donald, *Why the North Won the Civil War* (1960) and *Lincoln Reconsidered: Essays on the Civil War Era* (1966); Eric Foner, *Politics and Ideology in the Age of the Civil War* (1980); David Montgomery, *Beyond Equality: Labor and the Radical Republicans, 1862–1872* (1967); Phillip Shaw Paludan, *"A People's Contest": The Union and the Civil War, 1861–1865* (1988); David M. Potter, *Lincoln and His Party in the*

Secession Crisis (1942); Joel H. Silbey, *A Respectable Minority: The Democratic Party in the Civil War Era, 1860–1868* (1977); Kenneth Stampp, *And the War Came: The North and the Secession Crisis, 1860–1861* (1950); and Hans L. Trefousse, *The Radical Republicans: Lincoln's Vanguard for Radical Justice* (1969).

For more on politics and society in the Confederacy and border states, see: William Blair, *Virginia's Private War: Feeding Body and Soul in the Confederacy, 1861–1865* (1998); Carl Degler, *The Other South: Southern Dissenters in the Nineteenth Century* (1974); Barbara J. Fields, *Slavery and Freedom on the Middle Ground: Maryland During the Nineteenth Century* (1985); William W. Freehling, *The South vs. the South: How Anti-Confederate Southerners Shaped the Course of the Civil War* (2001); Steven Hahn, *The Roots of Southern Populism: Yeoman Farmers and the Transformation of the Georgia Upcountry, 1850–1890* (1983); Mark E. Neely, Jr., Harold Holzer, and Gabor S. Boritt, *The Confederate Image: Prints of the Lost Cause* (1987); James L. Roark, *Masters Without Slaves: Southern Planters in the Civil War and Reconstruction* (1978); and J. Mills Thornton, III, *Politics and Power in a Slave Society: Alabama, 1800–1860* (1978).

For more on slavery and emancipation, see: Ira Berlin et al., eds., *Free at Last: A Documentary History of Slavery, Freedom, and the Civil War* (1992); John Hope Franklin, *The Emancipation Proclamation* (1963); Mark E. Neely, Jr., *The Fate of Liberty: Abraham Lincoln and Civil Liberties* (1991); Benjamin Quarles, *The Negro in the Civil War* (1953); Willie Lee Rose, *Rehearsal for Reconstruction: The Port Royal Experiment* (1964); and Jean Fagin Yellin, *Harriet Jacobs: A Life* (2005).

For more on women's life and labor, see: Jeannie Attie, *Patriotic Toil: Northern Women and the American Civil War* (1998); John R. Brumgardt, ed., *Civil War Nurse: The Diary and Letters of Hannah Ropes* (1980); Virginia Ingraham Burr, ed., *The Secret Eye: The Journal of Ella Gertrude Clanton Thomas, 1848–1889* (1990); Victoria E. Bynum, *Unruly Women: The Politics of Social and Sexual Control in the Old South* (1992); Jacqueline Glass Campbell, *When Sherman Marched North from the Sea: Resistance on the Confederate Home Front* (2003); Drew Gilpin Faust, *Mothers of Invention: Women of the Slaveholding South in the American Civil War* (1996); Lori D. Ginzberg, *Women and the Work of Benevolence: Morality, Politics and Class in the Nineteenth-Century United States* (1990); Elizabeth Leonard, *Yankee Women: Gender Battles in the Civil War* (1994); C. Vann Woodward, ed., *Mary Chesnut's Civil War* (1982).

For more on military history, see: Bruce Catton, *A Stillness at Appomattox* (1954); Shelby Foote, *The Civil War: A Narrative,* 3 vols. (1958–1974); Ovid L. Futch, *History of Andersonville Prison* (1968); Joseph P. Glatthaar, *Forged in Battle: The Civil War Alliance of Black Soldiers and White Officers* (1990); James M. McPherson, *Battle Cry of Freedom: The Civil War Era* (1988); Annette Tapert, ed., *The Brothers' Civil War: Civil War Letters to Loved Ones from the Blue and Gray* (1988); Bell Irvin Wiley, *The Life of Billy Yank: The Common Soldier of the Union* (1952); Bell Irvin Wiley, *The Life of Johnny Reb: The Common Soldier of the Confederacy* (1943).

12

Reconstructing the Nation

1865–1877

He Wants a Change, Too
In the wake of the July 4, 1876, massacre in Hamburg, South Carolina (when local armed whites fired on outnumbered black militiamen who were participating in an Independence Day celebration, murdering five), Thomas Nast's cartoon was unusual in promoting armed self-defense by freedpeople. Thomas Nast, *Harper's Weekly*, October 28, 1876 — American Social History Project.

I N 1871, ABRAM COLBY, a former slave and an elected Republican representative in the Georgia legislature, testified before a joint congressional committee investigating the dramatic upsurge of racial violence against African Americans in the years following the Civil War. Colby told the senators and representatives that in October 1869, thirty members of the Ku Klux Klan had broken into his house and — in front of his wife, mother, and young daughter — dragged him out of bed. They "took me to the woods and whipped me three hours or more and left me for dead," Colby testified, adding that he received this punishment because he had demanded that the army protect freed slaves' personal safety and right to vote. When the committee members asked him to describe his assailants, Colby noted, "Some are first-class men in our town. One is a lawyer, one a doctor, and some are farmers." Colby never recovered from his injuries.

Abram Colby's harrowing experience illustrates the failures as well as the successes that were inherent in the task of rebuilding the nation following the Civil War: vigilante violence, often fatal conflict over the right of African American men to vote, courageous African American insistence on self-determination and participation in the political process, and federal intervention in the South to help assure freedpeople's rights. The Union victory in April 1865 had settled two major debates but left everything else in doubt. The United States of America was preserved; slavery was dead, and African Americans were now free. But who would hold and exercise economic and political power in the postwar South? What kind of labor system would replace slavery? Who would lead the South politically? What would freedom mean for the four million former slaves? Answers to these questions were widely contested and would emerge only after two decades of intense political and social struggle, a struggle that contemporaries hopefully called Reconstruction.

Racial conflicts in the former Confederacy continued to disrupt efforts at reunification, and a protracted financial crisis dashed hopes for a quick economic recovery. In response, northern political and business leaders focused their efforts on revitalizing the economy through reconciliation between North and South rather than protecting racial advancement in either region. Thus, as the nation approached its one-hundredth anniversary, the old planter aristocracy — under the protection of a revived Democratic Party — returned to power, controlling a nonslave but still exploitative system of agricultural labor.

The failure of Reconstruction to transform southern race relations shaped the nation as a whole. Still, it was freedpeople who paid the highest price. Outgunned, both figuratively and literally, they were left with few alternatives. Yet they did not give up. Those who remained in the South established a dense network of autonomous community-based institutions, including black schools, churches, and businesses, to keep their democratic hopes alive within an oppressive and racist system.

The Beginnings of Reconstruction

Reconstruction began not in 1865, but in the midst of the Civil War itself. Early in the war, the Union Army quickly captured and occupied several areas in the deep South, including the Sea Islands off of the South Carolina coast and much of southern Louisiana and the key port city of New Orleans. Slavery rapidly disintegrated in these areas under Union Army control. Yet the occupation by the Union Army seemed to fuel rather than calm sectional and racial tensions. Union troops in New Orleans, for example, under the command of General Benjamin Butler, served as a constant irritant to local whites; and Confederate women as well as men repeatedly harassed the soldiers. At the same time, the presence of federal troops in the city raised the expectations of African Americans, who assumed that Union forces would not only free and protect them, but also assure their rights as citizens. The federal troops met neither the worst fears of the Confederates nor the best hopes of the African Americans.

As in other southern cities, blacks in New Orleans faced segregation in nearly all public accommodations — theaters, restaurants, inns, streetcars, railroads, schools, and churches. For instance, African Americans were forced to ride only in streetcars that were marked with a black star. They were abused and harassed for demanding to be treated as equals or simply for failing to defer to whites by giving way on sidewalks, doffing their hats, and lowering their eyes. Because New Orleans had a large population of African Americans who had been free and had achieved some measure of

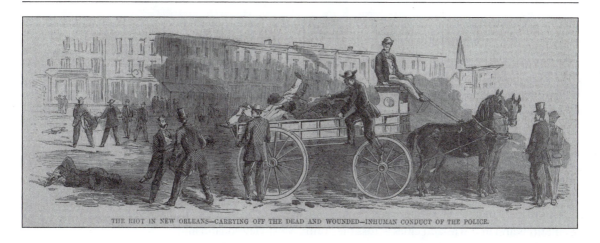

THE RIOT IN NEW ORLEANS—CARRYING OFF THE DEAD AND WOUNDED—INHUMAN CONDUCT OF THE POLICE.

Disrespecting the Dead

In the aftermath of the New Orleans riots, coverage in the illustrated press was critical of the city's police, including their "inhuman conduct" toward the victims of the violence. *Harper's Weekly*, August 25, 1866 — American Social History Project.

economic autonomy even before the Civil War, freedpeople in that city were quick to challenge such vestiges of slavery. In 1865, for instance, the local black newspaper, the *New Orleans Tribune*, published calls for direct action against segregated streetcars: "Let every colored citizen of New Orleans, on and after the fifteenth of August, enter into any car . . . and if ordered out— take a seat, and if afterwards ejected, sue the company." When open seating on the streetcars was finally achieved in 1867, the newspaper turned its attention to public schools and other segregated institutions.

Such challenges to southern racial norms occurred in many cities after the defeat of the Confederacy. African Americans often assumed that the presence of Union troops and federal officials would assure their protection as they asserted their humanity and sought equal rights under the law. Yet even as northern newspapers derided the "rebel rabble," outraged by Confederates' continued defiance, many white Union soldiers and officials stationed in the South were ambivalent about, or outright opposed to, blacks' pursuit of racial equality. In Memphis and New Orleans, local authorities stood by or actively participated as whites slaughtered blacks in orgies of racist violence.

Developments in New Orleans, Memphis, and other southern cities reflected both the promise and the limits of Reconstruction. Following a brutal civil war, no actions by individuals, groups, or the government could restore the nation to daily life as Americans remembered it. African Americans avidly sought change, hoping to gain the economic opportunities, political rights, and personal autonomy that had been denied them under slavery. Most southern whites hoped instead for a return to traditional ways. Although recognizing that slavery was gone, they nonetheless imagined a South in which whites regained economic, political, and social power and blacks remained subordinate in status and limited to manual labor. Among northern whites, many supported expanding rights for blacks in the immediate aftermath of war, in part to ensure the resurrection of the southern economy. Certainly, the Republican Party hoped to benefit at the polls from the surge of African Americans into electoral politics. Indeed, some Republican leaders viewed the punishment of Confederate leaders and the enhancement of black rights as going hand in hand. Still, their commitment to racial advancement generally fell well short of full equality.

African Americans Build New Lives After Emancipation

When the Civil War ended with the Confederacy's defeat and the abolition of slavery, the future seemed frighteningly uncertain to most Americans. Yet newly emancipated African Americans could savor the taste of freedom on plantations and in towns and cities across the South. Most viewed land and political participation as the two most important foundations for freedom, but they also sought to reunite families, legalize marriages, establish churches, gain an education, and earn a decent wage.

Freedpeople Explore the Meaning of Freedom   The meaning of freedom could be as specific and personal as the decision to take a new name or the ability to dress as one pleased, or it could take the form of refusing to be deferential to one's former owner. A Charleston, South Carolina, planter complained: "It is impossible to describe the condition of the city — It is so unlike anything we could imagine — Negroes shoving white persons off the walk — Negro women drest in the most outre style, all with veils and parasols, for which they have an especial fancy." In Richmond, Virginia, freedpeople held meetings without securing whites' permission. They also walked in Capitol Square, an area that had previously been restricted to whites, refusing to give up the sidewalks when whites approached. In countless ways, large and small, freedpeople demonstrated that the end of slavery meant the end of petty control by whites.

Freedom also meant the ability to reunite families. Thousands of freed slaves set out on searches for loved ones who had been sold away or displaced during the war's upheavals. A northern correspondent reported meeting a middle-aged ex-slave — "plodding along, staff in hand, and apparently very footsore and tired" — who had walked six hundred miles in search of his wife and children. As one government official noted, for many ex-slaves, "the work of emancipation was incomplete until the families which had been dispersed by slavery were reunited." Emancipation also made it possible for thousands of couples to formalize long-standing relationships. People who had been unable to marry before the war because of separation or their masters' objections, as well as those who had been allowed to "marry" only informally, sought out northern missionaries and Union officers to officially register and solemnize their unions. And many

"There Was Never Any Pay-day for the Negroes": Jourdon Anderson Demands Wages

For newly emancipated slaves, securing their liberty meant finding the means of support to obtain land or otherwise benefit from their own labor, as Jourdon Anderson made clear in this 1865 letter to his former owner. He addressed Major Anderson from Ohio, where he had secured good wages for himself and schooling for his children.

Sir: I got your letter and was glad to find you had not forgotten Jourdon, and that you wanted me to come back and live with you again, promising to do better for me than anybody else can. . . .

I want to know particularly what the good chance is you propose to give me. I am doing tolerably well here; I get $25 a month, with victuals and clothing; have a comfortable home for Mandy, — the folks here call her Mrs. Anderson), — and the children—Milly, Jane and Grundy—go to school and are learning well; the teacher says Grundy has a head for a preacher. They go to Sunday-School, and Mandy and me attend church regularly. . . . Now, if you will write and say what wages you will give me, I will be better able to decide whether it would be to my advantage to move back again.

As to my freedom, which you say I can have, there is nothing to be gained on that score, as I got my free papers in 1864 from the Provost-Marshal-General of the Department of Nashville. Mandy says she would be afraid to go back without some proof that you are sincerely disposed to treat us justly and kindly; and we have concluded to test your sincerity by asking you to send us our wages for the time we served you. . . . I served you faithfully for thirty-two years and Mandy twenty years. At twenty-five dollars a month for me, and two dollars a week for Mandy, our earnings would amount to eleven thousand six hundred and eighty dollars. Add to this the interest for the time our wages has been kept back and deduct what you paid for our clothing and three doctor's visits to me, and pulling a tooth for Mandy, and the balance will show what we are in justice entitled to. . . . Here I draw my wages every Saturday night, but in Tennessee there was never any pay-day for the Negroes any more than for the horses and cows. Surely there will be a day of reckoning for those who defraud the laborer of his hire.

In answering this letter please state if there would be any safety for my Milly and Jane, who are now grown up and both good-looking girls. You know how it was with Matilda and Catherine. I would rather stay here and starve, and die if it comes to that, than have my girls brought to shame by the violence and wickedness of their young masters.

Reprinted in Lydia Maria Child, *The Freedmen's Book* (Boston: Ticknor and Fields, 1865), 265–267.

children who had lost their parents during the war were now legally adopted by relatives or friends.

The postwar years also saw a tremendous upsurge in African American demands for education. Over 90 percent of black adults in the South were illiterate in 1860, and idealism and pragmatism now fueled their desire to secure an education. Some wanted to read "the word of God" on their own. Others wanted to read and do sums to protect themselves in a world of wage labor and signed contracts. In Savannah, a large number of black residents, led by a group of ministers, formed the Savannah Education Association in December 1864. Within three months, the association had raised nearly $1,000 and had hired 15 black teachers, who began their work with 600 pupils. Freedpeople built and maintained schools and hired black teachers all across the South in 1865 and 1866. Drawing on their own scarce resources and with help from northern missionary groups and the federal government, African Americans converted some places that symbolized the oppression of slavery—such as the old slave markets in New Orleans and Savannah—into schoolhouses.

Freedpeople also quickly established churches that were independent of white control. Religion had been a fundamental institution before the war, but most slaves had been forced to worship in biracial churches headed by white preachers. Freedpeople now challenged white domination of biracial congregations and even replaced white preachers with black ones, as did the African American members of the Front Street Methodist Church in Wilmington, North Carolina, early in 1865. When such efforts failed, as they frequently did, many black congregants pooled meager resources to construct new church buildings as permanent symbols of their desire to practice their religion as they chose. The African Methodist Episcopal (AME) Church was the most famous of these independent churches. But Baptist churches attracted the largest number of freedpeople after the war, mainly because this denomination's decentralized, democratic structure allowed for popular ministers, enthusiastic worship services, and local control of church affairs. "The Ebony preacher who promises perfect independence from White control and directions carries the colored heart at once," observed an officer of the American Missionary Association. The independent black church rapidly became the moral and cultural center of African American life.

But maintaining black freedom demanded continual struggle, especially in rural areas, which were still dominated by whites. On Henry

"The negroes migrate to Louisiana and Texas in search of paying labor."

Traveling

African Americans exercised their new freedom in many ways; one of them was traveling where and when they chose. This engraving was published in Edward King's *The Great South*, one of many postwar surveys of southern life. Northerners were curious to learn about the region that they had defeated in war. (J. Wells Champney [W. L. Sheppard, del.]), Edward King, *The Great South* . . . (1875) — American Social History Project.

Defying Stereotypes
After drawing a military wedding scene in Vicksburg, Mississippi, in June 1866, which subsequently was reproduced as an engraving in *Harper's Weekly*, pictorial journalist Alfred Waud showed the sketch to a local white "lady." Her immediate response was disbelief: "the decent appearance of the party and the taste shown in the bride's apparel [was] exaggerated for the sake of appearances." This, Waud assured the incredulous woman and *Harper's Weekly*'s readers in general, "was not the case; the scene is given just as it appeared." Alfred R. Waud, *Marriage of a Colored Soldier at Vicksburg by Chaplain Warren of the Freedmen's Bureau*, c. June 1866 — The Historic New Orleans Collection, accession no. 1965.71.

Watson's plantation in Alabama, for example, workers had chosen to remain on the plantation after emancipation, but they quit work in June 1865. Watson responded in January 1866 by proposing a harsh labor contract that set up strict work rules and limited mobility. But the freedpeople rejected this contract in a "most defiant manner." In disgust, Watson rented the plantation to his overseer, who leased individual plots to freed families.

That was not the only way in which Watson's workers demonstrated their interpretation of freedom. "The women," Watson complained in 1865, "say that they never mean to do any more outdoor work, that white men support their wives, and they mean that their husbands shall support them." All over the South, black women both embraced public efforts to gain a political voice and sought to move out of field labor and domestic service to concentrate on their own familial duties. Those who were employed in white households also tried to remove themselves from the dangers of sexual abuse that came with such employment. To black women, these were crucial efforts to erase remnants of their slave past, but Watson saw them only as reflections of a desire to be "idle."

Other whites, long accustomed to African American subservience, were enraged by the new assertiveness among blacks and resorted to violence to punish it. When, in the course of a dispute, an Arkansas ex-slave told her former white mistress, "I am as free as you, madam," the white woman struck her. Later that day, learning that a "negro had sauced his wife," the planter horsewhipped the black woman. A North Carolina planter shot an employee, his former slave, after a quarrel over food. He later justified the murder by noting that the freedman's "language and manner became insolent." Such incidents were symptoms of the deep conflict that was generated between black and white Southerners by the lack of agreement on the meaning of emancipation, particularly in relation to political and economic freedoms.

Freedpeople Need Votes and Land   To ensure that emancipation meant lasting change, southern blacks needed the power that was invested in the ballot and the independence that came with property ownership. Though in certain ways, this vision of political and economic independence echoed the republican ideals that many white Americans embraced, freedpeople imagined their advancement in collective as well as individual terms.

"It's Slavery Over Again": Martin Delany Urges Black Self-Determination

In this speech, delivered in the summer of 1865 to the freedpeople of the South Carolina Sea Islands, Martin R. Delany, a longtime black abolitionist, Union Army officer, and now a federal official, condemns the northerners who purchased cotton plantations in the area, and exhorts resident African Americans to resist wage labor. Delany's words were recorded by Alexander Whyte, Jr., a white Union Army officer who thought Delany's views too radical.

I came to talk to you in plain words so as you can understand how to throw open the gates of oppression and let the captive free — In this state there are [hundreds of thousands] of able, intelligent, honorable negroes, not an inferior race, mind you, who are ready to protect their liberty. The matter is in your own hands. . . . I want to tell you one thing: Do you know that if it was not for the black man this war never would have been brought to a close with success to the Union, and the liberty of your race . . . ? I want you to understand that. Do you know it? Do you know it? Do you know it? (Cries of "Yes! Yes! Yes!") They can't get along without you. [Yet,] yankees from the North . . . come down here to drive you as much as ever. It's slavery over again: northern, universal U.S. slavery. But they must keep their clamps off. . . . They don't pay you enough. I see too many of you are dressed in rags and shoeless. These yankees talk smooth to you, oh, yes! Their tongue rolls just like a drum. (Laughter.) But it's slavery over again as much as ever it was.

——————

Herbert G. Gutman Archive, American Social History Project.

Consequently, preachers, along with schoolteachers and ex-soldiers, emerged as community leaders, and churches often housed political meetings.

Religion and politics mixed easily in the first years after the war. In Richmond, Virginia, for example, African American men, women, and children met at the 4,000-seat African Baptist Church to discuss proposals to be presented to the 1867 state constitutional convention. In decisions made by standing votes or voice votes, women had their opinions counted alongside men. In Raleigh, North Carolina, a Freedmen's Convention was held at the AME church in 1865. Participants elected a black preacher from the North as their chairman and petitioned the white legislators to assist in the "education for our children," "protection for our family relations," and "the re-union of families which have long been broken up by war or by the operations of slavery."

African Americans held dozens of such conventions, meetings, and rallies across the South in 1865 and 1866. They raised demands for full civil equality and called for universal manhood suffrage, which, in the words of one delegate, was "an essential and inseparable element of self-government."

Plowing in South Carolina

An 1866 engraving portrayed a freedman as a farmer cultivating his homestead. For most mid-nineteenth-century Americans, the image symbolized honesty, responsibility, and independence. James E. Taylor, *Frank Leslie's Illustrated Newspaper*, October 29, 1866 — American Social History Project.

In some communities, African Americans organized militia companies and "justice committees" as a way of both embracing their responsibilities and claiming their rights as American citizens. The statewide freedmen's conventions and the communitywide attempts to craft a collective agenda were the first steps that ex-slaves took toward the independent political activity that characterized the era of Reconstruction.

Freedpeople were equally committed to obtaining land. They realized that without ownership of property, they would remain in a fundamentally subservient position to their economically powerful former masters. "Every colored man will be a slave, and feel himself a slave," a black soldier argued, "until he can raise his own bale of cotton and put his own mark upon it and say this is mine." Freedpeople argued that they were entitled to land in return for their years of unpaid labor. "Our wives, our children, our husbands, have been sold over and over again to purchase the lands we now locates upon; for that reason we have a divine right to the land," argued freedman Baley Wyat in a speech in Yorktown, Virginia, protesting the eviction of blacks from land they had been assigned by the Union Army during the war. "And then didn't we clear the land, and raise the crops of corn, of cotton, of tobacco, of rice, of sugar, of everything? And then didn't them large cities in the North grow up on the cotton and the sugar and the rice that we made? . . . I say they has grown rich, and my people is poor."

Many southern blacks firmly believed that the federal government would help them to achieve economic self-sufficiency. Just before the end of the war, the Republican-dominated Congress established the Bureau of

"The Presence of Some Authority": Eliphalet Whittlesey Speaks for the Freedmen's Bureau

Many agents of the Freedmen's Bureau viewed themselves as mediators between two deserving groups: former slaves and former masters. In the following report from October 1865, Colonel Eliphalet Whittlesey, an assistant commissioner for the Freedmen's Bureau in North Carolina, discusses the order imposed on black life and labor in the Raleigh area since his arrival the previous June, when he had found "much confusion." Then freedpeople, "exhilarated by the air of liberty," had "committed some excesses," while planters, "suddenly stripped of their wealth," looked "upon the freedmen with a mixture of hate and fear."

. . . [M]any freedmen need the presence of some authority to enforce upon them their new duties. . . . The efforts of the bureau to protect the freedmen have done much to restrain violence and injustice. Such efforts must be continued until civil government is fully restored, just laws enacted, or great suffering and serious disturbance will be the result. Contrary to the fears and predictions of many, the great mass of colored people have remained quietly at work upon the plantations of their former masters during the entire summer. . . . In truth, a much larger amount of vagrancy exists among the whites than among the blacks. . . .

The report is confirmed by the fact that out of a colored population of nearly 350,000 in the State, only about 5,000 are now receiving support from the government. . . . Our officers . . . have visited plantations, explained the difference between slave and free labor, the nature and the solemn obligation of contracts. The chief difficulty met with has been a want of confidence between the two parties.

. . . Rev. F. A. Fiske, a Massachusetts teacher, has been appointed superintendent of education, and has devoted himself with energy to his duties. . . . the whole number of schools . . . is 63, the number of teachers 85, and the number of scholars 5,624. A few of the schools are self-supporting, and taught by colored teachers, but the majority are sustained by northern societies and northern teachers. The officers of the bureau have, as far as practicable, assigned buildings for their use, and assisted in making them suitable; but time is nearly past when such facilities can be given. The societies will be obliged hereafter to pay rent for school-rooms and for teachers homes. The teachers are engaged in a noble and self-denying work. They report a surprising thirst for knowledge among the colored people — children giving earnest attention and learning rapidly, and adults, after the day's work is done, devoting the evening to study.

Report of the Joint Committee on Reconstruction, 39th Cong., 1st sess. (1866).

Freedmen, Refugees, and Abandoned Lands, known as the Freedmen's Bureau. It was created to assist freed slaves by issuing supplies, providing medical aid, establishing schools, dividing confiscated plantation lands, and supervising labor contracts. General Oliver O. Howard headed the bureau, and many of its 900 agents and officials were army officers. Committed to

"THE POPULAR IDEA OF THE FREEDMEN'S BUREAU—PLENTY TO EAT AND NOTHING TO DO."

The Popular Idea of the Freedmen's Bureau — Plenty to Eat and Nothing to Do

An 1866 cartoon lampoons popular misunderstanding about the policies of the Freedmen's Bureau as well as persistent racist beliefs about freedpeople's laziness. *Frank Leslie's Illustrated Newspaper*, October 6, 1866 — American Social History Project.

ideals of self-sufficiency, they did much to aid blacks with education and medical care. African Americans throughout the South turned to the bureau to protest brutality, harsh working conditions, and the hostility and inattention of local courts and police. Although such requests often went unanswered, most bureau agents were at least committed to guiding the South toward northern patterns of free labor relations, which one Tennessee agent called "the noblest principle on earth."

But there were limits on how far the bureau would go in supporting the economic interests of blacks against white planters. In fact, in many areas of the South, the Freedman's Bureau adopted extremely coercive labor policies. In the spring of 1865, for example, the bureau issued stringent orders that restricted blacks' freedom of movement and required them to sign one-year labor contracts with large landowners. If freedmen refused to sign, the bureau withheld relief rations. "Freedom means work," declared General Howard in 1865, and his policies ensured that African Americans would continue to work the lands of their former masters.

Despite the bureau's limitations, many southern blacks continued to believe that the federal government would confiscate the slave owners' land and distribute it among the freedpeople. "This was no slight error, no trifling idea," reported an observer in Mississippi, "but a fixed and earnest conviction as strong as any belief a man can ever have." General William Tecumseh Sherman's Field Order Number 15, which distributed confiscated plantation lands to African Americans during the final months of the war, only reinforced this heartfelt conviction.

It was unclear whether President Lincoln would endorse Sherman's order. Lincoln's assassination before he decided how to proceed left the matter up to Vice President Andrew Johnson. After Johnson, a southerner and a senator from Tennessee before the Civil War, was elevated to the presidency, he rescinded Sherman's field order. In doing so, he gave encouragement to recalcitrant planters and a bitter defeat to freedpeople.

Planters and freedpeople alike understood that black land ownership would destroy whites' basic control over labor and lead to the collapse of the plantation economy. "The negroes will become possessed of a small freehold, will raise their corn, squashes, pigs, and chickens, and will work no more in the cotton, rice, and sugar fields," concluded one Alabama newspaper. If even a few independent black farmers succeeded, concluded one Mississippi planter, "all the others will be dissatisfied with their wages no matter how good they may be and thus our whole labor system is bound to be upset."

For a century and a half, the South's labor system had been based on the regimentation of slavery, and maintaining a similar system of labor regimentation became the planters' most important objective. One northern observer concluded correctly that planters "have no sort of conception of free labor. They do not comprehend any law for controlling laborers, save the law of force." Planters looked to their state governments to secure this "law of force." Consequently, the struggle over the meaning and extent of freedom for African Americans shifted back to the arena of politics.

The Drama of Reconstruction Unfolds

Reconstruction was a process that unfolded in two intertwined arenas: in battles between blacks and whites across the South and in struggles among political leaders in Washington, D.C. Decisions that were made in the nation's capital expanded or constrained the rights that African Americans could claim and the level of protection they could expect in asserting them. Yet the demands of southern blacks also influenced debates in Washington. As poor white Southerners and freedpeople organized in support of the Republican Party immediately after the war, the radical members of that party gained important leverage to reject President Johnson's plans for reconstruction. He hoped to return southern whites to power with few protections for newly freed blacks. For a brief time, however, progressive forces in the South converged with radical Republicans in the North to map out a radical vision of reconstruction that promised significant gains for African Americans in the South and the nation.

President Johnson Versus Congress   Though Johnson was a Southerner, he had long viewed slaveholders as "an odious and dangerous aristocracy." A tailor by trade and entirely self-taught, Johnson resented the power that slaveholders held in his region, identifying personally and politically with the region's white yeoman farmers. When his state seceded from the Union, he remained in his Senate seat, the only senator from a seceding state to do so. This act led Lincoln to choose him as vice president in 1864. But Johnson's hostility to the planters did not make him a supporter of African Americans, who, he thought, as slaves, had participated with their masters in the oppression of yeoman farmers. One senator believed that Johnson

SOUTHERN SECESH (just pardoned)—" *Look here, Andy, if you want* Reconstruction, *you had better set me over the whole thing down in our State.*"
A. JOHNSON—" *Why, what are your qualifications !*"
SOUTHERN SECESH—" *Qualifications, eh ? I ought to know. I pulled the old machine to pieces !*"

Pardoned

A cartoon in an illustrated newsweekly portrayed Andrew Johnson poised beside a basket overflowing with pardons to be distributed to former Confederate officials. "Look here, Andy," says a recently reinstated southerner, "if you want Reconstruction, you had better set me over the whole thing down in our state." *Frank Leslie's Illustrated Newspaper*, August 1865 — American Social History Project.

was "as decided a hater of the negro . . . as the rebels from whom he had separated."

In May 1865, with Congress in recess, Johnson calculated that he could win broad political support in the South by offering total amnesty to all white Southerners who would swear basic loyalty to the Union. On May 10, Jefferson Davis, who had gone into hiding as the Confederacy collapsed, was captured in Irwinsville, Georgia, and imprisoned. He and other members of the southern social and political elite were excluded from Johnson's automatic amnesty. Still, Confederate leaders could petition the president for a pardon on a case-by-case basis, and many did. Even Jefferson Davis served only two years in prison and then lived in relative obscurity until his death in 1889.

Johnson also demanded that for full readmission to the Union, southern states hold constitutional conventions to ratify the Thirteenth Amendment, which abolished slavery; cancel Confederate debts; and nullify the ordinances of secession. Once they had complied, the states were free to organize elections and reestablish governments. In the interim, Johnson appointed governors for the southern states, often conservatives who were hostile to the gains that African Americans had secured since 1863.

The readmission process proceeded rapidly, and nearly all the southern states held elections in the fall of 1865. Meanwhile, planters and Confederate officials flooded Johnson's desk with requests for pardons, most of which were granted. Although pleased to wield power over the South's former aristocrats, Johnson also believed that only planters possessed the experience, prestige, and power to "control" the volatile black population and that planters were therefore the best hope for the South's future.

Although in Johnson's view, Reconstruction was now complete, the outcome of the 1865 elections shocked many northerners. Ex-Confederates were elected to office in large numbers. Representatives who were chosen to fill vacated southern seats in Congress, for example, included the vice president of the Confederacy, four Confederate generals, five Confederate colonels, six Confederate cabinet officers, and fifty-eight Confederate congressmen. More moderate elements—mainly former Whigs, Unionists, and "reluctant" secessionists—dominated the newly elected state governments in the South, but these men (all white) shared with the ex-Confederates a determination to rebuild the South's plantation society.

The Black Codes   Immediately after the elections in 1865, the new state governments began to pass legislation that became known as the Black Codes. These codes attempted to ensure planters an immobile and dependent black labor supply through a series of rigid labor-control laws. Most states embraced the same basic provisions: a freedman found without "lawful employment" could be arrested, jailed, and fined. If he could not pay the fine, he could be hired out to an employer, who would pay the fine and deduct it from the worker's wages. In practice, this meant that any freedman who refused to work at a prevailing wage could be arrested as a vagrant. Other provisions prevented African Americans from entering any employment except domestic work or agricultural labor, allowed black children to be apprenticed to white employers for indefinite periods of time without parental consent, and set severe penalties even for petty theft. The overall effect of the Black Codes was to set the status of newly freed African Americans as landless agricultural laborers with no bargaining power and restricted mobility.

SELLING A FREEDMAN TO PAY HIS FINE, AT MONTICELLO, FLORIDA.—FROM A SKETCH BY JAS. E. TAYLOR.—SEE PAGE 275.

Selling a Freedman to Pay His Fine

"Special artist" James E. Taylor toured the South for *Frank Leslie's Illustrated Newspaper* after the Civil War, when the notorious Black Codes were being enforced. He sketched this scene in front of the county courthouse in Monticello, Florida, during the winter of 1866–1867, showing the auction of a freedman for his inability to pay a fine for an unspecified crime. James E. Taylor, *Frank Leslie's Illustrated Newspaper*, January 19, 1867 — American Social History Project.

"We Are Willing to Take Our Muskets": Freedmen Protest the Black Codes

The following letter—from the black citizens of Yazoo City, Mississippi, to a U.S. army commander—complains about various aspects of the state's Black Codes.

Yazoo City, January 20, 1867

Dear Sir

By Request I Send you the Proceeding of this Place. The Law in regard to the freedman is that they all have to have a written contract. Judge Jones, mayor of this place, is enforcing the Law. He says they have no right to rent a house nor land nor reside in town without a white man to stand for them. He makes all men pay Two Dollars for Licenses and he will not give a License without a written contract. Both women and men have to submit or go to Jail.

His Deputy is taking the people all the time. Men that are traveling are stopped and put in jail or Forced to contract. If this is the Law of the United States we will submit, but if it is not we are willing to take our muskets and serve three years Longer to have more liberty. We the undersigned Look to you for Protection and hope you will give it. You can write to any white man of this place and he can testify to the same.

Yours Respectfully,

[signed by twelve men]

Ira Berlin, Joseph P. Reidy, and Leslie S. Rowland, eds., *Freedom: A Documentary History of Emancipation, 1861–1867, Series II: The Black Military Experience* (1982), 821.

The Black Codes were never effectively enforced, largely because of a labor shortage throughout the South and because of opposition from African American workers and Freedmen's Bureau agents. Their passage did have one important result, however. Many members of Congress and their constituents became enraged that such laws could be passed in the first place.

In 1865, the Republicans held a three-to-one majority over Democrats in Congress. Representative Thaddeus Stevens of Pennsylvania and Senator Charles Sumner of Massachusetts led a group of Republican congressmen called Radicals, whose political roots lay in the prewar antislavery movement. They sought a vast increase in federal power to obtain new rights for the freedpeople and to revolutionize social conditions in the South.

The Radical Republicans attracted only a minority of party members. The far greater number of "moderate" Republicans initially hoped for a rapid reunification of the nation and a return to good business relations between North and South. But like the Radicals, they were profoundly disturbed by the return of many ex-Confederate leaders to positions of

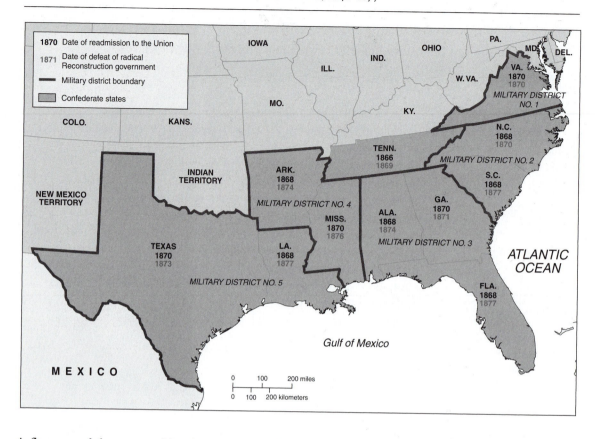

MAP 12.1 The Duration of Radical Reconstruction

The plan for Radical Reconstruction, including the establishment of military districts, was introduced in every state of the former Confederacy. But the duration of the Radical governments varied significantly. Radicals lasted only a few months in Virginia but held on for several years in Louisiana, Florida, and South Carolina. Because African Americans had much more access to voting rights and political office under Radical governments, they had significantly greater opportunities to engage in formal politics in the states where those governments maintained control for the longest period.

influence and the return of freedpeople to near-slave status by the terms of the Black Codes. Consequently, when Congress finally reconvened in December 1865, Radicals and moderates joined in refusing to seat the newly elected southern representatives, an act that initiated a confrontation with President Johnson and transformed the meaning of Reconstruction (Map 12.1).

Radical Reconstruction At the end of 1865, the Radicals established a joint committee of Congress to investigate the situation in the South. In the next few months, army officers, white southern Unionists, Freedmen's Bureau officials, newspaper reporters, and a handful of freedpeople testified to growing anti-Union sentiment, violence, and systematic oppression of the freedpeople. Joseph Stiles, a white Virginian who was loyal to the Union, complained, "It seems to me that the rapid promotion of rebels, the old politicians, to places of trust and honor, has had a great tendency to render treason popular instead of odious." Richard Hill, one of the few black witnesses, informed the joint committee that if the recently elected southern representatives were allowed to sit in Congress, "the condition of the freedmen would be very little better than that of slaves."

Mad Andy

An October 1866 *Harper's Weekly* cartoon views Andrew Johnson's Reconstruction policies as a betrayal of northern sacrifices during the Civil War.
Thomas Nast, *Harper's Weekly*, October 27, 1866 — American Social History Project.

Such evidence convinced many congressmen that the rights of the freedpeople had to be guaranteed. The Republicans in Congress passed a bill that extended the life of the Freedmen's Bureau and expanded its powers. In addition, they passed a Civil Rights Bill that defined "all persons born in the United States (except Indians) as national citizens," granted freedpeople "full and equal benefit of all laws," and gave federal courts the power to defend their rights against interference from state governments. In this sweeping act, Congress nullified the Supreme Court's 1857 *Dred Scott* decision (which had denied citizenship to African Americans), undermined the Black Codes, and expanded the powers of the federal courts. Both bills marked a dramatic break from the deeply rooted American tradition of states' rights.

An outraged President Johnson vetoed both bills as unconstitutional infringements of states' rights, arguing that the "distinction of race and color" had been "made to operate in favor of the colored and against the white race." For many Republicans, these vetoes were the last straw. "Those who formerly defended [the president] are now readiest in his condemnation," said one moderate Republican. On April 6, 1866, Congress overrode Johnson's veto of the Civil Rights Bill, the first time in U.S. history that a major piece of legislation was passed over the president's objection. Three months later, Congress also overrode Johnson's veto of the bill to extend the Freedmen's Bureau. And congressional Republicans were prepared to go

"The Whole Fabric of Southern Society Must Be Changed": Thaddeus Stevens on Land Reform

In this 1865 speech delivered to a Republican gathering in Lancaster, Pennsylvania, Radical Republican leader Thaddeus Stevens lays out a detailed case for redistributing southern land to freedpeople and others who had remained loyal to the Union.

We especially insist that the property of the chief rebels should be seized and appropriated to the payment of the national debt. . . . By forfeiting the estates of the leading rebels the government would have 394,000,000 of acres besides their town property, and yet nine-tenths of the people would remain untouched. Divide the land into convenient farms. Give, if you please, forty acres to each adult male freedman. Suppose there are 1,000,000 of them. That would require 40,000,000 acres, which deducted from 394,000 leaves 354,000,000 acres for sale. Divide it into suitable farms, and sell it to the highest bidders. I think it . . . would average at least $10 per acre. That would produce $3,540,000.

The whole fabric of southern society must be changed and never can it be done if this opportunity is lost. . . . How can republican institutions, free schools, free churches, free social intercourse exist in a mingled community of nabobs and serfs? If the South is ever made a safe republic let her lands be cultivated by the toil of . . . free labor. . . .

Nothing is so likely to make a man a good citizen as to make him a freeholder. Nothing will so multiply the production of the South as to divide it into small farms. . . . No people will ever be republican in spirit and practice where a few own immense manors and the masses are landless. Small and independent landholders are the support and guardians of republican liberty.

Speech of the Honorable Thaddeus Stevens Delivered in the City of Lancaster, September 7, 1865 (Lancaster, PA, 1865).

even further, preparing a constitutional amendment to guarantee civil rights to southern blacks.

The Radicals in Congress sought an even more sweeping approach. Stevens and Sumner envisioned not just civil rights for African Americans but a total transformation of southern society. Sumner wanted to make sure that blacks in the South, who were now citizens, would not be denied the right to vote because of a lack of property, for he believed that this was the only way to give the Republican Party political power in that region. Stevens argued that if the vote was to have any meaning, it needed to be backed up with economic power. Echoing the demands of freedpeople, he called for confiscating the land of planters and distributing it among the ex-slaves. "The whole fabric of southern society must be changed," he proclaimed, "and never can it be done if this opportunity is lost."

The best that the Radicals could achieve, however, was the Fourteenth Amendment, which passed both houses of Congress in June 1866. It granted full citizenship to African Americans and prohibited states from denying them "equal protection of the laws." This alone was a sweeping transformation of the constitutional balance of power. Until now, states had been seen as the guardians of the rights of their citizens against the power of the federal government. Now the roles were reversed.

Still, states were not required to grant black men suffrage. If they chose not to do so, however, their representation in Congress would be reduced in direct proportion. Most Republicans were not yet prepared to take the step of guaranteeing voting rights to black men, and the Radicals were forced to go along.

One group of political activists took a different position. As the members of Congress worked to pass the Fourteenth Amendment, women's rights activists called on them to place women and men—black and white—on an equal footing. Congress refused to pressure states to grant voting rights to women and instead, for the first time, inserted the word *male* into the Constitution. Although the movement for women's rights had long been intertwined with the abolitionist movement, women's rights' leaders Elizabeth Cady Stanton and Susan B. Anthony broke with the abolitionists and began searching for other allies in their drive for the vote. This would soon lead to a series of internal conflicts among suffragists and would complicate their relationships with advocates of both racial equality and labor advancement.

The concerns of woman suffrage advocates were overshadowed, however, by the president's appeal to southern legislatures to reject the Fourteenth Amendment. Encouraged by the president's position, all but one southern state (ironically, Johnson's home state of Tennessee) refused to ratify it. The congressional elections in the fall of 1866 thus became a referendum on the Fourteenth Amendment and Johnson's approach to Reconstruction. The Union had won the war, but it now appeared to be losing the peace.

In the months leading up to the 1866 congressional campaign, antiblack violence increased throughout the South. In Memphis, where a race riot erupted in May, the Union Army commander refused to intervene because, he claimed, "he had a large amount of public property to guard; that a considerable part of the troops he had were unreliable; that they hated Negroes too." Although he initially had many African American troops under his command, he demobilized most black soldiers who were stationed near the city in the months preceding the riot. A local white newspaper had then applauded the Union officer: "He knows the wants of the country, and sees the Negro can do the country more good in the cotton fields than in the [Army] camp." In July 1866, black laborers paraded in New Orleans to press

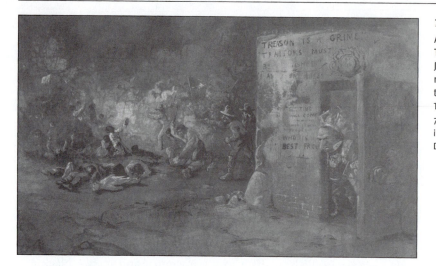

The Massacre at New Orleans
A panoramic painting by
Thomas Nast shows Andrew
Johnson as indifferent to the
murder of freedpeople during
the July 1866 New Orleans riot.
Thomas Nast, 1867, oil on canvas,
7 feet 10 3/4 inches × 11 feet 6 1/2
inches — Prints and Photographs
Division, Library of Congress.

their demands for equal suffrage to a convention writing a new state constitution. Hostile white mobs dispersed the marchers, and African American
convention delegates as well as spectators and marchers were beaten and
shot in the ensuing melee. A congressional investigation later that year concluded that what began as a "riot" ended as a "massacre," in part because of
the inaction of law enforcement agencies, army officers, and other government authorities. The Memphis riot took the lives of 46 African Americans; the one in New Orleans left 166 wounded and 34 blacks dead along
with three of their white supporters.

The riots revealed what one northern newspaper called "the demoniac
spirit of the southern whites toward the freedmen." This naked brutality
led to a stunning victory for the Republicans in the November elections.
They held their three-to-one majority in Congress and retained power in
every northern state as well as in West Virginia, Missouri, and Tennessee.
And among Republicans, the Radicals were the biggest winners.

The Republican mandate in 1866 encouraged the Radicals to present an
even more sweeping agenda. They failed to achieve their most radical
aim — the redistribution of land — but they did finally convince moderates
to join them in embracing black voting rights. The Reconstruction Act of
March 1867 — the centerpiece of what became known as "Radical" Reconstruction — passed over President Johnson's veto. The act divided the former Confederate states into five military districts. In each state, there would
be constitutional conventions in which blacks would participate, backed
up by protection from federal troops. These conventions were mandated to
draft new constitutions, which had to include provisions for African American suffrage. Newly elected state legislatures were also required to ratify the
Fourteenth Amendment as a condition for their readmission to the Union.

The guarantee of black voting rights seemed to many Americans to represent the final stage of a sweeping political revolution. In February 1867, a journalist writing in *The Nation* magazine summed up how the Civil War had revolutionized northern politics:

> Six years ago, the North would have rejoiced to accept any mild restrictions upon the spread of slavery as a final settlement. Four years ago, it would have accepted peace upon the basis of gradual emancipation. Two years ago, it would have been content with emancipation and equal civil rights for the colored people without extension of the suffrage. One year ago, a slight extension of the suffrage would have satisfied it.

Now Congress had overridden a presidential veto to enshrine African American suffrage in federal law.

African Americans Become a Force in Southern Politics   The onset of Radical Reconstruction inaugurated a massive and unprecedented movement of freedpeople into the political arena. They staged strikes, rallies, and protests in cities all over the South during 1867 — including Charleston, Savannah, Richmond, Mobile, and New Orleans — and small towns such as Meridian, Mississippi, and Tuskegee, Alabama. The first organized expression of freedpeople's political activity was the dramatic growth of the Union (or Loyal) League. The league had started as a national organization that encouraged the Union cause during the war. With passage of the Reconstruction Act, the Union League dispatched white and black organizers all over the South to found local chapters. They functioned as political clubs, providing a civics education for new members and encouraging support for the Republican Party and its candidates.

These local chapters soon broadened the league's mission to include more aggressive economic and political activities. They helped to build schools and churches, organized militia companies to defend communities from white violence, and called strikes and boycotts for better wages and fairer labor contracts. A number of local chapters were even organized on an interracial basis. One such racially mixed league in North Carolina debated questions such as disfranchisement, debtor relief, and public education, which members expected to be raised in the forthcoming state constitutional convention.

In the fall of 1867, Southerners, black and white, began electing delegates to these constitutional conventions. The participation of freedpeople was truly astonishing: women joined in local meetings to select candidates, between 70 and 90 percent of eligible black males voted in every state in the South, and a total of 265 African Americans were elected as delegates. These conventions were of tremendous symbolic and practical importance. For the first time in U.S. history, blacks and whites met together to prepare constitutions under which they would be governed. The constitutions they produced were among the most progressive in the nation. They established public schools for both races, created social welfare agencies, reformed the criminal law, and drew up codes that more equitably distributed the burden of taxation. Most important of all, the constitutions guaranteed black civil and political rights, completing what one Texas newspaper called "the equal-rights revolution."

The intensity of black political participation that was demonstrated in these elections represented a dramatic turning point in southern politics. After 1867, the southern Republican Party won elections and dominated all of the new state governments. African Americans were prominent in many of these governments. Although they represented an actual majority only in South Carolina's legislature, blacks held a total of six hundred legislative seats in southern states. Between 1868 and 1876, southern states elected fourteen black representatives to the U.S. Congress, two black U.S. senators, and six black lieutenant governors. In addition, thousands of African Americans served local southern communities as supervisors, voter registrars, aldermen, mayors, magistrates, sheriffs and deputies, postal clerks, members of local school boards, and justices of the peace.

Unlike its northern counterpart, the southern Republican Party was, in the words of one black Republican leader, "emphatically the poor man's party." Ultimately, the party came to include poor white as well as poor black southerners, but in 1867, nearly 80 percent of southern Republican voters were black. Because of the Republican Party's central role in emancipation and enfranchisement, freedpeople demonstrated a near fanatical loyalty to it, placing the party with the church and the school as a central community institution. George Houston, an Alabama Union League organizer and Sumter County voter registrar, proudly asserted: "I am a Republican, and I will die one." The intensity of Houston's commitment echoed across the South.

White Supremacy Forever!
An anti–Union League handbill, 1867. Prints and Photographs Division, Library of Congress.

"Remove This Vast Weight of Ignorance": Debating Compulsory Schooling in South Carolina

This debate among African American delegates to South Carolina's 1868 constitutional convention reflects the articulate, thoughtful, and pragmatic manner in which African Americans participated in politics during the Reconstruction period, despite racist claims about their inability to hold public office. The brief openness of southern politics during Reconstruction did succeed in bringing compulsory public education to all southerners, black and white.

R. C. DeLarge: The schools may be open to all, but to declare that parents shall send their children to them whether they are willing or not is, in my judgment, going a step beyond the bounds of prudence. Is there any logic or reason in inserting in the constitution a provision which cannot be enforced?

A. J. Ransier: I am sorry to differ with my colleague from Charleston on this question. I contend that in proportion to the education of the people so is their progress in civilization. Believing this, I believe that the committee has properly provided for the compulsory education of all children in this state between the ages named in the section.

J. A. Chesnut: Has not this convention the right to establish a free school system for the poorer classes? Then if there be a hostile disposition among the whites, an unwillingness to send their children to school, the fault is their own, not ours. Look at the idle youth around us. Is the sight not enough to invigorate every man with a desire to do something to remove this vast weight of ignorance that presses the masses down?

F. L. Cardozo: . . . some gentlemen . . . affirm that [the section of the constitution] compels the attendance of both white and colored children in the same schools. There is nothing of the kind in the section. It simply says that all the children shall be educated; but how, it is left with the parents to decide. It is left to the parent to say whether the child should be sent to a public or private school. There can be separate schools for white and colored. It is left so that if any colored child wishes to go to a white school, it shall have the privilege of doing so. I have no doubt, in most localities colored people will prefer separate schools, particularly until some of the present prejudice against their race is removed.

W. E. B. DuBois, *Black Reconstruction in America, 1860–1880* (1935), 397.

Moreover, although only African American men were granted the franchise, their wives and daughters considered voting to be a family affair. Some freedwomen continued to wield ballots in community meetings, and throughout the South, they influenced electoral politics by lobbying male voters, demanding that men use their new-found electoral rights, and accompanying voters to the polls on election day. Within African American communities, then, the ballot was seen as a collective rather than an individual possession, and the Republican Party was seen as an organization to which women as well as men declared their loyalty.

Most blacks who were elected to state and federal offices were educated, and many were freeborn. At the local level, however, black political leaders often emerged from the ranks of the freedmen. James Alston was a slave-born shoemaker and musician in Macon County, Alabama; he headed the Union League chapter in Tuskegee, became the county registrar of voters, and later represented Macon County in the state legislature. Such small-town artisans possessed the skill and independence to represent the growing African American population in southern towns and villages as well as their rural constituents. Moreover, their work experience, which involved a good deal of contact with whites, helped them to link the black community with potential white allies.

The First Vote

An 1867 *Harper's Weekly* illustration features three figures symbolizing black political leadership: a skilled craftsman, a sophisticated city dweller, and a Union Army veteran. Alfred R. Waud, *Harper's Weekly*, November 16, 1867 — American Social History Project.

Republican Party Activism in the South

White allies were essential. Only in South Carolina and Mississippi were blacks in the majority. To survive in the South, the Republican Party would need to develop a coalition that included some white support. Most visible among the white Republicans were those labeled "carpetbaggers." Carpet-covered valises were used as luggage in the mid-nineteenth century, and white Southerners used the term *carpetbaggers* to refer to white Northerners who traveled south to gain money and power. Yet some so-called carpetbaggers were black and anything but greedy. This was true of Martin Delany, who had risen to the rank of major in the Union Army and then served in the Freedmen's Bureau before settling down in Charleston. Many white carpetbaggers were similarly sincere in their commitment to black rights and Republican government.

Even more important to Republican successes in the South were the "scalawags" — native white Southerners who supported the Republican Party and were therefore viewed as traitors by many former Confederates.

Hiram Revels

In 1870, the Boston firm of Louis Prang and Company published a chromolithograph (an inexpensive type of color print) portrait of the first African American U.S. senator. One prominent admirer of the portrait was Frederick Douglass: "Whatever may be the prejudices of those who may look upon it," he wrote to Prang, "they will be compelled to admit that the Mississippi senator is a man, and one who will easily pass for a man among men. We colored men so often see ourselves described and painted as monkeys, that we think it a great piece of good fortune to find an exception to this general rule." L. Prang and Company (after a painting by Theodore Kaufmann), 1870, chromolithograph, 14 × 11 3/4 inches — Prints and Photographs Division, Library of Congress.

Some were wealthy planters who nevertheless believed that the South's future must be built on industrialization, urbanization, and the construction of a wage-labor system. They sought governmental support for railroads, industry, and the establishment of a stable banking and currency system. But far more of the southern white Republicans were poor yeoman farmers from the mountain regions who had long resented the large planters' monopoly on land, labor, and political power. The southern mountain region had been a stronghold of Unionist sentiment during the war, providing a vital link to postwar Republicanism.

Economic changes added a new ingredient to yeoman support for the Republicans. Before the war, many small southern farmers had lived largely outside the market economy, producing most of their own food and necessities of life. But after the war, many of them were drawn into cotton planting, just in time to be hit hard by catastrophic crop failures in 1866 and 1867. The passage of new state constitutions containing provisions for homesteading and debtor relief led these struggling white farmers to become Union League and Republican supporters.

Most of the Republican Party's southern adherents, then, were poor people, black and white, who had a strong hostility to the planter aristocracy. In Georgia, the Republicans called on "poor men" to vote for the party of "relief, homesteads, and schools"; their nominee for governor proclaimed himself the "workingman's candidate." The "bottom rail" among both races voted overwhelmingly in 1867 and 1868 to reconstruct state governments and design laws to benefit all citizens.

During their period in power — from two years in Tennessee to eight years in South Carolina — these Republican governments constructed the beginnings of a welfare state for their citizens. They created a public school system where none had existed before. These schools remained segregated by race and were better in the cities than in the countryside, but there was real progress nonetheless. By 1876, about half of all southern children — white and black — were enrolled in school. And not only children went to school: a northern correspondent reported in 1873 that in Vicksburg, Mississippi, "female negro servants make it a condition before accepting a situation, that they should have permission to attend the night-schools."

Although school integration made little progress, several Radical governments did pass laws banning racial discrimination in other public accommodations, notably streetcars, restaurants, and hotels. Arkansas, Mississippi, Louisiana, and Florida made it illegal for railroads, hotels, and theaters to deny "full and equal rights" to any citizen. After 1869, South Carolina, with a black majority in the Republican-controlled legislature, required equal treatment in all public accommodations and in any business that was chartered or licensed by municipal, state, or federal authority. Much of this legislation proved unenforceable, but it showed that Republicans were committed to ending legal segregation.

Laws that helped both black and white landless agricultural laborers were another achievement of Radical rule. Radical Republicans repealed the notorious Black Codes and passed lien laws that gave farmworkers (both black and white) a first claim on crops if their employers went bankrupt. South Carolina went further, creating a state Land Commission with the power to buy land and resell it to landless laborers on long-term credit. By 1876, despite this commission's initial mismanagement, 14,000 African American families (about one-seventh of the state's black population) had acquired homesteads, as had a handful of white families. Other states chose to increase the property tax rate that was paid by large landowners, shifting some of the burden of new programs from poorer to wealthier residents.

Having local officials who sympathized with the plight of landless farmers proved especially beneficial to the rural poor. Locally elected magistrates and justices of the peace, many of them black, negotiated contract disputes between planters and laborers and usually decided in favor of the laborers. The poor thus gained a significant bargaining edge in their economic relations with employers. This became particularly clear in the late 1860s, when the economy improved and black agricultural workers could command higher wages. With the repeal of the Black Codes by progressive state legislatures, "the power to control [black labor] is gone," lamented one white southern newspaper.

Their new bargaining power enabled freedpeople to negotiate compromises with planters on how the land would be worked and who would reap its bounty. Rather than working in gangs for wages, individual black families now worked small plots independently, renting land from the planter for cash or, more commonly, for a fixed share of the year's crop. By 1870, "sharecropping" had

Equal (If Begrudging) Treatment

Trafficking in racist caricature, this 1874 cartoon also captured the unprecedented nature of antidiscriminatory legislation. "But I don't want to sleep with a Negro," exclaims a guest when confronted by the proprietor of a crowded hotel. "Well, it's the only double bed in the house," is the response, "and if I don't give him half of it I shall have to pay him five hundred dollars damages. You may either sleep with him or go into the street." *Frank Leslie's Illustrated Newspaper*, June 13, 1874 — American Social History Project.

become the dominant form of black agricultural labor, especially in the vast cotton lands. The system was a far cry from the freedpeople's objective of owning their own land, and later in the century, it became connected to a credit system that drastically reduced the workers' economic freedom. But in the short run, sharecropping did free black workers from the highly regimented gang-labor system, allowing them a good deal of control and autonomy over their work, their time, and their family arrangements.

These very real economic and legal gains would be short-lived, however. Members and potential supporters of the southern Republican Party were constantly dissatisfied. Because the party was a fragile coalition of wealthy ex-Whigs, northern politicians, rural ex-slaves, free urban blacks, and poor white yeomen, it could not take any position without alienating at least part of its constituency. Its leaders, moreover, generally favored economic expansion. The promotion of transportation and industry, combined with large increases in state spending on schools and social programs, led to tremendous increases in taxes. This tax burden fell increasingly not only on the wealthy planters, but also on poor whites who owned little property. Revelations of political corruption among southern Republicans seeking to gain from the state's involvement in capitalist enterprise also contributed to the growing disaffection of white voters. And perhaps most important at this critical moment, the corruption provided Northerners with a rationale for losing interest in southern affairs. In 1869, Tennessee and Virginia became the first states to return to Democratic control, in a process that conservative whites called "redemption."

The End of Reconstruction

Two distinct forces converged to end Reconstruction. First, passage of the Reconstruction Act in 1867 had severely undercut the political power of the planter class, so they were now willing to turn to violence, economic intimidation, and fraud to regain political control of the South. Second, both northern public opinion and the northern Republican Party began to move sharply away from the original goals of Radical Reconstruction. Ordinary Northerners' commitment to the political and civil rights of African Americans had dwindled, as was indicated by Republican defeats in a number of northern states in 1867. Many Northerners were worn out by the long military and political battles and considered their obligation over when the most overt signs of southern resistance were removed. When a financial panic swept the nation in 1873, economic woes reinforced this sense of political exhaustion and caused many northern whites to refocus their attention on concerns closer to home.

Southern Democrats and the Klan "Redeem" the South
Economic issues loomed large even during Radical Reconstruction. Indeed, the first

official sign of retreat from Reconstruction occurred on the economic front when Congress refused to confiscate planters' lands and distribute them among the freedpeople. Throughout 1867, Radicals Charles Sumner and Thaddeus Stevens had proposed a number of confiscation schemes. Echoing Thomas Jefferson, Stevens proclaimed, "Small independent landholders are the support and guardians of republican liberty." But northern businessmen and moderate Republicans effectively blocked land redistribution efforts for two reasons. First, many of them firmly believed that government had no business redistributing property. Second, and perhaps more important, they feared the economic consequences of ending plantation production of raw cotton, which remained the nation's single largest export and an important source of foreign revenue.

Other indications of waning enthusiasm for Reconstruction were apparent in the nation's capital. In 1868, Radical Republicans persuaded the House of Representatives to impeach the president for his efforts to subvert the Reconstruction program. In the subsequent trial before the U.S. Senate, however, moderate Republicans cast the deciding votes, narrowly acquitting Johnson. His successor, Ulysses S. Grant, elected in 1868, was a popular Union Army general. Grant's ascendancy to the presidency coincided with the emergence of a new group of moderate leaders in the Republican Party following the death of Thaddeus Stevens in 1868. These men, known as the Stalwarts, had none of the idealism of the Radical Republicans. Their sole objective was to maintain the power of the Republican Party. By 1870, the Stalwarts had stripped Stevens's Radical Republican ally, Charles Sumner, of power.

By 1872, the end of Grant's first term of office, it was starkly obvious that national Republican leaders were willing to abandon southern blacks to cultivate northern business support—support that depended on a revitalized southern economy. Northern politicians were prepared to retreat from social and political experimentation and leave the South's economic revitalization in the hands of the former slave owners. Now black Republican voters were the only remaining obstacle to the return of conservative white rule.

Initially, large planters tried to use their economic power to limit freedpeople's political activities. In Alabama, for example, one landlord required two black laborers to sign the following contract before he would hire them: "That said Laborers shall not attach themselves, belong to, or in any way perform any of the obligations required of what is known as the 'Loyal League Society,' or attend elections or political meetings without the consent of the employer." Without land, African Americans depended on planters for employment, but even so, this economic pressure was not very successful. Another planter complained bitterly that the Civil War and the Radical program had totally destroyed "the natural influence of capital on

A Prospective Scene in the "City of Oaks," 4th of March, 1869.

" Hang, cure, hang! * * * * * * *Their* complexion is perfect gallows. Stand fast; good fate, to *their* hanging! * * * * * * If they be not born to be hanged, our case is miserable."

A Prospective Scene in the "City of Oaks," 4th of March, 1869

A September 1868 edition of the Tuscaloosa, Alabama, *Independent Monitor* proposes the treatment its Republican opponents should receive if they lose the upcoming presidential election. The editor of the Democratic newspaper was the Grand Cyclops of the Ku Klux Klan in Tuscaloosa. Tuscaloosa *Independent Monitor*, September 1, 1868 — Alabama Department of Archives and History, Montgomery, Alabama.

labor, of employer on employee." The result was that "negroes who will trust their white employers in all their personal affairs . . . are entirely beyond advice on all political issues."

When economic pressure proved inadequate, planters turned to more violent methods of intimidation. Their most important and effective weapon was the Ku Klux Klan. The Klan was, in essence, the paramilitary arm of the southern Democratic Party. Founded by Confederate veterans in Tennessee in 1866, the Klan grew rapidly after the advent of Radical Reconstruction. Although many of its rank-and-file members were poor men, its leaders were mainly prominent planters and their sons. As a white minister who traveled through Alabama reported in 1867:

They had lost their property, and worst of all, their slaves were made their equals and perhaps their superiors, to rule over them. They said there was an organization, already very extensive, that would rid them of this terrible calamity . . . the organization of the Ku Klux Klan . . . seemed to answer precisely the design expressed by these men.

By 1868, the Klan had a wide following across the South. The Klan terrorized individuals and freedpeople's organizations. Night riders targeted black Civil War veterans and freedmen who had left their employers or complained about low wages. Freedpeople who had succeeded in breaking out of the plantation system and were renting or buying land on their own were in particular danger because they defied white supremacist assumptions of racial superiority and were often physically isolated. According to one Georgia freedman, "whenever a colored man acquires property and becomes in a measure independent, they take it from him."

Hooded Klansmen broke up meetings, shot and lynched Union League leaders, and drove black voters away from the polls all across the South. The targets of Klan violence were rarely chosen at random. James Alston, an early Union League organizer and by 1870 a Republican member of the Alabama legislature, reported that he was shot by the Klan because of his political activities. Alston had been one of five African American Radicals from his area who had gone to Washington for President Grant's inauguration in 1869. When asked about the fate of the other four, he replied, "I am the only man that is living. Everyone [else] is killed that went there to the

"Kill Him, God Damn Him": Betsey Westbrook Testifies About Klan Violence

In the courthouse of Demopolis, Alabama, before a congressional committee investigating the Ku Klux Klan, Betsey Westbrook recounts the murder of her husband, Robin Westbrook. The testimony offered by freedpeople at the 1871 hearings on the KKK detailed a horrifying litany of brutal violence and intimidation.

They came up behind the house. One of them had his face smutted and another had a knit cap on his face. They first shot about seven [shotgun] barrels through the window. One of them said, "Get a rail and bust the door down." They broke down the outside door. . . . one of them said, "Raise a light." . . . Then they saw where we stood and one of them says, "You are that damned son of a bitch Westbrook." The man had a gun and struck him on the head. Then my husband took the dog-iron and struck three or four of them. They got him jammed up in the corner and one man went around behind him and put two loads of a double-barreled gun in his shoulders. Another man says, "Kill him, God damn him," and took a pistol and shot him down. He didn't live more than half an hour.

My boy was in there while they were killing my husband and he says, "Mammy, what must I do?" I says, "Jump outdoors and run." He went to the door and a white man took him by the arm and says, "God damn you, I will fix you too," but he snatched himself loose and got away.

Q—Did you know any of these men?

A—Yes, sir. I certainly knowed three.

Q—What were they mad at your husband about?

A—He just would hold up his head and say he was a strong Radical [Republican]. He would hang on to that.

House of Representatives Report 22, 42nd Cong., 2nd Sess. (1871).

inauguration of Grant." Such targeted violence profoundly affected postwar politics. Even though African Americans fought back valiantly, the Klan succeeded in destroying Republican organizations and demoralizing entire communities of freedpeople.

Despite the Republicans' general movement away from further intervention in the South, moderate Republicans were not yet ready to stand by and allow their party in the South to be terrorized and destroyed by violence. Congress finally acted in 1869 when members approved the Fifteenth Amendment to the Constitution (ratified in 1870). This time, however, federal officials, already in retreat from Radical Reconstruction, enacted only a lukewarm compromise. The amendment declared that the right of U.S. citizens to vote could not "be denied or abridged" by any state "on account of race, color, or previous condition of servitude." This careful wording left open the possibility of using numerous non-race-related means, such as

"Dedicated to the Men of the South Who Suffered Exile, Imprisonment and Death for the Daring Service They Rendered Our Country as Citizens of the Invisible Empire"

By the turn of the century, popular novels such as Thomas Dixon, Jr.'s *The Traitor* transformed the bloody record of the Ku Klux Klan (now softened by the euphemism "Invisible Empire") into tales of gallantry, sacrifice, and latter-day knighthood. (L. D. Williams) Thomas Dixon, Jr., *The Traitor: A Story of the Fall of the Invisible Empire* (1907) — American Social History Project.

poll taxes and literacy tests, to restrict black voting. Moreover, the amendment said nothing about the right to hold elective office.

In March 1871, a series of grisly events in Meridian, Mississippi, shocked the nation and galvanized Congress to act more forcefully. The Meridian authorities had arrested three African American leaders who were organizing freedpeople to resist Klan night riders. Charged with delivering "incendiary speeches," the men were put on trial. In the midst of the first day's proceedings, shots rang out in the courtroom—probably fired by a white spectator—killing two of the defendants and the Republican judge. In the rioting that followed, 30 African Americans were brutally murdered.

A joint congressional committee that was appointed to hear testimony in Washington and across the South (including in Meridian) listened while witnesses estimated that the Klan had killed or beaten thousands of freedpeople and their white allies in the previous four years. They heard the wives and daughters of black Republican leaders testify to being whipped and raped, often on more than one occasion and by more than one assailant.

Aghast at tales of such violence and fearing the demise of the Republican Party in the South, Congress passed a series of enforcement acts that imposed harsh penalties on those who used organized terrorism for political purposes. In April 1871, the Ku Klux Klan Act became law. For the first time, certain individual crimes against citizens' rights were punishable under federal law. Later in the year, President Grant declared martial law in parts of South Carolina and, though he had earlier removed federal troops from many parts of the South, dispatched U.S. Army units to the area. Hundreds of Klansmen were indicted and tried by the U.S. attorney general in South Carolina, North Carolina, and Mississippi. The federal government had broken the Klan's back, at least temporarily. The election of 1872, which saw Grant reelected, was the most peaceful in the Reconstruction period.

But other groups rapidly arose to replace the KKK. The Democrats gambled that neither Congress nor the president would act decisively to prevent further political violence and fraud. The gamble paid off. After the 1872 election, Republicans in the North continued their steady retreat from the defense of African American rights.

The national economy was expanding rapidly, and the Republican Party now became closely attuned to the interests of business. Concerned with investment possibilities in the South, businessmen and their political allies became increasingly weary of Reconstruction. A reunion between affluent whites in the North and South was finally within reach. For African Americans and poor whites, however, this newfound national unity among economic and political leaders meant that even the minimal protections afforded by federal troops and federal laws in the late 1860s and early 1870s were gradually withdrawn. Though small contingents of U.S. troops would remain in the South until 1877, Northerners and the federal government were clearly in retreat from their earlier support for Radical Reconstruction.

The large planters now engaged in their final battle to "redeem" the South, struggling largely against freedpeople who had declining resources and few allies. Planters initially justified their actions with overt appeals to racism. As one planter put it, "God intended the niggers to be slaves." But the racism of their rhetoric cloaked another motivation: planters wanted a government-enforced system that would help them to reassert control over agricultural workers. As one leading southern Democrat declared, "We must get control of our own labor." In many areas of the South, the effort to regain control of blacks' lives and labors met substantial resistance from African Americans, sometimes in coalition with poor whites, throughout the late nineteenth century. Still, planters and their new industrial allies gradually achieved their main economic and political goals. As they did so, the South became a much more dangerous place for African Americans.

Klansman

A captured member of the Ku Klux Klan posed for a Holly Springs, Mississippi, photographer after turning state's evidence in the prosecution of Klan members under the 1871 law. © National Law Enforcement Museum, Washington, D.C. (2007.24.2).

The Final Assault on Reconstruction   Beginning in 1873, Americans who still advocated the reconstruction of race and class relations confronted the longest period of uninterrupted economic contraction in U.S. history — fully sixty-five months, well over five years. The entire nation suffered as businesses failed, banks collapsed, and massive unemployment became

Colored Rule in the Reconstructed (?) State

Although Thomas Nast was an ardent supporter of equal rights, he often resorted to racial and ethnic stereotypes in his *Harper's Weekly* cartoons. Questioning the actions of some southern black Republican legislators, Nast drew the figure of "Columbia," symbol of the nation, chiding: "You are aping the lowest whites. If you disgrace your race in this way you had better take back seats." Thomas Nast, *Harper's Weekly*, March 14, 1874 — American Social History Project.

widespread (see Chapter 13). During the Panic of 1873, poor whites, new immigrants, and freedpeople alike saw their dreams of land ownership wither in the shadow cast by rapidly growing cities, wage labor, and long workdays. At the same time, many of the freedoms that southern blacks had gained in the late 1860s and early 1870s slipped away.

Southern landowners and employers, under the protection of the newly empowered Democratic Party, curtailed the potential for mass mobilization of poor whites and blacks in rural areas or their unionization in urban ones. New criminal codes in Georgia and elsewhere declared insurrection and incitement to insurrection to be capital offenses. Most southern legislatures increased penalties for theft, broadened the definition of arson, made it illegal to ride a horse or mule without the owner's permission, and restricted traditional access to land for the purpose of gathering wood, hunting, and fishing.

These codes were part of a larger pattern of discrimination that Democrats also directed against black Republicans and their white allies. In 1875, the Democrats' "Mississippi Plan" became a model for "redemption" in what was left of the reconstructed South: South Carolina, Louisiana, and Florida. The first step in this plan was to use economic pressure, social ostracism, and threats of physical violence to force the remaining white Republicans back into the Democratic Party. Democrats simply made it "too damned hot for [us] to stay out," explained one white Republican who gave in to the pressure. The second step was to use a combination of economic and physical coercion to prevent African Americans from voting. One Democratic newspaper pledged to "carry the election peacefully if we can, forcibly if we must." Landlords informed African American sharecroppers that they could expect no further work if they voted Republican. Democrats also organized rifle clubs and physically attacked Republican picnics and rallies. Such violence proved to be the Democrats' most effective tool.

Vicksburg, Mississippi, was the scene of the worst political violence since the 1871 Klan murders in Meridian, Mississippi. In December 1874, responding to the continuing harassment of Republicans, Vicksburg's African American sheriff called on local blacks to help maintain the peace. But they were outnumbered and outgunned. White terrorists attacked a group of armed black deputies, killing 35 of them. With black voters intimidated, the Democrats won the county elections that same month, and the violence continued. It was directed primarily at local Republican leaders such as Richard Gray in Noxubee County. According to a fellow black Republican, Gray was "shot down walking on the pavements . . . because he was nominated for treasurer, and furthermore, because he made a speech and said he never did expect to vote a Democrat ticket, and also advised the colored citizens to do the same."

In response to this reign of terror and to the appeals of African Americans, Mississippi governor Adelbert Ames organized a state militia. Black men all around the state volunteered to serve in it, but Ames hesitated to arm them, perhaps fearing that this step would only result in greater violence. Although Ames requested President Grant's administration to send in federal troops, his request was denied. On election day, Republican supporters were thoroughly intimidated. Many stayed away from the polls, and the Democratic Party carried the state by thirty thousand votes. Mississippi had been "redeemed."

The presidential election of 1876 brought down the final curtain on the long drama of political Reconstruction (Map 12.2). The Republicans nominated Rutherford B. Hayes, governor of Ohio, as their candidate. He was a moderate Republican with a respectable Civil War record and a reputation for honesty. The Democrats, focusing on the corruption scandals that had rocked the Grant administration, chose New York's reform governor Samuel J. Tilden. Tilden had helped to break the grip of the notorious Tweed Ring in New York City. Although initial returns gave Tilden the election—including victories in New York, New Jersey, Connecticut, Indiana,

I Wonder How Harper's Artist Likes to Be Offensively Caricatured Himself?

Nast received a taste of his own medicine in this answering cartoon on the cover of the *New York Daily Graphic.* Such consciousness in the press about offensive imagery would not last long. By the 1880s, with the end of a national commitment to black equality, racist stereotypes characterized most published cartoons and illustrations. Th. Wust, *New York Daily Graphic,* March 11, 1874 — American Social History Project.

"A Dead Radical Is Very Harmless": Democratic Military Clubs in South Carolina

In 1876, using the Mississippi Plan as their model, the Democratic Party in South Carolina organized a chilling campaign of violence to steal the gubernatorial election. Their strategy, excerpted below, succeeded with the election of former Confederate General Wade Hampton. Items 2 and 16 appeared in a first draft of the plan and were marked "omit."

2. [It is decreed] That the Democratic Military Clubs are to be armed with rifles and pistols and such other arms as they may command. They are to be divided into two companies, one of the old men, the other of the young; an experienced captain or commander to be placed over each of them. That each company is to have a first and second Lieutenant. That the number of ten privates is to be the unit of organization. That each captain is to see that his men are well armed and provided with at least thirty rounds of ammunition. That the Captain of the young men is to provide a Baggage wagon in which three days rations for the horses and three days rations for the men are to be stored on the day before the election in order that they may be prepared at a moment's notice to move to any point in the County when ordered by the Chairman of the Executive Committee. . . .

11. Every Democrat must feel honor bound to control the vote of at least one Negro, by intimidation, purchase, keeping him away or as each individual may determine, how he may best accomplish it. . . .

14. In speeches to negroes you must remember that *argument* has no effect upon them: They can only be influenced by their *fears*, superstition, and cupidity. . . . Treat them so as to show them, you are the superior race, and that their natural position is that of subordination to the white man. . . .

16. Never threaten a man individually. If he deserves to be threatened, the necessities of the times require that he should die. A dead Radical is very harmless—a threatened Radical or one driven off by threats from the scene of his operations is often very troublesome, sometimes dangerous, always vindictive. . . .

Francis Butler Simkins and Robert Hilliard Woody, *South Carolina During Reconstruction* (Gloucester, MA: P. Smith, 1966), 564–569.

and most of the former Confederacy—disputes about the votes from three southern states that were still in Republican hands (Louisiana, South Carolina, and Florida) threw his victory into question.

In February 1877, a specially appointed electoral commission composed of ten congressmen and five Supreme Court justices—eight Republicans and seven Democrats—ruled eight to seven that the disputed votes in the three states belonged to Hayes. But there was no guarantee that the Democratic majority in the House of Representatives would accept this decision, and many Americans believed that the nation faced another civil

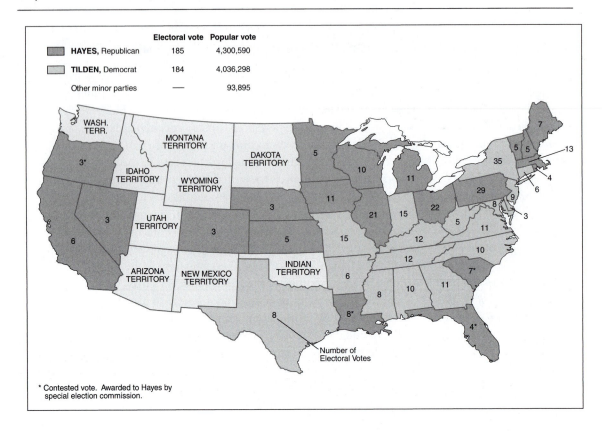

MAP 12.2 The Election of 1876
Initially, it appeared that Democratic candidate Samuel J. Tilden had won the election of 1876. He captured a majority of the popular vote and was leading in electoral votes. Only a series of political maneuvers and a compromise by Republicans that involved the final withdrawal of federal troops from the former Confederacy allowed Rutherford B. Hayes to gain all of the contested electoral votes in Florida, Louisiana, and South Carolina. With those votes in the Hayes column, he won the presidency by a single electoral vote.

war. Leading Republicans now moved to the fore, working out an understanding with southern Democrats in Congress to assure Hayes's inauguration. In exchange for Democratic support, the Republicans promised to give southern Democrats a fair share of federal appointments and to remove the remaining federal troops from the South. They also agreed to provide federal assistance for southern railroad development as a boon to industrialization and the creation of truly national markets.

Hayes was inaugurated in March 1877. In April, he pulled out the few remaining federal troops from the capitals of Louisiana and South Carolina, allowing Democrats to return to power. Neither the southern Republican Party nor the freedpeople who were its most ardent supporters could rely any longer on federal protection against violence and intimidation.

Conclusion: Still Searching for Freedom

As one southern state after another was "redeemed," those African Americans who could left the South behind. Beginning in the mid-1870s, colonization schemes, which proposed migration to Africa or to midwestern states

The Modern St. George
Republican president Rutherford B. Hayes is portrayed in this cartoon from the satirical weekly *Puck* as the savior saint, freeing the South from the "misrule" of Reconstruction.
Joseph Keppler, *Puck*, May 2, 1877 — New-York Historical Society.

such as Kansas, became popular among freedpeople. Henry Adams, a Union Army veteran from Louisiana and a colonization organizer, claimed to have signed up 60,000 blacks from all parts of the South. "This is a horrible part of the country," he wrote. "It is impossible for us to live with these slaveholders of the South and enjoy the right as they enjoy it." Although not many made the journey to Africa, tens of thousands of southern blacks did migrate to Kansas, taking their name from the Bible's Book of Exodus. Few of these Exodusters succeeded in establishing themselves on Kansas farmland, however, and most had to settle for menial jobs in the state's towns.

Life was indeed repressive in the South after Reconstruction ended, but the fact that thousands of freedpeople were able to emigrate at all indicates that they had at least succeeded in preventing the reinstitution of slavery. Moreover, many of the gains that had been secured during the Civil War and Reconstruction could not be erased by "redemption." African Americans came out of this era having won control over their family and religious lives; having secured, however briefly, national legal guarantees of equal rights, including suffrage; and, perhaps most important, having created a legacy of successful collective action on which their heirs would draw in future struggles for civil rights. Nonetheless, by 1877, the free-labor society that black Americans and their Radical Republican allies had tried to hard to create during Reconstruction had become but a distant ideal.

Growing numbers of African Americans entered the industrial labor force. Unfortunately, they joined the industrial age at the moment of its worst crisis of the century, which drastically limited African Americans' opportunities to secure employment, especially in skilled jobs, much less to join labor unions. Yet even after the Panic of 1873 subsided, the reconciliation of political and business leaders from the North and South ensured that few African Americans would benefit from the revitalization of commercial agriculture and industry. At the same time, the failure of the South and the nation to recognize the contributions that African Americans had made and could make economically, socially, culturally, and politically

"Let Us . . . Resolutely Struggle On": Frederick Douglass on Reconstruction

In his third autobio-graphical narrative, Life and Times of Frederick Douglass, *the nation's preeminent African American leader—whose career spanned the abolitionist crusade, the drama of war and eman-cipation, and, finally, the tragedy of the postwar era—summed up the political and moral les-sons of Reconstruction.*

History does not furnish an example of emancipation under condi-tions less friendly to the emancipated class than this American ex-ample. Liberty came to the freedmen of the United States not in mercy, but in wrath, not by moral choice but by military necessity, not by the generous action of the people among whom they were to live, and whose good-will was essential to the success of the measure, but by strangers, foreigners, invaders. . . . They were hated because they had been slaves, hated because they were now free, and hated because of those who had freed them. Nothing was to have been expected other than what has happened, and he is a poor student of the human heart who does not see that the old master class would naturally employ every power and means in their reach to make the great measure of emancipation unsuccessful and utterly odious. It was born in the tem-pest and whirlwind of war, and has lived in a storm of violence and blood. When the Hebrews were emancipated, they were told to take spoil from the Egyptians. When the serfs of Russia were emancipated, they were given three acres of ground upon which they could live and make a living. But not so when our slaves were emancipated. They were sent away empty-handed, without money, without friends, and without a foot of land to stand upon. Old and young, sick and well, were turned loose to the open sky, naked to their enemies. The old slave quarter that had before sheltered them and the fields that had yielded them corn were now denied them. . . .

Inhuman as was this treatment, it was the natural result of the bitter resentment felt by the old master class; and, in view of it, the wonder is, not that the colored people of the South have done so little in the way of acquiring a comfortable living, but that they live at all.

Taking all the circumstances into consideration, the colored people have no reason to despair. We still live, and while there is life there is hope. The fact that we have endured wrongs and hardships which would have destroyed any other race, and have increased in numbers and public consideration, ought to strengthen our faith in ourselves and our future. Let us, then, wherever we are, whether at the North or at the South, resolutely struggle on in the belief that there is a better day coming, and that we, by patience, industry, uprightness, and econ-omy may hasten that better day. I will not listen, myself, and I would not have you listen to the nonsense, that no people can succeed in life among a people by whom they have been despised and oppressed.

Frederick Douglass, *Life and Times of Frederick Douglass* (1882), 613–614.

assured that the nation as a whole would suffer from the deeply ingrained racism that thrived in the still unreconstructed United States.

The Years in Review

1862

- Union forces capture New Orleans in April and begin an occupation of the city.
- Northern reformers travel to the South Carolina Sea Islands, which have been under Union occupation since November 1861, to establish schools, churches, and self-government for the newly emancipated slaves there.

1863

- Newly freed black Sea Island residents purchase two thousand acres of deserted land from the federal government in an effort to distance themselves from the plantation system.
- President Lincoln's Proclamation of Amnesty and Reconstruction allows any Confederate state to seek readmission to the Union if 10 percent of its voters take an oath of loyalty to the Union.

1865

- On January 16, Union General William Tecumseh Sherman issues Field Order Number 15, which distributes confiscated Confederate plantation lands to African Americans.
- President Lincoln endorses limited suffrage for African Americans.
- On April 15, John Wilkes Booth assassinates President Lincoln at Ford's Theatre in Washington, D.C.; Booth's accomplices also attempt to kill Secretary of State William Seward. Vice President Andrew Johnson of Tennessee assumes the presidency.
- The Bureau of Freedmen, Refugees, and Abandoned Lands is created to assist freed slaves.
- President Johnson offers total amnesty to white Southerners who would swear basic loyalty to the Union.
- Ex-Confederate officials are elected in large numbers to federal and state positions. Enraged Radical Republicans establish a joint committee of Congress to investigate.

1866

- The Fourteenth Amendment, granting full citizenship to African Americans, passes both houses of Congress. Encouraged by President Johnson, all but one of the southern states refuse to ratify it.

- Confederate veterans in Tennessee found the Ku Klux Klan.
- White violence against African Americans rocks Memphis in May and New Orleans in July; nationwide, shocked northerners vote for Republicans' benefit in the fall elections.
- Congress passes a bill that extends the life of the Freedmen's Bureau and the Civil Rights Act of 1866, which gives federal courts the power to defend freedpeople's rights against interference from state governments.
- President Johnson vetoes both bills as a federal infringement on states' rights; Congress overrides both vetoes.
- Radical Republicans Charles Sumner and Thaddeus Stevens propose confiscating the land of ex-planters and redistributing it to freed slaves.

1867

- Large numbers of African Americans participate in politics by joining the Union Leagues that are spreading throughout the South.
- Congress passes the Reconstruction Act of March 1867 over President Johnson's veto. It mandates state constitutional conventions in which African Americans will participate, backed up by protection from federal troops.
- After two years of struggle by African Americans, New Orleans ends segregated seating on its streetcars.
- Radical Republicans are elected in southern states and pass laws supporting public education, the rights of landless laborers, and integration of public accommodations.

1868

- Republican Ulysses S. Grant is elected president.
- African Americans begin winning elected office in the South; between 1868 and 1876, fourteen black representatives are elected to the U.S. Congress, two are elected to the U.S. Senate, six are elected lieutenant governors, hundreds are elected to state legislatures, and thousands are elected to local offices.
- The U.S. House of Representatives impeaches President Johnson; the U.S. Senate acquits him.
- Radical Republican Thaddeus Stevens dies; a more moderate group of Republicans, known as the Stalwarts, gains control of the party.

1869

- Tennessee and Virginia revert to Democratic political control, beginning the state-level rollback of Reconstruction gains known as "Redemption."

1870

- The Fifteenth Amendment, granting all citizens the right to vote regardless of color, is ratified.

1871

- Shots ring out in the Meridian, Mississippi, courthouse during the trial of three African American men who had been accused of delivering "incendiary speeches"; a white spectator kills two of the defendants and the Republican judge, touching off rioting that kills 30 African Americans.
- The following month, Congress passes the Ku Klux Klan Act, making certain individual crimes against citizens' rights punishable under federal law.

1872

- Ulysses S. Grant is reelected; the Republican Party continues its retreat from the defense of African American rights.

1874

- In December 1874, whites in Vicksburg, Mississippi, attack a group of armed black deputies, killing 35 of them. Continued violence ensures a Democratic victory at the polls later that month.

1875

- President Grant denies Mississippi governor Adelbert Ames's request for federal troops to end the violence directed at Republican voters.

1876

- Initial returns in the presidential election give victory to Democrat Samuel J. Tilden, but in February 1877, a commission of congressmen makes Republican Rutherford B. Hayes president; to gain the presidency, congressional Republicans promise southern Democrats a fair share of federal appointments, removal of the remaining federal troops from the South, and federal assistance for southern railroad development.

1877

• President Hayes is inaugurated in March; in April, he pulls out the few remaining federal troops from the South.

Additional Readings

For overviews of Reconstruction, see: Ira Berlin et al., eds., *Free at Last: A Documentary History of Slavery, Freedom, and the Civil War* (1992); W. E. B. DuBois, *Black Reconstruction in America, 1860–1880* (1935); Eric Foner, *A Short History of Reconstruction, 1863–1877* (1990); Eric Foner and Joshua Brown, *Forever Free: The Story of Emancipation and Reconstruction* (2005); John Hope Franklin, *Reconstruction: After the Civil War* (1961); and James M. McPherson and J. Morgan Kousser, eds., *Region, Race, and Reconstruction: Essays in Honor of C. Vann Woodward* (1982).

For more on the political history of Reconstruction, see: Dan T. Carter, *When the War Was Over: The Failure of Self-Reconstruction in the South, 1865–1867* (1985); Laura Edwards, *Gendered Strife and Confusion: The Political Culture of Reconstruction* (1997); Michael W. Fitzgerald, *Urban Emancipation: Popular Politics in Reconstruction Mobile, 1860–1890* (2002); Ann Gordon et al., eds., *African American Women and the Vote, 1837–1965* (1997); Steven Hahn, *A Nation Under Our Feet: Black Political Struggles in the Rural South from Slavery to the Great Migration* (2003); Thomas Holt, *Black Over White: Negro Political Leadership in South Carolina During Reconstruction* (1977); Morgan J. Kousser, *The Shaping of Southern Politics: Suffrage Restriction and the Establishment of the One-Party South, 1880–1910* (1974); Peyton McCrary, *Abraham Lincoln and Reconstruction: The Louisiana Experiment* (1978); Eric L. McKittrick, *Andrew Johnson and Reconstruction* (1960); Michael Perman, *The Road to Redemption: Southern Politics, 1869–1879* (1984); and James Roark, *Masters Without Slaves: Southern Planters in the Civil War and Reconstruction* (1977).

For more on working people, see: Nancy Bercaw, *Gendered Freedoms: Race, Rights, and the Politics of the Household in the Delta, 1861–1875* (2003); Noralee Frankel, *Freedom's Women: Black Women and Families in Civil War Era Mississippi* (1999); William Harris, *The Harder We Run: Black Workers Since the Civil War* (1982); Jacqueline Jones, *Labor of Love, Labor of Sorrow: Black Women, Work and the Family from Slavery to the Present* (1985); Roger L. Ransom and Richard Sutch, *One Kind of Freedom: The Economic Consequences of Emancipation* (1977); Joseph P. Reidy, *From Slavery to Agrarian Capitalism in the Cotton Plantation South: Central Georgia, 1800–1880* (1992); and Julie Saville, *The Work of Reconstruction: From Slave to Wage Laborer in South Carolina, 1869–1870* (1994).

For more on newly emancipated African Americans, see: Carol Faulkner, *Women's Radical Reconstruction: The Freedmen's Aid Movement* (2003); Leon Litwack, *Been in the Storm So Long: The Aftermath of Slavery* (1979); William S. McFeeley, *Yankee Stepfather: General O. O. Howard and the Freedmen* (1968); Nell Irvin Painter, *Exodusters: Black Migration to Kansas after Reconstruction* (1971); Willie Lee Rose, *Rehearsal for Reconstruction: The Port Royal Experiment* (1964); Joel Williamson, *After Slavery: The Negro in South Carolina During Reconstruction, 1861–1877* (1965); and Jean Fagin Yellin, *Harriet Jacobs: A Life* (2005).

For more on the end of Reconstruction, see: Heather C. Richardson, *The Death of Reconstruction: Race, Labor, and Politics in the Post–Civil War North, 1865–1901* (2001); Nina Silber, *The Romance of Reunion: Northerners and the South, 1865–1900* (1993); Allen W. Trelease, *White Terror: The Ku Klux Klan Conspiracy and Southern Reconstruction* (1971); and C. Vann Woodward, *Reunion and Reaction: The Compromise of 1877 and the End of Reconstruction* (1951).

13

New Frontiers: Westward Expansion and Industrial Growth

1865–1877

FRANK LESLIE'S
ILLUSTRATED
RAILROAD RIOT EXTRA.
NEWSPAPER

NEW YORK, AUGUST 4, 1877.

"Railroad Riot Extra"
The burning Pennsylvania Railroad roundhouse illuminates the Pittsburgh nighttime sky on Saturday, July 21, 1877, as recorded by a local artist and disseminated by a leading illustrated newsweekly during the nationwide railroad strike. John Donaghy, *Frank Leslie's Illustrated Newspaper*, August 4, 1877 — American Social History Project.

IN 1876, THE UNITED STATES reached a venerable anniversary. The republic had survived for a century since declaring its independence from England. Although only a decade had passed since the end of the bloody Civil War, many of America's political and business leaders believed that their country deserved a spectacular birthday party that would display the nation's achievements in industry, science, agriculture, and the arts. Designed to meet these heady expectations, the Centennial Exposition opened on four hundred and fifty acres in Philadelphia's Fairmount Park on May 10, 1876. Ten million people, from every state and more than thirty countries, flocked to the celebration over the next six months.

The major exhibition buildings were gigantic. In this still largely rural nation, Agricultural Hall covered more than ten acres. Inside, visitors marveled at the latest mowing and reaping machines. But the centerpiece of the Exposition was the 700-ton, 40-foot-high Corliss Double Walking-Beam Engine, which generated 1,400 horsepower, enough to drive all the other machines in the enormous hall. Powered by a steam boiler in an adjacent building and running almost silently, the engine was an awesome creation, representing in the beauty of its motion, design, and power the very essence of the new industrial age.

Some Americans, however, were put off by the grandeur and pomp of the Centennial Exposition. They viewed it less as a celebration of the nation's achievements than as a diversion from hard and bitter daily realities. Neglected and sometimes stifled by the lavish festivities, these "other Americans" — including women, African Americans, American Indians, and workers—raised issues that would resonate far into the future.

■ 633

The Centennial's Women's Pavilion, for example, was fraught with division. Paid for with contributions from across the country, the pavilion presented visitors with crafts, inventions, and institutions established and conducted by women. Yet to many observers, the displays focused too much on the private, "domestic" sphere and too little on women's public achievements. As if to highlight this point, the National Woman's Suffrage Association held its founding meeting in New York City on the same day that the Women's Pavilion opened in Philadelphia. And at the Centennial's July Fourth ceremonies, feminists Elizabeth Cady Stanton and Susan B. Anthony disrupted the proceedings to read a Woman's Declaration of Independence that demanded equal rights for women in the family, the church, politics, work, and wages.

If women's role was limited at the Exposition, the contributions of African Americans were nearly invisible. African American women, who had helped to raise funds for the Centennial, found no place in the Women's Pavilion. No black men were hired on the crews that constructed the Centennial buildings, and visitors saw African Americans doing only menial tasks or performing in the Southern Restaurant, where (as a guidebook described it) "a band of old-time plantation 'darkies' . . . sing their quaint melodies and strum the banjo." This pervasive racism manifested itself again during the Centennial's opening ceremonies. Frederick Douglass—the militant abolitionist and acknowledged leader of the nation's African Americans—was invited to sit on the opening-day speakers' platform but not to speak.

Even America's Indian population played a more pronounced role than African Americans did, though not entirely by design. The Smithsonian Institution mounted a massive Centennial exhibit of Indian artifacts, replete with pottery, tepees, totem poles, and life-sized costumed mannequins. But if the exhibit suggested that Indians had vanished from American life, visitors were rudely reminded of their continued efforts to maintain sovereignty in the western United States. In July 1876, news reached the Centennial of the victory of Sioux and Cheyenne warriors at the Battle of Little Big Horn in the Dakota territory, where General George Custer and more than 200 U.S. Army soldiers perished.

White working-class men and women were among those who were shocked by news of Custer's defeat. Few saw any similarity between their own struggles for justice at the workplace and Indians' efforts to regain control of their native economy, government, and culture. Yet both Indians and workers found themselves at war with new economic and political forces. The Indians at the Centennial Exposition were brought as museum exhibits. The workers, however, were alive and well, if disgruntled. Indeed, some workers attended the celebration via excursions arranged by their employers, who hoped to ease workers' growing discontent with the ravages of industrial capitalism. Perhaps the defeat at Little Big Horn momentarily overshadowed class conflicts by reminding white Americans that they still had common enemies to confront on the western frontier.

Indeed, as travelers visited the exposition, there was plenty of evidence that the United States faced struggles on both the western and industrial frontiers. Custer's defeat highlighted the continued battles over western expansion. Northern workers, American Indians, western emigrants, and women found their opportunities restrained by some of the same forces that curtailed equality for blacks. Indeed, to many Americans, it seemed that the Civil War had been fought to destroy the power of one ruling class, southern slaveholders, only to produce another: an industrial oligarchy.

The trial of twenty coal miners in a Schuylkill County, Pennsylvania, courtroom that summer reflected the conflicts that erupted when big business and organized labor confronted each other. These developments, moreover, were not unrelated. Railroads and mining corporations, which were among the most important forces behind the rise of big business, sparked an endless demand for more western lands. At the same time, federal troops that honed their skills fighting Indians to protect these western investments would later turn their firepower against workers on strike. And most of those disgruntled workers, like the 20 on trial in Pennsylvania and the thousands that launched the Great Uprising of 1877, focused their anger on the owners of mines and railroads.

Change and Violence on the Frontier

Although the United States had gained legal authority over lands stretching to the Pacific Ocean before the Civil War, the nation had still not fully settled, much less conquered, this vast territory. American Indians and Mexicans, resident in the West for centuries, did not willingly relinquish their property or their rights. At the same time, white Americans, immigrants, and African Americans continued to look to the West for economic opportunities and the chance for a fresh start. All of these groups increasingly competed with big business, especially railroads, for land and authority on this contested terrain.

Railroads and Settlers Move West   By the late 1870s, thousands of African Americans across the South joined hundreds of thousands of new settlers—native-born and immigrant, black and white, women and men—and headed west, hoping for a new start on the "open lands" of the frontier. Some hoped for wealth from newly discovered mineral resources. Others sought land for farming. Still others searched for a refuge from the repression and conflicts of their former southern homes.

Heading West

A group of immigrants pose beside a Central Pacific train stopped at Mill City, Nevada, en route to California in 1880. American Association of Railroads.

The railroad turned these dreams of western expansion into a reality not only for eastern and southern migrants but also for corporate investors. Between 1867 and 1873, railroad companies laid 35,000 miles of track in the United States—as much as was built in the three previous decades. In 1862, in the midst of the Civil War, Congress had chartered the Union Pacific and Central Pacific corporations to construct a line between Omaha, Nebraska, and Sacramento, California. In 1869, a golden spike—hammered into place with great ceremony at Promontory Point, Utah—marked the completion of the link between the Atlantic and Pacific coasts.

The largest government subsidies in U.S. history financed the railroad boom. Between 1862 and 1872, Congress gave the railroad companies more than 100 million acres of public land and over $64 million in loans and tax breaks. The Republican congressmen who had voted for these huge grants linked assistance to the railroads with what appeared to be a pathbreaking land bill: the Homestead Act of 1862. This act opened the West to settlement and allowed any adult citizen or permanent immigrant to claim 160 acres of public land for a $10 fee; final title to the land would be granted after five years of residence on the land. (In 1862, Congress also passed the Morrill Act, which gave land grants to states to build state universities using profits from the sale of public lands to the railroads.) A law such as the Homestead Act had long been demanded by urban workers, and its supporters heralded it as the salvation of the laboring man. "Should it become

"Every Lick We Strike Is for Ourselves": A Homesteader Writes Home

In the fall of 1872, Union Army veteran Uriah Oblinger and two of his wife's brothers took advantage of the Homestead Act and migrated west; the following year, his wife Mattie and daughter Ella joined him in Nebraska. Borrowing techniques from the Plains Indians and earlier pioneers in Kansas, Mattie Oblinger and other homesteaders built sod houses. They cut the prairie sod deep and wide, laid it up like giant bricks, and fit the bricks together snugly without mortar. In this 1873 letter to her family back in Indiana, Mattie describes her community of neighbors and her sod house.

I have just as good neighbors as I ever had any where and they are very sociable. I was never in a neighborhood where all was as near on equality as they are here. Those that have been here have a little the most they all have cows and that is quite a help here. I get milk & butter from Mrs Furgison who lives 1/4 of a mile from us get the milk for nothing and pay twelve cents a pound for butter she makes good butter. Most all of the people here live in Sod houses and dug outs. I like the sod house the best they are the most convenient. I expect you think we live miserable because we are in a sod house but I tell you in solid earnest I never enjoyed my self better but George I expect you are ready to say It is because it is somthing new. No this not the case it is because we are . . . on our own and the thoughts of moveing next spring does not bother me and every lick we strike is for our selves and not half for some one else. I tell you this is quite a consolation to us who have been renters so long there are no renters here every one is on his own and doing the best he can and not much a head yet for about all that are here was renters and it took about all they had to get here. Some come here and put up temporary frame houses thought they could not live in a sod house. This fall they are going to build sod houses so they can live comfortable this winter a temporary frame house here is a poor thing a house that is not plastered the wind and dust goes right through and they are very cold. A sod house can be built so they are real nice and comfortable build nice walls and then plaster and lay a floor above and below and then they are nice.

Uriah W. Oblinger Collection, Nebraska Historical Society, from *Prairie Settlement: Nebraska Photographs and Family Letters*; American Memory, Library of Congress (http://memory.loc.gov/ammem/award98/nbhihtml/pshome.html).

a law," wrote the Radical Republican George Julian before it was passed, "the poor white laborers . . . would flock to the territories, where labor would be respectable, [and] our democratic theory of equality would be put in practice."

A vast expansion of farming in the West did follow closely on the heels of the railroads (Table 13.1). In the decade following the completion of the transcontinental line in 1869, Kansas attracted 347,000 new settlers. Similarly dramatic increases occurred in the other Plains states. Only about one-tenth of the new farms in these years were acquired under the Homestead Act, however. The land was free, but a city laborer, making perhaps $250 a year, could not even pay the entry fees to file a claim, let alone raise the

Railroad Mileage and the Expansion of Settlement, 1840–1860

State	1840 Railroads	1850 Railroads	1860 Railroads
New York	453	1,409	2,682
Pennsylvania	576	900	2,598
Massachusetts	270	1,042	1,264
New Jersey	192	332	560
Connecticut	94	436	601
Ohio	39	590	2,946
Indiana	20	226	2,163
Illinois	26	118	2,799
Missouri	---	4	817
Michigan	114	349	779
Iowa	---	---	655
Wisconsin	---	20	905
Virginia	341	341	1,731
North Carolina	247	249	937
Georgia	212	666	1,420
South Carolina	136	270	973
Maryland	273	315	386
Tennessee	---	48	1,253
Kentucky	32	80	534
Alabama	51	112	743
Mississippi	50	60	862
Louisiana	62	89	335
Texas	---	---	307

TABLE 13.1 Railroad Mileage and the Expansion of Settlement, 1840–1860

The spread of railroads throughout the Northeast and to the West and South sometimes followed the path of settlement and at other times helped to set that path. In the years between 1840 and the Civil War, rail lines were particularly important in establishing links between the Northeast and what we now think of as the Midwest. This chart illustrates the extension of railroad tracks to the West, particularly to Ohio, Indiana, Illinois, Missouri, Iowa, and Wisconsin in the mid-nineteenth century. Although the railroad also reached several southern states in this period, the number of miles of track laid there was considerably smaller, especially given the size of the states involved. *Hunt's Merchants' Magazine, 25* (September 1851), 381–382, for 1840 and 1850; and Henry V. Poor, *Manual of the Railroads of the United States* for 1868–69 (1868).

substantial funds that were necessary to buy farm equipment and move west. Indeed, many workingmen, including European and Asian immigrants, native-born whites, and African Americans, could make the journey to Kansas and similar destinations only by signing on as laborers with the heavily subsidized railroad companies.

Instead of western lands going mainly to individual small farmers, some people staked claims under the Homestead Act as a means of acquiring land for large mining and lumber companies. A provision of the act allowed homesteaders to obtain full and immediate title to land by paying $1.25 or $2.50 an acre for it. The large companies paid individuals to stake claims and quickly acquired huge tracts of land at prices that were well below their actual value. Later amendments to the act made the acquisition of western land by large companies even easier.

The dreams of small prospectors fared little better than those of small farmers. Major discoveries of silver and gold in Colorado and Nevada drew miners to the Rockies and eastern Sierras in the 1860s, as did subsequent discoveries in Montana, Idaho, Wyoming, and the Black Hills of Dakota. Unlike the veins of precious metals that had been found in California, however, those in Colorado and Nevada often ran three thousand feet deep or more and required extensive capital and technology to retrieve. As a result, individual prospectors who discovered veins of gold or silver, such as Nevada's spectacular Comstock Lode, were rapidly displaced by mining companies. These enterprises employed large numbers of wage-earning miners in impersonal (and often unsafe) settings. The subsequent industrialization of hard rock mining, the emergence of powerful mining syndicates, and the movement of independent prospectors into the ranks of wage-earning employees stood in stark contrast to the dream of a free and open West.

The development of hard rock mining also had devastating effects on the environment. In 1866, Congress passed the Mineral Act, which granted title to millions of acres of western land to mining companies, assuring their control over mineral deposits. Six years later, the Apex Mining Act gave rights to the entire vein of ore below the surface to the "individual" who discovered its apex (the point closest to the surface). Because large corporations already owned the land on which most apexes were discovered, mining companies could now freely blast through mountains as they worked the entire span of a particular vein. Trees that had not already been decimated by the passage of thousands of pioneers, by massive cattle drives, or by the movement of Indians into previously unoccupied lands were either felled for lumber to build deep mine shafts or lost in the efforts to demolish the rocky terrain in order to reach the rich ore below. Huge piles of broken rock, deep and dangerous abandoned shafts, and polluted lakes and streams were left in the wake of such operations as mining companies depleted a vein and moved on.

American Indians and Mexican Americans Fight for Autonomy During the 1860s, the dreams of American Indians as well as their lands were being destroyed. The rapid spread of railroads, mining companies, cattle ranchers, and settlers across the Plains and Far West led to violent conflict not only between tribal peoples and settlers from the East, but also among the various tribes themselves. These incursions pushed Sioux, Pawnee, Apache, Navajo, Comanche, and other native peoples off their ancestral lands and forced them into greater contact with one another. Nomadic tribes that had survived by hunting now overran lands on which other groups had settled to farm. As more and more American Indians were crowded into smaller and smaller areas, some tribes raided the stores and fields of others, touching off a series of mini-wars. Old animosities, such as those between the Navajo and the Mescalero Apache, flared when the U.S. government forced hostile groups to share the same reservation.

The clashes among the western tribes and between them and the growing numbers of white settlers ensured that the federal government would bolster the U.S. Army's presence on the Plains. Between 1860 and 1865, the number of U.S. troops stationed in the West increased from 11,000 to nearly 20,000. The battle at Apache Pass in 1862 in what is now Arizona and the campaigns against the Mescalero Apache, Navajo, and Sioux in 1863 in the New Mexico territory made it clear that not even the Civil War could deter the U.S. government's plans to conquer the West. In 1864, U.S. soldiers brutally attacked a sleeping village at Sand Creek, Colorado, killing some 200 Cheyenne — two-thirds of them women and children. As news of the massacre reached other Indian communities, confrontations with white settlers escalated.

In the spring of 1865, as the last battles of the Civil War were being fought, the Union Army mounted a new offensive on the Plains. Political leaders in Washington, D.C., now viewed the pacification or elimination of native societies as a necessary condition for the development of the West's economic potential. Army officers who were sent to quell uprisings included hardened veterans of the Civil War, men such as William Tecumseh Sherman and Philip Sheridan, firm believers in the kind of total war against enemy populations that had proven so successful against the Confederacy. In 1867, Sherman assumed command of the Plains division of the U.S. Army.

Also in 1867, Congress declared a new policy that it claimed would ensure peace. Although treaties that had been signed in the 1830s pledged much of the Great Plains to tribal peoples, the federal government now withdrew that pledge. The remaining "free" Indians would now be concentrated on two reservations in the Dakota and Oklahoma territories. Officials persuaded a number of tribal leaders to accept the new terms, and many American Indians felt that they had little choice.

This did not mean that Indians viewed the new reservations as a benefit. An Apache named Daklugie moved as a child to the San Carlos Reservation in the Arizona territory in the early 1870s. Interviewed in the 1940s, he recalled San Carlos as a terrible place: "The heat was terrible. The insects were terrible. The water was terrible." Cacti and mosquitoes thrived on the reservation, and many Apache died of the "shaking sickness" — malaria. Daklugie concluded that San Carlos was "considered a good place for Apaches — a good place for them to die."

Still, many Indians resisted the drastic reduction of their lands and, even worse, the destruction of their nomadic culture by the boundaries of the reservation system. To give just one example, an Apache warrior,

Ride the Train and Shoot a Buffalo!

One of the short-lived attractions of western railroad travel was the opportunity to join a buffalo hunt — often without having to leave the comfort of the railroad carriage. In this 1870 promotional photograph, the official taxidermist displayed his wares outside of the Kansas Pacific Railroad's general offices. Richard Benecke, Kansas & Pacific Railroad Album — Collection Number: Ag1982.0086.0060. DeGolyer Library, Southern Methodist University.

Victorio, led a group off the San Carlos reservation in the 1870s. He declared, "We prefer to die in our own land under the tall cool pines. We will leave our bones with those of our people. It is better to die fighting than to starve." Eventually, this band of Apache were chased into Mexico, where Victorio and many of his followers were killed in a two-day battle in Chihuahua. Throughout the 1870s and 1880s, these "nontreaty" Indians conducted guerrilla warfare against white settlers and U.S. troops. But U.S. soldiers resisted their attempts to circumvent the reservation system.

The battle to subdue Indians in the West was fought on many fronts. In 1869, the same year that Sherman was appointed commander of the entire U.S. Army, the *Army Navy Journal* reported his suggestion for undermining Indian culture. Sherman remarked that "the quickest way to compel the Indians to settle down to civilized life was to send ten regiments of soldiers to the plains, with orders to shoot buffaloes until they became too scarce to support the redskins." The bison that roamed the West in giant herds provided the raw material for survival among nomadic tribes, and their destruction would be fully as devastating as open warfare. The army regularly staged buffalo "hunts" by soldiers and civilians and applauded soldiers who reported large kills. "Sportsmen," many outfitted at army posts, also killed many buffalo on the northern plains, as did railroad crews in search of meat. Professional hunters joined the slaughter after a Pennsylvania tannery discovered in 1871 that buffalo hides could be used for commercial

"This Was to Be Our Land Forever": A Cheyenne Remembers Losing Her Land

Iron Teeth, a Cheyenne woman, provided a vivid account of the conflicts that arose in the 1870s between federal troops and the Indian tribes they were trying to relocate.

Soldiers built forts in our Powder River country when I was about thirty-two years old. The Sioux and the Cheyennes settled at the White River agency, in our favorite Black Hills country. This was to be our land forever, so we were pleased. But white people found gold on our lands [in 1874]. They crowded in, so we had to move out. My husband was angry about it, but he said the only thing we could do was go to other lands offered to us. We did this.

Many Cheyennes and Sioux would not stay on the new reservations, but went back to the old hunting grounds in Montana. Soldiers went there to fight them. In the middle of the summer [1876] we heard that all of the soldiers [led by General George A. Custer] had been killed at the Little Bighorn River. My husband said we should go and join our people there. We went, and all of our people spent the remainder of the summer there, hunting, not bothering any white people nor wanting to see any of them. When the leaves fell, the Cheyenne camp was located on a small creek far up the Powder River.

Soldiers came [on November 29, 1876] and fought us there. Crows, Pawnees, Shoshones, some Arapahoes, and other Indians were with them. They killed our men, women, and children, whichever ones might be hit by their bullets. We who could do so ran away. My husband and my two sons helped in fighting off the soldiers and enemy Indians. My husband was walking, leading his horse, and stopping at times to shoot. Suddenly I saw him fall. I started to go back to him, but my sons made me go on, with my three daughters. The last time I ever saw [my husband], he was lying there dead in the snow. From the hilltops we Cheyennes saw our lodges and everything in them burning.

Thomas B. Marquis, "Red Ripe's Squaw: Recollections of a Long Life," *Century Magazine*, 118 (June, 1929), 201–202, 206–207.

leather. By the mid-1880s, buffalo—which had once numbered over thirteen million—had all but disappeared from the Great Plains.

With the slaughter of the buffalo, the constant movement to either avoid or confront U.S. army troops, the periodic massacres of whole villages, the concentration of more diverse tribes in ever-smaller territories, and the disruption of normal patterns of hunting, agriculture, and trade, many Indian tribes found it impossible to sustain traditional ways of life. Others, whether within the confines of a reservation or amid the hazards of traveling the Plains, worked hard to maintain some aspects of their religious ceremonies and kinship ties and their sense of themselves as a sovereign nation.

Battle of the Little Bighorn
This is part of a series of pictures drawn by the Sioux warrior Red Horse recording his memories of the 1876 battle, drawn five years later at the Cheyenne River Agency. Tenth Annual Report, Bureau of Ethnology, #4700 — National Anthropological Archive, Smithsonian Institution.

The pacification of the American Indians was not an easy process, and Indians fought back even when they were badly outnumbered and literally outgunned. One of the most notable stands made by Indians to fight off the U.S. Army's control of the West was that of the Sioux and Cheyenne at the Battle of Little Big Horn, noted earlier in the chapter. The Sioux had begun openly resisting the reservation system in the mid-1870s when white miners had rushed into the Black Hills, the site of the Sioux reservation, after gold was discovered there. In late June 1876, just a week before the nation celebrated its centennial, General George Custer and the U.S. Seventh Cavalry were attempting to ferret out rebellious Sioux (led by chiefs Sitting Bull and Crazy Horse) when Custer stumbled into a Sioux camp. Though taken by surprise, the Sioux, with the aid of Cheyenne camped nearby, won a major victory when they cut down Custer's troops and kept possible reinforcements pinned down on a nearby bluff.

The news of the battle finally reached Philadelphia just as the Centennial Exposition opened in July. Unable to imagine that the fault lay with Custer, many visitors to the Exposition viewed the defeat at Little Big Horn as further evidence of Indian savagery. In any event, the victory was short-lived. Facing a shortage of food and supplies and the certainty that the army would send fresh troops to avenge Custer's loss, the Sioux and Cheyenne headed north. By fall 1877, U.S. Army troops had captured the renegade leaders and defeated the Sioux and Cheyenne warriors, forcing these once powerful tribes back onto reservations that continued to shrink in the face of white interest in settling the Dakota territory (Map 13.1).

Another group that had long been settled in the West—Mexicans and Mexican Americans—also found their ways of life changed by the entrance

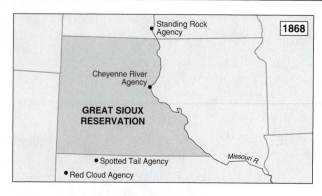

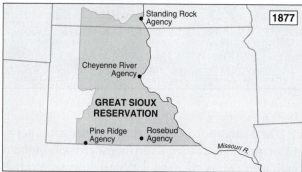

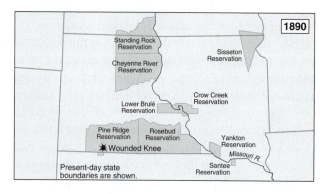

MAP 13.1 Reduction of the Great Sioux Reservation, 1868–1890

The Fort Laramie Treaty of 1868, signed between the Sioux Indians and the U.S. government, assured that the Sioux would henceforth confine themselves to a reservation, but it was a substantial reservation that covered roughly the western half of present-day South Dakota, with a portion also crossing the border into western North Dakota. With the discovery of gold in the Black Hills, however, the Sioux were forced to cede more territory, narrowing the lands on which they lived. A decade later, representatives of the federal government claimed that the Sioux, who had been forced to shift from holding land in common to individual homesteads and from hunting to farming, were not using much of the land that had been granted them. In February 1890, President Benjamin Harrison stunned Sioux leaders by announcing a new agreement that broke up the existing reservation into six smaller reservations and opened the remaining land to white settlement. Reductions in food rations, epidemic disease, and a summer drought made 1890 one of the most devastating years in Sioux history.

of large numbers of eastern whites into the region. For instance, people who had once lived in settled villages along the Mexico-U.S. border were forced to migrate ever longer distances to find work. During the 1860s and 1870s, Mexican American villagers established farming communities as far north as southern Colorado. The railroad, which had just begun to extend its reach into the Southwest in this period, offered seasonal wage labor for men in the region. This was new but also beneficial, providing a critical supplement to sheep raising and petty trade. Mexican and Mexican American women, who had traditionally been considered economic partners with their husbands and sons and shared the use of communal pasturelands, continued to do so. Thus, although the expansion of the Anglo fron-

All Colored People

THAT WANT TO

GO TO KANSAS,

On September 5th, 1877,

Can do so for $5.00

IMMIGRATION.

WHEREAS, We, the colored people of Lexington, Ky,. knowing that there is an abundance of choice lands now belonging to the Government, have assembled ourselves together for the purpose of locating on said lands. Therefore,

BE IT RESOLVED, That we do now organize ourselves into a Colony, as follows:— Any person wishing to become a member of this Colony can do so by paying the sum of one dollar ($1.00), and this money is to be paid by the first of September, 1877, in instalments of twenty-five cents at a time, or otherwise as may be desired.

RESOLVED, That this Colony has agreed to consolidate itself with the Nicodemus Towns, Solomon Valley, Graham County, Kansas, and can only do so by entering the vacant lands now in their midst, which costs $5.00.

RESOLVED, That this Colony shall consist of seven officers—President, Vice-President, Secretary, Treasurer, and three Trustees. President—M. M. Bell; Vice-President —Isaac Talbott; Secretary—W. J. Niles; Treasurer—Daniel Clarke; Trustees—Jerry Lee, William Jones, and Abner Webster.

RESOLVED, That this Colony shall have from one to two hundred militia, more or less, as the case may require, to keep peace and order, and any member failing to pay in his dues, as aforesaid, or failing to comply with the above rules in any particular, will not be recognized or protected by the Colony.

Exodusters

An 1877 handbill urged African Americans to leave Kentucky and join a new settlement in Kansas. Kansas State Historical Society.

tier in the 1870s transformed Mexican American ways of life, the negative effects of wage labor and private property were not yet widespread.

Mexican Americans faced problems, however, from the ongoing efforts by white politicians to establish racial supremacy. The majority of white settlers in the Southwest had migrated from the former Confederacy, and they sought to use the Black Codes that had been developed in the South to restrict the political and economic rights of Mexican Americans. In addition, Mexicans and Mexican Americans had intermarried with various American Indian groups during the centuries when they occupied the same region. The tribal peoples who had developed kinship ties with Mexican Americans may well have tried to bring members of their families into settled villages as an alternative to reservation life. But Mexican Americans were wary of becoming embroiled in the bitter warfare between the U.S. Army and Indians. By the 1870s, forts were scattered across the New Mexico and Arizona territories, from which army units did battle with renegade members of the Comanche, Kiowa, and Apache tribes. These Indian rebels, whose homes were in the Southwest, threatened to bring the fighting into Mexican American villages, increasing the disruptions initiated by white settlement, mining companies, and the railroads.

African Americans Seek Opportunity in the West Although relations between white Americans and Indians or Mexican Americans made clear that the West was no racial utopia, many African Americans rightly viewed the region as providing greater opportunities than the unreconstructed South did. Benjamin Singleton, for example, had been born into slavery in 1809 near Nashville, Tennessee, escaped to Detroit, Michigan, in the 1850s and then returned to Nashville to work as a carpenter after the Civil War. Although he had more resources than most newly emancipated blacks did, even his hopes for a peaceful life as a free worker in the South were dashed. As Singleton watched former masters force African Americans into wage labor or sharecropping during the late 1860s, he decided that the best hope for southern blacks was land ownership, preferably outside the South.

En Route to Kansas
While many newspapers described the southern African American migrants as desperate and destitute refugees, pictorial coverage emphasized the organization and orderliness of the migration, as exemplified in this engraving showing the arrival of Exodusters in St. Louis, Missouri, during 1879. *Frank Leslie's Illustrated Newspaper*, April 19, 1879 — American Social History Project.

In 1871, Singleton founded the Tennessee Real Estate and Homestead Association to recruit African Americans for emigration to Kansas. Kansas held great promise for freedpeople. The state contained vast tracts of undeveloped farmland that, under provisions of the federal Homestead Act, could be obtained in 160-acre lots for $1.25 per acre. Kansas was well known as a home to ardent abolitionists and as the site where the first black soldiers joined the Union Army. The Republican Party dominated the political life of postwar Kansas, and the state legislature had been one of the first to ratify the Thirteenth Amendment abolishing slavery. In addition, many white Quakers, Presbyterians, and Congregationalists from the Northeast, with a "sense of mission toward the Negro," had moved to Kansas during the 1860s, ensuring a warm welcome for freedpeople.

But by 1878, when Singleton arrived in Kansas with the first party of 200 African American emigrants, the railroad companies and speculators had already claimed the best land. The black homesteaders had to settle on less fertile lands, but even that proved difficult when, a year later, the Kansas Freedman's Relief Association sent 400 new settlers to the same area to which Singleton and his followers had gone. Because the plots that were offered to African Americans were too small to sustain families, many of the new settlers ended up working for wages for white ranchers and large farmers or moving into local towns, where most could find only menial employment.

There were still advantages for African Americans who moved West. Western states and territories were less likely to pass Black Codes, and some African Americans gained economic and political rights that were denied

"A Strong Desire to Emigrate to Kansas"

In this letter to the National Emigrant Aid Society, a group of North Carolina freedpeople lists their reasons for wanting to migrate to Kansas.

August 1, 1879

We the people of the 2nd congressional district, North Carolina, have a Strong Desire to Emigrate to Kansas Land Where we can Have a Home. Reason and why:

1. We have not our rights in law.
2. The old former masters do not allow us anything for our labor.
3. We have not our Right in the Election. We are defrauded by our former masters.
4. We have not no [right] to make and honest and humble living.
5. There is no use for the Colored to go to law after their Rights; not one out of 50 gets his Rights.
6. The Ku [Klux] Reigns. . . .
7. We Want to Get to a land Where we can Vote and it not be a Crime to the Colored Voters. . . .
8. Wages is very low [here.]

Nearly all of the laborers have families to take care of and many other things we could mention, but by the help of God we intend to make our start to Kansas land. We had Rather Suffer and be free, than to suffer [the] infamous degrades that are Brought upon us [here.] . . .

Rev. S. Heath
Moses Heath
Lenoir Co., N.C.

Senate Report 693, 46th Cong., 2nd Sess. (1880).

---

them in the South. Moreover, the mix of Indians, Mexican Americans, Chinese immigrants, and African American and white settlers ensured that no single racial group became the sole focus of racial hostilities. In some cases, other racial groups—such as the Chinese in California or the Comanche and Apache in New Mexico—bore the brunt of labor exploitation and political oppression. Still, while opportunities for blacks in the West were greater than those in the South, they were still severely restricted.

Industrialization and the Working Class

The railroads and mining companies that transformed life in the West also contributed to the acceleration of industrial growth after the Civil War. With this development, ideals of economic independence and self-sufficiency became less and less possible for most Americans to attain, whatever their race and whatever the region in which they lived. In 1860, there had been about as many self-employed people as wage earners. Twenty years later, far more people relied on wages. The number of workers in manufacturing and construction, for instance, leapt from two million in 1860 to more than four million in 1880 (Figure 13.1). The rise of big business in the late nineteenth century was thus accompanied by the emergence of an industrial labor force that included women and men from a wide range of ethnic and racial groups. The very diversity of this new labor force, however, made it difficult for workers to organize in the face of increasing demands and pressures from employers.

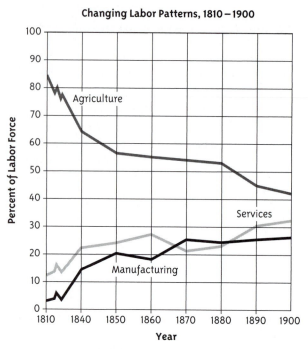

Changing Labor Patterns, 1810–1900

The Rise of Big Business   The railroads were central to changes in the very fabric of American economic life. Through large subsidies to the railroads, the federal government helped to create powerful corporations, which became America's first big businesses. The Pennsylvania Railroad, the nation's largest single business enterprise, employed over 20,000 workers by the early 1870s. The railroads' tremendous need for capital led them to adopt and popularize a variety of modern managerial methods. One was the limited-liability corporation, which allowed wealthy men to buy shares in new ventures while limiting their financial responsibilities if the business failed. The number of railroad stockholders expanded exponentially, and large boards of directors—usually including several powerful bankers—replaced old-fashioned individual entrepreneurs. This new separation of ownership and control gave the railroad corporation a permanence and impersonality that had previously been unknown, which made it more difficult for workers to negotiate problems and express their grievances.

The railroads were also the first businesses to face the problem of intense economic competition. This led periodically to disastrous rate wars. In some areas, groups of railroads formed "pools" that tried to end cutthroat competition by setting rates and dividing up traffic. From the standpoint of the railroad managers, pools seemed essential to survival. To other people, such practices undermined the "free competition" that some lauded as the key to American prosperity. Critics contrasted the bankruptcy of some companies with the rise of a small group of wealthy entrepreneurs who had built immense personal fortunes through railroad promotion and

FIGURE 13.1   Changing Labor Patterns, 1810–1900

Although agriculture continued to employ the largest percentage of the workforce throughout the nineteenth century, both the number and the proportion of women and men working in manufacturing and service increased steadily. The Civil War was an important catalyst for this industrial leap, increasing the demand for guns, uniforms, shoes, and other war materiel. In the postwar period, textile factories multiplied exponentially in both the North and the South. Laborers in the service category grew as a result of both the war and the expanding urban population. Government clerical workers, typists in city offices and factories, and sales clerks joined those workers who had long been employed in service such as domestic servants and laundresses.

"Money Monopolies": William Sylvis on Workers and the Vote

In this 1868 speech to the Labor Reform Party Convention, Iron Molders' Union president William Sylvis rails against the power of "money monopolies" and implores workers to use their vote to regain their rights and restore the virtue of the American republic.

Men talk to me of our independence and boast of our constitutional government, and all that it guarantees to us; but with these spread-eagle gentlemen I do not agree. These things will do very well for Fourth-of-July orations, but not for everyday life. Workingmen do not live in imagination, but upon cold, practical facts; and the facts are, that the workingmen of this nation are oppressed more than the same class in any other country. It is true, we have no king—no political king—but here we have monopolies, banking monopolies, railroad monopolies, land monopolies, and bond monopolies, that supply the place of kings, dukes, lords, etc., and their rule is getting to be more intolerable than is found anywhere else. If we have no political kings, we have money kings, and they are the worst kings in the world. We, by our labor, have been putting into motion millions of little streams of wealth, and a false financial and money system has been directing them into the pockets of a few individuals, while we remain poor and power-less. No, not powerless, for we have yet one way of escape. The ballot-box is still open. We in this State have yet no law allowing the Legislature to do our voting for us. If we will use the ballot effectively, we will soon be freed from the golden rule that now crushes the vitality out of the industry of the whole nation. This we are now trying to do. This is the object of the Labor Reform Party; and we are ready to make common cause with any other party or people who will adopt our principles and get on our platform.

James C. Sylvis, *The Life, Speeches, Labors, and Essays of William H. Sylvis* (1872).

---

consolidation. In the eyes of critics, these men—including Cornelius Vanderbilt, Jay Gould, Jim Fisk, and Collis P. Huntington, who together became known as the Robber Barons—symbolized all that was wrong with the capitalist system.

The industrial barons rapidly translated their economic might into political power. They hired armies of lobbyists whose activities gained the corporations even more subsidies and land grants and protected them from regulation and taxation. "The galleries and lobbies of every legislature," observed a Republican leader, "are thronged with men seeking . . . an advantage" for one corporation or another. These developments made many Americans doubt the future of their nation. Having fought a civil war to destroy the power of one ruling class, Americans were now confronted with an even more powerful industrial oligarchy. This new power was emerging in part as a result of the rapid and uncontrolled development of the West, the very region where the dream of a free and open republic should have been ful-filled.

Railroads, which led in the develop-ment of big business, were vital in the opening up of the West. They developed the rapid, reliable shipping that was needed to create a truly national market. This development, in turn, encouraged manufacturers to produce in larger quantities and to experiment with low-cost mass-production methods. Small producers that had once dominated local markets now faced competition from products that were made in distant factories and hauled by railroads to every corner of the United States. By the late nineteenth century, carriages, wag-ons, furniture, and other wood products, as well as shoes, textiles, and cereals, were all mass-produced.

The most dynamic industries, such as oil refining, were those that were involved in processing the natural resources of the rapidly developing West. In 1859, Edwin Drake drilled America's first oil well in Pennsylvania. The lucrative business of refining crude oil grew up in the cities of Pittsburgh, Cleveland, and Philadelphia, leading to a period of intense competition similar to that which plagued the railroads. John D. Rockefeller, whose Standard Oil Company dominated the Cleveland petroleum business by 1871, saw this competition as the main problem facing the industry. Rather than supporting price-fixing pools like those used by railroad companies, Rockefeller brought pressure on smaller refiners to sell out to him. By the late 1870s, Standard Oil was a virtual monopoly, controlling about nine-tenths of the nation's oil-refining capacity.

The American Frankenstein
Inspired by Mary Shelley's novel about a human-made monster who turned on its cre-ator, this cartoon depicted the railroad trampling the rights of the American people. "Agri-culture, commerce, and manufacture are all in my power," the monster roared in the cartoon's caption. "My in-terest is the higher law of American politics." Frank Bellew, *New York Daily Graphic*, April 14, 1874 — American Social History Project.

The Growth of Cities and a National Industrial Workforce   As industries grew, so did the need for workers. Many workers were still laboring in their homes under the old outwork system. Sewing women in particular still pro-duced clothing the old-fashioned way in the tenements of New York, Boston, and Chicago. Women outworkers also made paper flowers, cigars, and buttons, and many male tailors worked at home as well. Still, increased demand for such products did not improve the lives of these workers. For instance, between 1860 and 1880, textile manufacturers insisted that women homeworkers buy or rent newly invented sewing machines to speed up their work. Contractors then lowered the prices paid to the women for each piece of work completed, arguing that it was now easier to produce more. "I have worked from dawn to sundown, not stopping to get one mouthful of food, for twenty-five cents," reported a woman tailor in 1868.

Yet it was the factory, not the outwork system, that represented the wave of the future. The history of shoemaking in Lynn, Massachusetts, is typical. As the national market expanded along with transportation and population, the outwork system seemed less efficient. The idea of concentrating workers in shoemaking factories was made possible with the invention of the McKay stitcher (an adaptation of the sewing machine) in 1862. The McKay stitcher allowed manufacturers to employ more machine operators, centralize production, and thus end outwork. Discipline became tighter, and work was performed more steadily. "The men and boys are working as if for life," observed a visitor to one Lynn factory. So were the women and girls.

During this period, factory cities such as Lynn were extremely dynamic. A similar city — Paterson, New Jersey — grew from a market town of 11,000 people in 1850 into a sprawling city of over 33,000 by 1873. Many of its residents labored in the new locomotive, iron, machinery, and textile industries. In the late 1860s, industry grew faster in smaller cities such as Lynn and Paterson than in large cities such as New York and Boston. Industrial centers began to emerge in the South as well. In Augusta, Georgia, for instance, textile factories provided work for growing numbers of families — especially widows and their daughters — in the aftermath of the Civil War. By the 1870s, textile factories were opening across the South. Between the mid-1870s and the mid-1880s, six new mills opened in Augusta alone, and the workforce jumped from 700 to 3,000 workers.

Cities in the Midwest and Far West grew impressively as well. Chicago, which had 30,000 people in 1850, became the sixth-largest city in the world a mere forty years later, with a population of over one million. Linked by the spreading railroad network, cities such as St. Louis, Cleveland, and San Francisco also grew tremendously. The modern American city emerged in the first decade after the Civil War. During these years, city governments began to deliver services to their citizens, including public transportation, professional fire and police protection, and rudimentary sanitation and health facilities.

The Spread of Immigration   Large cities, with their expanding services and job opportunities, also attracted the most immigrants. Immigration had slowed during the Civil War. Now it picked up again — this time on an even more massive scale. About five million people entered the United States between 1815 and 1860, but more than double that number came between 1860 and 1890. As before, most immigrants came from Northern and Western Europe, where agricultural crises prompted them to leave home. Tens of thousands of farm people, including many Irish families, emigrated to the New World in the decade following the Civil War. Not all immigrants in this period were from the countryside, however; coal miners from Scotland and Wales and iron puddlers from England's Black Country brought crucial skills to the most dynamic sectors of the American economy. German immigrants worked as laborers and artisans in more traditional trades, such as baking, brewing, and upholstering. They made up the majority of skilled craftsmen in St. Louis, Chicago, and other large cities.

Most immigrants, however, ended up working in the least-skilled sectors of the workforce: hauling and loading and unloading goods on the docks and in warehouses, building roads and streetcar lines, and laboring at building sites. Most important, it was overwhelmingly immigrants who built America's railroad network—especially the Irish in the East and the Chinese in the West.

Chinese immigration to the Pacific Coast had surged in the 1850s, when famine in China had triggered an exodus to California. By 1860, nearly one Californian in ten was Chinese. When the Central Pacific began to build the western end of the transcontinental railroad in the 1860s, it recruited laborers directly from China. Its agents paid a person's outfitting and passage in return for a $75 promissory note, the debt to be repaid within seven months of beginning work on the railroad. However, new debts—for food, housing, and other necessities—generally replaced old ones. Thus, for most immigrants, their chances for financial independence receded into the distance right along with the railroad tracks. Despite the hardships, over 10,000 Chinese laborers found their way to the grading camps and construction crews of the Central Pacific.

As the United States extended its reach into the Pacific—purchasing Alaska from the Russians and annexing the Midway Islands in 1867—the Chinese continued to migrate eastward. By 1870, more than one in four people living in the Idaho territory was Chinese (Table 13.2). In mining towns, the Chinese had established their own communities and built businesses, particularly laundries. This allowed some to work for themselves rather than for American employers. Virginia City, Nevada, for instance, was home to about 1,000 Chinese immigrants and twenty Chinese laundries in the mid-1870s. Whether working in mining towns or on the railroads, Chinese men, isolated from their families, struggled to survive the most brutal work conditions then known in the United States. In the winter of 1866, heavy snows covered the Chinese encampments in the Sierra Nevada Mountains. The laborers had to dig chimneys and air shafts through the

TABLE 13.2 Chinese in the Western Mining Areas, 1870

The U.S. Census of 1870 demonstrated the massive impact Chinese men had on the mining industry. Their labor was critical to extracting the enormous mineral wealth of the western states and, in the process, providing raw materials for the entire nation's industrial development. Moreover, the number of miners represents only part of the contribution of Chinese immigrants to western and national economic growth. The Chinese also contributed by building railroads and serving as cooks, storekeepers, and laundry and domestic workers in the mining areas. John Kuo Wei Tchen, *The Chinese of America* (1980).

Chinese in Western Mining Areas (1870)			
State or Territory	Total Mining Workforce	Chinese Miners	Percentage
Oregon	3,965	2,428	61.2%
Idaho	6,579	3,853	58.5%
Washington	173	44	25.4%
California	36,339	9,087	25.0%
Montana	6,720	1,415	21.0%
Nevada	8,241	240	2.9%

snow and live by lantern light. Yet under orders from Charles Crocker, who directed labor for the Central Pacific, construction continued. On Christmas Day, 1866, a local newspaper reported that "a gang of Chinamen employed by the railroad were covered up by a snow slide and four or five died before they could be exhumed." Even when not facing such dangers, the Chinese labored for ten grueling hours a day at roughly two-thirds the wages paid to whites. The experience of the Chinese in America at this time was harsher than that of other immigrant groups — partly because they were "contract laborers" and were recruited on a basis much like that of the indentured servants of the colonial period.

The dramatic increase in immigrants and wage laborers and the enormous expansion of industry and wealth raised fundamental questions about the survival of traditional American ideals and values. Business leaders and their intellectual supporters tried to create a rationale for these vast changes in American economic and social life by combining two concepts: "laissez-faire" and "Social Darwinism." The theory of laissez-faire (which means, roughly, "leave it alone" in French) rested on a belief that economic growth could result only from the free and unregulated development of a market that was governed entirely by laws of supply and demand and kept free from any interference by government or unions. Social Darwinism applied British scientist Charles Darwin's ideas about the evolution of biological species to social relations. Its proponents used Darwin's concept of "the survival of the fittest" to explain the economic success of a few capitalists ("the strong") and the increasing impoverishment of many workers ("the weak"). They argued that this "natural" process resulted in society's continuing improvement.

Not all Americans agreed. Even the generally conservative *New York Times* expressed concern in 1869 that the increasingly rapid descent of the independent mechanic to the level of a dependent wage earner was

On Stampede Pass, After the Blizzard
Chinese workers constructing a tunnel on the Northern Pacific Railway were photographed sometime in the 1880s as they cleared a switchback (a zigzag, uphill road) in the Cascade Mountains of Washington. Special Collections Division, University of Washington Libraries.

producing "a system of slavery as absolute if not as degrading as that which lately prevailed [in] the South." In the North, the *Times* noted, "capitalists threaten to become the masters, and it is the white laborers who are to be slaves." More than any other single fact, the development of industrial capitalism and the attendant deterioration of working conditions lay behind the rapid growth of the American labor movement in the years after the Civil War.

An American Labor Movement Emerges

The period from 1866 to 1873 marked a new stage in the development of the American labor movement. A greater proportion of industrial workers joined trade unions during these years than in any other period in the nineteenth century, and more of them than ever belonged to unions that were national rather than local in scope. By 1872, there were thirty national trade unions in the United States and hundreds of local ones, with a total membership of over 300,000 workers.

The efforts to create more and larger unions was limited, however, by the refusal of many white working men to organize alongside African Americans, Chinese immigrants, and women. Then in 1873, a devastating panic swept the nation, shattering the hopes of workers and unions. Still, before the country had fully recovered from the Panic of 1873, workers in one key industry—railroads—managed to launch a massive strike. Although the Great Uprising of 1877 failed to achieve workers' demands, the strike suggested the power of collective national action to gain leverage for labor against the giants of industrial capitalism.

Workers Organize Trade unions emerged in the 1860s out of a series of intense local struggles with employers over wages, hours, and working conditions. The struggle to limit the length of the workday to eight hours was especially important, and it triggered union organization in a number of trades. Workers' ideological traditions also helped to spark the labor upsurge. Native-born workers, white and black, drew on the egalitarian ideals and republican traditions of the American Revolution and the early years of Reconstruction in building both individual unions and the labor movement as a whole. German, Irish, and British immigrants carried with them from their home countries new, often radical, ideas about collective action and forms of struggle and organization, including socialism and anarchism. The melding of these traditions shaped the politics and ideology of the post–Civil War American labor movement.

The National Molders' Union, founded in 1859, became one of the most important of the new unions. The power of the iron molders lay in their possession of valuable skills in a rapidly expanding industry. Led by president William H. Sylvis, they were also deeply committed to an egalitarian legacy. "We assume to belong to the order of men who know their rights, and knowing, dare maintain them," proclaimed a Troy, New York, molder. The iron molders had organized locals during the inflation-ridden Civil War, most notably among Chicago's giant McCormick reaper workers. Through a series of successful strikes, the union managed to maintain its members' real wages and even obtain wage increases for the unskilled workers in the plant. By 1867, the molders' union stood at the head of efforts to shorten the workday to eight hours.

Manufacturers were unified in their opposition to labor's demand for a shorter work day. "As long as the present order of things exists, there will be poor men and women who will be obliged to work," noted one employer who wanted to maintain a ten-hour workday, "and the majority of them will not do any more than necessity compels them to do." Concerned with the effect of a shortened workday on their profits, factory owners vowed to fight the eight-hour day.

The Illinois legislature presented a major test of employers' resolve. The Republican-controlled state legislature passed a law declaring eight hours to be "the legal workday in the State," and the governor signed it into law in March 1867. Employers were required to conform to the new legislation beginning May 1. Chicago workers, elated with the seeming victory, took to the streets on May first in a spectacular parade that featured 6,000 marchers, elaborate floats, and exuberant brass bands.

Serenading a 'Blackleg' on His Return from Work

Trade union organizing in the coal industry was a family affair, as indicated by this illustration from *Frank Leslie's Illustrated Newspaper* showing coal miners and their families harassing a scab (strikebreaker) during a strike in the Cherry Valley region of Ohio in 1874. Jonathan Lowe, *Frank Leslie's Illustrated Newspaper*, September 5, 1874 — American Social History Project.

Chicago employers, however, encouraged by the legislature's failure to institute a penalty for noncompliance, simply refused to comply. Workers once again took to the streets, this time in a massive citywide work stoppage, to demand that the new law be enforced. The iron molders led the way, followed by German and native-born machinists and Irish workers from the packinghouses and rolling mills. On May 6, a crowd of strikers estimated at 5,000, many of them armed, marched through the city's industrial areas, closing factories and battling police.

But the strike was badly weakened by hostility from the same politicians who had passed the law. Calling for the liberation of Chicago from "the riot element," Illinois Republicans united behind the mayor when he called out the Dearborn Light Artillery on May 7 to suppress the strikers. Chicago workers bitterly denounced Republican politicians, but by the middle of June, most workers, including the molders, had gone back to work on a ten-hour-day basis.

Coal miners also built powerful unions in this period. In 1868, miners organized an effective trade union, the Workingmen's Benevolent Association, under the leadership of Irish-born John Siney. A year later, the organization had a membership of over 30,000, including skilled and unskilled workers throughout the entire industry. By 1873, the Miners' National Association was formed, with Siney as its president, to organize all American mine workers into one great industrial union.

A third group, shoemakers, also built on traditions of struggle going back to the early 1800s. Forced into factories, they found themselves working under a new order, subjected to the control of manufacturers and

"Eight Hours and No Surrender!"

The following newspaper account describes a parade that was held in Chicago on May 1, 1867, to celebrate the passage of an Illinois law mandating an eight-hour workday. The description conveys not only a sense of the workers' elation at winning passage of the state law, but also a feeling of how momentous the victory seemed. The parade is reminiscent of similar parades of workers in support of the U.S. Constitution eighty years earlier.

MAGNIFICENT DEMONSTRATION BY CHICAGO'S WORKERS!
MOTTOES AND SLOGANS ON THE BANNERS.
THE MASS MEETINGS.

The Eight-Hour Bill became law yesterday, and to celebrate, the workers of the city turned out by thousand with bands, banners, and the badges of their trades. The demonstration was grandiose and impressive.

The procession . . . extending for more than a mile, made a deep impression on the thousands of onlookers who had gathered in the streets. . . . They covered the stairs, the windows, and even the roofs of the houses where the procession passed by. An almost countless number of banners, flags, slogans, etc. were carried by the marchers. Following are some of the mottos:

"In God We Trust."
"Eight Hours and No Surrender!"
"To the Advantage of the Next Generation."
"Illinois on the Side of Reform."
"The Workers' Millennium. . . . "

The day laborers were represented by a four-horse wagon, on which rode several day laborers with their various tools.

The Molders' Union participated with an eight-horse wagon on which were displayed all the materials, tools, and machinery needed for molding. . . .

Next was a delivery wagon with a coffin bearing the inscription "Death and Burial to the Ten-Hour System. . . . "

Then another delivery wagon appeared, again with a coffin on which were inscribed the words "Death and Burial of the Chicago *Times*"; above the coffin hanging from a gallows was a dummy with a veiled head.

Boston *Daily Evening Voice*, May 1, 1867.

machines. In 1867, the shoe factory workers organized the Knights of St. Crispin, named after the patron saint of shoemakers. Through a series of successful strikes, the organization grew rapidly, and by 1870, it had a membership of nearly 50,000, making it the largest labor union in the nation. Women shoe workers organized the Daughters of St. Crispin to fight what they called "the unjust encroachments upon our rights." Defying the wave of anti-Asian feeling that was sweeping the nation, the Crispins also

The Eight-Hour Movement
Workers demonstrate for the eight-hour day along New York's Bowery in June, 1872. The production of cigars (much in evidence in this engraving), one of the city's major industries, was undergoing rapid change in the 1870s as production moved from craftwork in small shops to manufacture in factories and tenement houses. Matthew Somerville Morgan, *Frank Leslie's Illustrated Newspaper*, June 29, 1872 — American Social History Project.

organized a local of Chinese workers who had been brought to Massachusetts to break a shoemakers' strike in 1870.

Despite the Chinese local, however, a number of racial and ethnic groups organized into separate unions. Ethnic concentrations in particular industries or workplaces, as well as language and cultural differences, proved difficult obstacles for unions to overcome, assuming that they were even willing to make the effort. Many foreign-born workers chose to join associations organized by their countrymen. German immigrants, for instance, created separate craft unions, trades councils, and political organizations. In 1868, Adolph Douai and Friedrich Sorge established a section of the International Workingmen's Association (IWA) in New York, and by 1872, there were twenty sections in the city.

Founded by the German revolutionary Karl Marx in London in 1864, the IWA held that "the final object" of the labor movement was "the abolition of all class rule." Members sought the abolition of private ownership of production and its replacement by a socialist system in which workers would hold political power. They would then run the nation's industries in a democratic fashion, allowing workers to participate in setting production quotas, wages, hours, and working conditions. German American socialists also played a leading role in the great eight-hour-day strikes. Despite the strong opposition of employers and politicians, the eight-hour strikes were partially successful, and organized socialism continued to grow.

Many native-born workers shared the German immigrants' distrust of industrial capitalism and the wage system, if not their more militant ideology. Some turned to cooperation as an alternative to capitalist competition. To circumvent the monopolistic power of the railroads, small farmers had organized in the late 1860s local chapters of the Grange, or Patrons of Husbandry, for the cooperative distribution and purchase of agricultural products. Worker-run cooperative stores and factories that mimicked the Granger co-ops appeared all over the nation in the early 1870s, particularly in textile, shoemaking, and mining towns.

Though members of the middle class hailed cooperation as an alternative to strikes, working-class cooperatives reflected a deep dissatisfaction with the unfettered individualism that was celebrated by industrial capitalism. Cooperation, argued one advocate, would make workers "independent of the capitalist employer," end "ceaseless degradation," and establish a new civilization in which "reason directed by moral principle" would prevail and universal brotherhood would flourish. Yet it was not clear whether such a brotherhood could bring together workers of different ethnic and racial backgrounds, different skill levels, and different sexes.

Racism Stalls the Labor Movement   The resurgence of working-class militancy was capped by the formation of a new federation of labor organizations, the National Labor Union (NLU), which covered workers in diverse craft and industrial occupations. It was founded in Baltimore in 1866 and was led initially by iron molder William Sylvis. The NLU marked a new stage in labor organization: the emergence of a nationwide institution that linked wage workers together in a broad community of interest. Its vision of this community was limited in crucial respects, however. Reflecting the racism and sexism of most white workingmen, the NLU condemned the Chinese and gave only lip service to the rights of African American and women workers. These very exclusions gave rise to alternative movements that both expanded organization among workers and tested the power of labor unions and the law to create a more democratic society.

Many of the trade unions that were affiliated with the NLU had policies that excluded blacks from membership, and in 1867, the NLU ground to a halt on the question of pushing these trade unions to organize African American workers. NLU head Sylvis took a pragmatic line, arguing that "if the workingmen of the white race do not conciliate the blacks, the black vote will be cast against them." But a committee that was assigned to study the question took no action, leaving black workers to fend for themselves.

African American workers had already set about creating their own labor institutions, calling the exclusion of blacks from trade unions "an insult to God and injury to us, and disgrace to humanity." In 1869, a national convention of African Americans created the Colored National Labor Union (CNLU). Led by onetime Baltimore caulker Isaac Myers, the new organization attracted the backing of Frederick Douglass and other prominent African Americans. The CNLU, like Douglass, also actively supported the Republicans, the party of Lincoln and Radical Reconstruction.

The NLU, hoping to create a working-class party, could not understand the political stance of African American workers. White labor leaders refused to recognize that the discrimination that their unions practiced had a far greater effect than did partisan differences in hindering class solidarity. At the same time, the NLU had good reasons for doubting the efficacy of labor's alliance with the Republican Party. Focusing attention on the central demand of white workers, the NLU attempted to obtain a national eight-hour-day law for industrial workers. It ran up against intense opposition not only from employers, but also from Republicans.

"WHAT SHALL WE DO WITH OUR BOYS?"

What Shall We Do with Our Boys?

Some of the most virulent anti-Chinese imagery of the 1870s and 1880s was published in *The Wasp,* a San Francisco illustrated satire magazine. In this cartoon, a grotesque, multi-limbed figure representing Chinese immigrant labor is shown depriving white working-class youths of jobs. George Frederick Keller, *The Wasp,* March 3, 1882 — Richard Samuel West.

Ira Steward, a self-educated Boston machinist and a leader in the eight-hour movement, met this opposition head-on. He maintained that the system of wage labor undermined freedom and civilization. Steward, a veteran of the antislavery movement, likened northern industrial capitalism to southern slavery. Just as the motive for "making a man a slave was to get his labor, or its results, for nothing," Steward argued, so "the motive for employing wage-labor is to secure some of its results for nothing." The eight-hour day, he said, would totally transform this system. As hours were shortened and wages rose, profits would decline, leading to the gradual elimination of the capitalist "as we understand him." Cooperation would replace the wage system, and "a republicanization of labor, as well as a republicanization of government" would occur.

Steward had taken a long step toward adapting the antislavery and republican traditions of thought to the new industrial age. White working people quickly took up his argument, stressing the comparison between southern racial slavery and northern "wage slavery." Only an eight-hour day would allow the worker to feel "full of life and enjoyment," asserted a Massachusetts boot maker, because "the man is no longer a slave, but a man."

Drawing this parallel to slavery, however, did not necessarily put white workers on the side of black workers. Although some farsighted leaders, such as William Sylvis, recognized the potential power of interracial coalitions, those who viewed unionization as a right for whites only drowned out calls for unity. Discrimination against Chinese workers was especially intense. Almost every important native-born labor leader opposed Chinese immigration and advocated instead the absolute exclusion of Chinese. The primary argument was that employers would use "docile" Chinese labor to lower the standard of living of U.S. workers and take away the jobs of native-born Americans.

"Narrow and Unjust": Joseph McDonnell Argues for Acceptance of Chinese Immigrants

In this 1878 editorial in the Labor Standard *attacking demands for Chinese workers to be deported, Irish-born socialist Joseph McDonnell reminds readers that the arrival of virtually every ethnic group in America had been met with the same "intolerant, silly and shameful cry" of "Go home!" Though voices like McDonnell's were exceptional, they serve as reminders that some late-nineteenth-century white Americans were able to pierce the veil of prejudice that others, including some labor leaders, erected against Asian immigrants.*

The cry that the "Chinese must go" is both narrow and unjust. It represents no broad or universal principle. It is merely a repetition of the cry that was raised years ago by native Americans against the immigration of Irishmen, Englishmen, Germans and others from European nations. It now ill becomes those, or the descendants of those, against whom this cry was raised in past years, to raise a similar tocsin against a class of foreigners who have been degraded by ages of oppression. . . . we have no right to raise a cry against any class of human beings because of their nationality. . . .

Let us organize and raise our voices against low wages and long hours. Let us use our organized power against the capitalistic combinations which carry on a slave trade between this country and China and elsewhere, by importing thousands for the purpose of reducing wages in America. Let our first stand be against those rich and intelligent thieves who strive to perpetuate and establish a system of overwork and starvation pay. And then against all those, whether they be Chinese or American, Irish or English, French or German, Spanish or Italian who refuse to co-operate with us for their good and ours, and that of the whole human family.

_____

Unsigned editorial, "The Chinese Must Go," *Labor Standard* (New York), 30 June 1878.

The "docility" of the Chinese, like the penchant for strikebreaking among blacks, was largely mythical. In the spring of 1867, for example, thousands of Chinese railroad workers in the Sierras went on strike, demanding higher wages and an eight-hour day. Management condemned the strike as a "conspiracy" and considered the possibility of transporting 10,000 southern blacks to replace the Chinese. But Charles Crocker, who managed labor for the Central Pacific Railroad, developed a more powerful strategy, similar to Sherman's policy of slaughtering the buffalo to defeat American Indians. Crocker decided to starve the workers into submission. "I stopped the provisions on them, stopped the butchers from butchering, and used [other] such coercive measures," Crocker bragged. The strike was broken within a week.

Most white workers argued for the exclusion of the Chinese from jobs on the same grounds that they argued against African Americans: economic competition. In most cases, the issue of competition was largely illusory, since Chinese immigrants generally occupied the lowest-paying jobs at the bottom of the employment ladder—the jobs that had largely been abandoned by whites. This fact mattered little, however, since the underlying hostility toward the Chinese had as its basis the same deep belief in racial supremacy that shaped white attitudes toward African Americans. Labor editor John Swinton, a humane working-class leader in other ways, spoke for many workers when he argued that the "Mongolian type of humanity is an inferior type—inferior in organic structure, in vital force or physical energy, and in the constitutional conditions of development." Such racial classification schemes were pervasive in the postwar period, when educated middle-class Americans used Social Darwinism and other pseudoscientific theories to justify their belief in the inevitability of their social and political dominance. Anti-Chinese sentiment was equally pervasive among white working-class labor leaders.

Working Women, Unions, and the Vote   Labor leaders also strongly opposed the organization of workingwomen—even white, native-born workingwomen. Nonetheless, wage-earning women, who formed nearly one-quarter of the total nonfarm labor force in 1870, used a variety of tactics to defend and improve their conditions and wages during this period. In 1869, for example, sewing women in Boston petitioned the Massachusetts legislature to provide them with public housing. Although the legislature ignored the request, the petition broke new ground in demanding state intervention to remedy oppressive working conditions.

Many workingwomen, however, turned to trade unions rather than the state to gain protection. Female cigar makers, umbrella sewers, and textile and laundry workers all formed short-lived local unions in these years, but they received little support from white male workers. Of the thirty national unions that existed in the early 1870s, only two—the cigar makers and the printers—admitted women into their ranks and even then not on an equal basis with men. Most organized workingmen believed that the presence of women in the paid labor force was either a temporary phenomenon or, like the employment of African Americans and Chinese immigrants, part of a strategy of employers to lower wages. Clinging to the myth that "all men support all women," they kept women out of their unions in an effort to keep them out of their trades.

This opposition came to a head in 1869, when the NLU, which initially welcomed women to its ranks, expelled women's rights advocate Susan B. Anthony. The conflict behind the expulsion was complex and stemmed in part from Anthony's efforts to train female workers to take the jobs of striking New York printers, who at the time excluded women from apprenticeships in their trade. But many workingmen opposed Anthony because her vision of total female equality—including women's right to vote and equal access to jobs and pay—threatened male domination. In arguing for

"Less Than Twenty-Five Cents a Day": Unskilled Work for Women

In a speech delivered on April 29, 1869, at a convention of Boston working women, a Miss Phelps describes the plight of wage-earning women employed in unskilled and low-paying jobs.

There are before me now women whom I know to be working at the present time for less than twenty-five cents a day. Some of the work they do at these rates from the charitable institutions of the city. These institutions give out work to the women with the professed object of helping them, at which they can scarcely earn enough to keep them from starving; work at which two persons, with their utmost exertions, cannot earn more than forty-five cents a day. These things, I repeat, should be known to the public. They do not know how the daughters of their soldiers fare. I do. They have a little aid, to be sure, from the state, but it is only a little, and they have today to live in miserable garrets without fire; and during the cold winters with scanty food and insufficient clothing, they go out daily to labor along these beautiful streets. Do not you think that they feel the difference between their condition and that of rich, well-dressed ladies who pass them? If they did not, they would be less than human. But they work on bravely and uncomplainingly, venturing all things for the hope of the life that is to come. . . . Last winter many of them did not get work enough at even ten cents a garment to live upon, and were obliged to ask charity. They get it doled out to them, but at what a loss of self-respect, of independence! How much better to have these girls independent, earning their own living, enjoying their own homes, than that they should be compelled to go to station houses for soup! That is what many of them had to do last winter. The people have wondered how these girls live.

Can you imagine how you should live upon twenty cents a day? Rent is one or two dollars at the lowest, and there is your clothes and your food. Count it up. Where does it come from?

Herbert G. Gutman Archive, American Social History Project.

Anthony's expulsion, one NLU member noted, "The lady goes in for taking women away from the washtub, and in the name of heaven who is going there if they don't? I believe in woman doing her work and men marrying them, and supporting them."

Women's rights advocates, rebuffed by union leaders, shared the interest of Boston's sewing workers in using state power to improve the lives of women. They argued that the Reconstruction era amendments to the U.S. Constitution could be interpreted in broad and inclusive ways that would gain rights for women without limiting the rights of African Americans or of white male workers. If women gained the right to vote, advocates of woman suffrage argued, then they could influence legislators to improve women's economic position. The legal strategy they wielded, known as the New Departure, was developed by a husband-and-wife team of Missouri suffragists, Francis and Virginia Minor, in 1869. The Minors emphasized the new idea of federal power as positive and as supportive of individual rights, broadly defined.

Hundreds of women tested the argument for universal suffrage backed up by the power of the national government. Between 1868 and 1872, freed-women, female antislavery veterans, women taxpayers, and women wage earners attempted to register and vote in South Carolina coastal communities; in Vineland, New Jersey; Detroit, Michigan; St. Louis, Missouri; Washington, D.C.; Santa Cruz, California; and dozens of other cities and towns. These attempts to vote led to a number of arrests, the most famous being that of Susan B. Anthony in Rochester, New York, in 1872. Anthony's case came to trial in a federal district court at Canandaigua, New York, in the spring of 1873. The judgment—rendered by a judge rather than a jury—repudiated an inclusive interpretation of the Reconstruction amendments.

The Thirteenth, Fourteenth, and Fifteenth amendments were relatively new additions to the U.S. Constitution and were just starting to be tested. The judge's narrow interpretation of the Fifteenth Amendment in the Anthony case boded ill for their use to broaden political and economic opportunity in the United States. Moreover, this ruling and others like it had important implications for African Americans and for white male workers as well as for women. In 1873, for example, the U.S. Supreme Court upheld both the right of Illinois to bar women from practicing law in the state (in *Bradwell v. Illinois*) and the right of Louisiana to regulate the work of butchers (in the three cases known as the Slaughter-House Cases). The two opinions, handed down on the same day, ensured that the federal powers granted under the Fourteenth Amendment would not be used to advance the interests of either women or workers. By 1875, the voting rights accorded under the Fifteenth Amendment would be similarly narrowed, with the U.S. Supreme Court arguing, in a case brought by Virginia Minor (*Minor v. Happersett*), that the Constitution "does not confer the right of suffrage upon any one." Shortly afterward, the Court used this logic in *United States v. Reese* and *United States v. Cruikshank* to reject the claims of two freedmen who sought protection of their political rights under the Fifteenth Amendment.

A Lady Delegate Reading Her Argument in Favor of Woman's Voting, on the Basis of the Fourteenth and Fifteenth Constitutional Amendments

A delegation of women, including Victoria Woodhull (standing) and Elizabeth Cady Stanton (seated behind her), argued for voting rights before the Judiciary Committee of the House of Representatives in January 1871. *Frank Leslie's Illustrated Newspaper*, February 4, 1871 — American Social History Project.

The Fifteenth Amendment Illustrated

A cartoon in an 1870 edition of *Die Vehme* ("The Star Chamber"), a short-lived St. Louis satirical weekly, supports woman suffrage by denigrating the voting rights of male African Americans, Chinese, and "illiterate" immigrants. Joseph Keppler, *Die Vehme*, April 2, 1870 — American Social History Project.

The judicial redress that women, workers, and African Americans sought in the early 1870s demonstrated that members of these groups viewed both the federal government and union organization as avenues for improving the lives of their families and communities. The rulings that the courts handed down, reinforced by Congress's retreat from the egalitarian implications of Reconstruction era laws, belied these hopes to forge broad alliances in the fight for equal rights. The failure of postwar coalitions across racial, gender, or class lines haunted efforts at collective action for decades to come.

The Panic of 1873   But working people in America faced an even more immediate challenge in the mid-1870s: five years of serious deflation and the longest and most severe depression of the century. An economic crisis of such magnitude not only dealt a heavy blow to labor activism, but also delivered a fatal blow to Reconstruction. In the South, the depression drove many black landowners and renters back into the ranks of laborers, sharply reduced wage levels for African Americans, and helped to transform sharecropping into a system of peonage. In the North, the depression encouraged northern businessmen and workers to focus their attention on problems at home and away from divisive racial politics in the South.

The crisis began on September 18, 1873, triggered by the collapse of Jay Cooke and Company, one of the country's great investment houses. In a matter of days, panic led to runs on a number of banks across the country, and for the first time, the New York Stock Exchange closed. By 1874, construction of railroads and buildings ground to a halt, and tens of thousands of businesses, large and small, went bankrupt. Two years later, in 1876, half the nation's railroads had defaulted on their bonds, and half the nation's iron furnaces were idle. The businesses that survived did so by engaging in cutthroat competition to keep customers, causing the prices of capital and consumer goods to spiral downward.

The nation had experienced economic downturns before, but this one differed in both kind and degree. Not only was it the longest period of uninterrupted economic contraction in U.S. history—a full sixty-five months—but it also exacted an extraordinary human toll. This was because so many more Americans were now dependent on

Panic, as a Health Officer, Sweeping the Garbage out of Wall Street
Despite the ghastly appearance of the figure representing financial panic, this *New York Daily Graphic* cover cartoon of September 29, 1873, subscribed to the belief that such financial "busts" cleansed the economy. Frank Bellew, *New York Daily Graphic*, September 29, 1873 — American Social History Project.

industry for wage labor for their survival. By 1874, fully a million workers were without jobs. City dwellers were hit hardest. In some cities, unemployment approached 25 percent of the workforce. New York alone counted some 100,000 unemployed workers in the winter of 1873–1874. "The sufferings of the working classes are daily increasing," wrote one Philadelphia worker the following summer. "Famine has broken into the home of many of us, and is at the door of all." Workers in small towns could—and did—tend little garden plots or engaged in hunting as a way to survive the hard times. The countryside was flooded, however, with urban men and a few women, wandering from town to town in search of jobs. The wanderers often used the network of railroads that earlier had linked the nation in a single prosperous market, which led to the birth of the popular image of the rail-riding "tramp."

The struggle for public relief now became far more pressing than that for the eight-hour day. In mass meetings, workers in cities across the nation demanded jobs. New York labor leaders in the winter of 1873 demanded to know what would be done "to relieve the necessities of the 10,000 homeless and hungry men and women of our city." They called on officials to create jobs financed by the sale of government bonds. Their request was denied,

NEW YORK CITY.—A TRAMP'S MORNING ABLUTIONS—AN EARLY MORNING SCENE IN MADISON SQUARE.—See Page 341.

A Tramp's Morning Ablutions

An early morning scene in New York's Madison Square during the summer of 1877. To the annoyance of more affluent urban residents, city parks all over the United States served as homes for many of the country's unemployed. *Frank Leslie's Illustrated Newspaper*, July 21, 1877 — American Social History Project.

and the police brutally suppressed subsequent meetings of the unemployed in New York. In Chicago, St. Louis, and other large cities, many in the West, socialists took a leading role in the protests of the unemployed. It was during this period that socialism moved out of its relative isolation in German neighborhoods and began to build a larger following among native-born workers. In these cities, too, demonstrators demanding relief and jobs were often met with violence from public officials and the police and open hostility from the press.

Employers and their supporters, drawing on Social Darwinist theories, viewed the depression as a necessary, if painful, process that would weed out inefficient businesses and allow only the strongest and most creative capitalists (and, by extension, workers) to survive. Business and government leaders were inclined to blame the suffering of working people on "the ignorance, indolence, and immorality" of the poor, and they attacked public works schemes as a form of imported "communism." Business leaders and editors spoke scornfully of the "debased bread of charity." The *Nation* magazine summed up this attitude when its editor, E. L. Godkin, wrote in its Christmas 1875 issue that "free soup must be prohibited, and all classes must learn that soup of any kind, beef or turtle, can be had only by being paid for."

The depression nearly destroyed the young labor movement. At the depression's beginning in 1873, there were almost thirty national trade unions, with 300,000 members. By the end of the decade, the numbers had dropped to eight or nine unions, with only about 50,000 members. Any wage gains that had been won since the Civil War were lost. New York building tradesmen, for example, had earned $2.50 to $3.00 for an eight-hour day in 1872; three years later, they were working a ten-hour day for $1.50 to $2.00.

Northern white working-class voters, preoccupied by the depression and still unconvinced by arguments for racial equality, turned away from their own earlier radicalism and that of Reconstruction. Capitalizing on this weariness, Democrats scored important victories in the North in the elections of 1874 and subsequently took control of the House of Representatives.

For African Americans in the South, the depression coincided with the end of Reconstruction. The political leverage of black workers collapsed, and they had no alternative now but to accept white rule and white control of the economy. One of the most significant effects of the depression in the South was, ironically, the consolidation of a capitalist economy in that region. After 1873, merchants who were unwilling to accept the financial risks of extending credit to poor farmers and farm laborers, black or white, instead charged goods to the accounts of large planters. The planters then resold the goods to workers, usually at inflated prices. Lien laws ensured that any debts that were owed to planters and merchants would be paid before small farmers could take profits for themselves. This meant that in a season of bad harvests or low prices, both of which were frequent in the 1870s, black farm families that had slowly and painfully accumulated a little capital, or even a piece of land, were likely to lose everything.

At the same time, southern manufacturers increased their holdings as falling cotton prices and a growing supply of unskilled wage labor created the possibilities for industrial profits. The Bibb Manufacturing Company in Macon, Georgia, for instance, opened a massive cotton mill in the midst of the depression. Between 1870 and 1880, the number of Macon's African American household heads who worked as artisans or professionals fell precipitously. Among their white neighbors, many men left the skilled trades as well. Some moved into clerical, professional, or proprietary positions. Others joined white women and children in the cotton mills, which flourished despite the economic crisis.

The dual transformation of black landowners, renters, and sharecroppers into day laborers and of poor whites into industrial wage earners created a southern workforce that mirrored, more closely than ever before, that of the North and West. This same transformation ensured that even in the midst of hard times, activism among some southern workers — white and black; rural and urban — would continue. The Readjuster movement in Virginia in the late 1870s and early 1880s typified such interracial cooperation, bringing together black and white small farmers and urban workers in a political coalition to change the state's economic policies. Such activism was largely local and short-lived, but its very persistence suggested the potential for a new labor and political insurgency that could respond to the needs of working people throughout the country. Particularly as industrial develop-

The Red Flag in New York — Riotous Communist Workingmen Driven from Tompkins Square by the Mounted Police, Tuesday, January 13th 1874
Demonstrations by workers and their allies demanding relief and job programs often were met with official violence and were treated with hostility by the nation's press. Matthew Somerville Morgan, *Frank Leslie's Illustrated Newspaper*, January 31, 1874 — American Social History Project.

The Molly Maguires

An illustration from *The Mollie Maguires and the Detectives*, Allan Pinkerton's self-serving account of his detective agency's infiltration of the secret society of Irish miners, shows a clandestine meeting in a bar adorned with pictures of the pope and numerous crucifixes (indicating the miners' allegiance to a foreign power). Pinkerton's work in the service of the Reading Railroad typified the widespread use of private police by railroads and other businesses to suppress unions. Allan Pinkerton, *The Mollie Maguires and the Detectives* (1877) — American Social History Project.

ment moved south and growing numbers of southern workers moved north and west, the preconditions were developed for the creation of a national working class and a national labor movement.

Workers Renew Demands for Economic and Political Power Though insurgencies that crossed lines of region or race were still rare, railroad workers launched a wave of strikes across the nation between November 1873 and July 1874. Engineers, brakemen, and machinists on eighteen railroads walked off their jobs, mainly in response to wage cuts. The workers effectively disrupted railroad traffic through a variety of actions: removing coupling pins from freight cars, tearing up sections of track, and cutting telegraph lines. Railroad companies in turn convinced a number of state governors to send in the militia, and nearly all of the strikes were eventually defeated. Despite those defeats, the strikes indicated the determination of rank-and-file workers to resist attacks on their livelihood.

More characteristic in the mid-1870s were regional labor protests, such as the dramatic Long Strike in the eastern Pennsylvania coalfields. Franklin Gowen, president of the Reading Railroad, had bought up small mines in the area and by 1874 had become the largest coal operator in eastern Pennsylvania. In a plan to break labor's power, he stockpiled coal and then, in the winter of 1874–1875, shut down his mines. The bitter struggle that followed lasted five months, caused tremendous hardships for the miners and their

---

"A 'Tramp and Vagabond'": Looking for Work in 1875

In a September 7, 1875, letter to the National Labor Tribune, *an unemployed mechanic describes his year-long search for work and the rejection he faced.*

Twelve months ago, left penniless by misfortune, I started from New York in search of employment. . . . During this year I have traversed seventeen states and obtained in that time six weeks' work. I have faced starvation; been months at a time without a bed, when the thermometer was 30 degrees below zero. Last winter I slept in the woods, and while honestly seeking employment I have been two and three days without food. When, in God's name, I asked for something to keep body and soul together, I have been repulsed as a "tramp and vagabond."

National Labor Tribune, September 7, 1875.

families, and was marked by violence on both sides. "Coal and Iron Police" hired by Gowen shot indiscriminately into crowds of workers, while members of the Workingmen's Benevolent Association (WBA), the union that represented the miners, attacked strikebreakers with clubs and stones.

Gowen also hired the Pinkerton National Detective Agency to infiltrate the miners' organization, providing further ammunition against the workers. Allan Pinkerton had formed a detective agency and private security company in Cook County, Illinois, in the 1850s after consulting with several midwestern railroad companies. Initially, his agents provided security for private businesses, since city police forces were generally small and underfunded. They also hired out their services to army contractors and tracked western outlaws such as Jesse James and his gang. In 1860, Pinkerton had gained national fame when he foiled a plot to assassinate President-elect Abraham Lincoln. By the 1870s, railroads and other corporations regularly hired Pinkerton agents to infiltrate labor unions and guard company property against strikers, such as the

Pennsylvania miners. Despite their courage and determination, the miners of the WBA could not overcome the combined power of the Reading Railroad Company and the Pinkertons. They finally had to concede defeat and reluctantly accept a 20 percent wage cut.

In the winter of 1876, Pennsylvania coal miners were again confronted by the anger of mine owners, now cloaked in the robes of law. James McParlan, a Pinkerton Agency operative who had lived among the Irish miners of eastern Pennsylvania for several years, stepped forward and became a leading witness in a series of sensational murder trials. McParlan testified that the murders of a mine boss and a miner were the result of a conspiracy by the Molly Maguires, a shadowy organization of Irish immigrant workers who were reputed to be willing to redress their grievances through violence. He also claimed that the "Mollies" dominated the WBA.

Greenback Candidate

The early craftworker career of the Greenback Party's 1876 presidential candidate, the businessman and philanthropist Peter Cooper, is featured on a campaign poster. Courtesy of The Cooper Union.

Despite questions about the validity of the testimony of McParlan and other Pinkerton agents, more than twenty miners were found guilty of murder and related charges in the spring of 1876. A year later, ten were hanged and over the course of 1878 and 1879 ten more would be executed. Because of widespread press coverage, these trials helped to link in the public mind trade unionism and terrorism. The perception destroyed unionism in eastern Pennsylvania mining for twenty years.

The lack of responsiveness to workers' needs on the part of the two existing political parties also increased working-class dissatisfaction with traditional politics during the depression years. With the growing disfranchisement of African Americans in the South and the disaffection of northern workingmen, the Republican Party increasingly emphasized business development and looked to businessmen as its most important social base. Politicians of both parties were accepting bribes from big business to guarantee the politicians' support on critical issues. Consequently, the two major parties, which had been diametrically opposed a mere decade earlier, now seemed indistinguishable.

As working-class activists grew increasingly dissatisfied with both parties, they looked for other, more independent roads to political influence. What they found was the Greenback Party, organized on a national level by farmers in 1875. The new party stood for governmental action to expand the currency with paper "greenbacks" that were not tied to the nation's gold reserves — a reform that was intended to inflate prices, thus benefiting debtors and providing capital needed for economic growth. Despite the protests of eight-hour advocates such as Ira Steward, many labor leaders — including Richard Trevellick, A. C. Cameron, and John Siney — rallied to the Greenback cause, marking their final rejection of the Republican Party.

Other workers, mainly from the cities and including a large core of immigrants, based their hopes on the Workingmen's Party of the United States. The Socialists who founded this party in 1876 put aside their differences and took a major step toward bringing immigrant and native-born workers together in the same political organization.

The Prohibition Party, inspired by grassroots campaigns against saloons in Ohio in 1874 and 1875, also began nominating candidates for state and national elections. Neither the Greenback nor the Workingmen's Party offered any real threat to Republican dominance, however. The Prohibitionists were limited by women's lack of voting rights, since it was women who had led the attacks on "rum sellers" across the Midwest. Nonetheless, the willingness of workers to experiment with alternative party affiliations suggested a new awareness of their place in national politics.

The Great Uprising of 1877   The very events that crushed the aspirations of many black and working-class Americans — the "redemption" of

The Philadelphia Militia Firing on the Mob, at the Twenty-eighth Street Crossing, near the Union Depot of the Pennsylvania Railroad, on Saturday Afternoon, July 21st A panoramic engraving based on an eyewitness sketch delineates the composition of the crowd that gathered to observe and protest the arrival of the Philadelphia militia. John Donaghy, *Frank Leslie's Illustrated Newspaper*, August 4, 1877 — American Social History Project.

southern state governments, the opening of new investment opportunities in the former Confederacy, the tainted victory of the Republican Party in the 1876 presidential election, and the defeat of labor radicalism by the trials of the Molly Maguires—buoyed the hopes of businessmen. Although the country had not yet emerged from the depression, the major problem of cutthroat competition was gradually being eliminated by the emergence of large monopolies in a number of basic industries. And unionism was clearly in retreat. The public hanging of ten Molly Maguires in June 1877 seemed to close the book on a defeated post–Civil War labor movement.

Within a month of the hangings, however, it would be clear that business confidence was profoundly misplaced. In July 1877, a massive railroad strike, the first truly national strike in the country's history, shook the very foundations of the political and economic order. On July 16, 1877, in Martinsburg, West Virginia, workers on the Baltimore and Ohio (B&O) railroad staged a spontaneous strike in response to yet another wage cut imposed by the railroad company. Three days later, as the strike intensified, President Hayes ordered federal troops into West Virginia to protect the B&O and the nation from "insurrection."

The use of federal troops in a domestic labor dispute incited popular anger across the country. In Baltimore, the Maryland state militia fired on huge crowds of angry workers, leaving eleven dead and forty wounded. Work stoppages rapidly spread north and west along the railroad lines to Pennsylvania, where, in Pittsburgh, the strike reached its most dramatic climax. Because many Pittsburgh citizens sympathized with the railroad workers, the Pennsylvania Railroad sought help from outside the city. But when the state militia reached Pittsburgh on July 21, a large and angry crowd

July 22, 1877

The interior of the Pennsylvania Railroad's upper roundhouse after the battle between the Philadelphia militia and Pittsburgh strikers. This picture was part of a series of forty-four stereographs by S. V. Albee that were sold commercially as "The Railroad War." Stereographs were cards with "double photographs" that, when viewed through a "stereoscope," looked three-dimensional. By the 1870s, stereoscope viewing was one of the most popular forms of home entertainment. S. V. Albee, "The Railroad War" — Paul Dickson Collection.

of strikers and sympathizers met them. Unnerved by their reception, the soldiers suddenly thrust their bayonets at members of the crowd. When rocks were thrown at the troops, they answered with a volley of rifle fire. When the gunfire finally ended, twenty Pittsburgh citizens, including a woman and three small children, lay dead.

News of the killings quickly spread. Pittsburgh residents, including thousands of workers from nearby mills, mines, and factories, converged on the Pennsylvania Railroad yards. By dawn, they had set fire to the railroad roundhouse to which the militiamen had retreated. Twenty more Pittsburgh residents and five soldiers were killed in the ensuing gun battle.

In the next few days, the strike spread across the Midwest. Workers took over entire towns, shutting down work until employers met their demands. The same railroad and telegraph lines that had unified the nation and laid the groundwork for the full emergence of industrial capitalism also linked and unified workers' protests. Without any central organization (most national unions were defunct as a result of the 1870s depression), the conflict spawned local committees, many led by anarchists and socialists, that provided unity and direction to the strike. In Chicago, for example, the strike quickly became a citywide general strike that touched off open class warfare. In St. Louis, by contrast, thousands of workers participated in a largely peaceful general strike that shut down virtually all of the city's industries, while government officials fled. Black workers in St. Louis took an active role in the strike, closing down canneries and docks. When an African American steamboat worker, addressing a crowd of white workers, asked, "Will you stand to us regardless of color?" the crowd responded, "We will! We will! We will!" In other strikes, however, racism prevailed, particularly in the Far West. In San Francisco, a crowd gathered to discuss strike action but ended up rampaging through the city's Chinese neighborhoods, killing several residents and burning buildings.

But the massive national strike was directed mainly against the railroads and the unchecked corporate power they typified. Most working people in 1877 were seeking not to overthrow capitalism as a whole, but to

"The Grand Army of Starvation": The 1877 Strike

At a rally called on July 23, Albert Parsons, a printer and a leader of the Workingmen's Party, addressed 10,000 striking Chicago workers and their supporters. Parsons's speech evoked widely held republican ideals; his opening image of a "grand army of starvation" recalls the Grand Army of the Republic, a name that had been used for the victorious Union Army in the Civil War.

We are assembled as the grand army of starvation. Fellow workers, let us recollect that in this great Republic that has been handed down to us by our forefathers from 1776, that while we have the Republic we still have hope. A mighty spirit is animating the hearts of the American people today. When I say the American people I mean the backbone of the country—the men who till the soil, guide the machine, who weave the material and cover the backs of civilized men. . . . [We] have demanded of those in possession of the means of production . . . that they not be allowed to turn us upon the earth as vagrants and tramps. . . . We have come together this evening, if it is possible, to find the means by which the great gloom that now hangs over our Republic can be lifted and once more the rays of happiness can be shed on the face of this broad land.

———————

Chicago *Inter-Ocean,* July 25, 1877.

set limits on the system's unbridled economic power and to assert workers' right to an equitable share of the extraordinary economic bounty they helped to produce. Despite the nationwide mobilization of workers in the first truly national strike in American history, in the end, the strike failed when faced with the massive power of the railroads and their allies in state and national government.

Conclusion: The Lessons of 1877

To fully engage in successful collective action, workers would have to create a labor movement in the future that would welcome a national and increasingly diverse labor force. Native-born and immigrant workers, men and women, African Americans, Asians, Indians, Mexican Americans, and whites, skilled and unskilled, industrial, agricultural, and domestic workers would have to find common cause in the same way that planters and industrialists, railroad magnates and coal operators, moderate Republicans and New South Democrats had. And they would have to do so in a nation that now embraced lands from the Atlantic to the Pacific Coast and beyond; that was increasingly defined by industrial and urban developments; and that was venturing ever further into international arenas of commerce, labor, and war. Moreover, workers would have to deal with a national—and international—economy that was marked by periodic panics and depressions.

Waiting for the Reduction of the Army

As this 1878 cartoon from the *New York Daily Graphic* indicated, in the aftermath of the "Great Uprising" of 1877, Indians, trade unionists, immigrants, and tramps were often grouped together in the press as symbols of disorder and opposition to the nation's progress. Ph. G. Cusachs, *New York Daily Graphic*, June 14, 1878 — American Social History Project.

By 1877, the United States had recovered from the Panic of 1873 and returned to prosperity. Still, as the 1877 strike made clear, even prosperity did not promise opportunity or equality for all Americans. Those were goals that generations of workers, from diverse backgrounds, would continue to seek.

The Years in Review

1859

- The National Molders' Union is founded as part of nationwide growth of trade unions.

1862

- Congress passes the Homestead Act, which allows any adult citizen or permanent immigrant to claim 160 acres of public land for a $10 fee; final title to the land is granted after five years of residence.
- Congress also passes the Morrill Act, which gives land grants to states to build state universities, using profits from the sale of public lands to the railroads.

1864

- U.S. soldiers massacre Cheyennes at Sand Creek, leaving 200 men, women, and children dead.

1866

- The National Labor Union (NLU), a federation of labor organizations covering workers in diverse craft and industrial occupations, is founded.
- Congress passes the Mineral Act, granting title to millions of acres of western land to mining companies.

1867

- Congress declares a new Indian policy that aims at concentrating Indians on two reservations in the Dakota and Oklahoma territories.
- Shoemakers organize the Knights of St. Crispin, named after the patron saint of shoemakers. By 1870, the Knights of St. Crispin is the largest labor union in the nation.
- The Illinois legislature passes a law mandating an eight-hour workday; after Chicago employers fail to uphold the law and workers strike in protest, the law is rescinded.

1868

- Republican Ulysses S. Grant is elected president.
- German immigrants Adolph Douai and Friedrich Sorge organize the socialist International Workingmen's Association in New York.
- Coal miners organize the Workingmen's Benevolent Association; five years later, they organize the larger Miner's National Association.

1869

- The transcontinental railroad is completed at Promontory Point, Utah.
- General William Tecumseh Sherman is appointed commander of the U.S. Army.
- A national convention of African Americans creates the Colored National Labor Union (CNLU) in response to exclusion from other labor unions.

1870

- The Fifteenth Amendment, granting all citizens the right to vote regardless of color, is ratified.

1871

- A Pennsylvania tannery discovers that buffalo hides can be used to make commercial leather.
- Former slave Benjamin Singleton founds the Tennessee Real Estate and Homestead Association to recruit African Americans for emigration to Kansas; in 1878, he arrives there with 200 African American emigrants.

1872

- Ulysses S. Grant is reelected president; the Republican Party continues its retreat from the defense of African American rights.
- Congress passes the Apex Mining Act, which allows mining companies to blast freely through mountains, disadvantaging individual miners and ravaging the environment.

1873

- An economic depression, triggered by the collapse of Jay Cooke and Company, begins; by 1874, fully a million workers are without jobs.
- The Miners' National Association forms under the leadership of John Siney.
- The U.S. Supreme Court hands down two decisions (*Bradwell v. Illinois* and the Slaughter-House Cases) ruling that the Fourteenth Amendment would not be used to advance the interests of either women or workers.

1874

- The Long Strike in the eastern Pennsylvania coalfields pits miners against the Reading Railroad; after five months of violence on both sides and hardship for the miners, the miners concede defeat.

1875

- Farmers looking to artificially inflate prices and create capital needed for economic growth organize the Greenback Party.

1876

- Initial returns in the presidential election give victory to Democrat Samuel J. Tilden, but in February 1877, a special commission makes Republican Rutherford B. Hayes president.
- The Centennial Exposition is held in Philadelphia.

- Sioux warriors defeat General George Custer's Seventh Cavalry at the Battle of Little Big Horn in the Dakota territory.
- More than twenty alleged members of the Molly Maguires are found guilty of murder and related charges.
- Socialists form the Workingmen's Party of the United States.

1877

- A railroad strike, the first national strike in U.S. history, spreads from coast to coast in two weeks. One hundred people die, and millions of dollars' worth of property is destroyed. President Hayes sends federal troops in to protect the interests of the railroad owners.
- U.S. Army troops defeat Sioux and Cheyenne warriors, forcing these once powerful tribes back onto ever-shrinking reservations in the Dakota territory.

Additional Readings

For more on immigration, race, and labor in the West, see: Susan Armitage and Elizabeth Jameson, eds., *Writing the Range: Race, Class and Culture in the Women's West* (1997); Colin G. Calloway, ed., *Our Hearts Fell to the Ground: Plains Indian Views of How the West Was Lost* (1996); Jerome A. Greene, ed., *Lakota and Cheyenne Indian Views of the Great Sioux War, 1876–1877* (1994); Stuart C. Miller, *The Unwelcome Immigrant: American Images of the Chinese, 1785–1882* (1969); Victor Nee and Brett de Barry Nee, *Longtime Californ': A Documentary Study of an American Chinatown* (1972); Alexander Saxton, *The Indispensable Enemy: Labor and the Anti-Chinese Movement in California* (1971); Ronald Takaki, *Iron Cages: Race and Culture in Nineteenth-Century America* (1979); Quintard Taylor, *In Search of the Racial Frontier: African Americans in the American West, 1528–1990* (1998); John Kuo Wei Tchen, *The Chinese of America* (1980); and Robert M. Utley, *The Indian Frontier of the American West, 1846–1890* (1984).

For more on industrialization and urbanization, see: Sven Beckert, *The Monied Metropolis: New York City and the Consolidation of the American Bourgeoisie, 1850–1896* (2003); Joshua Brown, *Beyond the Lines: Pictorial Reporting, Everyday Life, and the Crisis of Gilded Age America* (2002); Alfred D. Chandler, *The Visible Hand: The Managerial Revolution in American Business* (1977); John R. Commons, ed., *A Documentary History of American Industrial Society* (1958); Melvin Dubofsky, *Industrialism and the American Worker, 1865–1920* (1985); Herbert G. Gutman, *Work, Culture and Society in Industrializing America* (1976); William Harris, *The Harder We*

Run: Black Workers Since the Civil War (1982); Walter Licht, *Working for the Railroad: The Organization of Work in the Nineteenth Century* (1983); David M. Scobey, *Empire City: The Making and Meaning of the New York City Landscape* (2003); and Alan Trachtenberg, *The Incorporation of America: Culture and Society in the Gilded Age* (1982).

For more on the resurgence of the labor movement, see: Robert V. Bruce, *1877: Year of Violence* (1959); Philip S. Foner, *Organized Labor and the Black Worker, 1619–1973* (1974); Kevin Kenny, *Making Sense of the Molly Maguires* (1998); Sidney Lens, *The Labor Wars: From the Molly Maguires to the Sitdowns* (1973); and David Montgomery, *Beyond Equality: Labor and the Radical Republicans, 1862–1872* (1967).

For more on women's work and suffrage, see: Ellen Carol DuBois, *Woman's Suffrage and Women's Rights* (1998); Ann Gordon et al., eds., *African American Women and the Vote, 1837–1965* (1997); Jacqueline Jones, *Labor of Love, Labor of Sorrow: Black Women, Work and the Family from Slavery to the Present* (1985); and Alice Kessler-Harris, *Out to Work: A History of Wage-Earning Women in the United States* (1982).

Appendix 1
The Declaration of Independence

IN CONGRESS, July 4, 1776.

The unanimous Declaration of the thirteen united States of America,

When in the Course of human events, it becomes necessary for one people to dissolve the political bands which have connected them with another, and to assume among the powers of the earth, the separate and equal station to which the Laws of Nature and of Nature's God entitle them, a decent respect to the opinions of mankind requires that they should declare the causes which impel them to the separation.

We hold these truths to be self-evident, that all men are created equal, that they are endowed by their Creator with certain unalienable Rights, that among these are Life, Liberty and the pursuit of Happiness. — That to secure these rights, Governments are instituted among Men, deriving their just powers from the consent of the governed, — That whenever any Form of Government becomes destructive of these ends, it is the Right of the People to alter or to abolish it, and to institute new Government, laying its foundation on such principles and organizing its powers in such form, as to them shall seem most likely to effect their Safety and Happiness. Prudence, indeed, will dictate that Governments long established should not be changed for light and transient causes; and accordingly all experience hath shewn, that mankind are more disposed to suffer, while evils are sufferable, than to right themselves by abolishing the forms to which they are accustomed. But when a long train of abuses and usurpations, pursuing invariably the same Object evinces a design to reduce them under absolute Despotism, it is their right, it is their duty, to throw off such Government, and to provide new Guards for their future security.—Such has been the patient sufferance of these Colonies; and such is now the necessity which constrains them to alter their former Systems of Government. The history of the present King of Great Britain is a history of repeated injuries and usurpations, all having in direct object the establishment of an absolute Tyranny over these States. To prove this, let Facts be submitted to a candid world.

He has refused his Assent to Laws, the most wholesome and necessary for the public good.

He has forbidden his Governors to pass Laws of immediate and pressing importance, unless suspended in their operation till his Assent should be obtained; and when so suspended, he has utterly neglected to attend to them.

He has refused to pass other Laws for the accommodation of large districts of people, unless those people would relinquish the right of Representation in the Legislature, a right inestimable to them and formidable to tyrants only.

He has called together legislative bodies at places unusual, uncomfortable, and distant from the depository of their public Records, for the sole purpose of fatiguing them into compliance with his measures.

He has dissolved Representative Houses repeatedly, for opposing with manly firmness his invasions on the rights of the people.

He has refused for a long time, after such dissolutions, to cause others to be elected; whereby the Legislative powers, incapable of Annihilation, have returned to the People at large for their exercise; the State remaining in the mean time exposed to all the dangers of invasion from without, and convulsions within.

He has endeavoured to prevent the population of these States; for that purpose obstructing the Laws for Naturalization of Foreigners; refusing to pass others to encourage their migrations hither, and raising the conditions of new Appropriations of Lands.

He has obstructed the Administration of Justice, by refusing his Assent to Laws for establishing Judiciary powers.

He has made Judges dependent on his Will alone, for the tenure of their offices, and the amount and payment of their salaries.

He has erected a multitude of New Offices, and sent hither swarms of Officers to harrass our people, and eat out their substance.

He has kept among us, in times of peace, Standing Armies without the Consent of our legislatures.

He has affected to render the Military independent of and superior to the Civil power.

He has combined with others to subject us to a jurisdiction foreign to our constitution, and unacknowledged by our laws; giving his Assent to their Acts of pretended Legislation:

For Quartering large bodies of armed troops among us:

For protecting them, by a mock Trial, from punishment for any Murders which they should commit on the Inhabitants of these States:

For cutting off our Trade with all parts of the world:

For imposing Taxes on us without our Consent:

For depriving us in many cases, of the benefits of Trial by Jury:

For transporting us beyond Seas to be tried for pretended offences

For abolishing the free System of English Laws in a neighbouring Province, establishing therein an Arbitrary government, and enlarging its Boundaries so as to render it at once an example and fit instrument for introducing the same absolute rule into these Colonies:

For taking away our Charters, abolishing our most valuable Laws, and altering fundamentally the Forms of our Governments:

For suspending our own Legislatures, and declaring themselves invested with power to legislate for us in all cases whatsoever.

He has abdicated Government here, by declaring us out of his Protection and waging War against us.

He has plundered our seas, ravaged our Coasts, burnt our towns, and destroyed the lives of our people.

He is at this time transporting large Armies of foreign Mercenaries to compleat the works of death, desolation and tyranny, already begun with circumstances of Cruelty & perfidy scarcely paralleled in the most barbarous ages, and totally unworthy the Head of a civilized nation.

He has constrained our fellow Citizens taken Captive on the high Seas to bear Arms against their Country, to become the executioners of their friends and Brethren, or to fall themselves by their Hands.

He has excited domestic insurrections amongst us, and has endeavoured to bring on the inhabitants of our frontiers, the merciless Indian Savages, whose known rule of warfare, is an undistinguished destruction of all ages, sexes and conditions.

In every stage of these Oppressions We have Petitioned for Redress in the most humble terms: Our repeated Petitions have been answered only by repeated injury. A Prince whose character is thus marked by every act which may define a Tyrant, is unfit to be the ruler of a free people.

Nor have We been wanting in attentions to our Brittish brethren. We have warned them from time to time of attempts by their legislature to extend an unwarrantable jurisdiction over us. We have reminded them of the circumstances of our emigration and settlement here. We have appealed to their native justice and magnanimity, and we have conjured them by the ties of our common kindred to disavow these usurpations, which, would inevitably interrupt our connections and correspondence. They too have been deaf to the voice of justice and of consanguinity. We must, therefore, acquiesce in the necessity, which denounces our Separation, and hold them, as we hold the rest of mankind, Enemies in War, in Peace Friends.

We, therefore, the Representatives of the united States of America, in General Congress, Assembled, appealing to the Supreme Judge of the world for the rectitude of our intentions, do, in the Name, and by Authority of the good People of these Colonies, solemnly publish and declare, That these United Colonies are, and of Right ought to be Free and Independent States; that they are Absolved from all Allegiance to the British Crown, and that all political connection between them and the State of Great Britain, is and ought to be totally dissolved; and that as Free and Independent States, they have full Power to levy War, conclude Peace, contract Alliances, establish Commerce, and to do all other Acts and Things which Independent States may of right do. And for the support of this Declaration, with a firm reliance on the protection of divine Providence, we mutually pledge to each other our Lives, our Fortunes and our sacred Honor.

Georgia
Button Gwinnett
Lyman Hall
George Walton

North Carolina
William Hooper
Joseph Hewes
John Penn

South Carolina
Edward Rutledge
Thomas Heyward, Jr.
Thomas Lynch, Jr.
Arthur Middleton

Maryland
Samuel Chase
William Paca
Thomas Stone
Charles Carroll of
    Carrollton

Virginia
George Wythe
Richard Henry Lee
Thomas Jefferson
Benjamin Harrison
Thomas Nelson, Jr.
Francis Lightfoot Lee
Carter Braxton

Pennsylvania
Robert Morris
Benjamin Rush
Benjamin Franklin
John Morton
George Clymer
James Smith
George Taylor
James Wilson
George Ross

Massachusetts
John Hancock

Delaware
Caesar Rodney
George Read
Thomas McKean

New York
William Floyd
Philip Livingston
Francis Lewis
Lewis Morris

New Jersey
Richard Stockton
John Witherspoon
Francis Hopkinson
John Hart
Abraham Clark

New Hampshire
Josiah Bartlett
William Whipple

Massachusetts
Samuel Adams
John Adams
Robert Treat Paine
Elbridge Gerry

Rhode Island
Stephen Hopkins
William Ellery

Connecticut
Roger Sherman
Samuel Huntington
William Williams
Oliver Wolcott

New Hampshire
Matthew Thornton

Appendix 2
Constitution of the United States of America

Note: The following text is a transcription of the Constitution in its original form.

We the People of the United States, in Order to form a more perfect Union, establish Justice, insure domestic Tranquility, provide for the common defence, promote the general Welfare, and secure the Blessings of Liberty to ourselves and our Posterity, do ordain and establish this Constitution for the United States of America.

Article I

Section 1
All legislative Powers herein granted shall be vested in a Congress of the United States, which shall consist of a Senate and House of Representatives.

Section 2
The House of Representatives shall be composed of Members chosen every second Year by the People of the several States, and the Electors in each State shall have the Qualifications requisite for Electors of the most numerous Branch of the State Legislature.

No Person shall be a Representative who shall not have attained to the Age of twenty five Years, and been seven Years a Citizen of the United States, and who shall not, when elected, be an Inhabitant of that State in which he shall be chosen.

Representatives and direct Taxes shall be apportioned among the several States which may be included within this Union, according to their respective Numbers, which shall be determined by adding to the whole Number of free Persons, including those bound to Service for a Term of Years, and excluding Indians not taxed, three fifths of all other Persons. The actual Enumeration shall be made within three Years after the first Meeting of the Congress of the United States, and within every subsequent Term of ten Years, in such Manner as they shall by Law direct. The Number of Representatives shall not exceed one for every thirty Thousand, but each State shall have at Least one Representative; and until such enumeration shall be made, the State of New Hampshire shall be entitled to chuse three, Massachusetts eight, Rhode-Island and Providence Plantations one, Connecticut five, New-York six, New Jersey four, Pennsylvania eight, Delaware one, Maryland six, Virginia ten, North Carolina five, South Carolina five, and Georgia three.

When vacancies happen in the Representation from any State, the Executive Authority thereof shall issue Writs of Election to fill such Vacancies.

The House of Representatives shall chuse their Speaker and other Officers; and shall have the sole Power of Impeachment.

Section 3
The Senate of the United States shall be composed of two Senators from each State, chosen by the Legislature thereof for six Years; and each Senator shall have one Vote.

Immediately after they shall be assembled in Consequence of the first Election, they shall be divided as equally as may be into three Classes. The Seats of the Senators of the first Class shall be vacated at the Expiration of the second Year, of the second Class at the Expiration of the fourth Year, and of the third Class at the Expiration of the sixth Year, so that one third may be chosen every second Year; and if Vacancies happen by Resignation, or otherwise, during the Recess of the Legislature of any State, the Executive thereof may make temporary Appointments until the next Meeting of the Legislature, which shall then fill such Vacancies.

No Person shall be a Senator who shall not have attained to the Age of thirty Years, and been nine Years a Citizen of the United States, and who shall not, when elected, be an Inhabitant of that State for which he shall be chosen.

The Vice President of the United States shall be President of the Senate, but shall have no Vote, unless they be equally divided.

The Senate shall chuse their other Officers, and also a President pro tempore, in the Absence of the Vice President, or when he shall exercise the Office of President of the United States.

The Senate shall have the sole Power to try all Impeachments. When sitting for that Purpose, they shall be on Oath or Affirmation. When the President of the United States is tried, the Chief Justice shall preside: And no Person shall be convicted without the Concurrence of two thirds of the Members present.

Judgment in Cases of Impeachment shall not extend further than to removal from Office, and disqualification to hold and enjoy any Office of honor, Trust or Profit under the United States: but the Party convicted shall nevertheless be liable and subject to Indictment, Trial, Judgment and Punishment, according to Law.

Section 4

The Times, Places and Manner of holding Elections for Senators and Representatives, shall be prescribed in each State by the Legislature thereof; but the Congress may at any time by Law make or alter such Regulations, except as to the Places of chusing Senators.

The Congress shall assemble at least once in every Year, and such Meeting shall be on the first Monday in December, unless they shall by Law appoint a different Day.

Section 5

Each House shall be the Judge of the Elections, Returns and Qualifications of its own Members, and a Majority of each shall constitute a Quorum to do Business; but a smaller Number may adjourn from day to day, and may be authorized to compel the Attendance of absent Members, in such Manner, and under such Penalties as each House may provide.

Each House may determine the Rules of its Proceedings, punish its Members for disorderly Behaviour, and, with the Concurrence of two thirds, expel a Member.

Each House shall keep a Journal of its Proceedings, and from time to time publish the same, excepting such Parts as may in their Judgment require Secrecy; and the Yeas and Nays of the Members of either House on any question shall, at the Desire of one fifth of those Present, be entered on the Journal.

Neither House, during the Session of Congress, shall, without the Consent of the other, adjourn for more than three days, nor to any other Place than that in which the two Houses shall be sitting.

Section 6

The Senators and Representatives shall receive a Compensation for their Services, to be ascertained by Law, and paid out of the Treasury of the United States. They shall in all Cases, except Treason, Felony and Breach of the Peace, be privileged from Arrest during their Attendance at the Session of their respective Houses, and in going to and returning from the same; and for any Speech or Debate in either House, they shall not be questioned in any other Place.

No Senator or Representative shall, during the Time for which he was elected, be appointed to any civil Office under the Authority of the United States, which shall have been created, or the Emoluments whereof shall have been encreased during such time; and no Person holding any Office under the United States, shall be a Member of either House during his Continuance in Office.

Section 7

All Bills for raising Revenue shall originate in the House of Representatives; but the Senate may propose or concur with Amendments as on other Bills.

Every Bill which shall have passed the House of Representatives and the Senate, shall, before it become a Law, be presented to the President of the United States: If he approve he shall sign it, but if not he shall return it, with his Objections to that House in which it shall have originated, who shall enter the Objections at large on their Journal, and proceed to reconsider it. If after such Reconsideration two thirds of that House shall agree to pass the Bill, it shall be sent, together with the Objections, to the other House, by which it shall likewise be reconsidered, and if approved by two thirds of that House, it shall become a Law. But in all such Cases the Votes of both Houses shall be determined by yeas and Nays, and the Names of the Persons voting for and against the Bill shall be entered on the Journal of each House respectively. If any Bill shall not be returned by the President within ten Days (Sundays excepted) after it shall have been presented to him, the Same shall be a Law, in like Manner as if he had signed it, unless the Congress by their Adjournment prevent its Return, in which Case it shall not be a Law.

Every Order, Resolution, or Vote to which the Concurrence of the Senate and House of Representatives may be necessary (except on a question of Adjournment) shall be presented to the President of the United States; and before the Same shall take Effect, shall be approved by him, or being disapproved by him, shall be repassed by two thirds of the Senate and House of Representatives, according to the Rules and Limitations prescribed in the Case of a Bill.

Section 8
The Congress shall have Power To lay and collect Taxes, Duties, Imposts and Excises, to pay the Debts and provide for the common Defence and general Welfare of the United States; but all Duties, Imposts and Excises shall be uniform throughout the United States;

To borrow Money on the credit of the United States;

To regulate Commerce with foreign Nations, and among the several States, and with the Indian Tribes;

To establish an uniform Rule of Naturalization, and uniform Laws on the subject of Bankruptcies throughout the United States;

To coin Money, regulate the Value thereof, and of foreign Coin, and fix the Standard of Weights and Measures;

To provide for the Punishment of counterfeiting the Securities and current Coin of the United States;

To establish Post Offices and post Roads; To promote the Progress of Science and useful Arts, by securing for limited Times to Authors and Inventors the exclusive Right to their respective Writings and Discoveries;

To constitute Tribunals inferior to the supreme Court;

To define and punish Piracies and Felonies committed on the high Seas, and Offences against the Law of Nations;

To declare War, grant Letters of Marque and Reprisal, and make Rules concerning Captures on Land and Water;

To raise and support Armies, but no Appropriation of Money to that Use shall be for a longer Term than two Years;

To provide and maintain a Navy;

To make Rules for the Government and Regulation of the land and naval Forces;

To provide for calling forth the Militia to execute the Laws of the Union, suppress Insurrections and repel Invasions;

To provide for organizing, arming, and disciplining, the Militia, and for governing such Part of them as may be employed in the Service of the United States, reserving to the States respectively, the Appointment of the Officers, and the Authority of training the Militia according to the discipline prescribed by Congress;

To exercise exclusive Legislation in all Cases whatsoever, over such District (not exceeding ten Miles square) as may, by Cession of particular States, and the Acceptance of Congress, become the Seat of the Government of the United States, and to exercise like Authority over all Places purchased by the Consent of the Legislature of the State in which the Same shall be, for the Erection of Forts, Magazines, Arsenals, dock-Yards, and other needful Buildings;—And

To make all Laws which shall be necessary and proper for carrying into Execution the foregoing Powers, and all other Powers vested by this Constitution in the Government of the United States, or in any Department or Officer thereof.

Section 9
The Migration or Importation of such Persons as any of the States now existing shall think proper to admit, shall not be prohibited by the Congress prior to the Year one thousand eight hundred and eight, but a Tax or duty may be imposed on such Importation, not exceeding ten dollars for each Person.

The Privilege of the Writ of Habeas Corpus shall not be suspended, unless when in Cases of Rebellion or Invasion the public Safety may require it.

No Bill of Attainder or ex post facto Law shall be passed.

No Capitation, or other direct, Tax shall be laid, unless in Proportion to the Census or enumeration herein before directed to be taken.

No Tax or Duty shall be laid on Articles exported from any State.

No Preference shall be given by any Regulation of Commerce or Revenue to the Ports of one State over those of another; nor shall Vessels bound to, or from, one State, be obliged to enter, clear, or pay Duties in another.

No Money shall be drawn from the Treasury, but in Consequence of Appropriations made by Law; and a regular Statement and Account of the Receipts and Expenditures of all public Money shall be published from time to time.

No Title of Nobility shall be granted by the United States: And no Person holding any Office of Profit or Trust under them, shall, without the Consent of the Congress, accept of any present, Emolument, Office, or Title, of any kind whatever, from any King, Prince, or foreign State.

Section 10

No State shall enter into any Treaty, Alliance, or Confederation; grant Letters of Marque and Reprisal; coin Money; emit Bills of Credit; make any Thing but gold and silver Coin a Tender in Payment of Debts; pass any Bill of Attainder, ex post facto Law, or Law impairing the Obligation of Contracts, or grant any Title of Nobility.

No State shall, without the Consent of the Congress, lay any Imposts or Duties on Imports or Exports, except what may be absolutely necessary for executing it's inspection Laws: and the net Produce of all Duties and Imposts, laid by any State on Imports or Exports, shall be for the Use of the Treasury of the United States; and all such Laws shall be subject to the Revision and Controul of the Congress.

No State shall, without the Consent of Congress, lay any Duty of Tonnage, keep Troops, or Ships of War in time of Peace, enter into any Agreement or Compact with another State, or with a foreign Power, or engage in War, unless actually invaded, or in such imminent Danger as will not admit of delay.

Article II

Section 1

The executive Power shall be vested in a President of the United States of America. He shall hold his Office during the Term of four Years, and, together with the Vice President, chosen for the same Term, be elected, as follows:

Each State shall appoint, in such Manner as the Legislature thereof may direct, a Number of Electors, equal to the whole Number of Senators and Representatives to which the State may be entitled in the Congress: but no Senator or Representative, or Person holding an Office of Trust or Profit under the United States, shall be appointed an Elector.

The Electors shall meet in their respective States, and vote by Ballot for two Persons, of whom one at least shall not be an Inhabitant of the same State with themselves. And they shall make a List of all the Persons voted for, and of the Number of Votes for each; which List they shall sign and certify, and transmit sealed to the Seat of the Government of the United States, directed to the President of the Senate. The President of the Senate shall, in the Presence of the Senate and House of Representatives, open all the Certificates, and the Votes shall then be counted. The Person having the greatest Number of Votes shall be the President, if such Number be a Majority of the whole Number of Electors appointed; and if there be more than one who have such Majority, and have an equal Number of Votes, then the House of Representatives shall immediately chuse by Ballot one of them for President; and if no Person have a Majority, then from the five highest on the List the said House shall in like Manner chuse the President. But in chusing the President, the Votes shall be taken by States, the Representation from each State having one Vote; A quorum for this purpose shall consist of a Member or Members from two thirds of the States, and a Majority of all the States shall be necessary to a Choice. In every Case, after the Choice of the President, the Person having the greatest Number of Votes of the Electors shall be the Vice President. But if there should remain two or more who have equal Votes, the Senate shall chuse from them by Ballot the Vice President.

The Congress may determine the Time of chusing the Electors, and the Day on which they shall give their Votes; which Day shall be the same throughout the United States.

No Person except a natural born Citizen, or a Citizen of the United States, at the time of the Adoption of this Constitution, shall be eligible to the Office of President; neither shall any Person be eligible to that Office who shall not have attained to the Age of thirty five Years, and been fourteen Years a Resident within the United States.

In Case of the Removal of the President from Office, or of his Death, Resignation, or Inability to discharge the Powers and Duties of the said Office, the Same shall devolve on the Vice President, and the Congress may by Law provide for the Case of Removal, Death, Resignation or Inability, both of the President and Vice President, declaring what Officer shall then act as President, and such Officer shall act accordingly, until the Disability be removed, or a President shall be elected.

The President shall, at stated Times, receive for his Services, a Compensation, which shall neither be increased nor diminished during the Period for which he shall have been elected, and he shall not receive within that Period any other Emolument from the United States, or any of them.

Before he enter on the Execution of his Office, he shall take the following Oath or Affirmation:—"I do solemnly swear (or affirm) that I will faithfully execute the Office of President of the United States, and will to the best of my Ability, preserve, protect and defend the Constitution of the United States."

Section 2

The President shall be Commander in Chief of the Army and Navy of the United States, and of the Militia of the several States, when called into the actual Service of the United States; he may require the Opinion, in writing, of the principal Officer in each of the executive Departments, upon any Subject relating to the Duties of their respective Offices, and he shall have Power to grant Reprieves and Pardons for Offences against the United States, except in Cases of Impeachment.

He shall have Power, by and with the Advice and Consent of the Senate, to make Treaties, provided two thirds of the Senators present concur; and he shall nominate, and by and with the Advice and Consent of the Senate, shall appoint Ambassadors,

other public Ministers and Consuls, Judges of the supreme Court, and all other Officers of the United States, whose Appointments are not herein otherwise provided for, and which shall be established by Law: but the Congress may by Law vest the Appointment of such inferior Officers, as they think proper, in the President alone, in the Courts of Law, or in the Heads of Departments.

The President shall have Power to fill up all Vacancies that may happen during the Recess of the Senate, by granting Commissions which shall expire at the End of their next Session.

Section 3

He shall from time to time give to the Congress Information of the State of the Union, and recommend to their Consideration such Measures as he shall judge necessary and expedient; he may, on extraordinary Occasions, convene both Houses, or either of them, and in Case of Disagreement between them, with Respect to the Time of Adjournment, he may adjourn them to such Time as he shall think proper; he shall receive Ambassadors and other public Ministers; he shall take Care that the Laws be faithfully executed, and shall Commission all the Officers of the United States.

Section 4

The President, Vice President and all civil Officers of the United States, shall be removed from Office on Impeachment for, and Conviction of, Treason, Bribery, or other high Crimes and Misdemeanors.

Article III

Section 1

The judicial Power of the United States shall be vested in one supreme Court, and in such inferior Courts as the Congress may from time to time ordain and establish. The Judges, both of the supreme and inferior Courts, shall hold their Offices during good Behaviour, and shall, at stated Times, receive for their Services a Compensation, which shall not be diminished during their Continuance in Office.

Section 2

The judicial Power shall extend to all Cases, in Law and Equity, arising under this Constitution, the Laws of the United States, and Treaties made, or which shall be made, under their Authority;—to all Cases affecting Ambassadors, other public Ministers and Consuls;—to all Cases of admiralty and maritime Jurisdiction;—to Controversies to which the United States shall be a Party;—to Controversies between two or more States;—between a State and Citizens of another State;—between Citizens of different States;—between Citizens of the same State claiming Lands under Grants of different States, and between a State, or the Citizens thereof, and foreign States, Citizens or Subjects.

In all Cases affecting Ambassadors, other public Ministers and Consuls, and those in which a State shall be Party, the supreme Court shall have original Jurisdiction. In all the other Cases before mentioned, the supreme Court shall have appellate Jurisdiction, both as to Law and Fact, with such Exceptions, and under such Regulations as the Congress shall make.

The Trial of all Crimes, except in Cases of Impeachment, shall be by Jury; and such Trial shall be held in the State where the said Crimes shall have been committed; but when not committed within any State, the Trial shall be at such Place or Places as the Congress may by Law have directed.

Section 3

Treason against the United States, shall consist only in levying War against them, or in adhering to their Enemies, giving them Aid and Comfort. No Person shall be convicted of Treason unless on the Testimony of two Witnesses to the same overt Act, or on Confession in open Court.

The Congress shall have Power to declare the Punishment of Treason, but no Attainder of Treason shall work Corruption of Blood, or Forfeiture except during the Life of the Person attainted.

Article IV

Section 1

Full Faith and Credit shall be given in each State to the public Acts, Records, and judicial Proceedings of every other State. And the Congress may by general Laws prescribe the Manner in which such Acts, Records and Proceedings shall be proved, and the Effect thereof.

Section 2

The Citizens of each State shall be entitled to all Privileges and Immunities of Citizens in the several States.

A Person charged in any State with Treason, Felony, or other Crime, who shall flee from Justice, and be found in another State, shall on Demand of the executive Authority of the State from which he fled, be delivered up, to be removed to the State having Jurisdiction of the Crime.

No Person held to Service or Labour in one State, under the Laws thereof, escaping into another, shall, in Consequence of any Law or Regulation therein, be discharged from such Service or Labour, but shall be delivered up on Claim of the Party to whom such Service or Labour may be due.

Section 3

New States may be admitted by the Congress into this Union; but no new State shall be formed or erected within the Jurisdiction of any other State; nor any State be formed by the Junction of two or more States, or Parts of States, without the Consent of the Legislatures of the States concerned as well as of the Congress.

The Congress shall have Power to dispose of and make all needful Rules and Regulations respecting the Territory or other Property belonging to the United States; and nothing in this Constitution shall be so construed as to Prejudice any Claims of the United States, or of any particular State.

Section 4

The United States shall guarantee to every State in this Union a Republican Form of Government, and shall protect each of them against Invasion; and on Application of the Legislature, or of the Executive (when the Legislature cannot be convened), against domestic Violence.

Article V

The Congress, whenever two thirds of both Houses shall deem it necessary, shall propose Amendments to this Constitution, or, on the Application of the Legislatures of two thirds of the several States, shall call a Convention for proposing Amendments, which, in either Case, shall be valid to all Intents and

Purposes, as Part of this Constitution, when ratified by the Legislatures of three fourths of the several States, or by Conventions in three fourths thereof, as the one or the other Mode of Ratification may be proposed by the Congress; Provided that no Amendment which may be made prior to the Year One thousand eight hundred and eight shall in any Manner affect the first and fourth Clauses in the Ninth Section of the first Article; and that no State, without its Consent, shall be deprived of its equal Suffrage in the Senate.

Article VI

All Debts contracted and Engagements entered into, before the Adoption of this Constitution, shall be as valid against the United States under this Constitution, as under the Confederation.

This Constitution, and the Laws of the United States which shall be made in Pursuance thereof; and all Treaties made, or which shall be made, under the Authority of the United States, shall be the supreme Law of the Land; and the Judges in every State shall be bound thereby, any Thing in the Constitution or Laws of any State to the Contrary notwithstanding.

The Senators and Representatives before mentioned, and the Members of the several State Legislatures, and all executive and judicial Officers, both of the United States and of the several States, shall be bound by Oath or Affirmation, to support this Constitution; but no religious Test shall ever be required as a Qualification to any Office or public Trust under the United States.

Article VII

The Ratification of the Conventions of nine States, shall be sufficient for the Establishment of this Constitution between the States so ratifying the Same.

The Word, "the," being interlined between the seventh and eighth Lines of the first Page, the Word "Thirty" being partly written on an Erazure in the fifteenth Line of the first Page, The Words "is tried" being interlined between the thirty second and thirty third Lines of the first Page and the Word "the" being interlined between the forty third and forty fourth Lines of the second Page.

Attest William Jackson Secretary

Done in Convention by the Unanimous Consent of the States present the Seventeenth Day of September in the Year of our Lord one thousand seven hundred and Eighty seven and of the Independence of the United States of America the Twelfth In witness whereof We have hereunto subscribed our Names,

G°. Washington
Presidt and deputy from Virginia

Delaware
  Geo: Read
  Gunning Bedford jun
  John Dickinson
  Richard Bassett
  Jaco: Broom

Maryland
  James McHenry
  Dan of St Thos. Jenifer
  Danl. Carroll

Virginia
  John Blair
  James Madison Jr.

North Carolina
  Wm. Blount
  Richd. Dobbs Spaight
  Hu Williamson

South Carolina
  J. Rutledge
  Charles Cotesworth Pinckney
  Charles Pinckney
  Pierce Butler

Georgia
  William Few
  Abr Baldwin

New Hampshire
  John Langdon
  Nicholas Gilman

Massachusetts
  Nathaniel Gorham
  Rufus King

Connecticut
  Wm. Saml. Johnson
  Roger Sherman

New York
    Alexander Hamilton

New Jersey
    Wil: Livingston
    David Brearley
    Wm. Paterson
    Jona: Dayton

Pennsylvania
    B Franklin
    Thomas Mifflin
    Robt. Morris
    Geo. Clymer
    Thos. FitzSimons
    Jared Ingersoll
    James Wilson
    Gouv Morris

Note: The following text is a transcription of the first ten amendments to the Constitution in their original form. These amendments were ratified December 15, 1791, and form what is known as the "Bill of Rights."

The Preamble to The Bill of Rights

Congress of the United States

begun and held at the City of New-York, on Wednesday the fourth of March, one thousand seven hundred and eighty nine.

The Conventions of a number of the States, having at the time of their adopting the Constitution, expressed a desire, in order to prevent misconstruction or abuse of its powers, that further declaratory and restrictive clauses should be added: And as extending the ground of public confidence in the Government, will best ensure the beneficent ends of its institution.

Resolved by the Senate and House of Representatives of the United States of America, in Congress assembled, two thirds of both Houses concurring, that the following Articles be proposed to the Legislatures of the several States, as amendments to the Constitution of the United States, all, or any of which Articles, when ratified by three fourths of the said Legislatures, to be valid to all intents and purposes, as part of the said Constitution; viz.

Articles in addition to, and Amendment of the Constitution of the United States of America, proposed by Congress, and ratified by the Legislatures of the several States, pursuant to the fifth Article of the original Constitution.

The First Ten Amendments to the Constitution as Ratified by the States

Amendment I

Congress shall make no law respecting an establishment of religion, or prohibiting the free exercise thereof; or abridging the freedom of speech, or of the press; or the right of the people peaceably to assemble, and to petition the Government for a redress of grievances.

Amendment II

A well regulated Militia, being necessary to the security of a free State, the right of the people to keep and bear Arms, shall not be infringed.

Amendment III

No Soldier shall, in time of peace be quartered in any house, without the consent of the Owner, nor in time of war, but in a manner to be prescribed by law.

Amendment IV

The right of the people to be secure in their persons, houses, papers, and effects, against unreasonable searches and seizures, shall not be violated, and no Warrants shall issue, but upon probable cause, supported by Oath or affirmation, and particularly describing the place to be searched, and the persons or things to be seized.

Amendment V

No person shall be held to answer for a capital, or otherwise infamous crime, unless on a presentment or indictment of a Grand Jury, except in cases arising in the land or naval forces, or in the Militia, when in actual service in time of War or public danger; nor shall any person be subject for the same offence to be twice put in jeopardy of life or limb; nor shall be compelled in any criminal case to be a witness against himself, nor be deprived of life, liberty, or property, without due process of law; nor shall private property be taken for public use, without just compensation.

Amendment VI

In all criminal prosecutions, the accused shall enjoy the right to a speedy and public trial, by an impartial jury of the State and district wherein the crime shall have been committed, which district shall have been previously ascertained by law, and to be informed of the nature and cause of the accusation; to be confronted with the witnesses against him; to have compulsory process for obtaining witnesses in his favor, and to have the Assistance of Counsel for his defence.

Amendment VII

In Suits at common law, where the value in controversy shall exceed twenty dollars, the right of trial by jury shall be preserved, and no fact tried by a jury, shall be otherwise re-examined in any Court of the United States, than according to the rules of the common law.

Amendment VIII

Excessive bail shall not be required, nor excessive fines imposed, nor cruel and unusual punishments inflicted.

Amendment IX

The enumeration in the Constitution, of certain rights, shall not be construed to deny or disparage others retained by the people.

Amendment X

The powers not delegated to the United States by the Constitution, nor prohibited by it to the States, are reserved to the States respectively, or to the people.

Index

Page numbers in *italics* refer to illustrations or sidebar documents.